# DEVELOPMENT STUDIES REVISITED

## Twenty-five Years of The Journal of Development Studies

'Nations tolerably well advanced as to skill, dexterity and judgement, in the application of labour, have followed very different plans in the general conduct or direction of it; and those plans have not all been equally favourable to the greatness of its produce. . . . Though those different plans were, perhaps, first introduced by the private interests and prejudices of particular orders of men, without any regard to, or foresight of, their consequences upon the general welfare of the society; yet they have given occasion to *very different theories of political economy*; of which some magnify the importance of that industry which is carried on in towns, others of that which is carried on in the country. Those theories have had a considerable influence, not only upon the opinions of men of learning, but upon the public conduct of princes and sovereign states.'

Adam Smith, *The Wealth of Nations*, Vol. I, pp. 2–3.


'It is always depressing to go back to Adam Smith, especially on economic development, as one realises how little we have learned in nearly two hundred years.'

Kenneth E. Boulding, 'The Economics of
Knowledge and the Knowledge of Economics',
*American Economic Review*, May 1966, p. 6.

# DEVELOPMENT STUDIES REVISITED

## Twenty-five Years of The Journal of Development Studies

*With an Introduction by*
Charles Cooper and E.V.K. FitzGerald

Routledge
Taylor & Francis Group

LONDON AND NEW YORK

*First published in Great Britain by*
FRANK CASS AND COMPANY LIMITED

This edition published 2016 by Routledge
2 Park Square, Milton Park, Abingdon, Oxfordshire OX14 4RN
711 Third Avenue, New York, NY 10017, USA

First issued in paperback 2016

*Routledge is an imprint of the Taylor & Francis Group, an informa business*

Copright © 1989 Taylor & Francis.

British Library Cataloguing in Publication Data

Development studies revisited: twenty-five years of the
Journal of development studies.
1. Developing countries. Economic development
I. Journal of development studies, ISSN 0022-0388
330.9172'4

ISBN 0-7146-3376-3

ISBN 13: 978-1-138-96757-1 (pbk)
ISBN 13: 978-0-7146-3376-3 (hbk)

# CONTENTS

# The Journal and Development Studies: An Introduction

*Charles Cooper and E.V.K. FitzGerald*
*The Hague, June 1988*

'... very different theories of political economy ...'

## I. DEVELOPMENT STUDIES IN THE POST-WAR PERIOD

### Opening Remarks

*The Journal of Development Studies* was founded 25 years ago as a professional journal for what had by then become an established sub-discipline within British social science. It was unique in its field in the UK and has remained so: other parallel journals were either effectively US institutions, or aimed at a less academic readership. The Journal has consistently published a broad spectrum of British research on development studies – a catholicity that has been reflected in the composition of the Editorial Board over the years – and has always welcomed authors from the USA, the European Continent, and above all from the Third World.

To page through the first 25 volumes of the Journal is to survey the intellectual history of development studies itself. The 20-odd papers presented here represent less than three per cent of articles published since 1964, and thus can only represent what we feel to be a continuing tradition of empirical research based on sound analytical foundations and informed by a classical tradition of political economy.

We open this Introduction with a brief and unavoidably superficial account of development studies since the Second World War, within which the Journal, or rather its authors, can be located. We shall then sketch the institutional history of the Journal itself as one aspect of the establishment of an academic discipline in close relation to policy debates. Finally, we shall try to analyse and locate the contribution made by the articles we have selected here as representative of the best that the Journal has offered to its readership since its foundation. In the absence of a major scholarly study of the history of ideas in development studies, we have had to make a series of assertions which perhaps should be seen as a contribution to debate rather than an authoritative survey. As we hope this collection shows, such a history would constitute an extremely valuable research project.

### The Foundation of Modern Development Studies

Development studies as a distinct branch of social science can only be said to have emerged after the Second World War, justifying its separate existence on the grounds that the technological, geopolitical and institutional structures of Third World economies were sufficiently different from those of the First and Second Worlds as to justify a distinct approach to that of the paradigms derived from the industrialised capitalist and socialist societies. This distinction was expressed early on in the structure of the newly formed United Nations itself [*UN, 1951*], with its specialised development agencies. The theoretical underpinning of this approach was provided by a group of eminent social scientists who can be justly called the 'pioneers in development' [*Meier and Seers, 1984*].

The intellectual origins of modern development studies are, however, much older. They can – and should – be traced back to the founders of classical political economy; for Smith, Ricardo and Marx were concerned above all with early industrialisation [*O'Brien, 1975*]. However, more immediate roots are to be found in the economic debates of the inter-war period. The first such root [*Blackhouse, 1985*] was the Keynesian revolution, which effectively invalidated the optimistic belief in the capacity of market systems for automatic adjustment towards optimality or even equilibrium. Keynes himself had rebelled against the Old Orthodoxy of 'sound finance' based on balanced budgets and the gold standard, rather than against neo-classical theory as such, for there was much of Marshall's *Principles* in the *General Theory*. None the less, the Keynesian approach became associated with the rise of the welfare state in the post-war period (where socially acceptable living standards became a citizen entitlement) and the reform of the world system to the benefit of the poor through the Bretton Woods institutions and the UN itself in a post-colonial age. Economists such as Prest [*1962*], Nurkse [*1953*] and Reddaway [*1963*] can be identified with this approach.

Secondly, the Eastern European tradition of concern with the political economy of 'late' industrialisation and Marxian analysis itself contributed concerns for intersectoral relationships, for the problem of oligopoly and for the role of the peasantry as important themes in development studies. Indeed, many of the first generation of development specialists were themselves refugees from recently industrialised semi-agrarian dependent states of Eastern Europe. The Soviet debate in the 1920s on how to mobilise the investible surplus lies at the basis of the initial analysis of the industrialisation process of the Third World. In fact the debate was continued during the design of concrete development plans. The Second and Third Indian development plans, for instance, revived many issues which relate directly to those discussed by Preobazhensky [*1962*], Bukharin and Fel'dman. This tradition was directly continued in the work of development economists such as Kalecki [*1976*], Mandelbaum [*1945*], who was one of the founding editors of the Journal, Rosenstein-Rodan [*1943*] and Dobb [*1960*].

Thirdly, and perhaps most significantly, theorists from the periphery such as Lewis [*1955*], Prebisch [*1950*] and Mahalanobis [*1953*] stressed the problems of intersectoral balance and technological dichotomy within Third World societies, and provided a critique based upon the unequal trading relationships between North and South [*Arndt, 1985*]. In this context, it should not be forgotten that much of Eastern and Central Europe was still 'industrialising' before the War, which kept the tradition of classical political economy alive there. In an atmosphere of post-colonial pressure for economic independence, the 'peripheral theorists' began to develop their own theory of industrialisation based on the trans-formation of a backward agricultural sector, the absorption into modern industrial employment of the surplus labour among the peasantry, and the negotiation of technology transfer and integration into the world trading system. This theory can properly be called 'structuralism' [*Chenery, 1975*].

Industrial development was seen as central to economic growth, to overcoming poverty and to economic sovereignty and was held to require considerable state involvement. The role designated for the state was understood to be problematic, as it was not based on neo-classical concepts of 'market failure', but rather on the argument that what was required even in mixed economies was conscious transformation of the institutional structures within which the market works in the absence of indigenous classes willing and able to undertake this task [*Hirschman, 1958*]. History was held to indicate that the developing countries had this in common with the experience of other 'late capitalist' nations [*Gerschenkron, 1962*].

There persisted, nonetheless, a strong element of 'modernisation theory' in the approach to development studies of the first post-war decades [*Bernstein, 1973*]. The propositions that industrialisation would necessarily involve rapid proletarianisation, the elimination of traditional social organisation, and the emergence of bourgeois values and institu-tions was taken over from the classical political economists, including Marx. The novelty was the thesis that strong state leadership was neces-sary to allow this to come about on the periphery of world economy and society, albeit in support of private capital in the long run. Only in the USA, however, was the belief held that modernisation could be uniquely measured by reference to progressive approximation to the present situation of the 'Western Democracies' [*Rostow, 1960*].

Production structures were seen as relatively inflexible in the short run as they embodied a determinate technology; which could only be changed over time by investment [*Chenery, 1979*]. Even the early 'dualistic' development models were centrally concerned with the issue of income distribution, both as a question of social justice and in relation to savings, demand and labour supply. The pioneers also recognised class forces working to inhibit growth and technical change. For example, Lewis [*1954: 410*] remarked that, because of the link between modern sector wages and subsistence earnings in this kind of society:

> capitalists have a direct interest in holding down the productivity of the subsistence workers. Thus [they] have no interest in seeking knowledge of new techniques or new seeds conveyed to the peasants and, if they are influential in the government, they will not be found using their influence to expand the facilities for agricultural extension.

These principles of what we might reasonably term *modern development studies* became the accepted framework for United Nations agencies by the late 1950s. In the two post-war decades the political economy tradition dominated development studies as a whole, across a broad ideological spectrum and is clearly expressed in standard textbooks such as Kindelberger [*1958*]. However, the mode of analysis was based more on the exercise of reason, intuition and experience than on extensive empirical research, which was to come later with improvements in statistics and in analytical methodology.

In consequence, development economics had a different conception of optimality from the neo-classical tradition. Economic efficiency was not defined in terms of profitability at current world prices (that is 'comparative advantage') but, rather, in terms of effective contribution to long-term goals such as basic needs satisfaction or technological absorption. This contrasted sharply and explicitly not only with the neo-classical approach in economics but also with its libertarian or utilitarian equivalents in sociology and political science. The basic premises of the latter, such as the homogeneous and rational behaviour of individuals (unless impeded by bad government policies), were challenged by development theory's insistence upon the institutional context in which individuals operate, and the historical background to government intervention [*Toye, 1987*].

It was at this point in the intellectual history of the British tradition of political economy, that the Journal was founded. We shall survey the history of the Journal itself later on, but here it is sufficient to note that in the opening editorial statement of the first issue the founding Editors declared the need to reflect the reality of a new professional identity with its own intellectual tradition. Moreover, the outlook was to be consciously multi-disciplinary. The Journal was established in order to provide publication for 'work on development economics not easy to secure in general economics journals . . . [and promote] . . . research dealing with efforts of the developing countries to establish stable political systems and efficient government institutions, with their political thought, and with their international relations'.

## The Debate on Development

Once the foundations of modern development studies had been established, enquiry could advance into empirical questions in a number of areas of sectoral or microeconomic analysis. In this task, researchers were enormously assisted by the improvement of statistical sources, many of which had been established by the pioneers of development themselves.

On the one hand, the causes and consequences of domestic phenomena such as poverty, underemployment, agricultural and industrial enterprise organisation, migration, tax reform, and infrastructure bottlenecks were discussed. This gave rise, in turn, to elaborate models and methods of sectoral and project planning. On the other hand, detailed analyses of international phenomena such as technology transfer, international commodity markets, and multinational corporations allowed a more detailed picture of the insertion of developing countries into the world economy to be built up. We shall return to these themes in more detail below when we discuss the selected papers from the Journal, which mostly reflect this approach. There were good reasons to believe that development studies had become technically established as a professional discipline with agreed foundations.

Of particular normative importance was the idea that poverty could and should be overcome, and that this would be the central theme of development planning rather than industrialisation or growth as such. Of particular influence was the work of the ILO [for example, *ILO, 1972*] in this respect, which was subsequently supported by the IBRD [*Chenery, 1974*] and most aid agencies. The 'poverty approach' became key in debates over unemployment, agrarian development and the choice of technology [*Kitching, 1982*]. This was in part a reaction to the disappointing growth experience of the first two decades after the War and of decolonisation itself, neither of which seemed to reduce hunger and homelessness as fast as had been expected. Moreover, the pressure from a growing number of non-governmental organisations working in the Third World with religious or 'solidarity' ethics undoubtedly influenced bilateral and multilateral official aid agencies.

However, the so recently established theory of development soon came under attack from both ends of the ideological spectrum. The first assault was from the left, and was itself a result in part of the reappraisal of Marxian theory current in Europe [*Carnoy, 1984*]. Three relevant themes can be identified: the nature of the state in an industrial society; the international subordination of the Third World to the First (that is, 'dependency'); and the articulation of distinct forms of production in a heterogenous social structure. New state theories stressed both the role of public investment and social services as part of the 'logic of capital' (in the Marxian tradition) and class struggles around state intervention in the economy (in a more Ricardian sense), as well as refining the concept of 'relative autonomy' in state-led structural transformation. These European ideas were rapidly deployed in criticism of Third World optimism about the rational planning of development. The European revival of interest in the ideas of Gramsci also reintroduced the discussion of ideology and political hegemony in state intervention in civil society.

The other two themes were more closely directed at the development problem. On the one hand, the revival of the Leninist theme of imperialism as a frustration of capitalist development [for example, *Baran, 1957*] led directly to the concept of 'dependency'. This attack on the concept of industrialisation being supported by integration into the international division of labour was combined with a more sophisticated approach to the terms of trade problem through theories of unequal exchange [*Love, 1981*]. In a sense, this line of criticism had already been dealt with in the political economy tradition outlined above, in discussions of 'late development'. However, the remnants of dependency theory lived on in the 'global Keynesianism' of the Brandt Report [*Brandt Commission,*

*1980*]. What dependency *did* provide was a basis for a devastating attack on 'modernisation theory' in its simpler form of 'growth stages' following the historical progress of the US or the UK.

On the other hand, the empirical analysis of rural problems under-mined the 'dualist model'. Analysis moved from an initial critique in terms of 'marginalisation' – at best little more than an updated concept of the reserve army which was quite compatible with the Lewis model – to the more sophisticated and useful concept of articulation *between* forms of production where the subordination of small-scale production to large capitalist farmers (and industrialists) was seen as part of a complete social formation. The complexity and dynamic of the 'traditional' sector of the economy came to be recognised, rather than regarded as a static structure, unresponsive to market incentives and mainly useful as a source of unskilled labour. Ideas of a rather more populist (or rather, 'Narodnik') origin were associated with this major change of perception; such as the concept of 'urban bias' and 'appropriate technology' [*Kitching, 1982*].

Simultaneously, but perhaps less spectacularly at first, there began to appear a powerful neo-classical critique of development studies [*Little, 1982*]. Although this was to reach its peak in the nineteen-eighties, the seventies already saw a conservative critique of development studies – mainly at that stage in the form of particular criticisms of the policies of Third World governments which were held to have been influenced by structuralist principles – particularly import substitution and inadequate aggregate demand management. At this stage, the emphasis of the critics was on the need to apply neo-classical theory to investment planning [*OECD, 1968*] and the emergence of a distinct monetarist approach to balance of payments management and development finance [*McKinnon, 1973*].

Under these attacks, the central 'structuralist' tradition of development studies did not respond as vigorously (or as rigorously) as might have been expected; indeed there were even signs of a certain failure of nerve in concepts such as the 'crisis of planning' [*Faber and Seers, 1972*]. The Journal responded characteristically by regretting this polarisation, stating editorially in 1976 (more or less half way through its life) that the papers being published at the time:

> provided competent and interesting examples of work in their particular disciplines, reflecting the 'world view' of the authors: such world views as neo-classical economics, redistributive social demo-cracy, structuralism and *dependencia*, or marxism and neo-marxism. We now believe that this is no longer enough. Development studies have revealed and reflected the inadequacies of various schools of thought in the social sciences, which have found many of their basic assumptions undermined. As long as scholars, however efficient, operate uncritically within the confines of their particular theoreti-cal systems, the major questions of development theory and policy will remain unasked.

*The Defence of Development Studies*

Unfortunately, development studies did not generally heed sound advice. The wave of neo-orthodox counter-reformation gathered momentum [*Lal, 1983*]. In the wake of world economic crisis, the attention of the development economics profession shifted away from industrialisation and poverty towards short-term economic stabilisation. In many developing countries economic strategy mainly focused on financial stability indicators such as the fiscal deficit and the money supply, while trade and price liberalisation came to replace public investment and sectoral planning as instruments of development strategy. In development theory the established tradition was pushed aside by a 'New Orthodoxy' [*Little, 1982*] based on a neo-classical tradition of price-clearing markets and pre-Keynesian principles of 'sound finance'.

The immediate practical reasons for this sea change in institutional attitudes are not hard to discern. By the end of the 1970s many developing countries had built up large external debt positions, which in the early 1980s turned out to be unserviceable. The issue was no longer one of maximising the capital flow from North to South, but of minimising the flows of interest, amortisation, profits and capital flight from South to North. This reversal of trends created for most developing countries a huge and immediate adjustment problem as expected import capacities fell. The multilateral financial institutions charged with organising conditionality for debt alleviation, insisted upon the application of financial orthodoxy and trade liberalisation as a means of reducing domestic demand pressure and using installed capacity more effectively.

The immediate practical concern for macroeconomic stabilisation rapidly became transformed into a debate on the principles of economic development strategies themselves [*FitzGerald and Vos, 1988*]. The exponents of what we have labelled as the 'New Orthodoxy' of development thinking tend to emphasise the role of 'undistorted' markets and price signals as principal mechanisms that would not only lead to macroeconomic stability, but also to renewed investment, growth and, eventually, increased living standards. All that had been learned in decades of research and analysis of unbalanced growth, balance of payments difficulties, food shortages and high inflation was reduced to a critique of the public sector and price controls as the central problem of macroeconomic management.

This widespread emphasis on the monetary sector, financial stability and market-oriented policy solutions marks an abrupt shift away from the central themes upon which development economics had been built up over the previous three decades as a distinct branch of social science theory. The problem of development finance had indeed been one of the major issues that preoccupied the founders of modern development economics, but it was seen as a long-term development strategy which required both sectoral output adjustment and the redistribution of employment and incomes, such that industrialisation could take place without running into unsustainable imbalances. Early writers attached the insufficiency of market solutions in meeting structural and institutional factors (like asset distribution and alignment of class interests) in explaining observed immobility of resources in face of price signals. Indeed, a freely functioning market in one sector may produce perverse effects on stability even if price signals are 'correct'.

However valid this critique may be, the widely acknowledged weakness of the structuralist position had been the failure to provide a coherent and rigorous theoretical and policy framework to deal simultaneously with the long-term problems of economic development in the 'classical' tradition and short-term problems of stabilisation. Exponents of the 'New Orthodoxy' heaped scorn on the structuralist approach (as their colleagues were doing on related schools of thought such as Keynesian economics). To quote an authorative textbook [*Dornbusch and Fischer, 1984: 571*]: 'an eclectic collection of ideas, not a systematic challenge . . .'.

The classical tradition of development studies was not abandoned, but it turned from theory to empirical research, country case studies and a more historical approach. In this, the development economists had been preceded by at least a decade by the development sociologists, who had already extended their scope to include, in effect, social anthropology and political sociology. The growth of empirical analysis displaced general theorising to good effect but it implied, on the one hand, an increasing use of complex computable models to handle data and, on the other, the greater emphasis on area studies as the frame of reference. Both of these trends required, and received, the establishment of specialist journals which, although of scholarly merit in their own right, made the broad development debate more difficult to sustain in academic circles.

Although there was little debate at the more general theoretical level, an implicit response to the apparent neo-orthodox hegemony is reflected in the pages of the Journal in the 1980s by 'specialised' topics such as women's studies, peasant household behaviour, international trade theory, general equilibrium economics and investment appraisal. Each developed their own methodological tradition and debates, but generally carried into their specialisation the reformed structuralism hammered out in the previous two decades. Above all, such approaches clarified the institutional dimensions of all these areas and problems, stressing the need for interdisciplinary analysis and demonstrating the hollowness of any claim that simple reliance on market forces will lead to development.

It is too soon to evaluate the contribution made by the Journal in recent years and, in any case, the present authors are not, perhaps, in the best position to judge. What is clear, however, is that in its twenty-fifth year the Journal is still at the centre of the development debate.

## II. A BRIEF HISTORY OF THE JOURNAL

The idea of a *Journal of Development Studies* came under discussion for the first time in early 1964. At the time, Mr Frank Cass was interested in expanding his firm's involvement in the publication of academic journals –

an involvement which had started a short while before with the *Journal of Middle Eastern Studies*. The notion of a journal which would provide an outlet for 'specialised research in economic development' was first put forward in talks between Frank Cass and Terry Byres [*Editorial Note, 1964*]. At this time, Byres – who later worked with Cass to set up the *Journal of Peasant Studies* – was a relatively new appointee at the School of Oriental and African Studies (SOAS) in the University of London. A short while later, he and Cass brought Dr Edith Penrose – then in a joint appointment between the London School of Economics and SOAS – into the discussion. The first issue of the Journal under Dr Penrose's editorship appeared in October 1964.

These initiatives took place against a background of increasing academic and governmental interest in development issues and the early history of the journal reflects some of these broader currents.

*Changes in the Institutional Context of UK Development Studies in the Mid-1960s: The Universities*

By the early 1960s, in Britain, scholarly involvement in teaching and research on issues of Third World development was on the increase. Development economics was established in a number of Universities. At Oxford, Cambridge, Edinburgh and at the Queen's University, Belfast there were optional papers in development economics at Bachelor's level, and economics departments at a number of other universities were to move in the same direction in the course of the 1960s.

In 1964 there were also a number of postgraduate courses. The University of Manchester had set up a postgraduate diploma course in 1960, which was mainly taken by Third World students and which gave access to an MA course. Cambridge was considering the establishment of a postgraduate diploma course (and later added an M.Phil.); Oxford was planning a one-year Diploma course. In London, the teaching of development economics was mainly done at SOAS and the London School of Economics. It might well be argued that the involvement of SOAS was itself a sign of the times – a sign that is of a new importance attached to the study of development issues. In the late 1950s and early 1960s under Sir Cyril Phillips, SOAS had undergone an important change away from a traditional 'orientalist' concern with language, law and history of 'oriental societies' to what were called Modern Studies – namely economics, politics, anthropology, sociology and geography of contemporary societies in Asia and Africa. The members of SOAS who played key roles in the formation of the Journal were of course representative of this 'modernisation' of the traditional SOAS. They were involved in postgraduate teaching of economics and aimed 'to train postgraduates who had a knowledge of language . . . culture, history and economies of the countries they were studying as well as a sound knowledge of economics,' [*Martin and Knapp, 1967: 206*].

In addition to these teaching faculties there were in the early 1960s a few established research centres: for example, the Institute for Commonwealth Studies at Queen Elizabeth House, Oxford and the new Centre for African Studies at Edinburgh. Later in the 1960s, as we shall see, the Institute of Development Studies (IDS) was set up at the University of Sussex.

Along with the growth in numbers of university courses, there was much consideration of the type of economics which would best equip people who were to spend their professional careers working on development problems. The literature of the time, of course, reflects a preoccupation with the specific nature of developing economies. It was natural, therefore, that when Dudley Seers attacked the question frontally in *The Limitations of the Special Case*, he should have had an immediate impact [*Seers, 1963*].

Seers later explained that what he described as the 'rather rude and carping' nature of his paper was not due to 'natural bloodymindedness but . . . to some impatience at being confronted with conventional Anglo-Saxon economics after working for a number of years in Latin America' [*Martin and Knapp, 1967: 156*]. Only a few months after its first publication, the paper was the main stimulus for the Manchester Conference on Teaching Economic Development, which met in April 1964. The organisers of the conference remarked: 'the acceptance of invitations to attend on the part of a large number of distinguished British economists . . . showed . . . that there existed a widespread feeling that Mr. Seers had a case that needed to be discussed' [*Martin and Knapp, 1967: ix*].

That 'case' is well known. Seers argued that the way economic processes work themselves out is contingent upon the economic and social environments in which they happen. Since economics teaching by and large took for granted the existence of forms of economic organisation special to the industrialised countries, it was often unhelpful and inappropriate to the circumstances of Third World countries, if not actually harmful. The different forms of social and economic organisation encountered in the Third World, and the different relationships which Third World countries have to the international economy called for new theory – and, ultimately, a transformation of the way in which economics was being taught. There was a strong flavour of Latin American structuralism in the paper, about which Seers is explicit: 'A basic framework . . . (for appropriate theory) . . . exists . . . in the writing of the Latin American school of structuralists, and this is sufficiently flexible, I believe, to be extended to other parts of the world' [*Seers, 1963*]. Seers' paper was the clearest statement of the current of structuralist thought which had been growing in British Development Studies (see Part I of this Introduction).

*Changes in Government and Administration*

The growth of Development Studies in the UK was also to be influenced by the change of government which followed in the Autumn of 1964. Harold Wilson took office as Labour Prime Minister after a narrow victory in the General Election of that year. Barbara Castle was appointed Minister of Overseas Development with cabinet rank and the erstwhile

Department of Technical Cooperation (DTC) was integrated into the Overseas Development Ministry (ODM). There was a substantial 'migration' of academics to take up new advisory functions in government.[1] Amongst the economists who had been at the Manchester Conference and who now moved to London were Thomas Balogh, who became Economic Adviser to the Prime Minister, and Dudley Seers, who was called home from the UN Economic Commission for Africa by Barbara Castle to set up a staff of economists and statisticians in the new Overseas Development Ministry. Seers was accompanied at ODM by Paul Streeten. Development Studies had acquired a new importance and respectability though, as Seers was later to remark, the early ambition to create a ministry concerned with 'development' was never really realised and the ODM fairly quickly reverted to being an *aid* agency in a narrower sense [*Seers, 1976*].

Seers and Streeten had for some time been involved in official discussions about a 'special institution', to deal with development issues and the training of administrators [*Seers, 1976*]. This notion had first been put forward in 1962 by the Bridges Committee on Training in Public Administration for Overseas Countries. Lord Bridges' Committee reported to the then Department of Technical Cooperation. After various vicissitudes the 'Special Institute' was accepted and featured in the first White Paper of the new ODM in 1965 [*HMSO, 1965*]. It was to be set up at the new University of Sussex and called the 'Institute of Development Studies'. Paul Streeten took over as Acting Director in September 1966 at the time of the Founding Conference. Dudley Seers was appointed Director and took office in 1967. The IDS rapidly became the largest concentration of persons concerned with development studies in the country. Streeten and later Seers argued for a broad range of expertise from many disciplines as a basis for policy studies and this dictated a 'critical minimum size'. The new Institute had a much wider mandate than the special training institution which had first concerned the Bridges Committee. In time, the setting up of the IDS was to have important implications for the JDS, but this was not immediately apparent in the mid-1960s.

As far as the 'academic sector' in Britain was concerned, the setting up of the IDS was an important impact of Labour's policy on Third World development, but it was by no means the only one. In addition, the new ODM expanded scholarship support through the technical assistance programme, for Third World students seeking higher education and training in a number of British universities and institutes. Furthermore, the research sources available through the ODM (as well as other research funding committees) were considerably expanded. As a result, the number of British academics with direct experience of Third World economic, political and social realities grew considerably in this period – creating an enlarged academic constituency for development studies.

Later, in the ensuing Labour administration (1966–70) and in the Tory administration of Edward Heath (1970–74), growth of development teaching and research was slower. By the time Labour returned to power under Callaghan (1974–79), willingness to fund academic activities associated with Third World development was considerably tempered. With Mrs Thatcher's accession in 1979, development studies were not only clearly on the defensive – but, broadly speaking, put into retreat, especially as support *within* British universities weakened in the subsequent period of intra-university struggles for diminishing total resources.

## Twenty-five Years of the Journal

It is, hopefully, not too fanciful to subdivide the 25 years the Journal has been in existence, into three subperiods: a period of 'establishment' (1964–68); a period of consolidation (1968–78) and the most recent period (1978–present) during which the Journal's constituency has 'broadened' somewhat.

## Establishment years (1964–68)

In its foundation and early years the story of the Journal reflected the times. For one thing, most of those who were involved in the years of establishment were members of the recently 'modernised' SOAS, one of the new institutions of the 1960s which was to have a major role in British development studies. For another, the conception and orientation of the Journal in those initial years reflected to a considerable degree those preoccupations which were expressed in the Manchester Conference (which all of the founding members of the Editorial Board attended).

In its first year the *JDS* had a small Editorial Board composed of Edith Penrose as Managing Editor along with Kurt Martin – progenitor of the Manchester Conference – and Alec Nove from Glasgow. By October 1965 (that is, Vol.2, No.1), Arthur Hazlewood from Oxford had joined the Board and Terry Byres and Dennis Dalton had become Review Editors. Subsequently, Dalton left the Board and Byres continued alone as Reviews Editor. Edith Penrose and Terry Byres were mainly responsible for the Journal in these earliest years, which was, to some extent, a SOAS dependency. The SOAS link was strengthened when Christopher Howe joined the Board in early 1967. Others who are still remembered for their (less official) support were Paddy O'Brien and Ken Walker at SOAS – as well as Harry Johnson of LSE and Chicago – who contributed a paper to the first issue. (This paper is included in the collection.) In these years the Journal successfully established itself as a publication outlet for empirical and theoretical papers arising from 'specialised research in economic development'. The editors also sought to publish articles on political development since it was argued that 'problems of political development have an urgency equal to those of economic development, yet political development is a seriously neglected field [*Editorial Board, 1964*].

In the course of 1967, Edith Penrose resigned the Managing Editorship of the Journal. She was succeeded by Arthur Hazlewood and Christopher Howe. Penrose remained on as a Board member and Byres, who had been Reviews Editor since his return from India in 1965, continued in that role.

At the start of 1968 the Board, therefore, consisted of Alec Nove and Kurt Martin together with Edith Penrose, aside from the Managing and Review Editors. The original team was, by and large, still in place.

## Consolidation: (1968–78)

In this period the *JDS* gradually became fully accepted in the British academic community (and increasingly overseas) as an important scholarly journal in its own right. The period was also one in which the composition of the Editorial Board was to change considerably, as the recently formed IDS at Sussex became more involved. *JDS* changed from a 'SOAS dependency' to a 'SOAS–IDS dependency'.

By 1968 the IDS at Sussex had recruited a considerable number of Fellows and had started to form its research programmes. A discussion had started within the Institute about the desirability of starting a journal which would reflect the interdisciplinary approaches the IDS sought to promote in development studies. Against this, a number of Fellows thought that it would not be in the general interest of the Institute to compete with the *JDS* and that it would be preferable to explore the possibilities of a closer editorial relationship to the Journal. In the course of 1968 Paul Streeten started discussions on behalf of the IDS with members of the Editorial Board and with Frank Cass.

In January 1969, Michael Lipton (IDS) joined Arthur Hazlewood and Christopher Howe as a Managing Editor and the Board was increased in size by the addition of Dudley Seers and Bernard Schaffer from IDS and Paul Streeten who had recently returned to the Institute of Commonwealth Studies after his spell as Acting Director of the IDS. There was a further change in late 1969 when Christopher Howe relinquished the Managing Editorship and was replaced by Donal Cruise O'Brien. Subsequently, in 1970, Arthur Hazlewood resigned as a Managing Editor. There followed a period up till late 1973 during which Lipton and Cruise O'Brien were Managing Editors with Byres as Review Editor, and the Board was composed of Hazlewood, Howe, Penrose, and Nove along with de Kadt, Schaffer and Seers from the IDS.

The Board increased further in size in 1974 when Clive Bell and Scarlett Epstein from IDS were recruited, with Norman Long (then at Durham) and David Wall from the University of Sussex. At this time David Lehmann – who at that time had left the IDS for Cambridge – had joined Michael Lipton as Managing Editor, and Donal Cruise O'Brien had left the Board. The Lipton–Lehmann managing editorship continued in this form without major changes until mid-1976. P. Ayres of SOAS joined as Reviews Editor for a while (1974–75), and Mike Faber (then of the University of East Anglia) was recruited to the Board in 1975.

In mid-1976, John Toye from Cambridge joined the Managing Editors. The tripartite managing editorship of Lipton, Lehmann and Toye continued until the end of mid-1981. By this time Michael Lipton had been Managing Editor (for economics) for 12 years (1969–81) and Lehmann had been the 'soc/pol' Managing Editor for seven years.

*A widening constituency: (1978–88)*

By 1978, the *JDS* had a clearly defined place as a scholarly journal in its field. It was, to some extent, perceived as dominated by London and IDS – but, as far as we are aware, this was never an issue of importance or resentment. From 1978, however, this image was to change, as the membership of the Editorial Board was changed by new recruitment. Over the period 1977–78 the Board was 'diversified' by the addition of Alison Scott (Essex), Ashwani Saith (QEH, Oxford), Anthony Thirlwall (Kent), Penelope Roberts (Liverpool), Bryan Roberts (Manchester) and Carlos Fortin (IDS). In January 1980, David Booth (Hull) joined the Board and by April 1980 was functioning as Revies Editor. After 1978, when Michael Lipton spent a period working in Botswana, the Economics Managing Editorship was carried out increasingly by John Toye alone.

The next and most recent major change came in mid-1981. John Toye and Michael Lipton resigned the Managing editorship and the present Managing Editors (Economics), Charles Cooper and Valpy FitzGerald, were appointed. Booth continued as Reviews Editor and Lehmann as 'Soc/Pol' Editor. Bill Brugger (Flinders, South Australia), P.N. Junankar (Essex) and A.I. MacBean (Lancaster) joined the Board. In this period the Economics Managing Editors were based at the Institute of Social Studies in the Hague, Netherlands. In 1984, the Board appointed Karel Jansen of the ISS as an additional economics editor to deal with extended absences of one or other of Cooper or FitzGerald.

In this period the Board was sadly depleted by the death of two of its most distinguished members. Dudley Seers died in 1983 and Bernard Schaffer in 1984.

In early 1988, David Lehmann resigned as Soc/Pol Editor and David Booth left the Review editorship. They were replaced respectively by Mick Moore (IDS) and Barbara Harriss (QEH, Oxford). Lehmann had been a Managing Editor for 13 years; the longest period of office in the Journal's history.

In this period, membership of the Board has been considerably widened to include people from many more faculties and institutes than in the first 15 years or so of the Journal's history. At the same time, probably partly as a result of changing Board membership, the Journal has drawn on a somewhat wider group of scholars than before. There has been a slow though still insufficient increase in the numbers of papers from Third World scholars; and more papers have come from the US and continental Europe than before. It seems, in short, that the Journal has acquired a somewhat more international character.

Throughout its life and changing editorships the Journal has kept rather closely to the objectives with which it was set up. It has attempted to remain multidisciplinary – though it has often proved difficult to do so. From the outset, it has proved easier to meet one of the early objectives than the other: the Journal has been more an outlet for research in political economy and economics than in sociology, political science and anthropology. The Editorial Board has tried to meet this problem in various ways. In the first place, whenever Board appointments are made, a good deal of attention has been paid to disciplinary 'balance'. Second, all Managing Editors have sought to encourage submission of sociology/politics articles – though with limited success. Third, and perhaps most effectively, successive editorial teams have carefully maintained the Book Review section of the Journal and ensured that it covers an appropriately wide range of disciplinary topics.

Finally, from early on in the Journal's history editors have used the system of Special Issues – intended to widen disciplinary coverage (though the Special Issues have served other purposes too, such as review of rapidly expanding research fields, encouragement of new themes in research, etc.). Special Issues have appeared intermittently since the early days. They are edited by guest editors, on invitation by the Editorial Board. The list of Special Issues is substantial.

July 1970: *Social Planning*
Editor: Raymond Apthorpe
April 1972: *Measuring Development: Development Indicators*
Editor: Nancy Basten
October 1972: *Science and Technology*
Editor: Charles Cooper
January 1975: *Employment and Income Distribution*
Editor: Frances Stewart
January 1977: *Finance in Developing Countries*
Editor: P.C. Ayres
July 1978: *Population and Development*
Editor: Geoffrey Hawthorne
April 1979: *Trade and Poor Economies*
Editors: John Toye and Sheila Smith
April 1981: *African Women in the Development Process*
Editor: Nici Nelson
April 1984: *Development and the Rural–Urban Divide*
Editors: M. Moore and John Harriss
October 1984: *Third World Industrialisation in the 1980s.*
Editors: R. Kaplinsky and M. Schultz
October 1985: *The Agrarian Question in Socialist Transitions*
Editor: Ashwani Saith
July 1988: *Markets within Planning: Socialist Economic Management in the Third World*
Editors: E.V.K. FitzGerald and Marc Wuyts

It is some measure of the role of the Special Issues that just on a third of the articles presented in this collection were drawn from them, although the Special Issues have accounted for only 12 per cent of the total number of issues published since the Journal started.

III. SELECTED ARTICLES

## Criteria for Selection

Selecting some 20 articles out of almost 700 published in the first 25 years of the Journal's life, was a daunting task. The preliminary screening criterion was that those chosen should not only be outstanding in their own right and stand the test of time, but also be related to key topics in development debates. The resulting list contains an implicit bias towards theoretical pieces which make up half our collection. This undoubtedly understates the results of Journal policy of publishing the results of outstanding quantitative analysis and contributions on current policy issues.

A balance was also struck between articles of a more 'economic' nature and those originating in the other social sciences; although in all cases we tried to reflect the interdisciplinary tradition of the Journal and of the British approaches to development studies (although just under half of the papers come from abroad). We also tried to make sure that the range of analytical approaches among our authors was well reflected; ranging from those of a neo-classical persuasion to those working in the Marxian manner.

Out of this selection process the main themes began to emerge almost of their own accord, and they form the basis for the discussion that follows. The central theme has been the working out of various aspects of development models constructed by the 'pioneers' in the two post-war decades before the foundation of the Journal. We have selected papers on: intersectoral accumulation and income distribution; on foreign trade; on labour markets and wages; and on the organisation of production and distribution. As one of the central problems of development studies has been the nature and role of the state, we have included a group of papers on this topic, reflecting the range of this debate. Finally, as befits a professional journal, we have included a discussion of the nature of the subject itself – both its definition and its defence.

It might be argued that these (or other) articles might have been better grouped according to problem areas such as poverty, or by sector such as agriculture, but we felt that this would have obscured the essential intellectual continuity of the debates. Thus, although a selection of this kind is inevitably fairly subjective and has the advantages of hindsight in establishing patterns in the development of the subject, it does demonstrate, we believe, the existence of distinctive intellectual tradition. Whether the Journal has contributed thereby to the resolution of the problems of underdevelopment, we would hesitate to say.

## Intersectoral Issues in Accumulation: Dualism

The concept of dualism has of course had a profound influence on Development Studies in general and Development Economics in particular. Dualist economic structures – especially agriculture/industry forms – were characteristic of much Classical analysis. However, the first formulation as far as the Third World is concerned was by Boeke and other Dutch economists and related to the pre-independence Indonesian economy. The notion only attained general currency in development economics after publication of W.A. Lewis's analysis of development with 'unlimited supplies of labour'.

Lewis's achievement was essentially that he brought the concept of 'disguised unemployment' into a more coherent framework – which he explicitly drew from Classical economics. The idea of disguised unemployment itself was widely discussed at the time: Lewis himself had been a member of the UN Group of Experts responsible for the Report on *Measures for the Economic Development of Under-developed Countries* in 1951, which concerned itself with the mobilisation of 'excess labour' from the rural sector. Ragnar Nurkse's concept of surplus labour as 'virtual saving' which could be used to 'finance' public works and which antedated Lewis, was similarly based on a notion of 'unlimited supplies'.[2] Lewis's article, however, was distinguished by an attempt to link the 'unlimited supplies' idea to a more specific form of economic structures special to ex-colonial economic systems.

The article and, more broadly, the dualist labour surplus idea was a point of departure for a large literature. Some was predictably highly critical. Lewis may have made appeal to the Classicals in his formulation but was vigorously attacked for being very unclassical because ahistorical. Policy responses in dualistic economic structures made no sense unless the origins and hence causes of duality were understood as historic phenomena. Such criticisms became especially prevalent in the 1960s as *dependencia* thinking evolved in Latin America out of older theories of imperialism and as attention turned to the mechanisms of underdevelopment – that is, to what became called the 'development of underdevelopment'.

At the same time, despite these criticisms (and often without acknowledging them) dual economy concepts were widely used as organising principles in other areas of development economics. For example, they gave rise to a closely related large literature on optimal resource allocation, typified by Marglin's work on allocation in the labour surplus economy [*Marglin, 1976*]. Theoretical research on optimal allocation was the point of departure for project appraisal methodology and other practical attempts to use 'shadow prices' [*UNIDO, 1972; Little and Mirrlees, 1974*].

Dual economy structures have profoundly influenced attempts to model economic processes in developing countries. In part this arose from elaboration and development of Lewis's original theoretical formulation. A widely quoted and particularly well known example is the Todaro extension of the Lewis structure by incorporation of an economic theory of rural–urban migration [*Todaro, 1969*]. Equally well known is the work of Fei and Ranis who made a systemic exploration of the dynamics of the simple dual economy structure, by setting it in the framework of a comprehensive macroeconomic model [*Fei and Ranis, 1961*]. The Ranis–Fei model allows for what might be called a 'Lewis' period of capital accumulation, essentially through a perfectly elastic labour supply at a fixed wage – followed by a 'neo-classical period' when full employment prevails, and a marginal product theory of wage formation displaces the classical subsistence wage. In their 1975 article in this collection ('A Model of Growth and Employment in the Open Dualistic Economy: The Cases of Korea and Taiwan'), Ranis and Fei open up the 'traditional closed dualistic model of development' of Lewis.

The growth patterns of the initially labour surplus economies are characterised by 'turning points', which are exemplified in the article using data from South Korea and Taiwan. The first and basic turning-point is the 'commercialisation point' where the labour-surplus condition ends. After this real wages rise – with major impacts on local demand for consumer goods. After this point, the authors argue, industrial export will be based less on labour-intensity and more on skills and fixed capital; in addition there will be increasing pressure of local demand for manu-factured consumer goods. The 'reversal point' is the point at which an absolute decline in rural population starts, and labour-saving technology is increasingly required in the agricultural sector. Third, there is the 'ex-port substitution' point after which primary goods exports on the colonial model are replaced increasingly by labour-intensive manufactured exports. This export substitution point customarily follows a period of consumer goods import substitution. The export substitution phase (usually encouraged by state intervention), shortens the time needed to reach the 'commercialisation point'. Finally, there may be a switching point at which the country shifts towards agricultural imports as a result of rising domestic incomes (and constrained natural resources). This article is one of the earlier attempts to come to terms with patterns of economic growth in the NICs.

The influence of the dual economy concept is still noticeable despite increasing sophistication of model structures facilitated by widespread access to computers.[3] A recent example is Lance Taylor's analysis of two-sector systems in which lagging food supply from the 'traditional' sector induces inflation [*Taylor, 1983*]. This relates to the critical role of the traditional sector as a supplier of wage goods, originally emphasised by Kalecki [*Kalecki, 1972*].

The dual economy model continues to inform the wider span of development economics thinking despite the many criticisms it en-counters. Indeed, one measure of its contribution is precisely that the criticism has been extraordinarily fruitful of new ideas. Good examples of such criticism are found in two articles discussed in the section on 'Wages and Labour' in this collection: Arrighi's attack on Barber's application of the Lewis model to the issue of labour supply in colonial Rhodesia, which underlines the complexities of political economy by and large ignored in Lewis's formulation; and Bent Hansen's rejection of the model for Egypt. And equally good examples of extensions of dual economy thinking are the articles by Singer and by Galbis in the collection.

Singer, who made his own contributions to understanding of economic structures in the Third World [*Singer, 1950*], here develops the concept in two ways. First, at a general level he argues that there are four key elements in dualism: coexistence of 'superior' and 'inferior' conditions in a given space at the same time; a high degree of permanence ('. . . the coexistence is chronic, not transitional . . .'); if anything the 'degree of superiority' tends to increase; and finally, a tendency for (Myrdalian) 'backwash' effects to outweigh 'spread' effects. Singer then argues that these general features of dualism as a concept are as applicable to the international economy as to the national units which make it up – which, he says, explains why concepts used in the analysis of the international economy, turn up in dualist analysis (for example, internal terms of trade, net resource flows, migration, etc.). Finally, he argues that an international technological dualism of great economic importance is echoed in an intra-national dualism of the same type – and examines the forces making for both inter- and intra-national patterns. The particular contribution of Singer's paper is the introduction of the idea of an international 'dualism' in science and technology – with a corresponding intra-national dualism within the Third World countries, where evidently most science and technology resources are locked up in the modern sector.

The final article in this group – Galbis on 'Financial Intermediation and Economic Growth in Less-Developed Countries: A Theoretical Approach' – is of a different order. It reflects the growing pre-occupation in the 1970s with the effect of manifest dualities in the organisation of financial sectors between the 'modern' and 'traditional' parts of the economy. Galbis sets up a dual economy model in which the 'modern sector' has higher marginal productivities of capital and rates of return than the less efficient 'backward' sector. The 'backward' sector entrepreneurs are self financing without access to capital markets, though they may make 'financial' investments in the form of bank deposits. Firms in the modern sector may finance investment in high capital productivity technology through their own savings or by bank borrowing. The rate of interest facing 'modern sector' borrowers is kept low by policy and credit rationing prevails. Galbis analyses the effects of liberalisation with high real interest rates and shows that it would generate growth, primarily through favouring higher proportionate investments in high return modern sector firms.

*International Economic Relationships*

Decisions about trade and other aspects of international economic relationships have naturally played a critical part in development policies. Changes in the structure of production are nearly always at least implicit in development strategies and such changes nearly always entail transformations of international trading relationships. For example, Rosenstein-Rodan's 'Big Push' proposals for Southern and Eastern European industrialisation [*Rosenstein-Rodan, 1943*] put forward in the war years were argued partly on grounds of sub-optimality of private saving and mainly on grounds of external economies and increasing returns to scale which could only be captured by simultaneous investment in a number of industries. Nurkse used similar arguments in favour of 'balanced growth', which he quite explicitly counterposed to international specialisation [*Nurkse, 1958*]. The appeal to externalities and economies of scale as a basis for resource allocation had a substantial ancestry: in one of the earliest discussions of planned development strategy, Preobrazhensky raised the issue of dynamic scale economies of learning in support of local production of certain capital goods – and incidentally by implication at least accepted the efficiency advantages of international trade to a surprising degree [*Preobrazhensky, 1962*].

Some of the arguments which put the merits of trade in question were taken into the corpus of neo-classical literature, especially in so far as they related to the 'accepted' range of market failures [e.g. *Chenery, 1961*]. Others, particularly those which responded to market failure with protectionism, were vigorously rejected. The essay by Harry G. Johnson in this collection, taken from the first number of the Journal, 'Tariffs and Economic Development: Some Theoretical Issues', is an excellent example of the genre. Johnson finds the origins of post-war Third World protectionism in the 1930s. He quotes Keynes' endorsement of tariff arguments for employment and pre-war Central European concerns with the promotion of industrialisation by tariff policy on the German model: '. . . the economic philosophy underlying this approach was transfused into the mainstream of economic theory through the emigration of . . . outstanding European scholars induced by the political developments of the 1930s . . .'. The paper is a vigorous rejection of protectionism in all cases except those where optimum tariff rules apply – carried through in a comparative statics framework. With this framework, Johnson argues for the use of subsidies in preference to tariff protection in all cases where market failure can reasonably be held to apply. This is a style and pattern of argument which has become increasingly familiar in the 1980's with the revival of ancient orthodoxies – but the Johnson piece belongs to an earlier round in the debate. It is interesting, though, that Johnson does not reject or belittle the possibilities of market failure – as Little, Scitovsky and Scott were to in their influential OECD study [*Little, Scitovsky and Scott, 1970*]; he simply argues that such failures are most appropriately dealt with by subsidy.

The Little–Scitovsky–Scott study with its accompanying country analyses can with hindsight be thought of as marking a turning-point in the discussion of trade policy. By the mid-1970s, structuralist approaches to trade policy were in retreat. The excesses of some import substitution policies became the justification for rejecting all – and for blanket proposals for a switch to export promotion policies. Earlier trade debates which seem to have been resolved in a structuralist direction were re-opened – with the difference that latter day liberals are not as open to market failure arguments as were their predecessors. The new liberalism rejects deficient governments in favour of deficient markets – grounds which, incidentally, are considerably more difficult to counter than the older generation of theoretical argument.

Alongside of proposals for re-thinking trade policy in function of the need for structural change in the domestic economy, there have been at least two other traditions which questioned the benefits of international specialisation. The first is the empirical tradition which grew around the thinking of Raoul Prebisch and, especially, around the view that the international economy is so structured that gains from trade occur in the 'centre' (industrial) economies as opposed to the less developed periphery. Essentially, Prebisch's arguments rest on the view that First World industrial markets are oligopolistic whilst the international market primary (Third World) export is competitive. These arguments and the evidence on which they were based were hotly contested but, nevertheless, had widespread impact – particularly in Latin America (where they legitimised import substitution policies which, in many cases, antedated the Prebisch–Singer thesis by decades). This tradition of structuralist analysis of trade relationships is represented by two papers in the collection. James Love's 1979 discussion of 'Trade Concentration and Export Instability' and Gerry Helleiner's 'Structural Aspects of Third World Trade: Some Trends and Some Prospects'. The articles fall naturally into the field defined as structuralist by Hollis Chenery: '. . . the structuralist approach attempts to identify specific rigidities, lags and other characteristics of . . . structure . . . that affect economic adjustments and the choice of development policy'.

Love attacks an old topic in a new and convincing way. He re-opens the discussion on relationships between concentration of developing country export trade (by commodity and by geographic region) and the instability of export earnings. Love uses a statistic which measures the contribution to instability of export earnings coming from major export products (the 'proportionate contribution statistic'), and determines the proportion of total export instability which this product group accounts. Using data from 52 countries (and trade data at three-digit SIR grouping), Love finds that major products and markets contribute disproportionately to instability in total earnings in 46 countries. Love's results stand in contrast to those which have been obtained in the past using regression analysis based on Gini-coefficients and instability measures.

Helleiner (on 'Third World Trade: Trends and Prospects') is mainly concerned with analysing the incidence and implications of intra-firm trade. The increasing importance of trade *within* multi-national enterprises (or between large enterprises and more loosely affiliated Third World firms – for example, licensees) means that the basic assumptions of neo-classical trade theory – especially the immobility of 'factors' – are not met. Welfare and income impacts of this form of trade are unclear – though it is obvious that it raises important questions about gains from trade in the Singer tradition [*Singer, 1950*]. Helleiner distinguishes trade in primary goods from trade in manufactures: '. . . at the very time that primary product exports from the Third World are being sold increasingly *outside* the closed channels of transnational corporations, manufactured

exports from developing countries seem to be growing . . . inside them'.
These changing patterns raise new problems for Third World exporters –
in particular, they increase the relative bargaining position of transnational enterprises.

The second critical tradition in which questions have been raised about
the benefits of international specialisation for developing countries is
primarily theoretical. It is in the main radical, drawing a substantial
inspiration from Marxian theories of imperialism and it has from time to
time 'intertwined' with structuralist thought. 'Intertwining' is particularly
noticeable in the close connections between the Latin American
*dependencia* analyses of the impact of the international economy on
developing countries, and the Prebisch analysis. Criticism of Prebisch
as having merely exchanged 'trade dependency' for 'investment
dependency' were important points of departure in the development of
dependency thinking. In the final analysis the dependency school added
little real content to structuralism – but probably did something to
open the way to subsequent 'world system' analysis associated with
Wallerstein.

Also in the theoretical radical tradition is the body of scholarship on
'unequal exchange' and related concepts, which took A. Emmanuel's
*Unequal Exchange: A Study of the Imperialism of Trade* [1972] as its
main point of departure. Emmanuel's analysis is Marxist in inspiration,
but others have followed a neo-Ricardian line. Lyn Mainwaring's article,
in this collection, on 'International Trade and the Transfer of Labour
Value', responds to this line of trade theory. Mainwaring's theoretical
analysis deals with a single important dimension of 'unequal exchange'
(or, rather, non-equivalent exchange) theory – notably the effect of
including imported intermediate goods in the schema. He shows that
when these goods are included, key conclusions of the unequal exchange
theories no longer hold. In particular, it becomes possible that labour
value might flow from the centre economies *to* the periphery.

*Employment and Wages*

The process of transformation of the labour force during industrialisation
had been at the heart of the classical concept of development, the
objective being higher productivity and living standards. The means for
this were growing *wage* employment (that is, absorption into the so-called
'modern sector') as opposed to self employment or employment in family
enterprise; and the process of creating a proletariat was regarded as
central to the concept of social transformation. This assumption was
implicit not only in the 1951 UN *Measures*, but also in the ILO [1970]
*Towards Full Employment*, which laid the foundations for much of
the subsequent empirical work in the field. The evident *failure* of the
corporate sector to absorb the rapidly growing workforce (itself the result
of successful investment in health, incidentally) and the growth of the
urban 'informal' sector due to internal migration were seen to be related
fundamentally to technological choices in the tradition of modern

development economics. The arguments for greater employment creation in agriculture (via land reform, co-operatives, etc.) and public works followed the same logic.

Wage determination in the classical model had originally been Ricardian, in the sense that subsistence agriculture was held to set the supply price of labour or (in Kalecki's interpretation) determines the real wage through food supply. The Lewis model could also be adapted by allowing for the modern sector wage to be set in neo-Ricardian form by negotiation with employers, and indeed empirical research appeared to indicate fairly stable wage shares in value added at the branch level in LDCs.

This led to the construction of a distinct approach in terms of a 'shadow wage rate' to reflect the fact that the social cost of employment (that is, the production lost in the activity from which the labour was absorbed) was much less than the wage [*OECD, 1968*]. Urban underemployment could also be explained in terms of *expected* wage income [*Todaro: 1969*] derived from the probability of gaining stable employment, which would equalise with rural incomes as migration proceeds. From these approaches, it was but one (albeit logically and empirically unjustified) step to argue that high formal sector wages (set by misguided governments, trade unions, etc.) were responsible for underemployment and that the solution was to deregulate wages and employment conditions entirely.

The article by Hansen, 'Marginal Productivity Wage Theory and Subsistence Wage Theory in Egyptian Agriculture', in this collection, is a valuable early critique of wage determination in the Lewis model and the contemporary work by Fei and Ranis, based on the study of long-run trends in Egyptian rural wages. Hansen sets out to test a marginal productivity theory based on Cobb–Douglas income shares as against a formalisation of the dualist model where the marginal productivity of labour is very small so wages are stable, being set institutionally to relate to subsistence requirements (Lewis) or equal to average peasant product (Fei and Ranis). Within an institutional framework traced back to 1880, data for the 1914–61 period are analysed: even though the well-known shortcomings of the Cobb–Douglas method are glossed over, the results would apply equally to an *average*-product theory.

Hansen's results indicate that rural wages in Egypt were far from stable, oscillating with commodity prices and seasons, and exhibiting wide differentials. This indicates that prices of both outputs and wage goods, in combination with labour productivity itself, explain wage movements quite well; even though long-run trends may well be related to subsistence costs. Hansen suggests, moreover, that population trends are sufficient to explain surplus labour, thereby further undermining the dualist model. None the less, the real value of this article is as a demonstration of elegant analytics, particularly the relationship of wages to the internal and external terms of trade which is, in spirit at least, in the classical tradition.

The radical critique of the received model saw the labour process as an integrated phenomenon, where labour in the 'informal' sector serves as a reserve army in the Marxian sense, sustaining profit rates by holding down the wage rate and guaranteeing a flexible labour force. This contrasts with the more structuralist approach of labour market segmentation and 'marginalisation' of surplus urban labour indicated above.

Arrighi's 1970 piece is also an empirical test of the Lewis model, but from a rather different angle, as he is mostly concerned with the historical roots of the creation of the surplus labour system. In particular, he is concerned to explain why in Rhodesia, African responsiveness to wage employment opportunities increased continuously, irrespective of whether real wages were rising, falling or constant. Arrighi shows that after the slumps of the 1920s, disguised unemployment in the peasant sector (that is, lack of labour supply to the British mines) was no longer due to the lack of incentives, as it had been earlier, but rather to the structural disequilibrium between access to productive assets and the subsistence requirements of the peasantry.

In other words, dualism did obtain after the 1930s, but only because it was *created* by administrative mechanisms which *ensured* the required labour supply at the 'desired' wage rate. Finally, Arrighi identifies a 'post-Lewis' phase of rising African wages, *not* because surplus labour has been adsorbed (as in Ranis–Fei) but, rather, because of the need for skilled (that is, differentiated) labour in industry and services. As with Hansen, the result is to enrich our understanding of the structural foundations of labour markets.

Further research indicated that there was a far greater degree of 'articulation' between these forms of organisation than had been previously organised, finally undermining the dualist model by showing how households allocate their labour power between sectors and over time. One inference from this is that the wage as such becomes less relevant to poverty, being replaced by the bundle of entitlements generated by the various activities of the household. Alternatively, it could be argued that all this meant was that the costs of reproducing the labour force were not borne by employers (through wages, social security, etc.) but by the family, particularly women.

The third article selected in this group reflects this more recent strand of critique and introduces the essential gender dimension to the issue. Alison McEwen Scott, in her 'Women and Industrialisation: Examining the "Female Marginalisation" Thesis' [*1986*], has a double aim: clarifying what is meant by marginalisation and informality in the labour force as a whole; and examining in particular the hypothesis that women are first absorbed into manufacturing employment and then excluded as industrialisation moves from extensive to intensive stages. She provides detailed analysis of Brazilian and Peruvian labour statistics, but finds that the hypothesis is in effect untestable as conventionally defined. More positively, she points out how both segregation and substitution are involved in labour demand, the relationship between household and factory employment, and the gender structuring of labour supply in terms of 'quality' (that is, subordination, etc.) as well as price. Again, this is an example of constructive critique.

## Organisation of Production and Exchange

The received development model had assumed that while 'traditional' production was constrained by resources and attitudes; 'modern' production would expand as rapidly as investment permitted. There was also a tendency to assume that large-scale production was necessarily more efficient than small. Domestic prices were neo-classically determined by competitive market forces at home and abroad, except for the effect of surplus labour. Decisions were taken on well-behaved profit-maximisation principles in the modern sector; while the traditional peasants and artisans would maximise family consumption for given land and labour resources.

However, empirical research on enterprise behaviour indicated that these assumptions were not wholly convincing. In the corporate sector, multinationals were revealed to operate on world-wide product cycles; state enterprises to respond to government investment plans or managerial aggrandisement; and domestic business to be prone to speculation and capital flight. Small-scale production, on the contrary, was revealed as more entrepeneurial than had been assumed, both in terms of its own household logic and in supply response to market forces.

Lipton's 1968 article is an outstanding example of this empirical revisionism. He starts off from Schultz' characterisation of the peasant as 'efficient but poor' along neo-classical lines – itself a considerable shift from the original dualist model. This characterisation included perfect competition in product markets and continual adjustment of the input–output mix to equalise 'marginal product value equivalents'. Lipton argues that this behaviour is neither possible nor desirable for the peasant due to uncertainty about the future and systematic price distortions at the macro-level (for example, urban bias). Moreover, Schultz' econometric results are flawed by the assumption of perfect competition in their methodology; Lipton proposes an alternative 'survival algorithm' as an explanation of rational security-centred peasant behaviour. This is not only more consistent with field experience but, in addition, brought the economic debate on peasant behaviour back to a fruitful inter-disciplinary collaboration.

Research on the way in which technology choices are made in practice revealed that investment decisions in LDCs were more complex than had been thought and that, in particular, models based on continuous production function and homogeneous products were unrealistic. Income distribution and advertising were shown to be crucial determinants of demand patterns. The debate led not only to a revision of technology policy (which generally moved from 'absorption' of foreign technology towards 'appropriate technology' and 'learning by doing'), but also to a re-consideration of employment, income distribution and growth strategies.

This interplay between theory or practice is well illustrated by Stewart [1972] on *The Choice of Technique in Developing Countries*, itself a contribution to a Special Issue edited by Cooper on *Science and Techno-*

*logy*. The key factors are product choice and managerial objectives –
which include an aversion to large bodies of unskilled workers; while the
effect of technical choice must also be seen in terms of savings and growth.
This accumulation process does lead, however, to a determinate technological development path, the result of which is that labour-intensive
technologies are also *old* technologies. Much depends, of course, upon
definitions of the categories too: for the skilled labour constraint may
actually be reduced by machine pacing, while the inclusion of working capital when measuring capital-intensity usually mitigates against
apparently labour-intensive production methods.

The organisation of domestic commerce is not well researched;
although in contrast pricing policy is a matter for heated debate. An early
article [*1965*] by Bauer on 'Price Control in Underdeveloped Countries'
does recognise that markets are not only rendered imperfect by government intervention but also by concentration of ownership – particularly
among importers. Abnormal profits are generated, which are distributed
throughout the marketing chain, although retail traders tend to be fairly
competitive. Bauer sees considerable justification for price controls in
times of supply shortage, but is concerned that the main benefits will
accrue to wholesalers, or at best to those with access to regulated supplies
(that is, state employees) as opposed to those purchasing on the parallel
markets. In consequence, he suggests that in the absence of adequate
fiscal controls, state trading as equilibrium prices may be the best solution,
with the scarcity rents thus adsorbed being assigned to more worthy uses.

### The State and Development

As we have already seen, the initial faith in the state as the agent of
postcolonial development in general, and of economic transformation in
particular had come under serious question by the late 1960s The original
view had been based on *a priori* logic (that is, the absence of an industrial
bourgeoisie) and on a particular reading of late industrialisers such as
Japan. The cumulative experience of state intervention in the Third world
led to empirical research, usually of an independent academic nature,
which transformed the study of the politics of development from its
previous basis in modernisation theory. To this was added a new
dimension of 'dependency' thought which took up (via Baran) the Leninist theme of frustrated capitalism in neo-colonial situations. This spread
from Latin America (Furtado) to Africa (Amin, Leys) and Asia, forming
into a more sophisticated analysis which identified the role of the state as
an intermediary between the domestic and international spheres.

The 1969 article by Sunkel on 'National Development Policy and
External Dependence in Latin America', is a significant contribution to
this dependency debate. Sunkel does not see dependency as a stagnant
phenomenon, but rather the result of the subordinate insertion of a
particular social formation into the international division of labour. The
economic dimension is the failure of import substitution to progress
towards capital goods production, so that manufacturing only produces

for the consumer while traditional exports 'produce' investment goods through trade. This makes LDCs more dependent, more vulnerable and more unstable. The political dimension is that the domestic political formation around the developmental (that is, 'national') state, which must undertake industrialising tasks but cannot acquire sufficient control over local resources, leads to debt and inflation.

This criticism of dependency led to deeper analysis of domestic factors, particularly the subordination of the national state to sectional interests in the form of specific class structures and groups such as landlords and bureaucrats. None the less, it was difficult to eliminate a normative element as authors still searched for the constraint or class responsible for the failure to industrialise.

O'Donnell [1978] concentrates on domestic regime formation, explicitly linking economic development to the balance of class interests, in his 'State and Alliances in Argentina, 1956–76'. The relevant interest groups are clearly identified and their conflict/alliances traced over time by reference to major macroeconomic indicators. In particular, the trade-off between export growth (of wage goods in the Argentine case), capital accumuaation and income distribution is analysed in political terms; leading to a perceptive analysis of economic policy formation around problems such as wages, inflation and the balance of payments. Although this sort of analysis does assume the subordination of the national to the world economy, it is explicitly opposed to the dependency school as being too general a notion to have any useful explanatory power.

A completely different approach to the problem of the state involved looked in more detail at the political sociology (and the anthropology) of administration itself; both from the point of view of decision making and from that of microeconomic behaviour (corruption, access to services, etc.). Again, this gradually moved away from normative discussion of 'goals' etc. towards the study of the phenomenon in itself. Schaffer's 1970 paper on 'Social Planning as Administrative Decisionmaking' is part of the Special Issue on *Social Planning* which stressed the interest of the Journal in development administration and the social services. Schaffer makes a conscious move away from prescription towards a critical evaluation of the state itself: bureaucratic decisionmaking, administrative adaptation and popular access are studied in order to generate suggestions for the improvement of the information systems for social planning which would include political debate on options and the participation of those affected. This approach also provides a useful contrast to the somewhat 'economistic' political economy of the first two authors; and leads naturally into Schaffer's later work on 'development discourse' inspired by Foucault.

One of the more fascinating analyses of the micro-relationship between the state and civil society published in the Journal is the 1982 article on Indian canal administration by Wade: 'The System of Administrative and Political Corruption'. Wade describes how irrigation engineers generate bribes from farmers by discretionary control of access to water, and how this system is reproduced through the personnel promotion system. The value of this approach is double: first, in the meticulous gathering of data on a very sensitive question, and second, in the absence of censure or moralising. Wade also avoids the simplistic view that such problems arise from government distortion of markets, leading to the so-called 'rent seeking society'. In contrast, Wade sees corruption (and thus poor supply performance) as just one facet of Indian local politics, which could be counteracted by a combination of improved technical coordination (to overcome problems of joint access and supervision) at the centre and greater territorial control by organised farmers – the exercise of 'voice'.

The contribution of the Journal to the debate on the state in socialist LDCs probably merits comment. In the 1980s interest in liberalising economic reforms understandably grew, above all as a reaction against the 'soviet' model of central planning. The Special Issue edited by Saith on *The Agrarian Question in Socialist Transitions* [1985] took up the debate on the relation between state and peasantry in the rural sector; while the Special Issue edited by FitzGerald and Wuyts [1988] on *Markets Within Planning: Socialist Economic Management in the Third World* tackled the problems of macroeconomic policy in semi-liberalised poor economies.

*Definition and Defence*

Occasionally, practitioners of development studies have written papers 'defining' broad issues of importance for future research or defending important parts of the field of enquiry. Over the years, the Journal has attracted a significant number of contributions of this kind, which either set established wisdoms in place or, in some cases, defend the field of study. Some examples are included in the collection. They include Paul Streeten's 'Frontiers of Development Studies' [1967], Bernstein on 'Modernisation Theory and Sociological Study of Development', Seers on 'What are we trying to Measure?' [1972], and John Toye on 'The Disparaging of Development Economics' [1983].

Streeten's article is characteristically questioning of a wide range of set positions – regardless of their disciplinary or ideological origins. He discusses five areas. First, there is the Rostowian Stages of Growth approach to development, which enjoyed some attention in the 1960s (and which still creeps back into discussion from time to time). Stages simply ignore the crucial historical reality that growth in some countries 'at the centre' irreversibly changes the context for others in significant ways. If one accepts this it makes little sense to talk of stages since the objective conditions for accumulation are continually changing. Streeten then attacks in turn: simplistic approaches to education policy inspired by the 'sources of growth' and 'education planning' schools; overreactions in favour of agricultural development after the excessive concentration on industrialisation in the 1950s: the unquestioning use of shadow prices in investment evaluation; and 'single barrier' approaches to development policy.

Dudley Seers' article, 'What are we trying to Measure?', is an antidote to simple-minded reliance on per capita income measures of 'development'. It belongs in the questioning tradition of 'Limitations of the Special Case' (see Part I), though it has probably been less influential. This is probably because it has proved difficult to establish alternative measures – despite the research on 'social indicators'. Seers correctly starts from the position that measurement of 'development' (an intrinsically normative concept) must start from a knowledge of development objectives. The first puzzle is: whose objectives? Seers rejects 'government objectives' and 'other countries experience' on the grounds that the relevant values 'are staring us in the face'. The universally accepted aim is the realisation of the potential of human personality; the absolute necessity for this is obvious '. . . enough food . . .'. Seers then proceeds to tie together an argument focussing on elimination of poverty, provision of employment, and income redistribution as fundamental requirements. National income measures are 'not totally meaningless'. They are 'inappropriate as indicators of development', but useful as measures of potential. The limitations of national income measures are then explored in more detail – and alternative measures are discussed (poverty standards, infantile mortality, employment, inequality, etc.). The article ends with a characteristic statement on political requirements:

> There are, of course, political dimensions to international as to national development. A big step was taken in the first post-war decade with the creation of a whole system – the United Nations and its agencies. But since then progress has been very gradual, due basically to the unwillingness of the rich countries to limit their sovereignty and accept the authority of international organisations. The continued eruption of wars is an eloquent indicator of a lack of political progress which goes far to explain the negative development of the world as a whole.

Henry Bernstein's article, 'Modernisation Theory and the Study of Development', is focussed on 'methodological and macro-sociological issues'. Bernstein sets out with a discussion of the origins of the concept of development, in which he notes that the insufficiency of economic conceptualisation led to recognition of the need for participation of other social science disciplines. The paper then outlines constituents of the sociology of development and, in particular, stresses the dominance of the 'modernisation' concept. Bernstein then seeks to confront '. . . modernisation theory . . . with the question of the historical context in which the . . . impact . . . on indigenous 'traditional' societies is first located . . .'. For Bernstein, the concept of the dual society (which is useful for modernisation) obscures the critical issue: 'It is precisely the inaugural mechanisms . . . the intrusion of a market economy . . . (etc.) . . . which are the basis of the creation of underdevelopment within the frmework of the political economy of imperialism.' It is precisely through historical understanding of dual economy/society processes that understanding of underdevelopment will proceed.

The final article in the collection is John Toye's, 'The Disparagement of Development Economics'. This is in the form of a commentary on Peter

Bauer's book, *Equality, the Third World and Economic Delusion* [*Bauer, 1981*], though Toye points out that his purpose is to meet a wider issue: the disparagement of development economics in a wider context 'by academics of a conservative persuasion . . . [seeking to] . . . denigrate the standards of those (who) . . . criticise existing arrangements'. Toye's article is important as one of a few which have taken up this challenge head on (see also Stewart [*1985*]; also published in the *JDS*.

Toye takes up Bauer's criticisms – especially his accusations of lack of rigour – one by one and confronts them with arguments, drawing on scholarly research in development economics. Bauer's sweeping, and often facile, generalisations are revealed in a methodical way: development economists have not persisted with Malthusian doctrines for political reasons; nor have they, as a group, proposed commodity price stabilisation schemes for political reasons. Bauer's attacks on redistribution policies and economists who propose them, are met on their own terms (that is, that people have a 'right' to their incomes, and that costs of redistribution, especially disincentive effects, outweigh benefits) and effectively countered. So are arguments on the role of the state and on foreign aid. In his conclusions, Toye lists the defects in Bauer's arguments – a failure to discriminate economists' statements from those of politicians, UN agency spokesmen, and newspaper leader writers; presentation of a partial picture of real academic debates on international income distribution, and other issues; mistakes of logic; and reliance on unqualified generalisation.

It is appropriate that the selection should end with Toye's paper, for it reflects a current state of conflict, or rather – as Toye puts it, a 'campaign [which] could be very successful in draining public resources away . . . from those engaged in a wide range of social science disciplines, including development studies in general and development economics in particular. Unfortunately, the campaign is not a purely academic one, and in the final analysis cannot be countered by scholarship alone. It must, nevertheless, be met head-on.

NOTES

1. In some circles this migration was referred to as the Great Trek.
2. UN Department of Economic Affairs, *Measures for the Economic Development of Under-developed Countries*, New York, May 1951. There was, in addition, an earlier UN publication on *National and International Measures for Full Employment* in December 1949. Also R. Nurkse, *Problems of Capital Formation in Underdeveloped Countries*, Blackwell, Oxford, 1953, which was based on lectures which Nurkse gave in Brazil in 1951.
3. See, for example, Blitzer, *et al.*, *Economy-wide Models and Development Planning*, World Bank, 1975, pp.40, 42 and pp.66–70.

REFERENCES

Arndt, H., 1985, 'The Origins of Structuralism', *World Development*, Vol.13, No.2.

Baran, P., 1957, *The Political Economy of Growth*, New York: Monthly Review Press.

Bauer, P.T., 1981, *Equality, the Third World and Economic Delusion*, London: Weidenfeld & Nicolson.

Bernstein, H., 1973, *Development and Underdevelopment*, Harmondsworth: Penguin.

Blackhouse, R., 1985, *A History of Modern Economic Analysis*, Oxford: Blackwell.

Blitzer, C., et al., 1975, *Economy-wide Models and Development Planning*, World Bank.

Brandt Commission, 1980, *North–South: a Programme for Survival*, New York: Pan Books.

Carnoy, M., 1984, *The State and Political Theory*, New Jersey, NJ: Princeton University Press.

Chenery, H.B., 1961, 'Comparative Advantage and Development Policy', *American Economic Review* (March).

Chenery, H.B., 1975, 'The Structuralist Approach to Development Policy', *American Economic Review*, Papers and Proceedings (May).

Chenery, H.B., 1979, *Structural Change and Development Policy*, Oxford: Oxford University Press.

Chenery, H.B., et al., 1974, *Redistribution with Growth*, Oxford: Oxford University Press and IBRD.

Dobb, M., 1960, *An Essay on Economic Growth and Planning*, New York: Monthly Review Press.

Dornbusch, R. and S. Fischer, 1984, *Macroeconomics*, New York: Basic Books.

Editorial Board, 1964, 'Editorial Note', *Journal of Development Studies*, Vol.1, No.1.

Emmanuel, A., 1972, *Unequal Exchange: A Study of the Imperialism of Trade*, New York: Monthly Review Press.

Faber, M. and D. Seers, 1972, *The Crisis in Planning*, London.

Fei, J.C.H. and G. Ranis, 1961, 'A Theory of Economic Development', *American Economic Review*, Vol.51, No.3.

Fei, J.C.H. and G. Ranis, 1964, *Development of the Labour Surplus Economy: Theory and Policy*, Homewood, IL:

FitzGerald, E.V.K. and R. Vos (eds.), 1988, *Financing Economic Development: a Structuralist Approach to Monetary Policy*, London: Gower.

Gerschenkron, A., 1962, Economic Development in Historical Perspective, Cambridge, MA: Harvard University Press.

HMSO, 1965, *Overseas Development; the Work of the New Ministry*, Cmnd 2736, Annexe (Aug.).

Hirschman, A.O., 1958, *The Strategy of Economic Development*, New Haven, CT: Yale University Press.

ILO, 1970, *Towards Full Employment: A Programme for Colombia*, Geneva: ILO.

ILO, 1972, *Employment, Incomes and Inequality: A Strategy for Increasing Productive Employment in Kenya*, Geneva: ILO. Kalecki, M., 1972, *Essays on Developing Economies*, Cambridge University Press.

Kalecki, M., 1976, *Essays on Developing Economies*, Hassocks, Sussex: Harvester.

Killick, T., 1986, 'Twenty-five Years of Development: The Rise and Impending Decline of Market Solutions', *Development Policy Review*, Vol.4, No.2.

Kindelberger, C., 1958, *Economic Development*, New York: McGraw Hill.

Kitching, G., 1982, *Development and Underdevelopment: A Historical Perspective*, London: Methuen.

Lal: D., 1983, *The Poverty of Development Economics*, London: Institute of Economic Affairs.

Lewis, W.A., 1954, 'Economic Development with Unlimited Supplies of Labour', *The Manchester School* (May). Lewis, W.A., 1955, *The Theory of Economic Development*, London: Allen & Unwin.

Lipton, M., 1970, 'Interdisciplinary Studies in Less Developed Countries', *Journal of Development Studies*, Vol.7, No.1, pp.5–18.

Little, I.M.D., 1982, *Economic Development: Theories, Policies and International Relations*, New York: Basic Books.

Little, I.M.D.: T. Scitovsky and M. Scott, 1970, *Industry and Trade in Some Developing Countries*, Oxford: Oxford University Press and OECD.

Little, I.M.D. and J.A. Mirrlees, 1974, *Project Appraisal and Planning for Developing Countries*, London: Heinemann.

Love, J., 1981, 'Prebisch and the Origins of the Doctrine of Unequal Exchange', *Latin American Research Review*.

McKinnon, R., 1973, *Money and Capital in Economic Development*, Washington: Brookings.

Mahalanobis, P.C., 1953, 'Some Observations on the Process of Growth of National Income', *Sankhya*, Vol.15 (Sept.)

Mandelbaum, K., 1945, *The Industrialisation of Backward Areas*, Oxford: Blackwell.

Marglin, S., 1976, *Value and Price in the Labour Surplus Economy*, Oxford: Clarendon Press.

Martin: K. and J. Knapp, 1967, *The Teaching of Development Economics*, London: Frank Cass.

Meier, G. and D. Seers (eds.), 1984, *Pioneers in Development*, Oxford: Oxford University Press for IBRD.

Nurkse, R., 1953, *Problems of Capital Formation in Developing Countries*, Oxford: Blackwell.

Nurkse, R., 1958, 'The Conflict Between Balanced Growth and International Specialisation', Lecture at Istanbul University.

OECD, 1968, *Manual of Industrial Project Analysis*, Paris: Organisation for Economic Cooperation and Development.

O'Brien, D.P., 1975, *The Classical Economists*, Oxford: Clarendon Press.

Prebisch, R., 1950, *The Economic Development of Latin America and its Principal Problems*, New York: UN.

Preobrazhensky, E., 1962, *The New Economics* (translated by Brian Pearce), Oxford: Clarendon Press.

Prest, A., 1962, *Public Finance in Developing Countries*, London: Weidenfeld & Nicolson.

Preston, P.W., 1982, *Theories of Development*, London: RKP.

Reddaway, W., 1963, 'The Economics of Underdeveloped Countries', *Economic Journal*, Vol.73, No.1.

Rosenstein-Rodan, P.N., 1943, 'Problems of Industrialisation of Eastern and South-Eastern Europe', *Economic Journal*, Vol.53 (June–Sept.).

Rostow, W.W., 1960, *The Stages of Economic Growth*, Cambridge, MA.

Seers, D., 1963, 'The Limitations of the Special Case', *Bulletin of the Oxford Institute of Economics and Statistics* (May). Also reprinted in Martin and Knapp [1967].

Seers, D., 1976: *The IDS; Conception, Birth and Early Years: A Personal Interpretation*, Tenth Annual Report of the IDS, Sussex.

Singer, H.W., 1950, 'The Distribution of Gains from Trade between Investing and Borrowing Countries', *American Economic Review*, Papers and Proceedings (May).

Stewart, F., 1985, 'The Fragile Foundations of the Neo-classical Approach to Development', *Journal of Development Studies*, Vol.21, No.2.

Taylor, L., 1983, *Structural Macro-economics*, New York: Basic Books.

Thirlwall, A.P., 1987, *Keynes and Economic Development*, London: Macmillan.

Todaro, M., 1969, 'A Model of Labour Migration and Urban Unemployment in Less Developed Countries', *American Economic Review*, Vol.59, No.1.

Toye, J.F.J., 1987, *The Dilemmas of Development*, Oxford: Blackwell.

UNIDO, 1972, *Guidelines for Project Evaluation*, New York: UN.

United Nations, 1949, *National and International Measures for Full Employment*, New York: UN.

United Nations, 1950, *The Economic Development of Latin America and its Principal Problems*, New York: UN.

United Nations, 1951, *Measures for the Economic Development of the Underdeveloped Countries*, New York: UN.

# INTERSECTORAL ISSUES IN ACCUMULATION: DUALISM

# A Model of Growth and Employment in the Open Dualistic Economy :

## The Cases of Korea and Taiwan

### By John C. H. Fei and Gustav Ranis*

*In this paper, the pressing problem of unemployment in the con-
temporary developing world is studied from an historical perspective of transition growth, i.e. the process representing the
termination of economic colonialism and the initiation of modern
growth. This problem is investigated for a particular type of LDC,
namely, the open dualistic labour surplus economy. The post-war
(1950–70) experience of Taiwan and Korea were analyzed from
this viewpoint—emphasizing the fine differences as well as the
family resemblance among these countries. As ex-Japanese colonies,
both these countries shared a relatively strong agricultural infrastructure and the open dualistic and labour surplus characteristic
at the beginning of the transition in the 1950s. However, as we
show, Taiwan had an initially more favourable set of institutional
and economic conditions in agriculture.*

In the post-war decade, we indicate that both countries experienced
two sub-phases of transition: an import substitution sub-phase followed by
an export substitution sub-phase. In the former, entrepreneurial experience was accumulated along with a further strengthening of the rural
infrastructure, e.g. by land reform. In the latter, both countries rapidly
developed labour intensive manufacturing exports to the world market.
It was this latter development that contributed substantially to the solution
of the unemployment problem and permitted the labour surplus condition
to be gradually terminated. This major 'turning point', as well as other
turning points related to the historical role of the agricultural sector, are
deduced theoretically in the paper as well as verified empirically.

The overall experience of the '50s and '60s seems to indicate a worsening
of the unemployment or underemployment problem in the developing
world, even where per capita income growth has been quite satisfactory.
When this experience is then projected forward, given the knowledge that

*Economic Growth Center, Yale University. The authors wish to acknowledge the
substantial contributions of Professor Sung Hwan Jo of Sogang University, Korea and
Professor Chi-Mu Huang of National University, Taiwan to this paper, especially its
empirical portions. Portions of this research were financed by funds provided by the
Agency for International Development under contract CSD/2492. However, the views
expressed in this paper do not necessarily reflect those of AID.

even the most successful population control programmes cannot affect labour force size for some 15 years to come, the gloom thickens. Something has to be done for employment—even if it means sacrificing the GNP growth rate.

The purpose of this paper is to demonstrate, with the help of a theoretical framework applicable to at least one type of LDC, that the necessity of contemplating a trade-off between employment and GNP may, in fact, be illusory and based on a misinterpretation of the historical record. The model presented 'opens up' the traditional closed dualistic model of development [Lewis, 1954], based on the notion that the full potential complementarity between growth and employment is best demonstrated when the focus of analysis is broadened from the process of domestic 'labour' reallocation within the closed dualistic setting, to include the possibility of labour reallocation through trade. While we believe that the solution of the employment problem in the context of growth, as demonstrated by the model, applies to all but the very large (and therefore domestically-oriented) labour surplus LDCs, our empirical test is concentrated on Korea and Taiwan.

In historical perspective, the post–war performance of most LDCs is a transition between a long epoch of colonialism and a long epoch of modern growth.[1] Korea and Taiwan share the colonial heritage of a heavy dependence on traditional land–based production and exports, moving gradually to a non-traditional labour-based output mix as they successfully solve their employment problem, mainly through trade.

We shall accept the 'initial' period of transition as 1952–4 for Taiwan and 1953–7 for Korea,[2] with the 'terminal' period as 1968–70, in both cases. In Section I we present a comparative static model, with statistical evidence, to examine the initial and terminal structural characteristics of the two countries under observation. Section II identifies several important turning-points during the transition process. In Section III we present our conclusions and the implications of our analysis for employment and output policy in labour-surplus LDCs.

I. COMPARATIVE STATIC ANALYSIS

The basic purpose of our comparative static analysis is to identify the structural change within the economy between the initial and terminal years. In the open dualistic labour surplus economy this structure can be described by a set of indices such as shown in Table 1, including production, consumption, saving, investment, trade, labour allocation, each of which has its place in the context of the model we intend to develop in the course of this section.

Since countries of this particular type are overwhelmingly agricultural, at least at the initial point, we begin our analysis with relations focussing on agricultural productivity, the allocation of labour between sectors, and trade in agricultural goods. The labour surplus condition is eliminated by the reallocation of unemployed or inefficiently employed (underemployed) workers from the subsistence to the commercialized sectors, where they

TABLE 1

COMPARATIVE STATIC ANALYSIS*

| (1) | | (2) Taiwan 1952–54 a | Initial Period (3) Korea 1955–57 b | (4) Parity b/a | (5) Taiwan 1967–69 c | Terminal Period (6) Korea 1968–70 d | (7) Parity d/c |
|---|---|---|---|---|---|---|---|
| 1. | $v$ — agricultural labour productivity | $273·4 | $198·5 | ·73 | $668·0 | $386·8 | ·57 |
| 2. | $\theta$ — labour allocation ratio | 42·3% | 32·0% | ·76 | 58·0% | 49·5% | ·84 |
| 3. | $E\Delta$ — 'per capita' agricultural net exports | $19·4 | $—8·3 | — | $9·3 | —38·9 | — |
| 4. | $C_a^\Delta$ — 'per capita' consumption of agricultural goods | $138·5 | $142·4 | 1·04 | $263·2 | $223·14 | ·77 |
| 4a. | GDP/X — 'per capita' GDP | $131·2 | $83·4 | ·64 | $276·8 | $150·5 | ·54 |
| 5. | $w_a$ — agricultural real wage | 303·8 | 195·4 | ·64 | 472·5 | $317·3 | ·67 |
| 6. | $w_i$ — industrial real wage | $313·9 | $219·0 | ·69 | $529·2 | $367·8 | ·69 |
| 7. | — internal terms of trade $Pa/Pi$ | 95·5% | 96·1% | 1·0 | 96·5% | 119·7% | 1·24 |
| 8. | $C_i^\Delta$ — 'per capita' consumption of industrial goods | $221·0 | $139·5 | ·63 | $416·1 | $240·0 | ·57 |
| 9. | $K^* = K/W$ — industrial capital-labour ratio | $2543.0 | $4508·0 | 1·77 | $2372·0 | $3051·0 | 1·28 |
| 10. | $q = Y/W$ — industrial labour productivity | $659·6 | $541·3 | ·82 | $1442·9 | $906·2 | ·62 |
| 11. | $Y\Delta = Y/P$ — 'per capita' industrial output | $279·1 | $169·9 | ·61 | $837·5 | $453·0 | 1·84 |
| 12. | $E_i^\Delta$ — 'per capita' industrial exports | $16·0 | $6·8 | ·43 | $223·5 | $110·0 | ·49 |

| (1) | (2) Taiwan 1952-54 a | Initial Period (3) Korea 1955-57 b | (4) Parity b/a | (5) Taiwan 1967-69 c | Terminal Period (6) Korea 1968-70 d | (7) Parity d/c |
|---|---|---|---|---|---|---|
| 13. E/GDP export ratio | 11·2% | 4·1% | ·37 | 27·6% | 25·4% | ·92 |
| 14. EΔ 'per capita' exports | $43·8 | $11·0 | ·25 | $251·9 | $123·0 | ·48 |
| 15. Ei/E industrial share of exports | 37·2% | 61·6% | 1·65 | 88·5% | 89·8% | 1·01 |
| 16. Ea/Q agricultural export ratio | 12·2% | 3·1% | ·25 | 3·3% | 6·9% | 2·09 |
| 17. Mc/Cd import substitution potential index | 8·5% | 6·5% | ·76 | 10·2% | 6·5% | ·63 |
| 18. Mc/M industrial consumer goods share of imports | 23·0% | 13·3% | ·57 | 15·9% | 7·5% | ·47 |
| 19. Ma(Ma+Q) agricultural import fraction | 5·1% | 8·1% | 1·58 | 6·4% | 21·3% | 3·32 |
| 20. (Sa+Si)/GDP domestic saving rate | 10·0% | -4·1% | | 34·4% | 18·5% | |
| 21. I/GDP investment rate | 17·2% | 15·4% | | 33·0% | 35·4% | |
| 22. Sa/I agricultural saving contribution | 18·5% | 15·2% | | 23·5% | 2·1% | |
| 23. Si/I industrial saving contribution | 40·0% | —43·5% | | 80·7% | 49·5% | |
| 24. Sf/I foreign saving contribution | 41·0% | 128·3% | | —4·4% | 48·2% | |
| 25. X population | 8·438 mil. | 22·263 mil. | | 13·313 mil. | 32·056 mil. | |
| 26. P labour force | 2·828 mil. | 6·924 mil. | | 4·926 mil. | 9·886 mil. | |

*Cumulative Contribution to Investment During Transition*

| | Taiwan | Korea |
|---|---|---|
| agricultural saving ΣSa/ΣI | 25·9% | 8·6% |
| industrial saving ΣSi/ΣI | 68·6% | 29·7% |
| foreign saving ΣSf/ΣI | 5·7% | 61·6% |

*See Appendix for data sources.

U.S. $ figures for Korea are in 1965 constant prices, and those for Taiwan, in 1964 constant prices.

are efficiently or competitively employed.[3] In the early phase of the transition growth, 'this' is the heart of the employment problem.

Suppose the economy's total initial labour force (P) is divided into an agricultural labour force (L) and a non-agricultural labour force (W), i.e. $P = W + L$. Let us denote $\theta = W/P$ as the fraction of the total labour force in the non-agricultural sector (i.e. $1 - \theta = L/P$ is the fraction in the agricultural sector). Suppose the total output of agricultural goods is Q and the average productivity of agricultural labour is $v = Q/L$. Then the demand and supply of agricultural goods is

$$Lv = Q = C_a + E_a \qquad (1)$$
$$\text{(supply)} \quad \text{(demand)}$$

where the demand for agricultural goods is either for domestic consumption ($C_a$) or for export ($E_a$)—as is typical in the colonial pattern. Dividing throughout by total population (and letting $x^\triangle = x/P$, i.e. per capita x), we have

$$(1 - \theta)v = Q^\triangle = C_a^\triangle + E_a^\triangle \quad \text{or} \qquad (2a)$$
$$v = (E_a^\triangle + C_a^\triangle) / (1 - \theta) \qquad (2b)$$

From (2b) we can see that a higher agricultural productivity (v) can lead to a combination of a higher consumption standard of agricultural goods ($C_a^\triangle$), a higher per capita export level ($E_a^\triangle$), and a higher fraction of the labour force already allocated to industry ($\theta$).

Let us assume that land and labour are the only important traditional factors of production in agriculture.[4] If the supply of land is approximately fixed, the total productivity of labour, say for Taiwan, in the initial year. may be represented by the $Q_T$-curve in Figure 1a (i.e. the agricultural labour force $L_T$ is measured on the horizontal axis to the left). If the total population is represented by a point 'P' in Figure 1a, the industrial labour force is $PL_T$, while the agricultural labour force is $OL_T$, leading to an initial agricultural labour productivity $v_T$ represented by the slope of the straight line $Oa_T$ in Figure 1a. In Figure 1b (below 1a) with the same fixed initial population P, the per capita output for the economy as a whole is represented by the $Q_T^\triangle$ curve (i.e. $Q_T^\triangle = Q_T/P$). The initial supply of agricultural output per head for Taiwan is then equal to $L_T b_T$ as indicated in Figure 1b. For the case of Korea, in a similar way, the initial agricultural output ($Q_K$-curve in Figure 2a), output per head ($Q_K^\triangle$ curve in Figure 2b) and labour allocation point ($L_K$) are shown.

What we have just portrayed is a realistic comparative picture of the agricultural condition of the two countries at the initial point. Taiwan inherited a more favourable agricultural infrastructure, reflected in a higher initial productivity of agricultural workers (slope of $Oa_T$ in Figure 1a > slope of $Oa_K$ in Figure 2a).[5] As indicated in Table 1, row 1, Korea's initial agricultural labour productivity was only 70 per cent of that of Taiwan. However, possibly due to their common colonial experience, the agricultural consumption standard ($C_a^\triangle$) in both countries is seen to be

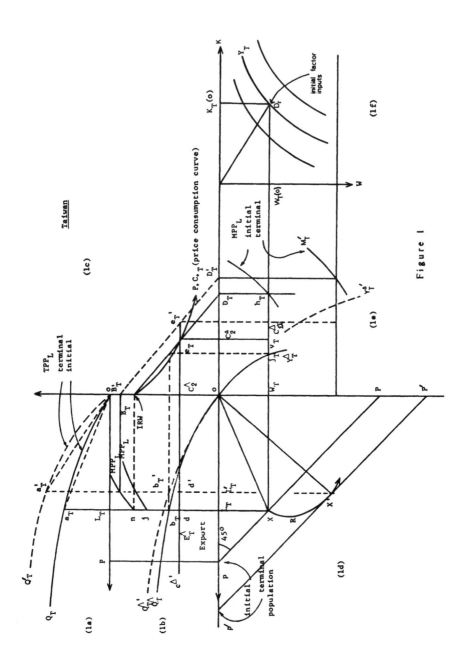

Figure 1

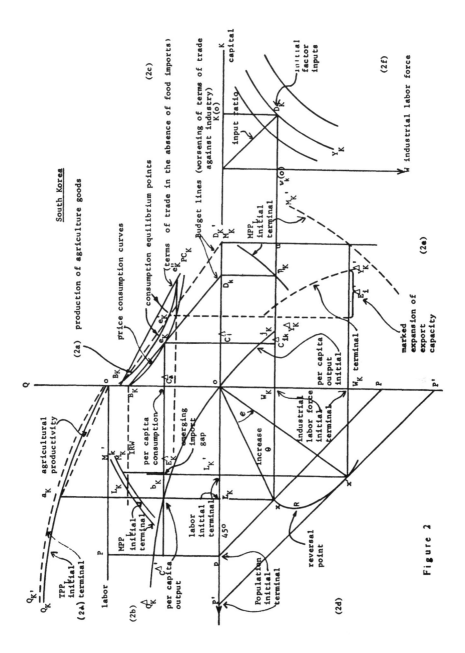

Figure 2

approximately the same (Table 1, row 4). Moreover, Table 1, row 2, indicates that initially Taiwan had already allocated 42 per cent of her labour force to non-agriculture, in sharp contrast to Korea with only 32 per cent. Thus, using equation (2b), the higher productivity in Taiwan led to *both* a higher fraction of labour in the non-agricultural sector ($\theta$) *and* a higher level of agricultural exports on a per capita basis.

Even more startling is the contrast summarized in row 3. While Korea was initially already a net importer of agricultural goods, Taiwan exported a hefty \$19 per capita and thus provided capacity to import capital goods and raw materials for the growing non-agricultural sectors.[6] This means that, from the very beginning, the agricultural sector in Taiwan played a much more positive role in fuelling the expansion of the industrial activities than Korea, in which the relative backward agricultural sector constituted a burden for industrialization. In the case of Korea, the agricultural sector was 'pulled along' by a dynamic non-agricultural sector rather than an important 'push' for industrialization, as in the case of Taiwan.

Since the individual worker consumes two kinds of commodities (agricultural goods, measured on the vertical axis of Figure 1c, and non-agricultural goods, measured on the horizontal axis), the agricultural real wage level for a typical Taiwanese worker may be represented by the budget line $B_T D_T$ (in Figure 1c). In other words, $OB_T$, ($OD_T$) is the level of the real wage in terms of agricultural (non-agricultural) goods, while the slope of the budget line represents the initial terms of trade. In a similar fashion, the budget line for Korea may be shown as $B_K D_K$ in Figure 2c. $B_K D_K$ is meant to lie below $B_T D_T$ since Korea's initial real wage in terms of agricultural goods, $OB_K$, is lower than Taiwan's, $OB_T$ (see row 5), as well as in terms of industrial goods (row 6). Since the wage parity in terms of both conditions are approximately the same ('·64' and '·69', column 4) the internal terms of trade are approximately the same for the two countries (row 7). This means that, in the context of an open economy, the possibility of the import of agricultural goods in Korea compensated for her relatively backward condition in agriculture and that, initially the internal terms of trade in both countries are governed by a common international terms of trade in the Japanese market.[7]

In the context of a labour surplus dualistic economy, the real wage in terms of agricultural goods (e.g. $OB_T$ in Figure 1c for Taiwan) may be thought of as the institutional real wage (IRW) which is determined by the institutional forces prevailing in the agricultural sector. In such an economy the IRW is likely to be above agricultural labour's marginal product ($MPP_L$), signifying the existence of surplus labour in the economy.[8] During the transition process, the IRW, moreover, is likely to increase only moderately, certainly less than the $MPP_L$, as long as $IRW > MPP_L$. However, once the labour surplus is exhausted and labour becomes scarce, $IRW = MPP_L$, and we can expect the wage to follow the $MPP_L$ thereafter.

In Figure 1c, given the fixed IRW at level $OB_T$, the price-consumption curve $PC_T$, for Taiwan, is shown.[9] Where this curve intersects the typical worker's budget line ($B_T D_T$), *i.e.* at point $e_T$, locates the initial consumption equilibrium point for Taiwan ($OC_2^a$ units of agricultural goods and $OC_1^a$ of non-agricultural goods). Similarly, for Korea, the price-consumption curve $PC_K$ may be drawn in Figure 2c. As we have noted earlier, virtually the same $OC^a$, is seen to prevail in both Korea and Taiwan initially. Thus, in the case of Taiwan, we can show (see row 3) the existence of a substantial agricultural export surplus per head ($E_T^a = b_T d$ in Figure 1b), while in the case of Korea, there exists a need to import agricultural goods at the outset.[10] Since Korea's budget line ($B_K D_K$ in Figure 2c) is lower than Taiwan's ($B_T D_T$ in Figure 1c) the fact that the two countries consume about the same amount of agricultural goods per capita, implies, moreover, that Korea's farmers initially consume substantially less non-agricultural goods on a per capita basis. This is confirmed by the data in row 8, columns 2 and 3.

Let us turn next to the production of and demand for non-agricultural (or, in shorthand, industrial) output. With respect to industrial output, there are two factors which differentiate the industrial from the agricultural sectors: first, the primary factors of production are now labour (W) and capital (K); and second, the industrial sector is assumed to be commercialized in that the real wage (in terms of industrial goods) may now be equated with the marginal productivity of labour. In Figures 1f and 2f, with labour (W) and capital (K) being measured on the vertical and horizontal axes, respectively, the production contour map, for Taiwan and Korea, for the initial period, is represented by the solid production contour maps indexed by $Y_T$ and $Y_K$. Given the initial capital stock, e.g. ($K_T(o)$) for Taiwan, the $MPP_L$-curve is represented by the solid $M_T$-curve in Figure 1e, 'below' 1f. To show the consistent equilibrium position for the case of Taiwan, let the 45-degree line PP be drawn in Figure 1d with the aid of which the initial industrial labour force $P_T^L$ (in Figure 1b) can be projected as $OW_T$ on the vertical axis (downward). Since the initial non-agricultural real wage in Taiwan is $OD_T$,[11] the $MPP_L$-curve (i.e. the $M_T$-curve) passes through the point $h_T$ in Figure 1e, indicating that $OW_T$ units of labour are demanded at the real industrial wage $OD_T$. Similarly, for Korea, with capital stock $K_K(o)$ in Figure 2f, the $MPP_L$-curve is represented by the $M_K$-curve in Figure 2e, with an employment equilibrium point at $h_K$ —indicating that $OW_K$ units of workers are demanded at the industrial real wage $OD_K$.

A possible important initial difference in the state of industrial technology in Korea and Taiwan should be noted. From the theoretical standpoint, if the initial production functions of the two countries were exactly the same, then the higher level of the industrial real wage in Taiwan would imply that Taiwan also has (1) a higher industrial capital-labour ratio ($K^* = K/W$) and (2) a higher average productivity of industrial labour ($q = \dfrac{Y}{W}$). However, the empirical evidence (rows 9 and 10) indicates otherwise. Korea has an initially higher industrial capital-labour ratio than Taiwan—in spite of the lower Korean real wage level—and nevertheless sports a lower level of labour productivity—than Taiwan.[12] The cause of this difference may be traced once again to the Japanese colonial heritage; while the Japanese lavished relatively more attention on agricultural infrastructure in Taiwan, they pushed industrialization more heavily in Korea, which probably led to a more capital intensive, less innovative industrial structure.[13]

With respect to the demand and supply of industrial goods a formula symmetrical to (2a) is

$$\theta \, q = Y^\Delta = C^\Delta + E_i^\Delta \qquad\qquad (3)$$
$$\text{(supply)} \quad \text{(demand)}$$

where $Y^\Delta$ ($= Y/P$) is the per capita output of industrial goods and q is industrial labour productivity. From row 11, we see that the initial $Y^\Delta$ is much higher in Taiwan than in Korea (the parity is ·61) in spite of a much smaller gap in q (row 10 with a parity of ·82), simply because a larger proportion of the population has already been allocated to the non-agricultural sector (see row 2). On the demand side, a much larger fraction of Korea's non-agricultural output is exported at the outset—i.e. the percentage $E_i/E$ is 50 per cent larger in Korea than in Taiwan (see row 15)—even though the actual magnitudes are small in both cases (see row 12).

Let us turn next to the overall magnitude and structure of international trade in the initial years in both countries. As far as the volume of total trade is concerned, given the already established fact that per capita GDP (row 4a) was higher in Taiwan initially, we would expect foreign trade to be quantitatively more important in Taiwan. Two indicators—exports as a fraction of GDP (row 13) and exports per capita (row 14)—are shown to corroborate this fact.

The contrast in the structure of the two countries' trade is even more dramatic than the difference in external orientation. While the initial export pattern of Taiwan was dominated by agricultural goods, Korea's modest exports were dominated by non-agricultural commodities (row 15). In fact, Taiwan inititally exported nearly 12 per cent of her agriculural output while Korea exported only 3 per cent of hers (row 16).

On the import side, during the initial years of transition growth total imports (M) consisted of imported industrial consumer goods ($M_i$) and producers' goods ($M_p$), i.e. capital goods and/or raw materials destined as productive inputs into the industrial sector ($M = M_i + M_p$). This breakdown will be seen to be significant for any analysis of the phenomenon of *import substitution (I-S) growth* which often characterizes the initial phase of transition.

By I-S growth we shall mean a sub-phase dominated by the development of the indigenous consumer goods industry with tradiional consumer goods imports ($M_i$) gradually being replaced. In order to build up these import substituting industries the LDC, however, usually needs to import more raw materials and capital goods $M_p$. Bearing this in mind, rows 17 and 18 attempt to describe the initial potential for I-S growth. Row 17, for example, shows that, while Taiwan initially imported 8.5

per cent of her total requirements for industrial consumer goods, the corresponding figure for Korea was $6 \cdot 5$ per cent. In the case of Taiwan, moreover, the imported industrial consumer goods accounted for $23 \cdot 0$ per cent of her total imports while the corresponding figure for Korea was only $13 \cdot 3$ per cent (row 18). Thus, both from the viewpoint of the domestic market and from the viewpoint of the allocation of foreign exchange, the importation of industrial consumer goods was more important in Taiwan than in Korea in the initial period under observation—allowing more scope for I-S growth.

The above description of the structure of trade reveals a contrasting pattern during the early phase of transition growth in the two countries under examination. In the case of Taiwan, there is in evidence a pattern of triangularism, i.e. the agricultural sector produces an exportable surplus which, in turn, provides the import capacity used for two types of industrial imports, consumer goods and producers' goods. The same agricultural exports, moreover, generate the incomes and demand for the larger volume of industrial consumer goods now produced at home. In this manner, agriculture fuels I-S growth as $M_p$ imports permit the continued building up of the domestic import substituting capacity that gradually replaces $M_i$ imports.

In the case of Korea, on the other hand, the growth dynamics represent more of a bilateral interaction between industry and the foreign sector as agriculture remains relatively stagnant. The industrial sector in consequence has to be depended upon to produce an exportable surplus which, together with the provision of capital from abroad, is used to import the capital goods and raw materials needed by the import substitution process. Moreover, as we shall see below, and especially during the later subphase of transition, the industrial sector, instead of being supported by agricultural exports, is saddled with the responsibility of diverting a part of the import capacity it generates for the purchase of food abroad.

The case of Taiwan is described in Figure 1e in which the $Y_T^\triangle$ curve is shown. The initial value of per capita output is seen to be $W_T j_T$, while the initial value of the per capita demand for consumer goods $C_T^\diamondsuit$ is $W_T C i_T^\triangle$ ($= OG^\triangle$).[14] Thus, there exists a shortage of $j_T C i_T^\triangle$ units of industrial goods which must be imported. Since, from Figure 1b, the initial per capita agricultural export is seen to be $E_T^\triangle$ ($= b_T d$), at the initial terms of trade, the import capacity generated by these agricultural exports is $C_T^\diamondsuit v_T$ (Figure 1e). The other portion of industrial goods required (i.e. $v_T j_T$ units on a per capita basis) is financed by foreign capital.

In the case of Korea, in Figure 2, the inital $Y^\triangle$-curve is labelled $Y_K^\triangle$ leading to an initial per capita output of $W_K j_K$ units. This output is actually higher than domestic demand $W_K C i_K^\triangle$, signifying that Korea's industrial sector is already producing an exportable surplus, to finance its own import needs. The agricultural sector, on the other hand, is not involved in the financing process; in fact, to the extent that there is a food deficit, it is already drawing on the import capacity provided by industrial exports and foreign capital inflow.

The above presents a fairly accurate picture of the comparative structural conditions of the two countries under observation at the initial point in time. The purpose of comparative structural analysis is to contrast these initial characteristics with those obtaining in the terminal periods. The forces that brought on the marked structural change observable in columns 5–7 of Table 1 include (1) capital accumulation, (2) population growth, and (3) technology change in both the agricultural and non-agricultural sectors.

Let us first concentrate on capital accumulation. The saving fund available to these entrepreneurs, in both the public and private sectors, was composed of three sources: foreign capital $(S_f)$, the reinvestment of industrial profits $(S_i)$, and agricultural saving $(S_a)$, i.e. [15]

$$I = S_a + S_i + S_f \qquad (4)$$

Turning once again to Table 1, we have indicated the relative contribution to the total investment fund of the three sources of saving, both for the initial and terminal period—in rows 22–24. In the same table, moreover, we have presented the cumulative contribution of each between the initial and terminal period. In terms of these cumulative figures, the dramatic differences between Taiwan and Korea during the transition period is demonstrated by the fact that foreign capital financed 61·6 per cent of total investment in Korea and only 5·7 per cent in Taiwan. Agricultural saving contributed about three times as much to a higher investment rate in Taiwan than in Korea. This lack of domestic saving capacity, especially in agriculture, to finance her own investment needs and the heavy continued reliance on foreign capital, remains the most serious problem facing Korea's development.

Other evidence of marked structural change can be analyzed in terms of a comparison of (1) the role of agriculture; (2) the behaviour of wages and consumption; (3) the progress of industrial technology and the structure of international trade. While there continues to exist a marked family similarity between these two countries, differences in observed structural change are also instructive for the understanding of the employment problem.

### The Role of the Agricultural Sector

To begin with the non-agricultural sector in both countries has grown rapidly enough to absorb the unemployed and underemployed in agriculture in spite of substantial population increase. Thus the centre of gravity of both economies, in terms of the allocation of labour between the two sectors, has shifted markedly. Returning to Figures 1d and 2d, the growth of population may be represented by the parallel and outward shift of the population lines PP to P'P'. At the same time the allocation points have shifted from $L_T$ ($L_K$ for Korea) to $L_T^1$ ($L_K^1$ for Korea), representing an increase in $\theta$ for both countries, as indicated. Rows 25 and 26 of Table 1 yield an average annual rate of growth between the initial and terminal period of 2·9 per cent in population and 3·7 per cent in the labour force for Taiwan, and 2·5 per cent and 2·7 per cent, respectively, for Korea. In spite of this, as we can see from row 2, Taiwan registered an increase in $\theta$ from 42 to 58 per cent and Korea from 32 to 49 per cent. This demonstrates the rapidity of the growth and industrial sector labour absorption process in both countries.

Associated with this marked structural change in terms of labour reallocation, is a markedly different role played by the agricultural sector. In the case of Taiwan, the initially more favourable agricultural infrastructure, and the encouraging policies led to dramatic advances in technology and agricultural labour productivity. This is depicted by the upward shift of the total output curve from $Q_T$ to $Q_T^1$ (in Figure 1a) and of the per capita output curve from $Q_T^\triangle$ to $Q_T^{\triangle 1}$(in Figure 1b). Coupled with the labour reallocation effect, agricultural labour productivity has thus advanced from the slope of $Oa_T$ in Figure 1a to the slope of $Oa_T'$.[16] The exportable per capita agricultural surplus in the terminal period is now $d'b_T'$, in Figure 1b, compared with $db_T$ earlier.

From row 1 we see that agricultural labour productivity in Taiwan advanced by more than 244 per cent. As a result, in spite of substantial gains in the per capita consumption of agricultural goods (row 4) agricultural exports, even on a net per capita basis, could be sustained at a high level (row 3). All this in the face of the fact (row 2) that the agricultural labour force is now a much smaller fraction of the total labour force than in the initial period, and, in fact, declined absolutely after a point.

In the case of Korea, the initially relatively unfavourable agricultural infra-structure, reinforced by the relative government neglect over time thereafter, has led to a situation of comparative agricultural stagnation. Agricultural productivity here also registered some gains. But, as seen from row 1, the gains were more modest leading to a further substantial decline in the relative position of the two agricultural sectors (see row 1, columns 4 and 7). Consequently, the increase in Korea's agricultural consumption standard is modest (row 4—note especially the decline in the parity ratio) from domestic sources; instead, increasing volumes of food imports have been required (see row 3).

To obtain a clear picture of the contrast we can look at the net import or export figure for food only over the relevant period. While Taiwan has been continuously exporting food during the entire transition period, Korea's food deficit problem has been steadily worsening, with more than $300,000 annually being spent on net food imports in recent years. The contrast is best summarized in Figure 3, showing food imports as a percentage of total food consumption in Korea and food exports as a percentage of total food consumption in Taiwan.

Thus, in the case of Taiwan, rapid growth, industrialization and labour reallocation were financed in considerable part by gains in agricultural productivity. In the case of Korea, on the other hand, rapid industrialization, growth and labour reallocation were financed in large part by the inflow of foreign capital. In the case of Korea the agricultural sector was 'pulled along' by a dynamic non-agricultural sector rather than providing an important 'push' for industrialization, as in the case of Taiwan. This contrast was also demonstrated vividly by our earlier analysis of the comparative cumulative sources of finance during the transition.

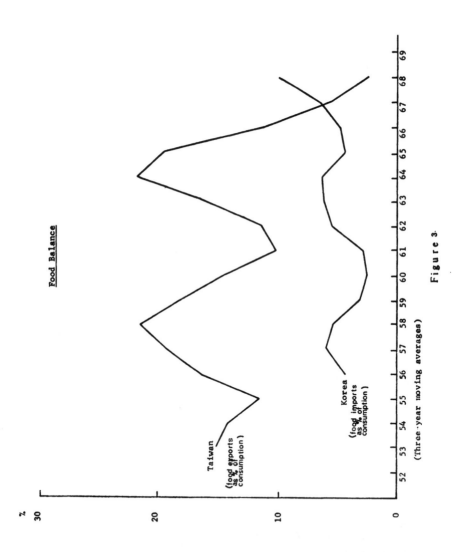

Figure 3·

## Real Wage and Welfare

From the viewpoint of welfare, the impact of economic development may be examined in terms of an economy's (1) consumption level, (2) saving capacity and/or (3) the distribution of income between labour and property-owning classes. All these dimensions are in turn closely related to the behaviour of the real wage through time. An increase in the level of the real wage can be described by an upward shift in the budget line of a typical worker in Figure 1c. In the case of both Korea and Taiwan two facts may be noted. First, the real wage did go up between the initial and terminal years (see rows 5 and 6).[17] This is due to an upward revision of the IRW in agriculture as productivity change occurs[18] and means that, for example, for Taiwan, the budget line has shifted, from $B_T D_T$ to $B_T^1 D_T^1$ in Figure 1c. Secondly, the terms of trade have remained about constant in Korea, but worsened slightly against the industrial sector in Taiwan (see row 7). As far as the consumption standard is concerned, both the consumption per head of agricultural goods (row 8) and of industrial goods (row 9) rises with the increase in real wage. Accordingly, the consumption equilibrium point moves from $e_T$ to $e_T^1$ and $e_K$ to $e_K^1$ in both cases. Large food imports made this possible without a deterioration of the industrial sector's terms of trade in Korea.

As far as income distribution is concerned, labour's distributive share in any sector is $\emptyset = (Lxw)/z$ where 'z' is the total output of that sector. Consequently the rate of increase of $\emptyset$ is

$$\eta_\emptyset = \eta_w - \eta_{z/L} \tag{5}$$

which is the difference between the rate of increase of the real wage ($\eta_w$) and the rate of increase of labour productivity in that sector. Thus, for each sector, the distribution of income moves against labour when the increase in the real wage lags behind productivity gains during the unlimited supply of labour phase.[19]

As the company moves through its transition, changes in income distribution and in the participation of medium and small scale entrepreneurs under a more market-oriented policy setting, enhance the economy's saving capacity. Row 2, Table 1, indicates that Taiwan's gross domestic saving rate had, in fact, increased spectacularly during the transition period. The same is true of Korea where negative saving rates initially gave way to a very satisfactory saving performance at the 18·5 per cent level at the end of the period. From rows 22, 23, and 24 we may, moreover, gather that these gains in domestic saving capacity were largely based on the increasing contribution over time of the non-agricultural sector which, especially in Taiwan, replaced foreign capital as the main source of developmental finance.

The relative failure of Korea's agricultural sector also resulted in a less dramatic increase in her domestic saving capacity as we have already noted (row 20). In fact, rows 22–24 permit us to see precisely how the agricultural sector's contribution to the economy's total investment fund declined dramatically during the transition period. Consequently, even in the terminal period, foreign capital still had to be relied on for close to 50 per cent of Korea's total investment fund. Thus, while the saving capacity of the industrial sector increased dramatically, the gap left by the failure of agriculture's contribution had to be filled largely by foreign capital.

### Industrial Sector and International Trade

Turning, finally, to a brief examination of the non-agricultural sector in the same comparative static setting, we should, first of all, note that it is the performance of this sector that has marked off the path of both Korea and Taiwan from that of other contemporary open dualistic economies. Recalling equation (3), we see that the dramatic increase in $\theta$ (proportion of the population already efficiently allocated or employed) and in q (non-agricultural labour productivity) has led to a large increase in the per capita output of industrial goods $Y^\triangle$. Although there has been some increase in the domestic use of that industrial output, the most conspicuous result of this development has been in the spurt of industrial exports.

Referring to row 11, the availability of industrial output per head ($Y^\triangle$) sustained an annual rate of increase of 8·0 per cent in Taiwan and 7·5 per cent in Korea during the transition period. This high rate of increase followed from both the increase in $\theta$ (row 2) and the increase in q (row 10). The spectacular change in the extent of external orientation of both countries' rapidly growing non-agricultural sectors is summarized in row 12. In Taiwan (Korea), industrial exports per head grew at the remarkable rate of 19·3 per cent (24·0 per cent) annually, yielding a 14-fold (16-fold) increase during the transition period.[20]

This dramatic increase in the external orientation of the industrial sector brought with it a corresponding change in the structure of foreign trade. First of all, in terms of the overall involvement in trade, as measured by the export ratio (row 13), while Korea participated much less in trade at the outset, the export ratio rose substantially in both countries so that, by the terminal year, more than 25 per cent of GDP was exported in both cases. Furthermore, as seen from row 15, in the case of Taiwan, the initial dominance of the agricultural sector in exports was completely reversed so that in the terminal year almost 90 per cent of exports are seen to be non-agricultural. In the case of Korea which had a relatively much more industrial orientation (including exports) to start with, exports are now also almost exclusively industrial in origin. The fact that agricultural exports lagged along with agricultural output is further confirmed in row 16, i.e. the fraction of agricultural goods exported remains small in Korea and substantial in Taiwan.

### II. LANDMARKS IN THE TRANSITION PROCESS

We have thus tried to compare and contrast the economic structure of the two countries under observation during both the initial and terminal periods of the transition process to obtain two flashlight exposures. But it is inadequate in the sense that we are still lacking a picture of the process of continuous change over more than a decade which, of course, brought about the structural changes observed. In this section we will attempt to describe the highlights of this process, in terms of the turning points by

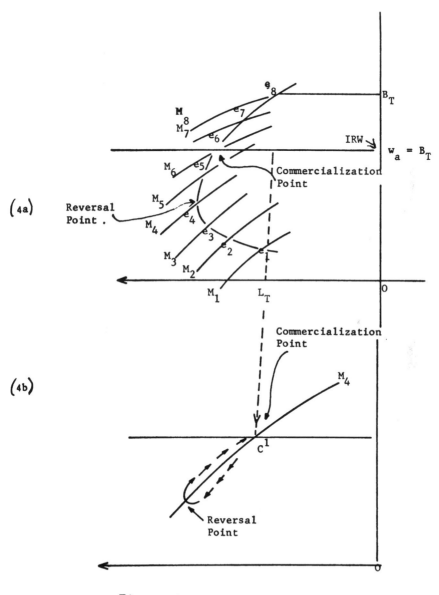

Figure 4

which the sub-phases of the transition process can be marked off.[21] In what follows we shall explore the economic significance of four turning points:

| Turning Points | Taiwan | Korea |
|---|---|---|
| (a) Commercialization point | 65–66 | 66–67 |
| (b) Reversal point | 64–65 | 66–67 |
| (c) Export substitution point | 60 | 64 |
| (d) Switching point | 75 (?) | 80 (?) |

For a closed labour surplus dualistic economy, the *commercialization point* indicates the termination of the labour surplus condition.[22] From this point on, real wage in the agricultural sector is equated with the marginal productivity of labour (i.e. determined by 'commercial principle' rather than 'institutional forces') which signifies that labour now becomes a scarce factor (from the economic standpoint) and tends to increase rapidly. This concept can be applied to an open dualistic economy.

In the case of Taiwan the causes of the arrival of the commercialization point must be found in a combination of the 'push' effects of continuous technology change in agriculture combined with the 'pull' of industrial demand for labour in a balanced fashion. In Figure 4, which 'blows up' Figure 1b, we indicate the changing marginal product of labour curves $M_i$ as technological change takes place in agriculture. Thus the movement from $M_1$ (i.e. the $MPP_L$ curve of 1b) to $M_8$ (the $MPP_L'$ curve of 1b) is replicated in Figure 4. The dynamic process of labour reallocation may then be depicted by a sequence of points $e_i$ which, consistent with a continuously rising $\theta$, or a relative decline in the size of the agricultural population, show, first, an absolute increase in agricultural population ($e_1$ to $e_4$), followed by an absolute decrease (from $e_4$ onward).[23] The commercialization point is reached at $e_6$.[23] Thus the commercialization point arrives earlier, the faster the upward shift of the $MPP_L$ curve, the slower the rate of population growth, the slower the upward creep of the institutional real wage and the faster the demand for labour increases in the industrial sector.[24]

The above thesis is supported by the actual long-term behaviour of the real wage in the two countries under observation. As shown in Figure 5, the real wage in both countries shows only a minor upward creep until very recently (i.e. after 1965). It thus appears that the commercialization point may have been reached in both Korea and Taiwan[25] towards the end of the '60s—with agricultural 'push' forces contributing much more in Taiwan, and industrial 'pull', fuelled by foreign capital, much more in Korea.[26] If so, we can also expect a further acceleration of real wage increases to characterize their development in the '70s.

The increase of real wages has a profound impact on income distribution, on saving capacity and on the economy's consumption pattern. As income distribution within each sector now shifts in favour of labour, any decline in the propensity to save will be accompanied by a more sustained expansion of the domestic market for consumer goods. In other words, the commercialization point heralds an end to the relative natural austerity typical of the 'unlimited supply of labour' condition. After the commercial-

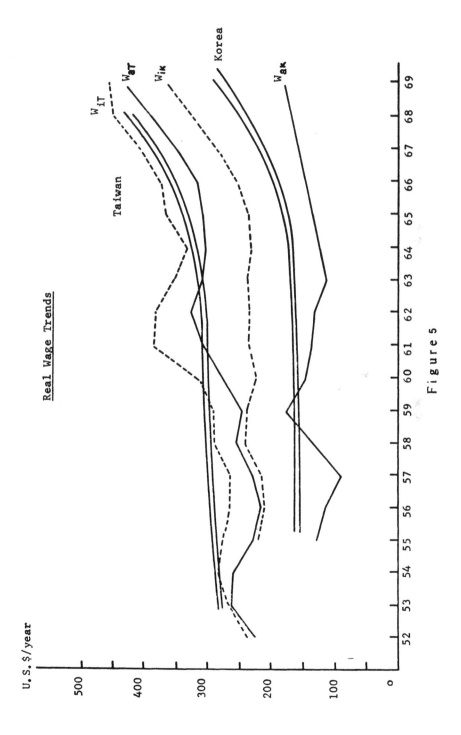

Real Wage Trends

U. S. $/year

Figure 5

ization point, *ceteris paribus*, we can expect the saving rate and the GDP growth rates to level off. Furthermore, in an open dualistic labour surplus economy the commercialization point is also likely to usher in changes in the structure of international trade. The external orientation of the industrial sector, which was previously based on the continuation of maturing entrepreneurs taking advantage of cheap labour,[27] now gives way gradually, to the incorporation of skills and capital goods as the basis for exports. Simultaneously we can expect a shift in the orientation of the industrial sector in the direction of satisfying the growing domestic market for industrial consumer goods, including more durable consumer goods.

The second turning point is the *reversal point* signifying an absolute decline in the agricultural population or labour force. It can be shown that when the rate of increase of the industrial labour force ($\eta_w$) is sustained long enough at a level higher than the growth rate of the total labour force ($\eta_w > \eta_p$), not only does $\theta$ ($=W/P$) increase continuously, as we have already observed, but a reversal point is reached after some time, when an absolute increase of the agricultural labour force gives way to an absolute decline. In Figure 1d, associated with an increase of the total population or labour force from OP to OP', the initial labour allocation point X changes to X' in the terminal years, representing an increase of $\theta$ (slope of OX' > slope of OX) as well as an absolute decline of the agricultural labour force. The movement of the labour allocation point through time is depicted by the locus XRX' in Figure 1d, where R is the reversal point. The same reversal point R can be observed in Figure 4. In the case of the two specific countries under observation here, our data indicate that the reversal point was reached in Taiwan a couple of years before commercialization, while in Korea both seem to have arrived more or less simultaneously, i.e. near the end of the '60s.[28]

When the supply of land is, for all practical purposes, fixed, the arrival of a reversal point signifies that the law of diminishing returns is beginning to work in a reverse direction, as both marginal and average productivities of labour begin to increase even when technology is stagnant. For Taiwan, this implies that the pressure is beginning to appear for the adoption of labour-saving technology (e.g. mechanization) in agriculture—as there is now an absolute shortage of manpower under the old technology. For Korea, this means that it is *possible* to solve the problem of agricultural stagnation by a strategy of 'pulling' this sector up by rapid industrial development. Whether or not this strategy will be successful remains to be seen.[29]

The third turning point is the *export substitution point*. During the long period of growth under colonialism, prior to transition growth, the economy was clearly a land based economy fuelled by primary product exports. During the import substitution sub-phase, which characterizes the initial period of transition growth, the system continued to rely on land based exports, to build up its import substitution industries. The meaning of 'export substitution' is that labour intensive manufacture export (e.g. textile) replaces (i.e. 'substitutes for') the traditional exports (e.g. rice and sugar in Taiwan and the traditional exports in Korea) as the dominant export items of the economy.

Turning to time series in our effort to identify sub-phases in the transition we see that the potential for primary (i.e. consumer goods) import substitution (measured by the share of total industrial consumer goods which is imported, $M_c/C_d$ is initially higher in Taiwan than Korea (see the $M_c/C_d$ curves in Figure 6). Moreover, this potential is being steadily explored (and thus reduced) until around 1960 in Taiwan and 1964 in Korea after which point these curves turn up. Similarly, if we trace the share of consumer goods imports to total imports ($M_c/M$ curves in Figure 6) we see the same turning points 1960 and 1964, respectively, occurring in the two countries. What lies behind these statistical results was the import substitution strategy adopted by the government (high tariff protection for domestic import substituting industries, overvalued domestic currency in the world market by the official exchange rate, artificially low domestic interest rates, etc.) to encourage the use of foreign exchange receipts (earnings by traditional exports) to build up import substitution industries.

When the domestic markets for industrial consumer goods is supplied almost exclusively by the new import substituting industries, the import substitution phase comes to an end (i.e. exhausted). In the case of a relatively small labour surplus economy, the natural development is the emergence of the export substitution phase—i.e. selling labour intensive manufacturing exports in the world market. This transition was facilitated by a change in government policy to promote exports (e.g. realistic foreign exchange rate or even undervaluation of domestic currency) based on labour efficiency (e.g. adoption of realistic interest rate through interest reform to eliminate the artificial 'capital cheapening' condition under the import substitution phase). The results are seen in Figure 7 which shows a marked shift in the composition of exports—with industrial exports as a fraction of total, shooting up in Taiwan after 1960 and a few years later in the case of Korea.[30] The change in export structure is nothing less than spectacular.

For a small labour surplus economy with a colonial heritage of primary product export, the emergence of the export substitution phase, replacing the import substitution phase is a highly significant phenomenon.[31] In respect to the unemployment problem, the import substitution phase was not a period conducive to full employment leading to the, by now popular, slogan of a 'necessary' conflict between 'employment and growth'. In reality, there is no such conflict when the export substitution phase arrives. For the embodiment of labour service in export to the world market is conducive to both rapid growth and full employment—as the country has, for the first time, found a way to make full use of her abundant labour supply. As this process continues it leads to both the 'commercialization point' and the 'switching point' signifying the termination of the labour surplus condition in the economy as a whole as well as in the agriculture sector in particular. For this reason, the export substitution point precedes the other turning point in both countries just mentioned.[32]

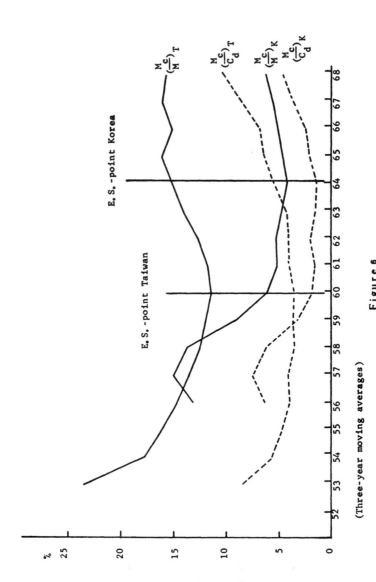

Import Substitution and Export Substitution

$M\left(\dfrac{c}{M}\right)_T$

$M\left(\dfrac{c}{C_d}\right)_T$

$M\left(\dfrac{c}{M}\right)_K$

$M\left(\dfrac{c}{C_d}\right)_K$

E. S. -point Korea

E. S. -point Taiwan

(Three-year moving averages)

Figure 6

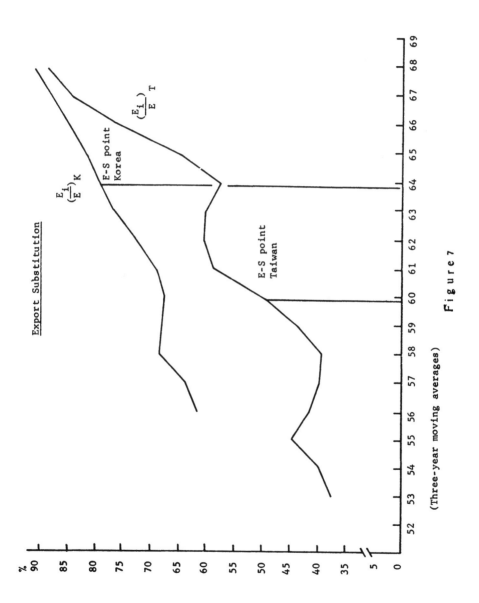

Export Substitution

$\left(\dfrac{E_i}{E}\right)K$

$\left(\dfrac{E_i}{E}\right)T$

E-S point
Korea

E-S point
Taiwan

Figure 7

(Three-year moving averages)

Another turning point in the transition of the open dualistic economy is the *switching point*. It is based on the notion that countries which are basically natural resources poor will at some point in their history have to become net importers of agricultural goods. This is as true of Korea and Taiwan as of historical Japan which became a net importer of agricultural goods from her colonies around the turn of the century.[33] Taiwan's agricultural sector, in spite of its superior performance, through the application of land reform, non-traditional inputs, etc., is, as we have already observed, reaching its natural limits—witness the determination of her industrial sector's terms of trade and the declining level of per capita agricultural exports (rows 3 and 7).[34] Korea, on the other hand, as we have also noted, became a net importer of agricultural goods virtually from the beginning of the transition period; her agriculture sector, we feel, has not fulfilled its historical mission.

The phenomenon of land-based exports at the beginning of the transition must be viewed as a temporary phenomenon in long run historical perspective. A 'switch' from an agricultural exporting to importing position is bound to occur at some stage in the development process in the future. But *when* it occurs and on the basis of *what* kind of agricultural performance remains an all important issue. It matters greatly for Korea whether or not existing reserves of agricultural productivity have been harnessed *en route* to the successful solution of the LDC employment problem. The alternatives may well be failure of the total effort—true for many contemporary LDCs of the type under discussion—or an unacceptably heavy reliance on foreign capital, as in the case of Korea.

### III. CONCLUSION AND IMPLICATIONS FOR POLICIES

In the transition process of a labour surplus open dualistic economy, the solution of the unemployment problem may be identified with the arrival of the commercialization point which signifies the termination of the labour surplus condition inherited from the colonial epoch. After commercialization, we can expect to observe a sustained increase in real wage; the 'unemployment problem' will then be of a different type.

The increase in real wage is expected to be accompanied by some reduction in the savings rate, a relative decline in the importance of trade and a shift toward a more skill and capital intensive technology and output mix—an increased concern with the provision of an adequate supply of high talented manpower. These are the major development issues confronted by Taiwan (and to a lesser extent Korea) at the present time and for the near future.

On the road to commercialization, the most important landmark is the export substitution point based on labour intensive export. There will no longer be a sharp conflict between growth and employment objectives— as was the case under import substitution growth. The arrival of the export substitution point 'facilitates' the arrival of the commercial point that terminates the labour surplus condition.

The whole array of government policy measures (e.g. high protective tariffs, exchange controls, low interest rates, overvalued currencies, price inflation) adopted to facilitate the import substitution process—via the exclusion of foreign competition and the augmentation of the profits of the domestic industrialists—are, of course, subject to changes. Both Taiwan and Korea, did, in fact, effect major changes in their policy environment around 1960 and 1963, respectively, to facilitate transitions to export substitution. Stabilization plus dismantling of the various existing direct control measures, on trade, interest rate and foreign exchange rates, thereby created a more market orientated economy most conducive to access for large numbers of domestic entrepreneurs seeking efficient utilization of the economy's relatively abundant resources via embodiment in labour-intensive industrial exports. The experience of Taiwan and Korea teaches us that unemployment problems can be solved through growth in 'this' way.

At some point during its life cycle, the open dualistic labour surplus economy is, moreover, likely to move from the successful exploitation of its agricultural potential to its 'natural' long term position as an importer of agricultural goods. The arrival of such a switching point signifies that the country will ultimately have to accelerate its industrial exports to acquire the needed food and raw materials—a phenomenon which may occur before commercialization point, as in historical Japan, or after commercialization point, as in Taiwan, or Korea in the future.

Finally, given the rates of population growth, a reversal point indicating an absolute decline in the size of the agricultural labour force is likely to occur before the switching point. Thus the policy focus may shift to labour saving techniques in agriculture in order to prolong labour using techniques in industry, while the economy gets ready for the skill and capital intensive phase. At the present time, this is precisely the central policy issue in Taiwan. In the case of Korea, however, due to its neglect of agriculture in the past, the country is still faced with the problem of first building up its rural infrastructure and utilizing the still unexploited slack in agricultural productivity—a process likely to release additional supplies of labour without the need to resort to extensive mechanization.

In Taiwan, the agricultural sector has already fulfilled its historical mission during the early phase of transition. In the case of Korea the story is quite different as it cannot be denied that Korea's agricultural sector has been relatively stagnant.[35] Consequently, throughout the import substitution sub-phase, while industrial entrepreneurial maturation took place, much of the potential domestic fuel for further growth was never generated. Consequently, after the export substitution point had been reached, a tremendous burden fell upon the industrial sector, fuelled largely by foreign capital, to continue to 'pull' the agricultural sector along with it, including the continuous 'pulling out' of agricultural workers.

The rather heavier burden which Korea's non-agricultural sector has consequently had to carry has, in turn, led to certain distortions in that sector. For example, industrial exports have undoubtedly been pushed, at least in some areas, beyond the point of efficiency, and that a good deal of 'premature' backward linkage type of import substitution has consequently taken place[36] (especially since 1968, with the help of a large assortment of special subsidies and other incentives). The simple reason is that, with agriculture's push not forthcoming,[37] industrial exports have had to 'run' ever faster, with the consequence that some fairly technology and capital intensive sub-sectors have been expanded, ahead of what the, admittedly changing, endowment picture would call for. Moreover, Korea was consequently forced to admit an unusually heavy flow of foreign aid, more recently private investment, to keep the process going.

As far as the future is concerned, it is, of course, 'mathematically' conceivable that the present trends continue during the decade ahead—until the non-agricultural sector and the non-agricultural labour force become so predominant that the Korean economy begins to operate something like the city-states of Hong Kong and Singapore, i.e. importing virtually all needed agricultural goods and depending entirely on her industrial exporting sector. Such a strategy is, however, not likely to be successful as a practical choice. Korea's agricultural sector and population remain too large relative to the total economy to permit the hinterland to be 'dragged along' into modernity in this fashion. It is difficult to conceive of trade able to expand fast enough in a competitive fashion; it is equally difficult to conceive of foreign capital as continuing to flow in at the rates required. The increasing import intensity of industrial exports, the heavy foreign debt structure, the growing food gap are all symptoms of difficulties ahead. Whether or not the commercialization point has already been reached, Korea will clearly have to reconsider its policy of agricultural neglect by pursuing a more balanced growth strategy in the years ahead.

## APPENDIX 1

In Figure 8bcde, we reproduce the initial equilibrium position of Taiwan described in Figure 1bcde. In Figure 3b, out of a total labour force OP, the agricultural labour force is $OL_T$ producing a per capita output of $L_T b_T$. Total agricultural output is represented by the area OPab. With respect to the allocation of this output, we see that, since the real wage in terms of agricultural goods is $OB_T$, labour's share is $OB_T cL_T (= B_1 + B_2 + B_3)$.[38] Let us assume that wage earners do not save; then the consumption by farmers of food is $B_1$ (at the consumption standard for agricultural goods Oe), while the income exchanged by farmers for industrial consumer goods is $B_2 + B_3$. To see the magnitude of the landlord or rent share, let the auxiliary straight line dc be drawn; then from point 'e' let a straight line parallel to cd be constructed, thus obtaining point 'f'. The area $B_4$ ($= dhgf$) then equals $B_2 + B_3$ by construction.[39] Since the wage share is $B_1 + B_4 (= B_1 + B_2 + B_3)$, the remaining total output or rent share is $B_2 + B_5 + B_6$. Under the assumption that all rental incomes are saved, this constitutes agricultural saving ($S_a$).

The total output of agriculture is thus allocated in the following way: $B_1$ is consumed by agricultural workers; $B_2 + B_5$ is exported ($hB_T$ being per capita exports); the remaining output $B_4 + B_6$ is destined for consumption by workers in the industrial sector. The latter two types of shipments summarize the contribution that agriculture makes to non-agricultural development, first in providing import capacity ($B_2 + B_5$) and second in providing food for industrial workers ($B_4 + B_6$).

Let us turn now to the industrial sector (in Figure 8e), where the equilibrium is established at point $h_T$, i.e. where the $M_T$-curve intersects the real wage level in terms of industrial goods, $OD_T$. With a given labour force ($OW_T$), the total industrial output is then divided into the wage share ($A_1 + A_2 + A_3$) and the profit share ($A_4$), the latter constituting industrial saving ($S_i$). Out of the total wage share, $A_1$ is consumed by industrial workers, while $A_2 + A_3$ is exchanged for agricultural goods for purposes of consumption. At the given terms of trade (slope of $B_T D_T$) the exchange value of $A_2 +$

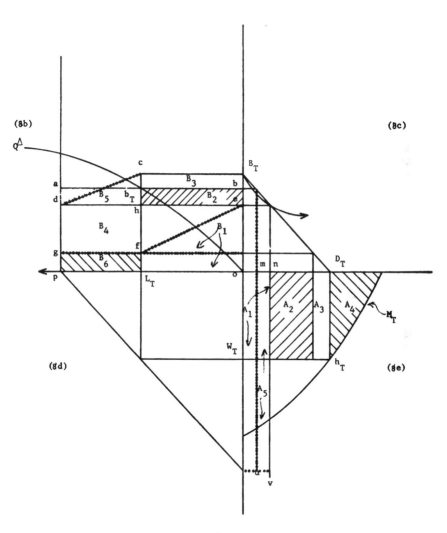

Figure 8

$A_3$ is $B_4 + B_6$. Notice that $A_2$ comprises industrial consumer goods exchanged for $B_4$ units of agricultural goods delivered by the farmers; $A_3$, on the other hand, represents investment goods exchanged for the landlord's agricultural saving $B_6$. Notice also that total agricultural export proceeds $(B_2 + B_3)$ which accrue to the owners of the agricultural surplus, enable the system to import $A_5$ (=mnuv) units of investment goods. [40] Thus the total domestic investment fund is $A_3 + A_4 + A_5$ and financed in the following way:

$$(A1) \quad \frac{I}{(A_3 + A_4 + A_5)} = \frac{S_a}{(A_5 + A_3)} + \frac{S_i}{(A_4)}$$

Since, in addition, there exist also inflows of foreign capital $(S_f)$, the finance equation may be slightly modified to obtain (4). [41]

What we have just presented is pertinent to the case of Taiwan and would have to be modified in a by now predictable fashion to capture realistically the case of Korea. As we indicated in the context of our discussion of Figures 1 and 2, the essential differences are (1) the agricultural contribution to the saving fund here is much lower because of the low level of agricultural productivity; (2) whatever contribution the agricultural sector does make to industrial finance is through the 'domestic route', i.e. inter-sectoral finance; (3) foreign capital plays a much larger role in the financing of domestic capital formation.

## APPENDIX 2

*Data Sources:* (Korea)

(a) *National Income Statistical Yearbook* 1968, 1969 (The Bank of Korea)

(b) *Korea Statistical Yearbook* (1960–69) (Economic Planning Board, Republic of Korea).

(c) *Annual Economic Review* 1955–1959 (The Bank of Korea)

(d) *Economic Statistical Yearbook* 1960–71 (The Bank of Korea).

(e) *Inter-Industry Relations Tables* 1960, 1963, 1966, 1968 (The Bank of Korea).

(f) *Price Statistical Summary* 1961, 1964, 1966, 1968 (The Bank of Korea).

(g) *Yearbook of Agriculture and Forestry* 1964, 1968, 1969 (Ministry of Agriculture and Forestry, Republic of Korea).

(h) *Foreign Trade of Korea* 1964–69 (Ministry of Finance, Republic of Korea).

(i) *Monthly Economic Review* (The Korea Development Bank).

(j) *Agricultural Cooperative Monthly Survey* (National Agricultural Cooperative Federation, Korea).

(k) *Estimates of Korean Capital and Inventory Coefficients in 1968* (by Kee Chun Han, Yonsei University).

(l) *Analysis of Household Spending-Saving Behaviour in Korea*, 1970 (by Sung-Hwan Jo, Sogang University).

*Data Sources:* (Taiwan)

(a) *National Income of the Republic of China*, 1951-1970 (Directorate-General of Budgets, Accounts and Statistics, Executive Yuan).

(b) *Industry of Free China* (CIECD), 1970

(c) *Commodity-Price Statistics Monthly, Taiwan District*, 1971 (Directorate-General of Budgets, Accounts and Statistics, Executive Yuan).

(d) *Monthly Statistics of the Republic of China* (Directorate-General of Budgets, Accounts and Statistics, Executive Yuan).

(e) *Input-Output Table* (CIECD), 1961, 1964, 1966.

(f) *Taiwan Agricultural Year Book*, 1962-1970 (Department of Agriculture and Forestry, Provincial Government of Taiwan).

(g) *Taiwan Economic Statistics* (CIECD).

(h) *Taiwan Statistical Data Book* (CIECD), 1970.

(i) 'Household Registration' of Provincial Department of Civil Affairs.

(j) *Taiwan Area Report on the Year-End Household Check and Population Registration Statistics* (of Provincial Department of Civil Affairs).

(k) *Export and Import Foreign Exchange Settlements Statistics*, 1970 (Foreign Exchange Department, the Central Bank of Taiwan.)

(l) *The Republic of China, Taiwan Industrial Production Statistics Monthly* (Ministry of Economic Affairs).

(m) *Quarterly Report on the Labour Force Survey in Taiwan,* 1963–69, (Labour Force Survey and Research Institute).

(n) *Taiwan Agricultural Price Monthly* (Department of Agriculture and Forestry, Provincial Government of Taiwan).

(o) *Monthly Statistics on Price Received and Price Paid by Farmer in Taiwan* (Bureau of Accounting and Statistics Provincial Government of Taiwan, Republic of China).

(p) *The Republic of China, Report on Industrial and Commercial Surveys,* 1954, 1962, 1966 (Ministry of Economic Affairs).

(q) *Taiwan Food Statistics Book,* 1970 (Taiwan Provincial Food Bureau)

NOTES

1. S. Kuznets [*1966*]; see also Fei and Ranis [*1969*]. This process, linked to the achievement of political independence, began earlier in Latin America.

2. These dates, coming a few years after the move from the Chinese Mainland, in the first instance, and after the Korean War, in the second, are commonly accepted as appropriate base years.

3. We recognize the incompleteness of the mapping between agriculture and subsistence, on the one hand, and non-agriculture and commercialized, on the other. 'Agriculture' is viewed as a proxy for sectors in which wages or income exceed the marginal product and are institutionally determined, and 'non-agriculture' as a proxy for sectors where there is an approximation to a competitive solution. The statistical problem remains and has not been solved in the context of this paper. It would require a careful disaggregation of the services sector, as well as of agriculture and even industry, into their commercialized and non-commercialized components.

4. If desirable, capital can be combined with land.

5. The reasons for this are complicated, but related to the greater attention paid by the Japanese to irrigation and organizational infrastructure in colonial Taiwan where a cash crop, sugar, was to be promoted, along with the staples.

6. In a predominantly agricultural economy, we would expect the relationship in relative agricultural productivities between the two countries to also be reflected in their relative per capita GDP levels. This is borne out by the parity calculations in Table 1, row 4a, column 4.

7. Thus, in column 7 of the statistical table, the internal terms of trade reflect the common international terms of trade.

8. This is shown by the distance nj in Figure 1b.

9. The absolute fixity of the IRW is, of course, only an approximation to reality The model could easily be amended to incorporate a more realistic upward 'creep' in the IRW level. The price-consumption curve (PC$_T$) is derived by taking the typical worker's income at OB$_T$ and determining his consumption of agricultural and non-agricultural goods at different terms of trade, i.e. it is the locus of tangencies between the worker's indifference map and a 'swivelling' budget line anchored at point B$_T$.

10. Given Korea's lower level of agricultural productivity (v) approximately the same level of per capita consumption of agricultural goods (C$_a$) and plus more people still in agriculture, if follows that E$_a$ must be smaller here (see equation 2b). This is not shown clearly in Figure 2b because the net export is negligible.

11. In the absence of a wage gap between the agricultural worker's real wage in terms of industrial goods and the industrial worker's real wage in terms of industrial goods. The existence, realistically, of a wage gap can be easily accommodated.

12. Suppose the production functions of the two countries were the same. Given the higher input ratio (at D$_K$, Figure 2f) for Korea than for Taiwan (at D$_T$, Figure 1f), the equilibrium point for Korea (h$_K$, Figure 2e) would have implied a higher level of both the marginal and average productivities of labour. For example, the Korean MPP$_K$-curve would have passed through a higher point such as 'u' in Figure 2e. Compared with such a point, the actual point 'h$_K$' indicates the presence of 'labour saving innovations' in Korea as compared with Taiwan.

13. Our understanding of the precise causes of such differences in colonial heritage

a phenomenon which must be traced to profit maximization under colonialism, given differential resource endowments in the two colonies—is clearly incomplete at this point. [see, however, *Samuel Ho 1971*].

14. The domestic demand for industrial goods which includes not only consumption but also industrial demands is actually higher than this (i.e. a certain multiple of $W_T C_i^\triangle$) We have, however, for simplicity's sake, assumed that $W_T C_i^\triangle$ represents the total per capita demand for industrial goods.

15. The forces that determine these contributions to the total saving fund may be traced to the distribution of income as well as to the rules governing intersectoral exchange in the context of our analytical framework. The theory of determination of savings in an open dualistic economy will be explained in Appendix 1.

16. While technological progress (i.e. the upward shift of the Q-curve) increases average labour productivity, the labour allocation effect itself will also increase labour productivity if the agricultural labour force declines absolutely. We shall examine this issue briefly below.

17. While agricultural productivity in Taiwan, for example, increases by 130 per cent during the period, agricultural real wages increased only 50 per cent (rows 1 and 5). The existence of labour surplus is indicated in Figure 1b, by point 'n' (corresponding to the IRW) lying above point 'j' (indicating $MPP_L$) in the initial year. This signifies the existence of disguised unemployment during much of the transition. In the case of Korea, agricultural real wages lag much less behind productivity gain. This signifies the more rapid 'pulling out' of agricultural labour with the help of foreign capital inflow and the earlier termination of disguised unemployment. We will return to both these points in the next section.

18. And/or, once the more realistic possibility of a wage gap (between agricultural and industrial workers) is admitted, due to a change in the size of that gap.

19. Nevertheless, for the economy as a whole, the distribution of income may well improve for labour, as a consequence of the existence of a wage gap between the two sectors and the shift of the economy's centre of gravity from one to the other. The full analysis of income distribution in the two-sector world under discussion is a complicated one and really beyond the scope of this paper.

20. In recent years, total industrial exports have been rising at close to 35 per cent annually in both countries.

21. In this paper we are not concerned with the formulation of a truly deterministic dynamic theory. Our analysis, it is hoped, can provide some guidelines as to how such a theory should be formulated and tested by time series.

22. For a fuller discussion of commercialization point, see Fei and Ranis [*1964*].

23. Before '$e_6$' there exists disguised unemployment in agriculture as the $MPP_L$ is below the institutional wage $w_a$; after '$e_6$' the labour surplus condition terminates as the wage now follows the $MPP_L$, signifying the fact that the reservoir of the unemployed has been 'mopped up' and wages are henceforth determined according to neo-classical rules. If, more realistically, the IRW itself rises, from $B_T$ to $B_T^1$ the commercialization point does not occur until productivity level $M_8$ (leading to point $e_8$) has been reached.

In the absence of technology change in agriculture, only a major absolute decline in the agricultural population could permit the commercialization point to be reached, i.e. by moving along a constant $MPP_L$ curve.

24. This is traced, in turn, to the rate of capital accumulation and the degree of labour using bias in the industrial sector.

25. This, in fact, has definitely been occurring in Taiwan. The question of whether or not the commercialization point and a condition of labour shortage has really been reached in Korea or whether the recent rise in real wages may be due to a short run deterioration of the industrial sector's terms of trade (as agricultural stagnation continues and P.L. 480 imports are becoming more expensive) is still not entirely clear and the subject of continuing investigation by the authors. One thing is clear, however, i.e. that, if the commercialization point has, in fact, already been reached in Korea it is more by moving upward along given M curves, while in Taiwan there was more of an upward shift in the M curve itself. On this general subject, see also Roger Sedjo (*1971*).

26. A similar pattern of the behaviour of real wages can be observed for historical Japan whose earlier experience as an open labour surplus economy is relevant here.

Here also the pattern of real wage increases shows a modest upward creep in the nineteenth century followed by a substantial acceleration after World War One [see *Fei and Ranis, 1971*].

27. See the discussion of the 'Export Substitution Point'.

28. In historical Japan the reversal point occurred during the last decade of the nineteenth century, thus preceding the commercialization point by at least several decades. It is also quite possible for the reversal point to occur after the commercialization point. A systematic investigation of the sequential order of all the turning points is the purpose of a more formal dynamically determistic theory yet to be developed.

29. The crucial factors are (1) the population growth rate (2) the relative size of the labour force in the agricultural sector, (3) the population size relative to the demand for the products of this country in the world market. Hong Kong can solve her 'agricultural problem' by this strategy because all these factors are favourable. There is a serious doubt in our mind that this strategy can be successful in Korea.

30. It should be noted that Korea's $E_i/E$ ratio is substantially higher from the very beginning, as a consequence of the economy's relatively weak agricultural base from the outset. Export substitution here means, in part, a shift from traditional non-agricultural exports (e.g. mining) to non-traditional non-agricultural exports (e.g. labour intensive textiles and electronics). The small differences in determining the E-S point from the import and export sides (in Figures 6 and 7) should not surprise us. 'Nature does not make jumps' and we are really talking about turning ranges rather than turning points. The change in trend and in the structure of the two economies is clearly established. In the case of Korea, there is more of an over lapping between the end of I-S and the beginning of E-S growth.

31. Many theoretical issues and interpretations can be raised, but not elaborated, in this paper. The phenomenon may be approached from the viewpoint of international trade and comparative advantage which emphasized the inefficiency of import substitution (see, for example, Little, Scitovsky and Scott [*1970*] which would view the emergence of export substitution phase essentially as correcting the mistakes of the import substitution strategy). On the other hand, from the growth theoretical point of view the import substitution phase may be viewed as an essential pre-requisite of the export substitution phase (see Paauw and Fei [*1973*] for a full exposition of this view; also see Ranis [*1972*] for an international comparison).

32. Again, these issues can only be explored with further study by dynamic models.

33. Before that point was reached, however, i.e. during the three decades following the Meiji Restoration in 1868, she had been very successful in generating substantial agricultural productivity increases. [see, for example, *Johnston, 1952; Ranis 1959; Ohkawa and Rosovsky, 1960*].

34. A full exploration of the relation between the 'international terms of trade' and the 'internal terms of trade' between agriculture and non-agriculture goods requires an understanding of whether 'free trade' prevailed in these countries and whether they are small countries. We feel that initially, 'free trade' prevailed in these two countries so that the internal terms of trade reflected the common international terms of trade. However, in the process of development in the last 20 years, internal terms of trade gradually diverged from the international terms of trade—a theoretical observation which needs to be investigated further.

35. While there admittedly exist important differences in the soil, climate and other elements of the natural endowment as between Korea and Taiwan—and no one is suggesting that every country has equal reserves of agricultural productivity ready for activation—there is ample evidence that much of the relative failure of Korea's agriculture to date is man-made. We know, for example, that the Japanese left a relatively inferior agricultural infrastructure in Korea, not only in terms of irrigation facilities, but also, and probably more important, in terms of organizational infrastructure. It is our distinct impression—though admittedly, it is risky to be categorical on this point—that much more could have been done to repair this differential. To cite one example, Korea's rural organization (the NACF) represents an attempt to do too many things in agriculture, including the provision of information, of inputs, as well as the power to tax. It is but a pale reflection of Taiwan's Farmers' Associations, hooked up with the JCRR structure, which farmers could view more as their own instrument. Moreover, agri-

cultural price policies in Korea are directed much more towards income redistribution objectives *after* production decisions have already been made rather than providing *ex ante* incentives for increased productivity, as in Taiwan. There seems, in short, to be a substantial consensus among agricultural economists and agronomists that while the 'Green Revolution' potential of Korea may be below that of Taiwan, the actual performance of Korea's farmers also remains substantially below that potential.

36. Research on this issue is currently under way. For the current use of a variety of special incentives ranging from tariff and tax reductions, to linkage systems, import wastage allowances, deposit rate preferences, differential interest, electricity and freight rates, see Kim Kwang Suk [*1971*].

37. Worse, with industry having to help pay for net agricultural imports.

38. $B_1 = oL_The$; $B_2 = hebb_T$; $B_3 = bb_TcB_T$. $B_1$, $B_2$ ... $B_6$ are rectangular areas.

39. $hf/he = ch/dh$. This means $hfxdh = chxhe$.

40. In Figure 8e total domestic output of the industrial sector is $A_1 + A_2 + A_3 + A_4$, with an output capacity for consumer goods of $A_1 + A_2$. For Taiwan, in fact, the domestic consumer goods production capacity is less than the domestic demand ($A_1 + A_2$) or the capacity for investment goods production is greater than $A_3 + A_4$. In that situation, a part of imports takes the form of industrial consumer goods.

41. When foreign capital inflows are admitted, the magnitudes of 'investment', 'supply of industrial goods', 'industrial imports' are all augmented by the value of '$S_f$'.

## REFERENCES

Fei, J. C. H. and G. Ranis, 1964, *Development of the Labour Surplus Economy: Theory and Policy*, Homewood, Ill.: Richard D. Irwin.

Fei, J. C. H. and G. Ranis, 1969, 'Economic Development in Historical Perspective', *American Economic Review*, May.

Fei ,J. C. H. and G. Ranis, 1971. 'On the Empirical Relevancy of the Fei-Ranis Model of Economic Development: A Reply', *American Economic Review*, September.

Ho, S., 1971, *The Development Policy of the Japanese Colonial Government in Taiwan, 1895–1945*, in G. Ranis (ed.), *Government and Economic Development*, New Haven: Yale University Press.

Johnston, B. F., 1952, 'Agricultural Productivity and Economic Development of Japan', *Journal of Political Economy*, 7: 2.

Kim, Kwang Suk, 1971. *Export Promotion and Industrial Incentive Policy in Korea*.

Kuznets, S., 1966, *Modern Economic Growth: Rate Structure and Spread*, New Haven: Yale University Press.

Lewis, W. A., 1954, *Development with Unlimited Supplies of Labour*, Manchester School of Economics and Social Studies.

Little, I., T. Scitovsky and M. Scott, 1970, *Industry and Trade in Some Developing Countries—A Comparative Study*, London: Oxford University Press.

Ohkawa, K. and H. Rosovsky, 1960, 'The Role of Agriculture in Modern Japanese Economic Development', *Economic Development and Cultural Change*, 9: 1, Part 2, October.

Paauw and Fei, 1975, *Development of the Open Dualistic Economy*, New Haven: Yale University Press.

Ranis, G., 1959, 'Financing Economic Development', *Economic History Review*, March.

Ranis, G., 1972, *Relative Prices in Planning for Economic Development*, in D. J. Daly (ed.), *International Comparisons of Prices and Output*, NBER, Columbia University Press.

Sedjo, R., 1971, 'The Turning Point in Korea', paper presented to the ILCORK Conference, Seoul, Korea, August 22–27.

# Dualism Revisited: A New Approach to the Problems of the Dual Society in Developing Countries†

## *By H. W. Singer**

SUMMARY

Dualism in the sense of persistent and increasing divergencies exists on various levels, internationally in relations between richer and poorer countries, and internally within the developing countries themselves. The following article focuses mainly on the internal dualism and growing inequalities within the developing countries, but links these to growing international inequalities in command over modern science and technology. Tendencies within the field of science and technology, including their increasing capital intensity and their increasing dominance by the needs of the richer countries and lack of direct relevance for the needs of developing countries are closely associated with growing unemployment and under-employment in various forms within the developing countries. More and more the relevant forms of dualistic fission run along the line of employed versus unemployed rather than the more traditional distinctions between rural and urban sectors, traditional versus modern sectors, etc. The tendency for technological developments to produce internal dualism in the under-developed countries is further strengthened by a number of factors, including the association of modern technology with foreign investment. The article also considers the argument by Professor Myint that dualism tends to be artificially induced and is due to prejudices in favour of a mistaken concept of modernization. The article concludes that the forces making for dualism in the contemporary world are deeply rooted particularly in science and technology, and that much more radical action than a mere redress of discriminatory practices or correction of prejudices will be needed. The limited applicability of western concepts is illustrated by issues arising from the wage and income structure in the developing countries. The better utilization of existing capital is a problem parallel in importance with a more appropriate technology and both together hold out prospects of approaching development problems along more Keynesian lines than is often realized.

A FIRST DEFINITION

Without claiming any refinement of definition, the concept of dualism clearly embraces four key elements: (1) different sets of conditions (of which one can in some meaningful sense be described as 'superior' and the other as 'inferior') coexist in a given space at the same time; (2) this co-existence is chronic and not merely transitional, i.e. it is not simply due to a necessary gradualism creating time lags in the displacement of the 'superior' element by the 'inferior' element; (3) the degrees of superiority or inferiority show no signs of rapidly diminishing—they may be con-

† This article was originally prepared for the Conference on the Dual Economy held at Glasgow in September 1969 with the assistance of a grant from Shell.
* The author is a fellow of the Institute of Development Studies (Sussex).

stant or even increasing; (4) the interrelations between the 'superior' and 'inferior' elements, or the lack of interrelations between them, are such that the existence of the superior element does not do much to pull up the inferior element (i.e. a weak 'spread'), or may even positively serve to pull it down ('backwash').

INTERNATIONAL DUALISM: DUALISM IN THE WORLD ECONOMY

When we reflect on this first definition, it becomes strikingly clear that these four elements also are an almost perfect description of the present situation in the world economy.

(1) Undoubtedly great differences in *per capita* incomes or standards of living, however measured, coexist at the present time between the different countries, continents, races and climatic zones of the world.

(2) These differences are clearly not short-term but chronic. Comparing North-West Europe with say India, they have persisted now for at least a century or more, and compared with Africa for perhaps three or four centuries.

(3) The differences show signs of increasing rather than diminishing. Adopting the somewhat doubtful measure of *per capita* G.N.P., this increased during the last decade by about 4–5 per cent per annum for the more developed countries (taking East and West together) but only by about 2·5 per cent per annum for the less developed countries. Moreover, within the group of the less developed countries there was a marked tendency for the better-off among them to advance faster than the poorest group, thus satisfying another criterion of dualism within the group of the LDCs. This is in sharp contrast to the more developed countries where the tendency was for the best-off among the developed countries to grow more slowly than the less well-off among the richer countries.

(4) The interrelations between the richer and the poorer countries in the world economy, in the judgement of a number of economists at least, contain elements which make the rapid growth of the former only doubtfully helpful and possibly positively harmful to the development of the latter. Such backwash elements have been seen variously in the following: colonialism, capitalism, export of unsuitable science and technology, brain drain, private foreign investment, one-sided or harmful international division of labour, harmful trade policies, harmful aid politices (or even harm done by the concept of aid itself), creation of élites in poorer countries, unsuitable methods of training for unrealistic professional standards, demonstration effect in luxury consumption, etc. We need only mention the name of Boeke to indicate how from its very introduction into economic thinking the concept of dualism has been interwoven with questions relating to the international relations between rich and poor countries.

It is not surprising, therefore, that the concept of dualism within the under-developed countries has been examined by methods of analysis often directly borrowed from international economics. Such concepts as the internal terms of trade, net flows of resources from one sector to the other, internal migration, etc., come to mind in this connection.

The undoubted existence of dualism in the world economy must not be taken too far. Most economists would agree that the high rate of growth and the maintenance of reasonably full employment by the richer countries in the post-war period on balance has been immensely helpful to the poorer countries. It has enabled them to maintain a growth rate of output which is high by historical standards and would, if maintained over a long period of time, improve their situation considerably. However, at the other extreme, very few would now say that the rapid growth of the richer countries, or even a rapid expansion of their trade with the poorer countries if it were associated with it, would be a sufficient as well as necessary condition for their continued or rapid growth. Moreover, and this is more directly relevant to our present purpose, it is at least arguable that the very forces which are set in motion by the rapid growth of the richer countries—specifically the development of ever more sophisticated, costly and capital-intensive technologies, and of mortality-reducing health improvements and disease controls—are such as to create forces within the poorer countries—specifically a population explosion, rising unemployment and inability to develop their own technological capacities, which may in fact assure that they will not have the time needed for the continued maintenance of current growth rates, let alone their acceleration, so as to result in acceptable levels of development.

INTERNATIONAL TECHNOLOGICAL DUALISM

The international dualism in the world economy discussed in the previous section is mirrored in the crucial field of science and technology Current discussion of dualism has concerned itself increasingly with this aspect, and this paper argues that it is the appropriate point of departure for an understanding of the nature of the problem.

International dualism in science and technology—in the sense of chronic widening inequalities can be seen in the following four dimensions:

(1) The process of scientific and technological advance in all its stages—basic research, applied research and blueprinting[1]—has been heavily concentrated in the richer countries. The best estimate we can make at the present time is that measuring the distribution of advance by the distribution of inputs in the form of research and development expenditures, we find that 70 per cent of world expenditure is in the U.S., 25 per cent in Europe, and 2 per cent in the less developed countries.[2] This unequal distribution would not matter if the direction of advance, the scientific and technological priorities and the methods of solving scientific and technological problems, were independent of where the work is carried on. This, however, is patently not the case. The 98 per cent of research and development expenditures in the richer countries are spent on solving the problems which concern the richer countries, according to their own priorities, and on solving these problems by the methods and approaches appropriate to the factor endowment of the

richer countries. In both respects—selection of problems and methods of solving them—the interests of the poorer countries would be bound to point in completely different directions. Yet the two-thirds of mankind with its different problems accounts for only 2 per cent of all expenditures—a discrepancy per capita ratio of no less than 100 : 1.

(2) The fact that the richer countries have such a virtual monopoly of research and development expenditures, as concretely expressed in terms of institutions, equipment, number of trained scientists and technologists, as well as a virtual monopoly of deciding where the existing frontiers of knowledge are, has the further consequence that the activites of the small number of institutions and people, represented by the 2 per cent of research and development expenditures in the poorer countries, is also itself largely devoted to the problems and methods determined by the richer countries. Much of the present expenditures of the poorer countries represent as hopeless attempt to compete from an inferior position in solving the same kinds of problems by the same methods, rather than those that would be suggested by their own conditions. In fact, the indigenous scientific and technological capacity of the poorer countries is even insufficient to determine the nature of their own problems and to determine how far they are susceptible to solution by applied science and technology with appropriate methods.

(3) The existence of the richer countries, with their immensely superior facilities, and the glamour associated with work on their self-defined 'frontiers of knowledge' exert a powerful attraction resulting in the well-known 'brain drain'. Although this brain drain—the external brain drain—has attracted a great deal of attention, in actual fact the diversion of their own effort mentioned in the preceding pargaraph—the internal brain drain[3] as we may call it—may in fact be a more serious and dangerous loss.

(4) The traditional remedy for the unequal distribution of research and development expenditures plus the two brain drains is, of course, the transfer of technology in ready-made form. However, this suffers from various difficulties. In the first place the technology is not always available for transfer, often being covered by secrecy, restrictive agreements, legal patent rights, etc. Perhaps under-developed countries may obtain this technological knowledge but only at an excessive price which they cannot afford for lack of foreign exchange, or perhaps only in the indirect form of imports of equipment or other commodities embodying the new technology which again possibly they cannot afford for lack of foreign exchange. The alternative of transferring technology as part and parcel of private foreign investment raises problems of its own, as will be seen in the next section. Perhaps most important of all, the transfer of technology may not be useful or even possible unless there is a domestic infrastructure available in the importing under-developed country capable of providing the capacity to select, adapt and introduce the appropriate technologies. This domestic capacity, as we have seen, is largely lacking.

FROM INTERNATIONAL TECHNOLOGICAL DUALISM TO INTERNAL DUALISM

This international imbalance, or dualism, in the field of science and technology explains to a large extent why the growth of the under-developed countries has not been as fast as one theoretically would expect. Theoretically—and a long line of classical as well as neo-classical economists were convinced of this—one would expect the development job to become progressively easier with the passage of time and the accumulation of knowledge. The late developing country would have an increasingly large stock of available scientific and technological knowledge to draw upon. Thus, the late-comers in development would be at an increasing advantage compared with their predecessors.

Now there is no doubt that the stock of available scientific and technological knowledge is increasing. In fact, it is increasing at an accelerating and unprecedented rate. Moreover, there can be no doubt that up to a point—perhaps we could say up to 1938—the theory actually worked. The early developers, specifically Great Britain and France, developed at a slower rate than say Germany and the U.S. in the second wave. The Scandinavian countries and perhaps Russia and Japan in the third wave developed even faster, and so again did the next wave of Australia, Canada, New Zealand, etc. (3, p. 20). But in the last few decades one cannot say that this trend has continued or become more pronounced, as one would have expected.

Evidently the accumulation of scientific and technological knowledge has not played the role that was hoped for from it. The chief reason for this is closely related to international dualism: although the total *volume* of available knowledge has rapidly increased, at the same time its *composition* has changed so as to become increasingly less relevant for the under-developed countries—and this in turn is due to international dualism, the fact that knowledge is accumulated by the richer countries, in the richer countries, and in respect of the problems of the richer countries. These are not the problems or methods of primary concern to the developing countries. The richer countries are mainly interested in sophisticated products, large markets, sophisticated[4] production methods requiring large inputs of capital and high levels of skill and management while saving labour and natural raw materials. The poor countries by contrast are much more interested in simple products, simple designs, saving of capital and particularly land, reduction in skill requirements, and production for smaller markets. The potential impact of the increasing stock of knowledge—no doubt still very important and on balance useful to developing countries—has been largely offset by a tendency for each unit of this knowledge to become less and less useful to the poorer countries.

So far we have talked about the impact of international dualism in science and technology on the rate of development in the poorer countries. For our present purposes it is also necessary to state why these conditions lead to internal dualism inside the under-developed countries, apart from retarding their rate of growth. There are four main reasons which can be distinguished.

(1) Most obviously, since virtually no research and development expenditure is devoted to problems of special concern to the under-developed countries, we find that technology tends to be much more up to date in those sectors (typically, modern manufacturing industry) in which the activities in the poorer countries are most similar to those in the richer countries. By contrast, there is little or no technological progress in areas where the problem does not exist in the richer countries (typically, problems of tropical agriculture, problems of small-scale production, problems of utilization of natural raw materials specific to the under-developed countries, problems of subsistence farming and of subsistence crops). This will be obviated only by delibe-rate countervailing international action, e.g. such technical assistance in the field as the work of the Rockefeller and Ford Foundations towards the development of new seeds or the endowment of the Tropical Products Institute by the Ministry of Overseas Development in Britain.[5] Barring such special efforts—at present on a minute scale—the end result will be that agriculture, rural, small-scale production as well as production utilizing indigenous materials and local labour, will be tech-nologically neglected and backward, while technology in industry or in fields otherwise corresponding to the situation in the richer countries (including also modern commercial farming) will be much more advanced.

(2) Since modern technology is imported from abroad by way of transfer, and for lack of an indigenous scientific and technological capacity inside the under-developed countries, the imported technology does not take root and is not adapted or sufficiently developed in line with the requirements of the country. This means that where modern technology is used its use remains limited to the specific area where it has been introduced, and it thus becomes an enclave of modernity. This point has been well expressed by Professor Stigler by saying that 'the small economies that imitate us can follow our methods of doing things this year, but not our methods of changing things next year; therefore they will be very rigid' (6). Although Professor Stigler attri-butes this rigidity more to the absence of a supporting network of auxiliary industries and educational facilities in the under-developed countries, this lack in turn is closely related to the lack of an indigenous widespread structure within the under-developed countries which could serve to propagate the type of improvements required by the local situation.

(3) The international dualism in technology leads to a situation where the transfer and foreign exchange difficulties are by-passed through modern technology being introduced into the under-developed countries to a high degree as part and parcel of the process of private foreign investment. In this way, the whole process becomes internalized within the big international firms. This arrangement, however, while it certainly helps to introduce modern technology and obviate some of the consequences of the concentration of innovation in the richer countries,

has other drawbacks for the under-developed countries. Quite specifically, through the repatriation of profits and dividends, a good deal of the reinvestment potential is lost to the under-developed country. Moreover, a foreign firm (and specially a large transnational company) is not likely to show any great interest in developing labour-intensive technologies—the handling of large masses of local labour is notoriously a difficult, politically touchy and unrewarding job for such foreign firms. In any case, the foreign firm is expected to pay 'decent wages'—the standard of decency being set with some reference to the firm's wages to its staff in its home base in the richer country or to the firm's size and profits—usually resulting in wages at a considerable multiple of average incomes (and certainly of rural incomes) in the under-developed country. This higher wage would in any case reduce much of the incentive for using local labour and for spending a lot of research and development money on production methods directed towards that end, even if the managerial and political reluctance to encourage masses of local labour did not exist. Moreover, in so far as the higher wage standards of foreign enterprise tend to spread to indigenous enterprise in the modern sector as well, the discouragement of indigenous labour-using technologies becomes even more general. A foreign firm also will normally have a preference for bringing in its skilled management and skilled personnel from abroad rather than to go through the lengthy process of training local people, particularly when it must assume that its days will be numbered. Management based on the assumption of getting out again or turning over to local management in a limited time will be weighted in the direction of using the known technology developed at its home base and its existing home-based staff rather than spending time and money on the necessarily gradual processes of local adaptation and local training. There is of course a danger of a vicious circle here: the foreign firms which do not develop local links or train local people, because they have only a limited time horizon, may find that the hostility which they thus generate will in fact shorten their days in the under-developed country; thus the initial short time horizon will have proved self-justifying. Enlightened foreign enterprise and enlightened governments can collaborate to break this vicious circle by combining confidence in long-term operation with application of development of local technology and local training (or alternatively providing for generous compensation for any expenditures on local research and development and training). But it would be short-sighted to deny that such a vicious circle does exist.

Thus it will be seen that there are many reasons why the association of modern technology with foreign firms may prove to be an obstacle to the spreading of modern technology into the economy of the under-developed countries beyond the original investment which will thus tend to remain an 'enclave'.

The need of the poorer countries for a wider spread of appropriate modern technology reveals one aspect of a 'divergence between the global planning of transnational corporations and the national planning

of the various host governments' when on the part of the large corporation 'its main loyalty must be to the parent country'.[7]

(4) The fourth reason why international dualism in science and
technology leads to internal dualism within the under-developed
countries is perhaps the most important. This refers to the rising
volume of unemployment in its various forms. Basically this is the combined result of a rapid increase in the population and labour force
(itself largely a result of the progress of science and technology in the
field of health and disease control) on the one hand, and the capital-
intensive nature of modern technology with its limited power of penetration, on the other hand. This combination means that the total
number of new jobs which can be created in the sectors reached by
modern technology is insufficient to cater for the increase in population
which cannot be productively absorbed in agriculture through the cultivation of more land. The artificially high wage rates in the modern
sector already referred to in the previous paragraph and further but-
tressed by welfare legislation, trade union pressures, etc., also mean that
it becomes quite rational, particularly for the younger people in the
under-developed countries, to migrate to the towns even on a remote
chance of a wage job in the modern sector. Since wage levels in the
modern sector may be perhaps two or three times the level of average
income on the small family farm—and many of the younger people
might not even have the chance of sharing in this average income—it
becomes rational to migrate even on a 50 per cent or 33 per cent chance
of a job in the town (8). Moreover, given the high skill differentials, the
prospect, however remote, of obtaining further training or experience
adds a further inducement, justifying the acceptance of even lesser
chances of a present job. Thus the acceptance of even extraordinarily
high rates of unemployment—far from being an irrational sociological
feature of 'Eastern' society in under-developed countries, à la Boeke—
becomes completely understandable.

This situation has created an employment crisis in the under-developed
countries which is probably the most important and dangerous source of
dualism in their economies and societies. On the one hand, we find a small
élite of regularly employed people. In sharp contrast with historical
experience, the share of the total population and labour force in regular
wage earning employment in the modern sector and using modern technology is not increasing in the under-developed countries, as it was
decidedly doing in all the previous instances of development, from the
U.K. to Japan and Russia. Typically, in an under-developed country
today, industrial output is increasing at the rate of 7–8 per cent per
annum which easily equals or exceeds the historical record of the now
developed countries. Employment, however, increases only at the rate of
about 3 per cent per annum—and even this may be a statistical exaggeration[8]—hardly more than the increase in the labour force itself. On the
other hand, we see an increasing number and an increasing proportion of
the total labour force relegated to a marginal existence: either casual
employment, intermittent employment, disguised unemployment or open

unemployment in the town, or else as a landless farm worker or marginal producer on a small farm in the country.

This is the most dangerous dualism of all. The older discussion of, dualism in its various categories—sociological, technological, economic etc.—seems to me to have faded in relevance by not focusing upon the central point, i.e. the employment crisis. This is perhaps understandable because the sharpening of the employment crisis and our realization of the seriousness of the situation are of comparatively recent origin. Professor H. A. Turner in a recent study (9, p. 7) has found that, in fourteen under-developed countries studied, unemployment is increasing at the rate of 8·5 per cent per annum. My own estimate is that the present level of unemployment in the under-developed countries on a moderate definition —not of course including low productivity employment except where the disguise of the unemployment is quite transparent—is 25 per cent or so,[9] more or less equivalent to our own experience in the depths of the Great Depression. At that time we would have had no doubt where the source of dualism in our own socieities was: it was between the men with work and the men without work. This is the situation in the under-developed countries today, except that the situation is statistically concealed since the notion of a 'job' is more complicated in countries where self-employment is dominant. If my estimate of a starting level of 25 per cent and Professor Turner's estimate of an annual rate of increase of 8·5 per cent are both correct, a projection into the future would yield frightening percentages of unemployment: 43 per cent by 1980 and 73 per cent by 1990. No doubt, drastic changes in policy, including the field of science and technology, would become inevitable in the face of such unthinkable exercises in futurology.

In the face of this present situation much of the previous discussion of where the lines of dualism should be drawn seem rather obsolete. Some of the dualistic models or theories contrast the urban and the rural sector; some the industrial and the agricultural sector; some the cash and subsistence sector; some the large-scale and small-scale sector, etc. All these distinctions are relevant for many other purposes, and they all place the activities with a prevalence of capital-intensive technology mainly on one side, with wage employment important, and on the other side activities carried out with little capital and with self-employment vastly predominant. However, in the light of the new situation it seems clear that the line of division does not run cleanly between the rural and urban sectors. Open and disguised unemployment of all types is as rampant in the towns of the under-developed countries today as it is in the countryside, and no simple rural/urban dichotomy will do. Similarly, those whom the available supplies of capital and land provide with reasonably full employment are to be found both in the country and in wage employment in the towns. It would not be easy to say whether the urban or rural proportions are generally higher on one side of the division or the other.

DUALISM—NATURAL OR ARTIFICIALLY INDUCED?

Some authors, including Professor Myint, maintain strongly that dualism tends to be artificially induced and is due to discrimination shown by planners and policy makers in the under-developed countries, and by aid donors and investors in the richer countries, in favour of a mistaken concept of 'modernization', mistakenly identified with 'capital-intensive' and 'large-scale'. One can comment on this at various levels, in the light of the preceding analysis.

At the most superficial level, one can question whether this alleged discrimination really exists. There are certainly countervailing forces at work which one should also not fail to mention. For instance, surely taxation is much more effective in the case of the urban modern sector, specially perhaps foreign enterprises, while it is very difficult to collect taxes from traditional producers? Surely also, while in the past very often a pro-urban and anti-rural bias existed among the planners, there has now been a considerable swing in the opposite direction? Surely, the policy of high urban wages squeezes the profits of the modern urban producer and helps to maintain the demand for agricultural products and other products from the traditional sector? Surely, while over-valued exchange rates and the tariff policies of developing countries may favour the import of capital at artificially cheap rates, other cases could also be cited where the balance of payments pressures on the developing countries result in general import difficulties which must surely hit the modern organized sector more severely than the traditional sector centred upon local inputs, and may in fact open up sales possibilities for the traditional sector? Surely, in many under-developed countries the social and political pressures arising from mass unemployment are now strong enough to enforce policies in the direction of creating employment by rural and urban public works, building of industrial estates for small-scale producers, etc.? Surely, the restrictive trade practices of the richer countries, such as the prohibitively high implicit tariffs on the processing stages, or their protectionist agri-cultural policies, may also bear as harshly or more harshly upon the development of the modern sector in the developing countries, and in some ways favour the traditional as against the modern sector?

But while at a superficial level one can debate whether the discrimination in favour of the capital-intensive sector is really as clear-cut as it is some-times presented, at a somewhat deeper level the argument certainly carries much weight. Our own analysis has placed the emphasis on factors which could be defined as 'artificial' or 'discriminatory'. It was pointed out that the scientists and technologists of the developing countries are themselves trained and conditioned to accept the frontiers of knowledge as being where they are for the richer countries—frontiers which may be as far removed from the problems of the poorer countries as the moon. This point certainly has much more general validity. It applies not only to the scientists and technologists but also to the economists, planners, skilled workers, business men and indeed the general population of the poorer countries. This used to be known as the 'demonstration effect'. Because the richer countries have come closer to the desired goal of development, their products, their way of life, their approaches are considered as superior, and it is forgotten that these approaches, products and technologies did not spring ready-made from the head of these various Zeuses, but rather are the end product of a long and painful development. When these standards are taken over, dualism results for two reasons: (*a*) the non-modern sector is excluded as being unworthy of attention and thus falls farther and farther behind; and (*b*) the resources of the poorer countries—both physical and human—are insufficient to do more than spread the forces of modernity over more than a limited and often exogenously controlled part of their economies. Thus, the discrimination involved in applying a concept of modernization, based on such a demonstration effect, does go a long way towards explaining the prevailing dualism.

Yet at an even more searching level one must say that it is not sufficient to change discrimination in day-to-day policies in order to avoid dualism. Rather, our analysis is aimed at maintaining that the forces making for dualism are deep rooted, particularly so in the field of science and technology. Much more positive action than a mere redress of discriminatory practices will be needed before balanced and widespread advance, indigenously fed and sustained, can permeate the economies of the under-developed countries in all their sectors.

Apart from the abandonment of mistaken concepts of modernization, mistakenly identifying progress with physical capital and with the large-scale unit, a positively new and different concept will have to be developed. Hence, the insistence in the earlier part of this paper on the vital necessity of creating an indigenously based problem-solving capacity in the field of science and technology. If the rising pressure of unemployment enforces on all of us reconsideration of present approaches it may yet turn out to be a blessing in disguise.

DUALISM—DO 'WESTERN' CONCEPTS APPLY?

In Boeke's original introduction of the concept of dualism into development analysis, this was closely linked with the idea that traditional western concepts, and quite specifically conventional western economics, do not apply to the under-developed countries particularly not to their traditional sectors. 'East is East and West is West and never the twain shall meet.' Any attempts to modernize the traditional 'eastern' (we would now call them southern) economies by the introduction of western ideas, western techniques or western-trained men only result in difficulties and in sharpening the dual character of their economies.

This viewpoint certainly has fallen into disfavour. Particularly such phenomena as the alleged backward sloping supply curve of labour, whether in agriculture or industry, or the alleged reluctance of the traditional farmer to migrate or accept new ways for raising his crops are fairly widely discredited, and rightly so. Obviously, east and west are in fact meeting in many places and many ways (although not always successfully), and the most ardent desire of the east does seem to be that the west would meet it more frequently and more intimately (although again not always in the same ways that it does now).

Our previous presentation of dualism as arising from the cleavage between the limited sector where modern regular wage employment obtains, and the sector where unemployment or under-employment in its various forms obtains, based on the lopsided nature of technological advance, in some ways serves to vindicate Boeke's position that conventional western concepts should not be applied too directly or uncritically. It was Keynes who demonstrated in 1936 with his General Theory that in a labour surplus condition many familiar and established tenets and relationships have to be re-thought, or even turned upside down. This is even more true in the special type of a labour surplus economy found in the under-developed countries of today.

A few illustrations may be given of how some apparently 'universal' economic propositions will have to be modified in the dual economies characterized by labour surpluses. The most obvious illustration can be provided in connection with the very first step in dealing with this unemployment problem. The 'universal' (including Keynesian) answer would be that the cure for unemployment is to create additional jobs by more public investment, more private investment, or by increasing the number of jobs connected with a given unit of investment through labour-intensive technologies, better utilization, etc. Ultimately that may be the answer—but more immediately and within the results of what can realistically be done, the creation of additional jobs may actually increase rather than diminish unemployment. This seemingly paradoxical or 'perverse' result follows directly from the previous explanation of high unemployment rates as arising from a willingness to accept a fractional share or chance of a wage job in exchange for marginal employment in agriculture or in other self-employed traditional occupations. This means that for any actual new job there will be a penumbra or cluster of the workers (larger than one) either actually sharing the job (through under-employment or intermittent employment or disguised under-employment in overstaffing), or sharing the earnings from the job (extended family-kinship-tribal system), or accepting unemployment or disguised unemployment (marginal employment) in view of the imagined chance of a future job. In the framework of this model (8) one can quite reasonably say that the creation of additional jobs creates more unemployment because for every available job two or three people are attracted by the prospect of obtaining it. It could be argued that this is not a real net addition to unemployment because the migrants would otherwise be unemployed in other forms either in rural unemployment or under-employment or else they would have migrated in any case even without the prospect of an additional job because of the attraction of the city lights', etc. This, however, is not necessarily so, and the Todaro model has a certain degree of realism.

Another economic relationship which looks to us perverse from the point of view of conventional economics, but which may well be true in the specific type of dualistic surplus economies with which we are now dealing, is that an increase in the supply of labour instead of reducing wage and salary levels, has the opposite effect of actually increasing them. Dr Jolly has pointed out that 'when salaries and qualifications are linked directly, increasing the supply may actually raise average remunerations' (2). The point here is that remunerations are determined not by the functions and requirements of the job actually performed, nor by market forces relating to supply and demand, but rather by the qualifications of the man holding the job. These qualifications may often be needlessly high, or have no relation to the job to be done, as a result of previous standards set by expatriate employees or colonial officials, under different types of administration or job classifications.

In the British-associated developing countries, the piling up of high educational or professional qualifications resulting in high standards of pay, can often be traced to the standards set by professional associations in the U.K., for instance the Society of Chartered Accountants, the Institutions of Civil, Mechanical and Electrical Engineers, the Joint Medical Council, the Royal College of Veterinary Surgeons, etc. The high standards set by these institutions—however unnecessary or even harmful in their application to under-developed countries—are to a large extent understandable. It must be remembered that under conditions of free Commonwealth migration persons having the required medical/engineering/accounting, etc., qualifications were also entitled to practise in the U.K. (7, especially Chapter XI.)

Additional training of skilled persons would tend to raise average educational standards, and thus average remuneration, since new trainees are likely to have higher formal qualifications than the existing stock of local jobholders—the first post-independence generation of jobholders. Furthermore, the higher the rate of unemployment, the more would trainees tend to postpone the date of entry into the labour market and pile up additional qualifications instead, thus further increasing the already high average rates of remuneration.

The high differentials in favour of skilled workers observed in the labour surplus under-developed countries—much higher differentials than in the richer countries—are conventionally supposed to encourage training and the acquisition of qualifications and thus serve to reduce the differentials to more reasonable proportions. Apart from other doubts on the effect of increasing supply previously discussed, this assumption further fails to take into account that many of the jobs are in the government sector where the present high differentials may often inhibit any further expansion of additional training on the grounds that it would be too expensive to employ the products when trained (2, p. 241). Moreover, in the case of governments specifically, but also of firms, the high salaries paid out to the middle and upper levels of their employees may absorb the funds that otherwise would have been available for the training of more people. In these and other ways, the effect of the skill differentials tends to become perverse rather than functional.

Another strand of 'western' theory which has played a long and important role in the development of economic analysis has derived from the idea that labour supplies arising from increases in population excessive in relation to demand for labour must produce something like a constant or subsistence wage level. This idea governs the development model of Ricardo with the proviso that wages, although remaining constant at subsistence level in real terms, would have a rising tendency in terms of wage cost to the industrial producer (as a result of diminishing returns in agriculture); this would exert a squeeze on profits and in the long run result in a slowing of development (the stationary state). In the analysis of Karl Marx, the industrial reserve army (labour surplus) would keep wages constant at or near subsistence level; but the squeeze on profits would be on the profit rate due to competition among producers while total profits would be constantly increased through constant replacement of labour with reproducible capital; this would go on until the situation became so antenably 'dualistic' (as we would now say), with rising unemployment and impoverishment, that the whole system of organizing production would have to be changed. In the work of Arthur Lewis, a much more optimistic turn appears. While also starting from a hypothesis of constant wages due to unlimited supplies of labour, Lewis assumes that the constancy of wages will lead to high and possibly rising rates of profits as the result of technical progress. This will increase capital formation and continuing reinvestment, thus raising the demand for labour and finally exhausting the labour surpluses in agriculture. The era of constant wages will then be superseded by one of rising wages; and the whole process would be accompanied by rising production, rising capital formation and modernization of technology, i.e. development. Moreover, wages, according to Arthur Lewis, while constant, would not be at subsistence level, but would include a differential over and above agriculture incomes—with rates of 30–50 per cent variously mentioned as minimum differentials.

In the light of the present situation in under-developed countries with a marked dualism governed by the existence of surplus labour, how does this major stream of western thinking look today? Superficially, facts do not agree at all with the theory. As previously stated, in spite of the existence of surplus labour wage rates in the modern sector are by no means constant but seem to be rising at a smart pace. Moreover, and as a result of such rises, the differential between urban wages and agricultural incomes seems a great deal higher than 30–50 per cent, although statistical comparisons of real agricultural incomes and real urban incomes are notoriously tricky. However, on the analysis presented earlier in this paper, and following the Todaro model logically through, the facts may not be as much in discord with the assumption of constant urban wages as we might think. We should perhaps take as our unit of labour, over which the wage rate for one job has to be divided, not only the person actually and regularly employed, but instead include also the penumbra or cluster of semi-employed or unemployed people connected with each job. If we then divide the going wage rate not by the one person who does the job, but by the number of persons who are either doing the job or hold themselves available to do the job (and who may in fact be directly sharing the earnings of the employed person), then our urban wage rate should be divided not by one but perhaps by two and three. And in that case the wage rate would in fact be pretty close to subsistence, pretty close to rural incomes, and (because of rising unemployment) pretty constant, even in Africa.

Thus, the classical Ricardo/Marx/Lewis analysis is not so much at variance with events as might be superficially thought. But what is happening, although not anticipated by the existing models, is that in fact the family system of self-employment which Boeke emphasized as leading to divergencies between average and marginal product and hence to divergencies for neo-classical marginalism, has in some ways invaded also the modern or urban sector in the under-developed countries. This leads to deviations in the allocation of resources away from marginal productivity which are similar to those always known to apply to family farms in a framework of extended family or communal systems.

Where Ricardo does seem to have gone wrong is in his projection—made, of course, for a closed economy—that rising wage costs would exert a squeeze on industrial profits. Wage costs have risen—just as he projected although not for the same reasons—but the squeeze was not on profits. Instead, it was partly on the farmers (this is where the anti-rural bias and discrimination emphasized by Myint and others comes in) and partly at the expense of the workers themselves, namely those not in regular employment. The effect of the squeeze on profits has been obviated by the capital-intensive technologies and by technological progress biased in that direction, both making high wage costs unimportant and acceptable as long as they served to avoid any labour troubles constituting threats to the spreading use of physical capital.

Where the Lewis model seems to have been wrong (at least in the earlier versions of his model), is in the assumption that unemployment and under-employment in its various forms and disguises would remain bottled up in the rural sector while development proceeded. The analysis of this paper, following Todaro, has on the contrary emphasized that in the urban sectors of the under-developed countries situations have arisen which are closely similar to and as serious as the structures which used to be associated with overcrowded farming communities on a family and communal basis under conditions of acute land shortage. In the light of this development, the old rural/urban dichotomy is no longer satisfactory as a basis for the analysis of dualism in the under-developed countries of today.

SOME FINAL REFLECTIONS

A further conclusion on the basis of the analysis of the type of dualism described here, is that it superimposes an additional type of inequality in income distribution over and above the familiar ones based on the categorization of factors of production or social classes. This additional inequality between the regular wage-earners and fully-employed farmers—i.e. those with sufficient capital and land—on the one hand, and the 'marginal' population of the unemployed and under-employed in town and country on the other hand, is largely dysfunctional. A high share of profits or high

professional skill differentials could be justified as serving the functions of
increasing the rate of investment and capital formation or encouraging
skill formation, although some analysts have expressed doubts about these
justifications. By contrast, the inequalities inherent in the cleavage between
the fully employed and the marginal population can hardly be said to
serve any such purpose. In fact, the fully employed urban group in the
under-developed countries is specially privileged in the sense that for
historical and sentimental reasons it is still considered to be among the
'economically under-privileged', and as such in need of special protection
against exploitation and special consideration in social service legislation,
etc. This includes also external support by international trade unionism
and international organizations promoting minimum wage legislation in
the developing countries. In fact, however, the regularly employed wage-
earner represents a comparatively privileged group in his own country by
comparison with the broad masses of the population, mainly marginal
farmers. The real justification for high minimum wages might be seen in
the fact that the benefit of the privileged full employment condition does
often in practice not go to the individual employee but is shared by him
with unemployed or under-employed relatives, kinsmen or neighbours. In
this case, the high minimum wage can be defended as an essential part of
the social service system, and the receiver acts more as a social service
agent than as an income-earner. In that sense the dysfunctional equality
is eliminated and can be *ex post* justified. But this is not the ground on
which the minimum wages are proposed.

In the preceding discussion, the main weight of the argument has been
upon lopsided development in the field of science and technology. In the
short run, however, there is another important factor producing high
capital intensity and explaining the heavy incidence of unemployment and
under-employment. I refer to the under-utilization of existing capital. It
seems paradoxical that in situations and countries in which the shortage
of complementary capital is such an obvious obstacle both to the increase
in production and to fuller employment of labour, existing capital should
be so heavily under-utilized. This is not the place to analyse the reasons
in detail. They include an identification of development planning with
new investment—symbolized by the Harrod-Domar model with its associated notions of the I.C.O.R.; the availability of external aid for new
capital investment under the fetish of 'project aid', but not for the utilization of existing capital, thus artificially lowering the apparent costs of new
investment from the point of view of the receiving country; the balance
of payments difficulties prevalent in the under-developed countries which
prevent the import of replacements, spare parts, etc.; inexpert management
or absence of complementary infrastructure such as transport, etc., which
prevents continuing operation at full capacity; failure to exploit the
possibilities of shift work, etc. All of these play their role here.

Those who identify the need for new technologies more appropriate to
the under-developed countries as the fundamental problem in reducing
dualism and achieving national integration in the under-developed
countries, must also feel under an obligation to pay equal attention to the

short-run problem of better utilization of existing capital. Although the concept of capacity utilization is statistically as tricky as the concept of employment in the under-developed countries, all the available evidence points in the direction of an extremely heavy degree of under-utilization of existing capacity—perhaps as high as the degree of under-utilization of labour. It is a commonplace for development economists to explain that the unemployment problem in the under-developed countries is not the Keynesian problem of lack of effective demand, because of the lack of complementary factors and inelasticities of supply. In some respects, however, the situation is much more Keynesian than we would imagine, and the complementary factors which are lacking to make Keynesian solutions relevant may be more in the field of planning policies and aid practices or in the field of entrepreneurship and administration than in inescapable shortages of physical capital. The utilization of existing capital together with the development of more relevant technology holds the key to solving what is presented in this paper as the most important type of dualism in the under-developed countries today.

## NOTES

1. For a discussion of these distinctions see Henry J. Bruton (1).

2. I am indebted for these estimates to my colleague Mr Charles Cooper. These figures exclude the eastern countries on the side of the richer countries, but they also exclude China on the part of the LDCs. With both categories included, the actual figure for the LDCs might possibly be higher, but at most 3 or 4 per cent instead of 2 per cent.

3. My colleague Oscar Gish informs me that he has used this same term previously.

4. The very use of this term, although it comes naturally, reflects this one-way standard setting. Intrinsically, an improvement to handlooms or 'simple' agricultural tools should be considered as potentially equal in sophistication to the development of the lunar module or the supersonic Jumbo Jet—but the plain fact is that it is not the case.

5. However, it may be noted that the total sum allocated for research in the U.K. within the British technical assistance programme fell from £2·8 million in 1967 to £2·7 million in 1968. This represents less than 0·01 per cent of the British national income, less than 0·5 per cent of total British research and development expenditures, and only a little over 1 per cent of total British aid. The United Nations has proposed a target of 5 per cent of all research and development expenditures to be devoted by the richer countries to problems of special concern to under-developed countries. One of the obstacles of giving research a proper place in technical assistance lies in the basis of country requests: many problems in this field are of considerable collective interest to many under-developed countries, but are not given national priority in its specific requests by any particular country. To some extent each may rely on the other. The Rockefeller Foundation did not wait for 'specific requests' when developing the IR-8.

6. It was this point which I emphasized in my paper for the American Economic Association in 1949 (5). In the more systematic context of the present paper, this aspect seems to me less important than it did at the time.

7. These are terms used by Mr Michael Shanks (4, p. 21). It may be noted that Mr Shanks feels that the bargaining position of the British Government *via-à-vis* these large corporations has declined with the stagnation of the British economy. If this is an 'unpalatable fact' for Britain, how much more so for the under-developed countries with their puny local markets?

## REFERENCES

(1) Henry J. Bruton, *Principles of Development Economics*, Prentice Hall, 1965.
(2) A. R. Jolly, 'Employment, Wage Levels and Incentives', from *Manpower Aspects of*

*Educational Planning*, International Institute of Education Planning, UNESCO. Reprinted in the Joint Reprint Series of the School of African and Asian Studies and the Institute of Development Studies at the University of Sussex, Number 26. (Dr Jolly gives interesting examples for the case of teachers in Uganda, p. 240.)

(3) Surendra J. Patel, *The India We Want*, Bombay, 1966.
(4) Michael Shanks, 'When Companies Span the Frontier', *The Times* Business Review, August 20, 1969.
(5) H. W. Singer, 'The Distribution of Gains between Investing and Borrowing Countries', *American Economic Review*, Papers and Proceedings, May 1950.
(6) G. J. Stigler, 'The Division of Labour is Limited by the Extent of the Market', *Journal of Political Economy*, June 1951.
(7) Richard Symonds, *The British and their Successors*, Faber and Faber, London, 1966.
(8) M. P. Todaro, 'A Model of Labour Migration and Urban Unemployment in Less Developed Countries', *American Economic Review*, March 1969.
(9) H. A. Turner, 'Can Wages be Planned?' Paper prepared for the Conference on the Crisis in Planning, University of Sussex, July 1969.

# Financial Intermediation and Economic Growth in Less-Developed Countries: A Theoretical Approach

by Vicente Galbis*

*In stressing the importance of financial intermediation in the development of the LDCs, neither the approach of financial deepening nor that of real interest rates has clarified the relationship between financial intermediation and real development. This paper shows—within a two-sector model, but extendable to the n-sector case—that high (equilibrium) real interest rates are growth-promoting, even if total real savings is interest insensitive (a controversial empirical question), because they bring about an improvement in the* quality *of the capital stock in a well-defined sense. The analysis also has implications for the theories of inflation and income distribution in the LDCs.*

## 1. INTRODUCTION

A number of recent writings [*Khatkhate, 1972; McKinnon, 1973; Shaw, 1973; Bhatia and Khatkhate, 1975*] have attempted to clarify the already established hypothesis [*Goldsmith, 1966, 1969; Gurley and Shaw, 1955, 1960; Patrick, 1966; Porter, 1966*] that improvements in the financial intermediation process are a precondition of economic growth. What is at issue is the development at an appropriate pace of financial savings as an alternative to consumption and to reinvestment in low-return enterprises, and the transfer of those savings from the surplus to the deficit sectors [*Khatkhate, 1972*]. Such a transfer appears to call for high interest rate policies as opposed to low interest rates to stimulate investment, following the Keynesian tradition [*McKinnon, 1973; Shaw, 1973*]. The emphasis of the theory of development in the context of the LDCs has therefore switched from concern with the lack of basic investment opportunities, to emphasis on the removal of financial constraints.

The theoretical postulates of the new approach rest on some 'stylised' facts, to use a Kaldorian expression, concerning the nature of the economies of the LDCs [*McKinnon, 1973, Chapters 1-3*]. First, developing economies are fragmented economies where the co-existence of old and modern technologies with strikingly different degrees of efficiency in using scarce physical and human resources result in enormously wide disparities in the rates of return to different investments. It makes therefore little sense in

* The author would particularly like to thank Prof. John Williamson, Warwick University (England) and Messrs. Deena R. Khatkhate and Delano P. Villanueva for their helpful suggestions on an earlier draft of this paper. However, they are absolved of any responsibility for remaining errors. The views expressed here do not necessarily represent those of the International Monetary Fund.

these economies to talk about an aggregate production function and uniform inputs; the spirit of the Cambridge school acquires particular relevance in the fragmented developing economy. Secondly, an important property of a large number of the more modern production processes is that they require comparatively large lump-sum investments so that indivisibilities in physical capital become an important element to be reckoned with in the process of development. These two facts concern properties of production processes.

A third element in the picture is the importance of self-financing of investment. Financial intermediation is in a rudimentary state, imposing serious financial constraints on external investment in new technologies which yield high rates of return, while investment proceeds in the older, self-financed sectors which yield low rates of return. It follows that improvements in the process of financial intermediation which tend to shift financial and real resources from the older low-yield investments to the new investments are likely to result in a dramatic acceleration in the overall rate of economic growth. Naturally, some costs will have to be incurred in the process, as development of the financial system is not a costless endeavour. However, it may well be that financial development is a prerequisite, if not a major determinant, of the take-off into self-sustained economic growth.

Finally, the role played by most governments in LDCs needs to be taken into account. In general, this has not been encouraging at all as a proliferation of regulations based on misguided principles has contributed significantly to the malfunctioning of the financial system and, to the inefficient use of real resources. Take for instance the widespread practice of regulating interest rates which credit institutions may pay for their deposit liabilities, which has resulted in very low rates being paid in the official markets, with the notable exceptions of Taiwan and South Korea. This has generally led (i) to a widening of the existing gap between the demand for and the supply of funds, thereby contributing to open or repressed inflation and (ii) to the perpetuation of an unofficial non-institutionalised financial market, itself a symbol of the segmentation of the economy.

Disparities in rates of return on different assets are not the exclusive property of LDCs. Technological advances even in today's more developed countries offer a more or less temporary advantage to those innovators who introduce them into the production process. So far as a country's economy shows signs of intense dynamism, such disparities may not only be unavoidable but necessary to fuel the entrepreneurial dynamism which characterises the process of economic growth [*Schumpeter, 1911*]. What is at issue in the case of developing economies, however, is the inability to profit from technological advance because of the constraints imposed by the nature of the financial processes.

This paper investigates the nature of the financial constraint in the fragmented developing economy. The analysis is simplified by assuming that the economy consists of two kinds of productive units which operate with quite different technological processes (and hence different real returns) and are subject to different financial constraints. Reality is undoubtedly much more complicated. However, the theoretical framework of this paper is sufficient to derive some important conclusions with regard to the influence of financial intermediation on the process of economic growth.[1]

Section 2 specifies a two-sector model of capital intermediation in a fragmented developing economy and discusses its basic properties. Section 3 discusses the effects of interest rate fixing on the efficiency of investment outlets, inflation, and the distribution of income. Finally, section 4 summarises the main conclusions and relates them to conditions in the LDCs.

## 2.  A TWO-SECTOR MODEL OF FINANCIAL INTERMEDIATION AND GROWTH

The model specified below captures in an essential way the main elements of the fragmented developing economy. Two production sectors with widely disparate technologies are assumed to represent in aggregate form the 'average' technology within each of two sectors into which the economy can be broken down.[2] Sector 1 is the backward or less efficient sector. Sector 2 is the modern or technologically advanced sector. For simplicity, it is assumed that both sectors produce the same output which is sold at a uniform price. This has the advantage that it emphasises the importance of differences in technologies. Even though changes in the composition of the output are also concomitant to the process of development, the model here does not centre on this other aspect. The two sectors are also different in their financial behaviour, but this is more conveniently explained as the various pieces of the model are fitted together.

### (a)  *Technological conditions*
Following standard theory, the production functions of the two sectors are specified in general form as follows:

$$(1) \qquad\qquad Y_1 = F_1(K_1, L_1)$$

$$(2) \qquad\qquad Y_2 = F_2(K_2, L_2)$$

These are assumed to be continuous and twice differentiable. The functions $F_1$ and $F_2$ embody technological factors such as mechanically different production processes, economies of scale, and embodied human capital.

It is assumed for simplicity that competitive conditions exist in each sector in the sense that productive factors are paid according to their marginal productivities. These determine, for instance, the returns to capital as follows:

$$\partial Y_2 / \partial K_1 = r_1$$

$$\partial Y_2 / \partial K_2 = r_2$$

In this context, the assumption that sector 2 embodies a technology with higher rates of return to the production factors than that of sector 1 means:

$$(3) \qquad\qquad r_2 > r_1$$

Equation (3) is a fundamental empirical assertion concerning the wide disparity in technological efficiency in underdeveloped countries. Since $F_1$ and $F_2$ represent quite different technologies to produce the same physical output (meaning that a unit of $Y_1$ is identical to a unit of $Y_2$), the greater return to capital in sector 2 does not imply a smaller wage rate. On the contrary, it appears to be empirically demonstrable that technologies with higher rates of return to capital typically also embody higher returns to labour for the same capital–labour ratio. In other words, it is also an empirical assertion that $w_2 > w_1$.[3] Though this paper does not focus on the labour aspects of the fragmented economy, the significance of this assumption is clearly to reinforce any conclusions derived from the disparity between the rates of return to capital in the two sectors.

The empirical assertion concerning the disparity of technologies 1 and 2 can easily be translated into a proposition concerning the growth of income. Under the assumption that the factors of production are fully employed and that they are paid their marginal productivities, Euler's theorem ensures the following income determination equation:

$$\text{(4)} \qquad Y = Y_1 + Y_2 = r_1 K_1 + w_1 L_1 + r_2 K_2 + w_2 L_2.$$

Equation (4) can be used to describe the result of redistributing capital from the backward to the advanced technological sector. Under the assumption that capital is fully employed and is given (at any moment in time) $K = K_1 + K_2$. An increase in $K_2$ at the expense of $K_1$, leaving $K$ constant, would imply a rise in $Y$, since this change in the structure of capital would be in favour of the higher capital returns (as $r_2 > r_1$) associated with $K_2$. This simple result provides the clue to understanding the efficiency aspects of an improvement in the allocative mechanisms of savings and investment.

The process of income growth can now be seen in this simple framework as one of growth of inputs and redistribution of the inputs toward the more advanced technologies, i.e. those technologies that provide for higher rates of return to the factors of production.

The growth of capital inputs is related to investment in capital goods. For simplicity it may be assumed that the rate of depreciation is zero. Then

$$\text{(5)} \qquad \dot{K}_1 = I_1$$

$$\text{(6)} \qquad \dot{K}_2 = I_2$$

(b)  *Savings, investment and financial intermediation*

The basic aggregate expenditure identity within this model is as follows:

$$\text{(7)} \qquad Y = C + I = C_1 + C_2 + I_1 + I_2,$$

where $C = C_1 + C_2$ and $I = I_1 + I_2$.

The determinants of expenditures by sector 1 are first specified. As regards consumption, it is assumed for simplicity that it is a simple linear function of income:

$$\text{(8)} \qquad C_1 = c_1 Y_1; \ 0 < c_1 < 1$$

Savings is defined as the difference between income and consumption—a residuum—so that

$$S_1 = Y_1 - C_1 = (1-c_1)\, Y_1 = s_1 Y_1$$

where $0 < s_1 = (1-c_1) < 1$.

Thus the functions $C_1$ and $S_1$ are not independent and the equilibrium of the model can be discussed in terms of either of the two.

The decision to invest by members of sector 1—the backward sector, which is further characterised as being composed of small self-financing units with no access to borrowing in the capital market[4]—depends on two rates of return, namely, the real rate of return on their own investment and the real rate of return on available financial assets. For simplicity, it is assumed henceforth that the only available financial asset is a deposit with the commercial banks. Complications arising from the existence of a securities market would not alter the essence of the arguments nor the conclusions derived from the model as both forms of intermediation are essentially similar.[5] The investment function is as follows:

(9)
$$I_1 = H_1(r_1, d - \dot{P}^*/P)Y_1;$$

$$\partial H_1/\partial r_1 > 0; \ \partial H_1/\partial(d - \dot{P}^*/P) < 0;$$

where $d$ is the rate of interest on commercial bank deposits (assumed for simplicity to be the weighted average of all bank deposit rates) and $\dot{P}^*/P$ is the expected rate of inflation.

The assumption that sector 1 is a self-financed sector with no access to borrowing implies that $Y_1 > C_1 + I_1$, i.e. $I_1 < S_1$, since units in sector 1 can save in the form of bank deposits. Indeed, ex-post savings-investment must be related by the following identity:

(10)
$$S_1 = I_1 + d(M_1/P)/dt$$

where $d(M_1/P)/dt$ is the accumulation of bank deposits in real terms by units in sector 1, or sector 1's real financial savings.

Identity (10) is the fundamental budget constraint of sector 1 and it means that the accumulation of financial savings by this sector is not independent of the consumption and investment decisions within that sector. This follows from Walras law.[6] Thus, for instance, a decrease in $(d - \dot{P}^*/P)$, which implies *ceteris paribus* an increase in $I_1$, means a smaller $d(M_1/P)/dt$ than it otherwise would have been. This completes the demand specifications for sector 1.

The consumption behaviour of individuals in sector 2 is assumed to be of the same simplistic type as in sector 1:

(11)
$$C_2 = c_2 Y_2; \ 0 < c_2 < 1$$

This function explains real savings in sector 2 as a residual:

$$S_2 = Y_2 - C_2 = (1-c_2) Y_2 = s_2 Y_2.$$

There are two sources of investable physical resources which may contribute to the growth of the capital stock in sector 2. First, there is its own non-consumed output, $S_2$. Second, there is the real physical counterpart of the increase in financial claims by units in sector 1, i.e. $d(M_1/P)/dt$, the difference between output in sector 1 and its own total absorption of physical resources for consumption and self-financed investment. In sum, the supply of investable resources in sector 2 is given by

$$(12) \qquad I_2^s = S_2 + d(M_1/P)/dt,$$

where $S_2$ is the non-consumed output from sector 2 and $d(M_1/P)/dt$ is the real value of the output produced but not used in sector 1.

The crucial question which arises now is whether the working of the economy can ensure that all these investable funds are effectively financed and invested by units in sector 2. Note first that, unlike in sector 1, units in sector 2 must invest their whole savings in the form of physical goods, thereby keeping no savings of their own in the form of financial assets. Moreover, if full utilisation of resources is to be maintained, sector 2 must also be able to invest the surplus of investable resources procured by sector 1. It therefore follows that sector 2 could neither finance the payment for the surplus of investable resources from sector 1 nor satisfy its complementary need for financial assets without recourse to bank credit.

Two separate but interrelated issues are thus distinguishable in the analysis of the determinants of equilibrium in the market for investable resources in sector 2. First there is the issue of the underlying technological characteristics of the economy which support the demand for investment. Second, there is the question of whether this basic demand is constrained, and in what way, by the financial characteristics of the economic environment.

As regards the first question, the technological conditions of the fragmented economy provide a clear-cut clue to the solution of the problem. It has been discussed earlier in this paper that real rates of return to capital in the technologically advanced sector can be exceedingly large. Moreover, they are not likely to be substantially reduced by even the largest amounts of investment, except in the very long run, i.e. when the economy becomes more mature. This is yet another way to state that the economy is starved for modern forms of capital and advanced technology. In these circumstances, it could not be expected that there will be a lack of basic demand for investment. On the contrary, one should expect that the demand for investable resources will largely exceed the supply. Nevertheless, a full understanding of this proposition also requires the specification of the financial constraints.

The decision to invest by units in sector 2 is not essentially different from that of units in sector 1; it is also based on the relative rates of return affecting this decision:

$$(13) \qquad I_2^D = H_2(r_2, b - \dot{P}*/P) Y_2;$$

$$\partial H_2/\partial r_2 > 0; \ \partial H_2/\partial (b - P*/P) < 0;$$

where $b - \dot{P}*/P$ is the real rate of interest on bank loans, a cost to investors who finance their investments by borrowing. What appears to be a crucial difference is that $r_2$ is rather large compared with $b - \dot{P}*/P$, so that a substantial edge exists for investment in this sector. As noted above, it appears empirically useful to think of $I_2^D$ as being vastly greater than $I_2^s$ under the conditions prevailing in a fragmented economy where an entrepreneurial élite is already in place.

Another crucial difference regarding the demand for investment in sector 2 as compared with sector 1 is that its validation is subject to the availability of credit. As noted earlier, investors in sector 2 cannot satisfy their complementary demand for financial assets nor pay for their invest-ment in excess of their own saving unless they have access to bank credit. Assume for simplicity that all their financial assets are required for trans-actions purposes alone. Then the following simple incremental demand for financial assets by individuals in sector 2 may be postulated:[7]

(14) $$d(M_2/P)^D/dt = \gamma I_2^D$$

The monetary authorities are assumed to control the incremental supply of money through the manipulation of the various policy instruments.

(15) $$dM_2^*/dt = d\bar{M}_2^*/dt$$

Now the role of financial intermediation and of monetary policy in the process of transferring real resources from the backward to the advanced sector can be analysed. It will be shown that various possible mechanisms of adjustment between the supply of and the demand for investment in modern technologies—and the failure or the success of monetary policy to do this within a stable financial environment—have crucially different implications for economic growth.

## 3. INFLATION, INCOME DISTRIBUTION AND GROWTH

Figure 1 pictures the market for investable resources in the technologically advanced sector in any given period. The kinked shape of the supply of investable resources is the result of the underlying assumptions of the model (equation (12)). Sector 2 invests at least its own surplus of physical resources since units in this sector cannot do better by putting it to alternative uses, namely, financial savings or investment in inferior tech-nologies. This is represented by the intercept of the $I_2^s$ curve with the horizontal axis, which is equal to $S_2$. The supply of investable resources from sector 1, on the other hand, depends crucially on the real rate of interest on financial savings as this represents an opportunity cost of self-investment in this sector. For simplicity it has been assumed in drawing Figure 1 that all savings of sector 1 are reinvested in that sector if the real rate of interest on financial savings is zero, and that no investment takes place in that sector if the real interest rate on financial savings rises to the level $(b - \dot{P}^*/P)_0$.[8] (The latter boundary results from the limitedness of yields on self-financed, backward types of investment.) No further increases in the supply of investable resources to sector 2 are possible, given the assumption that consumption behaviour is independent from the real rate of interest on financial assets and the return on physical investment. This simplifying assumption—which effectively implies that aggregate investment depends only on income and the distribution of income between the two sectors—could be altered to take into account the more

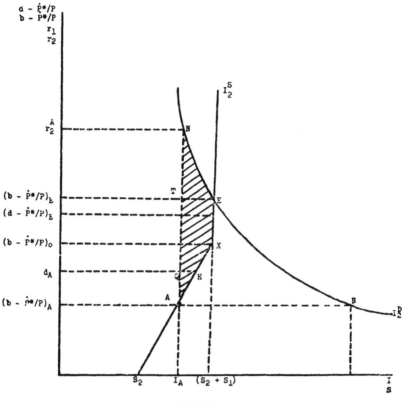

FIGURE 1

general case in which individuals respond to rises in the real rates of interest
on financial savings by reducing their propensity to consume [*Porter,
1966: 350–51; McKinnon, 1973*]. If this were so (a controversial empirical
question), the conclusions of the model would be reinforced.

The demand for investable resources in sector 2 is a marginal efficiency
of investment curve representing the various desired volumes of investment
in any given period which can be profitably undertaken at various rates
of real borrowing costs. As borrowing costs increase, fewer firms can undertake profitable investments. Thus the curve has a negative slope. Its
position is displaced to the right compared to that in Sector 1 as a result
of the assumption that the 'average' rate of return in the technologically
advanced sector is very high. Technological innovations tend to shift this
curve to the right.

It will be observed that the technological assumptions underlying the
model are not sufficient by themselves to undermine the existence of an
equilibrium solution in the financial market. For an equilibrium, $E$,
between the supply of and demand for investable resources is possible
provided that the real cost of borrowing can rise to the level $(b-\dot{P}^*/P)_E$.
However, various circumstances—either legal, political or institutional, as

well as monetary mismanagement—may prevent the real rates of interest on financial assets from rising to their equilibrium levels.

Assume that legal, political or institutional reasons prevent the real rate of interest from reaching its equilibrium level. Let $(b-\dot{P}*/P)_A$ be the 'acceptable' level of the rate of interest on financial assets. At this level there is a potential excess demand for investable resources, $AB$, so that the market is not automatically cleared. As the real rate of interest is kept at this lower level, two basic consequences can be observed.

First, not all saving units in the backward sector are now prepared to keep their savings in the form of bank deposits; the real rate of interest on these deposits is too small to induce them to do so as they foresee higher returns from their own self-financed investments. Thus, relatively low-yielding self-financed investments in sector 1 will be carried out while higher-yielding investments in the technologically advanced sector will be cut off at the point of the effective supply of investable resources, $A$. Indeed, the marginal rate of return to investment in sector 2 will be $r_2^A$, while investments in sector 1 in the amount $(S_2+S_1)-I_A$ will command yields ranging from their marginal yield (equal to the real rate on bank deposits, $(b-\dot{P}*/P)_A$) to the highest available yield, $(b-\dot{P}*/P)_0$. The investments foregone in sector 2 would have commanded higher yields than those carried out in sector 1, ranging from $r_2^A$ to $(b-\dot{P}*/P)_E$. The 'producer's surplus' lost as a result of this inefficient allocation of resources is measured by the shaded area NAXE.

Secondly, the disequilibrium between the real supply of and the demand for investable resources may itself lead to a kind of financial instability which will tend to exacerbate the initial effects from the imposed control on the real rate of interest on financial assets. Assume that entrepreneurs in sector 2 are allowed to satisfy their demand for loans at the prevailing borrowing cost. This means that with a price level of $P$ at time $t$ the incremental supply of money $dM_2^s/dt$ is such that it equals the effective incremental demand for money $d(M_2/P)^d/dt$ which is provided by the following relation:

$$(16) \qquad (d(M_2/P)^d/dt)_A = \gamma H_2(r_2, (b-\dot{P}*/P)_A) Y_2.$$

A peculiar state of simultaneous real and financial disequilibria results from this situation. On the financial side, the excess demand for loans is translated into a pressure for the banks to raise their lending rates, but this may be prevented for legal, political or institutional reasons.[9] On the real side, the excess demand for investable resources tends to drive the price level upward. To the extent that the upward pressure on lending rates materialises—as it is also fuelled by inflation and the consequent attempt of lenders to adjust to inflationary expectations—this tends to ease the state of disequilibria. However, inflation aggravates directly the potential disequilibria by reducing the *real* rates of interest on financial assets. In the event, unless there is a credit restriction such that it brings back the effective demand to the effective supply at the prevailing real rate of interest on financial assets, the system will not by itself have a tendency toward equilibrium. Resolution of the disequilibria will depend on the upward flexibility of interest rates in response to the disequilibria and the ability of the monetary authorities to effectively restrict the supply of credit.

It should be noted that, with an inflexible structure of interest rates, the kind of equilibrating credit restriction implied by the foregoing analysis is a system of credit rationing.[10] Assume that by denying a sufficient amount of loans to prospective borrowers at the prevailing real rate of interest on financial assets, $(b-\dot{P}*/P)_A$, the banking system brings down the effective (i.e. credit-rationed) demand for investable resources to the level of the effective supply, $I_A$. Two consequences follow from this credit restriction. First, inflationary conditions are suppressed. Secondly, as $\dot{P}*/P \to 0$ there is an increase in the real interest rate on financial assets. This results in an increase in the supply of investable resources to, say, $H$. At this new level of the supply of investable resources the authorities are required to ease correspondingly the initial tightening of the credit rationing measures to allow the effective demand for investable resources to reach the level of the expanded supply. If this action were delayed, the initial credit crunch would be followed by a period of under-utilisation of investable resources (in the amount $QH$), until the ease was established.

In the light of the above considerations it appears that credit rationing is in the nature of a second-best policy in a country with a rigid structure of interest rates on financial assets. Price level stability resulting from credit rationing ensures that real interest rates on financial assets are as high as they can be—given the restriction on nominal rates—with the consequent release of investable resources from the backward self-financed sectors of the economy. Optimal policy is, of course, to let interest rates rise to the level at which the supply of and demand for investable resources is equated, resulting in stability of the price level and making unnecessary the use of credit rationing devices. These propositions can be elucidated further by analysing the effects of interest rate restrictions on the distribution of income and economic growth.

Assume that starting from an initial equilibrium situation, at $E$, with no inflation and no credit rationing and with an equilibrium rate of interest on financial assets, a restriction is imposed on the interest rate at the level $(b-\dot{P}*/P)_A = I_A A$. Assume also that an effective credit rationing system is simultaneously introduced so that an inflationary outbreak is avoided ($\dot{P}*/P = 0$). For simplicity, assume that both before and after this change banks were forced to charge the same rate for their loans as they pay for their deposits. (Relaxation of this assumption is discussed below.) The effect of the interest rate and credit rationing restrictions is to reduce the volume of investable physical resources effectively traded in the capital market from $(S_2 + S_1)$ to $I_A$, resulting as already noted earlier in a loss of producer's surplus equal to the shaded area in Figure 1. The real income lost by individuals in sector 1 is given by the area TEXA which is equal to the difference between the equilibrium interest rate foregone and the average rate of return to investments carried on in sector 1 multiplied by the amount of self-investment in sector 1. The real income lost by individuals in sector 2 is given by the area TEN, equal to the difference between the average rate of return foregone by prospective investors which are rationed out of the market and the equilibrium cost of borrowing, multiplied by the volume of investment foregone in sector 2.[11] These losses may be only part of the overall real cost, as they only measure the opportunity costs of capital, not of labour. To the extent that inferior technologies are also associated with lower labour productivity, a real loss may also ensue on this account.[12]

In terms of equation (4), it may be seen that a decrease in $d$ or a rise in the expected rate of inflation, $P^*/P$, has the effect of impeding the process of real transfer of capital resources from sector 1 to sector 2 (and with it the transfer of labour resources). This means that $K_1$ will be rising faster than it would at the equilibrium rate at the expense of the growth of $K_2$. (Indeed the conditions depicted in Figure 1 would require $K_1 = 0$ for optimal growth.) Given the technological assumption that $r_2 > r_1$, this implies that the level of aggregate income will be growing at a slower pace than would be possible at the equilibrium rate of interest on financial assets.

In addition to the direct effect on economic growth from the failure of financial intermediation to secure the optimal allocation of investable resources in each period, other effects may result from the implications regarding the distribution of income. This can again be explored with the use of Figure 1. Assume as before that the banks charge a rate of interest for their loans equal to $I_A A$ and that an effective credit rationing system is monitored through the guidance of the monetary authorities to prevent the outbreak of inflation. If the system of credit rationing were perfectly efficient (see note 11 on page 71 below), the marginal rate of return to investments in sector 2 would be $I_A N$, with the average return being even higher. The distribution of income would be altered in favour of those entrepreneurs who would obtain the loans at a rate of interest below the equilibrium level, thereby reaping some 'windfall profits'. But the banks themselves could be the principal beneficiaries to the extent that they would respond by widening the spread between lending and deposit rates to take advantage of the effective situation of excess demand for loans. Indeed, under the simple assumptions made here, banks could, in principle, raise the lending rate up to the level $r_2^A$ while at the same time keeping the deposit rate at $I_A A$, appropriating all windfall profits. The losses would be suffered by those potential entrepreneurs in sector 2 who would be rationed out of the loan market and by the would-be bank depositors in sector 1 who would now be resigned to undertake their own self-financed lower-yielding investments.

If the assumption of a perfectly efficient credit rationing system is dropped in favour of the more palatable alternative hypothesis that banks have better information about, and give more importance to the net worth of creditors than about the returns from their prospective investments, then something more definite may be said concerning the distribution of income. However, it is not within the scope of this aggregate model to get but a glimpse of the consequences for economic growth derived from the implied redistribution of income toward the already affluent and possibly toward the banks themselves. This would require a detailed theory concerning the economic behaviour toward consumption and investment of the various economic groups—entrepreneurs and labourers—and bankers involved in each sector of the economy. Nevertheless, a further note on the implications of this theory for the behaviour of the banks as financial intermediaries is in order.

It has been assumed throughout the foregoing discussion that some legal, political or institutional restrictions were operating to prevent the interest rates on bank deposits and loans from reaching their equilibrium levels. However, it has also been noted that the banks could benefit, together with their preferred customers, from restrictions on interest rates paid on deposits, provided that limitations on lending rates are not imposed. It follows, therefore, that the banks as financial intermediaries have a veiled interest in perpetuating, if not initiating themselves, whatever restrictions there might be on deposit rates and in establishing a less-than-perfect credit rationing system by discriminating against customers with limited initial endowments.

All the above-mentioned considerations regarding the public and private behaviour leading to low interest rates merit further and more specific attention in a study of the influence of financial intermediation on economic development.[13]

## 4. CONCLUSIONS

The theory of financial intermediation in the context of LDCs presented above has proceeded on the assumption that the economies of LDCs are fragmented economies with wide disparities in the rates of return to physical investments and with substantial indivisibilities of physical capital. In this context, it has been demonstrated that improvements in the process of financial intermediation—such as those brought about by higher (equilibrium) real interest rates—which shift resources from the traditional low-yielding investments to investments in the modern technological sectors may result in a dramatic acceleration in the overall rate of economic growth [compare with Porter, 1966: 552–55].

In the experience of many LDCs, with notable exceptions such as those of Taiwan and South Korea [Chandavarkar, 1971], interest rates on financial assets appear to have been most of the time below equilibrium levels, a proposition which applies even more clearly to the real rates of interest, given the relatively high rates of inflation in most of these countries. This means that a state of excess demand for funds has generally prevailed. Appropriate correction of such imbalance would have required that interest rates rise to reach their equilibrium level.[14] It appears that this correction failed to materialise both because of misguided interest rate intervention policy and oligopolistic behaviour on the part of the banking and financial intermediation system.

The two consequences from this state of financial disequilibrium, which have been observed variously in LDCs, were: (a) perpetuation of high rates of inflation and (b) the establishment of some sort of credit rationing system. As credit rationing became necessary in many of these countries to halt increasing inflationary pressures, the issue turned to the efficiency and the practical implementation of rationing devices which are in the nature of a second best policy. However, the experience has been generally not encouraging in this area as this requires a comprehensive system of financial guidelines, which has rarely been set up, to ensure that firms with the highest potential rates of return have access to external finance rather than allocating financial resources according to conventional criteria such as the 'creditworthiness'—the initial capital endowment—of the prospective borrowers [*Park, 1973; Bhatia and Khatkhate, 1975*]. An all-too-frequent result of official credit rationing has been to encourage the further development of traditional curb markets operating outside the purview of the monetary authorities, with consequences for the allocation of resources which run contrary to the official design. Another consideration to be taken into account is that credit rationing could be converted into a force increasing the oligopolistic power of the banking system. The distribution of income has also deteriorated as a result of low interest rate policies and credit rationing.

It is important to stress that the above conclusions do not hinge on the simplifying assumption, made in this paper, concerning the insensitivity of the consumption function to interest rates. On the contrary, if consumption behaviour were sensitive to interest rates in LDCs,[15] it would tend to reinforce the arguments developed here. The rise in interest rates, by discouraging consumption, would increase the surplus of investable resources, thereby raising the rate of capital accumulation and mitigating inflationary pressures.

Introduction of a securities market into the model would not alter its basic conclusions. Securities may be viewed as a short cut to financial intermediation in that the savers pass their surplus funds directly to investors rather than depositing with the banks for them to lend to investors. Relative risk factors, costs of collecting information, and government regulations will influence the portfolio choice preferred by savers and investors as to the form of supply and use of funds [*Wai and Patrick, 1973*].

NOTES

1. The approach here is inspired by, but contrasts sharply with, McKinnon's [*1973, Chapter 6*]; it has similar implications and, hopefully, greater clarity. Surprisingly, he attempted to develop his basic propositions from a one-sector aggregative 'model' of economic growth, by assuming that the problem of financial intermediation could be discussed in terms of an 'average' rate of return to physical assets [*p. 59*]. Thus, he shut the door on the analysis of the effects of what he himself vaguely called 'improvements' in the quality of the capital stock and the financial intermediation process. Instead, he followed the path of neo-classical theorists which he himself criticised [*Chapter 5*].

2. 'Average' is used here to indicate that each of the two sectors is itself composed of productive units widely different among themselves. This makes possible the specification, which is made later on (section 3), of a declining marginal efficiency of investment in each sector. A similar notion was introduced by McKinnon [*1973: 63–64*] within his one-sector model.

3. To demonstrate that the existence of different technologies can result in a positive correlation between profits and wages across sectors, assume that the production functions are of the Cobb–Douglas type:

(1.a) $$Y_1 = A_1 K_1^\alpha L_1^{1-\alpha}$$
(2.a) $$Y_2 = A_2 K_2^\beta L_2^{1-\beta}$$

The rates of return to capital and labour are as follows:

$r_1 = \partial Y_1/\partial K_1 = \alpha Y_1/K_1; r_2 = \partial Y_2/\partial K_2 = \beta Y_2/K_2;$
$w_1 = \partial Y_1/\partial L_1 = (1-\alpha)Y_1/L_1; w_2 = \partial Y_2/\partial L_2 = (1-\beta)Y_2/L_2,$

and it is possible to simultaneously have

$$r_1 < r_2; \ w_1 < w_2$$

for the same values of the capital labour ratio, $K_1/L_1 = K_2/L_2$, if $A_2$ is sufficiently larger than $A_1$.

4. This extreme assumption is made for convenience, though it is recognised that in the real world some amount of borrowing may be undertaken by these units. The argument would then have to be modified to characterise this sector as a surplus sector or *net* supplier of funds, with gross flows running both ways [*Khatkhate, p. 547*].

5. One of the differences is that the securities market may provide a system of direct finance, while the intermediation through the banking system is indirect [*Wai and Patrick, 1973*]. However, the main difference between the role of the banking system and that of the securities market is that the latter acts as a purely intermediation market while the former is the source of expanding primary liquidity needed in order to finance the continued growth in income. This point is clarified below.

6. Alternatively, one could have specified a demand function for financial assets and let $I_1$ be determined as a residual. Such a demand function would take the general form:

$$(M_1/P)^d = L_1(Y_1, r_1, d - \dot{P}^*/P); \ \partial(M_1/P)^d/\partial Y_1 > 0;$$

$$\partial(M_1/P)^d/\partial r_1 < 0; \ \partial(M_1/P)^d/\partial(d - \dot{P}^*/P) > 0;$$

It is easy to show that this function implies (9), given the budget constraint (10). Nevertheless, McKinnon [*1973, Chapters 6 and 9*] appears to have overlooked this simple law in discussing the structure of his one-sector model.

7. This simplifying assumption is made here in order to avoid the complications arising from the interest sensitivity of the transactions demand for money.

8. For simplicity, it is assumed henceforth until page 68 that bank lending and deposit rates are strictly equal. Alternatively, the argument could be developed under the more realistic assumption that lending rates are above deposit rates by some constant fraction. But even this proportionality assumption could and indeed should be discarded to take account of the quasi-monopoly position of the banks.

9. The outcome will depend on the nature of the constraint. For instance, some countries have regulations concerning maximum deposit rates payable by the banks while lending rates are not controlled, thereby allowing for a response of lending rates to market forces. This situation is further analysed on pages 68–69 below.

10. The basic conclusion is in complete agreement with the literature on the role of money in LDCs. According to Park [*1973: 411*]: 'The effects of changes in the stock of money are transmitted to the real economy in part by portfolio substitution but primarily by credit rationing, which appears to be the most direct and powerful channel of monetary policy.'

11. This argument assumes that banks are fully efficient in their system of loan rationing in the sense that they provide loans only to those entrepreneurs who make investments with the highest rates of return. Clearly, this is a very strong assumption since banks may not be able to collect enough information to determine which entrepreneurs and which investments obtain the highest yields and, more important, it is not at all sure that they have an incentive to behave in a socially optimum way. Instead, banks may look at the creditworthiness of their customers primarily in terms of their net worth, which might not be correlated with the productivity of their investments. The failure of the credit rationing system as an *allocation* mechanism in this sense would further increase the producer's surplus loss.

12. This argument refers to the medium or long run. In the short run one would have to consider the possible loss of employment as a result of the transfer of labour to the advanced technological sector.

13. Another area which would require re-elaboration and integration in the framework presented here is that of international capital movements, because access to foreign borrowing by banks and large corporations provides an alternative source of finance at world-determined interest rates.

14. This conclusion is in agreement with McKinnon's [*1973*], though the reasons behind it are different.

15. It appears that no conclusive evidence is available in this area.

REFERENCES
1. Bhatia, Rattan J. and Deena R. Khatkhate, 1975, 'Financial Intermediation, Savings Mobilization and Entrepreneurial Development: The African Experience', IMF, *Staff Papers*, Vol. 22, 1, March.
2. Chandavarkar, Anand G., 1971, 'Some Aspects of Interest Rate Policies in Less Developed Economies: The Experience of Selected Asian Countries', IMF, *Staff Papers*, Vol. XVIII, No. 1, March.
3. Goldsmith, Raymond W., 1966, *The Determinants of Financial Structure*, Paris: Organization for Economic Cooperation and Development.
4. Goldsmith, Raymond W., 1969, *Financial Structure and Development* (Yale University Press).
5. Gurley, John G. and E. S. Shaw, 1955, 'Financial Aspects of Economic Development', *American Economic Review*, Vol. 45, September.
6. Gurley, John G. and E. S. Shaw, 1960, *Money in a Theory of Finance*, Washington: Brookings Institution.
7. Khatkhate, Deena R., 1972, 'Analytic Basis of the Working of Monetary Policy in Less Developed Countries', IMF, *Staff Papers*, Vol. XIX, No. 3, November.
8. McKinnon, Ronald I., 1973, *Money and Capital in Economic Development*, Washington: The Brookings Institution.
9. Park, Yung Chul, 1973, 'The Role of Money in Stabilization Policy in Developing Countries', IMF, *Staff Papers*, Vol. XX, No. 2, July.
10. Patrick, Hugh T., 1966, 'Financial Development and Economic Growth in Underdeveloped Countries', *Economic Development and Cultural Change*, Vol. 14, January.
11. Porter, Richard C., 1966, 'The Promotion of the "Banking Habit" and Economic Development', *Journal of Development Studies*, July.
12. Schumpeter, J. A., 1934, *Theory of Economic Development* (in German, 1911). First English version, 1934.
13. Shaw, Edward S., 1973, *Financial Deepening in Economic Development*, Oxford University Press.
14. Wai, U. Tun and Hugh T. Patrick, 1973, 'Stock and Bond Issues and Capital Markets in Less Developed Countries', IMF, *Staff Papers*, Vol. XX, No. 2, July.

# INTERNATIONAL ECONOMIC
## RELATIONSHIPS

# Tariffs and Economic Development:

## Some Theoretical Issues [1]

### *Harry G. Johnson* *

I. *Introduction*

In the course of the past thirty-five years, prevailing opinion among economists regarding the influence of commercial policy on economic development has changed radically. The central tradition of economics, set by the English classical economists, viewed free trade as a potent engine for economic growth, and protection as a policy making for waste of resources and the impediment of economic development. The classical advocacy of free trade evolved out of Adam Smith's attack on mercantilism. On the theoretical side it rested not only on the static theory of comparative advantage developed by Ricardo and Mill, but on a broader sociological recognition of the beneficial effects of exposure to foreign culture and foreign competition in generating the urge for social change and economic improvement. While two exceptions to the case for free trade were early recognised—the terms of trade argument and the infant industry argument—these were not regarded as of great practical importance. Nor did the heretics who advocated protection as a means of promoting the economic development of the relatively backward regions—notably Hamilton in the United States and List in Germany—have any significant influence on the central corpus of economic theory. Towards the end of the nineteenth century, the policies of using protection to promote the industrial growth of the United States and Germany attracted the scientific interest of

* *Professor Johnson is Professor of Economics at the University of Chicago.*

Marshall, and induced Taussig to undertake a major study of the economic effects of the United States tariff; but the results of Taussig's research were at best inconclusive, and both he and Marshall became increasingly sceptical about the efficacy of protection for promoting economic growth. Until the 1930s, free trade was the orthodox position of economists on questions of commercial policy, an orthodoxy based on the principle of comparative advantage and reinforced by the cosmopolitan perspective of the liberal tradition of classical economics.

In the 1930s, however, the orthodoxy of free trade was challenged by a new heterodoxy, associated with the economic problems and theoretical developments of the times. The great depression revived and gave point to mercantilist arguments for tariffs as a means of increasing employment, arguments made respectable by the personal endorsement of J. M. Keynes and subsequent Keynesian analysis of "beggar-my-neighbour" remedies for unemployment. New techniques of analysis and the questioning of the theoretical foundations of welfare propositions in economics revived the terms of trade argument for protection in the form of the "optimum tariff" theory, a theory more acceptable in the new climate of economic nationalism than it had been in earlier more cosmopolitan times, when Edgeworth had gone so far as to label it "poison". Finally, the national aspirations of the new states created by the dissolution of the Austro-Hungarian Empire had stimulated interest in the possibility of promoting industrialisation by tariff protection on the German model, and the economic philosophy underlying this approach was transfused into the main stream of economic theory through the emigration of many outstanding European scholars induced by the political developments of the 1930s. In addition, European thinking contributed a new argument to the case for protection, the Manoilesco argument, which rests on the existence of a differential between wages in agriculture and wages in industry that is alleged to call for compensation by tariffs on industrial products.

The reconsideration of the case for tariffs evoked by the developments of the 1930s laid the foundations for post-war analysis of the commercial policy aspects of the problem of promoting economic development in the group of countries, mostly newly independent, that have successively been described as "backward," "underdeveloped," and "poor". In the course of theorizing about that problem, not only have traditional arguments for protection been reformulated and sharpened, but the emphasis has shifted to new arguments and new versions of the older arguments. The purpose of this article is to review the most important of these arguments and set them in the context of a general theoretical framework, and to outline briefly an analysis of some aspects of tariffs that have heretofore received little theoretical attention, though they are of considerable relevance to the analysis of the effects of protection on economic growth. Specifically, Part II presents a classification of contemporary arguments for protective policies in underdeveloped countries based on a distinction between economic and non-economic arguments for protection. Part III analyses the economic arguments for protection, and shows that the only valid economic argument for protection is the optimum tariff argument, all other arguments, properly interpreted, being arguments for subsidies of one kind or another. Part IV is concerned with the non-economic arguments for protection and shows that whether the tariff is an economically efficient instrument of policy depends on whether the objective of protection is increased domestic production or increased self-sufficiency. Part V carries the analysis of tariffs further, by investigating the requirements of an optimum tariff structure for promoting domestic production. Part VI is concerned with some of the implications for tariff theory of the fact that raw materials and intermediate goods (including capital goods) as well as products for final consumption are traded internationally and subject to tariffs. Part VII dwells briefly on some aspects of the policy of import substitution as a means of economic development.

Throughout the article, as in this introduction, the term "protection" is used synonymously with the term "tariffs"; the purpose is to confine the term "protection" to policies that raise domestic prices to both producers and consumers above world prices, as distinct from policies such as subsidization that raise prices only to producers. While the analysis is explicitly conducted in terms of tariffs and subsidies, it should be noted that a variety of other devices such as multiple exchange rates or quota restrictions can be employed to achieve essentially the same effects as tariffs, and similarly tax concessions can be employed to produce the same effects as subsidies.

Finally, it should be noted that while the analysis is concerned primarily with tariffs on industrial products, since economic growth is implicitly or explicitly identified with industrialization in most of the contemporary literature, the analysis applies equally to arguments for the protection of domestic agriculture, such as is practiced particularly in the advanced industrial countries.

II. *Arguments for Tariffs in Underdeveloped Countries*

Contemporary arguments for tariffs in underdeveloped countries can be classified into three broad kinds: economic arguments, non-economic arguments, and non-arguments.

The economic arguments for protection comprise all those arguments that recommend the tariff as a means of increasing real output or real income above what it otherwise would be. The arguments for protection on these grounds include the traditional infant-industry and terms of trade (optimum tariff) arguments, and certain new arguments based on alleged distortions in the functioning of the economy that prevent competition from achieving the socially optimal allocation of productive resources among economic sectors. Among the new arguments, the most important are those derived from the assumed existence of external economies in manufacturing industry, and those derived from alleged distortions in the labour market which produce a disequilibrium characterised by an excess of the marginal product of labour in industry over its marginal product in agriculture. This last argument, which involves the modern formulation of the concept of "disguised unemployment" developed in the 1930s and applied somewhat uncritically to analysis of the development problem in the early postwar period, comes in two variants. One of these asserts that labour working on the land under peasant agricultural conditions receives its average product, which exceeds its marginal product by labour's share in the rent of the land, whereas labour in industry is paid its marginal product, so that equalization of wages in the two sectors through mobility of labour leaves labour's marginal product in industry above its marginal product in agriculture. The other asserts that for various reasons—convention, social conscience of employers, trade union action, social welfare legislation—wages in industry are fixed differentially above the wages of comparable labour in agriculture, so that though labour earns its marginal product in both sectors these marginal products are not equalised by labour migration. Both arguments are used to justify industrial protection, protection being recommended to offset the distortion in the labour market; but the difference in the alleged circumstances on which the case for protection is based implies a significant difference in the policies most appropriate for remedying the distortion, as will be shown in Part III.

Non-economic arguments for protection comprise arguments recommending protection as a means of achieving objectives with respect to the structure and composition of output that are desired for their own sake rather than as a means of increasing real income. Much of the argument for protection of industrial activity in underdeveloped countries is of this kind. Industrialization is frequently desired as a matter of national pride and self-respect or as a basis for military and political importance in the world, economic development being identified with industrialization as such rather than with rising real income. Similarly, protection of industry is frequently recommended as a means of promoting national self-sufficiency, self-sufficiency being desired for its own sake and identified with economic development. The distinguishing characteristic of non-economic as distinct from economic arguments for protection is that—at least if they are honestly advocated—they involve the willingness to forego potential real income in order to achieve other objectives of national policy. The non-economic arguments for protection may be divided broadly into those that identify economic development with industrialization, and those that identify economic development with self-sufficiency. As will be shown in Part IV, the economic policies appropriate for implementing these two objectives most efficiently are significantly different.

Non-arguments for protection comprise all arguments that purport to, but on logical examination do not, lead to the recommendation of tariffs. Two major types of arguments of this kind figure largely in the contemporary literature and discussion of economic development. One is concerned with the typical dependence of underdeveloped countries on the export of primary products, and argues from an alleged tendency of the terms of trade to turn against such countries or from the variability of the prices of and export earnings from such products to the recommendation of industrial protection. But secularly diminishing comparative advantage is not equivalent to proof of current comparative disadvantage, nor is it self-evident that the competitive adjustment to secularly changing comparative advantage needs to be supplemented by government intervention; analogously, greater variability of earnings in one occupation than in another is not equivalent to lower average earnings in the former than in the latter, and it is not self-evident that competition will attract producers into high-variability low-average-earnings occupations from which they need rescue by government intervention. The other major argument sees balance-of-payments difficulties as an argument for protection aimed at import-substitution. But balance-of-payments difficulties result from inflation or the maintenance of an overvalued exchange rate, for which the appropriate remedies are deflation or devaluation; and there is no argument for protection as a preferable policy in such circumstances that would not hold equally well in the absence of balance-of-payments difficulties.

III. *Economic Arguments for Protection in Underdeveloped Countries*

The economic analysis of the various arguments for protection as a means of increasing real income can be summarized in two central principles:[2]

(1) Only the optimum tariff argument provides an economic justification for tariffs: all other arguments for protection are arguments for subsidies.

(2) The use of the tariff on the basis of any of the other arguments may make matters worse rather than better, in the sense that whether in these cases the tariff increases or decreases real income depends on the relative magnitudes of various relevant technological and behavior relationships and cannot be determined by *a priori* reasoning.

The first principle is an application of the standard theory of Paretian welfare maximization. According to that analysis, the necessary conditions for a welfare maximum entail equality of the marginal social rates of substitution among goods with the marginal social rates of transformation among them in both domestic production and foreign trade. Where competition does not ensure fulfilment of these conditions, owing to divergences between private and social marginal rates of substitution and transformation, the analysis calls for the imposition of taxes and subsidies at appropriate rates designed to offset any (and all) such divergences. This recommendation has two implications for the economic arguments for protection. First, only where divergences between private and social marginal costs or benefits exist in foreign trade are taxes or subsidies on trade as such required to achieve the social optimum; these cases are precisely those with which the optimum tariff analysis is concerned. Second, divergences between private and social marginal costs or benefits in domestic consumption, production, or factor use require appropriate taxes on consumption, production or factor use, and not taxes or subsidies on international trade, which discriminate between goods according to whether they are of domestic or foreign origin or destination.

The second principle is an application of the modern theory of second best. In one version, that theory demonstrates that if the attainment of a welfare maximum is prevented by the presence of distortions that preclude the fulfilment of the necessary marginal equalities, there is no way of determining *a priori* whether a change to another set of distortions would move the economy closer to or farther away from the welfare maximum. Since the attempt to offset a distortion in the domestic economy by intervention in international

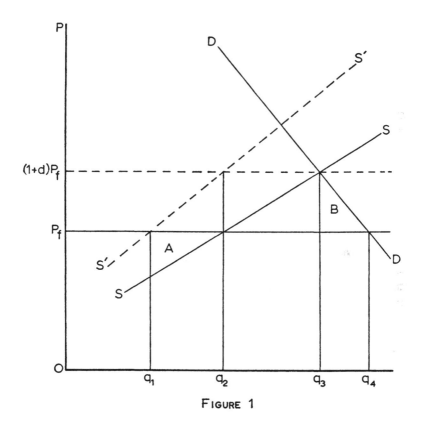

FIGURE 1

trade involves eliminating one distortion at the expense of introducing another, it follows directly that use of protection to correct domestic distortions may make the economy worse off rather than better off.

The economic effects of the application of tariffs to correct distortions in the domestic economy can be analysed with the assistance of the accompanying diagram (Fig. 1). The diagram depicts the demand and supply conditions of a good which is obtainable through importation at the price $p_f$, and is produced domestically subject to a distortion which makes the private cost of production and the supply curve in monetary terms $S'S'$ greater than the true domestic supply curve reflecting real costs of production $SS$ by a proportion $d$ of the latter. (It is assumed that this is the only distortion in the economy.)

Under free trade and in the absence of government intervention the economy will produce $Oq_1$ and import $q_1q_4$ of the good. It could however, replace $q_1q_2$ of imports by additional domestic production at a saving of real cost equal to the area $A$, which area represents the reduction of real income below the attainable maximum due to the distortion. In order to achieve this result, the government should give a subsidy on production at the rate $d$, the proportional excess of the monetary private over the real social cost of production. If instead the government levies a tariff on imports at the rate $d$, it will obtain the cost saving $A$; but it will also restrict total consumption by the amount of $q_3q_4$, and this will entail a loss of consumers' surplus equal to the area $B$. Area $B$ may be greater or less than the area $A$, depending approximately on whether $q_3q_4$ is greater or less than $q_1q_2$, that is, on whether the demand curve is less or more steep than the supply curve. If area $B$ is greater than area $A$, the correction of the domestic distortion by the imposition of the tariff results in a net economic loss by comparison with the situation under free trade.

As the foregoing analysis demonstrates, arguments for protection as a means of correcting domestic distortions that make private and social marginal costs or benefits diverge are really arguments for taxes or subsidies directed at the domestic economy. The nature of the required intervention in the conditions specified by contemporary arguments for protection in underdeveloped countries on these grounds may now be briefly indicated. In the case of external economies in manufacturing, the appropriate policy is a subsidy to manufacturing; if the precise source of the external economies can be specified—for example, training of labour, or research activity—the subsidies should be directed at the specific source. In the case of disequilibrium in the labour market, both variants of the argument require a subsidy on the use of labour in industry: it should be noted that a subsidy on output in industry will not meet the case adequately, since the need for a higher marginal product of labour in industry than in agriculture will induce employers in industry to choose less labour-intensive techniques than would be socially optimal. In the peasant agriculture variant, labour's participation in the rent of land implies the equivalent of a tax on the use of the co-operant factors in agriculture, and requires in addition to a subsidy on the use of labour in industry a subsidy on the use of other factors in agriculture. In the case of the infant industry argument, it is useful to begin by interpreting this argument as a contention that competition does not allocate investment properly among alternative opportunities: the nursing of an infant industry to viability is an investment of initial development costs for the sake of future profits, and a socially profitable investment opportunity of this kind will not be privately undertaken only if the social rate of return exceeds the private rate of return or if the private rate of discount (interest cost) exceeds the social rate of discount (interest cost). In either case, the appropriate policy calls for subsidization of the interest cost of investment. In any of the three conditions alleged to call for protection, the application of protective policies is certain to produce results worse (in welfare terms) than the application of the appropriate policies just described, and may produce either worse or better results than no intervention at all.

The analysis of the economic arguments for protection presented in this section leads to the conclusion that, except in the case of the optimum tariff argument, the appropriate policy involves a subsidy of one kind or another. The recommendation of subsidies as policy instruments in underdeveloped countries is frequently rejected as unrealistic, on the grounds that such countries lack the capacity to raise adequate revenue to finance such subsidies, and must instead use taxes. This argument is less relevant than it seems, for two reasons: first, the effect of a subsidy on a particular activity can always be obtained by imposing an appropriately designed set of taxes on other goods; and second, given that the state must levy taxes for its own purposes, subsidies can be given in the form of exemption from taxes normally payable. The recommendation of freedom of trade in underdeveloped countries is also frequently objected to on the ground that imports offer the only administratively feasible source of tax revenue; this objection, however, is not an argument for protection but rather asserts that fiscal expediency may necessitate violation of the requirements of an efficient competitive system.

## IV. *Non-Economic Arguments for Protection*

The discussion of non-economic arguments for protection in Part II distinguished between arguments whose objective is increased domestic production, and arguments whose objective is increased self-sufficiency. The economic analysis of these arguments can be summarized very briefly in two propositions:

(1) arguments that define the objective of protection as increased domestic production are arguments for subsidies and not for tariffs; this is so because tariffs impose a consumption cost (loss of consumers' surplus) that contributes nothing to achievement of the objective of protection.

(2) arguments that define the objective of protection as reduced dependence on imports are genuine arguments for tariffs, in the sense

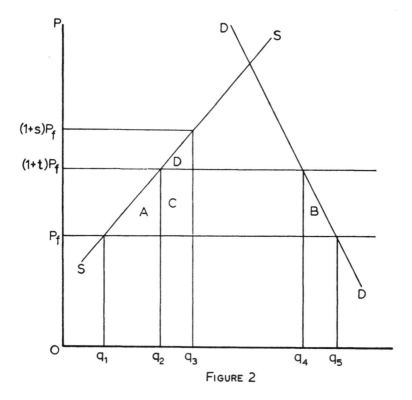

FIGURE 2

that the tariff involves less sacrifice of real income than alternative fiscal methods; the reason is that it is more efficient to reduce imports by both restricting consumption and increasing domestic production than by increasing production or reducing consumption alone. These propositions may be illustrated by reference to the accompanying diagram (Fig. 2), where DD represents the demand curve, $SS$ the domestic supply curve (there are no distortions between money and real costs in this case), and $p_f$ the price at which imports

TARIFFS AND ECONOMIC DEVELOPMENT

are obtainable. Under free trade, domestic production would be $Oq_1$, total consumption $Oq_5$, and imports $q_1q_5$. To increase domestic output to the level $Oq_2$, an excess production cost measured by the area $A$ must be incurred; this result could be secured by the granting of a subsidy on domestic production at the rate $t$. If instead a tariff were imposed at the rate $t$, the same effect on domestic production would be secured, but in addition to the excess production cost $A$ the country would incur a consumption cost (loss of consumers' surplus) measured by the area $B$. Thus the subsidy is more efficient than the tariff in securing an increase in domestic production.

Now consider the situation with the tariff in effect: imports are reduced from $q_1q_5$ under free trade to $q_2q_4$ under the tariff, at a cost in real income foregone of $A+B$. The same reduction of imports could be obtained by a production subsidy at the rate $s$ sufficient to increase domestic output to $Oq_3$, where $q_2q_3 = q_4q_5$; the cost in real income foregone in this case is $A+C+D$. Since $q_2q_3 = q_4q_5$, $C$ is necessarily greater than $B$ and $A+C+D$ greater than $A+B$. The tariff is therefore more efficient than the subsidy in securing a reduction in imports. By a parallel geometrical argument it can be shown that the tariff is more efficient than a third method of restricting imports, taxation of consumption of the commodity regardless of where it is produced. Thus the tariff is the most efficient method of securing a reduction of imports, or increased self-sufficiency. The reason is that the tariff equates the marginal costs of saving imports by increasing production and by decreasing consumption, whereas the two alternative methods do not, because each fixes one of these marginal costs at zero.

## V. *The Second-Best Optimum Tariff Structure*

It has been argued in the preceding section that, if the aim of protection is to increase domestic production of the goods to be protected, protection is an inefficient instrument for the purpose, the same results being obtainable by means of subsidization of production at a lower real cost in terms of foregone income. Supposing, however, that a country is determined to increase the output of a group of industries above what it would be under free trade, and chooses or has to choose protection as its means of achieving this objective. The question then arises, what tariff structure should it employ for this purpose; that is, what should be the relationship among the tariff rates levied on the various items to be protected? The answer to this question defines what may be termed the "second-best optimum tariff structure," so-called to distinguish it from the optimum tariff structure (which is derived from the Paretian welfare maximization conditions) and to emphasize its origin in the second-best welfare economics. Alternatively, the results may be thought of as a "scientific" tariff structure, designed to achieve the desired effects on the productive structure at minimum cost.[3]

The usual prescription of economists faced with this question is that the rate of duty should be the same for every item protected. This prescription is generally accompanied by the recommendation that the tariff should apply to a wide range of commodities, or to all manufactured goods, and that the rate of duty should be "low" or "not too high," estimates of what is "reasonable" varying from 10 or 20 to 50 or more per cent.

The logic of the recommendation of a single tariff rate employs the assumption that the cost or waste of protection is the excess of the cost of the protected production over the world price, and the principle that the total cost of protection will be minimized if the marginal cost of protection per value unit of protected output is

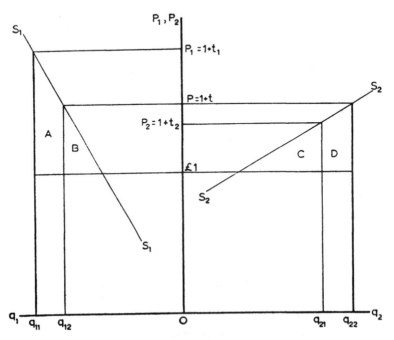

FIGURE 3

equal in the protected industries. This logic is illustrated in the accompanying diagram (Fig. 3). The diagram depicts the domestic supply curves $S_1S_1$ and $S_2S_2$ of two commodities subject to protection, the commodities being measured in units worth £1 at world market prices. At the unequal tariff rates $t_1$ and $t_2$, production of the commodities is $Oq_{11}$ and $Oq_{21}$ respectively, and total output of the two together $q_{11}q_{21}$, this total output being achieved at an excess cost over world market prices of $A+B+C$. By successively lowering the tariff on commodity 1, and raising the tariff rate on commodity 2 just sufficiently to replace the reduction in output of commodity 1 by an increase in output of commodity 2, a uniform tariff rate $t$ can be found that generates the same total output as $t_1t_2$, the excess cost over the world market prices now being $B+C+D$ and the difference from the previous cost $D-A$. Since $q_{11}q_{12}$ is equal to $q_{21}q_{22}$ and $t_1$ exceeds $t_2$, $A$ must exceed $D$, thus proving that the uniform rate involves a lower total excess cost of protected production than a system of differentiated rates.

A simple extension of this analysis can be used to show that extending protection to a third commodity would permit the same volume of protected production (excess of total output over what would be produced under free trade) to be produced at a lower total excess cost and lower tariff rate, through the replacement of high-excess-cost marginal output in industries 1 and 2 by lower-excess-cost marginal output from industry 3. This is the logic of recommending protection over as wide a range of commodities as possible. Similarly, the fact that the marginal excess cost of protected production is measured by the tariff rate accounts for the recommendation that the tariff should not be "too high," since presumably at some point the marginal excess cost of additional protected output becomes higher than the social benefit or gratification derived from it.

The answer to the problem of the second-best optimum tariff structure just discussed, however, is not theoretically valid. In the first place, it assumes the absence of any distortions in the economy of the type discussed in Part III. So far as distortions in the protected industries themselves are concerned, this is in principle a matter of secondary importance, since the recommended uniform rate could be modified to take account of any divergences of private from social costs in these industries; but if distortions exist in the unprotected sectors of the economy, correction for these will involve a complex calculation requiring detailed knowledge of the cross-relations among

protected and unprotected commodities in both production and
consumption. Second, and more important, the uniform rate rule
is incorrect even in the absence of distortions in the economy, since
it counts only the excess production cost of protection and fails to
take account of the loss of consumers' surplus, the consumption cost,
associated with protection.

This point can be illustrated by reference to Fig. 4, which repro-
duces the uniform-rate situation of Fig. 3 and introduces the demand
curves for the two commodities. With the uniform tariff rate,

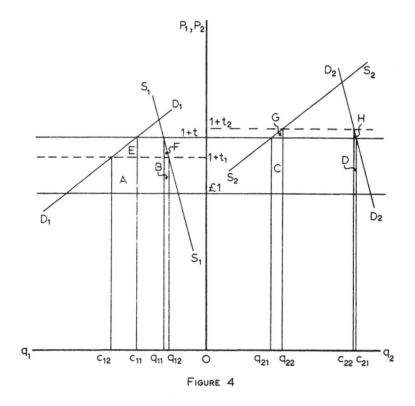

FIGURE 4

consumption of the two goods is $c_{11}$ and $c_{21}$, respectively, and
production $q_{11}$ and $q_{21}$ respectively. Assume that the tariff on commodity 2 is simultaneously raised by just enough to replace the lost
output of $q_{11}q_{12}$ of commodity 1 (caused by the reduction in the
tariff on it) by an equal increase $q_{21}q_{22}$ of commodity 2. The result
is an increase in the excess production cost of total protected output,
since the area $B+F$, the saving on excess cost of production of

commodity 1, must be smaller than the area $C+G$, the increase in excess cost of production of commodity 2. But the change also leads to an increase in consumers' surplus on consumption of commodity 1 equal to the area $A+E$, and a decrease in consumers' surplus on commodity 2 equal to the area $D+H$; and as the diagram is drawn, with $S_1S_1$ steeper than $S_2S_2$ and $D_2D_2$ steeper than $D_1D_1$ and the change in $t_1$ small, $A+E$ is sufficiently greater than $D+H$ to outweigh the excess of $C+G$ over $B+F$, so that a net gain results from lowering $t_1$ and raising $t_2$ in such a way as to keep output constant. It is obvious, however, that successive reductions in $t_1$ accompanied by matching increases in $t_2$ must eventually lead to $A+E$ becoming smaller than $D+H$, so that there must be an optimum relation between $t_1$ and $t_2$ that minimizes the total excess cost of the initial level of protected production. Assuming the various curves to be approximately straight lines, it can in fact easily be proved that the optimum relationship is given by

$$\frac{t_1}{t_2} = \frac{1+(d_2/s_2)}{1+(d_1/s_1)},$$

where $d_1$, $d_2$ and $s_1$, $s_2$ are respectively the (absolute) slopes of the demand and supply curves for the two commodities. In short, the second-best optimum tariff structure in this simplified case depends on the precise magnitudes of the slopes of the demand and supply curves for the commodities, and unless the two slopes bear the same ratio for every commodity subject to protection the second-best optimum tariff structure will not be a uniform tariff rate.

The conclusion that the uniform tariff rate will only be the second-best optimal tariff structure in special empirical circumstances can be established in a more general way by resort to the Meade-Fleming approach to second-best analysis.[4] Assume an economy in which the only distortions that exist are tariffs; the effect on welfare of small changes in these tariff rates can be expressed as

(1) $$dW = \sum_{i=1}^{n} \sum_{j=1}^{n} t_j(x_{ji} - c_{ji})\, dt_i,$$

where $t_i$ is the tariff rate on commodity $i$, and $x_{ji}$ and $c_{ji}$ are the partial derivatives of the quantities of commodity $j$ produced and consumed with respect to the price of commodity $i$. Assume further that tariff changes are constrained by the condition that the total output of a subset $k$ of the commodities is to be kept constant, and consider changes in two tariff rates $t_f$ and $t_g$ that satisfy this condition, so that

$$(2) \qquad \sum_{j=1}^{k} x_{jf} dt_f = \sum_{j=1}^{k} x_{jg} dt_g.$$

The effect on welfare is

$$(3) \quad dW = \sum_{j=1}^{k} t_j (x_{jf} dt_f - x_{jg} dt_g) - \sum_{j=1}^{k} t_j (c_{jf} dt_f - c_{jg} dt_g)$$

$$+ \sum_{j=k+1}^{n} t_j (x_{jf} dt_f - x_{jg} dt_g) - \sum_{j=k+1}^{n} t_j (c_{jf} dt_f - c_{jg} dt_g).$$

The second-best optimum tariff structure is the set of tariff rates $t_j$ that equates $dW$ to zero for any $dt_f$, $dt_g$. If the tariff rates on the $k$ commodities are all equal to $t$, the first term in (3) becomes equal to

$$t \left( \sum_{j=1}^{k} x_{jf} dt_f - \sum_{j=1}^{k} x_{jg} dt_g \right)$$

and vanishes; but the other three terms will in general not vanish. The last two terms will vanish if the tariffs on goods $k+1$ to $n$ are set equal to zero (i.e., the tariff is imposed only on the goods desired to be protected); but there is no reason to expect that zero rates on these goods are implied by the second-best optimum tariff structure, and in any case the second term would only be equal to zero by accident. In other words, the second-best optimum tariff structure will in general involve both differentiated rates on the goods whose production it is desired to encourage, and tariffs (or possibly subsidies, depending on the nature of the cross-effects) on other goods as well.

The recommendation of a uniform tariff rate on commodities whose production it is desired to protect therefore has no theoretical validity. To put this conclusion another way, the recommendation must assume both that distortions in the economy causing divergences between private and social marginal cost do not exist, or can be safely ignored, or are unknowable and on the principle of equal ignorance may be expected to cancel out, and that the consumption cost of protection can be ignored or on the same principle of equal ignorance can be expected to cancel out. Further, for consistency it must comprise all imports, since there are no grounds for believing that a uniform tariff on the imports it is desired to replace and a zero tariff on the remainder constitutes the most efficient tariff structure for encouraging domestic production of the desired commodities.

In conclusion, it may be observed that the uniform rate rule makes rather more sense as a guide for a protectionist policy aimed at increasing self-sufficiency. For in this case, as can be shown by a simple extension of the foregoing analysis, if there are no distortions apart from the tariff structure a uniform tariff rate applied to all importable goods will equate the marginal costs of import-saving (by increased production or reduced consumption) and so minimize the total excess cost of import-saving.

## VI. *Some Aspects of Differentiated Tariff Structures*

Most of the extant theory of commercial policy, including the theory employed in the analysis of the preceding Parts, is concerned implicitly or explicitly with tariffs levied on commodities destined for final consumption. In actuality, however, much international trade consists of the exchange of raw materials, semi-finished goods, and capital goods for utilization in the production of finished goods in the importing country; moreover, the rates of duty that make up tariff structures are usually differentiated according to the stage of production or place in the production process of the dutiable goods, as well as being differentiated among goods at the same stage of production. In particular, tariff rates are typically "cascaded," the rate increasing from the raw material to the semi-fabricated and from the semi-fabricated to the fabricated stages.

The fact that traded goods may be either inputs or outputs in the importing country's productive system means that a particular tariff may either tax or subsidize domestic production, depending on whether the tariff applies to an input or an output, and makes it necessary to distinguish between the protection accorded to *commodities*, and the protection accorded to the *processes of production* that produce those commodities by a given tariff structure. The latter may differ markedly from the former, and the rate of protection accorded, or the excess cost of protected production allowed, by the tariff structure to a particular process of production be very different from that indicated by the tariff rate on the commodity it produces. This Part presents a simple mathematical analysis of the relation between the tariff rates on commodities and the degree of protection accorded to processes of production—the rate of protection of value added, as it is sometime termed—incorporated in the tariff structure, and comments on some of the implications for economic development of tariff structures in which tariff rates are differentiated by production stages.

For purposes of analysis, assume that the productive system is characterized by an input-output matrix of the usual type; let $a_{ji}$ be the input coefficient for the $j$th commodity in the $i$th production process, and let $v_i$ be the coefficient of value added (or of "original factors" used) in that process, output being measured in unit values in world currency and the input coefficients being measured in values at world market prices, so that

$$\sum_{j=1}^{n} a_{ji} + v_i = 1,$$

where the input coefficients pertain to the technology employed in the world outside the country whose tariff structure is to be analysed. Let the tariff structure of the country in question be represented by $t_i$, $i = 1 \ldots n$; if the country is to take part in trade, at least one of the $t_i$ must be zero, or inoperative (effectively zero) because the relevant commodity is exported. Let $\tau_i$ represent the implicit rate of protection of value added or original factors used in the $i$th industry inherent in the tariff structure $t_i$, defined as the proportion by which the tariff structure allows the domestic cost of value added or value of original factors used in producing commodity $i$ to exceed the foreign cost or value $v_i$. The tariff structure allows the domestic price of the $i$th commodity to be $1 + t_i$, whereas its cost of production will be

$$\sum_{j=1}^{n} (1 + t_j)a_{ji} + (1 + \tau_i)v_i.$$

Equating price and cost to obtain the implicit rate of protection yields the formula

$$\tau_i = \frac{t_i - \sum_{j=1}^{n} a_{ji}t_j}{v_i}$$

It is evident from the formula that the implicit rate of protection on a particular productive process will be equal to the explicit rate of protection on the commodity it produces only if the weighted average tariff rate on the inputs it uses

$$\left( \sum_{j=1}^{n} a_{ji}t_j \bigg/ \sum_{j=1}^{n} a_{ji} \right)$$

is equal to the tariff rate on the commodity it produces. If the weighted average tariff rate on inputs is lower than the tariff rate on the output the implicit rate of protection exceeds the commodity tariff rate.[5] If the weighted average tariff rate on inputs is higher than the tariff rate on the output, the implicit rate of protection is lower than the commodity tariff rate, and may even be negative: that is, the tariff structure may tax rather than subsidize the production of certain commodities. [6]

The most obvious examples of this last possibility are export industries, which by definition are not protected but may use inputs subject to protection, and so be taxed by the tariff structure. This point has some relevance to the difficulties typically encountered by developing countries in expanding their traditional exports sufficiently to pay for the imports required for development: the heavily protective policies frequently used to promote development may tax the inputs of the export industries sufficiently severely to prevent their growth. In addition, since increasing productivity in agriculture hinges on increasing use of manufactured inputs, and taxation of such inputs discourages their use, protection may be a direct deterrent to agricultural progress. Protection may indeed produce a vicious circle of self-justifying policy measures, in which the planners start from the assumption that agriculture is incorrigibly backward, adopt a policy of heavy industrial protectionism to promote development, and by so doing throttle the development of agriculture and so provide evidence in support of the assumption of incorrigible agricultural backwardness from which their faith in industrialization is derived.

While export industries are the most obvious examples of industries taxed by a protective tariff structure, any tariff structure containing differentiated rates may involve such taxation of particular industries. This point also has relevance for underdeveloped countries, which usually go in for extensive protection of industrial activities of all kinds, from materials production through semi-fabrication to final production processes, and implement this policy not only by tariffs but by exchange controls, import licensing, prohibition of imports of "non-essentials," and bargains with foreign-owned companies or legislation making protection conditional on the use of domestically-produced components and materials. The effort to protect activities that produce inputs for other protected activities may use up all or more than all of the protection accorded to the latter, so that in spite of apparently heavy protection (as measured by the tariff rates on the commodities produced) these industries have difficulty in surviving and growing (because the implicit rate of protection they enjoy is low or negative). It is in this sense that protection may be said to "cancel itself out." [7]

The cases just discussed are ones in which the tariff structure, by imposing higher rates on inputs than on the finished product, reduces or eliminates the implicit protection accorded to the production process or subjects it to a net tax. Where the tariff on inputs is lower than the tariff rate on the output, the effect is to raise the implicit rate of protection on the process above the tariff rate on the commodity produced by it. This fact, in conjunction with the typical structure of tariff rates according to which tariff rates rise with stage of production, has important implications for world trade and economic development.

In the first place, the prevalence of such tariff structures in the advanced countries implies that the advanced countries grant much heavier protection to their manufacturing industries than their tariff rates by themselves suggest. The effect of "cascading" may be quite substantial: for example, suppose that materials constitute 50 per cent of the value of final output, and that final output is protected by a tariff rate of 30 per cent while materials enter free of duty; then the implicit rate of protection of value added will be 60 per cent, or double the tariff rate on the output. With a material content of 75 per cent, the implicit rate of protection would be 120 per cent, or four times the tariff rate on the output. The effect of implicit rates of protection of value added that rise sharply with stage of production is obviously to create a strong bias towards confining world trade as a whole predominantly to raw materials and semi-finished goods, and world trade in manufactures to capital goods and goods whose technological superiority or luxury nature enables them to overcome high protective barriers. Moreover, the pattern of trade fostered by such differentiated tariff structures itself disguises the protectiveness of those tariff structures, by giving a heavy weight in the conventional measurements of protection—tariff rates weighted by values of goods traded, or total duties collected divided by value of imports—to the very items whose entry at low or zero rates increases the protection afforded by the tariff structure to the higher stages of production. It is even possible for a country to increase the real protectiveness of its tariff structure while simultaneously reducing the degree of protectiveness as conventionally measured, by lowering or eliminating duties on imported inputs.

From the point of view of countries seeking to develop and industrialize, the heavy protection of final production processes implicit in the tariff structures of the advanced countries constitutes a major barrier to success. For it neutralizes part or all of the advantage of low wage rates that these countries possess, thereby debarring them from achieving the economies of scale and specialization that access to rich markets would permit, and forcing them if they insist on industrializing, to do so within the confines of their domestic markets, with all the disadvantages of small scale that that entails. That this can be a major barrier is illustrated by the following hypothetical example: suppose that in the advanced countries 50 per cent of the cost of a product is materials, 25 per cent capital charges, and 25 per cent labour cost, and that the tariff on the product is at the rate of 25 per cent. If the materials were available to the underdeveloped countries at the same prices and capital were freely mobile, the underdeveloped countries would have to have labour costs amounting to only 20 per cent of labour costs in the advanced countries for them to be able to land imports at the domestic market price in the advanced countries.[8] In view of the potential magnitude of the barrier to the industrialization of the underdeveloped countries inherent in the differentiated tariff structures of the advanced countries, it is somewhat surprising that the underdeveloped countries have devoted so much attention to the level and variability of the prices at which the advanced countries buy their primary products, instead of to the tariff differentiation that keeps them dependent on the sale of such products for their earnings of foreign exchange and deprives them of access to the large markets necessary for efficient industrialization.

In the second place, the underdeveloped countries in their own protective policies tend to follow the model of the advanced countries in differentiating their tariff rates and other protective devices according to stage of production. To the extent that they do this, the excess cost of the domestic production achieved by protection may be substantially higher than appears from the tariff rates on commodities or from the excess of the domestic price over the foreign price, and far higher than can be easily justified by presumed external economies, distorted wage rates, inelasticity of the demand for traditional exports, or *de facto* overvaluation of the currency.

Again taking a hypothetical illustrative example, suppose that the domestic price of the finished product is double the foreign price—an excess not outside the range of actual experience—and that 25 per cent of the total domestic cost consists of materials allowed entry duty-free; then the country will be paying three times as much for the working-up of the materials domestically as it would have to pay to have the working-up done abroad and incorporated in imports of the finished product. Such an arrangement would only be economically advantageous if the alternative opportunity cost of the domestic factors used were less than one-third of their money earnings, or if reallocation of them to export industries would increase foreign exchange earnings by less than one-third of their value. Moreover, given the complex interaction of tariff rates in determining the implicit rates of protection accorded to different industries, these rates may vary substantially from industry to industry, with no rational justification in terms of varying values of these industries to the economic development of the country. In other words, the implicit rates of protection may depart widely from the requirements of a second-best optimum tariff structure.

## VII. *Some Observations on Import Substitution and Economic Development*

Countries seeking to promote their own economic development generally employ tariffs and other trade barriers to encourage the establishment of domestic production of substitutes for imports. The attractions of a policy of import substitution are appealing—the existence of imports indicates the presence of a market for the product—especially when the country is in chronic balance-of-payments difficulties. Yet the results are commonly disappointing. Whereas the purpose of protection is to promote the development of locally owned and operated enterprises, it tends instead to encourage the establishment of subsidiaries or affiliates of foreign enterprises, generally the large international companies with headquarters in the United States or Europe, and so give rise to political anxieties about foreign "control" and "domination" of the economy. Moreover, whether the enterprises are domestically or foreign owned, their methods of operation prove objectionable in a variety of ways to those ambitious for economic development. Protected enterprises are frequently criticized for duplicating the market structure and marketing methods of the advanced countries—high distributive margins, heavy advertising, extensive product differentiation, rapid product changes, and so on; for using a technology that is backward by comparison with that of the advanced countries—for example, relying on second-hand or antiquated equipment; for using techniques adopted from the advanced countries and therefore inappropriate to the relative factor availabilities in the domestic economy; for failing to develop export markets; and for continuing reliance on extensive use of imported parts and machinery.

These subjects of criticism, far from being the demonstrations of the wilful perversity of capitalism that they are often alleged to be, are the natural economic consequences of pursuing economic development by a policy of import substitution implemented by protection. Goods are initially imported rather than produced domestically because the foreign producer possesses comparative advantages sufficiently strong to overcome the natural barriers to international trade imposed by transportation and communication costs; in the modern industrial world, these advantages generally stem from access to a large domestic market, which permits the exploitation of economies of scale and of specialization and fosters product improvement through research and development expenditure. The use of protection to promote substitution of local for foreign production does nothing to reduce the comparative disadvantage of local as contrasted with foreign entrepreneurship, and its main effect is therefore likely to be to induce the foreign firms to set up local production facilities to satisfy the demand previously satisfied by exports from their home country, rather than to create a domestically owned and operated industry capable of competing successfully with its foreign rivals. Where domestic ownership is insisted on, it is still likely to be most economical for the local entrepreneurs to come to an arrangement with the foreign firms that in the absence of the import-substitution policy would supply the market, to obtain access to the production and management methods the latter command. Hence the economic policy of import-substitution almost inevitably creates the political problem of foreign "control" of the economy.

Given that the policy of import-substitution by protection involves forcing industry to move from an economic to an uneconomic location, the methods of operation of the transplanted industries are likely to be objectionable to development enthusiasts on the various grounds previously mentioned. For, quite apart from any psychological and political implications of the fact that foreign enterprises are simultaneously coerced and bribed by protection to establish facilities that they otherwise would not establish, and so may feel no obligation to do more than the minimum necessary to satisfy the policy-makers of the developing country, there are strong economic reasons for adopting these methods of operation. The production and marketing methods of the advanced countries are known and familiar, and hence cost little to apply elsewhere, whereas the invention of new techniques of production and marketing adapted to the small markets, low income levels, and cheap but poorly trained labour of the underdeveloped countries would require an expensive investment in research that might not justify its cost. In other words, it is likely to be more efficient to adapt methods inappropriate to local conditions as far as possible than to invest in the development of the methods most appropriate to local conditions. Similarly, the use of second-hand equipment may be more efficient than either using up-to-date equipment designed for a higher-wage and larger-scale and more specialised economy, or designing and building new equipment tailored to the scale and factor prices of the under-developed economy. Again, given that the import-substitute industries are established to supply an existing market they are unlikely to become exporters, since the existing market typically demands small quantities of a large variety of goods whereas successful exporting for a small country typically demands concentration on quantity production of a limited range of standard lines. And given that the efficiency of industry in advanced countries frequently rests on tight control over the quality of material inputs and components and on the use of carefully designed precision machinery, it is likely to be relatively inexpensive to transplant the assembly or fabricating processes and relatively expensive to transplant the production of the materials and components themselves and of the machinery used in the process, so that industries transplanted by import-substitution policies are likely to remain dependent on extensive imports of material, components, and machinery.

All this suggests that a policy of import-substitution is unlikely to transform an underdeveloped country into a major industrial power, competitive in the world market for manufactured products. Instead, such a policy is likely to transform it into a miniature replica of the economies of the advanced countries, though less efficient and technologically laggard to an extent depending on the size of the domestic market and the degree of protection employed.

From the point of view of the economic welfare of the under-developed country this result may nevertheless constitute an improvement, at least in the longer run, especially if the policy of import-substitution attracts substantial amounts of foreign direct investment. For though the substitution of domestic production for imports entails an increase in cost and therefore a reduction in real income, the country may subsequently benefit from the resulting opportunity to learn modern industrial methods and participate directly in the progress of technology in the advanced countries.

This expectation, in one form or another, is of course the motivation of import-substitution as a development policy and the justification usually offered for it.

The attraction of foreign direct investment may be particularly beneficial in this regard for two reasons. First, under the usual double-taxation agreements the country in which investment occurs receives the first slice of profits taxation, so that foreign direct investment in an underdeveloped country enables that country to tax the capitalists of the advanced countries at the expense of the latter's own Treasuries; this is a tangible and important benefit derived by the receiving country from foreign direct investment quite apart from the benefits accruing through increased scale, improved technology, and increased competition in the domestic economy, Second, affiliation with an international parent company gives the local enterprise access to the research and development carried on by the parent and other affiliates, and so provides a flow of productivity-improving knowledge at relatively low cost to the country.[10]

It is not true, however, that a policy of import-substitution will necessarily prove beneficial in the long run, by giving the country a share in technical progress in the industries involved. It is, on the contrary, possible for a country to be made worse off by technical progress in its import-competing sector, because the reduction in the cost of currently-produced import-substitutes is more than outweighed by a consequent further replacement of imports by higher-cost domestic substitutes. This possibility is illustrated in Fig. 5, where the supply curve is to be thought of as a supply curve of import substitutes and the policy of import-substitution is represented by a tariff at the rate $t$ imposed on imports available at the world price $p_f$. Prior to the technical change the supply curve of import substitutes is $S_1 S_1$ and the excess production cost imposed by the import-substitution policy is the area $A + B$. Technical change shifts the supply curve to $S_2 S_2$, involving an excess production cost of import-substitution of $B + C$; as the diagram is drawn, $C$ is greater than $A$ so that technical progress in the import-substitution sector results in a net loss to the country.[11]

The foregoing analysis relates to import-substitution considered as a once-for-all measure, exemplified for example by the introduction of a protective tariff. A policy of progressive import substitution which seeks continually to expand the size of the import-competing sector by granting protection to more and more industries, such as has been pursued in several Latin American countries, may involve substantially slimmer prospects of economic growth, or nullify the prospect altogether. As has been demonstrated in Part VI, the excess cost of import-substitution may be high, appreciably higher than is

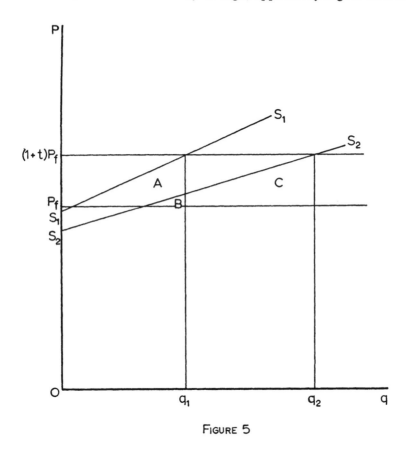

FIGURE 5

implied by tariff rates or the excess of domestic over foreign prices. Progressive import substitution could therefore easily absorb or more than absorb the potential increase in real income that would normally accrue from technical improvement and capital accumulation, and permit a country to accumulate capital at a substantial rate without achieving a significant increase in real income or in real income per head. In other words, potential increases in real income could easily be squandered on buying the luxury of high-cost local production of industrial goods previously imported. This situation could become a vicious circle, and the policy appear to be justified by its own consequences, if import-substitution were accompanied by inflationary development policies leading to chronic balance-of-payments problems.

[1] This article is a revised version of a lecture delivered at the Universities of Buenos Aires, Cordoba, Cujo, and Chile in the summer of 1963, when I was Visiting Professor at the Instituto Torcuato di Tella in Buenos Aires. Some of the analysis has subsequently been developed in greater detail in a series of five lectures on "Some Aspects of the Theory of Tariffs" delivered at the London School of Economics in January and February, 1964, and to be published by George Allen & Unwin. I am grateful to the Rockefeller Foundation for a grant in support of research on problems of trade and technical change, some of which are discussed in the concluding two parts of this article.

[2] For a statement and elaboration of these principles, see J. Bhagwati and V. K. Ramaswami, "Domestic Distortions, Tariffs and the Theory of Optimum Subsidy," *Journal of Political Economy*, Vol. LXXI, no. 1, February 1963, pp. 44-50.

[3] See my "The Cost of Protection and the Scientific Tariff," *Journal of Political Economy*, Vol. LXVIII, no. 4, August 1960, pp. 327-45.

[4] J. E. Meade, *The Theory of International Economic Policy*, Vol. I: *Trade and Welfare* (London, 1952).

[5] Even if the tariff rate on all imports is the same, implicit rates of protection will differ if the protected industries use inputs of exportable goods to different extents. This fact provides another reason why the uniform rate rule discussed in the preceding Part is unlikely to be optimal.

[6] These two propositions are exemplified by the following extreme examples of divergences between the tariff rates and the implicit rate of protection in the U.S. tariff schedule, taken from estimates prepared by Giorgio Basevi in connection with his doctoral study of the U.S. tariff and reproduced with his permission:

| S.I.C. No. | Industry Description | Tariff Rate (%) | Implicit Rate of Protection % | |
|---|---|---|---|---|
| | | | (a) | (b) |
| 2011 | Meat Packing | 3.8 | −31.9 | −30.9 |
| 2823 | Plastic Materials | 17.1 | −30.4 | −30.3 |
| 3111 | Leather Tanning and Finishing | 11.3 | −34.2 | −32.6 |
| 2561 | Screens, Shades and Blinds | 50.0 | +189.0 | +225.8 |
| 3491 | Metal Barrels, Drums and Pails | 35.0 | +107.1 | +115.3 |
| 3871 | Watches and Clocks | 39.3 | +88.1 | +102.9 |

NOTE: The input-output data used in the estimates included a residual category of "other material inputs" of unspecified origin; estimate (a) applies the average tariff rate collected on total imports (5.1 per cent) to these inputs, estimate (b) uses a zero tariff rate.

[7] Another way in which protection may cancel itself out is that wages in the protected industries may rise, under the shelter of the tariff, sufficiently to offset the competitive advantage of the tariff.

[8] Let $a$ = the ratio of underdeveloped to advanced country labour costs necessary for the former to compete in the latter's domestic market; then $(50 + 25 + a \cdot 25)(1 \cdot 25) = 50 + 25 + 25$, whence $a = \cdot 2$.

[9] By direct participation is meant participation as producers, earning higher incomes as a result of technical progress, in contrast to participation as consumers, enjoying higher quality and (or) lower prices of commodities as a result of technical progress. It is sometimes overlooked that underdeveloped countries dependent on imports of manufactured goods benefit from progress in the latter way without having to bear the research and development costs of progress.

[10] For analysis of the gains from foreign investment in the Canadian case, see the Foreword to my *The Canadian Quandary* (Toronto, 1963).

[11] This possibility, which results from "import-biased" technical progress in the presence of a tariff, is to be distinguished from the standard proposition originated by J. R. Hicks ("An Inaugural Lecture," *Oxford Economic Papers*, Vol. 5, no. 2, June 1953, pp. 117-35, reprinted in *Essays in World Economics*) that "import-biased" technical progress under free trade conditions benefits a country by turning the terms of trade in its favour. A full analysis of the effects of "import-biased" progress would require weighing the import-substitution and terms-of-trade effects against one another.

# Trade Concentration and
# Export Instability

by James Love*

*Conventionally commodity and geographic concentration are thought to be important factors contributing to the instability in export earnings of the developing countries. Empirical investigations have, however, provided little support for this proposition. Moving away from the customary cross-country methods of measurement, this paper examines the relationship between the forms of concentration and export instability for each country in a sample of 52 developing countries. The results obtained suggest that there are causal relationships for a wide range of countries.*

INTRODUCTION

A recurrent theme in discussions of the relationship between international trade and economic development is the importance of the problems created for the developing countries by fluctuations in their export earnings. Among the possible explanations of these fluctuations are those concerning the concentration of exports. Typically exports from African. Asian and Latin American countries are characterised by dependence on a narrow range of commodities which are sold to a small number of foreign markets. The concentration of exports on only a few commodities is often thought to be an important cause of export fluctuations because, as MacBean points out, 'it is always risky to put all one's eggs in a single basket. Concentration on a few products reduces a country's chances of having fluctuations in one direction in some of its exports offset or ameliorated by counter-fluctuations or stability in others' [*MacBean, 1966:41*]. An analogous argument is advanced with respect to geographic concentration. Massell argues that 'high geographic concentration is likely to imply greater dependence on economic conditions in one or a few countries. Fluctuations in demand in any recipient country will then have a more pronounced effect on receipts of the exporting country than if receipts were more diversified among recipients' [*Massell, 1970: 622*].

These arguments concerning concentration have the properties of simplicity and of immediate intuitive appeal, given that many developing countries are 'one-crop economies' and that trade patterns frequently reflect former colonial ties or simply the weight of the United States market in trade in primary products. Moreover, if the arguments are valid and if export

---

*Lecturer, Department of Economics, University of Strathclyde. The author is particularly indebted to A. I. MacBean, A. I. Clunies Ross, A. R. Gloyne and P. McGregor for constructive comments and criticisms.

fluctuations do have adverse effects on the economies of the developing countries, it follows that policies aimed at diversification are an obvious prescription. Surprisingly, however, empirical analyses by various authors have shown little association between either form of concentration and export instability.

Early studies into the effects of geographic concentration [*Coppock, 1962; Massell, 1964: 47–63; MacBean, 1966*] produced similar and largely unexpected findings. The results all indicated 'that if any association exists between geographical concentration and export fluctuations it is negative' [*MacBean, 1966: 44*]. More recent studies [*Massell, 1970: 618–630; Naya, 1973: 629–641; Khalaf, 1974: 81–90; Kingston, 1976: 311–319*] have found geographic concentration to be insignificant as an explanatory variable of, although positively related to, export instability. With regard to commodity concentration, MacBean noted that his results coincided with those of other authors[1] [*Coppock, 1962; Massell, 1964: 56–57; Michaely, 1962*] and concluded that 'all the correlation analyses yielded roughly the same answer of a very weak, if any, association between commodity concentration and export fluctuations' [*MacBean, 1966: 43*]. This conclusion is supported by the results obtained in the subsequent studies by Naya, Khalaf and Kingston. Only Massell found a significant relationship between commodity concentration and instability [*Massell, 1970: 626*]. The available evidence is heavily weighted, therefore, against accepting either form of concentration as an important cause of export fluctuations.

Despite the results of these empirical studies there does seem to be a considerable degree of *prima facie* soundness in the traditional arguments. Opening almost any textbook on problems of trade and development one finds reference to the extent of both geographical and commodity concentration in the exports of a wide range of developing countries. Given these characteristics, it is difficult to accept that whatever instability is experienced is not related to the concentration of exports and this paper sets out to examine the causal link between the two forms of concentration and export fluctuations.

I    GINI–HIRSCHMAN COEFFICIENTS AND REGRESSION ANALYSIS
The technique most commonly used in cross-country investigations into the association between concentration and instability is regression analysis. This approach requires that one has statistical measures of the extent of concentration and of instability. Customarily, concentration is measured by the Gini–Hirschman coefficient, which defines the degree of commodity concentration in a country's exports, $C_{xt}$, as

$$C_{xt} = 100 \sqrt{\sum_{j=1}^{n} \left(\frac{X_{jt}}{X_t}\right)^2}$$

where $X_{jt}$ is the value of exports of commodity $j$ in year $t$ and $X_t$ is total export earnings in that year.

The squaring of each commodity's share in total earnings prior to sum-mation is designed to place greater weights on the more important export items. The highest possible value of the coefficient is 100, which occurs when a country exports only one product. The value of the Gini–Hirschman coefficient will be lower the greater is the number of export items and the more even is the distribution of proceeds among these various products. When the shares of all products exported in total proceeds are the same, the lowest possible value of the coefficient will be obtained and is defined as

$$\frac{100}{\sqrt{n}}$$

where $n$ is the number of different commodities being sold abroad. Where $X_{jt}$ represents the value of exports to market $j$ in year $t$, $C_{xt}$ measures the degree of geographical concentration.

While each of the authors concerned with the question of export instability has employed the Gini–Hirschman index as a measure of concentration, they have not used any one single index of instability. The basic problem in the whole issue of export instability is the degree to which export earnings fluctuate around their trend values,[2] and the use of different indices reflects differences among the authors as to the appropriate trend correction and measure of dispersion. Indices which have been used to calculate the degree of export instability include (a) the standard error of estimate divided by the mean of the observations, (b) the standard deviation from a logarithmic trend and (c) the average proportionate deviation from a logarithmic trend. Clearly these instability indices will produce different numerical values from the same data series, although various authors [Coppock, 1962; Erb and Schiavo-Campo, 1969: 263–283; Leith, 1970: 267–272] have observed a high degree of correlation among results obtained using different indices.

After calculating instability indices and coefficients of geographic and commodity concentration for a sample of countries, the relationship between instability and concentration is estimated using a regression equation of the form

$$(1) \qquad I_j = a + bC_{xj} + cG_{xj} + \epsilon$$

where $I_j$ is the index selected to measure the degree of instability in total export earnings of country $j$, $C_{xj}$ is the coefficient of commodity concentration for country $j$ and $G_{xj}$ is the coefficient of geographical concentration for country $j$.

For an individual country the argument that the greater the dependence on one product or market, the more likely it is that fluctuations in earnings from the particular product or market will influence total export earnings, is nothing more than a tautology. When extending the argument to a cross-country study one moves from this tautology to a similar but different formulation which is implicit in the above approach, namely, that those countries with the higher indices of geographical and commodity concentration will also be those experiencing the greater degrees of instability in their export proceeds. Only if this formulation of the problem holds could one obtain significant results from regression analyses of the form above. There are grounds for believing, however, that this formulation is misleading.

The first problem arises because, whereas the various indices of instability involve measuring deviations from trend and provide one statistic summarising the degree of instability over the whole period of analysis, the Gini–Hirschman index measures concentration in one year. Most authors mentioned above have chosen to use indices of geographical and commodity concentration calculated for an arbitrarily chosen year.[3] The value of a coefficient for a particular country may change from year to year, however, and the choice of year is important where, as in the case of Brazil, exports have become more diversified over time. If one were to select an early year in a time series, the Gini–Hirschman coefficient associated with an instability index for total Brazilian export earnings would be higher than would be the case if a later year were chosen. Averaging the series of coefficients[4] may help to overcome this problem of arbitrary selection, but does not solve a more fundamental second problem.

Countries differ, on the one hand, in the commodities they export and the relative importance of different export items and, on the other hand, in the markets to which they export and the relative importance of their trading partners. These differences mean that greater concentration is not necessarily associated with greater instability. For example, Chad's exports of its major commodity, cotton, may be substantially greater relative to its total exports in each year than is the case for the Cameroons' major export item, cocoa, and, thus, indices of commodity concentration will be consistently greater for Chad. However, any one or some combination of a variety of factors, such as differences in the extent of demand- or supply-induced changes in aggregate quantities traded and in prices ruling on world markets, the relative effectiveness of commodity agreements and differences in domestic supply conditions, may cause Chad's earnings from cotton to be less volatile than cocoa earnings for the Cameroons. Consequently, the Cameroons may experience the greater degree of instability in total earnings.

Attempts to avoid specification bias and to raise the explanatory power of the model have led to the introduction of variables or proxy variables for factors other than the forms of concentration which may affect the stability of earnings, including some of those mentioned above. The fullest model was developed by Massell [*Massell, 1970: 618–630*]. There was, however, evidence of collinearity. Even in the simple model of equation (1) this problem may arise. If, for instance, Ethiopia's exports of coffee increase, *ceteris paribus*, this will raise the coefficient of commodity concentration, but since its coffee exports go principally to one market, the United States, this will simultaneously increase the coefficient of geographic concentration. If such behaviour is repeated in other countries in the sample, collinearity will result. The coefficient of geographic concentration was indeed one of the variables each of which Massell found to be collinear with several of the remaining independent variables in his model [*Massell, 1970: 626*].

While it is recognised that the use of regression analysis may obscure the true position for a few individual countries in a sample, the results obtained can usually be regarded as representing the general state of affairs. Thus, in the various empirical studies, statistically insignificant results are under-standably interpreted by the authors as showing that most developing countries do not suffer from the effects of geographical and commodity con-centration. The foregoing discussion, however, outlines difficulties which may arise from the use of Gini–Hirschman coefficients and instability indices in regression analysis, and it follows that the insignificant results of the empirical studies may reflect these problems rather than, as the authors have suggested, the absence of causal relationships.

Consequently, one may wish to avoid using Gini–Hirschman coefficients and instability indices in empirical investigations. Moreover, one might wish to move away from the use of cross-country regression analysis, since, even if such analysis were to provide satisfactory evidence of a statistically signifi-cant relationship between concentration and instability over a sample of countries, policy-makers in individual countries need to know the extent to which fluctuations in their export earnings are the result of commodity and/or geographic concentration.

## II   CONCENTRATION AND INSTABILITY

The approach adopted here begins from a reconsideration of the nature of the basic problem. Underlying the issue of concentration and the *a priori* case for diversification, say, of the commodity composition of exports, are two main assumptions. First, there is assumed to be a major product which simply as a consequence of its weight in total earnings can largely determine the degree of instability of total earnings. Secondly, the minor export items are assumed to contribute little to the instability in total proceeds because, as individual products, although they may exhibit relatively high degrees of instability, their shares in total earnings are relatively small and because, to the extent that the minor products are affected by different market forces, fluctuations in earnings tend to be offsetting. This latter point, which is the key to the arguments about diversification, means that the major product may contribute disproportionately to the fluctuations in total earnings. The implication of this is that, even where the major source accounts for a re-latively low export share, there might still be a case for diversification. For example, the major product and the remaining products as a group may have export shares of 25 per cent and 75 per cent respectively, but may be responsible for 45 per cent and 55 per cent respectively of the instability experienced. Then it may be argued that diversification, in the form of increased exports of each of the minor products, will tend to produce greater stability in total earnings.

In order to investigate the extent to which instability in a particular country's total earnings is related to concentration, total earnings are divided here into earnings from the major source ($M$) and the sum of earnings from all other sources ($S$).[5] As mentioned earlier, export instability is concerned with fluctuations around the trend of export earnings. Instability is defined here as the variance. This measure was selected because it is easily understood and because it provides the basis for many of the more specific indices of instability.

The variance of total earnings ($V_t$) is not determined simply by the vari-ances of earnings from the major source and of the sum of earnings from all other sources ($V_m$ and $V_x$ respectively) and their respective shares in total earnings ($x_m$ and $x_s$ respectively). It depends also on the degree to which $M$ and $S$ vary together,[6] i.e. on the covariance of $M$ and $S$ ($\text{cov}(ms)$). $V_t$ is a weighted average of the variance and covariance of earnings from the two sources and can be expressed as:

$$(2) \qquad V_t = x_m^2 V_m + x_s^2 V_s + 2x_m x_s \text{cov}(ms)$$

The contribution of the major source to instability in total earnings ($C_m$) can be written as:

$$(3) \qquad C_m = x_m^2 V_m + x_m x_s \text{cov}(ms)$$

What may be termed the 'proportionate contribution statistic' for the major source ($P_m$) is given as:

$$(4) \qquad P_m = C_m / V_t$$

The possibility that the major source may contribute disproportionately to total instability may be examined by estimating the ratio of the 'proportionate contribution statistic' to the export share of the major source. This ratio, $R_m$, is expressed as:

$$(5) \qquad R_m = P_m / x_m$$

Crucial to the debate on instability is the question of appropriate trend correction and, although various authors have observed similarity in the results obtained from indices based on different forms of trend correction, both a linear and an exponential trend were empoyed here for purposes of cross-checking.

## III  DATA
The sample covers 52 developing countries. In order to obtain a sample of this size the period chosen here begins in 1961. Reliable data are not available for all these countries before that date. The terminal year 1974 was determined by the availability of the latest data. For each country in the sample the major product was identified at the 3-digit level of the SITC.

## IV  RESULTS
Percentage contribution statistics were calculated for the major sources using a linear trend ($P_1$) and using an exponential trend ($P_e$). The associated ratios of the percentage contributions to the shares in total earnings were also estimated and are denoted by $R_1$ and $R_e$.

Values of $P_1$, $P_e$, $R_1$ and $R_e$ obtained for the major markets are presented in Table 1. From inspection of these results one can see broad similarity in the values of $P_1$ and $P_e$ obtained for each country. Those countries with high values of $P_1$ tend also to be those with high values for $P_e$. Clearly, however, the values of $P_1$ and $P_e$ vary considerably among countries. At one extreme, both $P_1$ and $P_e$ indicate that the major product was responsible for almost all of the instability experienced by the Gambia. At the other extreme, the major product accounted for only 0.13 and 0.09, as given by $P_1$ and $P_e$ respectively, of Mali's instability. For 19 countries the major product

## TABLE 1
### PROPORTIONATE CONTRIBUTION STATISTICS AND RATIOS OF PERCENTAGE CONTRIBUTIONS TO EXPORT SHARES FOR MAJOR PRODUCTS

| Country | Market share | $P_1$ | $P_e$ | $R_1$ | $R_e$ |
|---|---|---|---|---|---|
| Argentina | 0.29 | 0.27 | 0.14 | 0.93 | 0.48 |
| Bolivia | 0.50 | 0.44 | 0.44 | 0.88 | 0.88 |
| Brazil | 0.30 | 0.32 | 0.34 | 1.07 | 1.13 |
| Chile | 0.75 | 0.60 | 0.67 | 0.80 | 0.89 |
| Colombia | 0.58 | 0.60 | 0.77 | 1.03 | 1.33 |
| Costa Rica | 0.34 | 0.46 | 0.78 | 1.35 | 2.29 |
| Dominican Republic | 0.50 | 0.51 | 0.55 | 1.02 | 1.10 |
| Ecuador | 0.37 | 0.42 | 0.39 | 1.14 | 1.05 |
| El Salvador | 0.46 | 0.43 | 0.25 | 0.94 | 0.54 |
| Guatemala | 0.37 | 0.42 | 0.40 | 1.14 | 1.08 |
| Haiti | 0.41 | 0.43 | 0.43 | 1.05 | 1.05 |
| Honduras | 0.42 | 0.73 | 0.78 | 1.74 | 1.86 |
| Mexico | 0.11 | 0.13 | 0.12 | 1.18 | 1.09 |
| Nicaragua | 0.32 | 0.48 | 0.85 | 1.50 | 2.66 |
| Panama | 0.48 | 0.33 | 0.30 | 0.69 | 0.63 |
| Paraguay | 0.15 | 0.34 | 0.27 | 2.27 | 1.80 |
| Peru | 0.23 | 0.65 | 0.71 | 2.83 | 3.09 |
| Uruguay | 0.38 | 0.44 | 0.52 | 1.16 | 1.37 |
| Venezuela | 0.91 | 0.90 | 0.76 | 0.99 | 0.84 |
| Jamaica | 0.33 | 0.56 | 0.52 | 1.70 | 1.58 |
| Trinidad–Tobago | 0.82 | 0.86 | 0.93 | 1.05 | 1.13 |
| Guyana | 0.30 | 0.39 | 0.36 | 1.30 | 1.20 |
| Burma | 0.54 | 0.60 | 0.72 | 1.11 | 1.33 |
| Sri Lanka | 0.57 | 0.46 | 0.25 | 0.81 | 0.44 |
| Indonesia | 0.53 | 0.56 | 0.66 | 1.06 | 1.25 |
| Pakistan | 0.25 | 0.31 | 0.30 | 1.24 | 1.20 |
| Philipinnes | 0.25 | 0.27 | 0.44 | 1.08 | 1.76 |
| Thailand | 0.23 | 0.31 | 0.30 | 1.35 | 1.30 |
| Cameroons | 0.24 | 0.36 | 0.31 | 1.50 | 1.29 |
| Central African Republic | 0.41 | 0.44 | 0.45 | 1.07 | 1.10 |
| Chad | 0.75 | 0.92 | 0.90 | 1.23 | 1.20 |
| Congo, Peoples' Republic | 0.48 | 0.50 | 0.61 | 1.04 | 1.27 |
| Dahomey | 0.40 | 0.41 | 0.53 | 1.03 | 1.33 |
| Ethiopia | 0.50 | 0.35 | 0.25 | 0.70 | 0.50 |
| Gabon | 0.49 | 0.61 | 0.70 | 1.25 | 1.43 |
| Gambia | 0.94 | 0.95 | 0.97 | 1.01 | 1.03 |
| Ghana | 0.60 | 0.11 | 0.15 | 0.18 | 0.25 |
| Ivory Coast | 0.30 | 0.32 | 0.38 | 1.07 | 1.27 |
| Kenya | 0.26 | 0.33 | 0.28 | 1.27 | 1.08 |
| Mali | 0.20 | 0.13 | 0.09 | 0.65 | 0.45 |
| Mauritius | 0.90 | 0.82 | 0.89 | 0.91 | 0.99 |
| Morocco | 0.30 | 0.08 | 0.18 | 0.27 | 0.60 |
| Niger | 0.43 | 0.39 | 0.36 | 0.91 | 0.84 |
| Nigeria | 0.59 | 0.61 | 0.75 | 1.03 | 1.27 |
| Senegal | 0.55 | 0.43 | 0.51 | 0.78 | 0.93 |
| Sierra Leone | 0.58 | 0.56 | 0.52 | 0.97 | 0.90 |
| Somalia | 0.48 | 0.49 | 0.53 | 1.02 | 1.10 |
| Sudan | 0.17 | 0.13 | 0.10 | 0.77 | 0.59 |
| Tanzania | 0.16 | 0.48 | 0.50 | 3.00 | 3.13 |
| Togo | 0.44 | 0.58 | 0.66 | 1.32 | 1.50 |
| Tunisia | 0.20 | 0.49 | 0.52 | 2.45 | 2.60 |
| Uganda | 0.56 | 0.66 | 0.61 | 1.18 | 1.09 |

## TABLE 2
PROPORTIONATE CONTRIBUTION STATISTICS AND RATIOS OF PERCENTAGE
CONTRIBUTIONS TO EXPORT SHARES FOR MAJOR MARKETS

| Country | Market share | $P_1$ | $P_e$ | $R_1$ | $R_e$ |
|---|---|---|---|---|---|
| Argentina | 0.09 | 0.27 | 0.26 | 3.00 | 2.89 |
| Bolivia | 0.26 | 0.49 | 0.45 | 1.89 | 1.73 |
| Brazil | 0.26 | 0.40 | 0.50 | 1.54 | 1.92 |
| Chile | 0.19 | 0.35 | 0.51 | 1.84 | 2.68 |
| Colombia | 0.42 | 0.48 | 0.61 | 1.14 | 1.45 |
| Costa Rica | 0.42 | 0.43 | 0.44 | 1.02 | 1.05 |
| Dominican Republic | 0.76 | 0.66 | 0.58 | 0.87 | 0.76 |
| Ecuador | 0.43 | 0.53 | 0.52 | 1.23 | 1.21 |
| El Salvador | 0.10 | 0.50 | 0.47 | 5.00 | 4.70 |
| Guatemala | 0.33 | 0.35 | 0.42 | 1.06 | 1.27 |
| Haiti | 0.63 | 0.40 | 0.46 | 0.64 | 0.73 |
| Honduras | 0.56 | 0.51 | 0.50 | 0.91 | 0.89 |
| Mexico | 0.69 | 0.22 | 0.47 | 0.32 | 0.68 |
| Nicaragua | 0.30 | 0.26 | 0.27 | 0.87 | 0.90 |
| Panama | 0.59 | 0.57 | 0.41 | 0.97 | 0.70 |
| Paraguay | 0.24 | 0.18 | 0.08 | 0.75 | 0.33 |
| Peru | 0.20 | 0.50 | 0.49 | 2.50 | 2.45 |
| Uruguay | 0.13 | 0.43 | 0.28 | 3.31 | 2.15 |
| Venezuela | 0.39 | 0.50 | 0.48 | 1.28 | 1.23 |
| Jamaica | 0.39 | 0.62 | 0.52 | 1.59 | 1.33 |
| Trinidad–Tobago | 0.47 | 0.55 | 0.53 | 1.17 | 1.13 |
| Guyana | 0.24 | 0.31 | 0.27 | 1.29 | 1.13 |
| Burma | 0.19 | 0.26 | 0.20 | 1.37 | 1.05 |
| Sri Lanka | 0.17 | 0.15 | 0.10 | 1.13 | 0.59 |
| Indonesia | 0.19 | 0.30 | 0.21 | 1.58 | 1.11 |
| Pakistan | 0.10 | 0.11 | 0.11 | 1.10 | 1.10 |
| Philipinnes | 0.43 | 0.46 | 0.44 | 1.07 | 1.02 |
| Thailand | 0.23 | 0.41 | 0.37 | 1.78 | 1.61 |
| Cameroons | 0.37 | 0.44 | 0.54 | 1.19 | 1.46 |
| Central African Republic | 0.43 | 0.44 | 0.51 | 1.02 | 1.19 |
| Chad | 0.41 | 0.35 | 0.33 | 0.85 | 0.81 |
| Congo, Peoples' Republic | 0.21 | 0.31 | 0.23 | 1.48 | 1.10 |
| Dahomey | 0.48 | 0.56 | 0.50 | 1.17 | 1.04 |
| Ethiopia | 0.38 | 0.31 | 0.08 | 0.82 | 0.21 |
| Gabon | 0.37 | 0.33 | 0.24 | 0.89 | 0.65 |
| Gambia | 0.38 | 0.28 | 0.28 | 0.74 | 0.74 |
| Ghana | 0.22 | 0.25 | 0.30 | 1.14 | 1.36 |
| Ivory Coast | 0.33 | 0.34 | 0.41 | 1.03 | 1.24 |
| Kenya | 0.17 | 0.15 | 0.14 | 0.88 | 0.82 |
| Mali | 0.17 | 0.30 | 0.19 | 1.78 | 1.12 |
| Mauritius | 0.60 | 0.47 | 0.37 | 0.78 | 0.62 |
| Morocco | 0.35 | 0.33 | 0.25 | 0.94 | 0.71 |
| Niger | 0.55 | 0.59 | 0.63 | 1.07 | 1.15 |
| Nigeria | 0.19 | 0.20 | 0.25 | 1.05 | 1.32 |
| Senegal | 0.62 | 0.50 | 0.57 | 0.81 | 0.92 |
| Sierra Leone | 0.68 | 0.71 | 0.79 | 1.04 | 1.16 |
| Somalia | 0.36 | 0.32 | 0.29 | 0.89 | 0.81 |
| Sudan | 0.07 | 0.11 | 0.13 | 1.57 | 1.86 |
| Tanzania | 0.23 | 0.27 | 0.29 | 1.17 | 1.26 |
| Togo | 0.39 | 0.48 | 0.56 | 1.23 | 1.44 |
| Tunisia | 0.28 | 0.35 | 0.42 | 1.25 | 1.50 |
| Uganda | 0.22 | 0.26 | 0.23 | 1.18 | 1.05 |

contributed more than 0.5 of the fluctuations in total earnings as measured by both indices. The mean values of $P_1$ and $P_e$ calculated from the results in Table 1 are 0.47 and 0.49 respectively.

In 36 countries the major product contributed more than proportionately to fluctuations in total earnings. Within this group the lowest values of $R_1$ and $R_e$ were obtained for the Gambia. Thus, the high values of $P_1$ and $P_e$ reflect simply the high share of the major product in the Gambia's exports. The values of $R_1$ and $R_e$ were greatest for Tanzania and indicate that the contribution of the major commodity was in the region of three times greater than its export share. Unlike the Gambian case, therefore, the values of $P_1$ and $P_e$ for Tanzania result principally from the high degree of instability in proceeds from the major product relative to that of the sum of earnings from the other export items.

Values of $P_1$ and $P_e$ for the major markets are given in Table 2. The highest values of $P_1$ and $P_e$, 0.71 and 0.79 respectively, were recorded for Sierra Leone, while the major market contributed least, 0.11 as measured by both indices, in Pakistan. Only for 12 countries were both $P_1$ and $P_e$ greater than 0.5 and mean values of 0.38 for $P_1$ and $P_e$ respectively were estimated from the data in Table 2. Comparison of these results with those for the major products suggests that over the sample of countries geographical concentration is a less significant problem than commodity concentration.

For 35 countries the major market contributed disproportionately to fluctuations in earnings. Within this group $R_1$ and $R_e$ were just greater than unity for Costa Rica, while at the other extreme the contribution of El Salvador's major market was approximately five times as great as its market share.

Inspection of the results in Tables 1 and 2 shows that in 46 of the 52 countries in the sample the major product and/or the major market contributed disproportionately to instability in total earnings. Twenty-five countries experienced disproportionate contributions for both the major product and the major market.

CONCLUSION

The approach employed here differs from the use of Gini–Hirschman co-efficients in cross-country regression analysis in two important respects. First, it tackles the problem of the relationship between concentration and instability at the level of individual countries. Secondly, it allows one to focus directly on the degree to which one product or market is responsible for fluctuations in total earnings. The results indicate that the contributions of the major products and markets differ considerably among the 52 countries in the sample, but that for almost all of these countries the major product and/or the major market contributed disproportionately to earnings instability.

NOTES

1. It should be noted that Michaely's principal concern was not with the relationship between commodity concentration and fluctuations in export earnings, but with the relationship between commodity concentration and fluctuations in export prices [*Michaely, 1962*].

2. It has long been recognised that this is an arbitrary but convenient approach [*Massell, 1964*].

3. Coppock was concerned with the question of instability during the years 1946–58 and he calculated Gini–Hirschman coefficients for the year 1957 [*Coppock, 1962: 98 and Appendix Table A-2*]. In his study covering the period 1948–59 Massell estimated coefficients for the year 1959 [*Massell, 1964: 52*]. For his later study for the years 1950–66 Massell estimated coefficients for the year 1960 [*Massell, 1970: 624*]. MacBean took coefficients for the year 1954 from Michaely's study [*MacBean, 1966: 40*].

4. In a study covering the 1960s Naya attempted to overcome, at least partially, possible biases by averaging the ceofficients for two years, 1962 and 1967 [*Naya, 1973: 636*].

5. The major source is defined here as that product or market with the highest individual share in total earnings. While this paper deals only with the single most important product or market, it is recognised that concentration might be interpreted as dependence on a few products or markets.

6. Kingston attempted to examine the relationships between concentration and instability at the level of individual developing countries. He estimated a 'percentage contribution statistic' for the major source by:

      (*i*) weighting the average values of earnings from each source (*M* and *S*) by their respective instability indices, and

      (*ii*) calculating the result obtained in (*i*) for the major source as a percentage of the sum of the two results obtained in (*i*)

[*Kingston, 1973: 281–296*]. This approach ignores, however, the extent to which earnings from different products or markets vary together.

REFERENCES

Coppock, J. D., 1962, *International Economic Instability*, New York: McGraw-Hill.

Erb, G. F., and Schiavo-Campo, S., 1969, 'Export Instability, Level of Development and Economic Size of Less Developed Countries', *Bulletin of the Oxford Institute of Economics and Statistics*, Vol. 31.

Khalaf, N. G., 1974, 'Country Size and Trade Concentration', *Journal of Development Studies*, Vol. 11.

Kingston, J. L., 1973, 'Export Instability in Latin America: The Postwar Statistical Record', *Journal of Developing Areas*, Vol. 7.

Kingston, J. L., 1976, 'Export Concentration and Export Performance in Developing Countries, 1954–67', *Journal of Development Studies*, Vol. 12.

Leith, J. C., 1970, 'The Decline in World Export Instability: A Comment', *Bulletin of the Oxford University Institute of Economics and Statistics*, Vol. 32.

MacBean, A. I., 1966, *Export Instability and Economic Development*, Cambridge, Mass.: Harvard University Press.

Massell, B. F., 1964, 'Export Concentration and Fluctuations in Export Earnings: A Cross-Section Analysis', *American Economic Review*, Vol. 54.

Massell, B. F., 1970, 'Export Instability and Economic Structure', *American Economic Review*, Vol. 60.

Michaely, M., 1962, *Concentration in International Trade*, Amsterdam: North-Holland.

Naya, S., 1973, 'Fluctuations in Export Earnings and the Economic Patterns of Asian Countries', *Economic Development and Cultural Change*, Vol. 21.

# Structural Aspects of Third World Trade:
# Some Trends and Some Prospects

## by G. K. Helleiner*

*The changing role of the intrafirm trade carried out by transnational corporations deserves more attention. In Third World primary product exports the 'old order' of intrafirm trade is changing to one of more arms'-length relationships; and this is generating new problems in marketing. Transnationals are becoming more important than before in Third World exporting of manufactures, and the new protectionism of the OECD countries is encouraging this trend. Transnationals have easily adapted to changing economic and political circumstances; labour has had more difficulty.*

The New International Economic Order which has been so vigorously supported by Third World spokesmen in international conferences in recent years is not a target which, like landing a man on the moon, will be attained through a concentrated unidirectional push on the part of all those concerned with it. In the rough and tumble of international diplomacy it will only be achieved — if indeed it ever moves beyond rhetoric — by a series of reforms, most, of themselves fairly small in impact; progress is bound to be punctuated by many backward steps. While all the pulling and tugging goes on over a common fund, a code of conduct for technology transfer, the rewriting of article XIX of the GATT, the introduction of an aid-sdr link, etc., not to speak of the detailed deals on sugar price stabilisation, market access for footwear, revised Lomé Conventions and so forth, the world of international commerce and finance does not stand still. Changes in the international order may take place, without any particular reference to the agenda of the New International Order, which are important enough to dwarf in significance the negotiated agreements over which the diplomats strain. One must beware of devoting so much attention to the daily struggle to achieve slow and probably marginal improvements through North—South intergovernmental negotiation that one misses the significant changes which are occuring with a momentum of their own.

There have indeed been many major changes in the Third World's place in the international economy in recent years, some of which raise new policy

*Professor of Economics, Department of Political Economy, University of Toronto.
An earlier version of this paper was presented to the Twentyfifth Anniversary Conference of the Institute of Social Studies, The Hague, December, 1977; it will appear in *Development: the Next Twentyfive Years,* edited by Ken Post and published by the ISS in conjunction with Martinus Nijhoff, The Hague. I am grateful to participants in that conference and to Dudley Seers and John Toye for their helpful comments.

issues and concerns for those contemplating its future. This paper calls attention to some of those which seem particularly deserving of notice. My intention is not to denigrate in the slightest the effort to negotiate a series of international and multilateral agreements leading toward a New International Order. These efforts must continue. Rather, it is to sketch in part of the sometimes neglected backdrop to these negotiations, by standing back from 'the action' and looking for longer run structural trends. For those who are sceptical about the likely outcome of all these international conferences, these trends may be considered the most important to understand.

There have been significant changes in the composition of Third World trade over the past twenty-five years, which should be understood as a backdrop for any discussion of international structural change. On the *export* side, there have been two major developments: (1) the substantial and continuing increase in the share which manufactured products make up in the total Third World non-fuel export bill (43 per cent in 1975) [*World Bank, 1978: 50*], largely as a result of extremely high rates of export growth in fewer than a dozen of the more advanced developing countries (this includes a little noticed increase in the degree to which primary commodities are processed before export, about which more below); (2) the astonishing increase in the price of petroleum in 1973–74, which followed a period of steady decline in its real price (and has been followed by further erosion in the real price). Neither of these developments were foreseen by most development economists. Both raise broader issues for international economic policy, some of which will be discussed below. The structure of Third World *imports* has also changed substantially during the postwar period, in consequence of vigorous import substitution programmes in many countries; typically, the share of imports which is accounted for by manufactured consumer goods has fallen and those made up by intermediate inputs (including energy) and capital goods have increased. (In some cases, food imports have also increased in importance, and some analysts forecast continuing increases in the importance of food in particular developing countries' import bills.)

Commodity compositon of trade is only one dimension of the structural change which has taken place in the world markets which are of greatest concern to developing countries. No less interesting and important, although the data are frequently not as accessible, are the questions of 'market structure' — the degree of competition, the openness of markets, the unpackaging of what is being traded, etc. In the sphere of primary commodity markets, particularly those for minerals, there have been significant changes which can already be characterised as a 'breakup of the old order'. These changes have to do with the still imperfectly understood role of transnational corporations in world trade, of both primary and manufactured products. Some of the resulting policy issues will be addressed below.

There have also been important changes in the international policies of industrialised countries' governments, some of which have had and will continue to have profound implications for the structure of Third World trade and the international distribution of the gains therefrom. These are, in part, related to the changes in commodity composition and market structure to which reference has already been made, and will be considered in that context.

At least as important as these structural influences on Third World trade is the prospect of slower growth in conventionally defined income in the OECD countries over the next several decades. This prospect raises extreme dangers for the *entire* world economic system in the short run, because of the present fragility of the world financial system, and poses major political and economic problems for the Third World in the longer run. It would seem that there are now new grounds – based on hard projections of demand prospects, rather than romantic aspirations for 'solidarity' – for the stimulation and encouragement of South–South trade, and for various other forms of 'collective self-reliance'. But to consider these prospects would require a separate paper.

This article will focus primarily on those structural aspects of Third World trade which are related to the policies of the industrialised countries' governments, and to the activities of transnational corporations based in these countries. Section I outlines the changing (and still understudied) role of international intra-firm trade in the Third World. Section II considers other elements of transnational corporate practices and their relations with the governments of the industrialised countries. The arguments are sufficiently self-contained to require only a very brief conclusion.

## I INTRAFIRM TRADE AND THE THIRD WORLD

The most striking fact about the evolution of post-Second-World-War international trade is its phenomenal real rate of growth (in developing as well as industrialised economies). Much of this has been accomplished under the auspices of transnational corporations, often very large ones, active in many countries and many branches of trade. Moving their capital, technology and skill efficiently and flexibly about the globe, these large enterprises have effectively demolished the basis for one of the prime assumptions of traditional trade theory: that of factor immobility between nations. Perhaps even more important, they have also undermined the basis for the major underlying assumption of orthodox market theory: that transactions take place at arms'-length between independent actors. Increasing proportions of total world trade are being conducte' on an intrafirm basis; i.e. the transactors are related by ownership and/or other ties. Where there is intrafirm trade, both the volumes and prices of the transactions are likely effectively to be 'centrally planned' in the interest of the firm which is both buyer and seller.[1]

In 1975 nearly one-third of all US imports originated with majority-owned foreign affiliates (MOFAs) of US -based firms (compared with a quarter ten years previously). Those from developing countries were even more likely to originate in these affiliates (Table 1) and between 1971 and 1975 the proportion of this developing country MOFA trade which moved directly to US parents rose from 69 per cent to 82 per cent [*UN, ECOSOC, 1978: 221*]. Fully 45 per cent of total US imports in 1975 came from firms which are related by ownership (to the extent of 5 per cent of equity or more) to the importer. Such evidence as there is suggests that the proportions of US exports which take place on an intrafirm basis have been even higher. These are matters which are of potentially very great significance in the assessment of the distribution of the gains from trade, the interpretation of recorded trade statistics and the analysis of markets. The role of intrafirm

TABLE 1

AFFILIATE SALES TO THE UNITED STATES AS PERCENTAGE OF TOTAL U.S. MERCHANDISE IMPORTS BY AREA OF ORIGIN, 1966–75

| | 1966 | 1967 | 1968 | 1969 | 1970 | 1971 | 1972 | 1973 | 1974 | 1975 | 1966–75 Average |
|---|---|---|---|---|---|---|---|---|---|---|---|
| All areas | 25 | 27 | 26 | 27 | 25 | 28 | 25 | 28 | 31 | 32 | 28 |
| Developed countries | 22 | 25 | 24 | 25 | 25 | 27 | 24 | 25 | 24 | 28 | 25 |
| Canada | 49 | 54 | 53 | 54 | 55 | 59 | 55 | 55 | 51 | 58 | 55 |
| Europe | 10 | 11 | 11 | 11 | 11 | 12 | 11 | 12 | 12 | 14 | 12 |
| United Kingdom | 13 | 17 | 14 | 15 | 15 | 16 | 15 | 13 | 14 | 17 | 15 |
| European Communities (6)[a] | 7 | 9 | 9 | 9 | 10 | 11 | 11 | 13 | 13 | 15 | 11 |
| Other Europe | 11 | 12 | 13 | 10 | 10 | 11 | 9 | 9 | 10 | 12 | 10 |
| Japan | 1 | 1 | 1 | 1 | 1 | – | – | 1 | 1 | 1 | 1 |
| Australia, New Zealand, and South Africa | 10 | 12 | 13 | 14 | 13 | 12 | 9 | 9 | 11 | 8 | 11 |
| Developing countries | 30 | 29 | 28 | 28 | 23 | 30 | 27 | 32 | 36 | 35 | 32 |
| Latin America | 38 | 38 | 37 | 37 | 30 | 39 | 36 | 39 | 34 | 41 | 37 |
| Other Asia and Africa | 18 | 17 | 16 | 17 | 13 | 21 | 18 | 25 | 36 | 32 | 27 |

[a]Consists of Belgium, Luxembourg, France, Germany, Italy, and the Netherlands.
Source: Chung [1977: 35].

TABLE 2
AFFILIATE SALES TO THE UNITED STATES AS PERCENTAGE OF TOTAL AND
NON-PETROLEUM U.S. MERCHANDISE IMPORTS FROM DEVELOPING
COUNTRIES 1966–75

| | Total % | Total excluding petroleum % |
|---|---|---|
| 1966 | 30 | n.a. |
| 1967 | 29 | 20 |
| 1968 | 28 | n.a. |
| 1969 | 28 | 18 |
| 1970 | 23 | 14 |
| 1971 | 30 | 14 |
| 1972 | 27 | 11 |
| 1973 | 32 | 13 |
| 1974 | 36 | 12 |
| 1975 | 35 | 11 |

*Source:* Calculated from data in Chung [*1975: 35*], and OECD, *Foreign Trade. Commodity Trade: Imports,* various years.

international trade is likely to be great in developing countries where foreign firms have established a strong presence.

Yet a closer inspection of the data for Third World trade reveals that, as is so often the case, one cannot simply 'project' the recent global experience and draw conclusions for the developing countries. During the past decade, while the share of total US imports which originated with US majority-owned affiliates has risen markedly in Europe and Canada, this was not universally the case; when petroleum is excluded from the total, it has actually *fallen* in the developing countries. Whereas in 1967 20 per cent of US non-petroleum imports from developing countries originated in US affiliates there, by 1975 this had fallen to only 11 per cent (see Table 2).

What accounts for these perhaps unexpected structural trends in Third World trade, and what are their implications? In large part, they are un-doubtedly the consequence of the conscious 'delinking' policies of many developing countries. These policies have both sought to diversify their sources of capital, their trade links, etc., and introduced new institutional arrangements to replace primary resort to wholly-owned direct foreign in-vestments, particularly in the resource sector. The former (diversification) has led to the phenomenon of non-US-owned firms exporting from develop-ing countries to the US, thus lowering the measured proportion of US im-ports originating with US majority-owned affiliates, without necessarily reducing the proportions of imports taking place within firms. The latter has reduced the degree to which resource exports flow between majority-owned affiliates, without necessarily affecting the degree to which this trade con-tinues to take place between parties which are related in less obvious ways. Let us consider the emerging trends in intrafirm exports from developing countries on a more disaggregated basis.

*Primary Products Trade*
Two – somewhat contradictory – points may be made about the above-mentioned trend in US MOFA trade (which is primarily attributable to

events in the primary product sector). First, the data undoubtedly present a quite misleading picture of the trend in the role of transnational corporations in Thrid World trade. Minority ownership, technology contracts, management contracts, marketing contracts, etc., may be just as effective as indicators of close relationships (or 'nonarmslengthness') between buying and selling firms and of the potentiality for foreign control, as majority ownership.

Certainly the newly available data showing the extent to which US imports originate with firms which are related by ownership (5 per cent equity or more) to the buying firms suggest that intrafirm trade still dominates many primary product markets. While on average US importers acquired 45 per cent of their total imports from related parties in 1975, the equivalent shares of related-party imports in US purchases of some primary products from developing countries was much higher – 88 per cent in the case of bauxite, 80 per cent in rubber, 68 per cent in bananas and cotton [*Helleiner, 1977: 26*]. One must not be seduced by the more readily available direct investment data into believing that they tell one about the *total* role of transnational corporations. Many developing countries have learned by painful experience that nationalisation does not put an end to foreign control. What becomes necessary is a more sophisticated understanding of the detailed functioning of transnational corporations in circumstances where their 'control' is less total than it has traditionally been and is exerted through new institutional mechanisms.

The second point to be made about the downward trend in US MOFA trade with developing countries is that the breakup of the old order in world minerals 'markets' *is* now well under way.[2] The system in which vertically integrated transnational corporations controlled volumes and terms of flows within their own 'closed' systems provided a degree of security to the importing countries and their firms which is no longer there. Kissinger's proposal for an International Resources Bank to facilitate the continued flow of technology and capital for resource development in the Third World constituted implicit recognition that some type of 'new order' for these commodity markets was required. From the industrialised countries' standpoint what is most essential is that the old security of supply at reasonable prices be restored, or at least that the present uncertainty be reduced. The producing countries are clearly more concerned that they themselves acquire greater shares of resource rents, quasi-rents on capital and technology, and oligopoly rents, together with generally increased control and the prospect of developing forward-linked industries. New arrangements, in which commodity trade takes place at greater arms'-length but is nevertheless constrained as to fluctuations in its terms, must be developed – longer-term contracts, new 'rules for the game' combining price and supply guarantees, etc. If mutually satisfactory new rules are not developed there are predictable difficulties to be faced by Third World exporters of mineral and other primary products.

There are already some important 'unfriendly' reactions emanating from the developed countries in consequence of more effective Third World policies in this sphere. They aim, in effect, to 'residualise' those markets over which transnational corporations based in the developed countries do not have firm control. Moran has warned of this danger in world copper markets.

If Third World copper producers do not 'cooperate' with traditional buyers, he argues, they may find themsleves with 'a dual market system in which the CIPEC countries gradually become suppliers of last resort, outside the main network of semi-integrated ties between corporate producers and consumers, onto whom will be shifted the major costs of uncertainty about supply and demand for the entire industry' [*Moran, 1974: 233*]. Traditional copper interests have already begun to reshape their plans in accordance with the new realities. While CIPEC made up 35–40 per cent of world copper production in the early 1970s, it is estimated that by the late 1970s their share will have fallen in consequence of differential rates of expansion, to the extent that 70% of world demand will be met from 'secure' sources through 'sales between regular buyers and sellers in the historical semi-integrated pattern' [*Moran, 1974: 239*]. (For the immediate future, the power of the CIPEC countries is of course further reduced by the enormous privately held stocks of copper which now overhang the market.) Moran generalises his point as follows:

> the large industrial countries need secure sources of raw materials so badly that they will be willing to pay the price of neutralizing economic nationalists who threaten to upset the old and dependable system. There is nothing in history or logic to suggest that corporate boards of directors (or the governments they and their customers influence) will simply sit and let the price and terms of supply be dictated to them by outsiders, if they have other options available to them [*238*].

These rather ominous possibilities increase the need for careful assessment of the means of achieving greater benefits for the developing countries from their primary exports, without thereby acquiring new and potentially unmanageable marketing problems. They imply that strenuous efforts will have to be made to develop unified host government positions *vis-à-vis* foreign firms in the resource sectors; in some instances, the governments of developed countries (Canada, Australia) will have to be induced to cooperate if total success is to be realised.[3]

It is therefore likely that large transnational corporations will not forever be almost exclusively based in the industrialised countries. The advantages of scale in marketing and information-gathering, even if not always evident in production, seem likely to lead to larger transnationally-oriented firms in developing countries as well. Sometimes state-owned, sometimes private but working in close collaboration with the state, transnational enterprises are already beginning to emerge within the more industrialised segments of the Third World. Some have even bought into the oligopolies of the developed countries themselves, e.g. a private Brazilian firm's purchase of an American coffee processing firm which accounted for 12 per cent of the US market and the takeover by a Malaysian government-owned holding company (PERNAS) of a major transnational tin producer with activities in Nigeria, Thailand and Australia, as well as Malaysia. (More likely, for the present, are expanded transnational enterprise activities *within* the Third World; in Latin America such 'joint enterprises' are already attracting considerable interest.) [*Diaz-Alejandro, 1977; INTAL, 1977.*]

It is important to recognise that even where maximum (social) efficiency requires the retention of small productive units, as in most types of agriculture and in many areas of manufacturing (where scale economies are offset by the fact that increased capital-intensity is inevitably associated with increased scale) [*Felix, 1977; Morley and Smith, 1977*], there are still likely to be advantages obtainable from the creation of large-scale marketing agencies or boards, or what the Japanese would call trading houses. Not only are such arrangements efficient, but there is also increased market power for the sellers. Marketing Boards for agricultural products have a long history in the Third World. But the argument for their creation carries equal force when it comes to the export of manufactured products. In a world of increasing resort to 'voluntary export restraints', such marketing arrangements (or else private cartels) are willy-nilly being encouraged by the industrialised countries, which are content to pay slightly higher import prices in return for an assurance of reduced import volume.

It may therefore be that Third World producers and producer associations will increasingly conduct their business affairs in a manner very similar to that of the earlier foreign-owned oligopolistic firms. Specifically, in the minerals sector, they may calculate that 'their oligopolist position would be best preserved by a willingness to absorb short-run demand shocks through inventory variation or excess capacity' [*Moran, 1974, 236*], thus continuing to insure consumers somewhat against the risk of sudden scarcity.

At all events, there is obviously a great need for research on the relative merits of different types of institutional arrangements for the conduct of international trade in primary products, the politics and economics of producer alliances, and the potential for Third-World-based processing and marketing activities – perhaps through vertically integrated and oligopolistic transnational corporations of their own.

## Manufactured Goods Trade

The growth in importance of manufactured exports from developing countries has probably also contributed to the decline in the apparent importance of intrafirm US imports, since majority ownership is less frequent in this type of trade than it has been in primary products trade. (This is because it does not generate resource rents, its most crucial barriers to entry are at the marketing rather than the production end, it frequently involves little capital investment in production, and it has developed during the postcolonial period, when independent governments had become more sensitive to the issue of foreign control.) On the other hand, it seems that intrafirm trade in manufactures is growing exceptionally rapidly.

At the very time that primary commodity exports from the Third World are being sold increasingly outside the closed channels of the transnational corporations, manufactured exports from developing countries seem to be growing disproportionately quickly inside them. The latter phenomenon is illustrated by the extraordinary rate of growth (32 per cent per year in the 1970s) in US imports from developing countries under the encouragement of that country's value added tariff provisions (items 806.30 and 807.00 of the tariff, which require that duties only be paid on foreign value-added when inputs orginate in the US itself) (Table 3). Similar international subcontracting of component manufacture and assembly activities is increasingly being

TABLE 3
U.S. IMPORTS UNDER TARIFF ITEMS 807.00 AND 806.30, 1966–76
($ MILLIONS)

|  | Total value | | Dutiable value | | Value of US products | |
|---|---|---|---|---|---|---|
|  | Total | Developing countries | Total | Developing countries | Total | Developing countries |
| 1966 | 953.0 | 60.7 | 805.5 | 31.4 | 147.5 | 29.0 |
| 1967 | 1,035.1 | 99.0 | 837.2 | 42.6 | 197.9 | 55.8 |
| 1968 | 1,554.4 | 221.7 | 1,263.7 | 97.7 | 290.6 | 124.0 |
| 1969 | 1,838.8 | 394.8 | 1,396.7 | 177.3 | 442.1 | 217.6 |
| 1970 | 2,208.2 | 541.5 | 1,671.8 | 245.9 | 536.3 | 295.5 |
| 1971 | 2,765.8 | 652.5 | 2,105.9 | 314.1 | 659.9 | 338.4 |
| 1972 | 3,408.8 | 1.066.5 | 2,540.4 | 547.3 | 868.3 | 519.2 |
| 1973 | 4,247.1 | 1,557.3 | 3,238.3 | 845.4 | 1,008.8 | 711.8 |
| 1974 | 5,371.8 | 2,350.1 | 4,059.0 | 1,303.0 | 1,312.8 | 1,047.1 |
| 1975 | 5,161.2 | 2,261.7 | 3,895.5 | 1,238.7 | 1,265.7 | 1,023.1 |
| 1976 | 5,719.0 | 2,807.0 | 4,173.2 | 1,548.6 | 1,545.7 | 1,258.4 |
| 1977 | 7,188.1 | 3,306.8 | 5,212.0 | 1,721.4 | 1,976.1 | 1,585.3 |

*Source:* United States International Trade Commission.

undertaken with tariff encouragement from European bases as well; and these data do not tell the entire story, since some such activities do not qualify for these tariff provisions.[4] (On average, primary goods trade is nevertheless still probably more firmly under transnationals' ownership and control than is manufactured goods trade.)

Other things being equal, it will be easier for developing countries to penetrate the markets of the industrialised countries when they have powerful allies 'in court' than where they do not.[5] Even with final products, the established firms in the importing countries have information and marketing networks, all profiting from substantial scale economies and experience as well as the benefits of well known brand names, which render market penetration easier. There is thus some tendency for Third World trade — notably the rapidly expanding exports of manufactured products — to be driven into the marketing channels which are controlled by the established transnationals of North America, Europe and Japan. This channeling of the most dynamic aspect of developing countries' exports has two likely consequences: (1) the bargaining power of the transnational enterprises *vis-à-vis* the exporting firms or countries is rendered very great, and hence the terms of contracts — whether product prices or marketing, management or technology provisions — are likely disproportionately to favour the former; (2) that part of the trade which remains outside the established networks of the large transnational enterprises is rendered risker, because of the narrowing of the 'residual' market and the volatility and uncertainty which it implies. Third World exporters may therefore increasingly be confronted with a choice between low-risk/low-return trading arrangements negotiated with transnationals and high-risk/high-return ones which they develop for themselves. As Cohen has argued in the Far Eastern context, the choice made by particular countries may ultimately be determined by political calculations rather than economic ones [*Cohen, 1975: 135*].

As has been seen, the role of transnational corporations in Third World trade is not adequately represented by the data on trade between majority-owned foreign affiliates and their US parents. Their activities include the provision of management and marketing services, the sale of technology, and the supply of arms'-length or minority capital, as well as the continued participation in direct investment. Relationships between firms which are connected in any of these ways are likely to be different from those between transactors who deal with one another fully at arms'-length, in that there can be greater joint planning, cooperation (not to say collusion) with respect to prices, volume or directions of trade, etc.

## II TRANSNATIONAL CORPORATIONS, OECD GOVERNMENTS AND CHANGES IN TRADE STRUCTURE

The role of transnational corporations in the formation of trade policies, in the determination of actual trading practices, and in adapting to governmental policies, needs greater research attention. As a stimulus to further thought on these issues let me offer some brief reflections on: (1) the changed nature of protectionism in industrialised economies; (2) the phenomenon of private nontariff trade barriers, or what are more commonly known as restrictive business practices in international trade; and (3) the different capacities of actors in the industrialised economies to adjust to changing economic circumstances.

### (i) The 'New Protectionism' and the Third World

Changes in productivity generated by technological progress, changes in money wage rates and other costs, and changes in exchange rates, all operate to alter the competitiveness of the industries of the rich countries *vis-à-vis* those of the poor countries. The further effect of trade barriers on this competitiveness may therefore, by itself, be relatively small. Technological change and wage rate increases can probably be assumed to possess a momentum of their own. While it therefore does make some sense to focus on the level of trade barriers and changes therein, exchange rate changes have in recent years usually dwarfed those of tariff levels in importance. The most important policy-induced *changes* which have occurred lie in the realm of nontariff barriers and exchange rates. The former have been important for specific industries of interest to developing countries and thus to the overall structure of protection. The latter have been of greatest importance to the overall average level of 'protection' to tradeable goods sectors.

'Protectionism' has thus acquired a new face in the course of the last five years; or, more accurately, a formerly slightly blurred vision has now come into sharp focus. This change has been brought about by the appearance of flexible exchange rates in all the major industrialised countries. When one of these countries runs into balance-of-payments difficulties they are quickly reflected in its exchange rate; similarly, if short-term macro-economic (usually monetary) policy is brought to bear upon an unemployment problem it is likely to generate immediate effects on the exchange rate. Protective trade barriers have therefore been displaced as *generalised* policy approaches to short-run balance-of-payments and unemployment problems. (They were, in any case, never recommended for this purpose by most economists.) The generalised instrument for reallocating both consumption and production is the exchange rate, which has the further attribute, beyond the use of tariffs and nontariff barriers, of relating to *all* tradeables rather than simply to importables. As far as the major industrialised countries are concerned, the problem of uncoordinated adjustments is today more likely to be reflected in competitive exchange rate changes than in tariff wars.

Yet, that protectionism *is* on the rise seems to be a matter of general agreement and concern. It is important to recognise that the 'new protectionism' is *not* a matter of macro-economic policy response to employment or balance-of-payments problems. It has instead become, overwhelmingly, a matter of *structural* policy – indeed, perhaps even an imperfect form of 'adjustment assistance'. It is not the *overall* level of trade barriers which is rising (although this is difficult precisely to tell, in view of the well known problems of calculating tariff averages). Rather, trade barriers in *particular* industries are rising; while those in others continue, as proposed in the Tokyo Round of the GATT, to fall. The purpose of these industry-specific trade barriers is clearly to slow down the speed with which (inevitable) adjustment to new low cost imports takes place.

Those industries which are receiving increasing (or at least unchanged) protection, despite the increased potential role in readjustment which exchange rates now play, are those which were already benefitting disproportionately from trade barriers before the advent of flexible rates. In the last (Kennedy) round of tariff cuts, those which retained the highest levels of protection were unskilled-labour-intensive, stagnant and large in the US; unskilled-labour-intensive, relatively unconcentrated, and low in resource content in Canada; and unskilled-labour-intensive in West Germany,[6] [*Cheh, 1974; Helleiner, 1977; Riedel, 1977*]. Unskilled-labour-intensity is everywhere the dominant characteristic of the protected sectors.

Fluctuating exchange rates have introduced a new element to the structure of Third World international economic relationships. At present, of the more than 100 less developed member countries in the International Monetary Fund, fully 36 do not have their currencies pegged to major national currencies and several more maintain a peg, but change it very frequently. These countries either let their currencies float freely or peg them to the SDR (a particular basket of currencies with its own weighting system) or some other basket of currencies of their own choosing; in the latter cases, flexibility with respect to the currencies of individual industrialised countries is implied. Thus the 'competitiveness' of these countries' exports in their major markets can fluctuate within fairly wide ranges over fairly short periods. For those which maintain a peg to a major currency, which is likely to be that of their major trading partner, there will be short-term fluctuation with respect to all the other countries with which they trade. These continual alterations in the relative values of currencies dwarf the changes or, for that matter, the overall levels of overall import protection in individual countries. The recent rapid decline in the value of the US dollar *vis-à-vis* the mark and yen – in seven months of 1977, by 6 per cent and 11 per cent respectively – shows the extent of the possible change; the overall average tariff imposed on industrial products in 1973 was about 7 per cent in the US and the EEC, and a little higher in Japan [*GATT, 1974*]. (The precise figures depend on the weighting system chosen.) Again, to a degree never before seen, the 'protection problem' has become a matter of the *structure* of trade barriers rather than their overall level.

The 1977 annual report of the GATT states that:

> The spread of protectionist pressures may well prove to be the most important current development in international economic policies, for it has reached a point at which the continued existence of an international order based on agreed and observed rules may be said to be open to question [*GATT, 1977*].

In the words of the British Foreign Minister, 'The advanced industrialised countries should be starting to consider whether the basically free-market (i.e. free-trade) system can cope' [*Economist, 22 October 1977: 119*].

This burst of protectionism is *not* (at least not yet) reflective of a general inward-turning of the world's industrialised economies, such as typified the 1930s, but is very industry- and product-specific. At the highest level of generalisation, this protectionism is found disproportionately in (1) manufactured products exported by low-income countries, (2) products which flow at arms'-length across international boundaries rather than 'within' transnational corporations. (As has been seen, it is increasingly taking the form of administrative controls – 'the organisation of trade' – rather than tariffs.) These structural characteristics of emerging trade barriers impart a particular bias to the constellation of forces which shape the evolution of Third World trade. This is not to suggest that there is an inevitable path onto which the developing countries are being driven, but only to call attention to the influences against which they must struggle if they are to expand manufactured exports by autonomous Third World enterprises.

New trade barriers in the industrialised countries *can* effectively slow the rate at which particular types of export-oriented industrialisation proceed in the Third World. Their structure also influences the types of manufacturing for export which emerge. Physical controls on textiles and clothing, increasingly on footwear, and possibly soon on steel and other products, seem likely to limit opportunities for expansion to modest rates of annual growth which are considered low enough to prevent 'market disruptions' in the importing countries. The so-called semi-industrialised countries, rather than the poorest countries, are most severely constrained by these limitations in the short run.

Of greater immediate concern to the latter is the fact that tariff systems discourage the location in developing countries of raw material processing establishments, in which transnationals' capital and technology may often be involved. The escalation of tariffs with further levels of fabrication still generates high levels of effective protection for processing in industrialised countries. Of at least equal importance is the frequent similar escalation in transport rates with increased levels of processing of the products to be transported [*Finger and Yeats, 1976*]. (Thus, reductions in tariffs imposed on the products of less developed countries as they enter the industrialised countries are not necessarily beneficial to the former countries. When tariffs on raw materials are reduced proportionately more than those on processed products – as is indeed not so unusual a circumstance – the effective protection for processors in the importing countries is thereby *increased*. The

## TABLE 4
### TOTAL OECD IMPORTS OF RAW, SEMI-PROCESSED AND MANUFACTURED
### MATERIALS FROM DEVELOPING COUNTRIES, 1966 AND 1974

| | | Share of sectoral imports | |
| --- | --- | --- | --- |
| | | 1966 % | 1974 % |
| Cocoa: | Beans | 86 | 77 |
| | Paste & butter | 13 | 21 |
| | Powder and choc. products | – | 2 |
| | | 100 | 100 |
| Coffee: | Raw and roasted | 99 | 97 |
| | Soluble | 1 | 3 |
| | | 100 | 100 |
| Vegetable oils: | Oilseeds | 61 | 33 |
| | Oils | 39 | 67 |
| | | 100 | 100 |
| Sugar: | Raw | 50 | 57 |
| | Refined | 49 | 43 |
| | Sugar confectionery and preparations | – | – |
| | | 100 | 100 |
| Rubber: | Raw | 99 | 95 |
| | Semi-man, rubber products | – | – |
| | Rubber manufactures | 1 | 4 |
| | | 100 | 100 |
| Jute: | Fibres and waste | 40 | 29 |
| | Yarns | – | 4 |
| | Fabrics | 60 | 68 |
| | | 100 | 100 |
| Other vegetable fibres:[a] | Fibres & waste | 82 | 64 |
| | Yarns | 7 | 2 |
| | Fabrics | – | – |
| | Cordage | 12 | 33 |
| | | 100 | 100 |
| Wood: | Rough | 65 | 59 |
| | Shaped | 20 | 18 |
| | Manufactures | 15 | 23 |
| | | 100 | 100 |
| Bauxite: | Ore | 66 | 36 |
| | Alumina | 24 | 38 |
| | Alumina unwrought | 10 | 24 |
| | Alumina worked | – | 1 |
| | | 100 | 100 |
| Tin: | Ore | 28 | 15 |
| | Unwrought | 72 | 85 |
| | Worked | – | – |
| | | 100 | 100 |

|          |                              | *Share of sectoral imports* | |
|----------|------------------------------|------------|------------|
|          |                              | 1966 %     | 1974 %     |
| Copper:  | Ore & concentrates           | 12         | 30         |
|          | Unrefined                    | 32         | 15         |
|          | Refined                      | 54         | 54         |
|          | Copper plates, sheets, etc.  | 2          | –          |
|          |                              | 100        | 100        |
| Lead:    | Ore & concentrates           | 41         | 50         |
|          | Unwrought                    | 58         | 50         |
|          | Worked                       | –          | –          |
|          |                              | 100        | 100        |
| Zinc:    | Ore & concentrates           | 72         | 65         |
|          | Unwrought                    | 28         | 35         |
|          | Worked                       | –          | –          |
|          |                              | 100        | 100        |
| Nickel:  | Ore & concentrates           | 59         | 56         |
|          | Unwrought                    | 41         | 44         |
|          | Worked                       | –          | –          |
|          |                              | 100        | 100        |
| Iron:    | Ore & concentrates           | 97         | 83         |
|          | Unwrought                    | –          | –          |
|          | Worked                       | 3          | 17         |
|          |                              | 100        | 100        |

[a]Exclusive of cotton.
*Source:*   Helleiner and Welwood [*1978: 39*].

enthusiasm with which such tariff reductions are greeted must therefore be tempered by consideration of the implications for industrialisation prospects. Similar considerations apply to relative changes in transport charges. Reductions in rates on raw materials are not necessarily the 'good thing' which they might superficially appear.)

Other influences (the emergence of more skilled lcoal labour, more developed local infrastructure, continued widening of international wage gaps, anti-pollution laws in the industrialised countries, preferential tariffs in major markets and local governmental incentives or moral suasion) [*Helleiner, 1976: 201–3; Roemer, 1977*] are operating which, despite these impediments, have led to gradual relocation of processing facilities in most sectors (but not sugar, copper or lead) from rich countries to poor ones in recent years, often under the auspices of transnationals which can be expected to assist thereafter in campaigns to prevent future increases in protection. This has been so little remarked that I present the relevant data in Table 4.

### (ii) Restrictive Business Practices as 'Private NTBs'

As the average level of tariffs has fallen through successive rounds of GATT bargaining, the role of already existing non-tariff barriers (NTBs) has graduallly been thrown into sharper relief and there has been increasing resort to new ones. Discussions of NTBs among governments have so far been focused on those for which governments are directly responsible. Eventually the issue of NTBs imposed by private firms will have to be faced as well. This is, to some degree, a matter of international anti-trust policies to regulate restrictive business practices in the international arena, which may be outside individual nations' jurisdictions. It may also be necessary, however, to learn far more than we at present know about the decision-making practices of sellers and buyers of goods and services moving in and out of the Third World, whether or not they are strictly 'in restraint of trade'. It has been established, for example, that small countries pay more for imported machinery, iron and steel, and chemicals than do large ones [Hufbauer and O'Neill, 1972; Yeats, 1976; Yeats, 1978]. But the reasons for these phenomena are not clearly understood (and indeed the detailed data are few and far between).

As far as restrictive business practices are concerned, it is fairly clear that the developing countries are those most likely to be hit by their continued existence in their present form. This is not merely a matter of the frequently quite high levels of market concentration which confront their exports, where high levels of buyer concentration have long characterised petroleum and minerals markets, and markets for such agricultural products as bananas, cocoa, tea and rubber.[7] It is also a problem in the markets in which they buy. Arrangements to fix prices, allocate markets and customers, pool knowledge and plans, and predetermine levels of bids, are all quite frequent among selling firms from the industrialised countries. These practices, while illegal domestically, are frequently exempt as far as exports are concerned — as in the case of the Webb—Pomerene Act of the US — so that countries without the will or capacity to police the degree of competition in their markets are the only ones affected. It follows, as a recent paper written within the GATT puts it, that 'cartel arrangements and the abuse of dominant position are probably more widespread and damaging in exports to developing than to developed countries' [Tumlir and Robinson, 1975: 18].

*(iii) OECD Adjustment to Changes in the Structure of Trade*
Just as different economic and political actors differ in their capacity to influence changing events, such as trade policies and technical change, they also differ in their capacities to adapt, adjust and respond to them. Large, internationally oriented and experienced firms are much better able to adjust their activities than are smaller, less diversified, less mobile firms or individual workers. As governments in the Third World offer increased incentives for exporting, as many trade barriers in the industrialised countries come down, and as unit labour cost differentials and technologies change, transnational corporations can be expected relatively quickly to react. They will relocate their productive activities, redirect their international trade flows and change their composition, retool or diversify the plants which they prefer not to close and frequently even retrain their employees. Instead of investing their capital, where such investment is no longer wanted, they will happily sell their technology or other inputs. In many industries they have already made significant adjustments of this kind in response to changes in governmental policies, political climate or economic conditions. They can be expected to respond in a similarly flexible and pragmatic fashion to the

development of manufactured exports from developing countries to the industrialised countries. In fact, they have themselves been active promoters of a good deal of this international relocation of industry through their 'runaway plants' and international subcontracting activities. Opposition to 'the new international division of labour' tends to come from less internationally oriented, less diversified, less efficient and usually smaller firms – and from the labour movement. (Inefficient producing firms in the industrialised countries frequently begin to import from developing countries themselves, in order to retain their earnings while they increase their pressure for increased protection.)

The important role which transnational corporations seem likely to continue to play in the growth of manufactured exports is analogous to that which they played in much of the import-substituting industrialisation of the 1950s and 1960s. It is, after all, worth asking why there was so little reaction to the restructuring of world industry attendant upon the major industrial import substitution efforts in the Third World over the past thirty years. Tariffs, quotas, exchange controls and other measures were added to the 'natural forces' of markets and location economics to alter in quite a dramatic fashion the composition of the import-substitution countries' import bills. Firms accustomed to exporting to these markets were forced to 'adjust' to new market realities in which these opportunities had vanished. Yet there was nothing like the clamour over adjustment problems then that there is over manufactured exports from the Third World to Europe and North America today.

The principal reason for the 'benign neglect' with which transnational exporting firms viewed these import-substituting developments was, of course, that they were *not* thereby excluded from the profitable business of supplying Third World markets. On the contrary, these very firms were frequently significant *gainers* from protectionist policies which enabled them to extract high rates of return from local productive enterprises, while continuing to export intermediate inputs, equipment, technology, and marketing and management knowhow. Transnational corporations had no great difficulty in adapting their worldwide systems to these changing incentive structures; although the composition of their international trading operations and the product-mix of their developed country plants must have been altered thereby. In many instances, Third World markets were not of sufficient size, by themselves, to generate large such shifts; but internal readjustment in response to changing circumstances in a variety of different foreign economies (including those of the Third World) has nevertheless been an ongoing process. Developed country firms which had reached the point of exporting significant volumes to import-substituting Third World countries were typically of sufficient size, flexibility and power not to be hampered much by the emergence of new policies directed against their exports.[8]

Labour, on the other hand, has greater difficulty adapting to economic change. Even protection which is introduced purportedly in its defence is unlikely to be very effective in protecting its interest. Protection for an industry through a tariff or other devices, after all, provides no assurance that the labourers working in the industry thereby become better off. A recent study of the British jute products industry, for instance, shows that 'although protection postpones *trade* adjustment, it may precipitate *technological* adjustment' [*ODI, 1978: 00*]. Tariff protection which was ostensibly designed to protect jobs threatened by import competition actually made it possible for firms in the industry to develop job-destroying innovations (through the development of synthetics), leaving workers no better off than they would have been with continued imports. Only the *firms* benefitted from governmental protection.

Explanations of developed countries' tariff policies which are based on the purported objective of protecting labour from foreign competition — while perhaps reflecting some of the political realities — do not encompass them all. Governments which really want to assist labour will, one would think, do so directly — through adjustment assistance to workers and communities. [*Frank, 1977: 2–109*].

CONCLUSION

There are important structural changes under way in Third World trade. Those relating to market structure and institutional factors deserve more attention than they have received. While the data which would permit a complete analysis of the role of transnational corporations in Third World trade are not available, it is possible nevertheless to discern their changing relationship with developing countries in primary products trade, and their growing importance in manufactured goods trade. The governments of the developed countries seem to be working, through their trade policies, to channel as much of this trade as possible through the transnational corporations. Moreover, although transnationals are far more adaptable than labour to changing economic circumstances, governmental assistance programmes have not taken much account of this. What is now clearly required is more detailed research on the politics and economics of developed countries' trade policies, adjustment policies and experiences, and the emerging institutional structure of Third World trade. Only with the resulting knowledge of market structures and barriers to their entry into various activities will decision-makers in developing countries be able to construct successful policies for future trade.

NOTES

1. A more extensive treatment of the phenomenon of intrafirm trade may be found in Helleiner [*forthcoming*]. Much of the material in the succeeding two paragraphs is drawn from this source.
2. For an excellent exposition of the changing scene in the world minerals sector see Diaz Alejandro [*1976*].
3. Since this paper was written new and disturbing evidence has emerged on these possibilities. Between 1970 and 1973 more than 80 per cent of total expenditures on mineral exploration in the non-socialist world was concentrated in Australia, Canada, South Africa and the United States [*UN, Development Forum, 1978: 1*]. The developing countries' share of European companies total exploration expenditures fell from 57 per cent in 1961 to 13.5 per cent in 1973–75 [*Courier, Brussels, 1978, No. 49: 85*]. In the US the loss of control over production facilities abroad has generated strong copper industry pressure for protection.
4. For further discussion of this type of trade, see Helleiner [*1973*], Sharpston [*1975*], Finger [*1975*].
5. This argument is developed with special reference ot the US in Helleiner [*1977*].
6. In Germany the structure of nominal tariff protection for industry appears to have been changing in the direction of more uniform levels of protection for all. Other

non-tariff measures have increasingly been employed to achieve the same sort of interindustry discrimination as is found in theUS and Canada, but it remains true that total effective protection is moving in the direction of greater cross-industry uniformity [*Riedel, 1977*].

7.   For a much more wide-ranging assessment of 'imperfections' and 'concentrations' in markets of interest to developing countries, see Helleiner [*1978*].

8.   These firms are more threatened by the development of alternative technologies – whether of production or consumption – over which they do not possess market power. It is in fact in the very nature of many cheap consumer goods and unskilled-labour-intensive processes that they are easily copied; private returns from their development are therefore difficult to appropriate and firms in possibly affected sectors will not only refrain from developing them, but would also gain from resolutely suppressing them . . . . . . . . . . . . . . . . . . . . . . . . . . . . . . . . . . . .

## REFERENCES

Cheh, John H., 1974, 'United States Concessions in the Kennedy Round and Short-run Labor Adjustment Costs', *Journal of International Economics*, Vol. 4, No. 4.

Chung, William K., 1977, 'Sales by Majority-Owned Foreign Affiliates of US Companies, 1975', *Survey of Current Business*, Vol. 57, No. 2.

Cohen, Benjamin I., 1975, *Multinational Firms and Asian Exports*, New Haven and London, Yale University Press.

Diaz Alejandro, Carlos F., 1976, 'International Markets for Exhaustible Resources, Less Developed Countries, and Transnational Corporations', Economic Growth Center, Yale University, Discussion Paper No. 256.

Diaz Alejandro, Carlos F., 1977, 'Foreign Direct Investment by Latin Americans', in Tamir Agmon and Charles P. Kindleberger (eds.), *Multinationals from Small Countries*, Cambridge, MIT Press.

Felix, David, 1977, 'The Technological Factor in Socioeconomic Dualism: Toward an Economy-of-Scale Paradigm for Development Theory', *Economic Development and Cultural Change*, Vol. 25, Supplement.

Finger, J. M., 1975, 'Tariff Provisions for Offshore Assembly and the Exports of Developing Countries', *Economic Journal*, Vol. 85, No. 338.

Finger, J. M. and Yeats, A. J., 1976, 'Effective Protection by Transportation Costs and Tariffs: A Comparison of Magnitudes', *Quarterly Journal of Economics*, Vol. 110, No. 1.

Frank, Charles R., Jr., 1977, *Foreign Trade and Domestic Aid*, Washington, Brookings Institution.

GATT, 1974, *Basic Documentation for the Tariff Study*, Geneva.

GATT, 1977, *International Trade 1975/76*, Geneva.

Helleiner, G. K., 1973, 'Manufactured Exports from Less-Developed Countries and Multinational Firms', *Economic Journal*, Vol. 83, No. 329.

Helleiner, G. K., 1976, 'Multinationals, Manufactured Exports and Employment in the Less Developed Countries', in International Labour Office, *Tripartite World Conference on Employment, Income Distribution and Social Progress and the International Division of Labour, Background Papers, Volume II: International Strategies for Employment*, Geneva.

Helleiner, G. K., 1977a, 'Transnational Enterprises and the New Political Economy of U.S. Trade Policy', *Oxford Economic Papers*, Vol. 29, No. 1.

Helleiner, G. K., 1977b, 'The Political Economy of Canada's Tariff Structure: An Alternative Model', *Canadian Journal of Economics*, Vol. X, No. 2.

Helleiner, G. K., 1978a, 'Freedom and Management in Primary Commodity Markets: U.S. Imports from Developing Countries', *World Development*, Vol. 6, No. 1.

Helleiner, G. K., 1978b, 'World Market Imperfections and the Developing Countries', Overseas Development Council, Occasional Paper No. 11.

Helleiner, G. K., forthcoming, 'Intrafirm Trade and the Developing Countries: An Assessment of the Data', *Journal of Development Economics*.

Helleiner, G. K., and Welwood, Douglas, 1978c, 'Raw Material Processing in Developing Countries and Reductions in the Canadian Tariff, Economic Council of Canada, Discussion Paper No. 111.

Hufbauer, G. C., and O'Neill, J. P., 1972, 'Unit Values of U.S. Machinery Exports', *Journal of International Economics*, Vol. 2, No. 3.

INTAL (Instituto para la Integracion de America Latina), 1977, 'A Study on Latin America Joint Enterprises', Doc. 1, Progress Report, Buenos Aires.

Moran, Theodore H., 1974, *Multinational Corporations and the Politics of Dependence, Copper in Chile*, Princeton, N. J., Princeton University Press.

Morley Samuel A., and Smith, Gordon W., 1977, 'The Choice of Technology: Multinational Firms in Brazil', *Economic Development and Cultural Change*, Vol. 25, No. 2.

ODI (Overseas Development Institute), 1978, and Fraser of Allander Institute, *Trade Adjustment and the British Jute Industry*, London.

Riedel, James, 1977, 'Tariff Concessions in the Kennedy Round and the Structure of Protection in West Germany: An Econometric Assessment', *Journal of International Economics*, Vol. 7, No. 2.

Roemer, Michael, 1977, 'Resource-Based Industrialisation in the Developing Countries, A Survey of the Literature', Harvard Institute for International Development, Development Discussion Paper No. 21.

Sharpston, Michael, 1975, 'International Subcontracting', *Oxford Economic Papers*, Vol. 27, No. 1.

Tumlir, J., and Robinson S., 1975, 'What is Feasible in Legal Regulations of Restrictive Business Practices in International Trade', mimeo.

UN, ECOSOC (United Nations, Economic and Social Council), 1978, *Transnational Corporations in World Development: A Re-Examination*, New York.

World Bank, 1978, *World Development Report, 1978*, Washington.

UN Development Forum, 1978, 'Disturbing Trend in Minerals Search', Vol. VI, No. 4.

Yeats, A. J., 1976, 'An Analysis of Import Price Differentials Paid by Developing Countries', Geneva, UNCTAD Research Division, mimeo.

Yeats, A. J., 1978, 'Monopoly Power, Barriers to Competition and the Pattern of Price Differentials in International Trade', *Journal of Development Economics*, Vol. 5, No. 2.

# International Trade and the Transfer of Labour Value

## by L. Mainwaring*

*An accepted proposition of Marxist theories of non-equivalent exchange is that international trade involves a transfer of labour value from the low to the high wage country. It is argued that in systems in which intermediate goods are used and traded this proposition cannot be shown to hold of necessity, even though standard 'unequal exchange' assumptions are accepted.*

### 1. INTRODUCTION

The concepts of 'unequal' and 'non-equivalent' exchange are key features in some Marxist theories of underdevelopment. The definition of 'unequal' exchange varies from writer to writer, though there does appear to be agreement on what constitutes 'non-equivalent' exchange. This refers to the exchange of commodities between countries at prices which deviate from the ratios of labour embodied in those commodities. Initially, the various examples of non-equivalent exchange were displayed in terms of Marxian tableaux. A welcome development has been the substitution of the system of price determination proposed by Sraffa [*Sraffa, 1960*] for Marx's cumbersome and incorrect transformation procedure. It seems, however, that a central feature of the Sraffa system, namely the circularity of the production process (implicit in the title of Sraffa's book), has been neglected. Our purpose here is to show that this circularity in production has an important bearing on the direction of transfer of labour value. Indeed, it is our contention that, once the consequences of this circularity are taken fully into account, nothing *a priori* can be said about the direction of non-equivalent exchange.[1]

Because of the diverse nature of the writings on this subject a single model cannot possibly be fully representative of each contribution. Although we demonstrate our central proposition in the simple two-country, two-commodity model set out below, we shall go on to consider briefly the relationship between this model and some of the more important versions of unequal exchange theory.

### 2. PRICE RELATIONS

Suppose that each country is fully specialised in one commodity. Countries are referred to as A and B (which may be thought of as 'centre' and

---

* University College, Cardiff. I should like to thank Howard Nicholas for useful discussions on the subject of unequal exchange, but he should not necessarily be associated with the views expressed in this paper. I am also grateful for the helpful comments of a referee.

'periphery') and their respective commodities as 1 and 2. National wage rates are taken to be exogenously determined, in terms of some standard (which could be a basket of wage commodities), by institutional factors within each country. We begin by establishing some price-distribution relationships which will enable us to clarify certain initial premises of the argument.

Assuming no transport costs, the free-trade price equations are

$$(1) \quad p_1 = (1+r_A) (p_1 a_{11} + p_2 a_{21}) + w_A \ell_1$$

$$(2) \quad p_2 = (1+r_B) (p_1 a_{12} + p_2 a_{22}) + w_B \ell_2$$

in which $p_i$ (i = 1, 2) is the price of commodity i, $\ell_i$ and $a_{ji}$ (j = 1,2) are the unit labour and commodity input coefficients, and $r_Z$ and $w_Z$ (Z = A, B) are the rates of profit and wage rates in country Z.

Equation (1), for example, says that the price of commodity 1 is made up of wage costs, the prices of means of production and profits on the means of production at a rate $r_A$. The equation obviously refer to a circulating capital economy in which all production takes place in unit time periods. For simplicity, we take commodity 2 as the standard of value; then, since wages are given, the two price equations contain three unknowns, p ($= p_1/p_2$), $r_A$ and $r_B$. When international investment has become sufficient to equalise the rates of profit (so that $r_A = r_B = r$), the two equations form a wholly determinate system. Otherwise, demand conditions need to be known in order to determine relative prices and the rates of profit.

Solving equations (1) and (2) individually for p, and equating the solutions, gives

$$(3) \quad \frac{w_A \ell_1 + (1 + r_A) a_{21}}{1 - (1 + r_A) a_{11}} = \frac{1 - (1 + r_B) a_{22} - w_B \ell_2}{(1 + r_B) a_{12}}$$

The left-hand side of (3) increases as $r_A$ increases, while the right-hand side increases as $r_B$ decreases. It follows that, if both wage rates are constant, $r_A$ and $r_B$ are inversely related. This relationship is illustrated in the left-hand quadrant of Figure 1. Note that an increase in one or both wage rates reduces the income share of profits, thus drawing this $r_A - r_B$ trade-off in towards the origin.

The right-hand quadrant of Figure 1 is a relationship between $r_A$ and p derived directly from equation (1), for a given level of $w_A$. Whenever $w_A$ is fixed any change in $w_B$ or $r_B$ affects both the price ratio and $r_A$ and leads to a movement along this curve. For example, an increase in $w_B$ (with $r_B$ fixed) or an increase in $r_B$ (with $w_B$ fixed) leads to reductions in both $r_A$ and p which are reflected by a movement along the curve. On the other hand if $w_A$ should vary, the curve itself will shift: an increase in $w_A$ would reduce $r_A$ at any price, so shifting the curve in the direction of the p-axis.

A key element in all unequal exchange theories is that free international mobility of capital leads to the international equalisation of profit rates. It is precisely this mechanism operating between sectors of a closed economy

## Figure 1

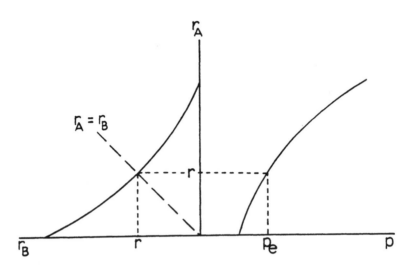

which, in the presence of unequal organic compositions of capital, leads to the deviation of prices from labour values,[2] and therefore to domestic non-equivalent exchange. This process is operating here in the world economy in which processes are located in different countries. But, as is apparent from Figure 1, whether the equalisation of profit rates improve or worsens country B's terms of trade depends on the pre-equalisation relationship of these rates. It is important to note that there is no presumption, on theoretical grounds, that the high wage country is also the low profit rate country. This may be seen by rearranging equations (1) and (2) to obtain national wage-profit frontiers.[3] Thus for equation (1)

(4) $w_A = [p_1 - (p_1 a_{11} + p_2 a_{21}) - r_A (p_1 a_{11} + p_2 a_{21})]/\ell_1$

which describes, *for given prices*, a straight-line trade-off between $w_A$ and $r_A$ of slope

$$q_1 = (p_1 a_{11} + p_2 a_{22})/\ell_1 ,$$

the price-weighted composition of capital (that is, the value of capital per worker) in country A. The two trade-offs are drawn in Figure 2, appropriate to pre-equalisation prices, first for the case in which $q_1 < q_2$, secondly for the case $q_1 > q_2$. When the high-wage country employs the less capital-intensive method, then, as can be seen in Figure 2(a) it is perfectly possible for $w_A > w_B$ and $r_A > r_B$. But this possibility also exists in what may be regarded as the more plausible case of $q_1 > q_2$ (Figure 2(b)). The intercepts, $y_Z$, on the vertical axis are values of net output per worker at the given prices. In the second case, the productivity of country A labour exceeds that of country B labour by an amount $y_A - y_B$. To rule out the possibility that $r_A > r_B$ in this

Figures 2

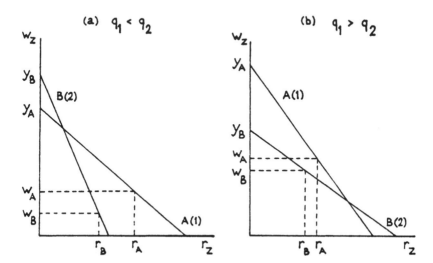

case it is sufficient that $w_A - w_B > y_A - y_B$, that is, that the difference in wages exceeds the difference in productivities. In the following we develop our analysis for the case in which $w_A > w_B$ *and* $r_A < r_B$. It should be emphasised that the conclusions reached should be regarded as possibilities only and the reader is left to decide for himself the plausibility of the underlying assumptions.[4]

From Figure 1, it follows that if $r_A < r_B$ equalisation of the rates of profit leads to a deterioration in country B's terms of trade; that is to reduction in p. In terms of the theory of non-equivalent exchange this should be regarded as a notional rather than an actual deterioration.

### 3. VALUE RELATIONS

So far the analysis has been conducted in terms of prices. We must now make reference to labour values. Non-equivalent exchange refers to the transfer of surplus value from one country to another. We therefore ask whether exchange at international *prices* is less favourable for B than exchange according to values. But we have to be very careful to specify exactly what is meant by 'exchange according to values'. For the relevant concept here is not the *total* labour embodied in the commodities exchanged but the quantity of country A's labour embodied in a unit of A's export commodity, etc. Remembering that each process may use imported means of production, these two concepts will not generally be the same. Thus non-equivalent exchange occurs if the amount of A-labour exported exceeds or falls short of the amount of B-labour imported when a unit of commodity 1 is exchanged for some amount of commodity 2.

To approach this problem we make the rather strong assumption (implicit in the literature) that units of labour in the two countries are qualitatively the same. Letting $\lambda_{Zi}$ be the quantity of Z-labour embodied directly and indirectly in a unit of commodity i (and remembering that $\ell_1$ is the quantity of A-labour embodied directly in a unit of commodity 1; $\ell_2$ the quantity of B-labour embodied directly in a unit of 2) we may write:

$$\begin{aligned}
\lambda_{A1} &= \ell_1 + \lambda_{A1}\,a_{11} + \lambda_{A2}\,a_{21} \\
\lambda_{A2} &= \quad\;\; \lambda_{A1}\,a_{12} + \lambda_{A2}\,a_{22} \\
\ell_{B1} &= \quad\;\; \lambda_{B1}\,a_{11} + \lambda_{B2}\,a_{21} \\
\lambda_{B2} &= \ell_2 + \lambda_{B1}\,a_{12} + \lambda_{B2}\,a_{22}.
\end{aligned}$$
(5)

The first of these equations says that the amount of A-labour embodied in commodity 1 is made up of labour used directly in production, plus the amount of A-labour embodied in the inputs of commodities into commodity 1. Since commodity 2 is not produced in A there is no direct A-labour embodied in it; $\lambda_{A2}$ (in the second equation) is therefore made up of solely from the indirect labour passed on through means of production. The second and third equations can be similarly interpreted. From (5),

(6)    $\lambda_{Zi} = (1 - a_{ii})\,\ell_i\,[(1 - a_{22})\,(1 - a_{11}) - a_{12}\,a_{21}].$

This allows us to define two separate labour embodied ratios:

(7)    $\eta = \dfrac{\lambda_{A1} + \lambda_{B1}}{\lambda_{A2} + \lambda_{B2}} = \dfrac{(1 - a_{22})\,\ell_1 + \ell_2\,a_{21}}{(1 - a_{11})\,\ell_2 + \ell_1\,a_{12}}$

and

(8)    $\lambda = \dfrac{\lambda_{A1}}{\lambda_{B2}} = \dfrac{(1 - a_{22})\,\ell_1}{(1 - a_{11})\,\ell_2}.$

The first of these, $\eta$, is the ratio of total labour, *irrespective of origin*, embodied in units of the two commodities. Once it is recognised that production normally requires imported inputs it becomes apparent that the relevant ratio for non-equivalent exchange is $\lambda$ which refers to the amount of each country's labour that is exchanged. This distinction is not normally made even in discussions which employ a circular production system and yet it is clearly of some significance for the concept of non-equivalent exchange: $\lambda$ and $\eta$ are equal if, an only if,

$$(\ell_1)^2\,a_{12}\,(1 - a_{22}) = (\ell_2)^2\,a_{21}\,(1 - a_{11})$$

(which is, of course, satisfied when the 'cross' coefficients $a_{12}$ and $a_{21}$ are both zero, that is, when there is no trade in intermediate goods).

Since centre wages are higher than periphery wages we may put $w_A/w_B = k > 1$. Then, weighting the $\ell_1$ terms in (7) by this relative wage factor we can define the relative wage costs of the two commodities as

(9)      $\mu \quad = \quad \dfrac{(1 - a_{22})k\ell_1 + \ell_2\, a_{21}}{(1 - a_{11})\,\ell_2 + k\ell_1\, a_{12}}$

From (9), $d\mu/dk > 0$ so long as $(1 - a_{11})(1 - a_{22}) > a_{12}a_{21}$, which is, of course, the Hawkins-Simon condition, which is naturally assumed to hold. When $k = 1$, $\mu = \eta$; it follows that when $k > 1$,

(10)     $\mu > \eta$

But we are unable to say *a priori* whether $\mu > \lambda$ or $\mu \leqslant \lambda$. Comparing (8) and (9), we have

(11)     $\mu < \lambda \Rightarrow (1 - a_{11})\, a_{21} > (1 - a_{22})\, a_{12}\, (k\ell_1/\ell_2)^2$

which inequality does not violate either the Hawkins-Simon condition or our own restriction on the relative compositions of capital: $q_1 > q_2$. It is, therefore, perfectly possible to have the set of inequalities:

$$\eta < \mu < \lambda$$

## Figure 3

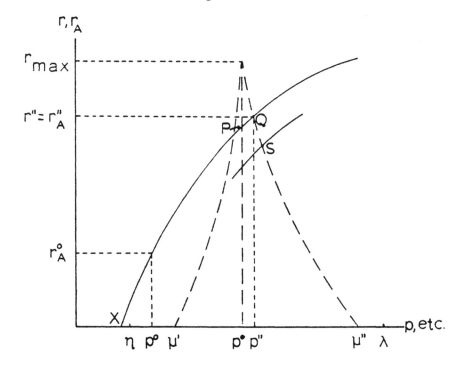

This particular ordering of these ratios is shown on the horizontal axis of Fig. 3; $\eta$ and $\lambda$ have fixed technologically determined magnitudes, but $\mu$ is dependent on the exogenously variable relative wage parameter k.

Consider in Figure 3, the broken line curves emanating from the horizontal axis. These curves relate relative prices to the post-equalisation rate of profit r, for various values of k. We shall refer to them as k-curves. It is a standard result that, when $r_A = r_B = r$ and $w_A = w_B$, the price ratio $(p_1/p_2)$ rises with r if the price composition of capital is greater for commodity 1 than for commodity 2. When, however, $w_A > w_B$ this result is slightly modified, as follows:

$$dp/dr \gtreqless O \text{ as } (pa_{11} + a_{21})/\ell_1 k \gtreqless (pa_{12} + a_{22})/\ell_2$$

or, alternatively,

(12)     $dp/dr \gtreqless O$ as $q_1/k \gtreqless q_2$

Now r attains its maximum, $r_{max}$, when $w_A = w_B = O$, and at a price ratio which we denote by $p^*$. This price $p^*$ holds at $r_{max}$ whatever the value of k, since $w_A = kw_B = O$. Thus the k-curves all meet at the point $(r_{max}, p^*)$. For k $= k^* = q_1/q_2$ it follows from (12) that prices are constant at $p^*$, for k = k' < $q_1/q_2$ prices begin at $\mu'$ (when r = O, and all costs are wage costs) and rise to $p^*$ (when $r = r_{max}$); similarly, for k = $k''> q_1/q_2$ prices fall from $\mu''$ to $p^*$ as r rises.

In Figure 3, the curve XQ is the function relating p to the pre-equalised rate $r_A$, taken from Figure 1. Notional variations in k can be brought about by varying $w_B$ with $w_A$ given, or by varying $w_A$ with $w_B$ given. The former case involves a shift in the XQ curve and to avoid this complication suppose that only $w_B$ is variable. Then obviously, for some given value of k, when $r_A = r_B$ the curve XQ will intersect a k-curve which is appropriate to that value of k. If, for example, k = k'' the curves intersect at point Q where $r_A'' = r_B'' = r''$ and p = p''.

The pre-equalisation price $p^\circ$ would have corresponded to a lower value of $r_A$, say $r_A^\circ$. This price may have been above or below the relative value $\eta$ (as it is drawn above), but in any event, the equalisation of the rates of profit has led to a deterioration in the terms of trade of country B. Moreover, after equalisation the price ratio is necessarily above the relative value $\eta$. This follows since, when k =k'' > k*, the corresponding price p'' must be greater than $p^*(= \mu^*)$. Since $k^* = q_1/q_2 > 1$ (by assumption) there are values of k satisfying $1 < k < k^*$, and corresponding values of $\mu$ such that $\mu < \mu^*$. It follows from (10) that $p'' > \eta$.

It is that result which has come to be known as non-equivalent exchange. Trade takes place at terms which deviate from relative value in a direction which is advantageous for the high wage country A, and to the detriment of the low wage country B. But the view that this trade necessarily involves a transfer of surplus value from B to A is mistaken, for the relevant ratio in this respect is $\lambda$. If the technical conditions of production are such that $\mu''$ satisfies (11), then it follows that $p'' < \lambda$, so that country A is engaged in a net transfer of its surplus value, though to a lesser extent than at the original price $p^\circ$. While the equalisation of the rates of profit has indeed worsened B's terms of trade, it has merely served to bring them into line with λ, but without completely closing the gap. Country A (the centre) therefore remains the victim of non-equivalent exchange. Of course, we are not saying that the centre necessarily suffers in this way; merely that this is a logical possibility. We have shown, however, that there is no presumption in favour of the proposition that the periphery inevitably suffers. To retain the proposition would require the use of additional assumptions which may be so restrictive as to leave the theory virtually empty.

## 4. ALTERNATIVE VERSIONS OF UNEQUAL EXCHANGE

We now consider briefly the implication of the result of the previous section for some of the more important versions of unequal exchange theory.[5] There are two basic distinctions we wish to focus on. The first concerns the definition of unequal exchange, as such; the second concerns assumptions about the extent of international specialisation. Although the theory of unequal exchange originated with Emmanuel, it is probably true to say that on the first of these his version is different from succeeding ones and we shall leave discussion of him till last. Other major contributors tend to regard unequal exchange as identical to non-equivalent exchange (as defined above). However, some like Braun [*Braun, 1974*], assume that commodities are 'specific' to countries; that is, that specialisation is complete. This is the assumption made above and so our conclusion applies directly. On the other hand, Amin [*Amin, 1976; 1977*], whilst in general approving of Braun,[6] and Saigal [*Saigal, 1973*] are insistent that commodities are 'non-specific'. They argue that periphery countries do produce the same (or similar) manufactured products as the centre. What then happens to our conclusions if (say) both countries produce both commodities? The answer is: nothing – provided that imports are not used solely for final consumption. So long as some imported goods are used as means of production there will still be a distinction between the two ratios $\eta$ and $\lambda$. Although the difference between them may be somewhat narrower than in the previous case, our conclusion that surplus value *may* move from A to B remains intact.

Our model is also directly applicable to Emmanuel [*Emmanuel, 1972*] in as much as he, too, assumes commodities to be specific. But for him unequal exchange arises not as a consequence of equalised profit rates but as a consequence of unequal wages (in the presence of equalised profit rates). Unequal exchange is, therefore, reflected not in the deviation of prices from values but in the deviation of prices, as they are, from prices as they would be had wages been uniform. Since Emmanuel's definition does not refer to values, only to prices, it is not affected by our result. What his basic proposition amounts to is that a widening of the wage differential (an increase in k) leads to a deterioration of B's terms of trade. This is easily seen in Figure 3: an increase in k, from say $k^*$ to $k''$, resulting from a fall in $w_B$ ($w_A$ constant) is reflected in a move from point P to point Q. The same increase in k resulting from a rise in $w_A$ ($w_B$ constant) is reflected in a shift from point P to S.

## 5. CONCLUSION

This paper is addressed to a specific logical question: In a two-country world in which profit rates are equalised, in which wage differences exceed productivity differences and in which the high wage country employs the more capital intensive technique, is it possible to say that international trade must lead to a net transfer of value from the low to the high wage country? A positive answer to this question would seem to be crucial to theories of non-equivalent exchange but we have tried to show that it is not possible to give an unqualified response. Our reasoning is directly analogous to that underlying the concept of 'effective protection': in circular production systems, that is, systems involving the use of intermediate goods, it is necessary to 'net out' that part of the gross (labour) value of a commodity which is contributed by imported means of production in order to obtain the true (labour) value-added in any one country. Once that is done, it is seen that a net transfer may occur in either direction.

Proponents of the unequal exchange theories may claim empirical support for their existing assumptions, but there can be no such support for the assumption that world trade in intermediate goods is insignificant. There may, of course, be patterns of trade in intermediates which are consistent with the accepted conclusions. But the onus is on the advocates of the accepted view to show what these patterns are and that they have some counterpart in reality. As it is, the concept of unequal exchange does not appear to be particularly useful in helping us to understand the process of underdevelopment.

## NOTES

1. The views expressed in this paper are not intended to prejudice the further question of whether net value transfers imply anything about more relevant economic magnitudes such as consumption levels and growth rates.
2. The inequality of wage rates is a further complicating factor which is of central importance for Emmanuel, but we put discussion on this aside for the moment.
3. The properties of these frontiers are discussed in [*Mainwaring, 1974*] where it is shown that their intersection defines a point on the w-r frontier for a world economy having equalised wages and profit rates. So long as the w's and r's are equal the curves must intersect in the positive quadrant, but otherwise intersections in the non-positive quadrants are possible. This does not affect our argument.
4. There is a strong similarity between the conditions $q_1 > q_2$ and $w_A - w_B > y_A - y_B$ with those often assumed by unequal exchange writers. For that reason they are deliberately adopted here.
5. Perhaps the best and most comprehensive critical survey of this literature is to be found in [*Evans, forthcoming*].
6. See, for example, Braun's numerical example reproduced in [*Amin, 1976:150*]. Whilst this example perfectly well demonstrates Emmanuel's proposition (see below) it is odd in that surplus value moves from the high to the low wage country (at $k = 0.7/0.12$, $p = 0.55$ and $\lambda = 0.583$), a circumstance which is largely attributable to the fact that $q_2 > q_1$ (2 = wheat, 1 = iron).

REFERENCES

Amin, S., 1976, *Unequal development*, New York: Monthly Review Press.

Amin, S., 1977 *Imperialism and Unequal Development*, New York: Monthly Review Press.

Braun, O., 1974, 'L'échange inégal', in G. Amoa and O. Braun, *Echanges Internationaux et Sous développement*, Paris: Anthropos.

Evans, D., forthcoming, 'Unequal Exchange Theory: a Critical Review', in D. Evans and R. Murray, *The Political Economy of Trade*, Hassocks: Harvester Press.

Mainwaring, L., 1974, 'A Neo-Ricardian Analysis of International Trade', *Kyklos*, Vol. 27.

Saigal, J., 1973, Réflexions sur la Théorie de L'échange Inégal', in S. Amin, *L'échange Inégal et la Loi de Valeur*, Paris: Anthropos.

Sraffa, P., 1960, *Production of Commodities by Means of Commodities*, Cambridge: Cambridge University Press.

# EMPLOYMENT AND WAGES

# Marginal Productivity Wage Theory
# and Subsistence Wage Theory
# in Egyptian Agriculture*

## *By Bent Hansen***

### 1. Agricultural Wages in Modern Growth Theory

In modern growth models various theories of wage determination have been applied. On the one hand, in particular in 'neo-classical' models inspired by Solow,[1] one meets the traditional marginal productivity theory according to which the money wage rate is equal to, or at least, governed by the value of the marginal product of labour. Sometimes a different formulation is used: that real wages equal the marginal productivity of labour.[2] If in the general model in connection with which the latter formulation is used only one commodity is produced and consumed, or a uniform price for all commodities is assumed, or prices are disregarded altogether, then the two

* In the statistical work I was assisted by Fathia Zaghloul who compiled the price information necessary for the calculation of the cost-of-living index for agricultural labourers, computed the index, and made the calculations behind the regression equations, and Mona El Tomy who helped me with some of the other statistical series. I thank both of them for their valuable help.

I acknowledge gratefully the permission to use some of the statistical material collected for the 'Survey of Rural Employment' of the Institute of National Planning, Cairo, jointly undertaken with the ILO, Geneva. In particular I thank Dr. Ulrich Planck, ILO-expert at the INP, for his helpfulness in making the material available to me.

I thank Professor Zvi Griliches, University of Chicago, who read the paper, for valuable comments.
** At the time of writing Professor Hansen was Consultant Expert to the Institute of National Planning, Cairo. He is now with the O.E.C.D.

formulations coincide. But if output prices and wage good prices differ we have to use the first formulation. For the following discussion it is important to keep this in mind.

On the other hand, we meet, in particular in growth models explicitly concerned with agriculture during the first phases of an industrialization process, the notion of 'conventional subsistence wages,' or 'institutionally' determined wages. The main source of inspiration for this line of thought is Arthur Lewis's well-known article on economic development with unlimited supplies of labour.[3] Lewis takes for granted that 'marginal productivity is zero or negligible'[4] and that 'the price of labour, in these economies, is a wage at the subsistence level (we define this later).'[5] Lewis himself was not too precise, however, in defining the subsistence wage level. 'The classical economists used to think of the wage as being determined by what is required for subsistence consumption, and this may be the right solution in some cases. However, in economies where the majority of the people are peasant farmers working on their own land,' Lewis said, 'the minimum at which labour can be had is now set by the average product of the farmer.' If, however, rents have to be paid, this 'objective standard' does not work because 'in overpopulated countries the rent will probably be adjusted so as to leave them just enough for a conventional level of subsistence.' He adds that 'It is not, however, of great importance to the argument whether earnings in the subsistence sector are determined objectively by the level of peasants productivity, or subjectively in terms of a conventional standard of living.'[6] Fei and Ranis[7] have presented a more precise version of Lewis's wage theory assuming that when development (i.e. industrialization) starts, wages are equal to the average agricultural product, and that wages (agricultural as well as industrial) stay at this initial level due to some unspecified institutional mechanism until agriculture becomes what they call 'commercialized,' i.e. until marginal productivity of farm labour begins to exceed this institutionally (or conventionally, whichever it may be) given level. From this 'stage' onwards the marginal productivity theory is supposed to hold.

The aim of the present paper is to study these notions of wage determination against the background of information available about wages in Egyptian agriculture.

## 2. Two Hypotheses of Agricultural Wage Determination

In order to confront the above-mentioned theories of wages with empirical data we have to specify the theories more concretely as statistical hypotheses.

The marginal productivity theory says that

$$(1) \qquad w = pf'_L$$

where w is the money wage rate, p is the (average) price for agricultural outputs, f is the production function for agriculture, and $f'_L$ is the marginal productivity of labour. For the sake of simplification in measurements, we shall assume that the production function is of the Cobb-Douglas type. This production function has the important property that the marginal product of any factor is a given fraction of the average product of the factor. In case of labour, we therefore have $f'_L = af/L$, $0 < a < 1$, L being the labour input, which permits us to write (1) as

$$(2) \qquad w = a\,\frac{pf}{L}\,,$$

in other words the wage rate is a certain fraction of the value of agricultural output per unit of labour. Adding a time subscript, t, to all variables in (2) and assuming a to be constant over time[8] we obtain after division

$$(3) \qquad \frac{w_t}{w_0} = \frac{p_t f_t/L_t}{p_0 f_0/L_0} = \frac{O_t/L_t}{O_0/L_0}$$

where O is the total value of output. Eq. (3) says that an index of wage rates, say $W_t$, and an index of the value of output per unit of labour, $(O/L)_t$, the two indexes having the same basis, i.e. $W_0 = (O/L)_0 = 100$, shall always be equal, i.e.

$$(3') \qquad W_t = (O/L_t).$$

We can then formulate the statistical hypothesis

$(4)\ W_t = a + \beta\,(O/L)_t + u_t,\ Ea = 0,\ E\beta = 1,\ \text{and}\ Eu = 0,$

where $u_t$ is a random variable. (4) is the hypothesis we are going to test. In order to avoid possible influences from trends, which do make themselves felt to some extent in the time series to be used, we shall alternatively test the same hypothesis formulated on the basis of the first-differences

$$(4^1) \qquad \Delta W_t = a + \beta\Delta\,(O/L)_t + u_t,$$
$$Ea = 0, \qquad E\beta = 1, \text{ and } Eu = 0.$$

To form a testable hypothesis corresponding to the conventional subsistence wage theory is more intricate. Its advocates usually avoid specifying exactly which conventional or institutional factors determine the real wages and how, and this makes it of course rather difficult to test the theory. Do, for instance, the wage determining institutional factors change over time?[9] Here we shall follow Fei and Ranis in so far as we simply assume that real wages, in the sense of money wage rates over a relevant cost-of-living index, P, are constant over time, i.e.

$$(5) \qquad \frac{w}{P} = k,$$

k being a positive constant. Egypt, on which we shall test our hypotheses has never (in historical time, at least, and this means 5,000 years) enjoyed the experience of a state where the majority of the people were peasants working on their own land. From ancient times until about 1880 the land belonged to the Sovereign and — directly or through feudal intermediaries of various kinds — exorbitant rents and taxes as well as corvé-labour were squeezed out of the majority of small peasants, who were no more than serfs and had at most an uncertain right of usufruct.[10]

Even after 1880,[11] when private ownership in land was definitely established and the corvé was subsequently abolished, a substantial part of the land was cultivated by tenants and share-croppers, and there has always existed a class of landless rural labourers. It is therefore impossible to follow the method of procedure adopted by Fei and Ranis, and indicated by Lewis, of letting the institutionally fixed real wages be determined by the average productivity of the farm population in an initial state[12] where the society consists of independent peasants.[13] The only thing we can do is to assume that real wages equal a certain given constant, k. Writing (5) as $w = kP$, adding time subscripts, and forming indexes we obtain

$$(5') \qquad W_t = P_t$$

where $P_t$ is a cost-of-living index with $P_0 = 100$. We reach in this way the statistical hypothesis

$$(6) \qquad W_t = a + \beta P_t + u_t,$$
$$E a = 0, \quad E \beta = 1, \quad \text{and} \quad E u = 0,$$

and alternatively,

(6¹)     $\Delta W_t = a + \beta \Delta P_t + u_t,$
$$E a = 0, \ E\beta = 1, \text{ and } Eu = 0.$$

Concerning the cost of living for agricultural labourers, two methods have been applied. The first one is to let the cost of living be represented by the price of maize, $P_M$, maize being the main item in the agricultural labourer's poor diet; in doing this, I have followed a method adopted by Colin Clark and M. R. Haswell,[14] namely to concentrate on the grain-equivalent of rural wages. This method, however, hardly does justice to the institutional subsistence wage theory when agriculture has become monetized[15] to the extent which it has in Egypt since the end of the last century, and when wages are paid in cash.[16] After all, even the most miserable agricultural labourers do spend on other things than grain and grain products, which in Egypt in 1958/59[17] seem to occupy less than half of their budget. I have therefore, secondly, used a regular cost-of-living index, $P_C$, for agricultural labourers, specially made for this study. We obtain in this way two different estimates (a) and (b) of (6) and (6').

In econometric studies of wage determination it is usual to assume lags between the explanatory variables and wages,[18] and it is natural to make experiments with lags also in this case. Since there are also strong trends between wages and the lagged explanatory variables, if we work with the original data, the lagged equations were only estimated on the first differences, and only for output value per man and cost-of-living. It will be understood that on a distributed lags hypothesis $\beta$ should be expected to be somewhat smaller than 1.[19]

## 3. RESULTS OF TIME SERIES ANALYSIS

In the Statistical Appendix I have explained the statistical material in some detail. The wage index is based on information on the annual averages of daily wages for agricultural labourers in 17 years (1914, 1920, 1928-29, 1933, 1934, 1937-39, 1941, 1943, 1945, 1950-51, 1955-56, 1959-61). The information about daily wages was compiled from various sources and is of varying quality. I have not been able to find serious, comparable wage estimates for other years than those listed above. The reader may even

find that I have gone too far in my efforts to piece together
a wage index from the scattered information available.
The value of output per unit of labour was arrived at by
dividing an index of the value of output by an index of the
total labour force in agriculture. Concerning the total
value of output very reliable estimates from 1914 to 1961
are available, their main defect being that from 1914 to
1939 vegetables and fruit, fodder and animal production
are not included. Since the area under vegetables and
fruit, as well as the number of animals, increased relatively
to the production of field crops during this period a certain
downward bias in our index of value of output per labour
unit seems likely before 1939; this bias is probably small,
the size of fruit and vegetable production being small at
that time, while the stock of animals seems only to have
increased slightly more than production of field crops. The
labour force index is based on the population census figures
for persons economically active in agriculture, and annual
figures, based on registrations, for rural and urban population; this is the only labour input index available and it is
obviously not an ideal index. The price of maize gave rise
to a special problem in that two different series were available: one which is used in calculating the value of agricultural output and shows the estimated average price
obtained by the producers, and another one which is used
in calculating the special cost-of-living index and is based
on the wholesale quotations at the grain markets in Cairo
(and Alexandria). Estimates were made with both series
and the latter one which showed by far the highest correlation with wages was preferred.[20] For the special cost-of-
living index, reference is made to the Statistical Appendix.

The estimates based on the original observations are then,
r being the estimated coefficient of correlation, $\sigma$ the
standard error of the estimate, and the figures in brackets
under the values of $\alpha$ and $\beta$ their estimated standard errors
(scatter-diagrams in Graph. 1 and Graph. 2):

(4)*    $W'_t = 31.31 + 0.88\ (O/L)_t$   $r = 0.973\ \sigma = 32.00$
              (15.21) (0.05)

(6)*  a) $W'_t = -5.09 + 1.33\ (P_M)_t$   $r = 0.907\ \sigma = 57.63$
              (32.74) (0.16)

      b) $W'_t = -21.5 + 1.41\ (P_C)_t$   $r = 0.941\ \sigma = 46.25$
              (26.88) (0.13)

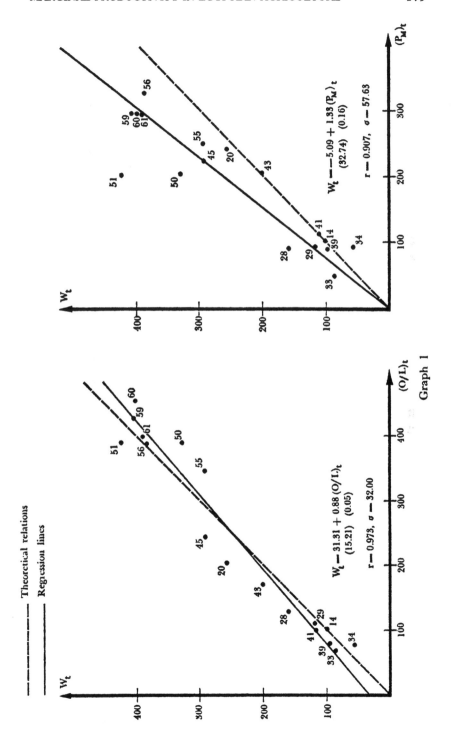

Graph 1

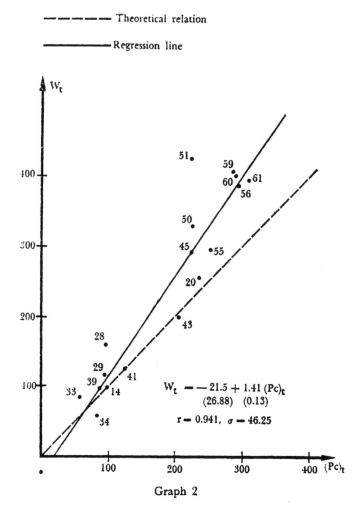

Graph 2

For the first-differences we get:

(4')*    $\Delta W'_t = 1.30 + 0.91 \, \Delta \, (O/L)_t$   $r = 0.712 \; \sigma = 55.18$
         (14.50) (0.24)

(6')* {
         a) $\Delta W'_t = 9.98 + 0.68 \, \Delta (P_M)_t$   $r = 0.584 \; \sigma = 63.80$
            (16.24) (0.25)
         b) $\Delta W'_t = 8.11 + 0.86 \, \Delta (P_C)$.   $r = 0.645 \; \sigma = 60.08$
            (15.43) (0.27)
}

We have here two sets of estimates, one on the original 17 observations and one on the 16 first-differences. Looking at the correlation coefficients we find higher values for the original observations than for the first-differences. This is of course what would be expected, particularly because there are trends in the original observations. A glance at the scatter diagrams shows that in all three cases the majority of dots are concentrated in two clusters, one for the pre-World War II years, one for the post-World War II years; within these clusters, however, there are no clear trends. The existence of trends makes the estimates on the original observations less interesting. We notice, anyway, that although for all three estimates the correlation coefficients are significant, the estimate with the value of the marginal productivity as the explanatory variable is the best from most points of view. The correlation coefficient is highest (and very high, indeed), while the standard error of the estimate is lowest; the estimated value of $\beta$ is much nearer[21] to the theoretical value, 1, and the estimated standard errors of $\alpha$ and $\beta$ much smaller than when the price of maize or the cost-of-living are used as explanatory variables. The value of $\alpha$ is, however, highest (numerically) in the first equation. Only in one case does the statistical material available permit an outright refutation of the hypothesis tested, namely in case of the cost-of-living where the estimated value of $\beta$ is larger than 1 by more than three times the standard error.

As to the more interesting first-differences estimates, the estimates also favour the marginal productivity theory. The correlation coefficient falls by about 25 per cent from 0.973 to 0.712 and is still highly significant, while with the maize price and the cost-of-living as explanatory variables the correlation coefficients drop by over 30 per cent, although they are still significant at the 5 per cent level. Concerning the coefficients $\alpha$ and $\beta$, the values found with the price of maize as the explanatory variable are quite different from the theoretical values, while the marginal productivity hypothesis leads to values much nearer to the theoretical values, and the cost-of-living hypothesis falls in between. The standard errors found with the marginal productivity hypothesis are slightly lower than with the cost-of-living and the maize price hypothesis. The first-differences do not lead to an outright refutation of any of the hypotheses since all correlation coefficients are significant and all estimated values of $\alpha$ and $\beta$ differ less than three

standard errors from the theoretical values, but looking at
the coefficient $\beta$ and its standard error, the estimate with
the price of maize as the explanatory variable is fully consistent also with a theoretical value of $\beta$ equal to zero, i.e.
with a hypothesis that there is no connection at all between
maize price and money wages.

Using the lagged first differences[22] as explanatory variables
the following estimates were obtained[23]

(7) $\quad \Delta W_t = 6.5 + 0.87 \; \Delta \; (O/L)_{t\text{-}1}, \quad r = 0.767, \quad \sigma = 50.4$
$\qquad\qquad$ (12.87)(0.19)

(8) $\quad \Delta W_t = 3.26 + 1.11 \Delta \; (P_C)_{t\text{-}1}, \quad r = 0.719 \quad \sigma = 54.63$
$\qquad\qquad$ (14.19) (0.29)

In both cases the correlation coefficient is somewhat
higher than with unlagged variables. This circumstance
points towards a distributed lag, and it would have been
desirable to carry out a multiple regression analysis with
both lagged and unlagged explanatory variables, in particular with lagged wages as an explanatory variable. Since,
however, the observations are not equidistant and the
unlagged and lagged explanatory variables turned out to
be highly intercorrelated[24] we abstained from making a
multiple regression analysis. Also with lagged variables the
marginal productivity hypothesis seems to be the superior
one.[25] Not only is the correlation highest and the standard
error of estimate lowest, but the value of $\beta$ found is theoretically more satisfactory than with the cost-of-living as the
explanatory variable. As pointed out above the value of
$\beta$ should here be somewhat smaller than 1.

To judge from the estimates now discussed, it would seem
fair to say then that the marginal productivity theory is the
superior hypothesis. Accepting this wage theory as the 'true
theory' it would be natural, however, that we should *also*
expect some correlation, although lower, between money
wages and the cost-of-living index, and a certain correlation, but even weaker, between money wages and the
maize price in full accordance with what we have actually
found. The reason for this is simple. From the point of view
of the marginal productivity theory we can divide the
explanatory variable into two components: the physical
marginal productivity (i.e. af/L, see equation (2) ), and the
output prices (p in equation (2)'). In Table I in the Statis-

tical Appendix these two components are shown separately. It turns out that although there has been substantial change in physical labour productivity over the 47 years embraced by our study — with a 20 per cent fall until the end of the 'thirties and a further fall by almost 15 per cent during World War II, followed by an almost 60 per cent increase after World War II[26] — the fluctuations of the output prices have been much stronger and dominate the development of the value of the marginal productivity, at least until the middle of the 'fifties. The output price index alone would therefore also show a good (although lower) correlation with money wages. Now, the cost-of-living index used here is composed mainly of agricultural prices (tea and kerosene being the only non-agricultural commodities entering the cost-of-living index and their combined weight is less than 0.1), and should therefore be expected to show some correlation with the general agricultural output price index. The same holds true, to a lesser degree, for the maize price.[27] The big difference between the agricultural output price index and our cost-of-living index is that the former includes the price of cotton (which before World War II had a weight of about 1/2 and after World War II of between 1/4 and 1/3) which does not appear in the latter.[28] Indeed, the different price development for cotton — the export crop — and cereals explains most of the difference between the agricultural price index and the cost-of-living index, and, accordingly, also a good deal of the difference in the explanatory power of the value of marginal productivity and the cost-of-living index. Incidentally it follows that a good deal of the changes in rural labourers' real wages is due to changes in the cotton price-cereals price ratio, see Graph 3. An increase in the price of cotton will, *ceteris paribus*, increase agricultural labourers' real wages; an increase in the price of cereals will, *ceteris paribus*, decrease agricultural labourers' real wages. But both will increase their money wages. Without this difference in the development and effects of cotton and cereals prices we would hardly have been able to test our theories.[29] The different price developments are partly due to the Government policies which at times have worked on the cereals prices — in the 'thirties through customs duties and in the war and post-war period through subsidies and forced deliveries at relatively low prices —

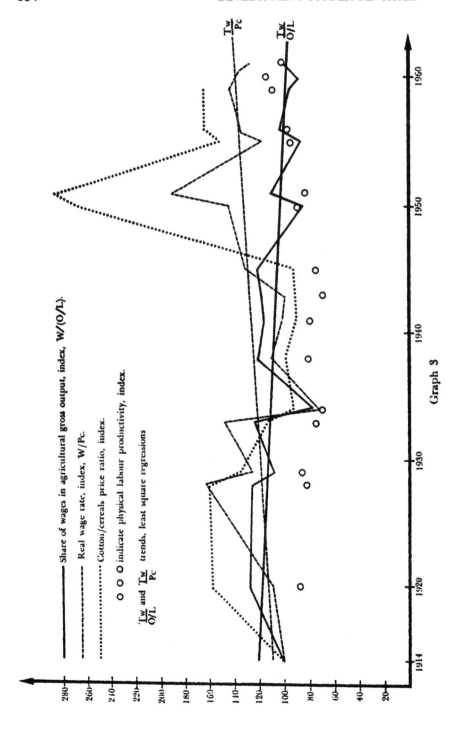

Graph 3

in order to counteract the effects of the dramatic fluctuations of the cotton prices on agricultural income. Although the Government's efforts have not sufficed to bring about a negative correlation between cotton prices and cereals they have at least worked in that direction.

It might be asked, finally, whether our simple unlagged least square regressions may not be biased due to interdependencies in the Egyptian economy. Through the demand for food, and as an element of costs, money wages might assist in determining agricultural prices and hence the value of agricultural output, at the same time as the output value is a determinant of money wages. I do not think that this is a serious source of error in the present case, however. After all the major agricultural prices have been determined either from abroad (through exports and imports) or through direct Government interference. Some interdependencies do of course make themselves felt. At given agricultural prices the wage level may affect the margin of cultivation and, accordingly, the product per man. With a sloping foreign demand curve for Egyptian cotton, the supply of Egyptian cotton on the world market affects the prices of cotton, and if the wage level affects the cotton production a relationship from wage rates to cotton prices is hereby established. For certain 'domestic' commodities like pulses and dates rural workers' demand may be sufficient to affect the prices, etc. But all these examples are probably of secondary importance.

## 4. Real Wages and Labour's Share in Agriculture, 1914-1961

In this section we shall analyse our data in a slightly different way, which, quite apart from the question of the 'true' wage theory, leads us to a discussion of two important phenomena: the share of wages in agricultural output value, and real agricultural wages. Looking back at equations (2) and (5), it will be seen that we can formulate our two theories as

$$(9) \qquad \frac{W_t}{(O/L)_t} = 1 \qquad \text{and}$$

$$(10) \qquad \frac{W_t}{(P_C)_t} = 1,$$

and the corresponding statistical hypotheses (multiplying
for the sake of convenience by 100) as

(11) $\quad \dfrac{100\,W_t}{(O/L)_t} = a + \beta t + u_t, \;\; Ea = 100, \; E\beta = 0, \; Eu = 0,$

and

(12) $\quad \dfrac{100W_t}{(Pc)_t} = a + \beta t + u_t, \;\; Ea = 100, \; E\beta = 0, \; Eu = 0.$

The estimated equations are

(11)* $\quad \dfrac{100W_t'}{(O/L)_t} = \begin{array}{c} 121.5 - 0.52\,t, \\ (8.6)\;(0.27) \end{array} \qquad \sigma = 15.13, \qquad$ and

(12)* $\quad \dfrac{100W_t'}{(Pc)_t} = \begin{array}{c} 108.9 + 0.62\,t, \\ (13.9)\;(0.43) \end{array} \qquad \sigma = 24.5$

The estimates together with a glance at Graph 3 show
immediately that the share of labour $(W_t/(O_t/L)_t = W_tL_t/O_t)$ is more constant over time than are the real
wages and this confirms our conclusions from the preceding
section.

In Graph 3 we have shown the development of the indexes of real wages, $W/P_C$, and the share of wages in the
value of output, $W/(O/L)$, together with indexes of the
cotton/cereals price ratio, and physical productivity of
labour.

The share of labour in gross output value does not show
any major change from before 1914 to the beginning of the
'sixties. There is a slight downward trend in the series
depicted in Graph 3. This trend is not statistically significant, however, and I do not think there is any reason for
considering it an established fact. First of all the share of
wages may have been relatively high in 1914 as compared
with the immediate pre-1914 years; the 1914 crop was
relatively bad and the prices temporarily depressed so
strongly,[30] and although money wages were probably relatively low in that year, it seems unlikely that they would
have followed the output-value fully (cf. the experience of
1961). Secondly, as mentioned earlier, a downward bias
makes itself felt in our index of output value from 1914 to
1939 due to the exclusion of fodder, fruit and vegetables, and
animal production for these years, and this bias may be
responsible for the relatively high share of labour from

1920 to 1937-39. Some authors, however, believe that the
Land Reforms of 1952 worsened the position of the remaining landless labourers by breaking up the big estates
and thereby diminishing the demand for outside labour
more than the supply. The persistent relatively low share
of labour after 1951 might be taken as an indication of this.
But, as already mentioned, statistically there is no significant
time trend.[31] We notice that the fluctuations around the
regression line show no systematic pattern.

Real wages seem on the other hand to follow a cyclical
pattern; real wages were high at the end of the 'twenties,
a trough during the 'thirties and World War II, and very
high around the Korean Boom. The period through the
'thirties and World War II was affected by the low physical
productivity from the end of the 'twenties till the end of the
forties, but seems also to have been influenced by the low
cotton/cereals price ratio for reasons already explained.
The development of real wages through 1929, 1933 and
1934 looks, however, a bit queer. As explained in the Statistical Appendix, the wage index for 1929 and 1934 may
(due to the method of building up the index) be too low.
With a correction in the upward direction the real wage
index might show a top in 1928 and thereafter a more
continuous fall to 1934, when real wages may have been
some 10-15 per cent below 1914. This is still, however, a
relatively modest fall, taking into account that the cotton/
cereals price ratio was about the same, but physical productivity was 20-30 per cent lower. Compared with the
pre-1914 'normal' real wages, the fall may have been bigger,
however; as already mentioned real wages in 1914 were
probably lower than in the immediate pre-1914 years due
to a relatively low productivity and a low cotton/cereals
price ratio that year. Real wages in the middle 'thirties
may therefore quite well have been some 20-30 per cent
lower than in the 'normal' pre-1914 years. Still the increase from 1934 to 1937-39 calls for an explanation. One
might perhaps also have expected a stronger fall in real
wages during World War II. The fall in real wages was
about 13 per cent. Physical productivity fell by almost
15 per cent to 1943, while the cotton/cereals price ratio fell
by some 10 per cent. One explanation is that our price
index does not measure the actual price increase (black

markets)[32]; another possibility is that the strong demand for unskilled labour from the Allied military forces operating in Egypt at that time contributed in keeping up money and real wages.

Finally, there is the question of possible trends in real wages. There is a slight upward (linear) trend, but it is statistically insignificant. Linear trends are not very interesting here, either, against the background of the development of the two main real wage determining factors: physical productivity and the cotton/cereals price ratio. The first one moved in a long swing downwards until the middle of World War II and from then on upwards. Today the level may be about the same as before World War I. The cotton/cereals price ratio has moved upwards in long swings and it needs a rather 'linear' mind to visualize a linear trend in this movement. Trend or no trend, it would seem as if the level of real wages around 1960 was somewhat above the pre-1914 level. 1960 was about 40 per cent above 1914 but taking into account the depressed level of 1914 (see above) the increase as compared with the pre-1914 'normal' level may only be some 20-30 per cent. Since physical productivity seems to be about the same, the increase is mainly to be explained by the improvement of the cotton/cereals price ratio, which in relation to 1914 is as much as 60 per cent, and in relation to the pre-1914 'normal' may be about 40 per cent.

## 5. WAGE DIFFERENTIALS IN EGYPTIAN VILLAGES

In the preceding sections we have tested our wage theories on the basis of time series of annual averages. We shall turn ourselves now to the wage differentials within the year, seasonal and otherwise, and see to what extent this kind of data can help us in the choice between wage theories.

In developed countries one may, as is well-known, find wage differentials which have their natural explanation in institutional or conventional circumstances; this is, for instance, sometimes the case with differentials between men's and women's wages. And trade unions do their best to influence the wage structure in most countries. On the other hand, wage differentials in developed countries can also to some extent be explained in terms of demand and supply, i.e. in terms of the marginal productivity theory. The concensus is that in developed countries market forces and institutional forces work together in determining wage differentials in a way which is perhaps not well understood. I know of no theory of wage differentials for rural workers in underdeveloped countries, but if the marginal productivity theory applies to underdeveloped economies there is no reason why we should not also here meet demand and supply induced wage differentials. Rural workers in Egypt are completely unorganized, but this should not prevent other institutions or conventions from exerting an influence on wage differentials, indeed, it would be strange if non-economic factors exerted no influence on wage formation in Egyptian villages. As already mentioned, the institutional (conventional) subsistence wage theory is unfortunately not very precise and concrete and it is not clear to what extent this kind of theory allows for the existence of wage differentials and if so, exactly which rural wage differentials should be expected in underdeveloped economies. All we can do therefore, is to look into the existing wage differentials in Egyptian agriculture and see if they can be explained by either of the two theories. Fortunately there now exists much statistical material on this problem in Egypt. It allows us to study wage differentials of four different types: seasonal, between men, women and children, geographically, and according to operations performed. In all cases it is a question of differentials for agricultural labourers which usually are classified as unskilled, although they have, of course, experience in performing agricultural operations.

Concerning the *seasonal differentials*, Graph 4 shows the relationship between seasonality of wage rates and the demand for labour on a monthly basis for men, women and children together. The series for wages is based on information communicated by the Ministry of Agriculture on the monthly averages of wages per day in 1950 and 1951. During 1950 and 1951 (the Korean Boom) there was a strong upward movement in agricultural wage rates. In order to isolate the seasonal movements a least squares regression line was therefore fitted to the (average) monthly figures for the two years and the (average) monthly deviations from this regression line were interpreted as the 'true' seasonal deviations from the average wage rate. Adding these

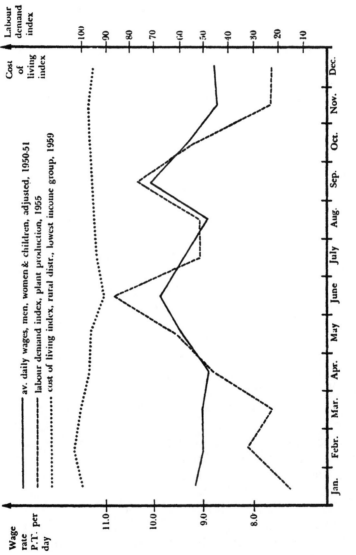

Graph 4

seasonal deviations to the actual average wage rate for 1950 and 1951 the monthly wage series in Graph 4 was obtained.[33] The index for labour demand was constructed on the basis of the monthly figures for labour requirements in plant production in 1955 as estimated by Hansen and El Tomy.[34] The labour requirements for plant production were estimated as the number of working days necessary per member of the *permanent* farm labour force. By measuring this number of days as a percentage of the total number of days in the month concerned the demand index was obtained.

The diagram shows clearly the two characteristic seasonal peaks in Egyptian agriculture, May-June and September. The demand index used here is based on labour requirements for plant production only and does not include work with the animals which is rather evenly distributed over the year, and work on cleaning and digging canals and drains which is concentrated in the slack winter season. There seems therefore to be little doubt that the seasonal variations of wages are fully explained by the seasonal variations in the demand for labour in relation to the supply.[35] With an unlimited supply of labour there should (presumably) be no seasonal variations in wages. Actually, it is a well-known observation that during the peaks there is regularly a shortage of labour in Egyptian agriculture. It might be asked, of course, whether the seasonal variations of wages are related to seasonal variations of the cost-of-living in accordance with our interpretation of the conventional subsistence wage theory. In the absence of more probing studies of the seasonal variations of prices in Egypt, a crude monthly index for 1959 was calculated with the same weights as the annual index. If anything, it shows a seasonal movement opposite to that of wages with a trough in June coinciding with one of the wage peaks, see Graph 4.[36]

The seasonal variations in wages are strong. The monthly averages on which Graph 4 is based show a difference of 17 per cent between the lowest and the highest monthly average. The monthly averages of Graph 4 which are overall, national figures including the whole country and lumping together men, women and children, hide the real strength of the seasonal movements. This comes out clearly in the weekly records of wages in certain villages collected for a

*TABLE 1*

Weekly Records of Wages in Three Egyptian Villages, 1964
PT (piasters) per day (hours worked per day almost constant)

| Date | Kilishan, Beheira | | | Abu El Gour, Gharbia | | | Bakour Abu Tig, Assiut | | |
|---|---|---|---|---|---|---|---|---|---|
| | Men | Women | Children | Men | Women | Children | Men | Women | Children |
| 8/6 | 20 | 10 | 6 | — | — | — | — | — | — |
| 15/6 | 22 | 10 | 7 | — | — | — | 20 | — | — |
| 22/6 | 22 | 10 | 6 | — | — | — | 21 | — | — |
| 29/6 | 22 | 10 | 6 | — | — | — | 20 | — | — |
| 6/7 | 20 | 7 | 6 | 12 | 8 | 6 | 18 | — | — |
| 13/7 | 20 | 7 | 6 | 12 | 8 | 6 | 20 | — | — |
| 20/7 | 20 | 7 | 6 | 12 | 8 | 6 | 18 | — | — |
| 27/7 | 20 | 7 | 6 | 12 | 8 | 6 | 18 | — | — |
| 3/8 | 15 | 7 | 6 | 12 | 8 | 6 | — | — | — |
| 10/8 | 15 | 7 | 6 | 12 | 8 | 6 | 18 | — | — |
| 17/8 | 15 | 7 | 6 | 14 | 9 | 7 | 17 | — | — |
| 24/8 | 15 | 7 | 6 | 14 | 14 | 7 | 15 | — | — |
| 31/8 | 15 | 7 | 6 | 14 | 14 | 7 | 17 | 16 | 12 |
| 7/9 | 12 | 8 | 8 | 24 | 15 | 15 | 18 | 16 | 14 |
| 14/9 | 12 | 12 | 12 | 24 | 15 | 15 | 20 | 18 | 15 |
| 21/9 | 15 | 15 | 15 | 24 | 15 | 15 | 22 | 20 | 16 |
| 28/9 | 20 | 20 | 20 | 23 | 13 | 13 | 30 | 20 | 18 |
| 5/10 | 18 | 18 | 18 | 16 | 10 | 8 | 30 | 20 | 18 |
| 12/10 | 15 | 15 | 15 | 16 | 10 | 8 | — | 13 | 12 |
| 19/10 | 15 | 12 | 12 | 14 | 8 | 6 | — | 12 | 12 |
| 26/10 | 15 | 12 | 12 | 14 | 8 | 6 | 15 | — | — |
| 2/11 | 20 | 15 | 10 | 15 | 8 | 5 | — | — | — |
| 9/11 | 20 | 15 | 10 | 15 | 8 | 5 | 15 | — | — |
| 16/11 | 20 | 15 | 10 | 13 | 7 | 5 | — | — | — |
| 23/11 | 20 | 15 | 10 | 13 | 7 | 5 | 15 | — | — |
| 30/11 | 20 | 15 | 10 | 12 | 6 | 5 | 15 | — | — |
| 7/12 | 12 | 6 | 6 | 10 | 8 | 5 | 15 | — | — |
| 14/12 | 12 | 6 | 6 | 10 | 5 | 5 | — | — | — |
| 21/12 | 12 | 6 | 6 | 8 | 5 | 5 | — | — | — |
| 28/12 | 12 | 6 | 6 | 8 | 5 | 5 | 15 | — | — |

Kindly communicated by Dr. Ulrich Planck.

*Note:* —indicates that no wages were recorded, which means that no 'contracts' were concluded on that day. When no employment is available the labour market simply disappears and it is impossible to say what the market wages are; they don't exist. The phenomenon is interesting and it has some bearing on the usual definitions of 'open unemployment': that there are workers who cannot find employment at the going market wages. There are no going market wages.

Survey of Rural Employment, jointly undertaken during 1964 and 1965 by the International Labour Organization (ILO), Geneva, and the Institute of National Planning (INP), Cairo. Table 1 contains such wage records for three villages, two in the Delta (Kilishan and Abu El Gour) and one in Upper Egypt (Bakour Abu Tig). The records available when this paper was written extend from the beginning of June to the end of December 1964. Concentrating for the moment on the seasonal differentials, we find from Table 1 that for men, the wages during the top season are three times those of the slack seasons in one of the villages, double in another, and in the third about 50 per cent higher. For women and children the seasonality is even stronger. The peak wages are up to three and a half times the wages in the slack seasons. The reason why these very strong seasonal variations are damped down in the national averages of Graph 4 is partly that men, women and children have different labour seasons (due to differences in the kind of work performed) partly because the seasons for the same crop differ by almost one month in the north and the south of the Nile valley. When all the information is collected by the Rural Employment Survey, it will be possible to study in detail (week by week, and village by village) the relationships between the level of employment and the wage rates, but there is no doubt that the strong seasonality in weekly data on the village level is closely related to the fluctuations in demand which the crop seasons give rise to.[37]

Turning to the *differentials between men's, women's and children's wages*, Table 2 shows the average per hour for the period June-November for four provinces.

TABLE 2

AVERAGE WAGES PER HOUR, JUNE-NOVEMBER 1964
(PT per hour)

|          | Men | Women | Children |
|----------|-----|-------|----------|
| Beheira  | 2.3 | 1.6   | 1.2      |
| Menoufia | 2.2 | 1.5   | 1.1      |
| Assiut   | 2.1 | 1.4   | 1.2      |
| Fayum    | 1.6 | 0.9   | 0.8      |

Kindly communicated by Dr. Ulrich Planck.

On average women's wage rates are about two thirds, and children's wage rates about half the wage rate of men, the proportions being the same in the Delta and in Upper Egypt.[38] These are the kinds of differentials on which one would particularly expect conventional and institutional factors to make themselves felt, but not even these differentials seem to be fully institutional (conventional). Looking back at the weekly records in Table 1, we find that in the village Kilishan, where on average the proportions are as above, in the peak season in September and the beginning of October, women and children earn the same daily wage as men do; from 14 September to 12 October the wage rates reported are identical for men, women and children with a strong seasonal movement from week to week. The same holds true for Albu El Gour 24-29th. August. And even in Bakour Abu Tig, a village in the south in a district which is notorious for its deep-rooted conservatism and where the traditional inferior social position of women is most obstinately preserved, there are weeks in September where the wages of women are comparable to those of men. September is the month of the cotton harvest — some weeks later in the Delta than in Upper Egypt — and represents in the majority of villages the most busy season with direct shortages of labour. The main operation performed is cotton picking, and for this work women, and especially children — with their small, rapid fingers and sharp eyes — are equally well, and perhaps even better, equipped than men. Equal work, equal pay ! In other seasons, when the operations performed require physical strength — ploughing, irrigation, threshing, etc. — men's wages are several times higher than those of women and children who may here only be useful for looking after the animals, etc. The stronger seasonality in the wages of women and children has a counterpart in the more strongly fluctuating requirements for women and child labour.[39]

Table 2 also gives some impression of the *geographical wage differentials*. In Upper Egypt the wage rates are on average some 20 per cent lower than in the Delta; this is clearly brought out in the Ministry of Agriculture figures in Table 3.

*TABLE 3*

|  | 1950-51 average | | 1960-61 average | |
|---|---|---|---|---|
| PT per day | Men | Children | Men | Children |
| Delta & Giza | 12.8 | 7.0 | 13.5 | 6.6 |
| Upper Egypt | 10.5 | 5.4 | 11.3 | 5.8 |

The geographical differentials seem to be closely associated with the density of agricultural population. In the Delta (incl. Giza) the cultivated area per person of the agricultural population is about 15 per cent higher than in Upper Egypt, and the difference in the crop area per person is somewhat larger.[40] This is, of course, what would be expected according to the marginal productivity theory. Other things play a rôle too, however, such as differences in fertility, irrigation, crop rotation systems, proximity to towns,[41] etc. (all this is fully consistent with a demand-and-supply theory of wages). As would be expected, the aggregation in Table 3 on the Delta and Giza and Upper Egypt, hides many of the geographical differentials. In 1945 the highest *provincial* average was almost double the lowest.[42] And on the village level the differences are even larger. Table 4 gives a snapshot of wage rates in 39 villages on the 22nd June 1964. For men the highest wage rate is 3 1/2 times the lowest. The differences here have, however, something to do also with the operations performed. The very high rates found in some of the Delta-provinces were paid for rice-planting, an operation which is fatiguing and has to be carried out very quickly at a certain point of time synchronized with the water supply.

6. THE STATUTORY MINIMUM WAGES

In 1942 the Government introduced statutory minimum wages for agricultural labourers at a level of 5 PT per day for men; in 1945 this minimum was raised to 10 PT. In connection with the Land Reforms of 1952 it was raised again to 18 PT for men, and a minimum of 10 PT for women was introduced. No attempt has been made, however, to enforce these minimum wages, and after the increase in 1952 it was openly admitted by the Government that agricultural wages would in practice be left to themselves.[43]

*TABLE 4*

<small>WAGES IN 39 EGYPTIAN VILLAGES ON THE 22 JUNE 1964 (PT PER DAY)</small>

|  | Men | Women | Children |
|---|---|---|---|
| *Beheira:* |  |  |  |
| Besentway | 20 | 18 | 10 |
| Abu El Kharaz | 35 | 25 | 12 |
| Kilishan | 22 | 10 | 6 |
| Safia | 25 | 10 | 7 |
| El Nigila | 18 | 12 | 8 |
| Mohalet Ahmed | 18 | 12 | 10 |
| Zawyet Sakr | 20 | 12 | 8 |
| *Gharbia:* |  |  |  |
| Kafr Kela | 25 | — | 10 |
| Kourama | 20 | — | 6 |
| Montamadia | 20 | 15 | 6 |
| Kiratia | 15 | 15 | 8 |
| Karanshu | 18 | 9 | 8 |
| Edsha | 20 | 12 | 9 |
| *Menoufia:* |  |  |  |
| El Mag | 25 | — | 6 |
| Kafr El Mouselha | 25 | — | 6 |
| Shatanouf | 18 | 13 | 12 |
| Helwasy | 15 | 8 | 6 |
| Kowesna El Mahatta | 25 | 15 | 10 |
| Mit Abu Shikha | 25 | 10 | 10 |
| Sirs Ellayan | 18 | — | 6 |
| Kafr Shoubra Zengi | 25 | — | 6 |
| *Assiut:* |  |  |  |
| Mousha | 14 | — | — |
| Awlad Ibrahim | 20 | — | — |
| Bany Mur | 18 | — | 6 |
| Nazhet Elassarah | 15 | — | — |
| Bakour Abu Tig | 21 | — | — |
| Nazhet Bakomr | 13½ | — | — |
| *Kena:* |  |  |  |
| El Ashraf El Keblia | 20 | — | 8 |
| Khouzam | 15 | — | — |
| Shanhour | 15 | — | 7 |
| Awlad Negm | 20 | — | — |
| *Fayum:* |  |  |  |
| Hawaret El Maktaa | 12 | — | 3 |
| El Azab | 10 | — | 4 |
| Abouksah | 12 | — | 5 |
| Kafr Abbud | 10 | — | 5 |
| Menyat Elhet | 10 | — | 4 |
| El Gaafra | 10 | — | 3 |
| Maasarat Sawi | 13 | — | 5 |
| Bablah | 10 | — | 3 |

Kindly communicated by Dr. Ulrich Planck.
Beheira, Gharbia and Menoufia are Delta provinces. The rest are Upper Egyptian provinces. As in Table 1, a dash indicates that no wages were reported.

The minimum wages have, however, been applied in public works and in certain public reclamation areas (not included in any of our statistics), and through the force of competition they may in this way have had an influence on wages paid in agriculture in general. But there is no reason to believe that the minimum wages have served as a norm for agricultural wages, or that they in other ways (than competition) have had any decisive impact on these wages.

## 7. CONCLUDING REMARKS

In social science it is seldom possible to reach very definite conclusions concerning the empirical validity of theoretical relationships. In particular this is true for theories concerned with growth in its early stages, for not only are the statistics available in underdeveloped countries scanty and of relatively low reliability, but also the theories themselves are often so woolly and vague that it is hard to know exactly which kind of facts could possibly refute them.

Nevertheless, it would seem that in the present case we do come out with something of an answer to our question. Both the development of agricultural wages over time and the general structure of wage differentials seem to be reasonably well explained, and also best explained, by the marginal productivity theory. The conventional subsistence wage theory in our specification can also to some extent explain the development over time of annual average money wages, but at least for those features of the structure of differentials, on which statistics have been presented here, the conventional subsistence wage theory has little to offer. Moreover, we do not at all need the conventional subsistence wage theory even to 'explain' those facts which actually to some extent support this theory, namely, the relatively high correlation between costs-of-living and money wages. This correlation follows, as we have seen, as a corollary of the marginal productivity theory itself. For an understanding of the data presented in this paper we simply do not need the conventional subsistence wage theory. Following the principle of Occam's razor, it would be tempting therefore to throw the conventional subsistence wage theory entirely overboard. Against this it would not be difficult to mobilize counter arguments.

First of all, the primary data on which our analysis is based are admittedly shaky. Only to a limited extent is the information collected under conditions which fulfil the basic requirements for the sampling of statistical data, and a purist might refuse to have anything to do with statistics like ours. I would like to point out, however, that with respect to the seasonal movements and the other differentials we are on quite firm statistical ground, and concerning the annual data, the results hinge mainly upon developments after 1937-39, from which time the quality of the data improves substantially.

Secondly, it might be argued that our statistical hypothesis (6), together with (6'), (8) and (12), does not do full justice to the conventional subsistence theory. The primitive version of the theory which we have used may be responsible for its lack of success. Although in our formulation it could to some extent explain the development of money wages over time, in general it is obvious that the hypothesis of a constant real wage, is a very poor one indeed. With annual real wages fluctuating as strongly as they actually have done — with an increase by more than half from 1914 to 1928, then a fall to less than the half until 1934, and thereafter more than doubling up till 1951 — and with daily wages within the year fluctuating by some 2-300 per cent, constancy of real wages seems to be a ridiculous assumption. And where exactly within this wide range of actually obtained real wage levels is the subsistence level? The proponents of the conventional subsistence wage theory have, however, usually something much more complicated in mind than just a constant real wage. This is quite clear when they talk about a 'historically determined' subsistence level. The problem is, how exactly does 'history' determine the level, and here we are left without much guidance.[44] Our primitive interpretation is based on a simplification made by two well-known authors in the field and if the proponents of the conventional subsistence wage theory want to have other, more sophisticated versions considered,[45] it is up to them to formulate their theory in such a way that it becomes empirically meaningful.

Thirdly, and in this I would agree fully, it might be said that the statistical data dealt with here are limited in scope and that data on other aspects of the wage problem might crop up where the marginal productivity theory would not suffice. In particular it could be expected that in a more detailed study of the wage structure, traditional demand and supply theory would prove insufficient. It would be strange if in such a study one would not have to have resort to conventional, institutional and sociological factors. But in this respect wage formation in Egyptian agriculture would not differ in principle from wage formation in developed countries although, of course, the concrete conventions, institutions and sociological factors may be very different in Egypt, and, say, England.

Finally, it might be argued that Egypt is a special case and may be the exception rather than the rule. Personally I feel that in development all cases are exceptions from a non-existent rule and there is no reason why Egypt should not be a special case, too, among all the others. Be this as it may, there is no doubt that development in Egypt exhibits some peculiar features which fit badly into the models of development constructed by Lewis and other proponents of the conventional subsistence wage theory. Most probably Egypt has never been overpopulated in the sense that the marginal (or, rather, differential) product of labour in agriculture is zero. It is the assumption of zero (or very low) marginal productivity which rules out the marginal productivity wage theory and calls for another kind of wage theory. The marginal product of labour in Egyptian agriculture is very low, but it is high enough to permit labourers to survive. In the old feudal times of the Mamelukes there were continuous complaints about shortage of labour in Egypt and one reads always about difficulties in cultivating all the cultivable land at that time. If anything, the labour shortage increased when in the first half of the 19th century a great extension of the perennial irrigation system was undertaken by the Government; quite apart from the work on digging the new deep canals, these canals required for their annual cleaning very large quantities of labour obtained through calling out the corvé. Curiously enough, it was a big capital investment — the Delta Barrage — which permitted the abolition of the corvé (1892) and thus signalized the final break-down of feudalism and the victory of capitalism in Egyptian agriculture. The barrage investments were extremely labour saving — through di-

minishing the annual cleaning work and the work necessary
for lifting water from the canals to the fields.

Although the increased crop area must have absorbed a
good deal of labour, and a good deal of the benefits from
these investments were handed over to labour through the
abolition of the corvé and the introduction of hired labour
for the remaining, very reduced cleaning work,[46] it seems
quite likely that the net effect was an easier labour market.

During the following decennia population increased
somewhat, and when we approach World War I complaints
about overpopulation began to be heard. But this is exactly
the point of time at which our study begins and when it
seems that agricultural money wages were governed by the
value of marginal productivity. This means again that
there was no overpopulation in the above-mentioned
special sense.[47] It was only after a period of almost fifty
years of capitalistic agriculture (technically primitive and
with some feudal remnants, of course, in particular widespread share cropping) propelled by Government investments
and foreign trade, and with wages governed by the value of
marginal productivity, that industrialization in Egypt finally
began. And when industrialization started in the 'thirties
it was against the background of a strong fall in agricultural
terms of trade, a strong fall in the cotton/cereals price ratio,
a strong fall in agricultural real wages, and a substantial
decrease in the cultivated area, all of which created a
surplus of labour and capital moving to the towns to be
available for industrialization and other non-agricultural
activities. With the agricultural labour force virtually unchanged since the middle of the 'thirties, the whole increase
in the economically active population has been available
for urban developments. These must, on the other hand,
have been able by and large to absorb the population increase at a higher real wage than could be obtained by an
agricultural labourer. How otherwise would real wages in
agriculture have been able to double between the 'thirties
and 1960 ?

All this obviously bears very little resemblance to the
Lewis model of unlimited supply of labour. Yet Lewis
himself insisted that unlimited supply of labour 'is obviously
the relevant assumption for the economies of Egypt, of
India, or of Jamaica.'[48] I do not know what evidence Lewis

had at his disposal for India and Jamaica. For Egypt it is pretty clear that the key to understanding the abundant supply of labour to industry since the 'thirties is neither Keynes nor Lewis, but rather neo-classical price mechanisms and population growth. I do not say this in order to belittle the importance of Lewis' model; it may be relevant in other parts of the world. But for the text-book case of Egypt available facts do not support it.

[1] R. Solow, 'A Contribution to the Theory of Economic Growth,' *Quarterly Journal of Economics*, 1956.

[2] See e.g. S. C. Tsiang, 'A Model of Economic Growth in Rostovian Stages,' *Econometrica*, 1964, p. 621.

[3] W. A. Lewis, 'Economic Development with Unlimited Supplies of Labour,' *The Manchester School*, 1954, here quoted from the reprint in B. Okun & R. W. Richardson, Ed., *Studies in Economic Development*, New York 1961. See also the penetrating analysis of Nicholas Georgescu-Roegen, 'Economic Theory and Agrarian Economics,' *Oxford Economic Papers*, 1960.

[4] Lewis, *op. cit.*, p. 281.

[5] *Ibid.*, p. 281.

[6] *Ibid.*, p. 284.

[7] G. Ranis & C. H. Fei, 'A Theory of Economic Development, *The American Economic Review*, 1961.

[8] Equation (3) holds even if we assume that the production function is dependent upon time according to the specification $f = g(t) La...$

Let it be added that the production functions which have been estimated on time series statistics from Egyptian agriculture have all of them, so far as I know, actually been of the Cobb-Douglas type and they show no significant influence of time, see M. M. El Imam, 'A Production Function for Egyptian Agricuture 1913-55,' *Memo. No. 259*, INP, Cairo 1962, Hanaa Kheir El Din, 'The Cotton Production Function in the UAR and its Relation to Technical Progress and to Disguised Unemployment,' *Memo. No 370*, INP, Cairo 1963, and Bent Hansen, 'Cotton vs. Grain: On the Optimal Allocation of Agricultural Land,' *Agricultural Research Papers*, Seminar on Economics of Industrialization of Cotton, Ministry of Scientific Research, Cairo 1964. That time does not show any significant influence does not necessarily mean that no technical progress has taken place in Egyptian agriculture since 1914 but rather that technical progress has been 'embodied' (in Solow's sense) in the factor fertilizer which is explicitly included in the production functions estimated.

On a cross-sectional basis linear functions have been applied, see Saad El Hanafy, 'Technical and Economical Study for the Optimum Utilization of the Underground Water', submitted to Regional Planning Project of Aswan.

[9] Georgescu-Roegen, *op. cit.*, p. 17, speaks about a 'minimum standard of living' which is supposed to be 'historically determined, and consequently susceptible of being changed by economic policy.'

[10] See A. N. Poliak, *Feudalism in Egypt, Syria, Palestine and the Lebanon, 1250-1900*, London 1939.

[11] Actually the introduction of private ownership in land in Egypt was a gradual process which had its beginning some fifty years earlier, but 1880 is the year when most landowners had obtained full ownership rights, see

G. Baer, *A History of Landownership in Egypt 1800-1950*, London 1962, p. 11. The general corvé was definitely abolished in 1892; before 1892 it is hardly possible to talk about a market for agricultural labour.

[12] This idyllic state seems to play something of the same rôle in modern growth theory as Robinson Crusoe played for early utility theory.

[13] Observe that in (2) we divide by the total labour force, L, including landless labourers.

[14] Colin Clark & M. R. Haswell, *The Economics of Subsistence Agriculture*, London 1964. Chap. VII.

[15] If Fei & Ranis, *op. cit.*, had not already used the word 'commercialized' in another meaning (see above), I would have preferred this term.

[16] Payment in kind occurs frequently, but payment in cash is more usual nowadays. Earlier, payment in kind of course dominated, but it is difficult to say exactly when the balance shifted in favour of cash payment, since this has been a gradual process. M. A. Lambert, 'Les salariés dans l'entreprise agricole égyptienne,' *L'Égypte Contemporaine*, 1943, mentions that at that time there was a strong tendency to replace payment in kind by cash payment. In the beginning of the period 1914-61, which we shall study, payment in kind may therefore quite well have been dominant. No information is available about the size and developments of payments in kind, however.

[17] This is the only year for which systematic information about household expenditure for the lowest income brackets in rural districts is available. Before and during World War II the Fellah Department collected information about expenditures of cultivators, but to judge from the size of total expenditures the information pertains to average cultivators with a standard far above that of the labourers, see M. A. Anis, 'A Study in the National Income of Egypt,' *L'Egypte Contemporaine* 1950, p. 756. The same holds true for the information given by W. Cleland, *The Population Problem in Egypt*, Lancaster, Penn., 1936, p. 119.

[18] See e.g., L. R. Klein, *An Econometric Model of the United Kingdom*, 1961, pp. 99, and 114f.

[19] The sum of all $\beta$'s should be equal to one.

[20] A priori this would also seem to be the appropriate price to use in discussions of the real wages of rural labourers. The reason why producers' average prices in certain years deviate seriously from the wholesale market prices is, *inter alia*, that the Government bought part of the crop at fixed support prices, higher or lower than the market prices. When labourers buy directly from farmers the prices charged may be supposed to follow the market prices rather than the Government's buying prices. It may be added here that although the wage data for the earlier years are rather shaky, the weakest part of the primary information on which this study is based is probably the price data behind the estimates of the output values.

[21] Actually the values of $\beta$ in (4) * and (4') * are likely to be downward biased. If the 'true' relationship is between wages and 'normal' or expected output per man, our independent variable in these equations, which is actual output per man, is subject to random errors of measurement and this may involve a downward bias in the estimates. I am indebted to Professor Griliches for this point.

[22] While $\Delta(O/L)_t$ is $(O/L)_t - (O/L)_{t-\tau}$, $\Delta(O/L)_{t-1})$ is defined as $(O/L)_{t-1} - (O/L)_{t-\tau-1}$, etc.

[23] Since the maize price estimates were clearly inferior in the other cases they were not repeated on the lagged differences.

[24] Due to the long intervals between some of the original observations, the unlagged and lagged first differences are in most cases overlapping, and this gives of course rise to a high degree of correlation.

[25] See note 21.

[26] Disregarding the exceptionally bad crop year 1961, productivity at the beginning of the 'sixties was about 10 per cent above 1914. Noting that 1914 was also a relatively bad crop year, labour productivity now is therefore practically the same as before 1914.

[27] The weight of maize in the cost-of-living index is 0.45.

[28] Indirectly the cotton prices ought of course to appear in the cost-of-living index, namely through the prices of cotton fabrics. Textiles, however, only occupy 3 per cent of the budget of the lowest income bracket in rural districts and no price information extending back to 1914 was available. This item was therefore left out of the cost-of-living index.

[29] It is important to notice that these special 'terms of trade' — cotton is an export crop, cereals on balance now an import crop — have improved a good deal compared with the pre-World War I normal, and were in 1960 about the same as in the 'twenties and much higher than in the 'thirties. From the agricultural labourers' point of view these are the terms of trade which matter.

[30] In connection with the outbreak of World War I the cotton prices fell by about one third.

[31] If it had been known in advance that the marginal productivity theory was applicable in Egyptian agriculture, the constancy in labour's share might have been taken to support a hypothesis of a constant-share production function. We have proceded the other way, however, taking for granted that the production function was of the constant-share type and using this to test the marginal productivity theory of wages. The production function has then to be based on other evidence. I hope in the near future to be able to publish a paper on the distributive shares in Egyptian Agriculture 1897-1961.

[32] M. A. Anis, *op. cit.*, p. 756.

[33] The method applied may have tilted the wage curve somewhat clockwise. But with only two full years available it is impossible to devise any fully satisfactory method of calculating the seasonal movements.

[34] Bent Hansen & Mona El Tomy, 'The Seasonal Employment Profile in Egyptian Agriculture,' *Journal of Development Studies*, July, 1965. Vol. I, no. 4.

[35] In Graph 4 men, women and children are grouped together. It should be mentioned that separate graphs for men and women and children revealed different peaks both in wages and labour for these two categories of labour. The timing of the peaks in wages and in labour requirements were, however, not so perfectly synchronized for the two individual groups as is the case in Graph 4. I feel that this has to do with the assumptions behind the distribution of work (in particular work related to rice planting) between men and women & children, see Hansen & El Tomy, *op. cit.*, p. 339. These assumptions are rather arbitrary and may not correspond well to reality. Since the labour requirement estimates for men, women and children together avoid all such assumptions I have found it better therefore to work on the totals only.

[36] The ordinary, official cost-of-living index shows the same seasonal pattern as the special cost-of-living index used here.

[37] After this article was written some of the detailed and reliable material from the Rural Employment Survey has become available. A series of weekly average wages for labourers (men) and a series for actual employment (hours worked per 8 day period) for all men in rural areas, collected from a sample of villages June 1964 to July 1965, and an inflationary trend, showed a correlation coefficient of 0.923 and a highly significant influence of actual employment on wages, the employment elasticity of money wages being around two-thirds. See Bent Hansen, Atef Sedki and Yousry Moustafa, *Wages, Income and Consumption in Rural Areas*, Report of Committee D,

Employment Problems in Rural Areas, U.A.R., Institute of National Planning, Cairo, Dec. 1965, p. 31 and Graphs 5, 6 and 7.

[38] The proportions seem to have been the same over the last fifty years.

[39] See Hansen & El Tomy, *op. cit.*

[40] A more systematic study in this respect will have to wait until the tabulations of the ILO-INP survey are ready. A tentative attempt to correlate average wages for men for the period June-November 1964 with value of crop output per man in 1960 for 18 Markazes (local districts) did not lead to any results. To explain the local geographical differentials a detailed study of a variety of causal factors is obviously needed.

[41] According to the Surveys of the Fellah Department (Anis, *op. cit.*) of 1943 and 1945, the province of Giza, bordering Cairo to the South and West had the highest agricultural wages, about 30 and 50 per cent above the average for all provinces. Kaliyubia, bordering Cairo to the North, came second.

[42] Survey of Fellah Department, see Anis, *op. cit.*

[43] Sayed Marei, *UAR Agriculture Enters a New Age. An Interpretative Survey*, Cairo, 1960, p. 59: 'it was decided to leave the fixing of agricultural wages subject to the normal economic laws of supply and demand.'

[44] From our time series analysis it would seem as if there may be a distributed lag between output per man and money wages, and in a sense this means, of course, a 'historical' determination. But I do not think that it is this kind of short term lag which the conventional subsistence theorists have in mind.

[45] Fei and Ranis, *op. cit.*, suggest a slight refinement of the conventional subsistence theory, namely that the conventional real wage level is related over time to actual average physical productivity. With a Cobb-Douglas function and with the same composition of agricultural output and consumption, the conventional subsistence wage theory would then become identical with the marginal productivity theory. At most there could be a difference in the absolute level of wages with the two theories and the statistical material studied here would not suffice for distinguishing between them. Actually, however, there is a fundamental difference in the composition of output and consumption in our case, due to the already described special rôle played by cotton, and we are therefore also able to test this particular version of the conventional subsistence wage theory. It turns out that the correlation, 0.514, between real wages and physical product per man, measured on the original observations, is not significant at the 5 per cent level (on the first differences there is no correlation at all), and we can therefore write off this specification of the subsistence wage theory.

Let me add also that although we have here only studied the proportionality of wages and value of marginal product there is evidence also for *absolute equality* of money wages and value of marginal product. Production function studies, (see note 1), show a Cobb-Douglas coefficient of labour of about 0.3. The value of output per man per year was in 1960 about £120. and the value of the marginal product should accordingly be about £35, This is about the annual income which a fully employed average labourer would have. Taking into account the existence of some open unemployment, the value of the marginal annual product seems perhaps even to be somewhat above the average annual wages, see H. K. El Din, *op. cit.* Harry T. Oshima, 'Underemployment in Backward Countries. An Empirical Comment,' *Journal of Political Economy*, 1958, has suggested that due to market imperfections this may be the situation in underdeveloped countries rather than the opposite with wages exceeding the value of the marginal product.

[46] The Earl of Cromer, *Modern Egypt*, London 1908, Part II, Ch. L, and W. Wilcocks, *Egyptian Irrigation*, 2nd Ed.. London & New York 1899, Ch. XIII ; see also Sir W. Wilcocks & S. J. Craig, *Egyptian Irrigation*, 3rd Ed., London and New York, 1913, Vol. II, Ch. XV.

[17] Egypt is a classical case of that confusion of seasonal underemployment and disguised unemployment which Harry K. Oshima, *op. cit.* has argued so convincingly against. See also T. W. Schultz, *Transforming Traditional Agriculture*, 1964, Ch. 4, and Colin Clark & M. R. Haswell, *op. cit.*, Ch. VII. In spite of the 'continuous cropping' in Egyptian agriculture there are very strong seasonal fluctuations in the demand for labour which reconciles the existence of large scale underemployment and a positive marginal productivity (measured on an annual basis) of labour in agriculture.

[18] Lewis, *op. cit.*, p. 401.

## STATISTICAL APPENDIX

a. *The index of the value of marginal productivity of labour,* $(O/L)$.—

Table I shows the calculation of the index of the value of marginal productivity of labour used in estimating (4) and (4'). In order to isolate the price component I have calculated for all years a separate index for the marginal physical productivity of labour which, through multiplication by a price index, leads up to the marginal value productivity. The index for physical marginal productivity of labour was obtained through dividing a production (output) index by a labour force index.

The agricultural production index, Table II, col. (10) and Table I, col. (1), was spliced together from a series for production of field crops (incl. onions, but excl. fodder, other vegetables and fruit) calculated by Dr. M. M. El Imam, 'A Production Function for Egyptian Agriculture 1913-55,' *Memo. No. 259*, INP, Cairo 1962, and an index for total agricultural output (incl. vegetables, fruits, animal production and fodder) 1935-39 and 1948-61 calculated by the Department of Statistics and Census, Cairo (communicated by the former General Director Abdel Fatah Farah). Dr. El Imam's volume index is a chained 'ideal' Fisher index, while the Department of Statistics and Census' index is a fixed weight index with weights from 1935-39. For the years 1914-39 El Imam's index was used and for the rest of the period the Department of Statistics' index which for the present purpose is preferable to El Imam's index. From the beginning of World War II the downward bias in El Imam's index— due to the exclusion of fruit and vegetables and animal production — begins to become serious.[1] For the years during World War II, I used an estimate of agricultural output (crops and animal production) 1940-45 at fixed 1939 prices, made by M. Anis, and for 1946 and 47 a F.A.O. index.[2]

The labour force index, col. (2), was taken over from Dr. El Imam, *op. cit.* El Imam calculated this index starting out from the population census figures for 1907, 1917, 1927, 1937 and 1947 for the total number of persons economically active in agriculture. The figures for years outside the census he obtained through interpolation on the basis of the ratio between urban and rural population as estimated from the registration statistics. On the basis of the 1960-census we revised El Imam's figures from 1948 and brought them up to 1960. It was assumed that the figure for 1960 applies to 1961 as well.

*TABLE 1*

| Year | Agricultural production index | Labour force index | Marginal productivity of labour index | Agricultural prices index | Value of marginal product of labour index | Price of Maize index | Ratio of cotton price to cereals price index | Cost-of-living index |
|---|---|---|---|---|---|---|---|---|
| | | | | | (O/L) | $P_M$ | | $P_C$ |
| | (1) | (2) | (3) = (1)/(2) | (4) | (5) = (3)/(4) | (6) | (7) | (8) |
| 1914 | 100 | 100 | 100 | 100 | 100 | 100 | 100 | 100 |
| 20 | 99.5 | 113.0 | 88.1 | 228.2 | 201.0 | 242 | 159 | 236 |
| 28 | 123.8 | 151.8 | 81.6 | 156.4 | 127.6 | 89 | 157 | 98 |
| 29 | 133.6 | 155.2 | 86.1 | 125.8 | 108.3 | 92 | 135 | 94 |
| 33 | 125.5 | 166.7 | 75.3 | 87.5 | 65.9 | 48 | 113 | 58 |
| 34 | 117.5 | 167.2 | 70.3 | 107.7 | 75.7 | 93 | 93 | 82 |
| 37-39 | 138.3 | 171.6 | 80.6 | 98.0 | 79.0 | 92 | 98 | 86 |
| 41 | 138.3 | 173.3 | 79.8 | 124.6 | 99.4 | 117 | 90 | 114 |
| 43 | 120.3 | 173.8 | 69.2 | 243.9 | 168.8 | 204 | 89 | 205 |
| 45 | 130.0 | 173.7 | 74.8 | 321.7 | 240.6 | 227 | 92 | 225 |
| 50 | 149.4 | 173.7 | 86.0 | 450.6 | 387.5 | 202 | 265 | 227 |
| 51 | 145.2 | 174.2 | 83.4 | 463.4 | 386.5 | 202 | 285 | 226 |
| 55 | 164.6 | 174.9 | 94.1 | 364.3 | 342.8 | 248 | 152 | 253 |
| 56 | 170.1 | 174.9 | 97.2 | 395.2 | 384.1 | 324 | 163 | 294 |
| 59 | 188.1 | 174.4 | 107.9 | 395.2 | 426.4 | 294 | 163 | 287 |
| 60 | 196.4 | 174.5 | 112.5 | 402.6 | 452.9 | 294 | — | 290 |
| 61 | 170.1 | 174.5 | 97.5 | 409.0 | 398.8 | 294 | — | 308 |

The agricultural prices index, col. (4), was spliced together from Dr. El Imam's price index (*op. cit.*) which was used from 1914 to 1939, and for 1939-60 an implicit price index obtained in Table II through dividing an index of the value of output (col. (9) ) by the production index of col. (10), (see Table II). El Imam's price index is a chained 'ideal' Fisher index corresponding to his production index.

The way in which the index for the value of output and the price index was derived for the period 1939-61 follows from Table II. Four different series for the value of output had to be used, one for 1937 to 1945 estimated by M. A. Anis, *op. cit.*, a second on gross value added (not output) from 1945 to 1954 estimated by S.H. Abdel Rahman, *A Survey of Foreign Trade in Egypt in the Post-War Period*, unpubl. doct. thesis, Cairo University, Faculty of Commerce, 1960, a third for the years from 1947 estimated by the Ministry of Agriculture (see *Agricultural Economics*, Monthly Review, published by the Ministry of Agriculture, 1961) and a fourth for the years 1950-60 estimated by the Department of Statistics (see *National*

TABLE II

| | Anis,[1] gross value of output £ E 000 (1) | Index (2) | Abdel Rahman[2] value added £ E mill (3) | Index (4) | Min. of Agriculture,[3] Gross value of output £ E mill (5) | Index (6) | Dept of Statistics,[4] Gross value of output £ E mill (7) | Index (8) | Index of value of output (9) | Index of volume of output[6] (10) | Index of agricultural output Prices (11) |
|---|---|---|---|---|---|---|---|---|---|---|---|
| 1937 | 91.342 | 88.4 | | | | | | | 88 | 100 | 92 |
| 38 | 91.160 | 88.2 | | | | | | | 88 } 92 | | |
| 39 | 103.354 | 100 | | | | | | | 100 ) | 104 | 91 |
| 1910 | 98.629 | 95.4 | | | | | | | 95 | 100 | 117 |
| 41 | 120.480 | 116.6 | | | | | | | 117 | 91 | 196 |
| 42 | 183.548 | 177.6 | | | | | | | 178 | 87 | 229 |
| 43 | 205.751 | 199.1 | | | | | | | 199 | 91 | 268 |
| 44 | 252.067 | 243.9 | | | | | | | 244 | 91 | 302 |
| 1945 | 293.490 | 284.0 | 215.6 | 100 | | | | | 281 | 84 | 260 |
| 46 | | | 189.8 | 88.1 | 283 | 100 | | | 250 | (96) | 263 |
| 47 | | | 203.4 | 94.4 | 330 | 116.6 | | | 268 | (98) | 281 |
| 48 | | | | | 403 | 142.4 | | | 312 | 111 | 350 |
| 49 | | | | | 483 | 170.7 | | | 382 | 109 | 423 |
| 1950 | | | | | | | 473 | 100 | 457 | 108 | 435 |
| 51 | | | | | | | 473 | 100.0 | 457 | 105 | 351 |
| 52 | | | | | | | 399 | 84.4 | 386 | 110 | 341 |
| 53 | | | | | | | 385 | 81.4 | 372 | 109 | 332 |
| 54 | | | | | | | 416 | 87.9 | 402 | 121 | 342 |
| 1955 | | | | | | | 421 | 89.0 | 407 | 119 | 371 |
| 56 | | | | | | | 472 | 99.8 | 456 | 123 | 362 |
| 57 | | | | | | | 487 | 103.0 | 471 | 130 | 363 |
| 58 | | | | | | | 492 | 104.0 | 475 | 131 | 371 |
| 59 | | | | | | | 522 | 110.4 | 505 | 136 | 378 |
| 1960 | | | | | | | 556 | 117.5 | 537 | 142 | 384[5] |
| 61 | | | | | | | | | 472[5] | 123[5] | |

[1] M. A. Anis, 'A Study of the National Income of Egypt,' *L'Egypte Contemporaine*, 1950, p. 740 and 741.

[2] S. H. Abdel Rahman, *A Survey of Foreign Trade in Egypt in the Post-War Period*, unpubl. doct. thesis, Cairo 1960.

[3] *Agricultural Economics*, Ministry of Agriculture, Cairo 1961.

[4] *National Income from Agricultural Sector*, Dept. of Statistics and Census, Cairo, no year.

[5] Preliminary figures. After this study was finished 'provisional' figures for 1961 have become available. They are for col. (7)–(11) resp.: 513, 108, 494, 123 and 401. With this correction the correlation between W and O/I would improve slightly.

[6] 1937/39 and 1948 to 1961: Dept. of Statistics and Census index. 1940 to 1945 are based on Anis's estimates of plant and animal production at fixed 1939-prices, Anis, *op. cit.*, 1946 and 1947 are based on the FAO production index, see FAO, *Production Yearbook*.

*Income from Agricultural Sector*, 1950-60, Cairo (no year) ). Considering, the quality of the estimates it was decided to use the Department of Statistics series as much as possible i.e. for the years 1950-61. Since Abdel Rahman's series is a gross value added series rather than a value of output series, it was on the other hand decided to use his series as little as possible. This led to an index consisting of four links: Anis from 1937 to 1945, Abdel Rahman from 1945 to 1947, the Ministry of Agriculture from 1947 to 1950, and the Department of Statistics for the remaining years. Division by the volume index, col. (10), led to the implicit price index. For 1961 only preliminary figures for quantity and price index were available.

b. *The Maize Price*, $P_M$.

In Table I, col. (6) an index of the maize price is included. The index is based on the prices at the Cairo cereals wholesale market at Rod El Farag for the quality Nab El Gamal, Zawati, which is the price used in the cost-of-living index; see *Annuaire Statistique* 1960-61, p. 388 and corresponding tables for earlier years.

c. *The Cotton/Cereals Prices Ratio.*

In Table I, col. (7) has also been added an index of the ratio between the average cotton price (*Annuaire Statistique*, 1960-61, Tableau XI, p. 252 and corresponding tables for earlier years) and a chained Laspeyres' index of cereals prices calculated on the basis of price information collected from *Annuaire Statistique* 1960-61, Tableau V, p. 193 and corresponding tables for earlier years, and with weights from 1913 (for 1914-38) and from 1951/52 (for 1939-59). The calendar year figures are averages of crop-year figures. See Bent Hansen, 'Cotton VS. Grain: On the Optimum Allocation of Agricultural Land,' *Agricultural Research Papers*, Ministry of Scientific Research, Cairo 1964.

d. *The Wage Index, W.*

For the years 1937-39 (av), 1950, 1951, 1959, 1960 and 1961 the Ministry of Agriculture has made estimates of agricultural wages. For 1937-39 only a rough estimate of the average for the whole country (men and children, resp.) was available, but for the years 1950 and 1951 (together with part of 1952) the Ministry has compiled monthly estimates with break-downs on men and children, and on Lower, Middle and Upper Egypt. For the years 1959-61 estimates have only been made for four seasons but with break-downs as above. These estimates are not based on systematic sampling but represent averages of wages reported to the Ministry by its inspectors. Nevertheless, they probably give a good picture of the wage level and its changes. Special Government surveys (quoted by C. Issawi, *Egypt in Revolution*, London, 1963, p. 155), were made in 1955 for the province Daqahlia and in 1956 for Minia. The figures obtained in these surveys were chained to the Ministry of Agriculture series via the averages from 1950 and 1951 for the Delta & Giza and Beni-Sueif, Fayum & Minia, resp.; this chaining is a bit doubtful.

For the years 1937-39, 1941, 1943 and 1945 the Fellah Department of the Ministry of Social Affairs made wage surveys, here quoted from M. A. Anis, *op. cit.*, p. 752. These estimates are based on reports from social workers. They are not based on systematic sampling, but the reports were believed to cover the whole country fairly well.

For the years 1914, 1920, 1928, 1933, 1939 and for the end of 1942 estimates of the average daily wages have been published by M. A. Lambert, 'Les salariés dans l'entreprise agricole égyptienne,' *L'Égypte Contemporaine*, 1943. It is not clear whether Lambert's figures pertain to men only or are an average for men, women and children (Lambert speaks about 'ouvriers à la journée'). Also he does not give any information about the methods of estimation, but obviously it is not a question of systematic sampling.[3] Lambert presents figures for the Delta and Upper Egypt separately; I have taken a simple average of these figures which have been chained to the Ministry of Agriculture figures and Fellah Department figures in 1939.

Finally, a set of figures for 1912, 1929 and 1934 and for the Delta only has been published by C. Issawi, *Egypt. An Economic and Social Study*, London 1946, p. 77, who gives a general reference to Abdel Wahab Pasha, *Memorandum on a Stable Cotton Policy*, Government Press, Cairo 1930, and *Rapport de la Sous-commission sur les moyens de réduire les frais de production*, Government Press, Cairo 1936. On Abdel Wahab Pasha's Memorandum (the full title of which is: *Memorandum on the bases of a stable Cotton Policy; submitted to H. E. the Minister of Finance*) the wage figures are from 1912 and 1929 and pertain to 'fully grown labourers on certain state domains.' The figures of Upper Egypt are based on 'statements supplied by dairas which keep regular accounts,' *op. cit.* p. 10. Concerning the *Rapport* I have only been able to find a report entitled *Rapport de la sous-commission de l'agriculture du conseil économique chargé de l'études des moyens de réduire les frais de production et d'écoulement du cotton et des autres produits agricoles*, le Caire, Imprimerie National, Boulac 1936, and this report explicitly abstains from discussing wages. For 1934 I have therefore had to take over the figures quoted by Issawi without being able to control the quality of the information behind them. I have then made the assumption that the wage rate was unchanged from 1912 to 1914.[4] It is clear that the wage estimates from 1937-39 onwards are of a much better quality than those for earlier years.

*TABLE III*

| Year | PT per day Abdel Wahab Pasha, men[1] | | Lambert Rapport, total Egypt[2] | Fellah Dept. Ministry of Social Affairs[3] Total Egypt | | | | Ministry of Agriculture[4] | | | | | Other Governm. Surveys[5] | | Index |
|---|---|---|---|---|---|---|---|---|---|---|---|---|---|---|---|
| | Delta | U.Egypt | | Men | Women | Children | Average[6] | Men Delta & Giza | Men Beni-S., Fayum, Minia | Men Total Egypt | Childr. Total Egypt | Average[7] | Daqhalia (Delta) Men | Minia Men | |
| 1912 | 4.7. | | | | | | | | | | | | | | 100 |
| 14 | (4.7) | 3.8[8] | 2.6 | | | | | | | | | | | | 258 |
| 20 | | | 6.7 | | | | | | | | | | | | 161 |
| 28 | | | 4.2 | | | | | | | | | | | | 117 |
| 29 | 5.5 | 4.5 | | | | | | | | | | | | | 85 |
| 33 | | | 2.2 | | | | | | | | | | | | 58 |
| 34 | 2.7 | | | | | | | | | | | | | | |
| 37–39 | | | 2.5 | 3.0 | 2.0 | 1.5 | 2.5 | | | 3.0 | 1.5 | 2.4 | | | 96 |
| 41 | | | | 3.6 | 2.4 | 1.8 | 3.0 | | | | | | | | 115 |
| 43 | | | 5.0 | 6.3 | 3.9 | 3.0 | 5.2 | | | | | | | | 200 |
| 45 | | | | 9.3 | 5.7 | 4.6 | 7.6 | | | | | | | | 292 |
| 50 | | | | | | | | 12.0 | 9.0 | 9.7 | 6.0 | 8.2 | | | 328 |
| 51 | | | | | | | | 13.6 | 10.5 | 12.6 | 7.5 | 10.6 | | | 424 |
| 55 | | | | | | | | | | | | | 10 | | 294 |
| 56 | | | | | | | | | | | | | | 10 | 386 |
| 59 | | | | | | | | | | 12.5 | 6.4 | 10.1 | | | 404 |
| 60 | | | | | | | | | | 12.5 | 6.2 | 10.0 | | | 400 |
| 61 | | | | | | | | | | 12.3 | 6.1 | 9.8 | | | 392 |

[1] From C. Issawi, *Egypt, An Economic and Social Analysis*, London 1947, p. 77. For Upper Egypt 1929 Issawi reports wrongly a wage figure of PT 4.0; corrected here.

[2] M. A. Lambert, 'Les salariés dans l'entreprise agricole egyptienne,' *L'Egypte Contemporaine*, Cairo 1943. Lambert gives separate figures for the Delta and Upper Egypt from which the figures of the table were calculated as simple averages. The 1943-figures pertain to 'end of 1942.'

[3] Quoted by M. A. Anis, 'A Study of the National Income of Egypt,' *L'Egypte Contemporaine*, Cairo 1950, p. 752f.

[4] Information communicated by the Ministry.

[5] Quoted by C. Issawi, *Egypt in Revolution*, London 1963, p. 135.

[6] In calculating the average, men were given a weight of 3, women 1 and children 1, corresponding roughly to the number of men, women and children in the permanent farm labour force as disclosed in the Agricultural census of 1950.

[7] Weights, 3 for men and 2 for children.

[8] 1913-14.

e. *The Cost-of-Living Index*, $P_C$.

The official cost-of-living index is based on weights which pertain to the big cities for middle class incomes and may accordingly be out of touch with realities in the villages. A special index was therefore calculated by Fathia Zaghloul who used the percentage distribution of expenditure for the lowest income class (under £ E 25) in rural districts found in the household surveys of 1958/59 made by the Central Department of Statistics and Census; see *Annuaire Statistique*, 1960-61, p. 405. For each one of 10 commodity groups a 'representative' commodity was chosen. For 80.4 per cent of the total expenditure, 'representative' commodities with price information extending back to 1914 could be found. The price information was taken from the *Annuaire Statistique* and the prices were in most cases wholesale prices in Cairo (and Alexandria). It was believed that the prices in the villages are more closely related to the wholesale prices than to the retail prices in the big cities. After all most of the commodities concerned are agricultural commodities. No price information from the villages exist. For tea the import prices (average) were used. For details see Fathia Zaghloul, 'A Cost-of-Living Index for Rural Labourers, 1913-1961,' *Memo. No. 571*, INP, 1965.

The commodity groups and the 'representative' commodities and their weights are as follows:

TABLE   IV

| Commodity Group | Expenditure[1] per cent of total | Representative Commodity | Weight |
|---|---|---|---|
| Cereals products | 36.22 | Maize, Nab El Gamal, Zawati | 45.0 |
| Pulses | 3.01 | Beans, nabati | 3.7 |
| Meat, fish and eggs | 10.88 | Beef, balady | 13.5 |
| Fats and oils | 2.31 | Cotton seed oil | 2.9 |
| Dairy products | 7.06 | Butter, samna | 8.8 |
| Vegetables | 5.67 | Onions | 7.1 |
| Fruits | 1.27 | Dates | 1.6 |
| Sugar etc. | 4.75 | Sugar, blocks | 5.9 |
| Sugar products | 2.43 | Tea, Ceylon | 4.3 |
| Drinks | 3.47 | Petroleum, Kerosene | 7.2 |
| Stimulants | 1.39 | | |
| Fuel and lighting | 5.79 | | |
| Personal & decoration | 0.12 | | |
| Products for house | 1.97 | | |
| Clothes | 3.12 | | |
| Furniture & kitchen utens. | 0.12 | | |
| Health | 0.35 | | |
| Transport | 0.23 | | |
| Various services | 1.85 | | |
| Total | 100.00 | | 100.0 |

[1] *Annuaire Statistique*, 1960-61, p. 404.

*f. Real Wages and Share of Labour.*

The indices of real wages and share of labour used in Graph 3 are calculated simply as money wage index (Table III) over cost-of-living index (Table I, col. (8) ), and money wage index over value of marginal product of labour index, O/L (Table I, col. (5)), resp.

*TABLE V*

| Year | Real Wages index W/P$_C$ | Share of labour index W/(O/L) |
|---|---|---|
| 1914 | 100 | 100 |
| 1920 | 109 | 128 |
| 1928 | 164 | 126 |
| 1929 | 125 | 108 |
| 1933 | 147 | 129 |
| 1934 | 71 | 76 |
| 1937-39 | 110 | 122 |
| 1941 | 101 | 116 |
| 1943 | 98 | 118 |
| 1945 | 130 | 121 |
| 1950 | 144 | 85 |
| 1951 | 188 | 110 |
| 1955 | 116 | 86 |
| 1956 | 131 | 101 |
| 1959 | 141 | 95 |
| 1960 | 138 | 88 |
| 1961 | 127 | 99 |

[1] Another index of agricultural production 1914-45 was calculated by Dr. Anis, 'A Study of the National Income of Egypt,' *L'Egypte Contemporaine*, 1950, p. 920. Anis's index covers only field crops like that of El Imam, but is a Laspeyres' index. Anis also presents a price index for field crops, but since this, unfortunately, is a Laspeyres' index, too, and Anis does not present any value index or figures, we cannot use his indexes for our purpose.

[2] Anis, *op. cit.*, p. 742 and 743. This fixed price estimate has nothing to do with the production index mentioned in note 1.

[3] Lambert was an inspector of the Credit Foncier Egyptien and may have had his information from big estates. Lambert's figures for 1914 are partly supported by Wilcocks, *op. cit.*, who mention 3 PT per day as typical for the Delta and 1 1/2 PT for Upper Egypt. Lambert has the same figures for the Delta, but 2 1/2 PT for Upper Egypt. The big difference between the Delta and Upper Egypt assumed by Wilcox does not correspond to the differences reported for later years in other estimates.

[4] In the light of the regression analysis this assumption is somewhat doubtful. The value of output fell strongly from 1912 to 1914. The outbreak of World War I had a temporary, but strong depressive effect on the cotton prices and this may quite well have reacted back upon the agricultural wages. Most probably therefore the wage index is too low for the years 1929 and 1934, for which years the index is dependent upon the assumption of the text. The figures for Upper Egypt which are from 1913-14 (Abdel Wahab Pasha, *op. cit.*, p. 10) slightly support this argument. The increase for Upper Egypt from 1913-14 to 1929 was a little higher, namely 20 per cent, than the increase in the Delta from 1912 to 1929, 17 per cent.

# Labour Supplies in Historical Perspective: A Study of the Proletarianization of the African Peasantry in Rhodesia*

## G. Arrighi†

SUMMARY

The article attempts to show that W. A. Lewis's model of economic development with 'unlimited' supplies of labour has a far more limited application to the Rhodesian experience of capitalist development than W. J. Barber has assumed. 'Unlimited' supplies of labour were to a large extent the result of a process of 'primary accumulation' in which political rather than market mechanisms predominated and through which the gap between labour productivities in the peasant and capitalist sectors was progressively widened.

Thereafter, supplies of labour did become 'unlimited' and, for a period of about two decades, the Rhodesian economy displayed the main features of the Lewis model. However, owing to structural changes initiated by World War II (growing dominance of the economy by foreign oligopolies, development of a manufacturing industry, growing 'superiority' of capital intensive techniques, etc.), Lewis's assumption that investible surpluses are reinvested *in loco* so as to 'widen' capital ceased to be valid in the post-war period.

Barber's failure to understand the real nature of capitalist development in Rhodesia is attributed to the general antihistorical bias of modern economics.

In an article that was to become a classic of modern development theory,[1] W. A. Lewis proposed a two-sector model of labour reallocation from a low productivity 'subsistence sector' to a high productivity 'capitalist sector'. In the former all individuals have a right to receive means of subsistence in quantities determined by custom and, in the last instance, by average productivity in the sector in question. In addition, Lewis postulates that in this sector there is a surplus of labour ('disguised unemployment') in the sense that part of the labour force could be withdrawn without causing a reduction in total output, or at least without causing a reduction greater than the amount of means of subsistence customarily allocated to them. Under these conditions, individuals are assumed to be prepared to leave the subsistence sector and seek employment in the capitalist sector when the wage rate in the latter is some 30–50 per cent higher[2] than the conventional subsistence income in the former. Since productivity in the capitalist sector is postulated to be sufficiently high to make the payment of the above wage rate consistent with the rate

* First published in Italian as Chapter 2 of G. Arrighi, 'Sviluppo economico e sovrastrutture in Africa' (Einaudi, 1969).

† The author lectures in Economic Development at the Istituto superiore di Scienze Sociali, Trento.

of profit that employers expect in order to undertake production, the capitalist sector is said to enjoy 'unlimited' supplies of labour in the sense that, at that level of wages, practically everybody in the subsistence sector is prepared to enter wage employment.

Provided that average productivity in the subsistence sector does not increase, pushing up the conventional subsistence income, the capitalist sector can therefore expand indefinitely without an increase in wages becoming necessary to attract growing amounts of labour. In this way, the *per capita* income of workers and peasants remains constant and the investible surplus increases absolutely and as a proportion of aggregate output. Since Lewis further postulates that the entire surplus is always reinvested in a way that increases the demand for labour, the process continues until the 'surplus of labour' in the subsistence sector disappears.

Lewis points out, however, that wages may rise before the process is completed, thus slowing down capitalist accumulation, if average productivity in the subsistence sector increases, something that may happen for any of the following reasons:

(a) because the expansion of the capitalist sector is rapid enough to reduce the *absolute* population in the subsistence sector;
(b) because of technological progress in the subsistence sector; and
(c) because the terms of trade turn against the capitalist sector (assuming that the subsistence sector supplies foodstuff and raw material to the capitalist sector).

As we shall see, the last named possibility is of special interest to our analysis.

The above theory has inspired a good many studies of concrete development experiences. One such study is W. J. Barber's interpretation of the development of the African wage labour force in Rhodesia. Barber distinguishes four stages of such development:

(1) To begin with, the indigenous African economy is organized so as to be self-sufficient: real incomes and output are low and tastes are modest.[3]

(2) The second stage is inaugurated by the introduction of the money economy from outside. Because of the narrow horizons of the traditional society, the response of the indigenous peoples to 'unfamiliar' opportunities for increasing their real incomes may be 'delayed'. Historically, 'a prodding from the tax-collector has been required'.[4]

(3) 'After a period of adjustment', however, the indigenous peoples have attempted to acquire cash either through the sale of agricultural surpluses or through the sale of their labour. The latter is attractive only when it increases the total real income—in other words, it must supplement more than it subtracts from the income achieved through agricultural production.[5] This opportunity cost of labour is determined by the social organization of production in the indigenous economies. According to Barber, the customary division of labour was such that the male's role was essentially one of providing at periodical intervals the development works of the community, besides hunting and the

care of cattle, while most of the routine tasks in peasant agriculture
were the lot of women.[6] Development works were undertaken periodically, so that rather than 'general disguised unemployment', as postulated
by Lewis in his model, there was 'periodic disguised unemployment' of
male labour in the sense that individual members of the family productive unit could be withdrawn for at least a full annual cycle without any
sacrifice in indigenous agricultural production. Barber assumes that the
proportion of the total adult male population required to maintain the
integrity of the indigenous economy is, and has always been, 50 per cent.
The capitalist sector could therefore expand without inducing an
increase in real wages until its African labour requirements rose above
this proportion. Up to the mid-1940s the employment of extraterritorial
African workers prevented the proportion of ablebodied indigenous
males in wage employment from rising above 45 per cent.[7] Consequently, in the period 1929–45, while real wages showed a tendency to
decline, the volume of African employment continued to expand.[8]

(4) The fourth stage is attained when the demand for African labour
of the capitalist sector rises above 50 per cent of the total adult male
population. An expansion of the supply to meet this level of demand
implies a fall in the agricultural output of the indigenous family and
therefore the supply of labour ceases to be perfectly elastic: 'To attract
additional indigenous workers, . . . the employer in the money economy
[is] obliged to offer a real wage which [offsets] the loss in the real income
of the family in indigenous agriculture, and to provide a further increment to the real wage sufficient to induce the African worker to make
this break with his accustomed way of life'.[9] This stage, which Barber
calls of 'quasi-full employment', was, according to him, attained in the
late 1940s when the proportion of able-bodied males claimed by wage
employment reached the 50 per cent mark. He then finds confirmation
of this in the fact that, after 1950, African real wages began to
rise.[10]

As we shall presently see, this interpretation of the development of the
African wage labour force is questionable on a number of grounds.
Before we proceed, however, it is interesting to point out some general
assumptions which underlie Lewis's and Barber's analyses. These authors
conceive of the underdevelopment of the African peoples as an original
state which the development of a capitalist sector gradually eliminates.
The development of capitalism thus emerges as an ultimately *beneficial
and rationalizing influence* notwithstanding the fact (acknowledged by
Barber) that, over long periods, African workers and peasants derived
little, if any, advantage from it. Moreover, the development of capitalism
is conceived of not only as an ultimately beneficial process but also as a
*spontaneous process* in the sense that it is induced exclusively, or almost
exclusively, by 'market forces' (i.e. the free choice of individuals on the
market place) with no or little role assigned to open or concealed forms of
compulsion.[11]

The purpose of this paper is to show that neither Barber's interpretation of the development of an African wage labour force in Rhodesia nor his and Lewis's general presumptions concerning the relationship between underdevelopment and the development of capitalism find much supporting evidence in the Rhodesian experience. At the same time an attempt will be made to organize the above critique into an alternative theoretical explanation of the development of the African wage labour force in Rhodesia.

I

The first of Barber's assumptions that is inconsistent with the facts is that up to the late 1940s a situation of excess supply obtained in the labour market. Before 1920, owing to the combination of a relatively sluggish response of indigenous Africans to wage employment opportunities and unreliability of extraterritorial sources of labour, acute shortages of African labour were normal in periods of rising demand, i.e. 1896–1903, 1905–11, and 1916–19.[12] Thus, the situation in the African labour market of the late 1940s and early 1950s was no more one of 'quasi-full employment' than that obtaining during the above-mentioned periods. Moreover, Barber's assumption that the situation of 'quasi-full employment' lasted through the late 1950s, when African real wages continued to rise, is equally unfounded.[13] In conclusion, far from starting off from a situation of normal labour abundance and ending up with one of normal labour shortage, the Rhodesian capitalist sector seems to have moved in the opposite direction.

Nor did real wages rise for the first time in the late 1940s. In the period 1896–1903 they rose markedly,[14] and if thereafter they became sticky upward and flexible downward—so that in 1922, after fifteen years of predominant labour shortage, they were lower than in 1904—the reason cannot be sought for in the operation of market forces. The different behaviour of African wages before and after 1903 must instead be traced to the structural changes that occurred in the Rhodesian capitalist sector during the 1903–04 crisis, a discussion of which is beyond the scope of this study.[15] Suffice it to say that, prior to that crisis, production was predominantly undertaken with a view to the speculative gains which a small group of promoters and financiers could reap by floating companies on the London financial markets. What mattered was the working of gold deposits *irrespective of the costs involved.* Profitability considerations did not therefore hamper the competitive upward pressure on wages resulting from the shortage of labour. The realization of the low profitability of Rhodesian enterprises, under existing cost conditions, led in 1903 to the collapse of the Rhodesian speculative boom in London and precipitated the above-mentioned crisis. The subordination of production to speculation ceased, and efforts were directed at reducing costs in order to enhance the profitability of those enterprises which had survived the crisis. One of the main aspects of this economy drive was to undertake the monopsonistic organization of the African labour market.[16]

This situation was at the roots of what Bettison has aptly called 'the tradition of a subsistence wage':[17] market mechanisms were largely dis-

DEVELOPMENT STUDIES REVISITED

carded in the determination of wages, and the real wage rate came to be customarily fixed at a level that would provide for a subsistence of a *single* worker while working in the capitalist sector and a small margin to meet the more urgent of the *cash* income requirements of his family (which continued to reside in the peasant sector). The problem then became one of expanding the supply of labour to match demand at this customary level of wages. Like British capitalists in earlier times, Rhodesian employers, 'when they spoke of plenty in connection with supply, [they] had in mind not only quantity but also price'.[18] Thus, as changes in wages were no longer to be the equilibrating factor in the labour market, political mechanisms became of crucial importance in closing gaps between supply and demand, and they must therefore figure prominently in any interpretation of the development of the African wage-labour force.

Since Barber ignores political mechanisms, the shortcomings of his analysis are immediately apparent. It might be argued, however, that the labour shortages of the first three decades of white rule in Rhodesia were due to a 'delay' in African response to market opportunities for increasing their incomes and that extra-economic factors played the role of leading the African peoples on to the 'path of rational behaviour . Once this had been attained, an excess of supply over demand appeared in the labour market and Barber's model became applicable. No evidence is, however, to be found to substantiate the assumption of so long a 'delay' in African response to market opportunities. It is possible that in the 1890s the African peoples showed some 'unfamiliarity' with such opportunities, but by the turn of the century this was no longer the case. Prior to 1904 European farming in Rhodesia was insignificant and the African peasantry supplied the bulk of the foodstuffs required by the mines. In 1903, for example, it was estimated that the annual amount received by Africans for sale of grain, other produce, and stock was in the order of £350,000,[19] and there is much evidence that trade with the African population was at the time the most, if not the only, profitable activity carried out by the Europeans.[20] Further, when the development of European mixed farming and ranching created a demand for African-owned cattle, Africans were ready to sell them in large numbers.[21] Though mainly limited to the sale of what may be called 'traditional' produce (grain, cattle and beer), African participation in the produce market also took other forms: the production for the market of green vegetables, potatoes, wheat, groundnuts and tobacco, for example, was either introduced or expanded, and the practice developed in the mining areas of deriving a regular income fom hiring out bullocks to the mines for purposes of transport.[22] And as we shall see Africans were equally prompt in investing and innovating in response to market opportunities.

As regards African response to opportunities for increasing their incomes through the sale of labour-time, the first point that has to be made is that there is no evidence to support the view that 50 per cent of the male labour force was in 'disguised unemployment'. Among the Shona peoples (who, at the end of the last century, represented over two-thirds of the African population in Rhodesia) and among lower-caste Ndebele,[23] men were not only in charge of development works, hunting and the care of cattle. They also helped the women in cultivating the land, especially at planting and harvesting time, and were in charge of a number of non-agricultural productive activities (weaving, net-making, iron-working, etc.) which must have absorbed a non-negligible amount of labour-time until they were supplanted by the importation of capitalist manufactures.[24] In addition, we should not ignore the fact that the labour-time of African males was not only absorbed by material production but also by activities which, though unproductive, were socially necessary. The point has been emphasized (perhaps over-emphasized) by J. van Velsen:

> There are several fallacies in [the notion of 'leisure']. Those who hold this notion seem to think that unless people are working manually they are not using their time gainfully. . . . If a similar view were adopted for an industrialised European society all judges listening to cases in court, all bankers or business managers concluding important contracts. . . . and all those who are not actually using muscle power or even pushing a pen would be considered to be enjoying 'leisure' instead of working for their livelihood. This would, of course, be wholly unrealistic. It is equally unrealistic to think that people in tribal societies are indulging in unprofitable leisure unless they are handling a hoe or an axe or are doing otherwise physical labour. When men and women are sitting together the chances are that they are not just wasting their time in idle talk but are in fact settling a dispute over, say, garden boundaries or are discussing the desirability of moving the village to a better site, or, again, are arguing about the merits of some new farming techniques. . . . These are *activities* which vitally affect the welfare of individuals or the community as a whole.
>
> In literate societies the knowledge of new laws, of new farming methods, of market trends, of new possibilities for earning money, and so forth, is very largely spread through the written word. . . . But in societies where many people cannot read such information is spread through the spoken word. . . .[25]

In view of the above, we cannot assume that much 'disguised unemployment' existed in traditional African societies, though it can be safely assumed that a certain amount of *seasonal underemployment* existed among both Shona and Ndebele.

As this study will attempt to demonstrate, 'disguised unemployment' in Barber's or Lewis's sense was itself the result of the process of capitalist development which steadily restructured and eventually disrupted 'traditional' African societies. The very imposition of white rule on the Shona and Ndebele peoples, which opened up the territory to capitalist penetration, was a first cause of the appearance of some 'disguised unemployment'. For the *Pax Britannica* and the pillage of the African people that followed the establishment of white rule threw Ndebele men belonging to the upper castes into what may be called a state of 'structural underemployment'. While the imposition of the *Pax Britannica* prevented them from engaging in martial pursuits, the expropriation from cattle and land prevented them from fully reallocating their labour time to productive activities *within* the peasant sector (care of cattle and cultivation of the land).[26] The type of underemployment that the imposition of white rule induced among the vast majority of the African people (lower-caste Ndebele and all the Shona) was, on the other hand, of a very different nature. The imposition of the *Pax Britannica* released the labour-time (and means of production) previously allocated by the Shona to production of the surplus appropriated by the Ndebele (tribute and raids) and to a variety of defence preparations. It also released the labour-time of lower-caste Ndebele which used to be absorbed by the labour services exacted by upper caste Ndebele. At the same time, expropriation of land did not *immediately* restrict the quantity of land available to this section of the population because, as we shall see, they were generally allowed to remain on their ancestral lands. Moreover, they were also less affected by the expropriation of cattle because of the smaller quantities involved in the expropriation and because of the less central role played by cattle in their economies.[27]

It follows that, in the short run and in as far as the vast majority of the African population (i.e. excluding upper-caste Ndebele) was concerned, the imposition of white rule did not lead to a structural disequilibrium between means of production and (given techniques, size of population, tastes and wants) subsistence requirements of the peasant producers and their families. As a consequence, if some labour-time remained unutilized *within the peasant sector* ('disguised unemployment'), this was not due to a shortage of means of production relative to the total labour-time available, but rather to seasonal variations in agricultural production or to a *lack of incentives* to apply such labour-time to agricultural production;[28] and if 'little' labour-time was sold on the labour market, this was more likely to be due to the fact that the effort-price of cash income earnable through the sale of produce was lower than that earnable through wage employment, rather than to an alleged lack of African response to market opportunities for increasing their incomes.[29]

Most contemporary observers did in fact agree that the effort-price of participation in the produce market was far lower than that in the labour market. For example, in 1903 it was estimated that the latter was generally three times as large as the fomer.[30] The conclusion that the behaviour of the African peoples during these early days was consistent with an allocation of labour-time aimed at increasing their incomes is further warranted by the existence of marked seasonal variations in the supply of African labour and by discrepancies in the Ndebele and Shona rates of participation in the labour market.[31] While the seasonal variations in labour supplies show that, to the extent that there existed underemployment in the peasant economies, Africans were ready to enter wage-employment to supplement their incomes, the greater participation of Ndebele men in the labour market shows that the more 'structural' in character the disguised unemployment (and therefore the lesser the possibilities of absorbing all labour-time within the peasant sector) the greater the amount of labour-time allocated to wage employment.

Besides misinterpreting the situation in the labour market at the initial and terminal points of the process of formation of the African wage labour force, Barber misses some significant tendencies in African response to wage employment opportunities. These tendencies can be perceived by comparing the relationship between changes in real wages and changes in the rate of African participation in the labour market at different points in time. A first set of relevant data has been collected in Fig. 1 which shows trends of three crucial variables during the period 1904–45. These variables are:

(a) The rate of African participation in the labour market (Li/Ni), i.e. the ratio of the average number of indigenous African males in wage-employment at any given time (Li) to the total number of indigenous African males over 14 years of age (Ni).

(b) The wage-employment/population ratio (L/Ni), i.e. the ratio of the total number of African males (indigenous and extra-territorial) in wage employment (L) to the total number of indigenous African males over 14.

(c) The proportion of extra-territorial Africans in the total African labour force (Lf/L).

Variations in the first ratio may be taken to reflect changes in the responsiveness of the indigenous population to wage employment opportunities, *provided that their participation in the labour market was not unduly restrained by difficulties of obtaining employment.* This condition can be assumed to have been fulfilled when the Li/Ni ratio was rising or when there was a labour shortage. For this reason we shall limit our intertemporal comparisons to five periods: 1904–11, 1915–22,[32] 1922–26, 1932–38, and 1939–43.

The scanty evidence on money wages and costs of living during these five periods has been collected in Table 1.[33] Though the data, especially those in brackets, are not sufficiently reliable to form the basis of accurate estimates of the magnitude of the changes in African real wages, they are satisfactory for our purposes, namely for identifying the *direction of change* of real wages and, secondarily, for a rough assessment of their comparative magnitude. Taking into account the fact that the European cost of living index shown in the table grossly underestimates the rise in African cost of living between 1914 and 1922 and between 1939 and 1943,[34] the figures of Table 1 show that African real wages decreased rapidly in the two periods 1904–22 and 1939–43, that they increased moderately fast in the two periods 1904–11 and 1922–26, and that they probably decreased (or at best remained constant) in the period 1932–38. In Table 2, these data on real wages are juxtaposed to the rate of African participation in the labour market for the corresponding periods.

The most striking fact emerging from this table is the changing relationship between the two variables. A few intertemporal comparisons will illustrate the point. A roughly similar increase in real wages was associated with a moderate increase in the Li/Ni ratio in 1904–11 but with an exceptionally large increase in 1922–26; a roughly similar decrease in real wages was associated with a constant Li/Ni ratio in 1914–22 but with a large increase thereof in 1939–43. Conversely, a moderate increase in the Li/Ni ratio was associated with rising real wages in 1904–11, but with falling

Figure 1: Trends in the African Labour Market, 1904-45

Sources: Derived from *Annual Reports of the Chief Native Commissioners* and *Annual Reports of the Chamber of Mines of Rhodesia*

(or at best constant) real wages in 1932–39; a large increase in the Li/Ni ratio was associated with rising wages in 1922–26 but with a fall in real wages in 1939–43.

These comparisons suggest that the conditions affecting the supply of African labour did not change once and for all after an initial 'prodding from the tax-collector', as Barber puts it, but that they altered *continuously* and in the direction of greater responsiveness to wage employment opportunities. Moreover, while before 1922 African participation in the labour market did not increase in periods of falling real wages, after that year it always increased irrespective of whether real wages were falling, rising or remaining constant. It is hardly necessary to emphasize that these phenomena have to be taken into full account in our analysis of the development of the African wage labour force.

## II

We have seen that available evidence does not support the view that the low rate of African participation in the labour market during the early days of white rule was due to an alleged lack of response on their part 'to unfamiliar opportunities for increasing their real incomes' as Barber and others have presumed.[35] The reasons for this low rate must be sought

TABLE 1

AFRICAN MONEY WAGES AND COST OF LIVING INDEXES FOR SELECTED YEARS

| Year | Average Wages | | | Cost of Living Indexes | |
|---|---|---|---|---|---|
| | Mining | | Agriculture | European Cost | African |
| | Including Rations s. | Excluding Rations s. | Including Rations s. | of Living (Food, Fuel and Light) 1914 = 100 | Imports Price Index 1914 = 100 |
| 1904 | 46/9 (a) | 39/– (a) | | | 148 (g) |
| 1911 | | (32/–) (b) | | | 94 (g) |
| 1914 | | (28/–) (b) | | 100 (f) | 100 (g) |
| 1922 | 45/– (c) | (28/–) (b) | 20/– (c) | 114 (f) | 195 (g) |
| 1926 | | | 21/8 (d) | 109 (f) | (168) (g) |
| 1932 | | 25/10 (e) | | 94 (f) | |
| 1938 | 32/6 (e) | 23/6 (e) | | 93 (f) | |
| 1939 | 34/– (e) | 24/11 (e) | | 94 (f) | |
| 1943 | 42/– (e) | 27/5 (e) | | 112 (f) | |

Notes and sources: (a) *Annual reports of the Chamber of Mines of Rhodesia.* (b) Estimated by the author on the basis of information on changes in African wages given in the following: *Annual Reports of the Chief Native Commissioners; Annual Reports of the Chamber of Mines of Rhodesia;* B.S.A. Co., *Directors' Reports and Accounts* (various years); S. Rhodesia, *Report of the Native Affairs Committee of Enquiry,* 1911; S. Rhodesia, *Report of the Cost of Living Committee,* 1921. (c) 'Natural Resources' (Summary of Lecture delivered by Mr. L. Cripps before the Rhodesian Scientific Association) in *Official Yearbook of the Colony of Southern Rhodesia,* No. 1, 1924. (d) S. Rhodesia, *Report on Industrial Relations in Southern Rhodesia by Professor Henry Clay,* 1930. (e) *Economic and Statistical Bulletins of S. Rhodesia,* II, 13; VI, 8; VI, 10; XIV, 4; and XIV, 5. (f) *Official Yearbook of the Colony of Southern Rhodesia,* No. 3, 1932; *Official Yearbook of Southern Rhodesia,* No. 3, 1952. (g) Calculated by the author on the basis of data taken from the *Annual Reports of the Controller of Customs.* The commodities included in the index are those which according to the Controller of Customs were purchased by Africans and for which physical quantities were available, i.e. biscuits, coffee, preserved fish, rice, sugar, candles, matches, soap, boots and shoes, hats and caps, hoes and picks. The weights used in the calculation of the index are not based on the amounts spent on them by the African population, about which we have no information, but on the value of imports (which includes consumption on the part of Europeans).

elsewhere, namely in the 'discretionary' character of African participation in the money economy and in the low comparative effort-price of income earnable through the sale of produce.

Let us distinguish between 'necessary' and 'discretionary' material requirements of a society—the distinction being based on custom and habits as well as physiological criteria. We may then assume that in these early days, and with the exception of some sections of the Ndèbele people, there existed a rough balance between means of production and means of subsistence (i.e. the 'necessary' requirements of the population) within the peasant sector of the Rhodesian economy. Participation in the money economy, *whatever its form,* was therefore 'discretionary' in the sense that

TABLE 2

CHANGES IN THE RATE OF AFRICAN PARTICIPATION IN THE LABOUR MARKET
(Li/Ni) AND CHANGES IN REAL WAGES, SELECTED PERIODS

| Period | Change in Li/Ni (Yearly Average) | Change in Real Wages (increase: +; decrease: —; no change: = .) |
|---|---|---|
| 1904–1911 | +1 | + |
| 1915–1922 | 0 | — |
| 1922–1926 | +4 | + |
| 1932–1938 | +1 | — (or = ) |
| 1939–1943 | +3 | — |

Notes and sources: The data of the first column have been derived from
Fig. 1 and represent the average yearly increase in the per cent values of the
ratio. The increase in the Li/Ni ratio for the period 1904–11 has been adjusted
downward (from 1·5 to 1) for two reasons: (a) because in 1911 'abnormal'
extra-economic pressure was exercised on the African people to induce them
to seek wage employment (cf. p. 14 below); and (b) because in this period there
was a reduction in the rate of participation of Rhodesian Africans in the South
African labour market so that the increase in Li/Ni recorded in Rhodesia
partly reflected a 'territorial shift', rather than an overall increase, in African
participation in the labour market. Available data do not permit an accurate
assessment of this 'territorial shift', but estimates given in the *Annual Reports*
of the Chief Native Commissioners indicate that the proportion of Rhodesian
African males working in South Africa declined from 3·9 per cent in 1905 to
2·7 per cent in 1910.

it was not essential to the satisfaction of the subsistence requirements of
the African population. In such a situation the stimulus to participate in
the money economy is obviously weaker than in a situation in which the
sale of labour-time and/or of produce fulfills subsistence requirements.
This is a factor, however, that affects the *intensity* rather than the *form* of
participation in the money economy. That is to say, whether such participation is 'discretionary' or 'necessary' is something that affects more the
*total* amount of labour-time allocated to it, than the *distribution* of this total
amount between wage employment and production for exchange. This
distribution, on the other hand, will be mainly determined, as previously
noted, by the comparative effort-price of cash income obtainable from the
two forms of participation.

We have already seen that the comparatively small effort-price of cash
income earnable through the sale of produce was in fact the main factor
restraining African participation in the labour market. We may now add
that this factor was in turn traceable to the lack of population pressure on
the land and the high prices paid for African produce. The latter is of
particular significance because it highlights one aspect of the relationship
between the development of capitalist agriculture and the development of
the African wage labour force. Lewis mentions this relationship by way of
qualification of his theory outlined at the beginning of this article:

The increase in the size of the capitalist sector relatively to the subsistence sector may turn the terms of trade against the capitalist sector (if they are producing different things) and so force the capitalist to pay workers a higher percentage of their product, in order to keep their real incomes constant. . . .

If the capitalists are investing in plantation agriculture side by side with their investment in industry we can think of the capitalist sector as self-contained. The expansion of this sector does not then generate any demand for anything produced in the subsistence sector, and there are therefore no terms of trade to upset [our theory].[36]

Thus in Rhodesia, the expansion of the mining industry and of tertiary activities without a comparable development of capitalist agriculture generated a demand for, and tended to raise the price of, African produce, and this discouraged African participation in the labour market at the wage rate fixed by 'the tradition of the subsistence wage'.

Against this background, and bearing in mind that political rather than market mechanisms were to be the equilibrating factor in the African labour market, let us see what measures were taken by the Government to eliminate the labour shortage.

Forced wage-labour was an obvious device for closing gaps between supply and demand in the labour market and it was widely resorted to in the early days of settlement:

Native Commissioners or Inspectors of Police called on the various chiefs and headmen, informing the villagers that a certain percentage must work for the white man in return for a minimum wage of 10s. per month as well as board and lodging; these orders were enforced by African policemen who often exceeded their authority.[37]

This practice was one of the causes of the African Rebellions of 1896–97 and was subsequently abandoned, at least in its crudest forms, in order to avoid a costly repressive apparatus. But even as late as the early 1920s 'a hint from the Native Commissioner to some of the headmen [would] usually bring out the desired number of young ones to work'.[38] In 1908–9 a 'hint' of this sort increased the supply of labour in two districts by 50 per cent, and the abnormally high rate of African participation in the labour market recorded in 1911 was largely due to pressures of this sort.[39]

Measures of a different order—less risky and costly and more permanent in their impact—were necessary if capitalist development in Rhodesia was not to be seriously restrained. Taxation seemed at first to provide the solution as it would reduce the 'discretionary' nature of African participation in the money economy. A hut tax of 10s. for every adult male and 10s. extra for each wife exceeding one was imposed as early as 1894, and ten years later it was replaced by a poll tax of £1 on each male over 16 and 10s. upon each wife exceeding one. When the hut tax was first introduced, payment in kind was accepted but it was soon discouraged in order to induce Africans to earn their tax by wage labour.[40]

Taxation had, however, some shortcomings. For taxation, by not discriminating between incomes obtained from sale of produce and incomes obtained from the sale of labour-time, did not alter the discrepancy between the effort-prices of the two types of income. It could therefore, as it did in many instances, simply lead to the extension of the acreage under cultivation and/or to more intensive cultivation of the land. This was not, of course, the case in those areas which were located far from the centres of capitalist development (mines, towns and lines of communication) and were not reached by traders. For Africans living in these areas the only way to earn money to pay taxes was to sell their labour-time.[41]

Our previous discussion of the causes of low African participation in the labour market suggests that those measures which would significantly increase the effort-price of participation in the produce market would also be the most effective ones in solving the labour problem. Land expropriation was undoubtedly the major such measure though, as we shall see, its effects materialized in a more complex way than is commonly assumed. By 1902 the African people had been expropriated from more than three-quarters of all the land in the country.[42] This expropriation did not, however, mean an immediate restriction upon the land resources available to the African peasantry, for they were generally allowed to remain on their ancestral lands upon payment of rent or commitment to supply labour services. Roder has remarked the 'feudal' nature of these relations:

> The moment a man had pegged his farm, he regarded the African villagers on it as his serfs, who would have to work for him. The chief means of mobilising this pool of labour in the first years was the *sjambok* or hippohide whip, and after 1908 labour agreements which committed tenants to work several months, usually three, for the privilege of remaining on their ancestral land.[43]

In 1909 the British South Africa Company (B.S.A. Co.) imposed a rent charge on the so-called unalienated land (i.e. land which had been appropriated, but not yet sold or granted to individuals or companies, by the B.S.A. Co.) so that all Africans residing outside the Native Reserves came to pay a rent.[44] In addition to rents and labour services, European land-owners exacted various fees (grazing fees, dipping fees, etc.) which were so exorbitant that 'within a few years [they went] far towards paying the purchase price of the farm'.[45]

The reasons why Africans were not removed from their ancestral lands at this stage are not far to seek. As the Native Affairs Committee of Enquiry (1911) pointed out, 'it would be very short-sighted policy to remove these natives to reserves, as their services may be of great value to future European occupants'. Land was abundant and labour scarce, so that land with no labour on it had little value. That is to say, the establishment of semi-feudal relations was the most effective short-term solution to the labour problem. Also valuable to the capitalist economy were the rents and other payments exacted from African tenants. Quite apart from the financial contribution that they made to the nascent European agriculture, companies and individuals who had acquired vast tracts of land for speculative purposes and who were still influential with the Government welcomed this source of revenue which did not depend on development efforts on their part. Another reason why the Administration allowed Africans to reside on expropriated land was in fact that the capitalist sector continued to rely heavily upon African supplies of produce, and any reduction thereof would have seriously hit the dominant mining interests. The development of capitalist agriculture had therefore a double significance for the expansion of African labour supplies, for it would at one and the same time eliminate the terms-of-trade effect of capitalist development (cf. pp. 212–13) and free the hand of the Administration in expelling Africans from expropriated land, thus further raising the *effort-price* of their participation in the produce market.[46]

Market forces were, however, hampering the establishment of capitalist agriculture on a sound economic footing: the low opportunity cost to the African peasantry of supplying surpluses of 'subsistence produce', the scarcity of cheap wage labour,[47] and the smallness of the financial resources at the command of would-be European farmers, were all factors that made the latter's economic position precarious. Moreover, capitalist agriculture was a highly risky enterprise. For the market was relatively small and prices, being mainly determined by African production of marketable surpluses, fluctuated widely from season to season.[48] It is not surprising, therefore, that the white settlers chose the more profitable opportunities offered by trading, transport work, and various occupations connected with mining, construction, commerce and speculation rather than farming. Prior to the 1903–4 crisis, those Europeans who were interested in agriculture were either part-time farmers devoting themselves to more profitable activities or, as it was the case with many Afrikaaners who had trekked to Rhodesia, they were subsistence cultivators indistinguishable (by style of life, techniques of production, and crops cultivated) from the African peasantry.[49] Even during the season 1903–4, when European agriculture had began to develop, there were only 948 holdings in occupation by Europeans who accounted for approximately 5 per cent of the total acreage under cultivation and for less than 10 per cent of the total marketed output.[50]

Under these circumstances, the 'take-off' of European agriculture after the 1903–4 crisis could only be brought about by other than market mechanisms. The establishment of semi-feudal relations, discussed above, was one such mechanism, probably the main one; while the exaction of labour services remedied the labour shortage, rents and fees were an important source of finance for capital accumulation. It also became customary for European landowners to market their tenants' produce, and often that of neighbouring peasants as well, a practice that must have effectively prevented Africans, or traders on their behalf, from underselling European producers.

State power was brought to bear in other ways upon the strengthening of the white farmers' competitive position. In 1904 there occurred a major shift of the burden of taxation, i.e. from the settlers and foreign capital on to the African population (cf. Table 3), and while government expenditure on African agriculture remained negligible for at least another decade, expenditure on European agriculture soon became one of the major items in the Government budget.

TABLE 3

DISTRIBUTION OF PUBLIC REVENUE BY SOURCES

| | Period 1.4.01 to 31.3.04 (Yearly Average) | | Year ended 31.3.05 | |
| | £ '000 | % of total | £'000 | % of total |
|---|---|---|---|---|
| Paid by Africans | 122·1 | 26·8 | 187·6 | 41·4 |
| Paid by non-African residents | 150·1 | 33·0 | 122·8 | 27·1 |
| Paid by foreign capital | 87·3 | 19·1 | 67·1 | 14·8 |
| Services rendered (Posts and telegraph, land sales, etc.) | 96·4 | 21·1 | 75·7 | 16·7 |
| TOTAL | 455·9 | 100·0 | 453·2 | 100·0 |

Sources: *Annual Reports of the Administrator of S. Rhodesia.*

A Department of Agriculture was set up in 1903 to assist European agriculture, and four years later the B.S.A. Co. established central farms, where settlers could acquire a knowledge of local farming before taking up their own holdings. Subsequently the technical work carried out by the Department of Agriculture greatly expanded: it distributed various kinds of improved seeds and plants; it advised on the cultivation of new crops; it carried out various experiments in collaboration with individual growers; it opened an experimental farm at Gwebi; it assisted in water boring works by providing equipment and expert advice at cost price.[51] White farmers also received significant financial assistance at subsidized interest rates.[52]

In the next section we shall analyse the process whereby the development of capitalist agriculture contributed to the solution of the labour problem and we shall see that that process took roughly two decades. In the meantime, however, such development, by increasing the demand for labour, intensified the shortage. The role played by the recruitment of extra-territorial African workers in making possible rapid capitalist development during a transitional period can therefore hardly be exaggerated. Since capitalist development in the southern African sub-continent generated demand only for the labour and not for the produce of the African peasantries of the northern territories, the extention of taxation to such territories, the recruiting activities of various government and private agencies, and, subsequently, the spreading of new tastes and wants, soon turned Northern Rhodesia (Zambia) and later Nyasaland (Malawi) and Mozambique into reservoirs of cheap labour which enabled Rhodesian employers to overcome the labour shortage of the first two decades of this century: as shown in Fig. 1, the proportion of extra-territorial Africans in the total African wage labour force rose from less than 50 per cent in 1904 to 68 per cent in 1922.

III

In analysing the process whereby the sale of labour-time became a necessity for the African population of Rhodesia, attention must be focused upon two tendencies: (a) the transformation of 'discretionary' cash requirements into 'necessary' requirements; and (b) an upward tendency in the effort-price of African participation in the produce market resulting from a growing disequilibrium between means of production (mainly land) and population in the peasant sector and a weakening of the peasantry's competitive position on the produce market.[53]

(a) The introduction of the compulsory payments discussed in the previous section was the main factor making necessary African participation in the money economy. In addition, there were forces which worked in the same direction in a more gradual way. As mentioned, the terms 'necessities' or 'subsistence' are not to be understood in an exclusively physiological sense: people get used to what they consume and 'discretionary' consumption items can, with the mere passage of time, become necessities whose consumption is indispensable.[54]

In *periods of rising incomes* the subsistence requirements of consumers tend to increase, for *new* goods are added to their budgets and, though in the short run their consumption remains discretionary, in time some of them become necessities. Thus, in the short span of ten years of intense participation in the produce market, the subsistence requirements of the African peasantry changed significantly, as the following observations referring to successive points in time seem to suggest:

> There is a steady increase in the demand for trade goods, of which the articles most in request are hoes, picks, cutlery, blankets, clothing, salt, beads, etc., with occasionally such luxuries as coffee, sugar, golden syrup, and corned beef. . . .[55]

> The natives' progress is becoming more marked each year. This does not apply to any great extent to requirements of articles of civilized manufacture, but of correspondence by post, railway travelling, cleanliness in dress and person. . . .[56]

> The large number of town and country stores catering for the native customer is a striking illustration of the increasing wants of the native. The stock-in-trade comprises agricultural implements . . . boots and shoes, ready-made clothing of all descriptions, hats, shirts, drapery, coffee, tea, jams, sugar, salt, flour, candles, paraffin, and such luxuries as golden syrup, cigarettes, confectionery and perfumery. . . .[57]

> Natives are noticeably dressing better, and on enquiry it is found that many of them demand better quality in suits, shirts, and boots than formerly.[58]

> There is amongst natives, an increasing demand for European medicines. . . .[59]

> That the natives are depending more and more on European goods to supply their wants is manifest by the increasing number of applications for general dealers' licences, in town and country. The class of goods stocked by Europeans for native trade formerly consisted of beads, blankets, limbo, and brass wire; this has now given place to ready-made clothing, woman's apparel, boots, bicycles, paraffin lamps, candles, cigarettes, sugar, coffee, tea, fish, tinned meat and other

groceries, and there is besides a ready demand for farming implements and carpentering tools. . . . [60]

In *periods of falling incomes*, on the other hand, while discretionary consumption tends to be cut, consumers resort to dissaving, to increasing their supply of labour, and, in the case of self-employed producers, to a more intense use of the means of production in order to preserve their consumption of necessities. The protracted period of sustained demand for African produce and the participation in the money economy that it induced can thus be said to have performed the function of making such participation increasingly indispensable for the African population: should the sale of produce become uneconomic or impracticable, the African people would be compelled to sell their labour-time in order to satisfy their *subsistence* requirements.

Many of the articles mentioned in the above passages were substitutes for the products of the traditional economies. And in fact the non-agricultural productive activities of traditional African society soon succumbed to external competition.[61] The main reasons for this were the superior quality and lower prices of capitalist manufactures and the fact that it was difficult for African craftsmen to obtain their *cash* requirements through the sale of non-agricultural goods within the peasant economy: trade had traditionally been a matter of barter, and the peasants were reluctant to pay cash for something that they could, if necessary, make themselves.[62] Despite the fact that during the two World Wars, when capitalist manufactures were in short supply or altogether unavailable, there was a revival of the African handicraft industry,[63] the African peasantry underwent an 'unlearning process' whereby they gradually lost their ability to produce non-agricultural goods,[64] a tendency that also contributed to increasing their dependence upon the sale of agricultural produce or labour.

The process of growing African dependence on exchange with the capitalist sector tended to be cumulative. As cash payments became an essential part of African society, traditional transactions, such as marriage payments, began to assume a cash value,[65] further increasing the necessary character of participation in the money economy. And gradually, the spreading of missionary education became one of the most powerful factors in altering the nature of such participation. Not only did education (even of a merely religious kind, as it often was) change tastes and wants;[66] in addition, as wage employment became more and more a source of means of subsistence, expenditure on education also lost its discretionary nature, and was later to become one of the major expenditure items in African families' budgets (cf. p. 219).

(*b*) The tendency towards greater African dependence on exchange with the capitalist sector was matched by an upward tendency in the effort-price of African participation in the produce market. Available official estimates of acreage under cultivation, yields, and population point to two broad trends in African peasant agriculture during the first half of this century: a constant grain output *per capita* of the rural African population and a steady increase in the acreage under cultivation, also *per capita* of the rural African population.[67] These two trends taken together imply a steady increase in the effort-price of a given quantity of produce and therefore an upward tendency in the effort-price of African participation in the produce market.

A first point that has to be made in tracing the causes of the above tendency is that, at least prior to the late 1930s, it was not due to an abnormally high rate of population growth. Taking the Chief Native Commissioners' figures of the number of indigenous African males over 14 as a basis for the calculation of the rate of growth of the African population, we find that that rate remained roughly constant at 1·6 per cent per year between 1906 and 1936, it rose to 2·7 in the period 1936–46 and to 3·4 in the subsequent decade. Given the low density of population existing in the country as a whole at the turn of the century, we can assume that, before the late 1930s, falling yields per acre were not due to an abnormally high rate of population growth that forced the African peasantry to bring under cultivation increasingly inferior land.

The main causes of the trends in question must rather be traced to the long-term effects of the institutional framework that had been established at the beginning of the century. For one thing, the high rentals, dipping fees and stringent labour-clauses on European land occasioned a widespread movement of Africans into the less fertile lands of the Reserves. Moreover, with the development of capitalist agriculture, land values steadily appreciated and the labour situation improved. In consequence, the advantages of retaining African tenants were reduced in many instances since labour was more easily obtainable on the market and competition for grazing between African-owned and European-owned cattle on European farms intensified. European farmers became anxious to have their former tenants removed and, as farms were alienated, the African occupants were given notice and told to leave.[68] As a result, the proportion of the African population residing on Reserves rose from 54 per cent in 1909 to 59 per cent in 1914 and 64 per cent in 1922.[69]

This shift of the African population into the Reserves was, owing to the inferior quality of land therein, a major cause of falling average yields in African agriculture. But other, less apparent, forces were also contributing to the tendency in question, an understanding of which presupposes an analysis of the pattern of surplus absorption in the peasant economy. Disregarding for the time being the problem of the terms of trade with the capitalist sector, the surplus is here defined as the difference between the aggregate net output (net, that is, of the means of production used up in the process in the peasant sector) and the means of subsistence consumed by the peasantry, both referred to a given period of time. For our purposes it is sufficient to distinguish three main forms of surplus absorption: discretionary consumption, socially necessary unproductive absorption, and productive investment. The significance of the *pattern* of surplus absorption lies in the fact that it determines the size of the surplus itself in subsequent periods. Thus, for example, the greater discretionary consumption, the faster the growth of future subsistence requirements and, other things being equal, the smaller the surplus in subsequent periods; the greater and the more 'efficient'[70] the productive absorption of the surplus, the greater, other things being equal, the size of future surpluses.

Bearing in mind previous observations, we may say that the imposition of white rule in Rhodesia had a contradictory effect on the surplus-generating capacity of the African peasantry. By generating a demand for their labour-time and produce, it tended to bring about an increase in peasant *per capita* output, though the limitations imposed on land use soon counteracted this tendency. At the same time, however, the development of capitalism tended to restrain the productive absorption of the surplus *within* the peasant sector. For one thing, much of the surplus was appropriated by the Europeans in the form of labour-services, taxes, rents, etc. In the second place, the confrontation of a pre-industrial society, producing a limited range of goods, with the sophisticated consumption pattern of an industrial society (while it led to the above-mentioned increase in the productive exertion of the African peasantry) also tended, as we have seen, to foster discretionary consumption and therefore a rapid increase in African subsistence requirements. Lastly, the development of capitalism did not, in any great extent, reduce the insecurity of existence of the African peoples since it substituted market uncertainty for ecological uncertainty (which, of course, was only partially eliminated). As a consequence, the necessity of certain unproductive forms of surplus absorption which enhanced social cohesion was only marginally lessened.[71]

A substantial amount of productive investment was none the less carried out by the African peasantry during the first two decades of the present century. Africans bought wagons and carts for the transport of produce to the towns and mining centres, some invested in corn crushers and in water boreholes, though the latter were rather exceptional and to be found only among those engaged in market gardening near the towns and mining centres or under conditions of acute water scarcity.[72] But by far the most prominent forms of productive investment were cattle and ploughs. In the period 1905–21 the number of African-owned cattle increased from 114,560 to 854,000 head, or at an average compound rate of 12·5 per cent per year; subsequently this rate fell drastically to 6 per cent in the period 1921–31 and to 1 per cent in the period 1931–45.[73] This rapid accumulation was partly traceable to the existence of traditional mechanisms of transformation of current surpluses into cattle[74] and to the role played by cattle in enhancing social cohesion. Equally important, however, was the conscious response of the African peasantry to the opportunities afforded by this form of accumulation for increasing their future incomes. For, with the introduction of the ox-drawn plough and the increased importance of transport, cattle had come to play a more significant productive role in African agriculture, and the development of capitalist agriculture was, as we shall see, steadily raising the market value of African-owned cattle. The Africans readily responded to these new opportunities by supplementing the above-mentioned traditional mechanisms of accumulation with improved methods of stock management, investment in dipping tanks, and purchase of imported cattle, breeding stock in particular.[75]

The other major form of productive investment was the plough, the number of ploughs in use by Africans increasing from 440 in 1905 to 16,900 in 1921, to 53,500 in 1931, and to 133,000 in 1945.[76] The common characteristic of these two main forms of productive surplus absorption was their 'land-consuming bias'.[77] Given the general absence of population pressure on the land before the 1920s, this bias was fully justified by the factor-endowment of the peasant sector. In the long run, however, it tended to eliminate the relative abundance of land, a tendency that was already being promoted by the population movements into the Reserves discussed above. As we shall see this tendency was soon to materialize in an actual shortage of land which radically altered the position of the African peasantry *vis à vis* the capitalist sector.

In previous sections we have discussed the relationship between the supply of African labour and the development of capitalist agriculture, as well as the role played by political mechanisms in the 'take-off' of the latter. The policy of vigorous encouragement of European agriculture pursued by the Government brought immediate and impressive results (cf. Table 4). Taking into account the fact that a considerable proportion (between four-fifths and nine-tenths, according to the season) of African grain production was not marketed, it can be stated that, in as far as grain supplies were concerned, the capitalist sector had become largely self-sufficient by 1915.

The immediate effect of the expansion of European maize production was a downward pressure on grain prices. The scanty available evidence suggests a decline in the price of maize in the order of 30–50 per cent between 1903–4 and 1911–12,[78] which by itself must have significantly raised the effort-price of African participation in the produce market. But the fall in prices received by the African peasantry was even more drastic than the above decline would indicate. For only 30 per cent of the land assigned to Africans—as against 75 per cent of that alienated to Europeans —was within 25 miles from a railway line (and therefore also from towns and mining centres),[79] while it was generally recognized that grain crops could not bear the cost of more than 15 miles of ox-wagon transport when railway costs were to be added.[80] In consequence, as the development of capitalist agriculture occasioned the migration of the African peasantry into the Reserves, not only were the land resources available to Africans reduced, but their ability to compete on the grain market was progressively curtailed.

The development of capitalist agriculture did, however, have some positive effects on African agriculture which, for a while, counteracted the above tendency towards a rising effort-price of African participation in the produce market. Since the stock of European-owned cattle was largely built upon cattle purchased from Africans and upgraded by the use of imported bulls,[81] the growth of European mixed farming and cattle ranching generated a demand for African-owned cattle whose price

TABLE 4

COMPARATIVE GROWTH OF EUROPEAN AND AFRICAN AGRICULTURE, 1904–1921

|  | 1904 | 1911 | 1915 | 1918 | 1921 |
|---|---|---|---|---|---|
| European maize production: |  |  |  |  |  |
| Total ('000 bags) | 46 | 393 | 743 | 807 | 1,001 |
| Retained for farm use ('000 bags) | n.a. | n.a. | 142 | 149 | 194 |
| African grain production: |  |  |  |  |  |
| Total ('000 bags) | 2,151 | 2,190 | 2,161 | 2,495 | 2,630 |
| External trade: |  |  |  |  |  |
| Imports of maize ('000 bags) | 50 | 17 | 44 | 37 | 162 |
| Export of maize ('000 bags) | — | 41 | 225 | 300 | 386 |
| Cattle population: |  |  |  |  |  |
| European-owned ('000 head) | 30 | 164 | 395 | 600 | 905 |
| African-owned ('000 head) | 105 | 330 | 446 | 610 | 845 |
| External trade: |  |  |  |  |  |
| Cattle imports ('000 head) | n.a. | 3 | 7 | 1 | 1 |
| Meat imports ('000 lb) | 1,715 | 669 | 151 | 28 | 22 |
| Cattle exports ('000 head) | — | — | — | 23 | 9 |

Notes: Crops are shown under the year in which they were harvested. Production figures for 1915, 1918, and 1921 are averages for three seasons. Figures of African-owned cattle and meats imports for 1904 are annual averages for the two years ended 31.3.1905.
Sources: *Censuses of the European Population*, 1904 and 1911. *Official Yearbooks*, op. cit. 1924 and 1932; *Annual Reports of the Chief Native Commissioners; Annual Reports of the Controller of Customs.*

steadily advanced from £1–£2 per head around 1905–06 to £4–£7 in 1909 and to £9 in 1918.[82] However, this counteracting tendency was necessarily of a temporary nature: after a time the natural increase in European-owned cattle would become large enough to supply the whole of market demand and the relationship between European and African agriculture would become an exclusively competitive one.

It is probable that this situation would have been reached some time in the mid-1910s were it not for the boom in external demand for Rhodesian cattle and maize brought about by World War I and lasting through 1920. During this period the downward trend in maize prices was reversed, and African-owned cattle came in great demand to supply the export market. The war and post-war boom thus delayed the full materialization of the effects of the development of capitalist agriculture upon the effort-price of African participation in the produce market. As we shall presently see, however, it also made such materialization all the more sudden and drastic in its impact when it came to an end in 1921.

IV

The various tendencies analysed in the foregoing section were precipitated by the slump in cattle and maize prices of 1921–23 which radically altered the position of the African peasantry in the structure of the Rhodesian economy. The extent to which the slump affected cash earnings from sale of produce can be gauged from the following data: in 1920 African sales of grain to European traders were estimated at 198,000 bags at 10*s.* per bag; in 1921, the average price fell to approximately 5*s.* per bag at which price trade became uneconomic in many districts, with the result that, notwithstanding a plentiful harvest, only 43,600 bags were purchased from Africans.[83] A similar reduction occurred in receipts from cattle sales: though no figures are available for 1920, it was estimated that at least 20,000 head of cattle were sold by Africans in 1919 at prices in the order of £7–£8; in 1921, the demand for African stock 'diminished' and in 1922 'practically ceased', a head of cattle being 'worth little more than a sheep'.[84] In 1924 there was a recovery followed by a short-lived boom that lasted until 1929 when prices collapsed again.

The immediate effect of the drastic increase in the effort-price of African participation in the produce market brought about by these slumps was a sharp increase in African participation in the labour market (cf. Fig. 1). As a result, the relative importance of wage-employment and sale of produce as sources of African cash earnings was reversed: while the sale of produce had accounted for some 70 per cent of the total cash earnings of the indigenous African population at the beginning of the present century (cf. fn. 30) it accounted for less than 20 per cent of such earnings in 1932.[85] It is important to note that *this change cannot be considered as merely a cyclical phenomenon. It rather was an 'irreversible' change in the sense that subsequent recoveries could not restore the previous position of the African peasantry* vis-à-vis *the capitalist economy.* In order to understand this it is necessary to analyse the short- and long-term impact of the slumps in question on the economy of the peasant sector.

Both slumps were followed by an acceleration in the movement of Africans into the Reserves.[86] One reason for this acceleration was that the financial stringency in which the slumps had thrown the African peasantry[87] had greatly diminished their ability to meet the various charges to which they were subject outside the Reserves. Moreover, since the fall in produce prices had made participation in the labour market the more economic way for many Africans to meet their cash requirements, the payment of such charges in order to reside close to the markets and lines of communication had become less justified than previously.

Once the migration had taken place, the future ability of the Africans who had migrated to obtain their cash requirements through the sale of produce was, of course, jeopardized. More important still, these migrations into the Reserves precipitated the appearance of land shortages therein: in 1926 it was observed that 'several Reserves' were becoming 'overcrowded';[88] in 1928 'general overstocking' was reported, especially from Matabeleland;[89] and in 1932 the first symptoms of 'a vicious and expanding circle of destruction' were detected:

> Already the first signs of [the possible deterioration of the land in native areas from cumulative evils in the shape of soil erosion, the drying up of springs, the extirpation of valuable pasture grasses through overstocking, and the exhaustion of fertility] are discernible in some of

our more congested native reserves, and it is plain that we must take
more positive control, if we are to see an increase, and not a reduction
in the life-supporting capacity of our native areas.[90]

The 'cumulative evils' of population pressure on the land soon materialized: in an attempt to maintain output, land began to be brought back
into cultivation before the soil had a chance to regenerate fully and
grazing areas were destroyed as the number of stock increased.[91] As a
result of this 'expanding circle of destruction', supplemented after the late
1930s by the acceleration in population growth, a general shortage of land
developed in the African areas: by 1943 the Department of Native Agriculture estimated that out of 98 Reserves 62 were overpopulated (19
more than 100 per cent overpopulated) and 50 were overstocked. Several
of the remaining areas were either in, or dangerously close to, the tsetse
fly zones and could not safely carry cattle.[92]

As the African peasantry began to be affected by a shortage of land, the
production of a marketable surplus on their part tended to become
'impossible', not just 'uneconomic', and a return to the *status quo ante*
in relative produce prices would not restore their previous ability to
participate in the money economy through the sale of produce. It is mainly
for this reason that the enhanced importance of wage employment as a
source of African cash earnings after the 1920s must be considered as
largely 'irreversible' rather than 'cyclical'. It may be argued, however, that
a land shortage is nothing more than a structural disequilibrium between
labour, capital and land, and that a 'land-saving bias' in accumulation
can in due course eliminate such disequilibrium. This is certainly true
and we must therefore analyse the qualitative and quantitative characteristics of peasant surplus absorption in the 1920s and 1930s in order to
trace the causes of the persistence, indeed aggravation of the land shortage.

The pattern of peasant productive investment did alter with the appearance of population pressure on the land. In the 1920s the rate of growth
of African-owned cattle fell to half what it had been in the previous 15
years (cf. p. 214) while greater attention began to be paid to the quality of
herds as witnessed by the increase in the number of grade bulls owned
by Africans.[93] There were also attempts to counteract the emerging land
shortage by substituting wheeled vehicles for the traditional sleighs which
caused soil erosion besides making marketing from distant areas uneconomic.[94] In the 1930s there occurred a further shift in a land-saving
direction: the rate of growth of African-owned cattle fell drastically (it
averaged only 1 per cent per year in the period 1931–45) and land began to
be manured, a practice that became 'common' by 1940.[95]

However, these changes were not significant enough to affect the trend
towards a general land shortage. Particularly striking was the absence of
any major shift from production of marketable surpluses of foodstuff
(mainly cattle and grain) to the production of purely commercial crops
such as tobacco (which was particularly well suited to the soil and climatic
conditions of Rhodesia). Given the more favourable market conditions
faced by, and the lesser land requirements of, tobacco production relatively to maize and cattle, a shift of this kind could have gone a long way

in counteracting the tendency towards a sharply increasing effort-price of African participation in the produce market.

This partial failure of the African peasantry to adjust production patterns to the market conditions and factor endowment must be traced in the first place to the worsening of their terms of trade with the capitalist sector during the 1921–23 slump and the Great Depression.[96] This worsening, on the one hand, reduced the means available to the peasantry to carry out the investment which must normally accompany innovation. On the other hand, when little surplus is produced, production is almost entirely directed to satisfying short-term subsistence requirements. Innovation in crops and techniques may therefore be highly hazardous as they divert labour and/or land from the production of means of subsistence, leaving no margin to meet a possible risk of starvation should something go wrong with their commercial crops or should a bad harvest occur before the full effects of land-saving innovations have materialized.[97] In other words, while before the 1920s the absence of a land shortage and the good prices of grain and cattle discouraged, respectively, a shift towards land-saving patterns of investment and the cultivation of commercial crops,[98] after the slump of the early 1920s (and especially in the 1930s) these changes were impeded by the smallness of the surplus.

There was, however, another factor at work. Low wages and lack of security in the capitalist sector maintained the African worker's interest in the security afforded by membership of a rural-based kinship group; at the same time, fading opportunities for African participation in the produce market made the peasantry at large more reliant on wage-worker's remittances for their cash requirements. There was therefore little incentive for all involved to break up traditional structures which in some ways tended to hamper innovation in techniques and patterns of production. For example, in the 1930s 'centralization' of arable land came to be considered as a measure necessary to prevent haphazard interspersing of arable and grazing land which was one of the main causes of soil erosion. This innovation, however, made it increasingly difficult to provide land for a growing family in the vicinity of the parents' kraal, with the result that either the family land holdings had to be fragmented, or the family itself.[99] As the latter alternative would undermine social cohesion, centralization was resisted or, if implemented, it led to excessive fragmentation of holdings and further deterioration in land fertility.[100]

These factors were preventing a radical reorientation of peasant production patterns in the face of a growing land shortage, which in the late 1930s began to be made more acute by an acceleration in population growth. Moreover, the process tended to become cumulative. For one thing, as the surplus-generating capacity of the African peasantry began to fade, a tendency developed among them to sell more of their crops than they could spare in an attempt to maintain their consumption of purchased necessities. They then had to buy food at enhanced prices from capitalist producers before the next crop was ready,[101]—presumably by parting with their accumulated wealth (mainly livestock) or by working for wages—thus further reducing their future surplus-generating capacity. The urge to maintain subsistence consumption also led to the degeneration of agricultural practices noted above and to the persistence of types of productive investment and innovations whose efficiency had been diminished by the changed conditions facing production. For example, the substitution of maize for traditional crops (millets, ground-nuts, sweet potatoes), which were less land-consuming but which had become more difficult to dispose of on the market, gained momentum in the 1930s, probably relieving the shortage of cash income in the short-run but leading to faster soil erosion in the long-run.[102] Similarly, as participation in the money economy through the sale of produce became increasingly uneconomic or altogether impossible, the plough acquired new importance as a labour-saving device necessary to release male-labour for wage employment. It thus remained one of the main forms of investment notwithstanding its land-consuming bias which could only worsen the land shortage.[103] Equally important was the fact that, since male labour was traditionally in charge of management and capital formation, the steady increase after 1920 in the proportion of indigenous males in wage employment (cf. Fig. 1) became a factor hampering the adjustment of techniques of production and composition of output in peasant agriculture to the changing factor endowment and market conditions.[104]

In the late 1930s a major reorientation in the pattern of surplus absorption in the peasant sector did occur. A considerable amount of labour-time and expenditure began to be allocated to education. The interest of the rural African people (with exceptions among the youth) in education had previously been lukewarm, but with the deterioration in the income-generating capacity of the peasant sector, education (owing to the advantages it conferred in the wage economy) must have become more and more a 'necessary' rather than a 'discretionary' expenditure item. The first sign of a changed attitude was a dramatic increase in school attendance, soon followed by an equally dramatic increase in enrolment: average attendance in mission primary schools, after stagnating at around 45,000 for over a decade, shot up from 46,000 in 1936 to over 86,000 in 1943, and to 140,000 in 1947, while enrolment rose from 87,000 in 1936 to 117,000 in 1943, and to almost 180,000 in 1947.[105] Whatever its long-term political and economic implications, this 'rush' for education, by diverting a significant proportion of the labour-time and financial resources of the African people away from investment in agriculture, added new and probably decisive momentum to the process of their proletarianization.

Throughout the period under consideration the Government continued to play an important role in undermining the African peasantry's ability to participate in the produce market. To be sure, Government policy towards African agriculture was modified in the late 1920s. In 1926 the Government appointed an 'Agriculturalist for the Instruction of Natives' and three years later it began to pursue the policy of centralization of arable land mentioned above. In conjunction with this policy the Government subsequently introduced other measures meant to check the degeneration of agricultural practices; these included extension services, irrigation schemes, culling of cattle and destocking, voluntary at first but compulsory after the war. Yet even official reports often admitted that these schemes failed to have any significant impact on the trends that we have been analysing. This failure can be partly traced to the already discussed difficulties of changing techniques and patterns of production in the peasant sector; but the main reason was the smallness of the financial resources allocated by the Government to African agriculture: approximately one-fortieth, in the period 1939–45, of what was being spent on European agriculture.[106] Moreover, Africans, quite justifiably, feared that 'any success [in raising land productivity] will be a reason for depriving them of a portion of the Reserves set aside for them or a ground for refusing their demands, which are insistent, for the extension of the Reserves.'[107] For this reason they opposed Government action in the peasant sector, thus contributing to its failure.

That African suspicions were fully justified is shown by the fact that the land resources available to the African people were further restricted in this period. Though in 1931 they were formally increased through the allocation of previously unassigned land, this *de jure* increase was not matched by a *de facto* increase since Africans were already residing on the land newly assigned to them. In addition, the *de jure* increase was accompanied by the introduction of the Land Apportionment Act (1931), which came to bar Africans from purchasing land outside designated areas at a time when the shortage of land in the Reserves was likely to induce them to enter the land market in greater numbers. More important still, population movements from the European to African areas, due to the factors discussed earlier on and increasingly also to Government-organized explusions, continued to reduce the *de facto* availability of land to Africans: 50,000 Africans moved to the Reserves between 1931 and 1941, and at least as many between 1941 and 1945.[108]

Government action in other spheres was equally *graphic*. With the decline in the importance of the African peasantry as suppliers of foodstuff to the capitalist sector, and with the rise of the European farmers to a position of hegemony among the ruling classes, the earlier reluctance of the Government to discriminate against African marketed produce largely disappeared. Thus in the early 1930s the Government monopolized the marketing of locally produced maize and instituted a two-price system which protected the small European producer and discriminated against the African;[109] and similar discriminatory practices were introduced in the marketing of cattle.[110] These formal checks on African competition in the produce market simply supplemented what had been and still was the main discriminatory device: the distance of African lands from the consumption centres and the lines of communication. The development of motor transport did not significantly change the situation in this respect, for unless an African area happened to be in the track of a main road between European areas there was no provision for the construction of a road to its boundaries. As a consequence, most African areas had to rely on tracks which were unsuitable at any time for motor transport.[111]

All this having been said, it is probable that political mechanisms were progressively losing their *dominant* role in undermining the peasantry's ability to participate in the produce market and in strengthening the competitive position of European agriculture. For, once capitalist agriculture has overcome the initial difficulties related to its competitive weakness in the produce market and to its low productivity relatively to the market wage rate, market forces themselves tend to widen the gap between productivities in peasant and capitalist agriculture. The main reason for this is that capitalist producers in reinvesting surpluses tend to choose those techniques which increase the surplus itself at some future date rather than current output as the peasantry can be expected to do.[112] In time this leads to a higher rate of accumulation[113] and faster growth of land and/or labour productivity in the capitalist sector. In the second place, capitalist agriculture is not subject to the constraints which we have seen to hamper certain types of innovation in peasant agriculture. It is therefore free—and indeed compelled under the pressure of competition—to innovate as trends in market conditions and factor endowment change. For these reasons we can assume that the contraction of the surplus-generating capacity of the African peasantry was matched by a steady increase in the surplus-generating capacity of capitalist agriculture, something that progressively reduced the importance of political mechanisms in deepening the dualism of the Rhodesian economy.

## V

We are now in a position to explain why, after the early 1920s, African responsiveness to wage-employment opportunities increased continuously, irrespective of whether real wages were rising, falling or remaining constant. Our analysis has shown that this tendency must be traced to the increasingly 'necessary' character of African participation in the money economy and to the steady increase in the relative effort-price of participation in the produce market which was in turn the result of the development of capitalist agriculture and of the pattern of surplus absorption in the peasant sector. The significance of the 1920s is that the slumps of 1921 and 1929 precipitated a qualitative change in the economic position of the African peasantry: thereafter African participation in the labour market ceased to be largely 'discretionary', i.e. a way of transforming *surplus* labour-time which could not be absorbed economically in agricultural production into a surplus of commodities (discretionary consumption, productive and unproductive accumulation), and became the normal and only way in which a growing section of the peasantry could obtain a significant proportion of their means of subsistence.[114] To put it differently, the disguised unemployment of the peasant sector was no longer due to a lack of incentives to apply unutilized labour-time to agricultural production *within* the peasant sector but to a structural disequilibrium between means of production and subsistence requirements of the peasantry.

An analysis of the supply of African labour in historical perspective has thus invalidated Barber's interpretation of the development of the African wage-labour force in Rhodesia. For one thing, dualism in Rhodesia (i.e. the technological, economic and political distance between the two races) was less an 'original state', progressively *reduced* by market forces, than it was the outcome of the development of capitalism itself.[115]

Related to this oversight is Barber's failure to see that market forces did not *ab initio* favour capitalist development. Real wages remained at a level which promoted capitalist accumulation not because of the forces of supply and demand, but because of politico-economic mechanisms that ensured *the 'desired' supply at the 'desired' wage rate.* Before the determination of wage rates and rates of accumulation could be 'safely' left to market forces, the Rhodesian capitalist system had to undergo the process of 'primary accumulation', a concept that has no place in Barber's analysis and to which Lewis refers to in an off-hand way.[116]

Broadly speaking, 'primary accumulation' can be defined as a process in which non-market mechanisms predominate and through which the gap between productivity in the capitalist sector and productivity in the non-capitalist sector is widened. The process is completed when the gap is so wide that producers in the latter sector are prepared to sell their labour-time 'spontaneously' at whatever wage-rate is consistent with steady accumulation in the capitalist sector. Once this situation has been attained, the Lewis postulate of the predominance of market mechanisms in the re-allocation of labour from the non-capitalist to the capitalist sector of the economy becomes realistic, though political mechanisms may continue to play a subsidiary role. The Lewis model, like any other theoretical model, must therefore be situated historically. In the case of Rhodesia, our analysis suggests that it begins to be relevant in the 1920s when the capitalist sector had become 'self contained' and the peasants' independence of wage-employment was being irreversibly undermined.

We must now determine whether the model retained its validity after World War II. We have seen that towards the end of the 1940s African real wages began to rise and that Barber's interpretation of this phenomenon is no more statisfactory than his explanation of why wages did not

TABLE 5

TRENDS IN AFRICAN WAGE EARNINGS AND EMPLOYMENT: 1946–61

|  | 1946 | 1951 | 1956 | 1961 |
|---|---|---|---|---|
| 1. Total number of Africans in wage employment ('000s) | 376 | 527 | 602 | 628 |
| 2. Proportion of indigenous African males in wage employment (per cent) | 48·0 | 61·0 | 57·5 | 55·5 |
| 3. Average annual earnings of African employees (£) | 26 | 43 | 75 | 102 |
| 4. European cost of living index (Oct. 1949 = 100) | 86 | 116 | 135 | 156 |
| 5. African real wages: (3)/(4) | 30 | 38 | 56 | 65 |

Notes and sources: The European cost of living index is taken as a rough approximation to changes in the African cost of living, as no index of the latter is available prior to 1960. The data are derived from: *The National Income and Social Accounts of Southern Rhodesia, 1946–51; Economic and Statistical Bulletin of Southern Rhodesia*, February 7, 1952; *Monthly Digest of Statistics*, February, 1966; *Censuses of the European population; Reports of the Chief Native Commissioner and Secretary for Internal Affairs.*

rise in earlier times. The exceptionally rapid growth of the demand for African labour in the late 1940s and early 1950s (the number of Africans in wage employment rising at an average compound rate of almost 7 per cent per year in the period 1946–51) was certainly a major factor in pushing up real wages. Yet this was no new phenomenon; before World War II, also, large increases in the demand for labour, after periods of falling real wages, normally led to increases in the latter to restore them to the 'single worker subsistence level'. This was the case, for example, in 1908–11 and 1924–29. What was new in the post-war situation was that real wages continued to rise even when the rate of growth of the demand for labour fell—as it did in the mid-1950s—causing a decline in the proportion of indigenous African males in wage employment (cf. Table 5). This increase must obviously be traced to factors other than a situation of 'quasi-full employment'.[117]

Available evidence suggests that the rise in average African real wages, especially in the 1950s, was mainly due to the 'upgrading' of a section of the African wage labour force. The rapid growth of secondary and tertiary industries, which had become the leading sectors of the Rhodesian economy, created a need for greater labour stabilization. For these sectors required a labour force with certain skills which, though simple, could not be imparted under conditions of high turnover.[118] The demand for semi-skilled labour was further enhanced by the spreading of mechanization and automation to the Rhodesian mining and manufacturing industries favoured by technological development in the metropolitan countries as well as by rapidly increasing concentration of production in Rhodesia itself.[119] But stabilization of African labour presupposed the abandonment of the tradition of the subsistence wage (still obtaining after World War II) whereby the level of African wages was customarily fixed so as to allow only the subsistence of *single* men.[120] The persistence of this tradition meant that wage workers continued to rely on the tribal economy for the support of their families, and of themselves during their old age, sickness and unemployment. Participation in the labour market thus left the worker's obligations and duties to his rural kinsmen and his general involvement in the tribal social system unchanged so as to retain his cultivation rights and to be able to claim support and succour when necessary.[121] The creation of a stabilized wage labour force which would not periodically move to and from the peasant sector required, among other things, a level of African wages and living conditions in the capitalist sector that would provide Africans with some security not only during their working life but also during their old age, and above all that would enable them to support their families outside the peasant sector. That is to say, 'stabilized labour' commanded a premium determined by the difference between the cost of the means of subsistence of single men during their working life in wage employment and the cost of the means of subsistence of the worker's family over his 'life cycle'.

Large enterprises—especially those operating in secondary and tertiary industries—which could introduce labour-saving methods of production began to find it profitable to pay the above-mentioned premium because higher wages were more than compensated by the higher productivity of a stabilized labour force. It was in fact in those sectors in which stabilization mattered most (manufacturing, transport and communication) that after 1954 most of the increase in real wages was concentrated (cf Table 6). In agriculture, on the other hand, where stabilization mattered least, the increase in money wages was just sufficient to compensate for the rise in costs of living.

The post-war trend of rising wages was not unrelated to the pre-war trends in the economic position of the African population which we have analysed in the previous sections. The 'rush' for education of the late 1930s and early 1940s, for example, was certainly a factor which facilitated the subsequent politicization of the African masses. After the war, African workers showed an awareness of their increasingly proletarian status, something that led them to seek an improvement of their living conditions *within the capitalist sector*, i.e. *qua* proletarians rather than *qua* migrant peasants. With this new consciousness came a wave of strikes that made the late 1940s a period of African labour unrest of unprecedented intensity

TABLE 6

(a) AFRICANS IN WAGE EMPLOYMENT, AND (b) AVERAGE ANNUAL EARNINGS: 1954–62

| | | 1954 | 1956 | 1958 | 1960 | 1962 | Average rate of growth 1954–62 (%) |
|---|---|---|---|---|---|---|---|
| Agriculture | (a) ('000) | 218·0 | 228·0 | 230·0 | 240·0 | 243·9 | |
| | (b) (£) | 48 | 52 | 57 | 59 | 61 | *3·1* |
| Domestic service | (a) ('000) | 76·1 | 85·4 | 90·9 | 94·1 | 95·2 | |
| | (b) (£) | 71 | 81 | 88 | 94 | 102 | *4·6* |
| Mining and | (a) ('000) | 62·4 | 60·9 | 57·1 | 52·3 | 44·1 | |
| Quarrying | (b) (£) | 83 | 97 | 106 | 115 | 124 | *5·1* |
| Transport and | (a) ('000) | 12·1 | 13·7 | 15·1 | 16·0 | 16·6 | |
| Communications | (b) (£) | 94 | 114 | 148 | 166 | 209 | *10·5* |
| Manufacturing | (a) ('000) | 62·5 | 70·0 | 72·4 | 75·0 | 73·4 | |
| | (b) (£) | 65 | 81 | 108 | 125 | 164 | *10·8* |
| All Sectors | (a) ('000) | 555·0 | 602·0 | 628·0 | 640·0 | 616·0 | |
| | (b) (£) | 64 | 75 | 88 | 94 | 109 | *6·9* |
| European cost of living index Jan, 1962 = 100) | | 80·6 | 85·5 | 91·2 | 96·0 | 100·8 | *2·8* |

Source: *Monthly Digest of Statistics*, February 1966.

and scale. This phenomenon, developing at a time when a manufacturing capitalist class with an interest in labour stabilization and in the expansion of the internal market was temporarily playing a hegemonic role in Rhodesian society, induced the Government to raise basic African wages and to introduce a system of grading in industry. And this contributed to the general increase in African real wages.

Our assumption that the main factors behind the post-war rise in real wages were the qualitatively new man-power requirements of capitalist production and, secondarily, the greater African militancy in wage bargaining does not of course exclude the possibility that mechanization, automation and increased concentration of production might have been partly due to rising wages. This was in all likelihood the case in the gold-mining industry and among large-scale European maize producers. What the assumption does imply is that the qualitatively new manpower requirements of the capitalist sector (a factor largely exogenous to the situation in the Rhodesian labour market), rather than a shortage of African labour, was the *dominant* factor in the 'rising wages–mechanization spiral' of the 1950s.

But if the relationship between shortage of labour, wages and mechanization had changed with respect to the pre-war period, the behaviour of the demand for African labour had also changed. A comparison of such behaviour during the slump of 1921–23 and during the recession of the late 1950s and early 1960s will illustrate the change. During the 1921–23 slump the growth of African wage employment proceeded at a sustained rate (cf. Fig. 1). The main reason for this phenomenon was the predominance of competitive market structures in the Rhodesian economy of the time. For the presence of competitive pricing and investment behaviour in most sectors ensured both a high' intersectoral mobility of capital' and a relative independence of the rate of investment from the current absorptive capacity of the market.

'Intersectoral mobility of capital' is here defined as the ease with which capital moves to and from branches of production in response to changes in relative profitabilities, and it is assumed to depend mainly on the financial and entrepreneurial 'entrance requirements' of the various branches of production. In 1921–23, the competitive pricing behaviour of capitalist producers led to the drastic fall in grain and cattle prices referred to in section IV. The relative profitability of farming geared to these chief staples was consequently reduced, and, given the smallness of the above mentioned 'entrance requirements', there occurred the development of other branches of production which used (either as intermediary products or as foodstuff for their labour force) these staples as inputs. In this way the slump led to the establishment or expansion of various industries (dairy industry, pig industry, tobacco cultivation, gold mining) which contributed to sustain the demand for labour.[122]

As noted, the other implication of the predominance of competitive market structures in the Rhodesian economy was the relative independence of the rate of accumulation from the current absorptive capacity of the market. Despite the depression, European farmers showed 'a more than wanted activity in the way of permanent improvements and development. Labour was exceptionally abundant and the normal work being largely in abeyance, the opportunity was largely taken of making bricks, building houses, sheds, dipping tanks, kraals and stockyards, constructing roads, dams, canals and silos, fencing, sinking wells, clearing scrub, and in other ways preparing for the better seasons which are confidently awaited.'[123] That is to say, sanguine expectations, a desire to strengthen their long-term competitive position, and the exceptional abundance of labour (itself a result, as we have seen, of the slump in produce prices) induced European farmers to reallocate labour from current production to capital formation, thus sustaining the demand for African labour.

The essential characteristics of a self-regulating competitive capitalism were thus present in pre-war Rhodesia, and this is an additional reason for taking the Lewis model as a rough approximation to the operation of the Rhodesian economy during the late 1920s and the 1930s.[124] By the late 1940s, however, the structure of the Rhodesian economy had altered radically. Foreign controlled oligopolies, characterized by considerable 'international mobility', had come to dominate important sectors of the economy (mining and secondary industries),[125] while the financial and entrepreneurial 'entrance requirements' in most branches of production had greatly increased. As a consequence, prices had lost much of their downwards flexibility and even when changes in relative profitabilities did occur little intersectoral mobility of capital could be expected. Moreover, the greater calculating rationality of the large oligopolies relatively to the atomistic producers of earlier times implied a greater dependence of the rate of accumulation upon the absorptive capacity of the market.[126] For these reasons the recession of the late 1950s did not lead to structural changes that could sustain the rate of accumulation and the demand for labour. It caused instead a fall in both rates and an acceleration in the outflow of investment income.[127]

Equally important was the fact that secondary industries *producing mainly for the internal market* had assumed a leading role in the Rhodesian economy, thus making the extremely unequal distribution of income a major constraint on accumulation in the capitalist sector. The acceleration in the growth of the demand for labour that was necessary for the absorption of a growing proportion of the African labour force into wage-employment came, therefore, to depend not only on structural changes in the economy which, as we have seen, market forces were ill suited to promote, but also on changes in the power structure of Rhodesian society.[128]

The problems of capitalist accumulation which we have just discussed have no place in Lewis's theory of development. In his model all profits are automatically reinvested in productive capacity and, in addition, they are reinvested in such a way as to 'widen' capital, i.e. to create new jobs rather than to increase the productivity of those who already have jobs. Neither assumption is, according to our observations, valid in the Rhodesian context of the 1950s and 1960s. Investment tended to 'deepen' capital (largely irrespective of the situation in the labour market) and, as the limits of growth within the existing politico-economic framework were approached, reinvestible surpluses were either exported or absorbed unproductively or not produced at all.

In conclusion, the historical relevance of the Lewis model to the Rhodesian experience is limited to a period of roughly 20 years, i.e. from the mid 1920s to the mid-1940s: before the 1920s supplies of labour were in no sense 'unlimited'; after World War II, though labour supplies could be said to be 'unlimited' in Lewis's sense, the capitalist economy had become structurally incapable of absorbing them.

Before we close our discussion we may well ask how was it possible for Barber to misinterpret so utterly the process whereby an African wage labour force was brought into being in Rhodesia. For Barber was not unaware of the two relationships which we have seen to be necessary for a proper understanding of the above-mentioned process. Thus he recognized that:

(a) Participation in the labour market depends not only on the level of real wages but also on the relative effort-price of participation in the produce market and that it is possible 'that population pressure may so intensify that the natural growth in numbers can no longer be absorbed on the land without reduction in *per capita* product. Should this occur, the African might be denied the option of dividing his time between the money and the indigenous economies. Instead he may be forced to accept whatever wage terms were offered in the money economy'; and

(b) 'If an African labour force is to be stabilised in wage employment and its productivity there increased, it may be necessary for the employer in the money economy to break from the traditional low wage pattern of the past. The price which he must expect to pay for a stable labour force is a real wage sufficient to support the entire indigenous family at a standard which would make it attractive to grow roots in the money economy. . . .'[129]

Yet he makes no use of these assumptions in his analysis of the past and considers them as possibilities which may become relevant in the future. This arbitrary rejection of assumptions enables him to advance a mystifying picture of capitalist development in Rhodesia.

In this, Barber exemplifies the ideological bent of the anti-historical approach which is the essence of modern economics. For in economics assumptions need not be historically relevant. In fact, they are often plainly untrue and recognized as such. Historical processes fall into the background and are summarized by statistical series of *ex-post* data, the 'stylized facts' as they are sometimes called, which by themselves reveal nothing about causation. Thus, all that Barber takes from the complex historical process which we have been analysing are a series of real wages and a series of rates of African participation in the labour market. Causal relations, on the other hand, are not derived from historical analysis, but are imposed from without, that is, through *a priori* analysis: and a set of assumptions which yields the 'stylized facts' is held to have explanatory value, irrespective of its historical relevance. But since there will normally be many such sets, this methodology leaves room for considerable arbitrariness of choice and therefore for mystifications of all kinds. In view of this, the low scientific standards attained by modern 'development economics' and, for that matter, by economics in general should surprise nobody.

1. *Economic Development with Unlimited Supplies of Labour* (Manchester School, 1954).
2. The difference in real incomes is postulated to be necessary in order to overcome the 'psychological costs' involved in the change to the more regimented environment of the capitalist sector and to offset differences in the cost of living.
3. *The Economy of British Central Africa* (London, 1961), p. 93.

4. Loc. cit.
5. Loc. cit.
6. Op. cit., p. 46.
7. Op. cit., pp. 212–14
8. Op. cit., p. 208.
9. Op. cit., pp. 186–87.
10. Op. cit., pp. 216–18.
11. The 'prodding from the tax collector' quoted above is seen by Barber as a device necessary to induce the Africans to seek their own interest.
12. On the existence of such shortages official reports were unanimous and public debate was almost entirely focused on the problems created by them. Cf., for example, P. Mason, *The Birth of a Dilemma: the conquest and settlement of Rhodesia* (London, 1958), p. 219.
13. All available evidence suggests that, after the mid-1950s, the situation in the Rhodesian labour market, far from being one of 'quasi-full-employment', was for the first time becoming one of *open* African (and European) unemployment. The situation began to cause concern in 1958 (*Memorandum on Unemployment in S. Rhodesia and Policy to Eliminate It*, by G. E. Stent, Adviser to the Labour Department, Salisbury, February 1959) and led to the passing of the Foreign Migratory Labour Act (1958), which made it illegal for labour from non-federal territories to seek employment in the main urban areas of S. Rhodesia. This was the first time in the history of S. Rhodesia that the Government took steps to discourage the inflow of foreign migrant workers.
14. In 1898 the Administrator reported that African wages on mines had risen from 5s.–10s. to 15s.–30s. a month. In 1902 the average African wage rate on mines (rations apart) stood at 38s. 6d. and in 1903 it had further risen to 44s., the range of wages being 30s.–80s. Figures taken from *Ninth Annual Report of the Chamber of Mines of Rhodesia*, for the year ended 31.3.1904; *Report of the Chief Native Commissioner* (henceforth, C.N.C.), *Matabeleland*, for the year ended 31.3.1904.
15. I shall discuss the consequences of the 1903–04 crisis in a study, now in preparation, on Rhodesian Economic Development, 1890–1962. The best available account of the 1903–04 crisis and of its implications is given in I. F. Hone, *Southern Rhodesia* (London, 1909).
16. In 1903 the Rhodesian Native Labour Board was established with the aid of Government funds in order to centralize and co-ordinate the recruitment of labour. Competition among employers was further restricted by the promulgation of a Pass Law which regulated the mobility of African labour *within* the capitalist sector as well as between the capitalist and the peasant sectors.
17. 'Factors in the Determination of Wage Rates in Central Africa,' *Human Problems in British Central Africa*, XXVIII, December, 1960.
18. The quotation is from M. Dobb, *Studies in the Development of Capitalism* (London, 1963), p. 274.
19. *Report of the Administrator*, for the two years ended 31.3.1904.
20. Hone, op. cit., chapter 12.
21. *Annual Reports of the C.N.C.* and *Annual Reports of the Director of Agriculture.*
22. Ibidem.
23. The Shona were cultivators rather than pastoralists. Their principal crop was finger millet (*Eleusine sp.*) and they grew many varieties of vegetables and fruit. Game and fish were also important items in their diet. Cattle were allegedly not killed for food (except in periods of necessity) but for ritual purposes. However, ritual did not prevent the people from enjoying their cattle as items of food as well as objects of ritual, and ritual killings were in all likelihood spaced out so that the people had a regular diet of beef. Non-agricultural productive activities included basket-making, wood-carving, weaving and net-making from bark-fibre, mat-making, pottery, and iron work for the manufacture of agricultural implements, knives and spears.

Social and economic differentiations were very limited compared to those obtaining in other African pre-colonial social formations. Every adult member was entitled to land (which was abundant) in amounts sufficient for his and his family's subsistence. Membership of a village also ensured emergency allotments of food from headmen and chiefs and gifts from kin in case of need. Division of labour was more developed *within* than *among* productive units (the families). All that is embraced in the term 'housekeeping' were peculiarly feminine occupations. The building of houses and grain stores, weaving, net making, iron work, breaking up of new land, hunting and the charge of livestock, came within a man's sphere of work. The cultivation of land, sowing, weeding, reaping and threshing were jointly performed by the two sexes, though with a probable predominance of female labour.

A significant share of the surplus produced by the Shona was appropriated by the Ndebele. The form of appropriation varied from those tribes who had been made subject to the Ndebele State and those who had not, but who were exposed to Ndebele raids: in the case of the former the appropriation was in the form of regular payments of tribute; in the case of the latter the appropriation had not been institutionalized and was made through raids. Some Shona tribes lay completely outside the Ndebele range of activities and were therefore subject neither to tribute nor to raids.

The Ndebele people had a much more differentiated system from both economic and social points of view, being divided into castes which arose as a result of the assimilation of conquered peoples. The ruler of the Ndebele State was primarily the commander of the armies and his authority depended upon the control of cattle and captives rather than on control of land, as was the case with the Shona chiefs. The basis of Ndebele social organization was military rather than territorial.

They derived their subsistence from animal husbandry, agriculture, tribute from subject tribes, and raiding parties. Cattle played a more significant political and economic role than among the Shona, and they were more frequently and admittedly killed for food. The division of labour was much more marked than among the Shona. Higher caste men concentrated their energies on hunting, raiding, and various martial pursuits, leaving many of the productive activities to the women. Cattle herding and the clearing and fencing of fields were masculine activities but even in their performance most manual work was done by individuals of the lowest caste which consisted of the original inhabitants of the country. The latter, being of Shona stock, probably continued to organize production in a way not dissimilar from that of the Shona with the difference that part of their labour-time was used up in certain public works in which they were periodically called upon to perform.

The above characterization of Shona and Ndebele pre-colonial societies is based mainly on the following: T. O. Ranger, 'The Nineteenth Century in Southern Rhodesia', in T. O. Ranger (ed.), *Aspects of Central African History* (London 1968,); H. Kuper, A. J. B. Hughes and J. van Velsen, *The Shona and Ndebele of Southern Rhodesia* (London, 1955); F. W. Posselt, *Fact and Fiction: a short account of the Natives of Southern Rhodesia* (Salisbury, 1935); A. J. B. Hughes, 'Kin, Caste and Nation among the Rhodesian Ndebele', *The Rhodes-Livingstone Papers*, No. XXI (Manchester, 1956); *Report of the Native Affairs Committee of Enquiry, 1911* (Salisbury, 1911); *Report of the Mangwende Reserve Commission of Enquiry, 1961* (Salisbury, 1961).

24. Cf fn. 23.

25. 'Some Sociological Aspects of Community Development', unpublished manuscript (Salisbury, 1964).

26. That the Ndebele were more affected by expropriation from cattle is shown, among others, by Ranger, op. cit. That they were also more severely affected by expropriation from land was a consequence of their more concentrated settlement on the Highveld, i.e. on those lands which most immediately attracted European settlement.

27. Cf. fns. 23 and 26.

28. The distinction between the two types of disguised unemployment is similar to that made by H. Myint (*The Economics of the Developing Countries*, London, 1964, pp. 44–45) in connection with his analysis of peasant production for the market.

29. By 'cash income' we shall understand income derived from exchange, as opposed to 'income' consisting of goods produced for auto-consumption. The category 'effort-price' is the only possible category of cost for an economy in which there is no social phenomenon of wages. It is here defined as the quantity of labour-time of given drudgery necessary to obtain a unit (measured in real terms) of cash income. We shall use the short-hand expression 'effort-price of participation in the labour market' and 'effort-price of participation in the produce market' to indicate the effort-price of cash income obtainable through the sale of labour-time and through the production and sale of

produce, respectively. On the concept of 'drudgery' and on economic calculation in a peasant economy, cf. A. V. Chavanov, *The Theory of Peasant Economy* (Homewood, 1966).

30. *Report of the Inspector of Native Compounds*, for the year ended 31.3.1903. We have already seen that indigenous Africans received in 1903 an estimated £350,000 from the sale of produce. On the basis of wage rates and employment figures given in the *Annual Reports of the Chamber of Mines of Rhodesia* and in the *Annual Reports of the C.N.C.s* I have estimated that the total wage earnings of indigenous Africans were certainly less than £150,000 per annum and probably more than £100,000. It follows that at the beginning of the century sale of produce provided Africans with some 70 per cent of their cash incomes.

31. An index of seasonal variations in indigenous African employment on Matabeleland mines, which I have calculated on the basis of data taken from the *Annual Reports of the Chamber of Mines of Rhodesia* for the period 1903–07 indicates that the supply of indigenous African labour probably doubled between November–December (the peak period in African agriculture) and May–June (the period of greatest underemployment). As for the discrepancy in Ndebele and Shona participation in the labour market, the Annual Reports of the C.N.C.s stated that in 1902, for example, the proportion of able-bodied males in the age group 18–40 who spent at least three months in wage employment was 13 per cent among the Shona and 48 per cent among the Ndebele; in 1903 the corresponding figures were 20 per cent and 50 per cent respectively.

32. Though no marked increase in the L/Ni ratio during the period 1916–19 is shown in Fig. 1, these years were characterized by an acute shortage of labour and must therefore be included in our analysis.

33. 1914 has been taken instead of 1915 owing to a lack of information on the European cost of living index in the latter year.

34. *Report of the Cost of Living Committee, 1921* (Salisbury 1921,) and *Report of the National Native Labour Board on its Enquiry into the Conditions of Employment in Industry and within the Area of Jurisdiction of All Town Management Boards* (Salisbury 1948).

35. Cf. for example J. C. Mitchell, 'Wage Labour and African Population Movements in Central Africa', in K. M. Barbour and R. M. Prothers (eds.), *Essays on African Population* (London, 1961), p. 199.

36. 'Economic Development,' op. cit.

37. L. G. Gann, *A History of Southern Rhodesia* (London, 1965), p. 124.

38. E. Tawse-Jollie, *The Real Rhodesia* (London, 1924), p. 148.

39. Report of the C.N.C., Mashonaland, for the year 1909; F. W. Witts, 'The Native Labour Question in Southern Rhodesia', *The Empire Review*, XXII, 131, December 1911, pp. 333–34.

40. Gann, op cit., p. 123.

41. According to Hone (op. cit., p. 64), it was actually far easier to obtain labour from these distant areas than from villages situated within a day's journey of a mine or town. Given the scatteredness of gold mines in Rhodesia, it is not correct to assume, as P. Mason does in his already cited work, that only a small minority of the African population could participate in the money economy through the sale of produce. This assumption, as we shall see, did become valid only after the development of capitalist agriculture which, on the one hand, made trade with the African population unprofitable and, on the other hand, occasioned widespread movements of Africans into the Reserves.

42. *Papers relating to the Southern Rhodesia Native Reserves Commision, 1915* (London, 1917).

43. 'The Division of Land Resources in Southern Rhodesia', *Annals of the Association of American Geographers*, XLIV, 1, March 1964, p. 51.

44. Around 1910 rents consisted of a charge of 20s. per annum per adult male on unalienated land and of a charge varying from 10s. to 40s. per adult male per annum on alienated land. In some cases an extra 10s. was charged for each wife exceeding one. (*Native Affairs Committee of Enquiry*, op. cit., p. 9.)

45. *Report of the C.N.C.* for the year 1926. Similarly, the Native Commissioner of

Belingwe was reported in the *Bulawayo Chronicle* of 17.11.1923 as follows: 'Mr Bullock instanced the case of a native paying 1*d.* per head a week for dipping. That was 4*s.* 4*d.* a year. The native beast was worth nominally 15*s.* so that the native was paying insurance at the rate of 30 per cent per annum.' He did not think any insurance company would have the audacity to ask such a rate.

46. An awareness of this relationship between the development of capitalist agriculture and the supply of labour is implicit in this passage taken from 'The President's Address', *Seventh Annual Report of the Chamber of Mines of Rhodesia*, for the year ended 31.3.1902:

> With this cheap form of labour [i.e. family labour] at his command, coupled with the fact that, provided he lives on Native Reserves, he has no rent to pay, and that his taxation is reduced to a minimum, the native is enabled year after year to produce a large amount of grain, which is in due course purchased from him by the trader, and eventually at an enhanced price by the mine owner, and in fact he continues year by year to become more affluent, less inclined to do any work himself, and to enter most successfully into competition with the white man in that most important of articles, namely, grain.
>
> I would suggest that a remedy can be found in two ways, namely, by taxation, and the adoption of a co-operative system of farming by the mine owners.
>
> . . . Having the main factor, namely a soil sufficiently good to grow the grain, and in the majority of localities an unlimited supply of farm lands in proximity to our mines, I am certain that . . . grain could . . . be produced and delivered at the mines at a figure not exceeding 15*s.* per bag. If I am right in my contention, three most important points will be gained:
>
> 1. It will be at once seen that grain at this price, coupled with the suggested special taxation, would enable us to successfully compete with the native, for it would practically leave no margin of profit to the middle man (the trader) . . . and, as a consequence, the main cause which at present enables a native to remain idle at his kraal would be removed.
>
> 2. There would be an immediate saving to the mines for every bag of grain consumed during the year of from 10*s.* to 15*s.* . . . .
>
> 3. If this scheme of co-operative farming was adopted, it must mean the peopling of Rhodesia with a class of inhabitants which it requires more, perhaps, than any other class, namely, a settled farming population.

The *main* motivation for the Administration's active encouragement of capitalist agriculture was not, however, that of solving the labour problem but the desire of the B.S.A. Co. to recoup earlier heavy outlets in overhead captial. Cf. G. Arrighi, 'The Political Economy of Rhodesia', *New Left Review*, 39, September/October 1966.

47. The shortage of labour was far more acute in capitalist agriculture than in the mining industry because the former's period of greatest demand coincided with the months of peak activity in the peasant sector (*Annual Reports of the C.N.C.s*).

48. For example, owing to a low rainfall, difficulties of transport consequent upon a cattle plague and a sharp increase in demand due to a spurt in the mining industry, a 200-lb. bag of mealies fetched 30*s.* The following year, on the other hand, owing to a large acreage of land having been put under cultivation by the white settlers, an extraordinary favourable season and a consequent large supply of African grain, the price per bag dropped to 10*s.* (Hone, op. cit., p. 200).

49. Tawse-Jollie, op. cit., pp. 131–6; Hone, op. cit., pp. 194–96. Tobacco cultivation, on a significant scale, was established only after the 1921–23 crisis had created a situation of 'unlimited' cheap labour supplies.

50. Calculated from estimates given in: *Report of the Administrator*, for the years ended 31.3.1904; *Report of the C.N.C., Mashonaland*, for the year ended 31.3.1905; *Report of the C.N.C., Matabeleland*, for the year ended 31.3.1905; *Report of the Secretary for Agriculture*, for the year ended 31.3.1905; *Returns of the Census*, held on the 17.4.1904.

51. B.S.A. Co. *Directors' Reports and Accounts*, various years; *Annual Reports of the Director of Agriculture*.

52. *Report of Cost of Living Committee* (Salisbury, 1913); B.S.A. Co. *Director's*

*Report and Accounts*, for the two years ended 31.3.1914.

53. Cf. the discussion of the causes of low African participation in the labour market at pp. 5, 8–9 above.

54. The concept of 'subsistence' used here is in some ways similar to J. S. Duesenberry's 'previous peak income' (*Income, Saving and the Theory of Consumer Behaviour*, Cambridge, Mass., 1949) and T. E. Davis's 'previous peak consumption' ('The Consumption function as a Tool for Prediction', *Review of Economics and Statistics*, Vol. XXXIV, 1952. The main difference is that the period after which consumption becomes indispensable here is not specified. Moreover, the above authors discuss only the implications of the 'incompressibility' of previous consumption on the propensity to save. Here, on the other hand, the possibility that households may (in the face of a fall in income below 'subsistence') increase their supply of labour or use more intensely the means of production (mainly land) under their control, is also taken into account.

55. *Report of the C.N.C., Matabeleland*, for the year ended 31.3.1903.

56. *Report of the C.N.C., Matabeleland*, for the year 1907.

57. *Report of the C.N.C., Matabeleland*, for the year 1909.

58. *Report of the C.N.C., Matabeleland*, for the year 1909.

59. *Report of the C.N.C., Matabeleland*, for the year 1910.

60. B.S.A. Co. *Directors' Report and Accounts*, for the year ended 31.3.1912.

61. *Report of the C.N.C., Mashonaland*, for the year 1912; Tawse-Jollie, op. cit., p. 252; *Report of the Native Production and Trade Commission of Enquiry* (Salisbury, 1945).

62. E. A. G. Robinson, 'The Economic Problem', in J. M. Davis (ed.), *Modern Industry and the African* (London, 1933), p. 197.

63. *Notes on the Mining Industry of S. Rhodesia*, compiled by N. H. Wilson (Salisbury, not dated); *Report of the C.N.C. and Secretary for Internal Affairs*, for the year 1943.

64. Tawse-Jollie, op. cit., p. 252.

65. *Mangwende Reserve Commission of Enquiry*, op. cit., p. 29.

66. Ibidem.

67. Cf. M. Yudelman, *Africans on the Land* (Cambridge, Mass., 1964), pp. 236–37.

68. *Report of the C.N.C., Mashonaland*, for the year 1909; *Southern Rhodesia Native Reserve Commission*, op. cit., p. 9; Gann, op. cit.

69. *Annual Reports of the C.N.C.*

70. Broadly speaking we shall say that the productive absorption of the surplus is 'efficient' when it takes into account existing scarcities of factors of production.

71. These forms of surplus absorption consisted of all labour-time directly or indirectly expended on religious and social activities whose main function was to foster social cohesion. There were, of course, many activities in traditional African Societies whose main function was productive, or administrative, but which contributed to strengthen social cohesion. The empirical distinction between the two would often be problematic if not impossible.

72. *Annual Reports of the C.N.C.; Native Affairs Committee of Enquiry*, op. cit.; *Southern Rhodesia Native Reserve Commission*, op. cit.

73. *Annual Reports of the C.N.C.*

74. The rate of consumption of cattle, and therefore their rate of accumulation, was related to the size of the surplus. The ritual aspect of cattle played a crucial role in this relationship. In periods of adverse natural conditions there would be more 'pretexts' for ritual killings, the rate of cattle consumption would increase and the rate of accumulation decrease. Conversely, in periods of large yields the rate of accumulation would increase.

75. *Annual Reports of the C.N.C.; Native Affairs Committee of Enquiry*, op. cit.; *Report of the Director of Agriculture*, for the year 1914.

76. *Annual Reports of the C.N.C.*

77. By 'land-consuming bias' we shall understand the tendency of an investment or innovation to lead to a greater use of land for a given output. Similarly, we shall talk of land-saving, labour-saving, labour-intensive, and capital-intensive biases. It goes without saying that these distinctions are not water-tight and that an investment or innovation may have simultaneously two or more biases.

78. *Annual Reports of the Director (or Department) of Agriculture*.

79. B.S.A. Co. *Directors' Report and Accounts*, for the two years ended 31.3.1914.

80. 'Statement of Case of Rhodesian Agriculture Union', in *Report by Brigadier General F. D. Hammond on the Railway System of Rhodesia*, vol. II, Ann. 'C' (Salisbury 1925).

81. *Annual Reports of the Director of (or Secretary for) Agriculture.*

82. *Report of the C.N.C., Matabeleland*, for the year 1909; *Report of the C.N.C.* for the year 1918.

83. *Reports of the C.N.C.*, for the years 1920 and 1921.

84. *Reports of the C.N.C.*, for the years 1918, 1919, and 1922.

85. Calculated from 'The Economic Position of the Native', in *Economic and Statistical Bulletin of Southern Rhodesia*, I (new series), 8, 1933.

86. Reports of the C.N.C., for the years 1921, 1922, 1923, 1925, 1926, and 1931.

87. The amount paid in dog tax by Africans, 'an unfailing barometer indicating the state of their cash holdings', as the C.N.C. put it in his Report for the year 1932, fell by almost 33 per cent between 1921 and 1923 and by over 43 per cent between 1930 and 1934 (calculated from the *Annual Reports of the C.N.C.*).

88. *Report of the C.N.C.*, for the year 1926.

89. *Report of the C.N.C.*, for the year 1928.

90. *Report of the C.N.C.*, for the year 1932.

91. G. K. Garbett, 'The Land Husbandry Act of Southern Rhodesia', in D. Biebuyck (ed.) *African Agrarian Systems* (London, 1963), p. 190.

92. *Native Production and Trade Commission*, op. cit.

93. The number of grade bulls owned by Africans purchased through the Native Department, i.e. excluding those bought privately, increased from 918 in 1925 to 3,737 in 1930 (figures taken from the *Annual Reports of the C.N.C.*).

94. According to the estimates of the C.N.C., the number of African owned wheeled vehicles more than doubled between 1926 and 1930.

95. *Reports of the C.N.C.*, for the years 1934 and 1940.

96. According to all available evidence, i.e. that contained in the sources cited in Table 1 the fall in maize and cattle prices that occured during the two slumps led to a drastic deterioration in the terms of trade of the peasant sector with the capitalist sector, notwithstanding the relatively moderate fall in money wages. In defining the concept of surplus (see p. 14 above) we disregarded its relation to the terms of trade between the peasant and the capitalist sector. In the present context this relation has crucial importance and must be briefly discussed. A worsening in the terms of trade tends to reduce the real value of the surplus for two reasons: (*a*) because it increases the quantity of output that must be foregone in order to obtain those means of subsistence which are produced within the peasant economy; and (*b*) because it reduces the unitary value of the surplus in terms of the commodities against which it has to be exchanged in order to be realized. The negative impact of worsening terms of trade on the peasantry's surplus-generating capacity will therefore be the greater the more dependent are the peasants on exchange with the capitalist sector for their subsistence requirements and for the conversion of the surplus in its desired forms. It follows that the steady increase in such dependence which, as we have seen, took place in Rhodesia during the first two decades of this century had, among other things, the effect of magnifying the negative repercussion of the depressions of the early 1920's and 1930s on the surplus-generating capacity of the African peasantry.

97. Cf. Myint, op. cit., pp. 45–46. Myint deals with innovations in crops only, but his remarks obviously apply to most land-saving innovations such as green manuring, conservation works, etc.

98. *Reports of the C.N.C., Matabeleland*, for the year ended 31.3.1905 and for the year 1910; *Report of the C.N.C.*, for the year 1920.

99. *Mangwende Reserve Commission of Enquiry*, op. cit., p. 40.

100. Ibidem.

101. *Native Production and Trade Commission*, op. cit., p. 26.

102. *Report of the C.N.C.*, for the year 1938; *Report of Commission to Enquire into the Preservation (. . .) of the Natural Resources of the Colony* (Salisbury, 1939), pp. 11–12.

103. The assumption of a changing role of the plough in peasant agriculture is

consistent with the fact that, while before 1920 the acreage under cultivation increased rapidly (at an average rate of almost 5 per cent per year between 1911 and 1920, according to the estimates of the C.N.C.) and the proportion of indigenous males in wage employment remained constant (cf. Fig. 1), after 1920 the rate of increase in the acreage under cultivation slowed down (it averaged only 2·2 per cent per year in the period 1920–45) and the proportion of indigenous males in wage employment rose sharply. The assumption is also consistent with observations of the Native Commissioners: in 1908, for example, the C.N.C., Matabeleland, reported that the introduction of the plough tended to reduce the supply of labour because it induced greater involvement of male labour in the cultivation of land; in 1927 ,on the other hand, the plough began to be referred to as a 'labour saving device'.

104. On this opinion the literature is unanimous. Cf., for example, A. Pendered and von Memerty, 'The Land Husbandry Act of Southern Rhodesia', *Journal of African Administration*, VII, 3, 1955; Barber , op. cit.; Yudelman, op. cit., pp. 132–33; G. Kay, 'The Distribution of African Population in Southern Rhodesia, some preliminary notes' *Rhodes-Livingstone Communication*, No. XXVIII, Lusaka, 1964.

105. *Report of the Native Education Enquiry Commission, 1951* (Salisbury, 1952).

106. Calculated from: *Annual Reports of the Commissioner of Taxes; Annual Reports of the C.N.C. and Secretary for Internal Affairs; and Southern Rhodesia Statistical Yearbook* (Salisbury, 1947).

107. *Native Production and Trade Commission*, op. cit., p. 25. These fears were fully justified in view of the continuous curtailment of the *de facto* availability of land to Africans and also in view of official statements such as the following:

It is intended to develop the native reserves so as to enable them to carry a larger population, and so avoid, so far as possible, the necessity for acquisition of more land for native occupation. . . .' (*Report of the C.N.C.*, for the year 1932.)

108. *Second Report of the Select Committee on the Resettlement of Natives* (Salisbury, 1960; and *Annual Reports of the C.N.C. and Secretary for Internal Affairs*).

109. R. W. M. Johnson, *African Agricultural Development in Southern Rhodesia* (Stanford, 1964), pp. 196–97; Yudelman, op. cit., p. 197.

110. *Interim Report on Livestock and Meat with special reference to Cattle and Beef* (Salisbury, 1936); Yudelman, op. cit., pp. 190–91.

111. *Native Production and Trade Commission*, op. cit., p. 50.

112. Cf. A. K. Sen, *Choice of Techniques* (Oxford, 1962), p. 30 and Appendix A in particular; see also Chayanov, op. cit., p. 7. This discrepancy in investment behaviour is largely traceable to differences in 'time horizons' in production and investment decisions. But the 'time horizon' of the peasantry is itself a variable depending on the latter's surplus-generating capacity: the smaller such capacity, and therefore the more are the peasants struggling to maintain a certain level of subsistence consumption, the shorter their time horizon in reinvesting surpluses. It follows that the reduction in the African peasant's surplus-generating capacity that occurred in the 1920s and 1930s must have widened the gap between their 'time horizon' and that of capitalist producers.

113. Thus, in the late 1950s the amount of *private* captial invested in European farms was estimated at £250m. (*Select Committee on the Resettlement of Natives*, op. cit., p. 49), while the gross value of *all* capital (i.e. including accumulated Government investment in infrastructure) in African agriculture was roughly estimated at £90m., over 35 per cent of which was accounted for by livestock. (Yudelman, op. cit., p. 155). At the time there were less than 4,500 European farms while the number of African Holdings was estimated at about 380,000. It is, of course, impossible to assess the extent to which this huge difference in capital invested has been brought about by market forces rather than political mechanisms owing to the interaction of the two in the historical process.

114. In the 1950s it was reckoned that only 235,000 families could derive a subsistence (as determined by a rather restrictive formula adopted by the Government) from the land available for African use. This meant that probably more than half of the African population had to obtain the bulk of its means of subsistence from wage-employment (*Select Committee on the Resettlement of Natives*, op. cit. p. 43) But even among the families who could derive a subsistence from agricultural production it was only a small minority that obtained its *cash* requirements from the sale of produce. In the Mangwende

Reserve, for example, it was found that the so-called 'Ordinary Farmers', under which category fell 70 per cent of all peasant holdings in the Reserve, had average net cash incomes (sales minus expenses) of only £3½ per annum as against the £40 earned by the 'Master Farmers' (rich peasants) who represented 4–5 per cent of all peasant holdings. (*Mangwende Reserve Commission of Enquiry*, op. cit., p. 32).

115. Cf. on this A. G. Frank's theses on Latin American underdevelopment in his *Capitalism and Underdevelopment in Latin America* (New York, 1967).

116. Lewis's reference to 'primary accumulation' runs as follows: '[The capitalists] will not support proposals for land settlement, and are often instead to be found engaged in turning the peasants off their lands (cf. Marx on "Primary Accumulation"). This is one of the worst features of imperialism, for instance.'

117. Cf. p. 2 and fn. 13 above.

118. *First Interim Report of the Development Co-ordinating Commission of Southern Rhodesia* (Salisbury, 1948); *Report of the Select Committee on the Subject of Native Industrial Workers' Union Bill* (Salisbury, 1956). The *Report of the National Native Labour Board*, op. cit. gives the following figure of labour turnover among the employees of the Bulawayo Municipality during the year ended 31.3.48:

| | |
|---|---|
| Number employed at 1.4.47 | 3,059 |
| Number engaged during the year ended 31.3.48 | 3,448 |
| Number discharged | 3,426 |
| Number employed at 31.3.48 | 3,081 |

119. Development Co-ordinating Commission, op. cit.; *Censuses of Industrial Production, 1938–1953; Annual Report of the Chief Government Mining Engineer and Chief Inspector of Mines*, for the year 1954.

120. *Report of the Urban African Affairs Commission* (Salisbury, 1958); D. G. Bettison, 'The Poverty Datum Line in Central Africa', *Human Problems in British Central Africa*, XXVII, June 1960.

121. Cf. Mitchell, op. cit., p. 223 also for references to the vast literature on the subject.

122. *Annual Reports of the Director of Agriculture.*

123. *Annual Report of the Director of Agriculture*, for the year 1922.

124. Throughout his article, Lewis implicitly assumes the operation of competitive forces in the capitalist sector.

125. Cf. Arrighi, op. cit.

126. I have discussed this problem more extensively in the essay 'International Corporations, Labour Aristocracies and Economic Development in Tropical Africa', to be published in a volume of readings on underdevelopment edited by R. I. Rhodes (Monthly Review Press, forthcoming).

127. The ratio of capital formation to G. D. P., which had averaged approximately 37 per cent in the period 1951–58, fell to 25·5 per cent in 1959–61 and to 15·4 per cent in 1962–64. (*National Accounts and Balance of Payments of Rhodesia, 1965*, Salisbury, 1966.)

128. Cf. Arrighi *The Political Economy of Rhodesia*, op. cit.

129. 'Economic rationality and Behaviour Patterns in an Underdeveloped Area: a case study of African Economic Behaviour in the Rhodesias,' *Economic Development and Cultural Change*, VII, 3, 1960, p. 251.

# Women and Industrialisation:
# Examining the 'Female Marginalisation' Thesis

*by Alison MacEwen Scott**

*This article examines the thesis that women are marginalised from production in the course of development, in the light of recent research which shows contradictory trends. The analysis reveals serious deficiencies in the theoretical and methodological underpinnings of the 'female marginalisation' thesis. The result is not that the FM thesis is wrong, but that it is untestable. These problems are discussed with reference to Peruvian and Brazilian material. The article argues for attention to be paid to the micro-level processes which give rise to women's marginalisation.*

This article is concerned with the status of theories about long-run changes in women's economic roles produced by capitalist industrialisation. Specifically, it addresses a commonly-held thesis that women are progressively marginalised from production in this process, particularly in developing countries. The article discusses the methodological problems involved in verifying this thesis, the theoretical ambiguities which are revealed by the attempt at verification and, ultimately, the feasibility and desirability of establishing general theories about the long-run position of women under dependent capitalism.

Any analysis of the changing position of women in the economy raises questions about the relationship between the general pattern of development and the sexual division of labour. It is possible to examine this relationship at different levels, focusing on particular local or conjunctural factors within relatively short periods of time, or on general long-run tendencies. In Latin America the literature of the past decade has tended to pursue the latter course even where specific cases were the object of enquiry. Theorisation has been oriented towards highly abstract system-level questions such as the relationship between production and reproduction [e.g. *Harris and Young, 1981; Benería, 1979; Benería and Sen, 1982*] and the ways in which this relationship varies under different modes of production [*Saffioti, 1977, 1978*] or as a result of changes in the international division of labour [*Safa, 1981; Nash and Fernández Kelly, 1983*].

The focus on system-level structures and tendencies is common to many types of analysis in social science. However, the emphasis on long-run changes in the economy has undoubtedly derived from neo-Marxist and socialist

*Department of Sociology, University of Essex. I am grateful to Diane Elson, Maxine Molyneux, Ruth Pearson and Ted Benton for comments on the first draft of this article.

feminist thinking about the nature of capitalist development in general and of dependent capitalism in particular. One of the distinctive features of this approach is an emphasis on the *essential* causes of social phenomena in different modes of production, as well as the long-run tendencies produced by their internal contradictions. The 'female marginalistion' thesis is part of this tradition, although some writers are less Marxist than others. Basically it seeks to explain women's economic position in terms of system-level contradictions and tendencies created by the development of capitalism.

The popularity of this approach in Latin America derives partly from the fact that there is a well-established radical tradition within development theory which shares many of the same premises. (Dependency theory originally emerged in Latin America.) It is also due to the high level of politicisation of debates about women and development there, and the strong socialist feminist influence in them. Finally, it has been helped by the fact that many Latin American countries industrialised relatively early in Third World terms, and census records are available from the nineteenth century which provide evidence of long run changes in female employment patterns.

Although the FM thesis has been established on the basis of empirical evidence from various Latin American countries (for example, Brazil, Guatemala, Mexico, Venezuela), it is necessary to submit it to further scrutiny because of the emergence of new, apparently contradictory evidence. Also, given its widespread influence in academic and political circles and its negative implications for policy, it is important to assess its scientific value as a basis for the explanation and prediction of women's role in the economy.

In this study I shall argue that there are substantial theoretical and methodological problems with this thesis which require careful examination. In brief, they have to do with the ways in which long-run tendencies are to be identified and explained, how they are to be related to deviations from these trends, and how the link between micro and macro processes is to be established. These difficulties are inherent in any Marxist analysis, and have become more apparent as Marxism has moved way from functionalist explanation and has tried to attach more importance to historical contingency. However, they are particularly acute in the analysis of the changing position of women under capitalism because, in addition to the problems of detecting the underlying trends in the economy, the processes whereby the sexual division of labour is integrated with the economy have not yet been sufficiently well theorised.

THE 'FEMALE MARGINALISATION' THESIS

The notion of women's marginalisation from production under capitalist development is by no means confined to Marxism. It has been employed by a number of authors writing within orthodox economic and sociological perspectives. However, they have not given it the theoretical prominence that it has enjoyed in the radical literature. Ester Boserup, for example, provided extensive evidence of the erosion of traditional female roles and the exclusion of women from industrial employment, as well as from other aspects of the development process [*Boserup, 1970, 1976*]. Yet the explanations offered were eclectic, ranging from conventional supply and demand factors, to colonial ideology and indigenous social customs (cf. critique by Benería and Sen [*1981*] ). Women's marginalisation was portrayed as the result of a mixture of historical, economic and cultural factors, and not as a necessary effect of any particular economic or political system. On the contrary it was thought to be remediable within the present system with the appropriate policies. Significantly, the term 'marginalisation' is barely mentioned in her whole book.

The FM thesis which emerged in the Latin American context (in works by non-Latin American authors as well as by Latin Americans)[1] has a more precise theoretical structure. Its distinguishing feature is that 'female marginalistion' is portrayed as a single process, albeit a complex one, and is viewed as an irreversible systemic tendency within dependent capitalist development. Curiously, despite the frequency with which this approach is used in the literature, it has rarely been set out as an explicit theoretical model (Saffioti [*1978*] (1969) is the most elaborated version). Rather it exists as an implicit assumption supported by a number of general and often imprecise hypotheses drawn from Marxism, feminism and dependency theory. My purpose in presenting it as a 'thesis' is to draw together some of these hypotheses more systematically in order to submit it to rigorous theoretical and methodological scrutiny.

The central idea, drawn from Marxist and socialist feminist writings in Europe and North America, holds that women's marginalisation is a product of the capitalist organisation of production and use of labour. The basic elements in this are: the separation between production and reproduction, the hierarchical structure of capitalist enterprises, the rise of surplus labour and the industrial reserve army, and the 'mutual accomodation between capitalism and patriarchy' [*Hartmann, 1976, 1979*] which results in women's confinement to the home, to inferior jobs and to the reserve army of labour.

The first effect of these processes is to produce a withdrawal of women from the labour force particularly in the early stages of industrialisation.[2] Second, the active female labour force is reconstituted as a secondary labour force and concentrates into the inferior positions in occupational hierarchies. Third, women's employment is destabilised and casualised because of their deployment as part of the reserve army of labour. These are all manifestations of women's marginalisation from production.

In Latin America, 'female marginalisation' has additional theoretical connotations because of the role of the general term 'marginality' in a long-standing debate about the excess of surplus labour produced by the dependent character of capitalist development.[3] 'Marginality' was seen as a structural phenomenon resulting from imbalances between the labour requirements of the capitalist sector and the available labour supply, which in turn was an effect of technological dependency and internal inequalities. Key aspects of this phenomenon were exclusion from the capitalist sector, particularly from manufacturing, and absorption into the subsistence fringe of the economy – formerly known as the 'marginal sector' and now commonly referred to as the 'informal sector'.

In this context, the notion of 'female marginalisation' was linked to the general problem of marginality and was thus particularly associated with dependency, dualism, informalisation and tertiarisation. The typical indicators of female marginalisation were: (i) a general fall in global female participation rates; (ii) a decline in the female share of capitalist employment (wage labour, manufacturing); (iii) concentration of women into the 'informal' and tertiary sectors; and (iv) increasing economic inequality between men and women workers.

Authors emphasised that the forms and degrees of marginalisation of women from production were different in the LDCs compared with advanced industrial societies [e.g. *Saffioti, 1975: 80 – 82; Saffioti, 1977: 33 – 35; Schmink, 1977: 154*]. Because of the unbalanced nature of the development process in the Third World and the higher general level of marginality in the population, women's exclusion from productive employment was greater, as was their concentration into the informal sector and 'transitional' forms of employment such as domestic service. Thus the trend towards marginalisation was more marked than in advanced industrial societies and less likely to 'bottom out' in the advanced stages of industrialisation.

There are some variations within this approach which can only be briefly mentioned here. One line of argument sees women's unpaid domestic labour and their paid informal activities as part of an overall process of articulation between different forms of production [*Jelin, 1974, 1980*]. Another maintains that these articulations subsidise the dominant process of accumulation by providing cheap wage goods and services, thus lowering the subsistence costs of labour and hence the wage level (an interpretation which is also made of the informal sector as a whole [e.g. *Portes and Walton, 1981*] ). Yet another argues that the subsidy takes the form of a direct supplement to the male wage provided by working wives [*Marulanda, 1982*]. More recently, studies have focused on the growth of 'world market' industries such as clothing and electronics in areas such as the Mexican border and Free Trade Zones [*Safa, 1981; Fernández-Kelly, 1983; Nash and Fernández-Kelly, 1983*]. However, in the latter case the focus is more on the structure of the industry workforce and the international organisation of production, than on its consequences for the structure of the national labour market and women's marginalisation within it.

THEORETICAL AND METHODOLOGICAL PROBLEMS

As long as there was a clear tendency for female participation rates to fall in the course of industrialisation there was little pressure to think rigorously about the appropriate criteria for the measurement of marginalisation, or about the causal mechanisms which underlay it. During the early stages of industrialisation, when peasant production and cottage industry were declining, female participation both in manufacturing and in the labour force generally did unambiguously fall. The problem has arisen in the recent period because, as the urban-industrial economy has grown in size and complexity, female participation has begun to rise again and women's share of formal sector employment has increased, not only in the tertiary sector, but in manufacturing also. As a result, some writers have shifted their attention away from a concern with the extent of women's economic participation to the *types* of jobs in which they work.[4] This has led to methodological confusion concerning the appropriate measurement of marginalisation, which in turn has revealed considerable ambiguity about the causal assumptions underlying the thesis. In the face of apparently contradictory evidence, the FM thesis will either be directly refuted or will be untestable[5] Either way, its status as a theory about the long-run position of women under capitalism will be threatened.

Below I briefly review some of these theoretical and methodological problems. These will subsequently be illustrated with reference to Peruvian and Brazilian material which provides some of the contradictory evidence.

## Criteria of Marginalisation

The identification of long-run trends in women's economic roles depends crucially on appropriate measurement criteria. There are three main problems here. First, there are many different dimensions of marginalisation. These have not been elaborated systematically and different authors give greater emphasis to some aspects than to others, so that the treatment is not consistent in the literature. Second, even where the same dimension of marginalisation is referred to, the criteria for measurement are ambiguous and sometimes inappropriate. Third, there is no theoretical or methodological procedure for relating the different dimensions of marginality to each other. Let us consider the following four dimensions of marginalisation:

*(i) Marginality as exclusion from productive employment:* The major problem here is: what constitutes productive employment? Some authors take this to mean employment in general, that is, the global female participation rate; others refer to all capitalist employment, that is wage and salaried labour. Others refer to manufacturing employment only.[6] The second problem is: what constitutes exclusion? Exclusion is a relative phenomenon which can be measured in a variety of ways depending on the reference point used (see third sub-section below).

*(ii) Marginalisation as concentration on the margins of the labour market:* This refers to the degree of concentration of all *working women* into marginal occupations, industries, sectors or types of employment. But what constitutes 'marginal'? Much of the literature relies on the dichotomous 'informal sector' model which defines as marginal all forms of small scale employment, outwork and domestic service. This definition of marginality is very dependent on the validity of the dualist model, which has been much criticised. One particular weakness is that it does not allow for marginalisation *within* either sector. In preference, criteria might be based on more detailed occupational data which identify jobs with low pay, low status, bad working conditions, etc. However, the combination of dual sector and occupational criteria can lead to serious confusion. For example, women in the 'world market' factories may be considered to be marginal on occupational criteria, but not according to the

informal sector model since factory employment forms part of the formal or capitalist sector.

*(iii) Marginalisation as feminisation or segregation:* One of the effects of the concentration of women on the margins is the feminisation of the margins themselves. The appropriate index is the female ratio within occupations, sectors or industries. Indexes of segregation can be calculated for sections of the labour market or the whole, although there is some debate amongst statisticians about which measures are most appropriate.[7] Segregation measures are an important aspect of marginality but they can be misleading unless used in conjunction with other measures which show the degree of concentration of the workforce in segregated occupations (see discussion of Humphrey below).

*(iv) Marginalisation as economic inequality:* This refers to the degree of economic inequality that accompanies occupational marginalisation, for example, wage differentials, casualisation, restricted access to fringe benefits, etc.

In most of the Latin American literature all of these dimensions of marginalisation are referred to simultaneously as if they were different aspects of a single phenomenon. It would be legitimate to do this if there was a systematic correlation between them but there is not.[8] For example, in the early stages of industrialisation there may be an overall fall in female participation rates at the same time as an increase in female factory employment (textiles); and there is an expulsion of women from this sector just as global participation rates are beginning to rise. Advanced industrial societies show that a rise in female participation rates can be accompanied by an increase in occupational segregation, and there are signs that this is also true for Latin American countries [*Schmink, 1977; Scott, 1984*]. The link between marginalisation within the labour market and exclusion from employment altogether is not straightforward. The fact that these different dimensions of marginalisation do not correlate well together lies at the root of the ambiguity of the FM thesis. It raises questions about whether marginalisation should be conceptualised as a single phenomenon.

## The Problem of Levels

One reason for these discrepancies is that marginalisation proceeds at different rates in different industries and occupations. It is therefore important to know whether it is being studied at the national, sectoral, industrial or occupational level. Aggregated data create special problems since they reflect the cumulative effect of different marginalisation processes, together with many changes which do not involve shifts in the relative positions of men and women at all (see discussion of substitution below).

## The Relativity of Marginalisation

Marginalisation is essentially a *relative* phenomenon as well as a *processual* one. It must be based on comparisons between the relative positions of men and women at any one time, as well as changes in those relative positions over time. Studies which focus only on the structure of female employment without mentioning the point of comparison, that is, male employment, cannot be used to demonstrate marginalisation.[9] When comparing changes over time, it is crucially important to bear in mind the different base figures. Since women's share of employment is so low in Latin America, quite small increases can show misleadingly high growth rates compared with men's. Once again, changes in female employment over time *must* be compared with men's since it would be possible for women's employment and incomes to rise as a result of general economic growth without producing any change in their relative position compared with men.

## The Interpretation of Trends

Even if these methodological issues could be resolved, there is the problem of how to interpret trend data. The reserve army hypothesis allows the possibility of a temporary reversal of marginalisation in certain circumstances, such as during the upswing of the business cycle. This means that data showing an increasing integration of women into productive employment could both confirm the marginalisation thesis (by demonstrating the action of the reserve army) *and* disprove it. There is no way of choosing between the two possibilities in the short run. The only basis for testing the FM thesis is by looking at all phases of the cycle and at a number of cycles, thereby enabling long-run trends to be distinguished from temporary fluctuations (cf. Breughel [*1979*] for such an operation based on British data). The problem then is how to determine the periodisation of the cycle. Historically Latin American economies have been prone to economic instability and exhibit a series of cycles within cycles. How do we distinguish between these cycles, and in which does the reserve army come into play?

## The Problem of Causality

These problems all point to a lack of clarity about the causal mechanisms which produce women's marginalisation in the economy. The FM thesis is based on a number of observed aggregate correlations which are explained in terms of system needs or functions. However, these correlations are the product of a number of diverse micro-level processes which must be clarified. First, we need to know what the actual *mechanisms* of exclusion, segregation or marginalisation are. Second, it is important to be able to explain variations in the effectivity of these mechanisms in particular situations.

In the analysis which follows, I propose to demonstrate some of these problems with reference to Peruvian and Brazilian material. Both cases present evidence which has recently been used to question the FM thesis [*Humphrey, 1984a; Scott, 1984*]. They therefore present significant empirical challenges to the thesis. However, as the analysis will show, they merely reveal its untestability. In the Peruvian case, this is because the data show contradictory tendencies, and in the Brazilian one, because contradictory interpretations can be read into the data. Both cases therefore show the need for theoretical and methodological clarification.

'FEMALE MARGINALISATION' IN PERU

In this section I shall examine the FM thesis in the context of Peru in the period between 1940 and 1981. The data refer to the capital city Lima, rather than to the national level. Hence they do not reflect changes in rural areas such as the decline of cottage industry. I shall examine the first three dimensions of marginalisation: the level of women's participation in productive emloyment, their concentration into 'marginal' activities such as domestic service and informal production, and the degree of segregation. Economic inequality will be omitted because of the lack of trend data and for reasons of space.[10]

Lima presents ideal conditions to test the FM thesis since it has had a long period of industrial expansion recorded by three censuses (1940, 1961, 1972), followed by a severe recession in the late 1970s, whose effects can be seen in the 1981 census. [11] (For an evaluation of these data interested readers are referred to the Appendix below.) The pattern of growth, moreover, has been dominated by foreign capital and imported technology;[12] there is a large informal sector and a high concentration of the labour force in the tertiary sector. Lima thus presents all the characteristics of dependent capitalist growth and might therefore be expected to show evidence of 'female marginalisation'. In addition, the experience of the recent recession also provides a basis for testing the effects of the reserve army hypothesis.

The problem presented by the Peruvian case is that the evidence contradicts some aspects of the FM thesis, but not others. Therefore the thesis can neither be validated nor invalidated. In brief, the Lima data show that:

(i) the global female participation rate fell – but not at the rate that might have been expected by the FM thesis, and not for gender-specific reasons;

(ii) the overall female share of manufacturing employment fell, although in certain branches of industry it rose;

(iii) there was a decline in female wage labour, but this was more than offset by growth in white collar employment, so that women's participation in capitalist employment rose;

(iv) there was no marked concentration of women into the informal sector, and the proportion in domestic service fell; and

(v) despite the severe recession of the 1970s, there was little evidence of women's deployment as a reserve army of labour.[13]

Despite these contradictory tendencies, cross-sectional studies show a high degree of gender segregation and of enonomic inequality between men and women. Thus women clearly *were* marginal to the economy, but not in the ways predicted by the FM thesis. Let us now examine some of these data in more detail.

At the national level, Peru experienced the massive decline in female participation rates typical of the early stages of industrialisation. This decline can be traced as far back as the 1876 census. Although there is some debate about whether it was due to definitional changes between censuses,there is no doubt that the collapse of cottage industry in rural areas, the mechanisation of agriculture, and internal migration played a crucial part [see Scott, 1985]. These changes were not reflected in Lima since they took place mainly in rural areas. The female participation rate there did fall, but at a much slower rate and from an already low figure. There was neither a large-scale exodus of women from the labour force nor the later upsurge in the participation rates of married women typical of advanced stages of industrialisation.

Throughout the period, women's participation rates were influenced more by cultural factors than by economic ones.[14] This is reflected in high rates of inactivity even amongst single women with relatively high levels of education (completed secondary schooling) [*Scott, 1984*]. The most significant point about changes in participation during this period is that the male rates behaved in the same way as the female ones; they also fell (indeed the fall was greater), the same groups were affected (the young and the old), and the rates fell for the same reasons – increased school enrolment and earlier retirement. These changes were not gender specific and, since they affected men and women similarly, women's share of employment remained stable throughout, at approximately 28–9 per cent (Table 1).

TABLE 1

LABOUR FORCE PARTICIPATION RATES IN METROPOLITAN LIMA*
(population aged 6 years and over)

| Date | Total | Men | Women | Female share of employment |
|------|-------|------|-------|----------------------------|
| 1940 | 46.9 | 66.1 | 26.5 | 28.9 |
| 1961 | 44.8 | 64.4 | 25.2 | 28.5 |
| 1972 | 39.2 | 56.3 | 22.2 | 28.5 |
| 1981 | 39.0 | 55.5 | 23.0 | 29.6 |

*Source:* National Population Censuses, 1940, 1961, 1972, 1981.
*Metropolitan Lima = Province of Lima + Constitutional Province of Callao.

Note that the female participation rate only rose marginally between 1972 and 1981. This change is probably within the margin of error associated with census figures so not much importance should be given to it. However, it is clear that the recession neither pushed women out of the labour force significantly nor encouraged them into it through increased informal employment. If there was any reserve army effect during this period, it was not reflected in the participation rates.

Let us now examine the broad dualist division in the labour market and see to what extent economic changes produced an expulsion of women from capitalist employment and a concentration into the 'marginal' or informal sector (see Tables 2 and 4). Taking all capitalist employment, that is, wage and salaried labour, first, the most notable fact is that the proportion of all working women in this category *rose* rather than fell – from 39 per cent in 1940 to 52 per cent in 1972 and 55 per cent in 1981. However, there was a significant difference between salaried and wage labour, that is between white collar and manual work. The former increased to the point where it included almost half the female labour force, while the latter steadily fell. Both trends appear to have been unaffected by the recession (Table 2, column ii).

Between 1940 and 1981, the average annual growth rates in female wage

TABLE 2

DISTRIBUTIONS OF NON-PRIMARY EMPLOYMENT (*) BY EMPLOYMENT STATUS, DEPARTMENT OF LIMA AND CALLAO

| Employment status | (i) MEN | | | | (ii) WOMEN | | | | (iii) % of women within category | | | |
|---|---|---|---|---|---|---|---|---|---|---|---|---|
| | 1940 | 1961 | 1972 | 1981 | 1940 | 1961 | 1972 | 1981 | 1940 | 1961 | 1972 | 1981 |
| Wage labourers | 43.8 | 46.0 | 37.4 | 34.5 | 19.6 | 15.3 | 9.4 | 8.4 | 15.4 | 11.7 | 9.1 | 9.3 |
| Salaried employees | 30.6 | 26.3 | 38.2 | 35.6 | 19.5 | 29.5 | 42.6 | 46.4 | 20.6 | 30.9 | 30.7 | 35.4 |
| Self employed ** | 17.4 | 22.4 | 21.6 | 25.4 | 16.9 | 18.2 | 18.6 | 20.1 | 28.3 | 24.4 | 25.5 | 25.0 |
| Family labour | 0.7 | 0.7 | 0.7 | 0.4 | 2.2 | 1.6 | 1.2 | 1.0 | 57.3 | 49.3 | 39.2 | 53.5 |
| Domestic servants | 5.1 | 2.2 | 1.2 | 0.9 | 37.7 | 33.9 | 27.4 | 19.0 | 75.0 | 85.8 | 90.4 | 89.7 |
| Unspecified | 2.4 | 2.4 | 0.9 | 3.3 | 4.1 | 1.5 | 0.8 | 5.1 | 40.4 | 19.7 | 25.6 | 39.7 |
| | 100.0 | 100.0 | 100.0 | 100.0 | 100.0 | 100.0 | 100.0 | 100.0 | 28.9 | 28.5 | 28.5 | 29.6 |

*Source:* National Population Censuses, 1940, 1961, 1972, 1981.
*Notes:* \* Economically active population of six years and over, excluding those in agriculture, livestock, fishing and mining. The unemployed are also excluded, except in 1961 when unemployed persons with previous employment are included, classified according to their previous job (3.5 per cent of total). See Appendix.
  \*\* Independents and patrons are grouped together because of definitional changes between Censuses.

TABLE 3

DISTRIBUTIONS OF NON PRIMARY EMPLOYMENT (*) BY ECONOMIC SECTOR (**) DEPARTMENT OF LIMA AND CALLAO 1940, 1961, 1970, 1981

| Economic sector | (i) MEN | | | | (ii) WOMEN | | | | (iii) % of women in each sector | | | |
|---|---|---|---|---|---|---|---|---|---|---|---|---|
| | 1940 | 1961 | 1972 | 1981 | 1940 | 1961 | 1972 | 1981 | 1940 | 1961 | 1972 | 1981 |
| Manufacturing | 26.2 | 29.4 | 29.4 | 27.0 | 22.2 | 18.0 | 16.3 | 13.7 | 25.6 | 19.9 | 18.1 | 17.5 |
| Construction | 10.7 | 10.1 | 10.1 | 8.0 | 0.8 | 0.3 | 0.3 | 0.5 | 2.9 | 1.2 | 1.0 | 2.7 |
| Transport | 11.1 | 9.1 | 11.5 | 9.2 | 1.6 | 1.2 | 1.3 | 2.1 | 5.5 | 5.0 | 4.4 | 8.9 |
| Commerce | 17.5 | 21.1 | 17.6 | 19.8 | 13.7 | 18.1 | 16.4 | 22.1 | 24.1 | 25.8 | 27.0 | 32.0 |
| Services | 30.5 | 25.6 | 27.1 | 31.2 | 57.5 | 58.9 | 61.4 | 55.1 | 43.3 | 48.3 | 47.3 | 42.6 |
| Unspecified | 4.0 | 4.7 | 4.3 | 4.8 | 4.2 | 3.5 | 4.3 | 6.5 | 30.1 | 23.0 | 28.5 | 36.4 |
| TOTAL | 100.0 | 100.0 | 100.0 | 100.0 | 100.0 | 100.0 | 100.0 | 100.0 | 28.9 | 28.8 | 28.5 | 29.6 |

*Notes:* 
* Economically active population of six years and over, excluding those in agriculture, livestock, fishing and mining. The unemployed are also excluded in all years.
** The classification of economic sectors has been adjusted in order to maximise comparability across censuses.

gas, electricity and water are included in manufacturing in all years to give comparability with 1940.

the figures for 1972 and 1981 have been adjusted at sub-group level, in line with the 1940 and 1961 censuses as follows:

Manufacturing now includes manufacturing repairs (groups 9511–9519).

The new category of 'financial establishments and insurance' has been redistributed into commerce and services.

Commerce now includes banks, insurance etc. (groups 8101–8310) and loses restaurants & hotels (6310, 6320).

Services now includes business services (8321–8330), restaurants and hotels (6310, 6320) and loses manufacturing repairs (9511–9519).

*Source:* National Population Censuses. 1940. 1961. 1972. 1981.

TABLE 4
GROWTH RATES IN EMPLOYMENT BETWEEN CENSUSES, DEPARTMENT OF LIMA PLUS CALLAO

| | % increase in total employment 1940-81 | share of net increase going to women 1940-81 | average annual growth in women's employment (compound rates) | | |
|---|---|---|---|---|---|
| | | | '40-61 | '61-72 | '72-81 |
| Employment status* | | | | | |
| Wage labour | 347% | 7.6% | 3.7 | -7.8 | 3.6 |
| Salaried employees | 771 | 37.3 | 7.0 | 7.2 | 5.8 |
| Self employed | 746 | 24.5 | 5.3 | 3.9 | 5.7 |
| Family labour | 204 | 51.6 | 3.5 | 0.8 | 2.6 |
| Domestics | 165 | 98.5 | 4.4 | 1.7 | 0.7 |
| Economic sector | | | | | |
| Manufacturing | 466 | 15.8% | 3.8 | 2.9 | 2.8 |
| Construction** | 355 | 2.6 | -0.03 | 2.8 | 13.2 |
| Transport** | 424 | 9.6 | 3.4 | 4.8 | 10.5 |
| Commerce | 664 | 33.2 | 6.2 | 3.0 | 8.3 |
| Services | 513 | 42.5 | 4.9 | 4.3 | 3.6 |
| TOTAL*** | 514 | 29.7 | 4.8 | 3.9 | 4.8 |

*Source:* Adjusted Census figures [*Scott, 1985*]
*Notes:* *employment status figures include the experienced unemployed in 1961.
**note small numbers.
***includes persons in unspecified categories.

work were amongst the lowest of any category, and they were negative between 1961 and 1972. Women received only 7.6 per cent of the net increase in this type of work (Table 4). As a result the female ratio there declined and wage work came to be over 90 per cent 'male' (Table 2, column iii).

It should be noted that the rates of growth did not fall dramatically during the recession period, but rather during the period of growth fuelled by import substitution in the 1960s. This suggests that women's expulsion from wage work owed more to indirect substitution due to technological innovation than to the expulsion of the reserve army during the recession. In contrast, the growth of female white collar work has been truly staggering; between 1940 and 1981 it grew faster than any other category of employment, even during the recession years. Consequently the female ratio within the category rose – the only case where this was so, apart from domestic service.

These data clearly confirm one part of the FM thesis – the steady expulsion of women from capitalist wage work. But what of the increase in white collar work? Although the expansion of this category of employment has been noted by several authors [e.g. *Safa, 1977; Schmink, 1977*], it has been given little significance on the grounds of representing only a small proportion of total female employment. While this might be true at the national level, it clearly is not the case within cities. White-collar work is increasingly dominating all female urban employment, and is responsible for maintaining women's participation within the capitalist sector. Moreover, it does not seem to be subject to booms and slumps in the economy in the same way that wage work may have been.

Turning now to 'non-capitalist' employment, that is, domestic service, self-employment and family labour, Table 2 shows that the proportion in this category as a whole *declined* from 57 per cent to 47 per cent between 1940 and 1972 and fell even further to 40 per cent after the recession. The proportion of women in domestic service and the growth rates in this occupation have declined steadily since 1940, a tendency which has also been found in other Latin American cities. Even during the recession, the absolute numbers barely increased.[15]

On the other hand, the proportion of women in self-employment rose, although not nearly as much as might have been expected from the FM thesis. Although the rates of growth have been high relative to other categories of employment, and the proportions of self-employed women have increased, the share of total female employment remains small (20 per cent) and the female ratio within self-employment is low (25 per cent). Surprisingly, these trends appear to have been only marginally affected by the recession. Despite the rise in the growth rate between 1972 and 1981, the proportion of women in self-employment did not increase spectacularly, but rather was in line with an earlier trend. Moreover, the role of self-employment in the female labour market was closely paralleled in the male one – both the proportions and the rates of growth behaved similarly. Thus, there is little evidence for a gender-specific rise in informal employment deriving from women's role as subsidisers of the male wage. Therefore this version of the reserve army thesis also appears to be inapplicable in the Peruvian case.

Let us now examine the sectoral distribution of employment. Table 3 shows that, as predicted by the FM thesis, the proportion of women in manufacturing declined between 1940 and 1981, as did the female ratio within the sector. This was mainly due to the fall in women's manufacturing wage work, although it was somewhat offset by a sharp increase in white-collar labour.[16] Interestingly, the proportion of women in self-employment within manufacturing remained relatively stable throughout.

Table 5 shows the changes in the distribution of women within sub-branches of industry between 1940 and 1972 (unfortunately the data are not available in the 1981 census). Here we can see the overwhelming preponderance of women in textiles and clothing which persisted throughout the period despite a trend towards non-traditional industries. The fall in female employment in the textile industry, which has been the basis for much of the FM thesis, is evident here.

The slight redistribution of female employment towards non-traditional industries could be the result of new light assembly work, but may also reflect an expansion in clerical work. The increasing role of 'diverse industries' in the share of total female manufacturing employment, together with its marked increase in feminisation, merits comment since it is the only case where the female ratio increased. This branch includes many products made in 'world market' factories which have been noted for their gender-specific demand for labour, for example, assembly of scientific instruments, toys, sports and photographic equipment, etc.

Turning now to the proportion of women in tertiary employment (Table 3), it should be noted that the overwhelming predominance of commerce and services in the female labour market *predated* the period of industrial expansion, and though the proportion increased afterwards, it did not do so markedly.[17] The combined figure rose from 71 per cent in 1940 to 77 per cent in 1972 and 1981. Within the tertiary sector, the proportion of women in services grew only slightly up to 1972, although there was an internal switch from domestic service to public sector white collar employment. The fall in the proportions in service employment after 1972 was entirely due to the decline in domestic service. On the whole women's commercial employment grew faster than service employment and its share of total female employment rose consistently. However, contrary to expectation, the proportions in self-employment within this sector remained relatively stable, and the dynamic growth came from white-collar work. In summary, then, the high proportion of female employment in the tertiary sector cannot be attributed to concentration in 'marginal' occupations such as street selling or domestic service.

There is ample evidence of gender segregation in Tables 2–4, both in the degree of over- and under-representation of women in different categories of employment in each census and in the changes in these distributions over time. Despite small variations in the female shares of employment within categories, the sex distributions have remained very unbalanced. If we consider that a 'fair' distribution would be one that reflected women's overall share of employment that is, 28–9 per cent, we may note that the data show marked deviations from this figure in most cases (Tables 2 and 3, column iii). Manufacturing, construction and transport all have a significant under-representation of women, while women are over-represented in services. Only

TABLE 5

CHANGES IN THE SEX-COMPOSITION OF THE MANUFACTURING LABOUR FORCE*, DEPARTMENT OF LIMA PLUS CALLAO, 1940-72

| Industry | Female % distributions | | Change in industry share of women 1940-72 | Female % share within industries | | Change in female share within industry 1940-72 |
|---|---|---|---|---|---|---|
| | 1940 | 1972 | | 1940 | 1972 | |
| Food, drink, tobacco | 8.2 | 5.7 | -2.5 | 13.3 | 9.4 | -3.9 |
| Textiles | 18.1 | 10.2 | -7.9 | 34.1 | 21.4 | -12.7 |
| Footwear, leather, clothing | 60.1 | 54.1 | -6.0 | 47.1 | 47.6 | +0.5 |
| Wood, wooden furniture | 2.0 | 1.0 | -1.0 | 4.5 | 1.8 | -2.7 |
| Paper and printing | 3.0 | 3.2 | +0.2 | 12.4 | 10.8 | -1.6 |
| Chemicals | 3.1 | 6.6 | +3.5 | 28.8 | 20.8 | -8.0 |
| Minerals | 2.3 | 2.7 | +0.4 | 10.8 | 6.5 | -4.3 |
| Metal working | 1.6 | 3.3 | +1.7 | 5.4 | 3.3 | -2.1 |
| Diverse | 1.6 | 13.2 | +11.6 | 14.7 | 19.3 | +4.6 |
| TOTAL | 100.0 | 100.0 | | 26.1 | 18.2 | -7.9 |

*Source:* National Population Censuses, 1940, 1972.
*Economically active labour force of 6 years and over, excluding the unemployed. Manufacturing repair workers, classified in the services sector in the 1972 census, have been added in according to industry.

commerce approaches a proportional share. Similarly, wage work and domestic service show extreme under- and over-representation of women, and salaried work and self-employment are the only ones which approach a proportional distribution. As a result, the structure of men's employment differs quite markedly from women's, being more heavily weighted towards secondary sector employment and wage and salaried work (Tables 2 and 3, column i).

The second column of Table 4 shows that women's share of the net increase in employment in different categories was not comparable to their overall increase in employment; thus they did not usually receive a 'fair' share of new jobs. Apart from the transport and construction sectors from which they have traditionally been excluded, women received a less-than-proportional share of manufacturing employment and a more-than-proportional share of service employment. Only in commerce did they receive approximately their 'fair' share of jobs. The effect of this was to raise the female/male ratio in the service sector, and to lower it in manufacturing, construction and transport, thereby *increasing* the degree of over- and under-representation in each sector.

As far as employment status is concerned, the most marked deviations from a proportional share of employment growth were in wage work and domestic service. As already noted, women were not over-represented in the growth in self-employment and the female/male ratio there declined slightly. However, they did receive more than their 'fair' share of white-collar work, and by 1981 they were relatively over-represented in this category.

Note that the calculation of a 'fair' or 'proportional' share of jobs is relative to the overall share or increase in *female* employment. The fact that this figure falls far short of a half share (29-30 per cent) means that in all cases many more jobs went to men than to women. In the case of salaried work, for example, the very rapid and more-than-proportional increase in female employment was not sufficient to overturn men's majority position there.

These levels of over- or under-representation of women in broad categories of employment are the product of two more disaggregated distributions, the sex ratio *within* occupations and the distribution of men and women *between* these occupations. In order to understand the structures that underly the patterns of segregation discussed above we need to know about both these distributions. This information is not yet available from census data, but an analysis of 1974 survey data provides some indications [*Scott, 1984*]. In this study segregation was analysed at the three-digit level of occupational classification.

In that year, nearly two-thirds of the metropolitan labour force worked in occupations that were over 90 per cent male or female, and four-fifths were employed in occupations that were heavily dominated (over 50 per cent) by one sex or the other. There were only a few jobs with low levels of segregation, and they accounted for very little of male or female employment.[18] The degree of segregation was extreme both within occupational classes and within formal and informal sectors. The number of 'female' jobs was only a fraction of the number of 'male' jobs, and they provided employment for the majority of women.[19]

Since these data were collected at the end of the long period of growth, we can only assume that in previous times jobs were as segregated as they were in

1974 or less so. It would have been difficult for them to be more so. Thus it is fairly certain that growth did not produce desegregation; most probably the reverse.[20] However, some of these highly segregated 'female' jobs provided considerable employment for women, particularly within the capitalist sector, while others such as domestic service declined in importance. Therefore, although there were no marked changes in the degree of occupational segregation, there was a redistribution of women between the different parts of the female labour market. This produced an overall upward shift towards middle class employment and increased women's chances for mobility across the manual/non-manual divide.

Nevertheless, the majority of these 'female' jobs were located at the bottom of the hierarchies within capitalist enterprises and within broad occupational classes. Over half of non-manual women were concentrated on the lowest rungs of white-collar work compared with only a third of men, and 53 per cent of manual women were concentrated in unskilled and service work compared with only 17 per cent of manual men. This placed limits to women's upward mobility *within* manual and non-manual hierarchies. Moreover, it resulted in a high degree of economic inequality between men and women. Overall, women's average monthly earnings were about half that of men, and there were substantial male–female differentials within each occupational class.[21]

What does this analysis tell us about the processes of 'female marginalisation' in Lima? We have seen that women were not expelled from productive employment (if defined generally), nor were they increasingly confined to the informal sector, nor were they affected by the recession in ways that would confirm their role as a reserve army of labour. In certain cases they were incorporated into various parts of the labour market in ways that improved their occupational position. However this incorporation was predicated upon segregation and economic inequality. Thus women were marginalised on some dimensions, but not on others. In the absence of clear criteria of marginalisation, it is impossibile to select between these dimensions and therefore the FM thesis can be neither proved nor disproved.

This case indicates that the key to women's position in the labour market is not the *general* process of exclusion from or peripheralisation within the labour market but the *variety* of processes of selective incorporation and segregation which are continually being re-constituted in different parts of the labour market in the course of industrialisation. These variations clearly cannot be explained by system-level theories. Rather it is necessary to analyse them at the micro-level. This involves coming to grips with the issues of segregation and substitution.

MICRO-LEVEL UNDERPINNINGS OF MARGINALISATION: THE SEGREGATION AND SUBSTITUTION ISSUES

At the micro-level, processes of marginalisation and exclusion are the result of segregation and substitution between men and women in particular labour markets. There is considerable theoretical disagreement over these issues and different interpretations can be read into data which show changes in the sex composition of the labour force. Because the FM thesis has been pitched at the macro-level, it has failed to engage with these micro-level debates. However, it contains many implicit assumptions about labour market behaviour which are ambiguous and even contradictory. It is therefore necessary to consider some of these issues.

The literature on sex segregation in the labour market is wide-ranging and diverse (see Blau and Jusenius [1976] and Amsden [1980] for reviews). The conventional distinction is between supply-based and demand-based theories (neo-classical versus segmentation theories). However, another important distinction is between those who consider the market to be structured by 'pure' economic factors, and those who view it as a product of political, ideological and economic factors in combination.

Members of the first group, who may be referred to as 'substitutionists', may emphasise either demand or supply variables, but they share a common assumption that jobs are sex-neutral, and that demand and supply are structured by economic rationality alone, so that if market conditions were to change, patterns of segregation would alter. According to theorists within this group, gender segregation persists either because women's supply characteristics remain unchanged due to the prevailing family structure or biological differences, or because firms continue to use male-based technologies or segmentalist employment strategies. However, in both cases the theoretical possibility exists that if supply and demand conditions were to change, for example, through a rise in female qualifications or a change in entrepreneurial strategy, patterns of gender segregation might change. Since these factors *have* been changing in recent years,[22] the expectation is that segregation will diminish. However, research has consistently shown that neither the degree nor the pattern of gender segregation has altered significantly [*Oppenheimer, 1970; Gross, 1968; Hakim, 1979*].

The second group, who may be called 'segregationists', consider that political and ideological forces within the market produce inertia over time, so that it is unable to respond to changes in supply and demand as flexibly as might be assumed. This inertia is caused in two ways: by the stereotyping of men and women as particular categories of labour; and by the sex-typing of jobs. There is thus a two-fold segmentation, between male and female workers, and between 'male' and 'female' jobs. This segmentation is to a certain extent independent of the decisions of individual workers and employers. It has a structural force of its own which constrains the market through the process of stereotype formation and through political actions which reflect these stereotypes. Because of inertia, segregation is expected to be stable over time, unless deliberate policies are pursued to dismantle the ideological and political factors which support it.

These two approaches thus have different hypotheses about the way in which segregation (and, hence, marginalisation) changes over time. They also differ about the forms of substitution between men and women that are produced in the process. It is useful to identify three different kinds of substitution:

(i) *Direct substitution (of individuals):* The substitution of men by women or vice versa in *the same job.*

(ii) *Indirect substitution (of jobs):* The process whereby *jobs* are transformed through job re-design, technological change, or geographical relocation, changing the gender composition of the labour force in the process.

*(iii) Industrial or occupational substitution:* Changes in the relative distributions of men and women which result from differential rates of growth amongst industries or occupations rather than shifts in the relative distributions of men and women within them.

The 'substitutionist' approach emphasises direct substitution. It is reflected in the simple version of the reserve army hypothesis which assumes that when women are drawn into the labour market during the upswing of the cycle, or as substitute labour during strikes, etc., they do the *same* jobs as the men. These jobs are not constrained by sex-typing since they revert to men during the downswing of the cycle or after a strike.

The 'segregationist' approach considers that ideological and political pressures prevent direct substitution from taking place, except in isolated cases, and that for this reason women may actually be protected from market fluctuations [e.g. *Milkman, 1976*]. Gender substitution therefore takes place indirectly through the restructuring of jobs, changes in technology, etc., and this is more likely to happen in the medium or long run. The reserve army function of women can only take place through industrial and occupational changes, or by incorporating women indirectly through subcontracting.

The FM thesis is unclear or contradictory on these issues. For example, the processes which led to the expulsion of women from productive employment in the first phases of industrialisation are unspecified. Were women pushed out by men who took over their jobs through direct substitution, or did their jobs just become obsolete?[23] Does the reserve army operate on the basis of direct or indirect substitution? (Most analyses suggest the former.) Much of the discussion of the exclusion of women from modern sector employment in Latin American cities relies on standard supply variables such as lack of skills. Does this mean that if women were to acquire such skills they would get the jobs? Other writers have a more segregationist perspective [e.g. *Chaney and Schmink, 1980; Schmink, 1977*]; they emphasise the sex-typing of jobs and the male bias of imported technology. However, we need to know how the association between men and machines arose in the first place and what mechanisms perpetuate it. Finally, because of lack of clarity over the forms of substitution which give rise to marginalisation, evidence is often produced which is in fact due to industrial or occupational substitution, and does not reflect gender substitution at all.

In the next section, I shall discuss a recent article by Humphrey [*1984a*] which addresses the question of women's marginality from manufacturing employment in Brazil through an analysis of processes of segregation and substitution. I shall attempt to show that a lack of clarity over the theory of segregation and over appropriate indicators of substitution undermines the author's argument about the re-integration of women into manufacturing. This opens the way for a contradictory interpretation of the data which ultimately means that it is impossible to say whether Brazilian women have become less marginal or not.

'FEMALE MARGINALISATION' IN BRAZIL

Articles by Saffioti[*1969, 1975, 1978, 1982*], Madeira and Singer [*1973,*

*1975*], and Vasques de Miranda [*1977*] have become classic statements of
the FM thesis, based on Brazil. Through an analysis of changes in female
employment dating from the 1872 census, they document the fall in female
participation rates up to 1960, following the collapse of cottage industries and
the exodus from agriculture, and the reintegration of women into the urban
economy on the basis of tertiary sector activities, especially domestic service.
Alongside this is a demonstration of economic inequalities between men and
women workers. Amongst the many dimensions of marginalisation referred to,
the major emphasis is on women's exclusion from manufacturing employment
and the low rate of increase in female participation rates during the rapid urban
and industrial expansion of the 1960s.

Humphrey's study [*1984a*] aims to demonstrate that during the period of
rapid industrial growth referred to as the 'Brazilian miracle' (1967–73) these
tendencies were reversed. Not only did the global female participation rate and
the female share of industrial employment rise, but they rose faster than the
rates for men. He claims to show that these increases were not the result of the
temporary action of the reserve army, but represented structural changes
which were likely to endure beyond the conjuncture of the 'miracle'. Note that
the author is concerned only with the issue of marginalisation from industrial
employment, and his analysis is almost exclusively focused on manual
workers. He does not refer to other aspects of marginalisation such as
concentration into the tertiary or informal sectors, and he provides no data on
economic inequality.

The study is a useful contribution, first, because it calls attention to the
possible invalidity of the FM thesis, and second, because it departs from the
earlier style of analysis which relied on highly aggregated long-run data, and
examines the processes of segregation and substitution which underpin
women's marginalisation. To be fair, Humphrey does not set up his analysis as
a test of this thesis; he merely assumes that his evidence contradicts it and then
proceeds to examine why this should be so. However, the study suffers from
some of the methodological and theoretical ambiguities outlined above, so that
the interpretation is open to doubt. The problem is not so much that
Humphrey's analysis may be wrong, as that there is no way of choosing
between his and an alternative interpretation in the absence of clearer criteria
for measuring marginalisation and a more consistent theory of segregation. In
this case, then, the untestability of the FM thesis derives from contradictory
interpretations arising out of different theoretical and methodological
assumptions, rather than from contradictory evidence. In examining
Humphrey's analysis I shall focus on three inter-related issues: first, the
validity of the counter-marginalisation evidence; second, problems in the
interpretation of statistical data; and third, theoretical ambiguities in the
analysis of segregation processes.

Humphrey examines two hypotheses which might explain the increase in
female manufacturing employment during the 'miracle': (a) an expansion in
female-dominated industries and/or a process of feminisation through indirect
substitution (induced by technological change and deskilling); and (b) a
scarcity of male labour resulting from the acceleration of growth combined
with an increase in the supply of women to the labour market. In setting up the

hypotheses in this way, Humphrey implicitly distinguishes between the two competing approaches to gender segregation outlined above. In favouring the latter, he aligns himself with a substitutionist position: 'Scarcity of male labour has encouraged its substitution by female labour' [237]. Despite the disclaimer, his conclusion fits the simple reserve army hypothesis which posits that women are drawn into production during the upswing of the cycle as a result of shortages of male labour. He departs from this thesis only in his predictions as to what will happen in the downswing.

First let us examine the claim that there was a substantial rise in female manufacturing employment and significant changes in the sex composition of industry. Humphrey writes of a 'massive' influx of women into the economically active population' [241], and of 'sharp and widespread increases in female employment'[226] These statements are based on a comparison of the growth rates of the male and female workforces which shows the latter to be considerably greater than the former. The relatively better performance of women occurs in all broad industry groups and in all the major regions of Brazil. However, these rates are meaningless without the base figures from which they were calculated, for if the base was low, the absolute increases in women workers would still be low relative to those for men, and the overall sex distribution of the labour force would change very little. This is indeed suggested by the data for São Paulo in Table 4 [229].[24] The widespread occurrence of the relatively high female growth rates could be a result of the fact that the base was similarly low in all industries and regions. The extent of increases in the shares of female employment within industries also appears to have been exaggerated. A comparision between the 1960–70 and 1970–75 periods [Table 4] indicates considerable fluctuation in the share changes, cancelling each other out in some cases and producing an overall downward trend in others. It seems therefore that we are talking about small fluctuations around a low share of total manufacturing employment and variable changes in the sex composition of different industries, which is a rather different picture from the one Humphrey portrays.

The supposed evenness of the expansion in female employment constitutes the major grounds for rejecting the 'female job' hypothesis. Humphrey argues that an increase in female-specific demand would require a similarity in technological change which is unlikely to have occurred across industries and regions simultaneously. However, this argument would only be valid if the female-specific demand for labour had a single cause (deskilling). It is equally possible for a general rise in female employment to have been produced by a variety of factors, all of which were gender-specific.

Humphrey's observation that the changes were widespread is based on the fact that the female shares in manufacturing went up in all cases. However, he pays no attention to the fact that they did not go up *uniformly*. On the whole, the largest share increases were concentrated in industries which already had high proportions of female labour.[25] Humphrey discounts the possibility that the increases were due to the expansion of 'traditional' female industries, basing his observation partly on the poor performance of the textile industry. Although the female share of textile employment fell between 1960 and 1975 it was still almost twice women's overall share of manufacturing employment.

Moreover, the data show increases in other areas of traditional female employment. Over the whole period, the biggest change was in the footwear and clothing industry, surely the most traditionally female industry of all. Although its share increased by less in the second period than in the first, the overall rise was greater than in any other industry, and by 1975 the female ratio there was the highest in all manufacturing, almost three times the overall sectoral share.

It is possible that many of the non-traditional industries which show increases in female employment were of the 'world market factory' type (e.g. electronics and clothing), or relied on female labour for light assembly parts of the production process (e.g. perfumes and pharmaceuticals). Humphrey makes no mention of these questions. Yet it is known that much of the industrialisation of the 'miracle' period was export-led and dominated by multinational companies which did have a female-specific demand for certain jobs.[26]

Unfortunately, Humphrey does not give data on the distribution of women workers between different industries, but only on their shares within each industry. So it is difficult to assess the degree of concentration of the total female labour force in segregated industries. However, Table 5, assembled for a different purpose (based on enterprises with 50+ employees), shows a considerable concentration of manual women in industries which are known to have a gender-specific demand for labour, be it of the traditional type, or in the newer labour-intensive assembly factories. Sixty-nine per cent of them were concentrated in five such industries,[27] and 38 per cent were in textiles and clothing alone. The fact that these industries were also amongst those that showed increases in the female share of employment suggests that segregation was increasing both within industries and – as a result of their monopoly of female labour – within the sector as a whole.

Humphrey rejects the 'female job' hypothesis on the grounds that the association between total and female employment changed during the period. His argument is that if the gender shares of industrial employment had remained the same throughout the period, the levels of female employment would have been lower than they were. Thus the shares must have changed, indicating substitution. But this effect could also have been produced by a rise in female-specific demand for labour resulting from increases in segregation. Alternatively, they could have resulted from faster growth rates in industries that were employers of women – thus involving no gender substitution at all. This methodology therefore fails to distinguish between the two hypotheses because it cannot differentiate between the various types of substitution outlined earlier.[28]

Let us turn now to the 'labour supply' hypothesis favoured by the author (and by conventional reserve army theory). The first point is that scarcity of labour cannot be demonstrated by a rise in the aggregate volume of employment, since this could merely reflect growth in the economy. It would have to be supported either by a rise in wage levels, or by a fall in levels of employment in the 'reserve army'. In an economy like Brazil's the best indicator of the latter would be a fall in informal sector employment or in open unemployment. The increased female participation rate, used by Humphrey in the absence of adequate wage and employment data, is synonymous with the aggregate level of female employment and is therefore tautological. Moreover, it could reflect a shortage of female rather than male labour resulting from growth in female-specific industries.

In the absence of adequate data, then, the 'labour shortage' hypothesis remains unproven. Furthermore, there are some grounds for doubting its applicability. First, Humphrey's assertion of a *generalised* labour scarcity, affecting all skill levels [*236*] does not fit with his remarks about declining household incomes at certain points in the period studied, and amongst particular groups. He asserts, for example, that the 'desperate need for income' explains the rise in the participation rates of married women [*244*]. If household income varied over time and amongst groups despite the increasing labour force participation of secondary workers, we must assume that individual incomes were more variable than is suggested by the notion of a generalised scarcity of labour. This variation is consistent with some of the other literature on the effects of the 'miracle' on the distribution of income, which showed that while real earnings rose for most groups, there was increasing dispersion between them [*Pfefferman and Webb, 1979; Morley, 1982; Wells, 1983*]. The incomes that rose fastest were amongst skilled workers, suggesting that this is where the labour scarcity was to be found. However, Humphrey states that manual women were predominantly employed in the *unskilled* sections of the labour market. These women could not therefore have substituted for male labour directly. Indirect substitution could have taken place through the deskilling process, but this hypothesis was rejected.

All the evidence suggests that the pattern of female employment continued to be highly gender segregated and that relatively little direct substitution of men by women occurred during the period under review. This is supported by Humphrey's observations of strong workplace segregation [*235*] which he has taken up in more detail in subsequent articles [*Hirata and Humphrey, 1985; Humphrey, 1984b*]. How could he arrive at this contradictory interpretation, having rejected the 'female job' hypothesis?

Throughout Humphrey's article there is a confusion about the causes and extent of gender segregation in manufacturing. This confusion appears to reside in the notion that gender segregation occurs within the workplace *after* recruitment has taken place.

> While it is quite possible that when women were drawn into the labour force, certain changes in machinery and work organisation were made to facilitate their entry, or that women were predominantly recruited into those industries where such changes could be made, such changes would have been a *result* of the entry of women into the labour force, not its *cause*. [*235*, emphasis added].

This leads Humphrey to argue that market processes will be less flexible in the future, so that the conjunctural phenomenon of temporary labour shortages will be converted into a structural feature of the labour market: 'There will not therefore be any long-lasting reversal of the trend towards increasing female shares in industry'[*244*]. This suggestion is much more in line with a

278 DEVELOPMENT STUDIES REVISITED

segregationist perspective than a substitutionist one, since it indicates that future demand *will* be constrained by the 'female job' hypothesis. The contradiction in this argument could only be resolved if (a) pre-recruitment demand was separable from the jobs for which labour was recruited, and/or (b) there was a temporary suspension of gender-specific demand during the miracle period. No evidence is presented to support either of these possibilities, nor are they likely to have occurred.[29]

Humphrey's prediction has not been borne out by later events. In a recent article, Hirata and Humphrey [*1985*] mention that women suffered a disproportionate loss of jobs during the 1979–81 recession compared with men. Ironically this could have supported his earlier substitutionist position, demonstrating the disposability of women once the shortage of men had eased. (A segregationist interpretation would argue that this was due to the vulnerability of female-dominated industries to recession.)

What then of the marginalisation process in Brazil? Does Humphrey's evidence refute the FM thesis or not? The answer is that we cannot tell on the basis of the data provided because they are open to different interpretations. It is possible to argue, as I have done, that the increases in women's employment in manufacturing were relatively small given the low base, and that consequently women's overall share of sectoral employment remained low compared with men's. Such increases as did occur were based on high growth rates in female-specific industries and occupations and produced an overall increase in segregation. Moreover these industries were unstable over the complete phase of the economic cycle so that women suffered disproportionately from the later recession. These arguments would all be consistent with the FM thesis. However, in the absence of more accurate measures of segregation and the necessary evidence to support Humphrey's 'labour scarcity' hypothesis, the case must remain open.

The fact that Humphrey's data are open to contradictory interpretations means that the FM thesis cannot be tested without greater precision in the measurement of segregation and marginalisation. It also shows that methodological procedures have to be grounded in an internally consistent theory of segregation and substitution, and one that can take into account industry and occupation specificities. In the absence of these tools, the FM thesis is untestable.

CONCLUSION: BEYOND 'FEMALE MARGINALISATION'

This study has had two objectives: first, to reveal the theoretical and methodological weaknesses of the FM thesis; and second, to argue for a more consistent theoretical analysis of the role of gender in segmenting labour markets. Without this it is impossible to explain and predict the effects of economic development on women's position in the labour market.

I have argued that because of methodological imprecision the FM thesis fails to distinguish the different ways in which women are marginalised from employment, and cannot explain changes in these dimensions over time. Since almost any change in the pattern of female employment produces some degree of marginalisation, the thesis continues to be supported despite contradictory evidence. This is a serious problem for its status as a theory. 'Female marginalisation' will no doubt continue to be used for descriptive or political purposes, but it should not serve as a basis for theorisation.

Some critics may argue that official statistics are not sufficiently reliable as records of women's employment to serve as a basis for the analysis of their changing position in the labour market. Some of these issues have been addressed in the Appendix. However, if census data cannot be used to disprove the FM thesis, neither can they be used to support it, and alternative evidence must be found. Otherwise we are being asked to accept a theory in blind faith. This is clearly unacceptable not only because it is unscientific, but because it *is* important to understand how industrialisation affects women.

However, if the FM thesis is unsatisfactory for these purposes, we must ask what kind of theory should replace it? At what level should such a theory be pitched? Is a general theory of women's employment under capitalism possible, given the complexities discussed above? Is it desirable?

My own view is that a general theory *is* desirable, because the search for basic causes is irresistible, because I suspect that there *are* regularities in the ways in which gender structures labour markets in industrial societies, and because these regularities may have important implications for the analysis of class and politics. However, a general theory will only be possible (a) if it is built upon a firm foundation of micro-level analysis, and (b) if it adopts a multi-causal structure.

The Peruvian and Brazilian material has shown that while women may be marginalised from some forms of employment, they are selectively incorporated into others. The *selectivity* of these processes of exclusion, marginalisation and incorporation must be explained. The explanation will require a micro-level analysis that is specific to particular industries, occupations and perhaps localities. It may have to take into account historical and cultural factors. Studies which have proceeded along this route[30] have revealed the *variety* of ways in which gender is incorporated into and constructed by the labour market. This variety is absent from the FM thesis because besides being too general, it is essentially mono-causal. It relies on the notion of surplus labour and wage competition. But gender plays a role in structuring labour markets not just as cheap labour, but as subordinate labour, docile labour, immobile labour, domesticated labour, sexual labour, and so on. Thus it is not just dimensions of marginalisation that need to be distinguished, but dimensions of gender. The use made of these different aspects by employers extends far beyond pressure on wages.

However, while it is important to differentiate these micro-level processes, we should remain alert to the risk present in all differentiation analyses (cf. peasants, urban workers), of overstressing contingent factors and producing sterile typologies. It is therefore important to look for the regularities in these different situations in order to arrive at a set of more general propositions about the way in which gender is incorporated into capitalist labour markets. Only thus will it be possible to reconstitute long-run tendencies and system level structures that are not plagued with theoretical and methodological problems.

*final version received October 1985*

NOTES

1. See Arizpe [1977], Chinchilla [1977], Madeira and Singer [1973, 1975], Nash [1977], Saffioti [1969, 1975, 1978, 1982], Schmink [1977], Towner [1977], Safa [1977], Sautu [1980], and Vasques de Miranda [1977].
2. Evidence from advanced industrial societies shows that female labour force participation rises in later stages of industrialization. In Latin America also this trend has appeared since the 1950s and 1960s [Elizaga, 1974].
3. See Nun [1969, 1972], Cardoso [1971], Quijano [1974], Kowarick [1979], and Portes and Walton [1981].
4. See Schmink [1977], and Safa [1977] on white-collar labour, and Safa [1981], Fernández-Kelly [1983] Nash and Fernández-Kelly [1983] on women in 'world market' factories.
5. The term 'testable' is used here in a broader sense than that charcteristic of empiricist methodologies so as to include non-ad hoc postulation of consistent and plausible explanations which would account for the departure of empirical trends from initial expectations.
6. There is an extended debate within Marxism about what constitutes productive employment. The confusion largely resides in the rigour with which the labour theory of value is applied to categories of employment.
7. See Duncan and Duncan [1955], Gibbs [1965] and Gross [1968].
8. This is not to say that they are not sometimes associated together, but that this is not always and certainly not necessarily the case.
9. For example, it is often forgotten that men's participation rates have been falling as well as women's, and that men's real earnings have suffered during the recession as well as women's.
10. See Scott [1984] for data on earnings differences between men and women in Lima.
11. Between 1940 and 1972 real growth in GDP averaged around 5.5 per cent per annum, and per capita GDP doubled in spite of an increase in population growth. Manufacturing output rose at approximately seven per cent per annum and its share of GNP increased from 14 per cent to 22 per cent in the period. Most of the new manufacturing production was concentrated in Lima. The labour force in Lima quadrupled, reaching just over a million by 1972.
There has been continuing recession since 1975, which was particularly marked during 1977–78 and 1982–83. GDP growth rates were halved during 1975–76, and they were negative in 1978–79, recovering to around three per cent per annum in 1979–81. Manufacturing growth rates plunged to –2.3 per cent between 1975 and 1978, and they rose slightly during 1979–80, only to return to negative again between 1981 and 1983 [FitzGerald, 1979; IADB, 1984]. By 1981 real salaries had fallen by nearly half and wages by a third compared with 1973. Minimum wages had fallen by a third.
12. The dominance of foreign capital up to 1968 has been documented by FitzGerald [1979]. During the Velasco regime (1968–75), it was considerably weakened by a series of nationalisations, although continued reliance on foreign technology has maintained segmentation in the labour market.
13. A study of women's employment in Lima between 1974 and 1978, based on survey data does provide evidence of a reserve army pattern for women. As more families were concentrated into the poorest levels of household income, women's labour force participation did rise, and it was concentrated mainly in informal commercial employment [Jurado et al., 1982]. However, the figures presented in this study are considerably at variance with other reports, based on the same data, published by the Ministry of Labour. According to the former study the female participation rate for Lima in 1981 was estimated at 41.0 per cent, while the figure reported by the General Directorate of Employment was 29.2 per cent [Análisis Laboral, 1983:15]. This is much more in line with the census figure for that year. Therefore, although the possibility exists that a different methodology might reveal evidence of a reserve army effect, the question of error cannot be discounted in this particular study.
14. Cultural factors include gender ideologies derived from Roman Catholicism and family structure. My previous study showed that family structure had changed little in the period in terms of family size, age at marriage, and type of marriage. Gender roles also show remarkable stability, except amongst professional families where there is greater acceptance

of women working before and after marriage [*Scott, 1984*].

15. The shortage of domestic servants was also manifested in the preference for living out and working shorter hours.

16. Within the category of female manufacturing employment, white-collar work grew at ten times the rate of wage work.

17. Since the same pattern also held for men, questions may be raised about the general applicability of the dualist model to Peru. Aggregate data show little evidence of marked informalisation or terciarisation after the major period of industrialisation. My view is that this is because of the high selectivity of migration in Peru.

18. Jobs with low segregation were, for example, chemists, laboratory technicians, translators, librarians, telephonists, sales workers and assembly workers in certain industries. These occupations accounted for 21 per cent of all women workers. Note that many of them were segregated internally.

19. Sixty-three per cent of all women were employed in just 13 out of a possible 107 occupations.

20. The major exception to this is teaching. As in other countries, teaching began as a male profession, except in convents. But with the expansion of mass compulsory education, the lower echelons became filled with women.

21. These earnings differentials could not be put down to part-time employment, since the average working week for women was only just below the men's (42 hours compared with 46). Although about a quarter of women worked less than 35 hours per week, an equal number worked over 55 hours, and these tended to be the worst paying jobs (e.g. domestic service).

22. There has been a rise in the level of female qualifications and an increasing preference on the part of some employers for women workers (e.g. in light assembly industries).

23. It appears that some women's jobs did become obsolete, for example where cottage industries were replaced by mass produced goods, or where women acted as family helpers within factories or as outworkers. Equally there is evidence of women being pushed out of employment by male unions [*Hartmann, 1976; Kenrick, 1981*].

24. These data show that women's share of total manufacturing employment in the state of São Paulo (the most highly industrialised state) averaged only 23 per cent; it actually fell by two percentage points during 1960–70, and rose by less than one percentage point during the post-1970 expansion.

25. These were electronics, pharmaceuticals, perfume and soap, shoes and clothing, leather and hides, tobacco, and plastics.

26. TNC presence in Brazilian manufacturing was encouraged during the miracle period by policies designed to promote export of manufactures [*Balassa, 1979; Newfarmer, 1979*]. Typical 'female' industries such as footwear and clothing, leather goods and electronics, were major participants.

27. These were: metallurgical, electronics, plastics, textiles, and footwear and clothing industries.

28. Ultimately the only way of assessing whether substitution has taken place is by using (a) standardised measures of segregation which take into account changes in the aggregate level of female employment, and (b) statistical techniques such as shift share analysis which control for the differential growth of sub-sectors of industry [e.g. *Joseph, 1983*]. However, even these techniques cannot differentiate between direct and indirect substitution. This can only be determined at plant level.

29. The matching of people to jobs presumes that there is no disjuncture between the hiring and placement processes. While gender segregation certainly evolves and rigidifies over time, these processes are continually occurring in different parts of the labour market and have done so over a period of time. It is unlikely that such practices would or could have been suddenly suspended, even if employers had wished it.

30. Examples are Elson and Pearson's work on women in multi-national companies [*Elson and Pearson, 1981; Pearson, 1985*], Cockburn's work on printers [*1983*], etc.

## REFERENCES

Amsden, Alice H., 1980, *The Economics of Women and Work,* Harmondsworth: Penguin.
*Análisis Laboral,* 1983, Vol. VII, No. 68.

Arizpe, Lourdes, 1977, 'Women in the Informal Sector: The Case of Mexico City', *Signs,* Vol. 3, No. 1.

Balassa, Bela, 1979, 'Incentive Policies in Brazil', *World Development,* Vol. 7, Nos. 11/12.

Benería, Lourdes, 1979, 'Reproduction, Production and the Sexual Division of Labour', *Cambridge Journal of Economics,* Vol. 3.

Benería, L., and G. Sen, 1981, 'Accumulation, Reproduction, and Women's Role in Economic Development: Boserup Revisited', *Signs,* Vol. 7, No. 2.

Benería, L., and G. Sen, 1982, 'Class and Gender Inequalities and Women's Role in Economic Development – Theoretical and Practical Implications', *Feminist Studies,* No.1, Spring.

Blau, F., and C. Jusenius, 1976, 'Economists' Approaches to Sex Segregation in the Labour Market: An Appraisal', in M. Blaxall and B. Reagan (eds.), *Women and the Workplace,* Chicago: Chicago University Press.

Boserup, Ester, 1970, *Woman's Role in Economic Development,* London: Allen and Unwin.

Boserup, Ester, 1976, 'Employment of Women in Developing Countries', in Leon Tabah (ed.), *Population Growth and Economic Development in the Third World,* Vol.1, Belgium: Ordina Editions.

Breughel, Irene, 1979, 'Women as a Reserve Army of Labour: A Note on Recent British Experience'. *Feminist Review,* No. 3.

Cardoso, F.H., 1971, 'Comentarios sobre los conceptos de sobrepoblación relativa y marginalidad', *Revista Latinoamericano de Ciencias Sociales* (Chile), Nos. 1/2, Junio/ Diciembre.

Chaney, Elsa, and Marianne Schmink, 1980, 'Women and Modernization: Access to Tools', in June Nash and Helen Safa (eds.), *Sex and Class in Latin America,* New York: Bergin.

Chinchilla, Norma, 1977, 'Industrialization, Monopoly Capitalism and Women's Work in Guatemala', *Signs,* Vol.3, No.1.

Cockburn, C., 1983, *Brothers: Male Dominance and Technological Change,* London: Pluto Press.

Duncan, O.D., and B. Duncan, 1955, 'A Methodological Analysis of Segregation Indexes', *American Sociological Review,* Vol.20. pp.210–17.

Elizaga, J.C., 1974, 'The Participation of Women in the Labour Force of Latin America: Fertility and Other Factors', *International Labour Review,* Vol.109, Nos.5/6.

Elson, D., and R. Pearson, 1981, 'The Subordination of Women and the Internationalisation of Factory Production', in Kate Young, Carol Wolkowitz and Roslyn McCullagh (eds.), *Of Marriage and the Market,* London: CSE Books.

Fernández-Kelly, M.P., 1983, *For We Are Sold, I and My People: Women and Industry in Mexico's Frontier,* Albany: State University of New York Press.

FitzGerald, E.V.K., 1979, *The Political Economy of Peru, 1956–78,* Cambridge: Cambridge University Press.

Gibbs, Jack P., 1965, 'Occupational Differentiation of Negroes and Whites in the United States', *Social Forces,* Vol. 44, Dec.

Gross, Edward, 1968, 'Plus ça change . . .? The Sexual Structure of Occupations over Time', *Social Problems,* Vol.16, Fall.

Hakim, Catherine, 1979, *Occupational Segregation,* London: Department of Employment. U.K., Research Paper No.9.

Harris, O., and Young, K., 1981, 'Engendered Structures: Some Problems in the Analysis of Reproduction', in J. Llobera and J. Kahn (eds.), *The Anthropology of Pre-Capitalist Societies,* London: Macmillan.

Hartmann, Heidi, 1976, 'Capitalist Patriarchy and Job Segregation by Sex', in Martha Blaxall and Barbara Reagan (eds.), *Women and the Workplace,* Chicago: University of Chicago Press.

Hartmann, Heidi, 1979, 'The Unhappy Marriage of Marxism and Feminism: Towards a More Progressive Union', *Capital and Class,* No.8, Summer.

Hirata, Helena, and John Humphrey, 1985, 'Economic Crisis and the Sexual Division of Labour: The Case of Brazil', *Capital and Class,* No.24, Winter.

Humphrey, John, 1984a, 'The Growth of Female Employment in Brazilian Manufacturing Industry in the 1970s', *Journal of Development Studies,* Vol.20, No.4.

Humphrey, John, 1984b, 'Gender, Pay and Skill: Workers in Brazilian Industry', University of Liverpool, Department of Sociology (mimeo).

IADB (Inter-American Development Bank), 1984, *Economic and Social Progress in Latin America,* Washington, DC: IADB.

Jelin, Elizabeth, 1974, 'Formas de organización de la actividad económica y estructura ocupacional: el caso de Salvador, Brasil,' *Desarrollo Económico,* Vol.14, No.53, Abril–Junio.

Jelin, Elizabeth, 1980, 'The Bahiana in the Labor Force in Salvador, Brazil', in June Nash and Helen Safa (eds.), *Sex and Class in Latin America,* New York: Bergin.

Joseph, George, 1983, *Women at Work,* Oxford: Philip Allan.

Jurado, Joel, *et al.,* 1982, 'Informe técnico final del projecto: "Analisis y promoción de la participación de la mujer en la actividad económica"', Lima: Ministry of Labour (mimeo).

Kenrick, Jane, 1981, 'Politics and the Construction of Women as Second Class Workers', in Frank Wilkinson (ed.), *The Dynamics of Labour Market Segmentation,* London and New York: Academic Press.

Kowarick, L., 1979, 'Capitalism and Urban Marginality in Brazil', in Ray Bromley and Chris Gerry (eds.), *Casual Work and Poverty in Third World Cities,* Chichester: John Wiley.

Madeira, Felicia, and Paulo Singer, 1973, *Estrutura do emprego e trabalho femenino no Brasil, 1920–70,* São Paulo: Caderno CEBRAP No.13.

Maderia, Felicia, and Paulo Singer, 1975, 'Structure of Female Employment and Work in Brazil, 1920–70', *Journal of Inter-American Studies and World Affairs,* Vol.17, No.4. (translation of Madeira and Singer [*1973*], abbreviated).

Marulanda, Nohra Rey de, 1982, 'Empleo, pobreza y condiciones de vida de los hogares urbanos en donde el jefe es una mujer: el caso de Colombia', paper presented to the Congress of Americanistas, Manchester, September.

Milkman, Ruth, 1976, 'Women's Work and the Economic Crisis', *Review of Radical Political Economics,* Vol.8, No.1.

Morley, Samuel, 1982, *Labor Markets and Inequitable Growth,* Cambridge and New York: Cambridge University Press.

Nash, June, 1977, 'Women in Development: Dependency and Exploitation', *Development and Change* Vol.8, No.2.

Nash, June, and M.P. Fernández-Kelly, (eds.), 1983, *Women, Men, and the International Division of Labour,* Albany: State University of New York Press.

Newfarmer, Richard S. 1979, 'TNC Takeovers in Brazil: The Uneven Distribution of Benefits in the Market for Firms', *World Development,* Vol.7, No.1.

Nun, José, 1969, 'Superpoblación relativa, ejército industrial de reserva y masa marginal', *Revista Latinoamericana de Sociologic* (Argentina), Vol.5, No.2.

Nun, José, 1972, 'Marginalidad y otras cuestiones', *Revista Latinoamericana de Ciencias Sociales* (Chile), No.4, Diciembre.

Oppenheimer, Valerie, 1970, *The Female Labor Force in the United States,* Berkeley: University of California, Institute of International Studies.

Pearson, Ruth, 1985, 'The "Greening" of Women's Labour: Multinational Companies and their Female Workforce in the Third and First World', in Sheila Allen *et al.* (eds.), *The Changing Experience of Work,* London: Macmillan.

Pfefferman, Guy, and Richard Webb, 1979, *The Distribution of Income in Brazil,* Washington, DC: World Bank Staff Working Paper, No.356.

Portes, A., and J. Walton, 1981, *Labor, Class and the International System,* New York and London: Academic Press.

Quijano, Aníbal, 1974, 'The Marginal Pole of the Economy and the Marginalised Labour Force', *Economy and Society,* Vol.3.

Safa, Helen, 1977, 'The Changing Class Composition of the Female Labor Force in Latin America', *Latin American Perspectives,* Vol.4, No.4.

Safa, Helen, 1981, 'Runaway Shops and Female Employment: The Search for Cheap Labor', *Signs,* Vol.7, No.2, Winter.

Saffioti, Heleieth, 1969, *A mulher na sociedade da classes: mito e realidade,* São Paulo: Editora Quatro Artes.

Saffioti, Heleieth, 1975, 'Female Labor and Capitalism in the United States and Brazil', in Ruby
    Rohrlich-Leavitt (ed.), *Women Cross-Culturally: Change and Challenge,* The Hague:
    Mouton.
Saffioti, Heleieth, 1977, 'Women, Mode of Production, and Social Formations', *Latin American
    Perspectives,* Vol.4, Nos.1/2.
Saffioti, Heleieth, 1978, *Women in Class Society,* New York: Monthly Review Press.
    (Translation of Saffioti [1969].)
Saffioti, Heleieth, 1982, 'La modernización de la industria textil y la estructura de empleo
    femenino, un caso en Brasil', in Magdalena León (ed.), *Sociedad, Subordinación y
    Feminismo,* Bogotá: Asociación Colombiana para el Estudio de la Población.
Sautu, Ruth, 1980. 'The Female Labor Force in Argentina, Bolivia and Paraguay', *Latin
    American Research Review,* Vol.15, No.2.
Schmink, Marianne, 1977. 'Dependent Development and the Division of Labor by Sex:
    Venezuela', *Latin American Perspectives,* Vol.4, Nos.1/2.
Scott, Alison MacEwen, 1984, 'Desarrollo dependiente y la segregación ocupacional por sexo',
    *Desarrollo y Sociedad* (Colombia), No. 13, and *Debates en Sociologia* (Peru), No.10. An
    extended version of this article is to appear in English in Richard Anker and Catherine Hein
    (eds.), *Sex Inequalities in Urban Employment in the Third World,* London: Macmillan,
    1986.
Scott, Alison MacEwen, 1985, 'On the Adequacy and Comparability of Peruvian Employment
    Statistics, with Special Reference to Metropolitan Lima', University of Essex, Department
    of Sociology (mimeo).
Towner, Margaret, 1977, 'Monopoly Capitalism and Women's Work during the Porfiriato',
    *Latin American Perspectives,* Vol.4, Nos.1/2.
Vasques de Miranda, Glaura, 1977. 'Women's Labor Force Participation in a Developing
    Society', *Signs,* Vol.3, No.1.
Wells, John, 1983, 'Industrial Accumulation and Living Standards in the Long Run: The São
    Paulo Industrial Working Class 1930–75 (Part II)', *Journal of Development Studies,*
    Vol.19, No.3.

APPENDIX

ON THE ADEQUACY OF PERUVIAN CENSUS DATA

The analysis of historical trends in women's employment via the National Population
Censuses is subject to several possible weaknesses: first, problems in the coverage of
women's employment levels, that is, participation rates; second, changes in definitions
of employment between censuses; and third, changes in the levels of aggregation of
data. I shall discuss these in reverse order. (These issues have been considered in detail
in Scott [1985]).

*Levels of Aggregation*

Unfortunately, the 1940 census was the most highly aggregated census, and since this
is the base year, certain categories have had to be amalgamated in subsequent years.
The more serious problem is that the geographical area used for some of the tables is not
the Metropolitan area of Lima, which consists of the Province of Lima plus the
Constitutional Province of Callao, but the Department of Lima. This is because data on
employment status are only provided at Departmental level in the 1940 census. The
population outside the Metropolitan area (12 per cent of the total in 1981), lives in four
small coastal towns and scattered villages. Most of the workforce there is engaged in
primary sector activities so that when the non-primary workforce is excluded from the
Departmental figures, they very closely approximate the Metropolitan ones. Thus the
inclusion of the non-Metropolitan population does not distort the figures much.

## Changes in Definitions of Employment

The most important changes in definitions between censuses relate to the classification of employment by economic sector. Other inconsistencies are to be found in the treatment of the unemployed and in the distinction drawn between self-employed workers and owners. Because of the latter problem, the two categories have been amalgamated in all tables. The unemployed were classified as outside the active labour force in 1940, and information was only gathered on those who had previously been employed; thus those seeking work for the first time were excluded from both the active and the inactive labour force. A further problem arises in the 1972 and 1981 censuses, in that certain data are not provided for the unemployed. To avoid these problems, the unemployed were excluded from all tables. This was possible because in later censuses data are provided separately for the employed and the unemployed. However, the exception to this is the 1961 census which presents difficulties in eliminating the unemployed at the same time as the primary sector workforce. This is because the cross-tabulation of economic sector by employment status is not provided separately for the employed and unemployed labour forces as in 1972 and 1981. That is provided for the total EAP, with the experienced unemployed distributed within the table according to their previous job. Only first-time job seekers, who are all placed in unspecified, can be removed from the table. Since the extraction of the primary sector workforce is necessary for consistency with other tables, all data on non-primary workers' employment status must necessarily include the experienced unemployed. Fortunately this is only 3.4 per cent of the total workforce.

Economic sector classifications have been regrouped in order to permit maximum comparability between censuses. Broadly speaking the 1940 and 1961 censuses were comparable, as were the 1972 and 1981 ones. However, since the latter two are highly disaggregated, it was possible to relocate the relevant sub-categories as necessary. For details see footnotes to tables.

## Levels of Female Labour Force Participation

Much has been written about the change in definitions of economic activity which occurred between the 1940 and 1961 censuses, which resulted in a dramatic decline in female participation rates. It is likely that real social changes were important as well as changes in definitions, and in any case, it was the rural population that was primarily affected. The source of the definitional change was a change in the format of the schedules that were applied to the rural population. However, the schedule applied in Lima and other main cities had similar categories and wording to the 1961 and subsequent censuses. A different problem is presented by the fact that from 1961 on a minimum limit of hours worked per day or week was applied to unpaid family workers. This limit is rather high (15 hours per week) and may have led to some underestimation of informal employment.

There is no doubt that the form of words used on census schedules, the lack of probing on unemployment or inactivity, and the lack of training of census enumerators must produce some underestimation of female employment rates. However, a comparison of Ministry of Labour survey data collected in 1973 and 1974 with the 1972 census data suggests that the degree of underestimation may not be great. The Ministry of Labour has extensive experience of labour force surveys, their questionnaires have many probes for informal employment and their interviewers are specially trained to be aware of the ambiguities of employment data. Nevertheless, their surveys reported a female participation rate of 32.3 per cent in 1974 (based on a population of 14 years and over), which is only slightly above the 1972 census figure when based on the 15+ age group (29.3 per cent). A comparison of the age structure of the two labour forces suggests that the Ministry of Labour survey picked up more women in the older age groups (25–50) years. A comparison of the distributions of the labour force by economic sector and employment status shows slightly higher proportions in self-employment jobs in manufacturing and commerce. This would be consistent with the types of jobs held by married women, probably working from their homes.

It is possible that the extent of the discrepancy between census and survey data would have been greater in recession years if it was indeed the case that informal employment increased then. Against that argument is the fact that even in the growth years there were a considerable number of women living in poverty, who would have had good reason to work in the informal sector. The fact that they did not (according to survey data) suggests that there were some constraints – economic, cultural or otherwise – which prevented them from doing so. In any event, the discrepancies were not great in 1972, or in 1981, and the fact that the trends were so consistent over the years, suggests that useful information can be gathered from the census data.

# THE STATE AND DEVELOPMENT

# National Development Policy and External Dependence in Latin America

## By Osvaldo Sunkel*

### I. ANALYSIS OF THE PROBLEM

In an adequate historical perspective, development appears as a process of transformation of economic, social, political and cultural structures and institutions. National development policy, to be effective, must therefore stimulate and promote the institutional and structural changes essential for the achievement of desired social goals. This implies changing what is traditionally accepted, and challenging entrenched interests, both domestic and foreign. Therefore, the objectives, intensity, instrumentalization and efficiency of development policies are limited within certain margins of flexibility; their freedom of manoeuvre will depend principally on internal conditions but also on the international relations of the country concerned.

The domestic situation is affected over a period of time by the changes which the process of development itself brings about: industrialization, urbanization, occupational differentiation, changes in social structure, alterations of attitudes and values, modifications of the patterns of political participation, transformation in the social function of women, technological changes in mass media, changes in the size and functions of the State, etc.

The influence which external relations exercise on national development policy derives from the fact that the Latin American countries are enmeshed in the system of international relations of the capitalist world. This system is characterized by the presence of a dominant power, a series of intermediate powers and the underdeveloped countries ascribed to it. Like the domestic situation, this system is also essentially dynamic. Significant variations are experienced both because of changes inside the countries and as a result of the confrontation with the other principal system of international relations, that of the socialist world. Variations in this world-wide confrontation also affect the limits within which national development policy may move.

All this, of course, is not novel. Most people know perfectly well that policies in general, and development policy in particular, can range within a spectrum which at certain times is limited and at others enlarged by external conditions. Public officials, statesmen, and politicians are as conscious of this external conditioning as they are aware of the internal political situation.

* Osvaldo Sunkel is Professor of Economic Development at the Economics Faculty and Research Fellow of the Institute of International Studies of the University of Chile. He was formerly with the U.N. Economic Commission for Latin America and the Latin American Institute for Economic and Social Planning. This article is a revised version of a lecture delivered on November 17, 1966, at the University of Chile during the series of Inaugural Lectures of the Institute of International Studies.

Nevertheless, if one examines the writings of economists, sociologists and political scientists in Latin America, external dependence as a subject is remarkably absent.[1] It would appear that sociology, economics, and political science in the post-war period have not been concerned with this question.

One wonders if this extraordinary phenomenon is not in itself a first manifestation of dependence. The fact is that we dare not touch this theme, either because of the political risks and connotations, or because it has not been consecrated as part of the aseptic and formalistic range of topics which today serves as academic standard of reference for specialists in the social sciences. To find serious analyses of this theme one must go back to the classical theories of imperialism, either in their Marxist[2] or non-Marxist[3] versions, but it is evident that these theories, which were elaborated almost entirely during the first three decades of this century, are largely out of date because of the profound internal changes which both developed and underdeveloped countries have experienced, and the radical transformations which have taken place in their relations with one another.[4]

Also related to the theme of dependence are the critical analyses of the classical theory of international trade by Prebish, Singer, Myrdal and others, which are represented institutionally by the work of the U.N. Economic Commission for Latin America and more recently by that of the Secretariat of U.N.C.T.A.D. Nevertheless, these touch only partially on the theme of external dependence.

In contrast with the lack of serious research on this very important topic, public discussion and partisan controversy abound. Dogmatic and anecdotical approaches to the problem of external dependence occupy much of the casual conversation of the same social scientists who refuse to be concerned with it as a topic of research. It is not surprising that if the social scientist refuses to accept responsibility for offering information, analysis and objective interpretations of a problem of serious concern to the community, the dominant attitudes in public debate are extremist, biased and superficial.

Thus for some, private foreign investment, gifts, private and official credits and other forms of transfer of resources from the developed to the underdeveloped countries are 'foreign aid', 'a disinterested sacrifice which the rich countries make to help their poor brothers'. For others, this flow of foreign resources represents the 'new face of imperialism' through which 'the monopolies and international cartels have found new ways of sucking the blood of the backward countries in order to keep them permanently oppressed'.

Likewise, the treaties and international agreements in the economic, financial and military spheres which lead to the adoption of international and domestic policies other than those which would have been freely adopted, constitute for some 'the defence of liberty, democracy, and the traditions of Western Christian Civilization', while for others they represent the 'return to colonialism and imperialism'.

Less attention has been paid to the massive and rapidly increasing transfer of attitudes, values, patterns of consumption and styles of living, forms of artistic expression, social organization and technological development. Some see in all this the 'process of modernization and rationalization which constitutes the base and prerequisite of economic development'. Others see in it 'the most dismal process of cultural alienation in which our own values and traditions are sacrificed in the pursuit of a well-being which is mistaken with the consumption of more or less superfluous material goods'.

Like all schematic descriptions, this one is also exaggerated and something of a caricature, but it corresponds in its essentials to the actual opinions about the foreign ties of our countries. It would certainly be difficult to use this as a base for a serious discussion. I propose therefore to begin from quite a different angle. An examination of the development programmes of many Latin American countries, especially in their political versions, reveals that self-determination, independence and a reduction in foreign dependence are among the fundamental objectives. Moreover, if one analyses the policies of development and industrialization of Latin America—and of other underdeveloped areas of the world as well—one observes that an essential element is precisely the desire to overcome foreign dependence. Therefore, it is possible to accept the premise that this is one of the basic objectives pursued by economic development policies.

The question arises: is every development policy conducive to the fulfilment of this objective? The answer is clearly negative. There are exceptional cases of development policies—understanding development in the sense of economic growth—which have been very successful from this point of view, but which have meant not only the emigration of an important part of the population, but also the denationalization of these countries, their absorption into other cultures and the creation of what has been aptly named 'a dependent country' ('*país sucursal*'). I believe that this is not the ideal model to which Latin Americans aspire. In fact, one of the objectives of an ideal development policy seems to be, on the contrary, the affirmation of the national personality.

It is important, therefore, to examine Latin American development policies to see if they do lead towards the fulfilment of this essential objective or if, on the contrary, they are leading towards greater foreign dependence.

The study of conventional development policies reveals the existence of contradictory tendencies, some of which reinforce the situation of dependence, while others provide a start for a policy of greater independence. The analysis of these tendencies leads me to sketch certain alternative strategies and lines of action which, in my opinion, permit the scale to tip in the direction of reducing dependence, without conflicting with the necessary acceleration in the rhythm of economic growth.

In order not to be utopian or excessively idealistic, it is necessary to evaluate the viability of such alternative propositions starting from the situation of dependence in which we now find ourselves. All this, of course, is not more than a first attempt to explore the area of research on foreign dependence, an area which until now has been considered taboo for serious analysis, in terms which will make a fruitful discussion possible. Moreover, I must make it very clear that I shall examine the long-range tendencies which, in my opinion, influence the phenomenon of dependence, and not the particular changes derived from more or less temporary and partisan-political situations.

II. FOREIGN DEPENDENCE AND INTERNAL CHANGES

*Internal Socio-Political Changes and their Significance*

To gain a better understanding of the essence of the phenomenon of dependence in Latin America, it is useful to begin with a brief examination of the socio-economic evolution in very broad outline and starting from certain significant periods, because the present economic, social and institutional structure has characteristics whose origins date from different key formative periods.

The traditional rural structure, which was consolidated in Latin America partly before Independence and partly during the 19th century, is one which many voices from all directions have been insisting for years ought to be altered through an agrarian reform.

Between the end of the 19th century and the 1930s the characteristic structure of export and import trade and the financial links with the industrialized countries were established. It was during this time that, on the basis of foreign investment, most of Latin America developed the production of primary materials for export which still characterizes its foreign trade.

From the 1930s onwards, and especially in the major countries of the southern tip and in Mexico, a new historical phase was superimposed: this was industrialization, accompanied by rapid urbanization and the rise of social policies; systems of social security, housing, health, and education. As all of these developments imposed heavy burdens on the public sector, it was also a period during which the state expanded considerably and acquired new functions.

Each of the successive transformations experienced during these three phases influenced the pre-existing structures, but the opposite phenomenon was more striking; the stubborn resistance of the agrarian structure and that of foreign trade to the successive dynamic influences, first of the expansion of trade and later of industrialization. It is as if the development of our societies had been achieved by the addition of new structures rather than through the internal transformation and evolution of their original social forms.

The increasing diversification of Latin American societies during these periods had important effects on the social and economic structure. In terms of social structure, they variously passed from simple dual social systems—with a dominant oligarchy and a rural mass which was not even a political body—to a much more complex system of social differentiation. This was the result of modern export activities, industrialization, the growth of cities, expansion of the state apparatus, advancement of education, etc. The greater complexity of the social structure reduced the dominant role of the traditional oligarchy. The rural and urban masses were at least marginally incorporated into the process of political participation. Between the two extremes characteristic of traditional Latin American society there appeared a varied range of social strata, groups, classes, and estates. This was particularly true of the urban sector with its industrial entrepreneurs, professionals and technicians, white-collar workers of both public and private sectors, organized labour, students, etc.[5]

In so far as these different middle groups and the rural and urban masses increasingly influence the political process, a tendency can be discerned towards greater representation of the community in the State; towards higher levels of participation by increasing numbers of the national population in public affairs. If this tendency is a fact and is associated with the process of development, then it is possible to suggest that the differentiation of the social structure and the greater participation of the national community in the political process mark the beginnings of a broadly based and decisive assertion of the national and collective interest. Therefore, efficient political alliances of certain groups of the middle class with the great rural and urban masses become possible.

These new alliances (which ought not to be confused with the ones that have occurred in the past in Latin America) represent national collective interests and objectives in a better and different way from that which was the case in traditional, dual societies. Nationalism, development, and organized mass participation are the ideological pillars of such alliances. From this point of view it would seem, therefore, that at least potential conditions exist for a national development policy to be translated into programmes, strategies of action and concrete political movements in some of our countries.

This requires that certain middle groups be willing to assume the leadership in the organization and integration of the marginal urban and rural masses into the political process and into the economic, social and cultural life of the nation. Since a programme of this nature necessarily implies a redistribution of income and wealth, a transfer of political power and a reordering of social opportunities, as well as a considerable effort of saving and mobilization of resources, the middle groups which are now benefiting from privileged positions are naturally opposed to such a policy. But such middle groups as have not been able to take advantage of the process of development so far and which do not see in its orientation and sluggish rate prospects for future realization are likely to support it. In those countries where import substitution industrialization begins to falter, frustration is evident, especially among certain groups of professionals and technicians and technocrats of the public and private bureaucracy; amongst some of the national entrepreneurs displaced by foreign private enterprise[6] and in institutions concerned with collective and long-term interests rather than with immediate objectives—the intellectuals, youth and the Church.

The potential 'Nasserist' and reformist role of the armed forces in Latin America has been largely frustrated to the extent that these institutions have been functionally incorporated into a Cold War situation through their acceptance of the doctrine of the ideological frontier, which lends itself marvellously to equate, either deliberately or unconsciously, a national programme of basic transformations with a subversive process with respect to the dominant domestic groups. Thus imbued with this doctrine, the armed forces become a powerful instrument placed in the hands of those ready to resist change at all costs.

Another phenomenon which can lessen the possibility of certain middle groups assuming the leadership of a truly national development policy is found in the degree of cultural alienation of these groups; the intensity of their immediate aspirations to assimilate 'modern' ways of life and consumption and the extent to which they feel that these aspirations can only be realized by associating with foreign economic or cultural entities of various kinds. On the other hand, to the extent that these middle groups are victims of mass propaganda—which has reached the point of poisoning even children's literature, films and television—and accept the doctrine of the cold war and the ideological frontier, they can be easily frightened and led to reject a national development policy.

The preceding analysis reveals contradictory tendencies. On the one hand, basic changes are taking place in the social structure with the incorporation of the rural and urban masses, the growth and differentiation of the middle groups, the enlargement of the process and mechanisms of political participation and the greatly enhanced importance and functions of the central State. On the other hand, there are interest groups and sectors associated with foreign activities, as well as tendencies towards cultural and ideological alienation, particularly in the middle groups, which hinder the transformations implicit in a national development programme. Therefore, if our analysis is correct, there would not seem to be inevitable historical laws or tendencies at work in one direction or another but, rather, contradictions which open possibilities of choice and of alternative action.

Given certain foreign and domestic circumstances and an adequate analytical knowledge of the process of change, the formulation and implementation of national development policy appears as a distinct possibility. In the absence of such knowledge and of a concrete programme it is unlikely that such a policy could be achieved even if a favourable opportunity were forthcoming; worse, even the perception of the opportune moment would become impossible. I believe that, at this stage, our incapacity to lessen, modify and finally overcome the situation of dependence in which we find ourselves is fundamentally the result of a lack of intellectual and scientific effort to understand our historical reality and our possibilities of autonomous action, and a lack of creative effort to find adequate solutions to our problems.

The formulation of a strategy of national development requires, therefore, a precise diagnosis of the mechanisms of dependence in all its forms: economic, political, military, and cultural. That I shall refer only to certain economic aspects does not mean that the others are not as important.

*Development and the Mechanisms of Economic Dependence*

The historical evolution of our economies has left as vestiges certain characteristic features which must be pointed out in considering the problem of dependence and national development policy.

First, the traditional agrarian structure has largely been preserved, seriously limiting modernization and technological improvement of rural production. Agriculture has been unable to respond efficiently to the demand for farm produce which has been strongly stimulated both by the growth of population and of urban incomes and by the development of industry itself, which, at least in its initial stages, is based largely on primary agricultural materials. Among other serious consequences[7] this situation has contributed to the worsening of the balance of payments deficit, either because exports have been reduced or because agricultural imports have increased considerably.

Second, we have inherited a structure of foreign trade which, in open defiance of policy pronouncements repeated for the last 20 years, still relies principally on the export of a handful of primary commodities. Since the Second World War there has been increasing insistence on the necessity of diversifying exports and extending local processing of primary materials, but the figures show that in the majority of the Latin American countries, the degree of concentration of exports on very few products has in fact slightly increased.[8]

Third, industrialization has not produced all the expected benefits; in particular, it has not resulted in a lessening of foreign dependence which, after all, was one of its basic objectives. Even if industrialization has permitted the reduction of the proportion of the value of imports with respect to G.N.P.—the import coefficient—it has also resulted in a change of great importance in the structure of imports. If several decades ago a large proportion of available foreign exchange was devoted to purchasing non-essential consumer goods, today—at least in the most industrialized economies of the region—imports are made up almost exclusively of essential goods: tools, machinery and equipment, to maintain and expand productive capacity; primary materials and intermediate products to assure a normal level of economic activity; and basic foodstuffs to maintain popular consumption. That is to say, we have arrived at a situation of extreme external vulnerability because any alteration of foreign markets or any problem of foreign financing causes very grave difficulties. These difficulties may arise from the resulting scarcity and higher prices for essential consumer goods, from the restrictions on the import of primary materials and their effect on the normal development of manufacturing activity, or from the delays in imports of machinery and equipment and the resulting influence on productive capacity.

This curious result is largely the consequence of the way in which the policy of industrialization has been carried out in Latin America, the so-called process of import substitution. In situations in which foreign exchange is insufficient the importation of consumer goods has been limited. But, since the internal demand for these goods was not reduced, nor was the importation of the machinery and goods necessary to produce them limited, conditions were created which made it possible to begin to produce them within the country. Apparently protection favoured national industry, but the traditional foreign connections, by a sort of acrobatic leap, overcame the protectionist tariff and the policies of prohibition of imports. Far from disappearing, they increased. Goods which had previously been imported began to be produced domestically, but this meant not just importing equipment and machines—and even a considerable proportion of the components for the finished manufacture —but also incurring financial costs in foreign exchange which now constitute an overwhelming burden in many countries. This is due not only to the fact that a large part of this domestic industry is foreign-owned—subsidiaries of large multi-national companies—and that many products are manufactured under licence or technical assistance contracts which are paid for in various ways, but also to the fact that public and private financing from abroad was necessary in order to accelerate industrialization and investment in infrastructure. Thus the process of import substitution has resulted, on the one hand, in great vulnerability of our balance of payments and, on the other, in foreign financial commitments which in some Latin American countries represent a considerable proportion of current foreign exchange receipts.

Finally, another of the characteristic features inherited from this stage of industrialization is the establishment, during the period from 1930 to the present, of a very large and active Central State, which fulfils three basic functions. Based on the appropriation of a considerable part of the financial resources of the export activity—which because of its high productivity was the only sector of the economy to generate an abundant surplus of taxable income—the State has come to fulfill three new principal functions: *as a financial intermediary*, which transfers financial resources and subsidizes the development of private industry, usually by means of development institutions; *as a mechanism for income redistribution*, allocating resources to the expansion of social security and to the extension of educational, housing and health services; *as a mechanism of public investment*, which adapts and enlarges the economic infrastructure: transportation, communications, power and also some basic industrial enterprises. As can be appreciated, the process of industrialization and development begun in the decade of the 1930s in the now most industrialized countries of Latin America, and more recently in the others, depended on a fundamental support, the public sector. After the Great Depression the public sector began to fulfil a strategic function in development policy: the appropriation of resources in the highly productive export activities and their reassignment in order to promote industrial and social development.

In this new function the State has been confronting two contrary tendencies which are becoming more acute. On the one hand, there is an insatiable thirst for appropriating resources in order to use them in programmes of industrialization and infrastructure and especially in the area of social services. On the other hand, the goose which lays the golden eggs—the export sector—has remained relatively stagnant, due partly to heavy taxation but mainly to policies and technological developments in the world's developed industrial economies, over which the Latin American countries have little influence. Therefore, once the principal base of the taxation system stagnated and tax rates reached a certain level, revenues no longer grew at a rhythm commensurate with the rapidly increasing necessities of the public sector. The political and administrative problems of quickly and efficiently extending the taxation system to the rest of the economy, and the problems derived from the characteristics of the economic structure itself, thus determined a systematic and permanent tendency to deficit in the public sector. Moreover, given the instability of the income derived from the export sector, the deficit becomes more acute when foreign markets are depressed and lessens when the situation is prosperous, while the new functions that the State has acquired have meant new permanent financial commitments which have a dynamic of their own.

As a result of the four characteristic processes just outlined[9]—the stagnation of traditional agriculture, the structure of foreign trade, the type of industrialization and the function which the State is fulfilling—our countries are, from the point of view of the structure and functioning of the economy, entirely dependent on their foreign economic relations. An important and not always recognized fact is that this extreme dependence is rooted in several conditions: the vulnerability and structural deficit of the balance of payments; the type of industrialization and the form of exploitation of the export sector which have not permitted our countries— with a few exceptions—to acquire the ability to adapt and create their own technology; the fact that an important and probably growing part of industry and of the export activities are either foreign owned or depend on licences and foreign technical assistance, all of which weighs heavily on the availability of foreign exchange; and the fact that both the fiscal sector and the balance of payments persistently tend to deficit, which leads to the necessity of foreign financing. In certain conditions this foreign financing can mean the accumulation of such considerable debts and such a structure of maturities that the very servicing of the debt requires resort to additional foreign financing[10]—a genuine vicious circle. It is this aspect—the overbearing and implacable necessity to obtain foreign financing—which finally sums up the situation of dependence; this is the crucial point in the mechanism of dependence.

From what has been shown it can be deduced that even if the social structure has been differentiated and the middle groups and the masses have acquired more representation and participation in the political functioning of the countries, demanding in consequence a growing attention to the general interests of the nation, it is no less certain that an extremely delicate situation of foreign financing has been created which— independent of other forms of dependence—places our countries in a particularly weak position in the face of any pressure which may be exercised on them—and not only, obviously, in regard to development policy.

III. NATIONAL DEVELOPMENT

*The Nature of National Development*

If the preceding analysis is correct, what are the possibilities of re-orienting traditional development policy? This reorientation must lead to the reduction of the forms of dependence which are rooted in the structure and functioning of the economies; such tendencies have become increasingly acute and have been concretely translated into extreme financial dependence. In other words, it must be recognized that economic independence cannot be the magical consequence of an heroic political act. Rather, it will be the medium, or long-term, result—depending on the case—of the construction of a national economy which is both efficient and flexible, and also capable of generating a large and rapidly increasing surplus of resources for investment. This reality, in the technical-economic sense, is not essentially different from the reality which confronts those underdeveloped countries which are attempting to attain national development by the socialist path. Nevertheless, while in these cases the aspiration to national development is an essential part of the definition and social base of the political régime, in the underdeveloped countries of the capitalist area the very possibility of national development must be raised as a preliminary and decisive question mark. It is a crucial question mark that we want to elucidate, for the reply to it will reveal whether the construction of an independent nation is in the final analysis a viable and possible objective or if it is pure idealism. This question seems to me both basic and pertinent, since I believe that the alternatives which one or the other of the ideological camps wants to impose dogmatically on us—socialist revolution or 'dependent country' (*país sucursal*) —are not real alternatives.

One of the possibilities, a radical-socialist revolution, seems to me a very improbable historical event in the near future in Latin America, owing to a combination of external and internal circumstances of a geographic, military, political and economic nature. It is possible that there will be eruptions and even widespread guerrilla movements in some areas, but this will almost certainly tend to reinforce the *status quo* and foreign dependence, rather than the reverse. On the other hand, the 'dependent country' does not seem viable to me in the long run for the majority of Latin American countries. Apart from the negative elements of a general kind already mentioned, the experience of the region in the last two decades seems to suggest: (*a*) that the existing model requires a volume of foreign resources which the industrialized world—particularly private enterprise—is not interested in transferring to the periphery; (*b*) that the model of industrialization by import substitution, after a period of great dynamism, tends to stagnation even in the larger countries of the region; (*c*) that in spite of the industrialization efforts and social policies, a large sector of the population remains unable to integrate itself into economic, social, cultural or political life.[11]

Therefore, while the revolutionary route is currently blocked, to persist in the 'developmentism' of the last decades—when its positive stage seems to have already been completed—is obviously leading to frustration. I am therefore convinced that these alternatives present a false dilemma: the real option lies with a truly national development policy.

In order to avoid confusion, I must at this stage reiterate what I understand by national development. The nationalism I refer to is obviously not the autarchic, xenophobic, racist, fascist, imperialistic phenomenon familiar to Europeans and North Americans. This is 'developed nationalism'. The nationalism of the underdeveloped countries arose or was accentuated as a result, in part, of the struggle against the manifestations of developed nationalism. The underdeveloped countries not only sent their quota of forces to the allied powers during World War II, but they also resisted and confronted similar manifestations which—under a false internationalism—these same powers exhibited in their colonies and dependencies. The nationalism of development is a force of national affirmation, an aspiration to self-determination and sovereignty, a desire to participate in the benefits and creation of modern and universal culture and science, the desire to attain liberty, democracy, equality of opportunities and well-being, which the more industrialized countries enjoy to a greater or lesser extent.[12]

The advance of the process of development increases the socio-political participation of groups and social classes making it also more representative of the nation, its traditions, culture, values, institutions and history. These are the ingredients which the nation must utilize to create and achieve its own process of development and national realization. To substitute imported ingredients is to destroy the essence of the nation and to convert its inhabitants into outcasts, both from their own history but also from that of the advanced societies. What is required is a process of modernization which is imitative and creative at the same time, based on a deliberate and conscious selection of what is authentically universal in modern civilization and culture, and based on an imagination which can construct with these elements the politics, the institutions, the ideologies and other instruments of national development.[13] But there is no doubt that all this will necessarily result in the rupture, rejection or reform of all those internal and external circumstances and situations which interfere or block not only the realization of democracy, liberty, well-being and equality of opportunity, but also the free choice of the route and the methods of a national development policy. It would be easy to confuse these healthy and positive manifestations of nationalism with xenophobia, autarchy and patriotic arrogance. It is not a question of this, but rather of recognizing in a realistic manner that dependence is structurally inherent in underdevelopment. In order to be genuine development must tend to replace dependence with interdependence, that is, a situation in which the nation which has to confront outside pressures or limitations in its development can by itself create or choose alternative ways of responding to these situations.

*The Role of Latin American Integration*

There arises, nevertheless, a fundamental doubt: is a national development policy possible or viable in all the countries of Latin America? In even cruder terms: are the countries of the region viable nations in the economic-technical sense? There are those who maintain that they are not, and with powerful reasons. In this nuclear age, of the second industrial revolution, development seems to require vast markets, huge resources dedicated to scientific research, a labour force of highest technical qualifications, etc., conditions which few, if any, of the Latin American countries can fulfil before being incorporated as dependent areas in larger economic spaces.[14]

Faced with such a prospect, the necessity of Latin American integration acquires its real dimension and *raison d'être*. Integration, in fact, can be either a basic instrument of national realization in Latin America; or it can be the instrument of accelerated dependence ('*sucursalizacion*') of the region. Present conditions and existing policies of integration would seem to favour this latter tendency, since it is the subsidiaries of non-Latin American multinational mother companies, located in various countries of the region, which are in the best position to plan their activities with a view to the optimal exploitation of a free trade zone, and at the same time to displace the national industries even in the domestic markets. This would particularly be the case with respect to the new industries of great capital intensity and technological complexity which would be attracted as soon as a free trade zone is organized.

In order that integration should fulfil the aims of national development policies, the paths to follow must obviously be different. Unfortunately, those just mentioned are the ones which naturally tend to be followed, and which are already being put into practice. However, an integration directed towards the objective of Latin American national realization and to a lessening of foreign dependence for the region as a whole and for each country in particular, requires multinational initiative in order to develop—at least in the first stage—sectors of basic production (steel, petro-chemical, electronic, mechanical, etc.) under Latin American control. It would seem to be a condition *sine qua non* for Latin America to acquire: (*a*) its own capacity of technological creation, (*b*) large-scale production in sectors with high and increasing productivity, (*c*) sectors capable of generating substantial surpluses of resources for the expansion of the productive capacity, (*d*) a structure of production which allows her to change and increase exports—diversifying them with manufactured products—and diminishing the rate of growth of its imports, substituting the import of capital goods. In other words, the immediate efforts for integration must be concentrated on the establishment of production agreements, particularly in relation to the expansion of those sectors which produce basic goods and by means of multinational Latin American enterprises or consortiums which may be either public or mixed; that is to say, on the multinational planning of existing and additional basic industrial activities.[15]

Instead of this, the present integration efforts are concentrated on the liberalization of intra-Latin American trade. These efforts have barely managed to re-establish the relative importance which this trade had in relation to the total foreign trade of Latin America during the periods of war and the period of bilateral agreements in the middle 1950s. In fact, inter-Latin American trade managed to surpass the absolute levels of 1955 only as recently as 1964. Moreover, having reached the levels of these last years, trade concessions have become continually less significant and more difficult, and the growth of trade has slowed down.[16] In any case this increment of trade has been mainly in traditional products. It is almost entirely between countries which border on each other and it is not significant from the point of view of contributing to the process of development through the stimulation of industrial growth, the utilization of idle capacity, the gains of large scale economies, specialization of production, overcoming foreign exchange constraints, etc.

All the above refers particularly to the process of integration in the L.A.F.T.A. area and not to the Central American Common Market, which differs precisely in its emphasis on planning related to productive capacity and additional infrastructure, and in which the traditional process of import substitution is taking place in the context of an integrated market, with a rapid expansion of trade and important changes in the structure of production. But here also the difficulties inherent in the process of import substitution which the larger and more advanced countries of the region have already faced, will sooner or later have to be met, since the process there is also taking place on the basis of production of consumer goods and an indiscriminate participation of foreign private capital. On the other hand, the Central American Common Market is surely very limited either as a base for manufacturing activity capable of competing in the world market, or as a means of making these economies more dynamic. The above observations on the problem of integration may well be superficial and partial, but my intention is not to enter in depth into the study of this complex topic, but rather to illustrate to what extent a Latin American development policy implies the necessity of adopting completely different strategies from the ones which have been propounded until recently with so much determination and such limited success.[17]

### Overcoming the 'Centre-periphery' Model

National development policy also demands substantial readjustments in domestic development strategy. As I am not in a position to make an exhaustive analysis, which in any case could not be general, since the circumstances of each country must be taken into account, I am going to refer only to certain essential aspects in relation to which I believe a reorientation is possible and would be significant.

In the preceding pages I have put forward an explanation of the structural nature of the problem of dependence, which in fact results in a tendency to a balance of payments and budget deficit and problems of foreign financing. For many years there has been concern in Latin America to change the pattern of foreign trade, and more recently, as a result of the period of deterioration of terms of trade from 1954 to 1962, this concern, echoed in other quarters, has led to the creation of an international body dedicated to this problem: the United Nations Conference on Trade and Development. The requests of the developing countries refer principally to: access for their manufactured products to the markets of the industrialized countries; elimination of internal taxes, tariffs, and other obstacles to the importation of primary products exported by the periphery; agreements on the stabilization of the prices of primary products, or mechanisms for financial compensation; higher levels of processing of primary products within the underdeveloped countries; less burdensome terms of foreign financing; larger private foreign investment; more financial and technical foreign aid, etc.

Notwithstanding the efforts which have been devoted to these objectives, it must be recognized that up to now they have been almost entirely fruitless. The probabilities of future success are very low. The roots of this situation are to be found, in my opinion, in the fact that all these objectives represent some concrete sacrifice for the industrial countries. I do not believe that they are going to make these sacrifices for nothing especially if one bears in mind that the resulting measures would have important economic and political repercussions domestically on certain interests, groups or regions. Even public foreign aid, in which moral motives of international solidarity are important, often reflects the economic, cultural and, above all, political interest of the donor countries. And the greater the aid, the greater the temptation and possibility of using it for ulterior ends.[18]

Even if these measures put forth with such insistence by the underdeveloped countries should be successful, the result would only contribute to a precarious survival of the traditional 'centre-periphery' model. This is confirmed even by the most optimistic estimates of the size of the future 'trade gap', which assume various degrees of success for these policies.

The fundamental question, therefore, which a national development policy seeks to tackle is not the viability of the traditional 'centre-periphery' model, but rather the reverse, the need to overcome it. For this it seems to me that the transformation of the internal structure of production of the underdeveloped countries is as important as the nature of their foreign ties. If this is achieved, then the concessions, advantages and aid to the underdeveloped countries can yield their real fruits: a contribution to the achievement of a national development policy. But without the requisite *sine qua non* of internal transformation and changes in the nature of foreign ties, they can only result in preserving and even stimulating the 'dependent country' (*país sucursal*) model.

### Agrarian Policies

One of the most significant changes in the internal structure of production concerns agricultural activity. The development process typically means a highly dynamic increase in the urban demand for rural products. This arises for several reasons: the urban population frequently grows at rates of 5 or 6 per cent, the *per capita* income in urban areas rises more than the national average, a high proportion of the industrial sector—

which grows faster than any other—utilizes materials of agricultural origin. Moreover, food represents a large proportion of family expenditure for the low income urban sectors which constitute a substantial proportion of the urban population. Thus, one of the essential tasks of agrarian policy must be to speed up the growth of rural production available for the cities, at constant or decreasing *relative* prices for the urban consumer. As this must be compatible with an income rise for the peasants—the rural and urban poor being the political base of this strategy of development—it will be necessary to emphasize: (*a*) a substantial increase in yields per hectare; (*b*) the maximum efficiency and reduction of costs in the process of marketing; (*c*) a lowering of the cost of agricultural inputs; and (*d*) a redistribution of income within the rural sector itself.

These are the basic aspects of the formidable task which must be carried out in agriculture for this sector to make a substantive economic and political contribution to the process of national development and—by enlarging the exportable surplus and through import substitution—to diminishing foreign dependence.

Given the present land-holding situation in most Latin American countries, and the corresponding economic, technological, social and political circumstances prevailing in agriculture, agrarian reform will usually be an indispensable part of such an agrarian policy; but at the same time this reform must fulfil the general objectives of agrarian policy and of the national development policy itself.

### 'Export or Die'

One of the most important of these general objectives is an increase in exports and their diversification, not just because of the well-known instability which results from dependence on a single product, but also because the process of import substitution has led to a rigid import structure through what Prebisch has called 'the elimination of the margin of imports'.[19] That is to say, with such a limited availability of foreign exchange (after deducting the servicing of foreign financial commitments) only the importation of production goods and essential consumer goods is possible. Then, should an unfavourable situation arise in foreign markets or in export production, the only alternatives are the contraction of essential consumption and economic activity, or additional foreign indebtedness.

On the other hand, as the import of production goods has come to represent a high and ever-growing proportion of total imports, the traditional export activities have been transformed *de facto*, into our capital goods industries. The increase of exports, therefore, whether agricultural, fishing, mining, or manufacturing, is the essential requisite for the expansion of real national saving and investment capacity. The rapid increase of exports is thus the only possibility of basing growth progressively on national savings or on nationally-owned industry, which amounts to the same thing. Conversely, the stagnation of exports, if the rhythm of growth is to be maintained, demands more foreign savings and investment with the resulting additional indebtedness. But this implies an increasing denationalization of national wealth, either of

304 DEVELOPMENT STUDIES REVISITED

the actual ownership of industries when the savings are brought in as foreign private capital, or as a financial claim on the wealth of the nation as a whole, when the foreign savings take the form of a loan.

In countries without a sufficiently developed national capital goods industry and with a rigid import structure, any possibility of national development depends on the expansion of exports. In fact, this is the root of the central failing of the import substitution policy: *The import of capital and intermediate goods necessary to produce consumer goods has been substituted for the import of consumer goods themselves. The structure of manufacturing production is now organized basically to produce for the consumer and the traditional export sector has been left to 'produce' the investment goods. This seems to me the fundamental reason why our economies have become more dependent, more vulnerable and more unstable.*

This is also the fundamental reason why a radical reorientation of development strategy is needed. From a strategy based unilaterally on import substitution, we must move in a decisive way to another which rests on three principal supports: (*a*) the expansion and diversification of exports, (*b*) internal structural changes in the agricultural sector and in manufacturing activity, and (*c*) basic changes in the nature of foreign financial ties.

In the case both of traditional products and of manufactured goods, the expansion and diversification of exports meets with difficulties which are well known. They cannot be overcome merely with lyrical appeals to international solidarity. Moreover, there is a very important element which is rarely referred to, which has a decisive influence on the possibility of increasing and diversifying exports. I refer to the fact that almost all the traditional export activities of our countries belong to foreign private capital, not always in the production phase, but certainly in the marketing phase. They are usually subidiaries producing primary materials for the mother processing company located in an industrialized country; that is, vertically integrated international oligopolies. Therefore, international trade in these cases is simply the transfer of partly processed products from the 'extraction' or 'cultivation' section to the 'processing' section. In these cases neither a proper market nor price exists and it is impossible to determine the amount of profits realized in the primary activity. These will depend on internal decisions of the industry and will be mainly the function of the tax policies of the countries in which the mother company and the subsidiary are located.[20]

As the taxation of this type of industry in the underdeveloped countries is frequently higher than in the industrial countries, the export price tends to be fixed by adding a reasonable profit margin to local costs, while all the rest is profit attributed to the processing phase in the industrial country. On the other hand, given the greater external economies and economies of scale for processing in the industrialized countries, the companies always tend to leave it to be done there. Moreover to protect themselves against each other, the industrialized countries typically establish a high tariff for the finished product and a low one for the primary material. This, then, serves as an additional justification for not developing the processing phases in the primary producing countries.

Thus it is clear that a conflict of interest exists between the exporting country, which wants to maximize its export income, and the international oligopoly, which wants to maximize its own profits *as a whole*. This conflict can only be overcome by some sort of intervention in the industry—in its policy of production, processing, sales, markets and prices—either by nationalization, through its association with local private industry or the national State, by State supervision or some other form of effective intervention.

In addition it should be possible for countries which export primary materials to develop formulae of international co-operation which would allow them to increase their capacity to negotiate with big industry, to formulate co-ordinated tax policies, intervene in the markets, regulate supply, and negotiate changes in the tariff and tax structures of the developed countries, etc. These forms of co-operation could be highly significant if they were to result in an improvement in the terms of trade which would in turn lead to a permanent transfer of additional resources to the underdeveloped world.

In other words, the incapacity to improve the terms of trade, a greater stability in world markets for basic products or a higher degree of elaboration of primary export products is largely determined by the relationship between the mother processing companies in the developed countries and their extractive subsidiaries in the underdeveloped countries. Therefore, an objective of a policy of national development should be to change this relationship in favour of the exporting country. Various means of achieving this objective are already in the hands of national governments and in fact they have abundant experience in them. But in all these cases it is a question of national intervention in traditional international practices which have been accepted since the middle of the last century. It would therefore evoke strong resistance from the interests affected. This is the logical international corollary of a national programme of basic structural transformations. In the case of Latin America, the countries which have had a national revolution—Mexico, Bolivia, Cuba—have nationalized their basic export sector. In the case of more moderate national development policies, among them the Argentinian, Venezuelan, and the Chilean, the degree of national State control over the basic export activity has been enlarged substantially by various means: marketing boards, control over the operations of the export industries, intervention in prices and sales policies, formation of mixed enterprises, development of a national export industry, both public, private or mixed, agreements among producing nations, etc.

It has already been widely recognized that development demands profound internal structural changes. But it is now time to recognize as well that this is inseparable from profound transformations in the traditional patterns which characterize external economic relations. It must also be recognized that the adoption of new policies cannot be left entirely to the good will of the industrial nations, who for a century have been the principal beneficiaries of the traditional system. Rather it must increasingly depend on the will of the affected governments and nations themselves. There is an area of great importance in the elucidation of this problem to which the social sciences in Latin America and other regions could dedicate a creative and imaginative intellectual effort: in the creation of formulae for transition to national control of the basic export sector, in the examination of possible means of reprisals and their effects, in the collection of basic information, in the analysis of related experiences, in technical advice for negotiations, in organizational and administrative advice for the creation and functioning of the new institutions. In all these areas the specialized international organizations could render distinguished service if the governments of the interested countries were so to direct them.[21]

In the field of technology, too, there is a national and international task of great importance to be fulfilled which must be a fundamental part of a new policy. The traditional export activities have not had the stimulus to develop an intensive and dynamic policy of innovative technological exploitation of our countries' natural resources—except in the case of activities or natural resources which do not exist in the industrial countries —certain tropical crops for example. In other cases, the large international companies which exploit primary materials have an accumulated technical knowledge, derived from their experience with a particular manifestation of a natural resource, which makes them prefer it to other varieties. For example, if a certain mineral is found without the particular characteristics which the exploiting company is looking for, then that mineral does not have any interest for foreign capital, even if from the national point of view it could be an important resource if the appropriate technology were developed. In other words, to the extent that technological progress is the fundamental determining factor of dynamic comparative advantage, it is absolutely essential to stimulate it, not just to make our own natural resources more valuable, but also to assure their optimum utilization.

### Private Foreign Investment

Diversification through the export of manufactured products has also had very serious limitations as a result of relations maintained by a large part of domestic industry with foreign business enterprises. Whether it is a question of subsidiary firms or of companies which manufacture under foreign licence and trademarks, the policy of the mother companies limits the dependent firms to the national market, thus not only preventing the export to markets in the developed countries, but also to other countries of the underdeveloped area. In these countries either a parallel subsidiary company will exist, or one which has acquired the same licence and trademark, or else the product will be obtained by importing it from the country in which the mother company is located. There are well-known examples of this market-sharing practice in Latin America.

Therefore, even if tariff and other concessions could be obtained for the export of manufactured goods to the industrial countries—and even to the underdeveloped countries—the dependent character of a large part of manufacturing activity will seriously limit the possibilities of taking advantage of available opportunities.

Classic foreign private investment, moreover, and the national imitation of foreign products under licence and patented trademarks, have other serious drawbacks. On the one hand, it strongly inhibits the creation of technological and scientific capabilities in national manufacturing activity. Remember, for example, that a world war was necessary before the North American automobile industry produced a vehicle, the jeep, appropriate to the necessities of rural life in underdeveloped countries. On the other hand, it gives rise to an industrial structure geared very largely to the more or less superfluous consumption goods, which the policy of import substitution was supposed to eliminate.

Another potentially serious problem, which is already beginning to appear in many countries, is the high percentage that the financial commitments for remittance of profits, dividends, interest, royalties, payments for administrative services and technical assistance, etc., can come to represent in the balance of payments. Simple arithmetic illustrates the problem. Suppose that manufacturing activity comes to represent a third of national income, that about half of industrial capital is foreign-owned or is producing under foreign licence, that normal fees are paid on royalties, profits and remittances abroad, and that foreign trade continues to expand only moderately. We can then conclude that the remittances abroad of the industrial sector could reach 20–30 per cent of the total available foreign exchange, to which the remittances of the export sector and of other activities, and the servicing of the public foreign debt would have to be added. Requiring the foreign companies to reinvest their profits in the country would seem to be an alternative, but this would lead to the denationalization of existing national industries and/or to a rapid and considerable increase of new foreign industry relative to the national industries; in any case, it would produce a considerable outflow of resources once foreign companies had reached their limit of expansion within the domestic market. It is a problem which has been raised with great heat both in an academic context and in very sharp public debate in precisely those countries in which foreign private capital has been massively invested during the last decade; this is the case of Canada, Australia, and of various European countries.

Thus, in this aspect of our economic links with foreign countries as well, we seem to have arrived at the moment for seeking mechanisms to replace or modify the traditional forms of incorporating modern technology and foreign savings.

Very interesting in this regard are the investment, trade and loan agreements which the socialist countries have been approving with capitalist countries of Europe.[22] These agreements, called co-production or industrial co-operation, are being rapidly enlarged and extended. They have developed between France and Algeria (petroleum agreement) and with Egypt (growing and marketing of fruits and vegetables); Japan and also the United States are seeking to realize similar agreements with Yugoslavia, Roumania and the U.S.S.R. The traditional mechanisms for orientation and decision-making with regards to trade and international investment are at present rooted principally in the big multinational, vertically integrated, oligopolies. These existing mechanisms must be replaced by direct agreements between a genuinely national entity and multinational businesses or other foreign centres of decision.

'Industrial co-operation links two centres of decision which, after negotiations tending to safeguard mutual interests, agree with the need to attain, through commonly determined conditions and defined supplies of capital, one or more determined objectives . . . what interests us most here are the types of industrial co-operation which create durable flows of international trade which make possible a balanced international growth.'

According to Professor Byé, industrial co-operation presents the following characteristics:

1. Institutionalized links between centres of decision.
2. Participation by the centre of decision on the side of the receiving country, of an institution which represents the general interest (State or decentralized body of public capital).
3. Participation by the centre of decision on the side of the country of origin, of either a private firm or an institution of public capital (State or decentralized body).
4. Installation of the institutions of industrial co-operation as a result of international agreements, which either includes the possibility of the creation of such an institution and suggests its general conditions (trade agreements of 'co-operation' signed between countries of Eastern Europe); or binds them in a specific creation (agreement between States, granted by the Franco-Algerian hydrocarbon association, for an ammonia factory).
5. Definition, by means of the decree which creates the association, of a certain number of conditions, which in general would be: mode of establishing plans and programmes; financing, including eventual advances from one side; technical supplies and common research; the position to be adopted with respect to markets; distribution of the financial returns; manner of reinvestment.
6. Definition of the value attributed to the various supplies of capital as elements submitted to control; appreciation of the supplies of 'natural resources' which are not rented, but rather associated; appreciation of the supplies and the percentages of supplies in goods of different kinds (land, building, infrastructure, transport . . .); appreciation of the supply of labour. The national supplies are understood in the sense of stock and flows accounts and not as simple financial statements (a 'firm's or a State's budget').
7. Examination of the aid expected from national or international institutions. If, in particular, the state from which the capital comes understands that it must encourage the operation, it will adapt its system of foreign credit to the necessities of the new creation. A general review of credit conditions with the object of suiting them to aid would be necessary to establish an international statute of industrial co-operation.

'We must make clear that we do not mean to present industrial co-operation as the exclusive mode of regulating the movement of capital and aid; rather we consider it as one essential strategic means for the establishment of new and more effective links in the world, but with private investment on one side, and different forms of aid on the other, each conserving its own important functions.'

The experience indicated above and this concept of industrial co-operation open the doors to new ways of association with private foreign enterprise which may overcome the disadvantages mentioned before while preserving the very positive elements which foreign private enterprise brings; financial resources, experience and capacity in technology, administration and organization. Concretely, it would be a question of ensuring that the new productive activity, created in association with foreign State or private enterprise, is transferred to the country, pro-gressively and within a stipulated period of time, both in property and management and in technological capacity, and that the payment for foreign capital investment should be made by exporting part of the enterprise's own production or through other non-traditional exports. This latter is one of the characteristics of these agreements, and also of the loans for the installation of new productive activities, which the U.S.S.R. and other socialist countries are making to underdeveloped countries. Furthermore, this is the fundamental characteristic which made viable the 19th-century model of foreign investment in the peripheral areas. The massive transfer of capital resources from the centre to the periphery was possible precisely because foreign private investment created an export surplus in the periphery with which this foreign in-vestment was repaid. The industrialization process, on the contrary, has been attracting foreign capital to the development of domestic activities which do not directly contribute to create an exportable surplus. A growing imbalance between the inflow of foreign capital and the capacity ade-quately to service it has therefore been appearing. The new formula here described might overcome this problem.

*Industrial Policy*

Finally, it is also necessary to introduce new concepts in the field of industrial policy and to modify customs and policies which have been copied automatically from other countries and which consequently lack both sense and function in our conditions.

The insistence on the sacred principle of competition, for example, has permitted the indiscriminate proliferation of factories producing the same article, which has led to an atomization of a small and highly stratified market. Therefore, industrial production is characterized by very high costs and substantial idle capacity. Moreover, owing to its dependence on foreign technology, it is characterized by the production of articles whose size, design, capacities, maintenance, etc. are suited to the North American or European consumer, rather than by the production of manufactured goods within the means of and suited to a large potential market of a low income and largely rural population. Instead of an open-door policy and excessive stimulus to substitution industries and the absorption of foreign technology, a restrictive policy should be initiated which prohibits new activities where idle capacity already exists and fosters industrial concentration in large specialized productive units, instead of the small units turning out large numbers of different products which are common at present.

I believe that only the concentration in enterprises of economic size, with adequate scales of production and specialized in certain kinds of production or processes, can lead to the adequate utilization of existing capacity, a substantial increase in productivity, considerable reduction of costs, and the creation of productive units which can accumulate a sufficiently large volume of resources to be able to dedicate part of them to technological research and innovation and to a cumulative process of increasing productive capacity. There is no country in the world which has had success in the process of industrialization which has not entered into this phase of great industrial concentration and large enterprises. Moreover, the great productive potentialities of capitalism did not produce progressive and substantial increases in national income until they entered into the phase of big business and mass production. This, in my opinion, is a stage into which Latin American industrialization must enter if it is going to make a really significant and dynamic contribution to development. Here again we come up against the problem of the limitation of the national markets. On this point the strategy of industrial development is linked on the one hand to the agrarian policy to which we have already referred, and on the other to the role which integration can play in the consolidation and specialization of efficient national or multinational productive units.

The deliberate promotion of industrial concentration raises a considerable difficulty: the problem of the political and economic power of these large concentrations. Here is another challenge to our capacity for devising new forms of social control over big business which will function efficiently without effecting its administrative flexibility, or burdening its personnel with bureaucratic demands, or introducing anti-innovative or excessively conservative biases in its policies, as frequently occurs with traditional State companies. It is also a challenge to the organization of compensatory social forces with the power to negotiate effectively in the area of small and medium industrial and agricultural entrepreneurs, in that of consumers, in that of the urban and rural masses, etc., so that all these can have a voice in and influence on the conduct of national economic and social policy.

It has already been indicated that one phase of the policy of import substitution has been exhausted and that it becomes necessary to advance to the production of basic intermediate products and to mechanical industry. The possibility of developing these industries under efficient conditions will depend on the expansion of the markets for the national industry producing consumer goods—which in turn depends on the concentration and specialization of the latter—and the capacity to export to other countries of Latin America or to the developed countries. The latter will largely depend on the formation with other countries of Latin America of multinational companies and the achievement of industrial co-operation agreements with advanced countries.

Many other important aspects must be developed in relation to the strategies of development in the area of agrarian policy, external relations and industrial policy, to which I have briefly referred. The implications of these strategies in other key sectors must also be developed; for example, educational policy.

## IV. THE EXTERNAL CONDITIONS

There remains, however, a last fundamental question: to what extent will the limitations imposed by the web of international relations within which our countries exist, permit us to adopt policies and strategies of national development such as those suggested? Or, in other words, given the repercussions which a policy of national development would necessarily have on the nature of our external relations, would the affected foreign and domestic interests be sufficiently powerful to block these policies?

I believe that, with respect to this, we are in a better position than a few years ago. From the domestic point of view it has already been suggested that conditions could be such that ideas of this nature might form part of a programme, a strategy and an ideology of development. With respect to the capitalist world, within which we are, the adoption of strategies and institutional forms such as those which have been suggested would probably have been unacceptable up to eight or ten years ago. But today it is possible to air these problems openly and new solutions seem feasible. There have been fundamental changes in the international scene [changes which were referred to by some of the participants in the inaugural series of lectures of the Institute of International Studies of the University of Chile].[23] These changes relate to the relationship between the two principal world blocks and in particular to the relationship between the two super-powers. Since the Cuban crisis made clear that the direct influence of one of the great powers in the sphere of influence of the other carried the risk of nuclear war, they have arrived at a kind of *détente*. The nuclear balance of power has eliminated the immediate danger of war between the two great powers. This threat having disappeared, the hegemonic powers have lessened their rigid control and the perfect alignment which each had demanded from the intermediate powers and the underdeveloped countries inscribed within their spheres of influence. This has permitted the rise of intermediate countries relatively free of their respective hegemonic powers, and the adoption of important innovations in the development policy of these countries designed to arrive at forms most suited to national conditions. This is the case of the transformations which have occurred in the socialist economies of Eastern Europe and of the reorientation of the policy of international co-operation which the Alliance for Progress represents for Latin America. The intermediate, relatively advanced countries were surely not comfortable within the rigid norms of complete and total alignment. Even internally, within each super-power, there has been liberalization, a decrease of rigid control. So much so that the Soviet Union is trying new forms of organization of production, tending towards a relative liberalization of the system. Moreover, control over the satellite powers has been lessened so that the socialist countries of Eastern Europe have greater degree of freedom of decision on domestic questions, and even to a certain point on matters of international policy. The same has happened within the capitalist bloc, in part because of the rise of Western Europe as a strong economic power, particularly in the case of France. Even within America the programme of the Alliance for Progress, at least in its original conception and in the vestiges which remain, approved of this desire to try new formulae. The adoption of positive attitudes towards change in the underdeveloped countries is without doubt linked to the fact that direct nuclear confrontation between the great powers is impossible. What then are the forms in which this confrontation can take place? Obviously one is the ideological struggle, particularly at the level of development policy, each side showing the world that development can best be achieved in a capitalistic or, conversely, a socialist way. Therefore it is now in the interest of the dominant powers, even though they are conscious of running certain risks, to try out formulae which might lead to rapid and satisfactory development *without rupturing the prevailing political system*. This is in fact the argument given by both the U.S. and the U.S.S.R. to justify Santo Domingo and Czechoslovakia. Situations like these are clearly possible but I believe that they are only temporary and partial setbacks in the context of a long-term process of liberalization; internal pressures for liberalization and for decreasing the world-wide commitments of super-powers continue, and nationalistic voices are mounting in the satellite nations and everywhere.

This process has had the effect not only of a thaw within each system, but has also led to the rapid prolifertion of relationships between the countries of each block. The last five or six years show a clear evolution in this direction, both in international trade, in political relations, and also in international cultural relations. The countries of the under-developed world, each of which was before directly and exclusively affiliated with its own hegemonic power, have now wider possibilities of international trade, foreign aid, cultural contact, technical assistance and consultation, ideological discussion, exchange of students and professors, and of research, with the countries of the other bloc.

The thaw between the blocs was initiated primarily by and acquired most of its vigour—as would be expected—from the intermediate coun-tries of each bloc, gradually extending to the hegemonic powers themselves and later to the dependent countries. The latter, which are the most numerous and include a large proportion of the world's population, find themselves today in a very special situation. On the one hand, since direct military intervention by one of the hegemonic powers in a country in-cluded within the sphere of influence of the other could lead to a nuclear conflagration, it can be supposed that revolutionary movements in an underdeveloped country cannot count on open and declared economic or military support from the respective great power, while the government of the country in question will be able to count on massive and declared support from its respective hegemonic power. In other words, the pos-sibility of guerrilla movements expanding and converting themselves into victorious revolutionary movements seem remote, at least in Latin America. Would this mean the maintenance of the *status quo*? I think not. The possibility of implementing progressive policies in Latin America will obviously depend, in the first place, on the social structure and political forces, the degree of national integration, the legitimacy of the government and other internal circumstances. But when positive circumstances are present to a greater or lesser extent, the limits of development policy can, in my opinion, expand considerably beyond the traditional boundaries.

The principal considerations which support this thesis are:

(a) The danger of internal revolutionary change has been practically eliminated, both because of the Great Power *détente* and because of the reorganization of national armies for 'internal defence'. The possibility of foreign war is excluded, both between the Great Powers, for the reasons already pointed out, but also between satellites of one super-power; these would not tolerate it and, given the position of economic and military dependence of the satellites, are in a position to prevent it.

(b) It has become evident—as even the declarations and conceptions of the Alliance for Progress indicate, although never very seriously applied— that the revolutionary dangers and tensions in Latin America have their fundamental origin in the economic and social structure of these countries. Therefore, these must be modified, but only where the political capacity exists to accomplish this transformation without risk of letting loose a revolution. Because it has also been understood that the process of change itself contains potentially revolutionary tensions similar to the pressures which arise when trying to maintain the *status quo* beyond what is reasonable.

(c) Contacts of all kinds between our countries and *all* the others have been expanding to the detriment of the exclusive ties with the hegemonic power; increasing contacts with the intermediate and satellite countries of one's own bloc, as well as contacts with the alternative dominant, intermediate and satellite countries of the other bloc. Concretely, this means alternative sources of trade, finance, technical assistance, human resources, consultation about certain policies, education, research and cultural vision, as well as greater contact within blocs, whether geographic (Latin American integration) or of interest (U.N.C.T.A.D.).

(d) The hegemonic power itself will put all its weight behind achieving the following two objectives, in decreasing order of importance: to avoid pre-revolutionary situations, and to promote development. In the first place it will be a question of stabilizing, containing and freezing potentially explosive situations, deliberately promoting military control of the situation in extreme cases, but at any rate trying to have these military groups play a 'progressive' role. Naturally, only the first part of such a programme can be accomplished—the military take-over—since the presence of the military in power necessarily means in Latin America the gathering of reactionary forces around them and the neutralization of the intellectuals, trade unions and mass parties which might support a progressive policy. In countries without a solid and effective internal progressive political constellation, external support would probably lead to the opposite situation, a strengthening of the conditions for the preservation of the *status quo*. Countries which have a political situation which is under control and which seriously attempt policies of development and structural change, have the most favourable case from the point of view of the hegemonic power, and these countries can probably depend on ample support and foreign aid, even when their methods depart from orthodoxy.

Finally, then, given the changes in the international political scene, it seems to me that the possibility of carrying out a national development policy depends fundamentally on the domestic situation, that is to say, the degree of differentiation of the social structure, the degree of political participation, and the existence or possible formation of new political movements which would constitute a functional response to the concrete socio-political problems in terms of a programme, a strategy and an ideology of national development.

To summarize what I have wanted to suggest in these reflections—the only aim of which is to stimulate a more positive debate on these matters than that which we have had up to now—what I have tried to do is the following: to accept that *national* development is the fundamental objective of the policy of development; second, to indicate that the fulfilment of the objective of reducing external dependence requires very important re-orientations in traditional development strategy, particularly relating to agrarian policy, integration, foreign relations, and industrial policy; third, to indicate that in some countries of Latin America economic, social and political changes and transformations have been occurring which seem to indicate the possibility that such new policies could be formulated and applied; fourth, to suggest that in these particular cases, the changes in the international situation would seem to have created conditions which are sufficiently tolerant and flexible to permit the application of policies of national development.

[This paper owes much to the ideas which Anibal Pinto has elaborated on this topic, and to his specific comments on an earlier version. Nevertheless, the opinions expressed here are my responsibility.]

1. A notable exception, which confirms the rule, is the article signed: Espartaco, 'La crisis latinoamericana y su marco externo', *Desarrollo Economico*, July–December 1966, Buenos Aires.

2. Rosa Luxemburg, *Die Akkumulation des Kapitals, Ein Beitrag zur oekonomischn Erlarung des Imperialismus*, 1912; Rudolf Hilferding, *Das Finanzkapital*, 1910; V. L. Ulyanov (N. Lenin), *Imperialism: the Superior Phase of Capitalism* (original Russian edition in 1917); N. I. Bukharin, *World Economy and Imperialism*, 1918.

3. J. A. Hobson, *Imperialism*, 1902; J. A. Schumpeter, 'Zur Soziologie der Imperialismen', *Archiv für Sozialwissenschaft und Sozialpolitik*, Vol. 46, 1919 (English translation in: J. A. Schumpeter, *Imperialism and Social Classes*, 1951); Jacob Viner, 'International Finance and Balance of Power Diplomacy, 1880–1914', *South Western Political Science Quarterly*, 1929; Eugene Staley, *War and the Private Investor*, 1935; William L. Langer, *The Diplomacy of Imperialism*, 1890–1902, 1935; Lionel Robbins, *The Economic Causes of War*, 1939; B. M. Winslow, *The Pattern of Imperialism*, 1948.

4. See, for example, John Strachey, *The End of Empire* (London, Gollancz).

5. See Fernando H. Cardoso and Jose Luis Reyna, 'Industrialización, estructura

ocupacional y estratificación en América Latina', in F. H. Cardoso, *Cuestiones de sociología del desarrollo en América Latina* (Editorial Universitaria, Santiago, 1968).

6. It is not possible to generalize about the attitudes of the national business communities in the light of recent development as examined, for instance, by Celso Furtado in his article: 'La concentración del poder económico en los Estados Unidos y sus proyecciones en América Latina' (*Estudios Internacionales* Año I, Nos. 3–4, Octubre 1967; Marzo 1968, Santiago, Chile).

7. The significance of this phenomenon from the point of view of inflationary pressures and the effects on the distribution of income and industrial expansion, can be seen in my papers 'Inflation in Chile: An Unorthodox Approach', *International Economic Papers*, No. 10 (International Economic Association, London and New York, 1960); and 'El Fracaso de las políticas de estabilización en el contexto del proceso de desarrollo latinoamericano', *El Trimestre Económico*, No. 120 (October–December 1963, Mexico).

8. Instituto Latinoamericano de Planificación Económica y Social, *La Brecha comercial y la integración latinoamericana*, Siglo XXI Editores, Mexico, 1967, p. 25, able 5.

9. For a more complete analysis, see my article 'The Structural Background of Development Problems in Latin America', *Weltwirtschaftliches Archiv* (Band 97, Heft 1, 1966, Hamburg).

10. C.E.P.A.L., *El Financiamiento externo de América Latina*, Mexico, 1964; and International Bank for Reconstruction and Development, *Annual Report, 1965–66* (Washington, 1966).

11. See, among others, Pablo Gonzalez Casanova, 'Sociedad plural y desarrollo: el caso de Mexico', *América Latina*, Year V, No. 4, (October–December 1962, Rio de Janeiro); Andrew Frank, 'La inestabilidad urbana en America Latina', *Cuadernos Americanos* (January–February 1966); Celso Furtado, 'Desarrollo y estancamiento en America Latina', *Desarrollo Economico* (July–Decemner, 1966, Buenos Aires); C.E.P.A.L., 'El proceso de industrialización en América Latina' (Mexico, 1966).

12. Leopoldo Zea, *America Latina y el mundo* (Buenos Aires, 1965).

13. Jose Medina Echavarria, *Filosofía del desarrollo*, Siglo XXI y (Editorial Universitaria, 1967); Celso Furtado, 'Hacia una ideología del desarrollo', *El Trimestre Económico*, No. 131 (1966).

14. Helio Jaguaribe, *Desenvolvimento Economico e Desenvolvimento Politico* (Rio de Janeiro, 1962); also, *Political Models and National Development in Latin America*, a paper presented at the Sixth Inter-American Planning Congress (Caracas, October 1966).

15. Inter-American Development Bank, *Factores para la integración latinoamericana* (Mexico, 1966); see especially pp. 12–70 and appendices B (Coordinacion de las políticas de inversiones, by Aldo Ferrer) and F (Coordinación de las políticas nacionales, by Helio Jaguaribe).

16. Miguel S. Wionczek, 'Apreciaciones sobre el desastre de Montevideo', *Comercio Exterior* (December 1966 Revista del Banco Nacional de Comercio Exterior de Mexico).

17. The Andean Group (Zona Andina) established by Bolivia, Chile, Colombia, Ecuador, Peru and Venezuela, with its emphasis on industrial co-operation and the creation of a regional development corporation, appears as an interesting alternative strategy. C. Diaz Alejandro, 'El grupo andino en el proceso de integración latinoamericana', *Estudios Internacionales*, Año 2, No. 2 (Santiago, 1958).

18. See the excellent study by Goran Ohlin, *Foreign Aid Policies Reconsidered* (Development Centre of the Organization for Economic Co-operation and Development, Paris, 1966); also, M. Kalecki and I. Sachs, 'Formas de la ayuda exterior: un analisis economico', *Comercio Exterior* (December 1966 Revista del Banco Nacional de Comercio Exterior de Mexico).

19. Raul Prebisch, 'Desarrollo Económico o estabilidad monetaria: el falso dilema', C.E.P.A.L., *Boletín Económico de America Latina* (March 1961).

20. Francois Perroux, *L'economie du XXeme siecle* (Paris, 1964); Maurice Byé, *Relations economiques internationales*, Paris, 1965. Stephen Hymer, 'Direct Foreign Investment and the National Economic Interest', in Peter Russell, ed., *Nationalism in*

*Canada* (Toronto, 1966).

21. See, for example, the proposal of Dudley Seers, 'Big Companies and Small Countries: a practical proposal', *Kyklos*, Vol. XVI, 1963, No. 4.

22. This information and the comments which follow are based in the extremely interesting article by Professor Maurice Byé, 'Cooperacion en la producción y convergencia de los sistemas económicos', *Boletín de la Integración* (July 1966, I.N.T.A.L., Buenos Aires.

23. See the articles of Richard Gott and Claudio Veliz in Vol. I, No. 1, and of Jacques Vernant and Alain Joxe in Vol. I, No. 2, of *Estudios Internacionales*.

# State and Alliances
# in Argentina, 1956–1976

*by Guillermo O'Donnell\**

*In this paper an analysis of the relationships between the pattern of
economic development and the nature of class interests in Argentina
shows that changes in the balance of power follow closely the cycles
of economic activity, of foreign trade and of inflation and deflation.
An account of the insecure alliances between political forces, of their
uncertain ideological orientations and of the low relative autonomy
of the state is then combined with that analysis in an overall
interpretation of Argentine politics from the emergence of Perón to
the present.*

This paper pursues the historical perspective which I have employed in a
recently completed book. In that book I study the attempt, begun in 1966,
to implant and consolidate in Argentina what I have called a 'bureaucratic-
authoritarian' (BA) state.[1] I have compared the modalities of its alliance
with the large bourgeoisie and with international capital, its social impact
and, finally, its collapse, with those of Brazil since 1964 and Chile after
1973. Rather than pointing out similarities between the Argentine case and
the others, I shall stress here some differences, for these offer a basis for
understanding why, in recent decades, attempts to establish any type of
political domination have failed in Argentina.[2]

The following pages contain no analysis of specific conjunctures. This
work places itself at the level of the long-term tendencies which link the said
conjunctures with the historical process in which they have emerged and
dissolved. In the book already mentioned I indicate some specific
differences between the 1966–73 Argentine case of 'bureaucratic-
authoritarianism' and other Latin American cases. Briefly, the principal
differences were: (1) the smaller threat[3] level before the implantation of the
BA state; (2) the less severe repression imposed on the popular sector and
its political allies; (3) the greater autonomy of the popular sectors (and,
within them, of the working class) and of the trade unions, with respect to
the state and the dominant classes; (4) the moderate fall of industrial wages
and the more pronounced decline in the incomes of a sizeable proportion of
the employed middle sectors; (5) the rapid formation of an alliance of the
popular sector and the unions with the domestic bourgeoisie,[4] against the
new state and, particularly, against its 'efficientist' and internationalising

*CEDES, Buenos Aires, Argentina. The first version of this paper was prepared for the
Conference on the State and Economic Development in Latin America, Cambridge
University, 12–16 December 1976. It has been translated by Guillermo Makin and David
Lehmann.

policies; (6) the conflict between the government—and, with it, the large bourgeoisie—and the pampa bourgeoisie; and (7) the decisive role of *peronismo* as the expression and mobilisation channel of a heterogeneous constellation of forces in opposition to the BA state. These elements are fundamental in an explanation of the unusual conflicts which arose within the state's institutions and, also, of the social explosions which provoked a collapse unparalleled so far in the other Latin American BA states.[5] These factors account for the short-term differences between the fate of the BA state in Argentina in the period 1966–73 and other comparable experiences. But these, in turn, call for an explanation, which requires a longer historical perspective.

## I HISTORICAL BACKGROUND

In this section I shall point out certain features of Argentina's incorporation into the world capitalist system which gave rise to the country's peculiarity in comparison with the rest of Latin America.[6] These differences continue to bear upon certain characteristics of Argentine capitalism and class structure and also—centrally for our subject—on the power resources and on the political alliances available to the popular sectors.

The following are the most crucial features for our analysis:

(1) As in the rest of Latin America, the pace and characteristics of Argentine capitalist expansion were fundamentally determined by the incorporation of some of its regions as exporters of primary products. This allows us to make an initial distinction between those vast regions of Latin America with no direct linkage[7] to the world market (such as the Andean *hacienda*) and those which were directly linked to such a market as exporters of primary products. Among these the *estancia* of the Argentine pampas and Uruguay differed substantially from the enclaves and plantations which were the principal form of incorporation elsewhere in the continent. The main differences were: (1.1) The *estancia* was less labour-intensive than the plantation and the *haciendia*; (1.2) It was also less capital- and technology-intensive than the plantation and the enclave; (1.3) Largely because of the latter, the control of the principal productive resource (land) was left, in the Argentine pampas and in Uruguay, in the hands of an early domestic agrarian bourgeoisie, whilst the enclave and the plantation were usually directly owned by international capital, and the *hacienda* was left in the hands of an oligarchy with hardly any capitalist traits; (1.4) This pattern, combined with a high differential rent, endowed the pampean and the Uruguayan bourgeoisie with an important capital accumulation base of their own; (1.5) this bourgeoisie did not escape dependence on European capital *via* the transport, finance and international marketing of its products; but its base of capital accumulation did foment a significantly wealthier and more diversified urban, commercial and incipient industrial sector than was to be found in those economies which revolved around the *hacienda*, the enclave and the plantation. These characteristics are well known[8] but others, to which less attention has been given, stem from them.

(2) The cereal, wool, and later also beef-exporting, economy covered a relatively larger portion of the national territory than the exporting sectors

of other countries. Above all, in Argentina the areas not directly incorporated with the world market carried much less economic and demographic weight than in the rest of Latin America. Furthermore, in Argentina and Uruguay there was only a very small peasantry subject to precapitalist relations of production, as compared with much of the continent. The insertion of a much larger proportion of the population into the export economy meant that, from the end of the nineteenth century, Argentina exhibited a significantly greater homogeneity than the rest of Latin America, [9] which, in spite of later mishaps, continues to be noticeable.[10]

(3) Besides the sizeable base of local accumulation due to direct control of land, the high productivity of land in international terms until approximately 1930[11] and the low labour requirements of 'extensive' farming contributed decisively to the greater diversification and prosperity of the pampa region and its urban centres—compared to the regions dominated by the enclave, the plantations and the *hacienda*. Suffice it to say that wages in the pampa region and the Argentine urban centres, until approximately the Second World War, were higher than in many European countries,[12] whilst those of the rest of Latin America—if and when wage relationships were established—were much lower. Thus, not only was intranational homogeneity higher, but also the region of Argentina which was directly incorporated into the world economy was more diversified and generated a significantly higher income for its popular sector than in the other Latin American countries. This, in turn, has other consequences: (3.1) Around the beginnings of the twentieth century the existence of a fully capitalist and relatively wealthy urban (and, largely, also pampean) consumer market induced an industrialisation which received further stimulus from the import restrictions resulting from the First World War. Argentine industrialisation did not 'begin' with the world crisis of 1930; it began earlier and proceeded faster than in the rest of Latin America;[13] (3.2) An early working class therefore also emerged, which developed organisational patterns autonomous both of the state and of the incipient industrial bourgeoisie, although it entered the political arena only later.[14] In the absence of a large peasantry providing cheap labour, the strong demand for labour could only favour such an outcome. Because of the specific characteristics of Argentina's insertion in the world capitalist system, its economic growth was powered fundamentally by its civil society and its relationships with the international market. The dynamising impulse did not depend on the state, as generally tended to happen—with many difficulties— in the other Latin American economies. This point must be developed in greater detail.

   In the period between roughly 1870 and 1930[15] the Argentine state had certain features in common with the liberal state of the great world centres: although a more ostensibly fraudulent political democracy, the level of electoral participation was not lower,[16] and the state machine did not go beyond providing crucial, though limited, general conditions for the functioning of the economy.[17] But this state was the creation of the pampa bourgeoisie and its financial and commercial appendages, by means of a process which also entailed the making of that bourgeoisie, and of the system it dominated, in a marginal yet integral corner of the world capitalist market. To clarify this statement we must resort to some comparisons.

The pampa bourgeoisie and its urban branches directly constituted a national state, not the regional state[18] which was the main political power base of the dominant classes in so many Latin American countries. The Argentine national state also eliminated—earlier, and with greater ease and completeness— the autonomy of the regions not directly linked to the world market, largely because those regions carried much less weight in the country as a whole than in most other Latin American cases.[19] This implied that the state was an expression of changing power-relationships between regions directly incorporated in the world market and others marginal to it to a much smaller extent than in the rest of Latin America.

Thus the pampa bourgeoisie and its urban tentacles held both a central economic position and, through the national state, a central political position as an internally dominant class burdened by other regions. Furthermore, the shifts in the relative importance of export products took place within the pampean zone and its bourgeoisie[20] and not, as in most other cases, by means of the incorporation of new products from new regions leading to shifting alliances with existing locally dominant classes and established segments of international capital.

Nevertheless the pampa bourgeoisie and the national state became the principal channels of the internationalisation of both society and economy, because of the nature of their insertion in the world market. The 'liberal' characteristics of the Argentine state and the strong relative weight of its civil society can only be understood as consequences of the position of the state at the intersection point of the pampa bourgeoisie with international capital—which had deeply penetrated the economy through its control of the financing, transportation and external marketing of pampa production. Paradoxically, therefore, this original internationalisation of an economically dynamic and internally homogeneous region, including a decisive part of a country with barely any peasants, through the local retention of capital accumulation shares enabled a highly internationalised state to become devastatingly national with respect to the regions marginalised from the pampean system. In contrast, the Andean oligarchy or that of Brazil's north-east could directly and diaphanously control 'their' regional state apparatus, while international capital, based on enclaves and plantations, controlled a state which was less an emanation from than a graft imposed upon a society which lacked a local bourgeoisie endowed with its own accumulation base. Instead, in Argentina, the existence of such a bourgeoisie arising from the very process of incorporation into the international market generated a situation in which the regional states were of little weight; furthermore, the national state was one of the crucial channels of the rapid and early internationalisation, which, due to the weight of the pampa economy, covered much more of the country than in other Latin American cases. That is why—not in spite of, but as a very condition of, its centrality—the relationship between the pampa bourgeoisie and the state did not exhibit the transparency and immediacy which the regional oligarchies and international capital imposed in a large portion of Latin America's regional and (for a long time, mostly nominal) national states.[21]

Although the liberal Argentine state did not survive the crisis of the thirties, the factors summarised above allowed it to recover from the economic impact of the world crisis more quickly and easily than most other Latin American countries. The crisis induced a new wave of industrialisation through import substitution (helped by a comparatively broad internal market[22]) and the absorption of a large part of the still available work force from the non-pampa regions, thus reducing their relative weight even further. However, this is not the place to analyse how this affected the emergence of *peronismo*; instead, we turn to the central theme of the paper.

## II. DILEMMAS

I have already mentioned the emergence in Argentina of a popular sector, which included a politically significant working class, with larger economic and organisational resources than those of the rest of Latin America.[23] This in turn resulted from the combination of large available economic surpluses and the negligible pressure exerted on the urban labour-market by an almost non-existent peasantry. If this was an advantage for Argentina's capitalist development, it also strengthened its popular sector. When the bonanza disappeared and the economic conditions approached zero-sum, there was no sizeable peasantry to bear a substantial part of the costs of agreements negotiated between the classes located within the fully capitalist region.

The second point to be singled out arises from another peculiarity of this economy: its main export products—cereals and beef—are wage goods, foodstuffs which constitute the main consumption item of the popular sector. Let us initially note some general consequences of this peculiarity. Other Latin American primary export products have less influence on the consumption of the popular sector and therefore, on the relative prices of their consumption baskets. Furthermore, the way in which their price changes influence popular consumption is, in most cases, indirect, generated by mechanisms which are difficult to apprehend; in contrast, a change in the relative prices of foodstuffs is immediately perceivable. In addition, this perception arises in a popular sector with a significantly higher level of income (and, presumably, of expectations) and organisational autonomy (and therefore greater capacity for resistance) than in the other Latin American cases. We are now in a position to analyse more concrete processes.

The world-crisis of the thirties depressed the prices of pampean goods. Subsequently the *peronista* government (1946–55) offered a foretaste of the problems which would explode later. First (1946–50) the state appropriated a substantial part of the proceeds of pampean exports, kept internal foodstuff prices depressed, and thus increased the income of the popular sector and provoked an expanding demand for other goods, especially industrial ones. But this was to generate a balance-of-payments squeeze, due to the 'discouragement' effect of low prices on pampa production and to increasing internal consumption of exportable foodstuffs. Subsequently

(1952–55) agricultural prices improved, whereupon—because of the operation of the inverse joint effect—the balance-of-payments situation improved. But this in turn generated political troubles, due to the regressive redistribution of income it entailed and to the reduction of the domestic demand on which the urban bourgeoisie depended.

Following this, around 1960, a wave of direct foreign investment in industry and services provoked a rapid internationalisation of the urban productive structure[24] (by means of capitals and activities different from those involved in export activities). Contrary to the 'developmentalist' hopes, this new stage resulted in a marked increase in demand for imports, which outran the growth rate of GNP, exports and pampa production.[25] Faced with this situation the only economically 'evident' solution— repeatedly expounded—lay in a large increase of exports, which would have provided the urban productive structure with the imports necessary for 'self-sustained development'. Assuming the capitalist parameters of the situation, this solution entailed, fundamentally, an increase in pampean production (and productivity) and/or a reduction in real wages, so as to 'free' exportable surpluses of food. But the Cartesian simplicity of these solutions—which were indeed attempted—ran into political complications which we must now analyse.

### III. CYCLES

Several consequences arose from the fact that wage goods were also the main export products. In the first place, it offered an objective basis, which was also subjectively acknowledged,[26] for repeated alliances between a sizeable part of the weaker fractions of the urban bourgeoisie and the popular sector. These alliances were forged around the defence of the internal market against the recessive effects (*via* the increase of domestic food prices) of every significant rise in the price of pampa products. In the second place, the mobilisations of the popular sector in defence of its consumption levels reinforced its capacity for organisational and political action through partial but repeated victories. A third consequence was that the above-mentioned alliance again and again provoked and revivified a deep horizontal cleavage within the urban bourgeoisie, between its oligopolistic fractions and those weaker ones which found a welcome ally in the popular sectors. Fourth, these same processes determined the appearance of another fundamental intrabourgeois cleavage, by separating the economic interests and political goals of the urban bourgeoisie (including its oligopolistic fractions) from those of the pampean bourgeoisie. These changing alliances lie at the basis of the economic and political cycles on which students of Argentina have fastened their attention.[27]

The solution of Argentina's balance-of-payments bottlenecks requires a substantial increase of pampean exports. However, when, around 1960, the demand for imports rose rapidly, the exports themselves rose much less. This was partly the consequence of an increase in the internal consumption of exportables and, also, of slow improvements in the pampean region's production and productivity.[28] Neither the space available nor my knowledge allow for a satisfactory explanation of this failure, but it seems obvious that, assuming the capitalist parameters of the context, a necessary (but not sufficient) condition for rising production of pampean goods lies in 'satisfactory' prices for the pampean bourgeoisie. The meaning of 'satisfactory' is complex, but it includes at least two further necessary conditions: one is that prices should make feasible the investments necessary to increase the capital density of the pampean region and its productivity. The second condition—less obvious but more important—is that those prices should be stable and that they should be perceived as such at the microeconomic level. I do not know of any studies which establish this, but there is no reason to suppose that, in the 1956–76 period, the profit rates of the pampa bourgeoisie were lower than that of the urban bourgeoisie. However Figure 1 clearly shows the enormous instability of the main pampean wholesale prices (cereals, linseed and beef), measured in relation to wholesale urban prices.

A substantial increase in pampean production (and exports) cannot take place without converting the *estancias* into a much more capital-intensive agribusiness. Discarding explanations based on the economic 'irrationality' of the pampa bourgeoisie—which are an implicit avowal of their authors' ignorance—it seems clear that the answer must be found at the level of the parameters which govern microeconomic decisions. These parameters do not spring from some economic 'necessity' but from political struggles and from the swings of the state, which in turn result from the specificities of a class structure whose origins I have summarised in the previous sections. This is what we must analyse.

The conversion of the pampean *estancia* into a capital- and technology-intensive agribusiness[29] entails making rather long-term investment decisions. The instability of pampean relative prices, the historical awareness of this and, above all, the difficulty of forecasting future price instability[30] have prevented those decisions. Thus, the pampa bourgeoisie, once dynamic (even in international terms, during the period before 1930), has become less and less so in recent times. The basic reason is that relative prices made it microeconomically rational to maintain the 'extensive' exploitation of the land.[31]

In the short term the rise in relative internal prices of pampean production entails an almost equivalent net loss for the whole of the urban sector. The income redistribution and the recessive effect on the urban economy which (*ceteris paribus*) this entails, increases the export surpluses (*via* their immediate effect on the internal consumption of exportables) and might induce a medium-term increase of pampa production by satisfying the necessary condition of 'satisfactory' prices. This would not be too onerous for the oligopolistic fractions of the urban bourgeoisie. They have an objective interest in increasing the balance-of-payments surplus because of their high import coefficient.[33] The recessions and redistributions of income which usually accompany increases in food prices are less harmful for these oligopolistic fractions than for the weaker ones. In effect, the former have economic resources and preferential access to internal credit,[34] which enable them to shoulder the burden of the recession and, indeed, to promote capital concentration to their advantage at the same time.[35] Besides, the urban bourgeoisie's oligopolistic fractions aim much of

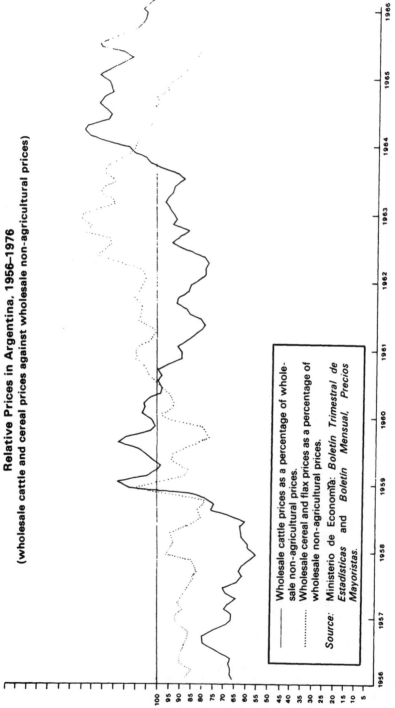

**FIGURE 1**

**Relative Prices in Argentina, 1956–1976**

(wholesale cattle and cereal prices against wholesale non-agricultural prices)

Wholesale cattle prices as a percentage of wholesale non-agricultural prices.

Wholesale cereal and flax prices as a percentage of
wholesale non-agricultural prices.

*Source*: Ministerio de Economía: *Boletín Trimestral de
Estadísticas and Boletín Mensual, Precios
Mayoristas.*

**FIGURE 1 continued**

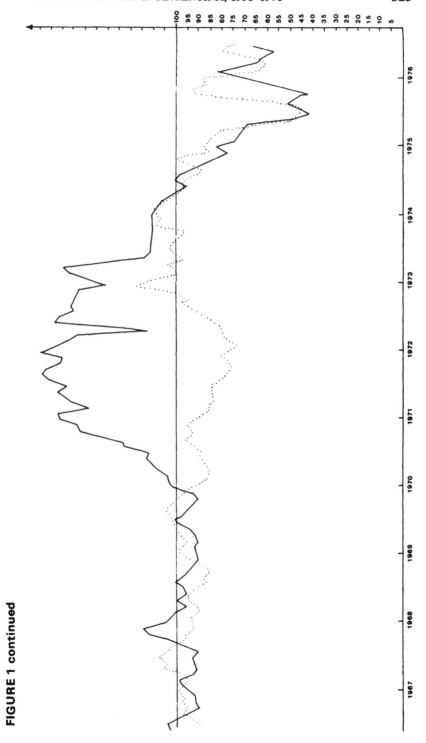

their production and supply of services at the relatively high income strata, whose income is less affected, absolutely and proportionately, by rises in food prices.

Although this generalisation would require qualification in a more refined analysis, it provides the objective basis for a long-term alliance between the large urban bourgeoisie and the pampa bourgeoisie, which could guide the 'modernisation' of Argentine capitalism simultaneously through capital concentration in the urban sector and the development of capital-intensive agribusiness in the countryside. However, at least until 1976, this alliance only lasted for short periods, dissolving rapidly in situations which repeatedly put these two dominant fractions of the Argentine bourgeoisie in different political camps.

Why this deviation from economic 'logic'? Fundamentally because this alliance has been confronted again and again by another—basically made up of the popular sectors and the weak fractions of the urban bourgeoisie— which, in spite of its economic subordination, has been able to prevent it from holding together beyond the short term. In the Latin American context this has been one of Argentina's (and, with its own characteristics, Uruguay's) peculiarities, which can only be understood in terms of the historical perspectives summarised in the previous sections. But we still have new elements to introduce into our analysis.

Which processes posed these dilemmas and conflicts? The periods of low internal prices of foodstuffs and stable foreign exchange rates have, not by chance, been those of the highest growth rates and—until the approach of the end of the cycle—lowest inflation rates.[36] But they have also led to balance-of-payments crises, which brought about the introduction of controls, especially on internal prices and the foreign exchange movements, although these were not enough to stave off the crises. Once the balance-of-payments crises was unleashed, it was dealt with by means of devaluations which (with the exception of the 1967–69 period) implied a correlative increase in the internal prices of exportables. These devaluations formed part of stabilisation programmes which accentuated the recessive and redistributionary effects of the devaluation by means of a restriction of money supply, reduction of the budgetary deficit, wage freezes and increases in the real interest rate, tending, on the one hand, to consolidate the transfer of income to the exporting sector and, on the other, to adjust the internal level of economic activity to meet the balance-of-payements restrictions.

The effects were not only recessive and redistributive but also inflationary ('stagflation' is no novelty in Argentina), through the rise in domestic food prices caused by the growth of their export value, and the rising cost of imported goods and credit—at times when, on the other hand, wages and salaries were kept frozen or systematically lagging and recession increased unemployment. In the short term (and, as we shall see, in these processes there was never more than a short term), the transfer of income towards the exporting sector did not induce an increase in pampean production,[37] but the stabilisation programmes were instrumental in easing the balance-of-payements squeeze.

True, such successes were due to factors very different from those proclaimed in official speeches, in the 'recommendations' of the International Monetary Fund and in the exultant statements of the organisations of the pampa bourgeoisie. They were achieved not by an increase of exportable production but by recession, which diminished the demand for imports and increased the exportable surplus, especially of foodstuffs. But this generated resistances among the many penalised by these policies, while the resulting easing of the balance of payments made possible economic reactivation policies. Consequently, the liquidity increase, the relaxing of controls on the fiscal deficit, the availability of foreign exchange, the growth in employment and the salary increases ended the downward phase of the cycle and inaugurated the upward phase. But the latter led into a new balance-of-payments crisis[38], after which further devaluation, and the consequent stabilisation programme, opened up another downward phase . . .[39].

IV. PENDULUMS

In each phase of the cycle, the large bourgeoisie has played on the winner's side. I have already pointed out that the recessions provoked by stabilisation programmes have, at the very least, not damaged that fraction: at the same time, as a direct appendage of (or intimately linked to) international capital, it is the large bourgeoisie which best perceives—and most fears—the costs of international insolvency[40]. It has the most direct interest in an improvement of the balance of payments[41]. Furthermore, the free international movement of capital enhances the privileged position, in an ever narrower domestic credit market, of this most internationalised (and therefore internally dominant) fraction, while at the same time reopening the 'normal' channels for the transfer of capital accumulation towards the centre of the system,[42] of which it is the most intrinsic part. In the final stretch of the upward phase of the cycle, these factors turn the large bourgeoisie into an ally of the pampa bourgeoisie (and of the whole of the exporting sector) in the clamour for the devaluation and deflationary policies which launch the downward phase. Thus, faced with the onset of the balance-of-payments crisis, the large bourgeoisie swings towards the objective interests of the pampa bourgeoisie, favouring and supporting stabilisation programmes which transfer a mass of resources toward the latter, mostly at the expense of the urban sector.

But the regressive and recessionary impact of these measures generated a reaction among the weaker fractions of the urban bourgeoisie and of the popular sector[43] at the same time as the improvement in the foreign exchange position made feasible the economic reactivation measures for which they were clamouring. Faced with this, the large bourgeoisie did repeatedly what all bourgeoisies do in the absence of a tutelary state to induce them to adopt longer-term strategies: they looked to their short-term economic interests, supported the economic reactivation policies, and thus rode the crest of the wave of economic recovery—from which, we may safely assume, they were able to profit in a privileged manner.[44] In this it covered a full swing of the pendulum, joining the rest of the urban sector and abandoning the pampa bourgeoisie to a solitary lament for the deterioration of its relative prices;[45] all of which produced the great fluctuations of relative prices observable in Figure 1.

Although this describes the recurrent pendulation of the large bourgeoisie, I have still to explain it. However, it must be added that, apart from their economic consequences, these displacements had political implications of the greatest importance: they repeatedly broke up that intra-bourgeois cohesion essential for its stable political domination. More precisely, they broke the cohesion of its two superior fractions (the urban oligopolistic and the pampa bourgeoisie), whose respective capital accumulation base made them potentially capable of 'modernising' Argentine capitalism. Another aspect, no less important and to which I shall shortly turn, is that such swings not only generated the political space for, but also were to a large extent the consequence of, an alternative alliance which encompassed the weaker fractions of the bourgeoisie and the popular sector.

Let me insist on a crucial point. The alliance of the dominant fractions of the bourgeoisie could have borne fruit if it had lasted long enough to bring about significant productivity increases in the pampa region. This was prevented by the large fluctuations in relative prices. But in their political demands the pampean bourgeoisie concentrated on the level and not the stability of their prices, thus contributing to the pendulations I have already mentioned. The productivity increases could have taken place with relatively depressed but stable pampean prices (thus meeting the necessary condition of stability stated above), combined with public policies which would have forced them through by more structural measures. This was the motivation behind the various projects designed to tax the difference between the potential and the actual productivity of pampa land.

Such an alternative, obviously conflicting with the short-term interests of the pampa bourgeoisie in its present composition, is not against those of the urban sector as a whole (since it does not presuppose a fall in their relative prices), and in the medium term it could have achieved the sought-after increase in pampa production and productivity. However, the attempts to impose such a tax on the 'potential rent of the land' repeatedly failed. This must be contrasted with what has happened in many other Latin American countries, where the state—impelled by and allied with the large bourgeoisie—has usually been able to force through the 'modernisation' of agrarian regions and their dominant classes[46]. But those agrarian classes were fundamentally regional ones[47] and, although their production might temporarily fall, their contribution to total exports was not comparable to that of the pampa bourgeoisie. That is why other Latin American states have been able to subordinate those classes, and the regional states which they controlled, without simultaneously worsening their balance-of-payments problems.

The case of the pampa bourgeoisie has been very different. I have pointed out its early position as a national class, even with respect to its linkage with a national state. This meant that intrabourgeois struggles usually occured, in contrast with other Latin American cases, at the very heart of a national state which was continually fractured by them. Besides, the 'discouragement' of the pampa bourgeoisie[48] caused by the fall in its prices and attempts to 'restructure it' by means of tax mechanisms, had strong immediate repercussions on the balance of payments—at the same time that, in the upward phase of the economic cycle, the increase in domestic consumption of exportables further diminished the potentially available exports, before pampean productivity had undergone any substantial improvement. Thus a balance of payments crisis ensued, and its alleviation by means of devaluations not only turned relative prices against the urban sector but also entailed the expulsion from the governing alliances of the sectors which had impelled the reactivation of the cycle.

As long as the stabilisation programmes lasted, the immediate interests of the pampa bourgeoisie weighed heavily in the institutional system of the state. Naturally enough, it opposed any prospect of its own 'restructuring', centring the issue on a sharp increase in its prices and thus creating the conditions for a renewal of the cycle . . . In other words, although it has long lost its position as the dynamic vanguard of Argentine capitalism, the pampa bourgeoisie, compared with other Latin American agrarian classes, has retained an unusually central economic and political position. This position was sufficient both to block any attempt to 'restructure' it and to use periodic balance-of-payments crises to bring about massive income transfers for its benefit. Meanwhile, and as a consequence, channels for capital accumulation in Argentina were repeatedly short-circuited and the state danced to the pendular tune of civil society.

This accounts for some of the characteristics of the period beginning in 1966, especially the economic policies followed between March 1967 and May 1969. The Economics Minister, Krieger Vasena, transparently carried out the policies of the large bourgeoisie. This entailed, among other things, a large devaluation which for the first time did not benefit the pampa and exporting sector. On the contrary, the March 1967 devaluation (40%) was wholly appropriated by the state, which withheld a percentage of the value of pampa exports equivalent to the devaluation. This fiscal revenue was used in a substantial programme of investment in physical infrastructure and communications. A fixed *peso* price of pampean production depressed the internal price of pampean foodstuffs, as can be seen in Figure 1. It also allowed a rapid reduction of inflation and—in contrast with other cases of bureaucratic-authoritarianism—only a moderate fall in industrial wages. (See Figures 2 and 3.)

Even so, this situation could not be maintained and, as can be seen in Figure 1, after 1970 pampean prices (especially those of beef) rebounded until they reached a very high level in 1971–72. Krieger Vasena's was the only clear and sustained attempt by the large bourgeoisie unilaterally to subordinate the pampa bourgeoisie[49] to its own accumulation needs. But the result was an internal rupture in the cohesion of the BA state and a political and economic collapse impelled from outside by other social actors. While this attempt marked the limits of a unilateral enforcement of supremacy by the large bourgeoisie, the history of previous devaluations, by pushing the big bourgeoisie into alliances with the urban sector, had shown that it was impossible to return to the good old times of pampean supremacy.[50]

330 DEVELOPMENT STUDIES REVISITED

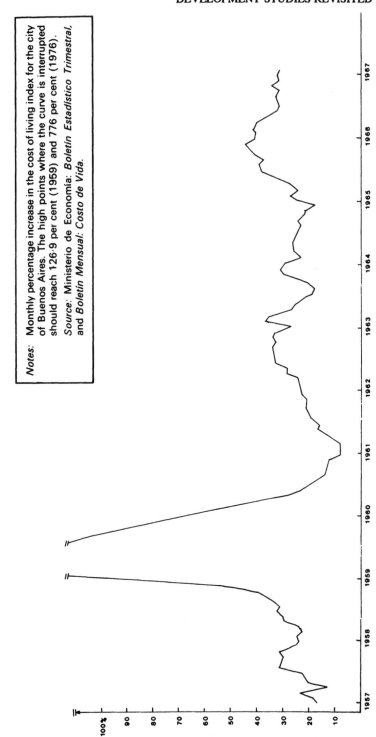

**FIGURE 2**
Inflation in Argentina, 1956–1976

*Notes:* Monthly percentage increase in the cost of living index for the city of Buenos Aires. The high points where the curve is interrupted should reach 126·9 per cent (1959) and 776 per cent (1976).

*Source:* Ministerio de Economía: *Boletín Estadístico Trimestral,* and *Boletín Mensual: Costo de Vida.*

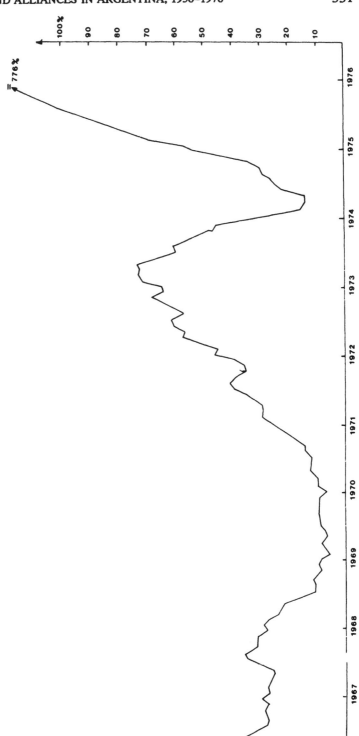

FIGURE 2 continued

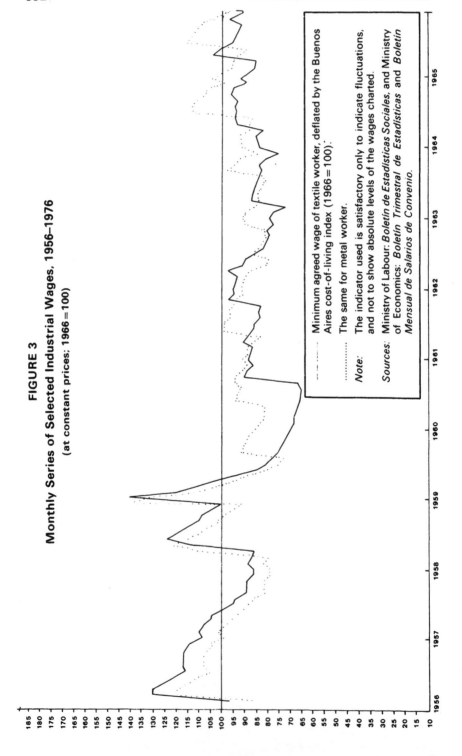

FIGURE 3

Monthly Series of Selected Industrial Wages, 1956–1976

(at constant prices: 1966 = 100)

Minimum agreed wage of textile worker, deflated by the Buenos Aires cost-of-living index (1966 = 100).

The same for metal worker.

*Note:* The indicator used is satisfactory only to indicate fluctuations, and not to show absolute levels of the wages charted.

*Sources:* Ministry of Labour: *Boletín de Estadísticas Sociales,* and Ministry of Economics: *Boletín Trimestral de Estadísticas* and *Boletín Mensual de Salarios de Convenio.*

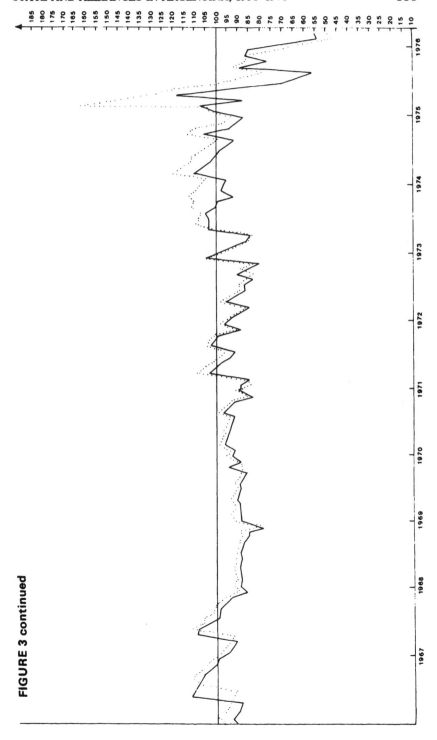

**FIGURE 3 continued**

## V. THE DEFENSIVE ALLIANCE

If the political and economic centrality of the pampa bourgeoisie marks an important difference with respect to other Latin American countries and their agrarian classes, a no less important difference stems from the greater political vulnerability of the weaker (and genuinely national) fractions of the urban bourgeoisie in those countries when faced with the expansion of the large bourgeoisie. The growth of the dominant productive structure, oligopolistic and internationalised, has occurred at the expense of many fractions of national capital, weakening its position *vis-à-vis* international capital and the state. This has caused complaints and strains, but has not, so far, been translated into serious political challenges to such 'development' patterns. No such development has taken place in Argentina. The reason for the local bourgeoisie's comparatively greater political capacity is to be found not so much in itself as in the characteristics of the popular sector and in the country's relative national homogeneity. Elsewhere, a weaker urban sector, less organised and autonomous, deprives the weaker fractions of the Latin American bourgeoisie of the extremely important ally they had in Argentina. This is a crucial point.

Not only is the Argentine popular sector endowed with greater autonomy and organisational capacity than in most other Latin American countries. It also so happens that the medium- and long-term alliance of the upper fractions of the bourgeoisie depends on the level and stability of the relative prices of the main internal foodstuffs. This gave the popular sector a precise target for its political action, which has interrupted the accumulation circuits of those upper bourgeois fractions. These are necessary but not sufficient conditions for the recurrent breakdown of the latter's alliances. To account for the specificity of the phenomena with which we are concerned we must also see how the popular sector associated itself with the objective interests and political action of the weaker fractions of the urban bourgeoisie.

These fractions are usually penalised by devaluations and stabilisation programmes. Given an alleviation of the balance-of-payments squeeze, their immediate interest lies in economic reactivation policies which increase employment, liquidity and credit availability, and give the state an expansionary role once again. This is also a direct effect of wage and salary increases; thus, it is not surprising that the bourgeois fraction in control of the most labour-intensive enterprises should support these increases, when the even greater costs to them of recession are taken into account. The concurrence with the unions in demanding wage increases is, besides, a token which it offers the popular sector to forge the alliance.[51] Such a bourgeoisie – more or less weak and more or less penalised by the expansion of oligopolistic and internationalised capital—exists in other Latin American countries, but only in Argentina has it found a popular ally whose immediate short-term interests are compatible with its own, and which possesses a significant capacity for political action.[52]

The main organisational supports of this alliance have been the CGE, the CGT and the national leadership of the main unions. Its first, principal, and possibly last expression has been *peronismo*. It was not the only one, since—above all in the periods in which *peronismo* was proscribed—it was channelled through other parties and within state institutions by diverse 'nationalist' military and civilian groups. Their banner has been the defence of the internal market, in the sense both of raising the level of its activity and of limiting the expansion of international capital in it.

The characteristics of this popular sector and of this local bourgeoisie cannot be understood in isolation from each other. It has been their conjunction in the multiplying effect of their alliance which has made it possible to impose, again and again, the satisfaction of their immediate demands. We can now examine the characteristics and principal consequences of this alliance.

(1) The alliance was sporadic but recurrent. It only appeared in the downward phases of the cycle, when demands for wage and salary increases and for diverse measures to relieve 'the suffocation of the small and medium-sized national enterprise'[53] concurred in the reactivation of the internal market at the expense of the pampean exporting sector. Once the cycle revived the alliance dissolved, partly due to the attempts of the local bourgeoisie and the unions to negotiate special agreements individually with the state and with the large bourgeoisie, partly because of the return of more 'normal' class cleavages.

(2) The alliance was defensive. It arose against the offensives of the upper fractions of the bourgeoisie. Its ideology of 'nationalist' and 'socially just' development overlooked what it was unable to *problematise:* the deeply oligopolistic and internationalised structure of the capitalism of which its members were the weakest components. It was defensive because in its victory it could not create an alternative capital accumulation system; all it achieved was the transition from the downward phase to the upward phase, in conditions which were doomed to provoke the repetition of the cycle.

(3) But despite its defensive nature, and although its victories signified the completion and not a way out of the cycle, this alliance was quite successful. It scored repeated victories in annulling the stabilisation programmes, limiting the domestic expansion of international capital, and launching economic reactivation policies and new 'discouragements' for the pampa bourgeoisie. Thus, it is not surprising that the wage series of Figure 2 should also show erratic behaviour; its peaks are the result of victorious struggles which soon led to marked reductions in wages. The upward movements of wages were accompanied by growth of the GNP and, in general, by higher profit rates for the industrial bourgeoisie as a whole—although, being also subject to the overall cycle, profits also seem to have undergone marked fluctuations.[54] The consequence of these processes may be seen in a phenomenon as intrinsically political as it is economic: the inflation which, as can be seen in Figure 3, is even more remarkable for its fluctuations than for its generally high level.

More basically, the defensive alliance was victorious because it managed to destroy the alliance between the two dominant fractions of the bourgeoisie. The large bourgeoisie, when the time came to weigh the immediate benefits from a revival of the economy against the political abyss entailed by aligning with the pampa bourgeoisie and the exporting sector when the remainder of civil society had joined forces against them, opted to support a new upward phase. Repeatedly the defensive alliance—

politically—broke 'from below' the cohesion of the dominant fractions and—economically—blocked the only alliance which could implant a new capital accumulation system and move the economy off its cyclical path.

(4) The alliance was polyclassist, in the sense that it included the popular sector (with a strong working-class component) and various bourgeois fractions. Its repeated successes were based on this conjunction. But, on the other hand, this ensured that its orientations were nationalistic[55] and capitalist. Its polyclass character, based on the achievement of shared tactical goals, offered a popular base for the demands of the weak bourgeoisie. This fraction thus appeared as a 'progressive' one which, contrasting with the large bourgeoisie's 'efficientist' orientations and the 'landholding oligarchy's' archaism, seemed to embody the possibility of a 'development with social justice'. On the other hand, the popular sector (especially the unions and the working class) gained, through the polyclassist nature of the alliance, access to resources and mass media which it could not otherwise have had.

In particular, the bourgeois respectability of the alliance made more difficult the harsh repression which has been directed at the popular sector elsewhere in Latin America when it has acted in isolation and/or in pursuit of more radical goals. The impact of this alliance stemmed from the multiplying effect of the concurrence of social actors who had their own resource base and who could co-operate in very concrete and short-term goals. In other Latin American countries, the absence of these joint conditions has meant that the local bourgeoisie has lacked popular support and that the popular sector (weaker, in any case, because of greater intranational heterogeneity) has not enjoyed the political protection of a bourgeois ally. This, in turn, has made it possible for the large bourgeoisie to advance unhindered, naturally encountering protests and conflicts, but not the limits and oscillations which this peculiar alliance imposed in Argentina.

(5) Locked in capitalist parameters, the principal political channel of the defensive alliance, *peronismo*, did not transcend these limits. This limitation also arose from the experience of repeated victories and subsequent defeats. The political activation of the popular sector in pursuit of the goals of the defensive alliance, the protection granted by its bourgeois component and the changes in public policies which it achieved, led, on the one hand, to a positive reinforcement of that activation and, on the other, to the solidifying of the organisational basis—above all the unions—which articulated the popular sector's action. Let us take a closer look at this.

(6) In historical terms, the alliance stemmed from the fresh memory of previous mobilisations which had managed to reverse the downward trend of real wages and of economic activity. It was also a function of the low deterrent effect of a repression which tended to cease the moment the state, indicating a shift in the governing alliances, launched a new upward phase of the cycle. This increased the popular sector's capacity for and disposition to political activation, but it also led to an equally repetitive experience of defeat: periods of low wages and salaries, and of mounting unemployment,

during which the spokesmen of the defensive alliance were removed from the governing coalition.

However, in contrast with the transparent stimulus entailed by rising food prices and falling salaries and wages, the reversal of the cycle took place because of problems (such as balance-of-payments crises) and through mechanisms (such as devaluations and restrictions in the money supply) whose functioning and impact were harder to grasp. The benefits derived by the pampa bourgeoisie and the exporting sector, and the initial support lent by the large bourgeoisie to each downward reversal of the cycle, fostered the hostility of the popular sector against both fractions and against the internationalisation and big business which they embodied. At the same time, the defensive alliance could not abandon its capitalist ideology and goals.

Thus, the interpretation of the sequences of such successes and defeats became a mythology of conspiracies of 'powerful interests' which had a magical ability to defeat the 'people' and hinder 'development'. Failure and tension generated in some cases a fascist ideological syndrome and in others a challenging of the capitalist parameters of the situation. But against these centrifugal tendencies a powerful centripetal force operated: as the CGT, the CGE and *peronismo* tirelessly repeated, since 1955 they had been prevented from carrying out the kind of 'socially just' capitalist development which, 'placed on the people's side' and exercising wide control of the state's institutions, the local bourgeoisie and the unions seemed to offer.

The feasibility of uniting the 'national and the popular' against the 'landholding oligarchy' and the 'international monopolies', which the short-term coincidences of the defensive alliance seemed to confirm, were expressed in *peronismo's* unusual appeal and were a decisive element in the great wave which in 1973 returned it to government. A further condition for this was that in the previous period the large bourgeoisie had ignored the limits of its supremacy and had tried to impose it unilaterally, even on the pampa bourgeoisie. The social explosions of 1969 and 1970 sealed the defeat of that attempt and, impelled by a great popular activation, forced the political withdrawal of the large bourgeoisie which, in 1973, lost its place in the governing alliance for the first time. Only then could the alternative which the main spokesmen of the defensive alliance claimed to embody be positively put to the test.

(7) Rather than cycles we must now speak of spirals, inasmuch as— politically, above all—each swing of the pendulum, with its succession of temporary victories and defeats, sharpened the conflicts from which they derived. The actors were not classes, fractions and organisations which retained their 'structural' characteristics unchanged, beyond these struggles. Rather, they were the political, organisational and ideological expression of classes and fractions created and transformed during and through this pattern of alliances and oppositions. In particular, the popular sector found in the unions and—politically—in *peronismo*, an organi- sational, ideological and political expression which corresponded closely to the limits of the situation. The mobilisation behind the defensive alliance's demands, with its precise aims and polyclass framework, achieved frequent

and spectacular victories. This explains the peculiar combination of impressive popular activation with economistic demands, which emphasised—as a token of its alliance with the local bourgeoisie—its rejection of any leap beyond capitalism. Precisely this militant economism, combined with the weaker fractions of the bourgeoisie, permitted repeated defensive victories and perpetuated the illusion of an alternative path of capitalist development.

On the other hand, the moments of political victory and reversal—at any point in the economic cycle—were those when the temporary victors took the state apparatus by storm, seeking to strengthen institutional positions from which they would fight future battles when the situation was once again reversed—as experience taught them it would be. Of course, the unions were no exception to this: the history of the defensive alliance is also that of the extraction from the state of important institutional concessions. These, in turn, reinforced the possibility of renewing the mobilisation of the popular sector. The conquest of institutional positions enabled the unions to cover the popular sector with a fine organisational net, from which they could direct it repeatedly toward a militant economism, towards the polyclass alliance and towards the mirage of the 'other' capitalist path which *peronismo* proclaimed.

(8) These multiplying fusions of the defensive alliance forced the large bourgeoisie repeatedly to abandon the pampa bourgeoisie to a solitary lament at the falling prices of their products. Such fusions both impelled economic reactivation and opened up the political abyss of a wide and active 'national and popular' mobilisation which had somehow to be reabsorbed. By swinging from support of the pampean bourgeoisie to support of a new upward phase of the cycle, the large bourgeoisie closely followed its short-term economic interests and managed to remain the only stable member of the governing alliance. It did not lose its dominant position, but the peculiar conditions outlined meant that its domination had to shift continuously backwards and forwards. At the same time and for the same reasons, the channels of capital accumulation were repeatedly short-circuited. These clues enable us to understand Argentine politics as a less surrealistic phenomenon than its 'political instability' and erratic 'development' might lead one to believe.

As I hope is clear, insofar as this discussion refers to the constitution of the classes, it also refers to the state. It is from this viewpoint—starting from and returning to civil society—that the problem of the state must be approached.

VI. THE STATE
The state is not merely a set of institutions. It also includes—fundamentally—the network of relationships of 'political' domination activated and supported by such institutions in a territorially defined society, which supports and contributes to the reproduction of a society's class organisation. In the Argentine case the pendular movements of the large bourgeoisie and the difficulties it has faced in subordinating civil society as a whole are a tangible indication of a continued crisis of the state as a system of political domination. So are the defensive alliance's recurrent

and partially victorious fusions. Out of this was born a democratisation by default, which resulted from the difficulties in imposing the authoritarian 'solution' that seemed to offer a chance of extracting Argentine capitalism from its political and economic spirals.

By 'governing alliance' I mean an alliance which imposes, through the institutional system of the state, policies conforming to the orientations and demands of its components. The large bourgeoisie was the stable member of the governing alliance, but each phase was marked by a temporary change in its partners and by an alternation of scarcely consistent circuits of capital accumulation. That is why public policies were continually changing and hardly ever implemented, as the state danced to the tune of the dynamics of civil society.

The state was recurrently razed to the ground by civil society's changing coalitions. At the institutional level, the coalitions were like great tides which momentarily covered everything and which, when they ebbed, washed away entire segments of the state—segments which would later serve as bastions for the piecing together of a new offensive against the coalition which had just forced its opponents into retreat. The result was a state apparatus extensively colonised by civil society. The upper fractions of the bourgeoisie were not the only ones to hang on to it; its weakest fractions and part of the subordinate classes did the same—another fundamental difference from other Latin American examples. Civil society's struggles were internalised in the state's institutional system in a way which expressed not only the weight of the bourgeoisie's upper fractions but also the peculiar characteristics of a defensive alliance endowed with a remarkable capacity for partial victory. As a consequence, this colonised state was extraordinarily fragmented, reproducing in its institutions the complex and rapidly changing relationships of dominant and subordinated classes—classes which could use these institutions to fuel the spiralling movements of civil society.

Such a state could not 'keep at a distance' from the governing alliance's immediate demands and interests; it could only reinforce the cycles and swings. It was, quite clearly, a weak state; as a support of social domination, because of the recurrent (and increasing) weakening of such domination implied by the popular sector's mobilisations and the unions' bargaining power; as an institutional sphere, because it was deeply colonised and fractionalised. This meant that one possible way out of the cycles—a shift towards some sort of state capitalism—was blocked; the fairly stable and consolidated bureaucratic apparatus, with non-negligible degrees of freedom *vis-à-vis* civil society, which would have been a necessary condition for such a solution, was not available.

Another obstacle arose from the fact that at times when the large bourgeoisie was in alliance with the pampa bourgeoisie, the stabilisation programmes entailed an 'antistatist' offensive aimed not only to slash the fiscal deficit but also to dismantle the advances which had taken place in a statist direction during the previous phase, when the defensive alliance had been part of the governing alliance. Those attempts blocked any trend towards state capitalism, by dismantling the institutions which could have encouraged it and by dismissing the 'technicians' who could have carried it out, replacing them with others who would issue a string of 'antistatist' pronouncements and decisions.

In addition, any movement towards state capitalism by the defensive alliance encountered the ambivalence (and, frequently, the opposition) of the governing alliance's permanent member—the large bourgeoisie. Feasible or not, this possibility was blocked *ab initio* by the dynamic of civil society.[56] It can be said, then, that at all levels the Argentine state of the 1956–76 period was an example of extremely limited autonomy. Its peculiarity was not only that it basically moved in time with the upper fractions of the bourgeoisie, but also that it reflected the fluctuating political strength of the subordinate classes in their alliance with the weaker fractions of the dominant classes. The limit of the alliance—which shows that it must not be mistaken for an equilibrium of forces—arose from the fact that, on the other hand, it had to co-operate in the governing alliance with the large bourgeoisie and, on the other hand, that it could only be a defensive alliance.

Could this defensive alliance constitute an independent governing alliance, excluding the large bourgeoisie (and, of course, the pampa bourgeoisie)? Only a crude mechanism could lead us to believe this to be impossible on the grounds that the defensive alliance contained Argentine capitalism's weakest and least capitalist fractions. In fact, it did happen in 1973, when the defensive alliance achieved an extraordinary but pyrrhic victory.

## VII. PROVISIONAL EPILOGUE

The experiment initiated in 1966 sought, on the one hand, to rebuild capital accumulation mechanisms which subordinated the whole of society to the large bourgeoisie and, on the other hand, necessarily and correlatively, to introduce a system of political domination which, reversing the preceding situation, would aggressively impose itself on civil society. I have mentioned the collapse of that attempt and how this made possible, for the first time, the conquest of the state's institutional system by the defensive alliance, independently of the large bourgeoisie. Recent history cannot be written here. But it is necessary to point out that this alliance could only briefly ignore the economic supremacy of the large bourgeoisie and the pampa bourgeoisie; a glance at the data already presented demonstrates how, after a brief truce in 1974, the cyclical fluctuations were repeated much more violently. Even before Peron's death, the intrinsically defensive content and limitations of the alliance had been shown beyond question. The old crisis reproduced itself with unusual acuteness and the local bourgeoisie had to abandon ship without even rescuing its organisation. On the other hand, the exacerbation of 'union power' could not go beyond a repetition, with increased force after the retreat of the local bourgeoisie, of the practices which had made it what it was: an aggressive economism and a search for new institutional advantages—pursued now from the very heart of the state institutional system. This cumbersome heritage of past victories created ominous gaps between the union leaders and their own class. It also generated conservative reactions, which threatened the substantial autonomy which the unions and the popular sector had retained throughout this complex process.

Peron's death, a peculiar 'palace' irrationality, and a violence which speedily fed on itself, helped to shake the foundations of a society and accelerated the spirals of its crisis; this happened with a state that too obviously failed to gaurantee the survival of this capitalism. But beneath those factors was the fact that, when the defensive alliance managed, at last, to become the governing alliance, it ran up against its own limitations; the very reasons which had brought about its extraordinary victory precipitated an unprecedented crisis. The promise of a 'nationalist' and 'socially just' path of capitalist development was subjected to a positive test and the alliance's centrifugal tensions fired off in their opposing directions.

The great victory of the defensive alliance led to the paroxysm of the political and economic crisis, to the ebbing away of the nationalist ideology, to the implantation of a new bureaucratic authoritarian state and to the dissolution or subjection to government control of the main organisations of the popular sector and the local bourgeoisie. As a result, for the first time, the defensive alliance's political, ideological, and organisational supports have been neutralised. This has enabled the dominant fractions of the bourgeoisie to explore the possibilities for a long-term reaccommodation on more egalitarian terms—between themselves—than those prevalent in 1967–69. The implication of and precondition for such a reaccommodation is the dispersal of the defensive alliance. This does not entirely preclude a return of that alliance or of the spirals we have studied. But for such a thing to happen, the local bourgeoisie would have to set itself on a hazardous 'road to Damascus' towards a renewed alliance with the popular sectors; and it is not certain that, by then, the popular sector will still be confined within the ideological and political parameters which cemented the defensive alliance before its greatest and most catastrophic victory.

NOTES

1. For an already published characterisation of this type of state see O'Donnell [*1972* and *1975*].

2. For a conception which considers any kind of political domination preferable to 'political instability', this cannot but seem the consequence of an acute pathology. Listing the dysfunctional psychological traits of Argentine 'masses and elites' has been one of the favourite occupations of influential currents in the social sciences [Kirkpatrick, *1971*] and of the apocalyptic elements of the Argentine right. Neither has much been contributed by visions of the problem of dependency as a *deus ex machina* which only has to be invoked to explain everything away. Reflections on the 'stalemate', or mutual blockings of political and social forces in Argentina, have been more fruitful, above all those which have connected it with the Gramscian view of hegemonic crisis [cf. Portantiero, *1973*]. But beyond describing the stalemate and outlining some of its consequences, the question still remains: what are the power relationships which have produced that stalemate?

3. The 'threat' concept refers to the degree to which internal and external dominant classes and sectors considered that the breach of the capitalist parameters and of the society's international alignments was imminent and willingly sought by the leadership of the popular sector [O'Donnell, *1975*].

4. I define 'domestic bourgeoisie' as the fractions of the urban bourgeoisie which control enterprises mostly or totally owned by nationals. The definition excludes, therefore, the local subsidiaries of transnational firms and the agrarian bourgeoisie. Within the latter, the 'pampa

bourgeoisie' is that which controls the grain and beef-exporting region of the Argentine pampas. The domestic bourgeoisie must in turn be disaggregated, since it ranges from the urban bourgeoisie's fully national and weakest layers to oligopolistic corporations intimately connected—by diverse mechanisms—with international capital. Making a different distinction, I shall also further speak on the 'large (urban) bourgeoisie', when referring to the set formed by the branches of transnational corporations and by the domestic bourgeoisie's oligopolistic action. 'Below' the large bourgeoisie, what I shall call the 'local'—or simply 'weak'—bourgeoisie is left, made up of capitalists controlling non-oligopolistic firms, smaller and usually less capital-intensive than the large bourgeoisie's. I shall also refer to the Confederación General Económica (CGE), an organisation which throughout invoked the representation of the local bourgeoisie. The 'popular sector' means the working class and the employed and unionised middle sectors; the Confederación General del Trabajo (CGT) is the national organisation of the working class and middle sector unions and federations of unions.

5. Such a collapse happened in Greece, a case which has significant similarities with the one we shall examine here, especially the combination of a low threat-level, a fairly autonomous popular sector and a relatively moderate earlier economic crisis.

6. And of Uruguay, to which I shall briefly return.

7. When I speak of direct incorporation or linkage I refer to the role which some regions had as (an exporting) part of the world capitalist system. This of course does not imply that regions not linked to the world capitalist system were not importers of products from the centre, nor subject to the effects of world capitalist expansion, often through directly incorporated regions.

8. Above all since Fernando H. Cardoso's and Enzo Faletto's book, *Dependencia y Desarrollo en America Latina*, where we find the characterisation of the types of exporting economy I have mentioned; an important recent contribution is that of Albert Hirschman, who adapts elements of staple theory to his concept of 'linkages', widened to include not strictly economic relationships, and from there explores the consequences of the type of export product through which incorporation into the international market took place; unfortunately this author does not deal with pampean and Uruguayan products. See Hirschman [1976].

9. With exception of Uruguay, a case of even greater intranational homogeneity, since practically all its territory and its population were incorporated in the world market in conditions similar to those of the Argentine pampean region. Another exception, though partial and more complicated, is that of Chile; here, in the last third of the nineteenth century, the highly homogeneous agrarian economy of the central valley, partly oriented towards the export of foodstuffs, underwent (in contrast with Argentina and Uruguay) a decline, and the mining enclaves of the north emerged. But in contrast with other cases, those enclaves were inserted in a national market and a national state already constituted around the central agrarian region. See Cavarozzi [forthcoming]. Uruguay's greater intranational homogeneity allowed the earlier and fuller development of a 'liberal' and 'welfare' state. But for this very reason the problems concealed by the initial bonanza exploded earlier than in Argentina. Besides, the smaller absolute size of the Uruguayan internal market was decisive in interrupting its industrialisation much earlier and thus, in recent decades, the relative weight of its working class has been significantly less than in Argentina.

10. For data and references on Argentina's greater intranational homogeneity with respect to most of Latin America, cf. O'Donnell, [1972], ch. 1. For an analysis of the differences in the distribution of income and of its political correlates in Latin America, see Graciarena [1971].

11. Since then the increasingly capital-intensive modalities of the production of wool, cereals and beef in the world market implied that agrarian productivity in Uruguay and Argentina rapidly fell behind in comparison with other exporters; cf. Díaz Alejandro [1970].

12. Geller [1975].

13. The exception to this generalisation is Brazil's Sao Paulo industrialisation, based on the dynamising stimulus of the coffee economy, which does not correspond to any of the generic types I have employed (see Hirschman [1967]). But its original use of slave labour, its labour-intensive character compared with the pampa economy and—most important for our argument—its location in a national context in which the slave system weighed overwhelmingly, contributed to the lower degree of autonomous organisation and political weight of the Brazilian working class compared with Argentina's.

14. This is related to the Spanish and Italian immigration which nourished that class and the anarchist ideology that prevailed in it until approximately 1920. The main source on this

point continues to be Germani, especially *Política y Sociedad en una época de transición* [*1962*].

15. That is, between the strong exogenous impulse of the incorporation of the pampa region in the international market and the world crisis which altered the main basis of the system.

16. Cf. Borón [*1972*].

17. Above all the transport and warehouse network necessary for shipping the pampa's production, the capture of which by international capital was generously subsidised by the state. If the small technology requirements of direct exploitation of the pampean region permitted domestic control of the land, the much greater requirements of such a network (and later on, of the meat-packing industry) determined a high and early inflow of international capital.

18. I am not concerned here with the details of the respective historical processes. In paricular the imposition of the nationalisation of Buenos Aires by a coalition of provinces of the interior against the opposition of a sizeable part of the pampa interests was no obstacle, once the vigorous exogenous impulses of the European demand for foodstuffs were felt, to the processes alluded to in the text.

19. Even in a case such as Brazil, characterised by relatively early industrialisation and by the great weight of the state bureaucratic apparatus inherited from the imperial period, the subordination of the dominant classes of the north east and the elimination of the barriers interposed by the regional states to the effective functioning of a national market were only completed after 1930; cf. CEBRAP [*1976*]. It should be borne in mind that I am excluding Chile and Uruguay from these generalisations.

20. Of course economic factors were not the only ones operating in this. Its greater weight, condensed in the national state, with respect to the oligarchies of other regions, allowed the pampean bourgeoisie to 'discourage' the emergence of other dynamic exporting industries by means of diverse economic and political mechanisms.

21. Of course, if instead of making these comparisons with other Latin American cases we had made them with Australia and New Zealand, the dimensions Argentina and Uruguay had in common with the other Latin American countries would be more noticeable. For some comparisons in that direction, see Geller [*1975*] and Dieguez [*1969*].

22. The effective market is a function not so much of the total population as of that part of the population subject to capitalist relationships and with a monetary income sufficient for the purchase of mass consumption industrial goods; cf. O'Donnell [*1972*], ch. 1.

23. As always with the exception of Uruguay and partly—and too complicated to be dealt with here—of Chile.

24. It is impossible to quote here all the pertinent bibliography. The data and main sources can be found in Gerchunoff and Llach [*1975*], and Sourrouille [*1976*].

25. See, above all, Ayza, Fichet and González [*1976*].

26. This was one of the constant themes of the CGE and the CGT after 1955.

27. The subject of the stop-go cycle has elicited important contributions from various theoretical perspectives. Cf. above all, Díaz Alejandro [*1966*] and [*1970*]; Diamand [*1973*]: Brodersohn [*1974*]; Sourrouille and Mallon [*1974*]; Ferrer *et al.* [*1969*] and Villanueva [*1972*]. Canitrot [*1975*] has a different viewpoint, but is nevertheless an important contribution. For attemps to connect this type of analysis with a more specifically political level, see Braun [*1973*] and O'Donnell [*1972*]. From another angle, the literature already mentioned on the political 'stalemate' in Argentina is relevant to this subject. However, not much has been done so far to capture the formation and shifts of political alliances which have stimulated those cycles.

28. On this subject the principal source is Díaz Alejandro's important book [*1970*], where the slow growth of the physical quantity of these exports and the spectacular lag of pampean productivity with respect to its principal competitors in the world market are shown. Also see Sourrouille and Mallon [*1974*].

29. I hope it is clear that I am speaking at the class level. That is, the change towards an agribusiness would surely displace more than the few individuals who at present constitute the pampa bourgeoisie.

30. The pampa bourgeoisie's demands and declarations, at least of the last twenty years, constitute a repeated complaint that it does not receive profitable or stable prices.

31. Cf. the microeconomic studies quoted in the works I mention below. The issue is however more complicated, as appears from the controversy which took place in *Desarrollo Económico* between Flischman [*1970* and *1974*] Braun [*1970* and *1974* ]and Martínez *et al.*

[*1976*]. The central point of these for our analysis is that the differential rent which the pampean region still enjoys and, especially, the great fluctuations of the whole economy and the high (and erratic) inflation rate, made the purchase of pampa land an excellent speculative investment—and a defence against the effects of inflation—for the urban and agrarian capital surpluses. This combines to reinforce the microeconomic rationality of maintaining the region's extensive exploitation. But, from the perspective of this analysis, the subject which these authors discuss seems to be a consequence (although in time it nourishes them in turn) of the economic and political factors I analyse here.

32. Further on I shall complicate this matter by introducing other factors.

33. Not only is the coefficient high but it grows with an elasticity greater then 1·0 with increases in its production level; cf. Ayza *et al.* [*1976*].

34. For data on this point cf. esp. FIEL [*1971*], and Brodersohn [*1972*].

35. On this point and others closely connected with it, see O'Donnell and Link [*1973*].

36. Cf. the pertinent data in Brodersohn [*1974*].

37. Actually, the price elasticity of pampean production is nil or slightly negative in the short term. This is because for cattle 'an increase in relative prices reduces supply and increases the stocks. Besides, an increase in the cattle stock implies a greater use of land due to the rigidity in the supply of land . . . Therefore, an increase in the relative prices of beef also negatively affects the production of cereals since to the lesser supply of beef is to be added the smaller area for cultivation' (Brodersohn [*1974*], p. 28).

38. In contrast with what I noted above concerning exports, the income-elasticity of imports is extremely high. It was estimated at around 2·6 for the 1947–67 period (cf. Díaz Alejandro [*1966*], p. 356); for the period after 1966, Ayza *et al.* [*1976*, p. 13], with a different methodology, estimate an elasticity of 1·8. One piece of information which indicates how internal consumption causes this pincer movement to close on the balance of payments in the upward phase of the cycle is that the wage earners' marginal propensity to consume exportable goods (foodstuffs, drinks and tobacco) is 0·36 and that of nonwage earners is 0·16; Díaz Alejandro [*1974*], ch. 4.

39. This is the briefest of summaries of the principal theme of the works quoted in n. 27, to which I must refer. A useful presentation of the economic mechanisms operating in the upward and downward phases of the cycles—which unfortunately came to my attention only when this work was substantially finished—is Diamand [*1976*].

40. As the upward phase approached the balance-of-payments crisis, state controls were imposed on prices and foreign exchange, thus particularly troubling this fraction. I cannot deal with these points at greater length; suffice it to point out that, as far as price controls, which are typical of the final moments of the upward phase, are concerned, they could only really be attempted with the 'leading firms'. In other respects, when the balance-of-payments crisis occurred, the imposition of foreign exchange controls and of restrictions on capital transfers abroad became serious hindrances, particularly to firms more closely connected with the centres of world capitalism. Admittedly, none of these controls achieved their goals, nor did they prevent massive flights of capital, but many of the high-ranking staff of large firms (national and transnational) whom I interviewed in 1971 and 1972 said that for that reason they 'had' to act 'excessively' beyond the pale of Argentine legislation, with consequent uneasiness at times when, during the upward phase of the cycles, 'demagogues' and 'nationalists' with access to state institutions were not lacking.

41. In terms of their high import coefficient and demand for foreign exchange, and in spite of their better access to international finance, which allows them to make excellent deals in pre- and post-devaluation periods of acute scarcity of foreign exchange.

42. Even within private capital's oligopolistic fraction, the more fully and directly internationalised firms—the subsidiaries of the transnational corporations—are usually the largest (in capital and sales), the fastest growing, and the most capital intensive; cf. especially Sourrouille [*1976*]. Of course this is not peculiar to Argentina; on Mexico see Fajnzylber and Farrago [*1976*] and Von Doellinger and Cavalcanti [*1975*].

43. These in turn carried with them a large part of the nonpampean regions, which also had to 'contribute' to these income transfers.

44. At least, the more concentrated and internationalised industrial branches usually responded with greater dynamism to the reactivation.

45. Maintaining a fixed exchange rate—or systematically allowing it to lag behind domestic prices—was the main mechanism which turned relative prices in favour of the urban sector (including wages and salaries).

46. This of course did not prevent these processes from being acutely conflictive. The point is that the capacity of these classes to resist was less than that of the pampa bourgeoisie and that, besides, the cost of such policies—in terms of their short-term impact on the level of internal economic activity and exports—was lower.

47. In the case of the enclaves it obviously was not a matter of modernising the economy's most capital and technology-intensive sector, but of renegotiating with international capital the percentages which could be retained locally. In the cases in which (1) 'excessive' pressures was exerted (reaching or threatening nationalisation, above all) and (2) the enclave's product was as important as the pampa production for total exports (Bolivia and, more recently, Chile) the familiar falls in production and/or prices—equivalent in this sphere to the pampa bourgeoisie's recurrent 'discouragements'—unleashed the consequent balance-of-payments crisis.

48. For the pampa bourgeoisie's insistence on its 'discouragement' because of its internal prices and the attempts to 'smother it' with taxes, it is enough to consult collections of documents of the Sociedad Rural Argentina (SRA) and the Coordinadora de Asociaciones Rurales de Buenos Aires y La Pampa (CARBAP).

49. Even by trying to introduce a tax on potential rent which, like so many other things, faded away with the social explosions of 1969.

50. Another exception—less clear, but also a telling one—can be found in the economic policy followed during 1964 and 1965. Then, as it can be seen from Figures 1 and 2, high pampean prices coexisted with an improvement of real wages. But this attempt ran into its own limitations, since it entailed the reduction of profits for the urban bourgeoisie—which actively contributed to the 1966 coup— a large increase in the fiscal deficit and severe restrictions on imports.

51. Since these wage and salary increases encourage economic activity at the same time that other policies, made possible by the transitory easing of the balance of payments, raise the employment level, the orthodox warnings that all this feeds inflation matter little—particularly since inflation, with a fixed or systematically lagging exchange rate, accelerates the reversal of relative prices in favour of the urban sector.

52. In Uruguay the lower level of industrialisation, fundamentally due to the smaller internal market, weakened both agents much more; the local bourgeoisie has in itself been weaker and in the popular sector the working class has had relatively less weight. In Chile the political expression of the working class in Marxist parties (and the absence of a direct target in the relative price of foodstuffs as in Argentina and Uruguay) made this alliance more ambiguous and discontinuous. In the remaining countries of the region the relative weakness of the popular sector—due to a greater intranational heterogeneity—deprived the local bourgeoisie of that fundamental ally.

53. These are subjects and terms which recur in the CGE's demands and declarations; cf. e.g., its *Memorias Anuales*.

54. At least using as a proxy the relationship between urban wholesale prices and wages.

55. Basically, it was prevented from uniting to defend the domestic market against the internationalised character of export-related activities and of the large bourgeoisie.

56. Even ignoring possibilities which would pressuppose a change in the capitalist parameters of the situation, tax policies might have cushioned the cycles to an extent which would have modified many of the political aspects we have analysed. But the ability to extract and reallocate resources by means of fiscal instruments (not only taxes on pampean land) also presupposes the medium-term stability of those instruments and their implementation and a fairly consolidated bureaucracy which can 'ignore' immediate pressures from the interests involved. These conditions could hardly be met in the midst of the pendular motions and the consequent colonisation and fractionalisation of the state's institutional system.

## REFERENCES

Ayza, Juan, Fichet, Gerard, and Gonzalez, Norberto, 1976, *América Latina: Integración Económica y Sustitución de Importaniones*, Mexico, CEPAL and Fondo de Cultura Economica.

Borón, Atilio, 1972, 'El estudio de la movilización electoral en América Latina: movilización electoral en Argentina y Chile', *Desarrollo Económico*, Vol. 12, no. 48, July-September.

Braun, Oscar, 1970, 'Comentario al trabajo de Guillermo Flichman', *Desarrollo Económico*, Vol. 10, no. 39–40, October-December.

Braun, Oscar, 1973, 'Desarrollo del capital monopolista en la Argentina', in Braun, (ed.) *El Capitalismo Argentino en Crisis*, Buenos Aires, Siglo XXI.

Braun, Oscar, 1974, 'La renta absoluta y el uso ineficiente de la tierra en la Argentina', *Desarrollo Económico*, Vol. 14, no. 54, July-September.

Brodersohn, Mario, 1972, *Financiamiento de Empresas Privadas y Mercados de Capital*, Buenos Aires, Programa Latinoamericano para el Desarrollo de Mercados de Capital.

Brodersohn, Mario, 1974, 'Política económica de corto plazo, crecimiento e inflación en la Argentina, 1950–1972', in Consejo Professional de Ciencias Economicas, *Problemas Económicos Argentinos, Diagnóstico y Política*, Buenos Aires, Macchi.

Canitrot, Adolfo, 1975, 'La experiencia populista en la redistribución de Ingresos', *Desarrollo Económico*, Vol. 15, no. 59, October-December.

Cardoso, F. E. and Falettoe, E., 1969, *Dependencia y Desarrollo en América Latina*, Mexico, Siglo XXI.

Cavarozzi, Marcelo, forthcoming, *The State and the Industrial Bourgeoisie in Chile*.

CEBRAP (Centro Brasileiro de Analise e Planejamento), 1976, *Estado y Sociedad en el Brasil: la Planificación regional en la época de de SUDENE*, São Paulo.

Diamand, Marcelo, 1973, *Doctrinas Económicas, Desarrollo e Independencia*, Buenos Aires, Paidos.

Diamand, Marcelo, 1976, 'El péndulo argentino: empate político o fracasos económicos?' mss.

Díaz Alejandro, Carlos, 1966, *Devaluación en la Tasa de Cambio en un Pais Semi-industrializado: la Experiencia Argentina, 1955–1961*, Buenos Aires, Editorial del Instituto.

Díaz Alejandro, Carlos, 1970, *Essays on the Economic History of the Argentina Republic*,

Diéguez, Héctor, 1969, 'Argentina y Australia: algunos aspectos de su desarrollo económico comparado', *Desarrollo Económico*, Vol. 8, no. 32, January-March.

Fajnzylber, Fernando, and Farrago, Trinidad, 1976, *Las Empresas Transnacionales: Expansión a Nivel Mundial y Proyección en la Industria Mexicana*, Mexico, Fondo de Cultura Económica.

Ferrer, Aldo, et al., 1969, *Los Planes de Estabilizacion en la Argentina*, Buenos Aires, Paidos.

FIEL (Fundación de Investigaciones Económicas América Latina), 1971, *La financiacion de las empresas industriales in la Argentain*, Buenos Aires.

Flischman, Guillermo, 1970, 'Modelo de asignación de recursos en el sector agropecuario', *Desarrollo Económico*, Vol. 10, no. 39–40, October-December.

Flischman, Guillermo, 1974, 'Neuvamente en torno de la eficiencia en el uso de la tierra y la caracterización de los grandes terratenientes', *Desarrollo Económico*, Vol. 14, no. 54, July-September.

Geller, Lucio, 1975, 'El crecimiento industrial argentino hasta 1914 y la teoria del bien primario exportador', in Marcos Giménez Zapiola (ed.), *El Regimen Oligárquico: Materiales para el Estudio de la Realidad Argentina (hasta 1930)*, Buenos Aires, Amorrortu.

Germani, Gino, 1962, *Política y Sociedad en una Epoca de Transición*, Buenos Aires, Paidos.

Gerchunoff, Pablo, and Llach, Juan, 1975, 'Capitalismo industrial, desarrollo asociado y distribución del ingreso entre los gobiernos peronistas', *Desarrollo Económico*, Vol. 15, no. 57, April-June.

Graciarena, Jorge, 1971, 'Estructura del poder y distribución del ingreso en América Latina', *Revista Latinoamericana de Ciencia Política* Vol. 2, no. 2, August.

Hirschman, Albert, 1976, 'A generalised linkage approach to development, with special reference to staples', Princeton, Institute of Advanced Study.

Kirkpatrick, Jean, 1971, *Leader and Vanguard in Mass Society*, Cambridge, Mass., MIT Press.

Martínez, Carlos, et al., 1976, 'Nuevamente en torno al problema de asignación de recursos en el sector agropecuario pampeano , *Desarrollo Económico*, Vol. 16, no. 61, April-June.

O'Donnell, Guillermo, 1972, *Modernisation and Bureaucratic Authoritarianism*, Berkeley, University of California, Modernisation Series.

O'Donnell, Guillermo, 1975, 'Reflexiones sobre las tendencias generales de cambio del estado burocrático-autoritario', Buenos Aires, CEDES (Centro de Estudios del Estado y la Sociedad) Documento CEDES G. E. CLACSO, no. 1.

O'Donnell, Guillermo, and Linck, Delfina, 1973, *Dependencia y Autonomia*, Buenos Aires, Amorrortu.

Portantiero, Juan Carlos, 1973, 'Clases dominantes y crisis politica en la Argentina', in Braun, Oscar (ed.), *El Capitalismo Argentina en Crisis*, Buenos Aires, Siglo XXI.

Sourrouille, Juan, 1976, 'El impacto de las empresas transnacionales sobre el empleo y los ingresos: el caso de Argentina', Geneva, International Labour Office.

Sourrouille, Juan, and Mallon, Richard, 1974, *Economic Policy-Making in a Conflict Society*, Cambridge, Mass., Harvard University Press.

Von Doellinger, Carlos, and Cavalcanti, Leonardo,1975. *Empresas Multinacionais na Industria Brasileira*. Rio de Janeiro, IPEA/INPES.

Villanueva, Javier, 1972, 'Una interpretación de la inflación argentina', *Revista de Ciencias Económicas*, April-September.

# 2. Social Planning as Administrative Decision-making

## By Bernard Schaffer*

SUMMARY

This paper defines a particular sense of social planning as a problem about data, anticipation and decisions by officials concerned with social instruments. Certain special difficulties are indicated about the differential impact of such official action and about areas, variations and clientele relations and so about anticipations by the official decision-makers. Some assistance in these difficulties might come from network analysis, machinery of government checklists and categorizations of types of social instruments or services. Such devices have their limits, and difficulties remain, e.g. about just when and why innovation (rather than adaptation) would be needed, about relations with innovating groups, about bureaucracy (especially in clientele relations) and about measurements. Hence there is a special need for analysing and organizing the information system for social planning and an approach to this, in terms of certain sorts of triggers, data categories and indicators, is outlined.

Whatever else we may have in mind when we talk about planning, we must certainly be thinking about decision-making. The implication is that there is a better way of going about decision-making, by allowing it to take into account more data about events, or outcomes which are farther off into the future. Social planning, then, must be about this notion of better decision-making in some limited area indicated by the word 'social'. It is about the problem of anticipation by decision-makers in some specific area. The questions are what this area is, how does the need to improve decision-making in such an area tend to emerge or be perceived by decision-makers, and then, thirdly, what are the problems in consequence and what are the possibilities of suggesting help about the problems? Why do the decision-makers want to improve their anticipations and how could they be helped?

Now, there are certain immediately obvious difficulties here. Should one not be thinking of the context as one of greater or lesser poverty and not some absolute category of less developed countries or traditional societies? If one thinks about administrative decision-makers, is one not identifying with them or their wants and may one not simply be thinking of their choices as rational factors in growth and of other elements in society as obstacles? How far is one entitled to abstract mere administrative action as one sub-system from the seamless web of interactions between, say, technological change, social custom and the wishes and choices of this or that group, be they public administrators or others?

At any rate, this discussion begins by taking one sort of special administration: decision-making about public policy on the use of social instruments. We can grant that a concept of administrative decision-

* The author is a Fellow of the Institute of Development Studies and Reader in Politics at the University of Sussex.

making is simply one abstracted view of a sub-system, distinguished by certain structural requirements (about supports, control, interests and access) for the performance of agent-like functions of demand reception and of allocation choices. We can also look at those structural problems in the more particular context of social policy. Then, in this generalized region of less developed or poor societies, are there some particular problems which demarcate the ways in which administrative decision-makers there will come to see and to face social planning in that one sense, such as problems of space, of sequential change, or of co-option? What can be done about these problems? How can social planning in this sense be 'improved'? The problem is to break the cycle of sub-system relations so as to anticipate the costs and the structural needs. Some general methods for assisting anticipation are discussed in Part II of this paper. Certain special difficulties, in particular about a necessary system of information, are discussed in Part III.

I

Two overlapping areas of meaning of social planning can be identified: first, an effort to anticipate and hence to programme and cost the effect of using different sorts of social instruments like education, health, housing or other services, or various sorts of payments; secondly, an effort to anticipate the social consequences of other policies or to detect their social premises and content. The second area of meaning has received more discussion in the literature of development studies; the first will be concentrated on here. Our topic is, of course, an abstraction. It may well be that social planning is a problem for administrative decision-makers because of the web of interaction between policies and changes. The family may be relied on less and public authority more. Once the decision-makers perceive this interaction they attempt to make choices about social instruments in a 'planning-like' fashion (whatever the objective validity may actually be) about any transfers between kin and public functions. This is, then, an area to be discussed.

That is not at all the same as arguing that actual machineries of government should, themselves, necessarily recognize a single specific function which should be called social planning. Although for example one might wish to distinguish conceptually between politics and administration, this is no argument for separating, actually or institutionally, the functions of politics and administration into specific and universally valid categories. Still less is there an argument for the setting up of a specific office or organization for social planning or social planners. What is being discussed is how certain needs which we call social planning come to emerge as a problem for administrative decision-makers; and, secondly, what devices are available, and particularly what information problems confront them, when they attempt to fulfil this perceived function.[1] It is thus a matter of thinking about ways of improving the anticipation of the consequences of actual or recommended economic and other structural or environmental changes, and thinking that social planning should go beyond the presently dominant fields of education, health and, perhaps, housing,[2] to the whole range of possible instruments.

Social planning could well include the effort to become aware of the social consequences of economic change. There is a long history of endeavour in this direction.[3] So far it has been vitiated by a tendency by administration and its advisers to think of some types of structural change as 'growth factors', and others as characteristically 'obstacles'.[4] That has happened to coincide with an over-reliance on generalizations about traditions, tribes and peasants. The fact is, of course, that any comparative or long-term study of significant degrees of alteration in one sub-system is likely to reveal more or less unexpected demands and effects in other systems.[5] A change in agrarian technology may be associated with a change say, in sex relations. A change in access rules in public offices may, equally, be associated with a change in village leadership, and so on. These interactions may well include social effects produced by alterations in the law and its administration which are part of the initial changes in economic policy, and requirements for different sorts of administrative performance as a consequence of either planned or unanticipated changes.

One may think, for example, of a tighter definition and stricter enforcement of proprietary land rights—an administrative change—producing changes in squatting and share-cropping. But, equally, specific, limited or even isolated technological changes can produce a need for radical and quite unexpected alterations in administrative systems and provision. For example, a different sort of seed may mean a different sort of harvesting and so a need to deal with both seasonal unemployment and a much wider scatter of labour recruitment and migration for the concentrated harvest. Even in terms of protective, defensive or regulatory administrative performance, that will need structural alterations: isolated village administration becomes inadequate. It is likely that administration will have to do more than negative regulation in this situation. Thirdly, the profits of legislative and administrative intervention are extremely unevenly distributed between social groups. The more interventionist and developmental the administration, the more this is likely to be so. The village's acceptance of the neutrality (to a large extent, a function of the social distance) of the previous regulatory administrative structures will tend to disappear.

Let us suppose that the district administration is recruited from categories who are separate, ethnically, educationally, or in other ways, from the villagers. As Max Weber said in a famous generalization, 'the actual social position of the official is normally highest where, as in old civilized countries, the following conditions prevail: a strong demand for administration by trained experts; a strong and stable social differentiation; where the official predominantly derives from socially and economically privileged strata because of the social distribution of power; or where the costliness of the required training and status conventions are binding upon him'.[6] He pointed out that certain aspects of this status element in the social position of the official, its 'explicit and impassive acknowledgement' will be found in modern bureaucracy with its exclusive guild-like nature, and also in past patrimonial and, especially, prebendal official systems.

Let us say social distance or distinct social esteem can be created, and that will be related to a more or less bureaucratized position. The official is accepted as neutral because of that distance, esteem or distinctiveness. But suppose the distance is removed. The official is to try to distribute benefits or to encourage alterations of behaviour. These may be meant as, or at least seem to mean, a general or even radical change in ways of life. But it is unlikely that the benefits will be distributed evenly. Some categories will be in a better position to harness them. They are almost bound then to be seen as differential. One factional group seems to be favoured, to capture the benefit or even the official as a resource, another to lose out. The official will no longer be seen impassively and distinctively but rather as part of the familiar and close competition of life. Whatever the administration had in mind to begin with, it is now in a very difficult position; complaints and claims seem to flood in from some sides, to be shunning from others. The official is surrounded with a strange and inconvenient mixture of familiarity, anger and silence. In this situation, the administration in its turn will have to alter so as to sustain itself. It will need different sorts of supports and resources and responses to control, different sorts of relations within its own structures and between its own officials and employees and different sorts of rules about the access to be given to clients.

But, even then, if one were to see the variations as flowing from technological change to social consequences and so to administrative implications, one could not very well begin the analysis at that point. Something will be said later about the administration's own needs for data and the problem of control. The general point is that while we can observe the interactions between administration and other changes, and while we might say that social planning ought indeed to develop methods for being aware of these interactions, administrators themselves will inevitably be affected by a special series of difficulties about decision-making on social instruments. It is with those difficulties that the discussion of social planning as decision-making could well begin.

In the first place, the physical areas for planned administrative operations are likely to have to be considerably larger than before (as for example in the registration and management of labour recruitment and seasonal migration). Yet at the same time, within any one such area the outcomes of technological changes are likely to be extremely varied. Tighter administration itself may lead, say, to a movement away from pastoral migration to land settlement and cash cropping. Together with various social policies, like malaria eradication, this may in one place mean fragmentation and small peasant holdings. But in another, quite nearby, it may mean ownership concentration and absenteeism. It may mean a re-enforcement of the practice of share cropping by family groups, or increases in specialization; decreases in, say, the availability of draught animals and the standards of animal husbandry, or mechanization and the collapse of share cropping elsewhere; or a move to new types of social stratification between a mass of seasonally unemployed casual wage labour and a limited group of mechanically skilled and relatively highly paid manpower.

All this is familiar. But what one is arguing is that there will be conflicting choices which administration may normally expect to be faced with in addressing itself to social planning. The conflict is increased by the coincidence of the need to enlarge the physical areas of administration with an emergence of an extremely wide scattering of the factors affecting the demands for administered social policy, as this is a characteristic of change. In the second place, the way in which the administration will be seen and its services received by the clientele will vary sharply. In addition to the sorts of situations cited above, there may be problems of adaptation in a move from extended to nuclear family structures. In another, the reaction to change, need and hardship may simply have been expressed in an alteration and indeed an increase of lineage and extended family functions. In some sections, the village or hamlet may have become wealthier and more self-sufficient as a whole; but that may be associated with more or less stratification. In other sections there may be more seasonal migration into the village, regular—even daily—movements out of the village for employment, and close urban connections within the family for marketing, education, services, credit or patronage. This is precisely what affects not only the *demands* but also the *perceptions* of the clientele.

It is not merely, then, that technological change will produce demands for social services. The point is rather that the areas of administration will have to alter in response, for example, to new factors controlling clientele access and reception. Moreover, the administration is likely to be involved in a sequence rather than a once-for-all change. In one phase, for example, it may be the distinction between those who own draught animals and relatively simple equipment and those who do not, which may be the key piece of evidence for social administration; in a second, the distinction between those who own land and those who do not, or between different categories of land rights; and in a third, those who have mechanical, artisanal or other sorts of trained or educated skills and those who do not. It is, in particular, the changes in social stratification which will be the key evidence for decision-making in social policy. Its planning should try to seek to anticipate precisely those sorts of changes: where, for example, will the demand for education and urban migration possibilities come from?[7] Institutionalized social action like public administration has severe problems in constantly changing the premises of its allocations and procedures.

We may discuss later some of the general problems around organizing the types of information which decision-making about social policy will then require. We can see at once that there will be two problems for the administrators. One is the need to adapt the structures in social policy to constant changes in the sorts of data being used and around which the structures are, in fact, organized; the second is the sheer sensitivity of some of the key indicators, particularly about clientele demands.

As we have argued, the problem of access and of perception is in part that administrative intervention will have differential benefits and will be seen to have them in the recipient structures. That is particularly so in relatively enclosed village situations. Where those situations are themselves changing, the problem of contact between the administration and the recipient is certainly no less. It is not, simply, that the available techniques for co-optation are now quite different.[8] Interventionist social administrations must seek to make themselves more acceptable by identifying themselves with resourceful elements in the receptive social structure. That will usually mean an identification with one side rather than another in an on-going dispute. But in periods of change, in any case, there will be new sorts of local resource which will constantly compete for co-optation; the new *literati*, the climber (rather than the traditional leader) who may specialize in contact with the local official of the social administration, the village-level labour negotiator and job awarder, will appear not merely as evidence for the planning of social provision, but as means through which the provision can be established, (and, at the same time, controlled). Sometimes this will be very direct indeed, as with the appearance of State paid, examined and controlled village-level teachers or social workers. Sometimes social administration will come to mean a conscious effort to adapt existing institutions, as when rural development academies attempt to train village headmen. Village leader training and, in that sense, adaptation then becomes the main technique of social administration. The same sort of difficulties arise here. The administration's use of one co-optant rather than another may be seen as further evidence of its partiality and may actually have important, if unanticipated, consequences in the flow of benefits. Another difficulty is that control will not, in fact, be that simple, as co-option implies a sharing of decision-making, even when those potential co-optants may have emerged as a more or less direct consequence of administrative action itself.

Administration, then, may mean (a) providing new institutions (b) adapting existing institutions or (c) adapting itself to the emergence of new institutions or to the change of existing ones. That is not an easy situation for administration: it is very expensive to be involved in institution building or adaptation like this, and constant adaptation does not come easily to decision-making in any organization. The consequences of its choices are obviously important but uncertain. Should it, for example, encourage or discourage new realms of expense and of brokerage (and if so which ones)?[9] The difficulty is in part the coincidence and interaction and then the constant flux of demands on decision-making. In part, it is, no less, the calculation and balancing of the costs of co-optation among the alternatives available, and the need for constant adaptation to new alternatives. In part, it is the further consequences of those choices.

We began by distinguishing between social planning as thinking about the use of social instruments and the social consequences of other non-social planned changes. The demand for administrative change may of course come from social sectors[10] and environmental change as well as from economic and technological changes. Another difficulty in an era of radical change is the need to start adapting to previously unheard of groups. It is also partly the uncertainty about the feedback effects of the administered allocations. The administrative decision-making becomes a part of the changes, in fact. Social planning thus alludes to the possibility of devices for working out the demands to be placed on administrative instruments by other planned programme changes (e.g. associated with

village level primary teachers) and from both those changes in demand
from the new groups.

It is to this that our distinction referred. We may abide by our conception of social planning as a sort of administrative decision-making
which is special insofar as it is concerned, say, with public choices about
social instruments in the context of poverty and change (while perceiving
the need to improve its ability to anticipate). The second sense of social
policy is not at all irrelevant to the first. But for the administrator thinking
about these public choices, social planning might come to appear merely
as a very desirable way out of specific difficulties which he comes more
and more to experience. Social planning might simply represent techniques
for improving his decision-making, so as to face these difficulties better,
by seeing farther ahead, by looking at a wider range of data, or at least
in the first instance by giving him the hope of making his decisions more
efficacious. That is not to say that everyone in administrative decisional
roles will necessarily have these actual wants in mind; but this is, at least,
how the need for social planning may come to appear to people in these
positions.

## II

So far we have been talking about the problems in decision-making as
social planning. The second question is what sort of help can be given or
where, at least, it can be looked for? This is a matter both of anticipating
structures and of anticipating costs. One hope here might lie in some
combination, for administrative planning, of network analysis with other
more conventional management services (like staff inspection), used for
anticipation, rather than for *post hoc* inspection, and for actual costing.
By network analysis here I mean thinking about a complex situation in
which some range of programmes are to be introduced, or are likely to be
demanded, and then thinking about the whole list of likely *activities* so that
they can be put together in some logistical order of *events*. The ordering
depends on the notion that many activities can conveniently occur independently of each other. Some can occur concurrently. Others again
are conditional or dependent. For some types of analysis, decision or
planning, there are great ranges of detail about any particular event which
may be needed; for others much less elaboration is required. So a hierarchy
of networks can be established providing information for decision-making
at different levels.

For example, one level in the organization may need to know when its
authority will be required for certain large-scale external and political
negotiations. It will need to prepare for that series of moments and amend
its preparations as the actual events require. Another level will need a
more detailed network, for example, about labour recruitment. These two
networks would be mutually dependent and in one sense part of a single
whole, but in another separate in terms of requisite authority and detail.

The network indicates the timing. What it can also serve to do (but for
the most part has not yet been employed for) is to indicate requisite
organizational structuring. Its use in operational control is familiar enough
with the design of bar charts from network charts showing activities against

a time scale. Target dates or latest event times can be indicated. Granted information procedures and the use of a regular such as a weekly moving cursor line, a focusing of management attention or control is possible.

That may be, at once, to say too much and too little. It may say too little since the technique of building network hierarchies and indicating necessarily coincident events can, in conjunction with the use of management services for planning, give a very clear indication of organizational demands. That is at least halfway to actual organizational planning. Let us suppose that a some single moment there will be a coincident need in some new social programme for (i) local authority liaison, (ii) setting up rules and procedures for clientele access, (iii) deciding on the location and area of field offices and (iv) recruiting certain sorts of staff. Then one can begin to see that at that point, certain sorts of organization demands will be felt and a certain sort of organization will have to be present. One could also go on to cost the meeting of those demands and to design the structures. That much staff recruitment, for example, might mean a readiness to take certain decisions, a flow of information to trigger the decisions, and that much dislocation and that much training, apart from anything else. Although not all parts of those demands could be costed, certainly some could be and this would represent much more costing than is normally done. Even such a relatively simple calculation for a new programme as total new staff requirements, times average time cost, times average training time per new member of staff is rarely undertaken, partly perhaps because the results would be so disturbing.[11] In the end, structural design should provide for a capacity to take decisions about meeting costs and demands. Capacity is a matter of information, interest and resource. Perhaps in this way something can, at least, be done about costing and about location.

At the same time this may also be saying too much. For one thing, network analysis has to use formulae for estimating the duration of activities. The existing formula may be quite inappropriate for any particular programme or system. Further, the meaningfulness of the analysis and its uses for control do depend on those assumptions about information flow. Information flow itself has its own problems of design,[12] severe costs and unanticipated consequences. Indeed, these may lie at the heart of the problem of the sort of programmes we are considering here.

There are also some problems about the network hierarchies. For example, the premiss is that the over-all network is inconveniently detailed and complex. Since it is in the end meant for communication, information and control, there is no need to inform the participant beyond what he will employ, for example, to time his own actions. So when the participant is at a high point in the pyramid, when his participation, that is to say, will be very important and authoritative, but very occasional and generalized, the relevant network for his role will be in a summary, or outline form. This is, however, to assume simple and self-contained organizational hierarchies. Such a participant will, in fact, certainly be involved simultaneously in many networks. It is also, secondly, to assume that high level participation is, in fact, effectively and exclusively done in terms of broad, sweeping, but powerful acts motivated by occasional and general signals. But this, for example, in external or inter-organizational or political negotiation, is often the very opposite of the case. The theory of network hierarchy assumes a simplification which may be too unrealistic.

We need more than network analysis alone, then. Perhaps it can be supplemented and specialized. That is to say one might think not simply about the general aids for administrative decision-making as such, but aids which might be particularly related to specific experiences of actually using social instruments of various kinds. For example, is there anything in the experience of this field which would suggest what sort of hierarchy of decisions is, in fact, likely? Less problematic at the present stage of study is the matter of a checklist of the type of over-all organizational or machinery of government problems about which social policy decisions are likely to have to be made. One could give three short examples of elements on that list.

In the first place, there are likely to be several sources of pressure towards decisions to establish *ad hoc* or non-ministerial organization in the field of social service provision. Three main operative factors have been found. The first is the increasing adequacy, and the acceptance of the objectivity, of some of the relevant ranges of data from, for example, demographic and employment data through nutrition and educational data. This may not be very apparent in any one place and in short periods of time, but it becomes vivid looked at comparatively and over long ranges of time. The second factor has been the professionalization of social service employees: medicine, first, and then other fields like school teaching. Such professionalization has tended to mean the emergence of non-ministerial or *ad hoc* structures as an actual vehicle of professionalization. It has also meant very powerful demands for the institutionalization of the special skill and for a separateness of careers in actual social administration itself. The third factor has been the ease and speed with which any particular social programme has tended, in fact, to become institutionalized. A social policy, in the sense of a decision to use certain social instruments, may mean the training of some field workers in diffusing one particular technology. The workers, the training and the technology will tend to become a 'set' factor. Alternatively, the programme might be recruited by or attached to an existing profession. The attachment again will become set. Or again some premiss, in social work or community development, say, will be entrenched in training and will be an unanalysed commitment. In this aspect, indeed, social administration can only be compared with the military, and the more the training the more this is so.

In the second place, the usual government problems about deciding the allocation of functions and departmentalization are peculiarly severe in this field. Various sorts of recurrent problems in establishing a central administration for social policy include the choice between amalgamation and specialization. Characteristically, there is a move from the provision of policy about basic health services and primary education to a wider social provision. The choice, then, is between remaining with something like the initial secretariat and the build-up of very large central services of a scale and status requiring separate departmental organization.

At the same time technical developments, political pressures and legislative changes tend to provoke highly erratic or unexpected departmental developments. This has perhaps been particularly so in central organizations for health, for housing and central-local relations, for the social policy sides of physical and regional planning. Any particular social policy function may be regarded either as a prize or as a bane in the inter-departmental struggles about the machinery of government and the allocation of functions. This is another source of problems. Responsibility for child welfare has been a marked case in point. The actual priority of one or another policy aspect in determining the department to which a particular function will be allocated has always been exceptionally erratic. Some systems, for example, separate the departmental responsibility for more advanced or for more specialized parts of education from those for other parts, or separate the responsibility for fringe services, like health within education, from the primary service. Decisions about functional allocations—and even about nomenclature—are, in fact, decisions about policy and resource allocations, and hence subject to disputes and upsets. In terms of our later nomenclature, policy or evaluation indicators are affected by political indicators, both in the politics of the machinery of government itself and in the politics of a more open or public arena.

The third part of the checklist relates to the inescapable need to decide about the design of procedures and relations between levels of administration, and between administration and clientele. This relates to certain problems of information flow, control and decision-making, of access and of diffusion. It can also be understood in terms of another sort of checklist —a set of criteria for the classification of the services themselves from the point of view of administration — particularly from the point of view of central–local allocations, and administrative–clientele relationships. One may, for example, distinguish between services which mean the provision of assistance or service in kind, and those which are essentially expressed in cash transfers. Again, some services are relatively guaranteed according to some stable and publicly available categorization of clientele or groups. Others depend, and are seen to depend, on relatively high degrees of administrative discretion. These classifications are related to others: for example, those which establish regular or recurrent administrative–clientele relations and those which are much more occasional; those which are providing basic and those which are providing marginal services; and those which deal with very broad and those which deal with very specialized *categories* of people.

At the same an occasional, a once-for-all, or an initiating service may have very different administrative demands and costs from a permanent provision. Some aspects of welfare services, for example, which may be either social casework, or the initiation of treatment, or the sponsorship of institution-building in a particular community, may have very high occasional costs. These may be over-all very much lower, more controllable, costs than the provision of a basic service regularly required at some guaranteed standard to very large categories like the aged or the unemployed. Secondly, administrative-clientele contact presents a different picture according to whether one is thinking of the provision or the taxation side of its administration and (apart from necessary increases in revenue *per se*) some aspects of social policy do have a taxation-like aspect.

We may assume that where social provision has to do with the idea of equalization or of minimum standards, the forces of centralization will be very strong indeed. We may also see that other generalizations would be much less reliable: assumptions about local roles in education are a case in point. In any case, the interpretation of centralization is extremely complex as between, at one extreme, the actual takeover of functions by central administration and, at the other, very subtle forces expressing central influence over local administration. There is, for example an important difference between the imposition of national and centrally enforced scales of provision by local administrations on the one hand, and, at somewhere near the other end, the recommendation of standard methods, for example, by which local authorities can actually tackle the objective assessment of local requirements. There is a difference between central guidance on the techniques which the local authority can use to assess and measure requirements, and the setting up of other common features of administrative methods, as distinct from an actual standardization of provision.

One can see that several of these points will express themselves differently according both to the degree and the rates of developments in the individual society concerned, that is according to its comparative poverty and its rates of change, whether one looks at the services or the recipients. For example, will the distinction between kind and cash or the distinction between guarantee and discretion fail to apply, or simply apply differently? What do local administration, central–local relations and the forces of centralization mean in a situation where the financial resources for local administration and the local administrative structures are thin, and where the exchanges looked for are scarcely those of central grants for local social provision save in very special senses?

Again, professionalization and the emergence of careers may be a factor not only in separating organizations but also, somewhat dramatically, in social mobility and urbanization. We have argued that institutionalization tends to operate rapidly and powerfully in social administration and that there are peculiar factors determining the allocation of functions. This has been vivid and perhaps disfunctional in some of the key areas of social policy in less developed conditions. Population policy has come to mean family planning and so to be allocated, almost always, to health departments with their peculiar political weaknesses and technical characteristics. There has been a commitment to some particular sorts of contraceptive techniques rather than others, especially where family planning administration has required very limited, *ad hoc* and specific training: I.U.C.D. insertions in one case, say, or vasectomies in another.[13] Yet the latent functions of institutionalization may in practice be a most important part of social policy in less developed conditions.

Whatever qualifications one may express about other points, the general rule remains that discretionary services are administratively expensive, that guaranteed services are difficult to control, that services in kind have distinctive problems of control, that guarantees tend to mean centralization and that institution-building has distinctive costs.

## III

One might argue that the normal problems of decision-making in administration in developing conditions are peculiarly heightened by social policy, as the normal problems of social administration are heightened by developing conditions. For example, the relationship between certain sorts of output or programmed achievement and the available technology is much more reliable in one sort of service than another: as between the eradication of yaws and the administration of antibiotics, say, compared with population control and family planning programmes. That is partly because of the technical uncertainties, partly because of the problems of control and partly because of the need for social as well as technical diffusion. Generally speaking, in administration in developing societies there may be both peculiar needs and peculiar problems in achieving decisions about administrative change. One can attempt to overcome organizational tendencies to institutionalization by adopting exceptional measures for feedback and for the referral of information and data which may make adaptive or even critical decision-making possible. One can also adopt research and evaluation techniques which may make crucial or innovatory decision-making more possible.[14] We have already discussed this in relation to such basic decisions as co-optation, and such basic features as the sequence of sub-system interactions in conditions of change. Where the matter in hand is the administration of a social programme with a degree of technological uncertainty in a society with a combination of scarce resources and peculiar vulnerability to disfunctional institutionalization, the need for control, and for adaptive and for innovative procedures in decision-making may be all the greater, but all the more difficult to achieve.

The point is not simply to repeat some general suggestion that administration in less developed countries needs to be innovative. Adaptation is very difficult for any institutionalized system, and what one really needs to explain is how either adaptation or innovation are to be done. Furthermore, there are questions about why and when, precisely, actual innovative administration is needed, since that is certainly not always what is required. As it happens, we do have here at least one criterion for recognizing a situation in which innovative administration may be required. Something will be said below about how innovative administration could be established. Broadly, innovative decision-making is more likely to occur when the choices are perceived as not merely critical—that is a matter of the possible alternative between innovation and adaptation or more or less radical changes in service—but crucial, when the choice is, in fact, between innovation and very severe political and institutional costs. In the one case the issue is seen as being about the institution, in the other about the service.

The field of social policy does seem to suggest at least one criterion for knowing when decisions about organizing for innovative decision-making may be needed; but even then it is another matter to see how that need can be met. And there are various reasons for the heightening of the difficulties of administration with social programmes in developing conditions. Now we have discussed the fact that clientele access to social administration is peculiarly difficult and significant.[15] Administrative systems adopt various combinations of bureaucratization and discretion to deal with it. In the case of social administration in developing conditions, there are, however, at least three extra degrees of difficulty to deal with.

We have already argued that there are extra problems of clientele perception and acceptance and of social diffusion. The administration cannot be quite neutral, objective or indifferent. It needs to distinguish the innovators and the early adapters from the opinion followers, the late adapters and the laggards.[16] Other processes of change, including other administrative programmes, might have identified or led to available contacts of this sort, but there are heavy political costs in contact administration or co-option, not merely because it will be seen and, in fact, be likely to operate as a strengthening of one faction as against another, but also because of its effects on the programme itself. As it happens, in the case of social administration in population policy or social assistance, say, delicate problems of access have characteristically to be handled by village level and other rank and file officials,[17] from whom a maintenance of a balance of objectivity and co-option is barely possible.

Secondly, there are characteristic solutions for these administrative problems. For example, fixed and objective but alienating rules for access are imposed as in 'queueing'. Similarly, decision-making is compartmentalized, rules for referrals and for the detection of critical data have to be learnt, some of the participants in policy decision-making will be relatively severely affected by institutionalization and responsibility will be discontinuously imposed. One has to see when one is deciding to set up the administration of some social provision in developing conditions that one is also deciding to face the peculiar difficulties either of using these sorts of solutions or of discovering alternatives. Social planning in our sense of administrative decision-making about the use of social instruments must include providing for these choices. Some of them will be choices about the system of information and control, and as such they will have implications for other areas of administrative behaviour; about official interests and incentives for example. Some of the choices will amount to decisions about how to handle the difficult problems of access.

Is 'queuing', for example, an available technique (in the sense that it can be more or less cheaply and peacefully administered and accepted) for governing the access between the clientele and the resources of the service? Is one not faced rather with a problem, in the first place, of actually initiating the demand or diffusing the acceptance of the service and then, in the second place, of choosing an appropriate set of access rules? The alternative might be a combination of a research and development strategy with something like a cafeteria rather than a queue model for access. What one is arguing is that there are alternative sets of rules, styles or systems of access. In particular one might define two separate models, one 'the queue' and another 'the cafeteria'. Of course, one does queue at a cafeteria when more than one person comes at a time. But the terms are used here to distinguish two defined models so as to indicate certain characteristics to be taken into account in the choice. The cafeteria provides a vivid and often a very much wanted service very cheaply, well within the resources usually available to the clients. It does so in part by using simple but key contributions from the clients which would otherwise be very expensive to provide. The 'queue' model maximizes the distinction between the compartmentalized official and the client. A community development model pretends that the official is not there. The cafeteria does, in fact, reduce the distinction.

What we are arguing is that there might be certain types of criteria in social policy for indicating special organizational needs and for indicating, therefore, where planning decisions will be needed. A decision for example to provide a new social service means setting up an organization and recruiting appropriate staff or setting up training programmes for developing an intermediate technology for the particular social administration. Amongst the recruited and trained staff, one is undertaking something much more difficult and expensive than apparently equivalent processes of recruitment and training in more settled or wealthy conditions. But there is at least one exceptional difficulty in social policy. This is connected with that problem of fixing quantitative objectives for various sectors in social planning and programming which was discussed in a paper of the social affairs division of the Economic Commission for Latin America (E.C.L.A.).[18] Costing the introduction of social programmes involving the use of social and administrative instruments must include the selection and design of measurements for the programme operation. It is patent that more work has been done on this in some sectors than in others, and that it is easier in some than others. However, there is a whole range of specifically administrative problems not considered in that paper.

It makes no sense to select a measurement without also selecting some organizational structure which can service it. It would be quite meaningless, for example, to say that one had decided that central assistance for a service would be distributed between areas according to some weighted population formula (a typical feature of equalizing and also of direct services beyond very limited points) unless one saw that there was also an organization for the collection of the data and the enforcement of its application to the distribution. However, while that might be obvious enough (though often, in fact, neglected, in the planning phases) there are distinctive problems there.

The first problem is that the setting up of any sort of measurement at all in administration tends to have wholly unexpected and frequently dysfunctional consequences, sometimes by way of becoming an unintended influence on performance (and in that sense a programme control). The classic case in social administration is the imposition of a mere measurement of numbers of counter cases dealt with which, in fact, tends to lead to a concentration on the treatment of what the rank and file or counter administration perceives as the merely *more easily dealt with* cases.

Secondly, data collection is in any case very costly. Thirdly, the collection and release of data from time to time is inevitably seen by administrative bosses as a considerable resource in their hands which they must want to bargain with. Fourthly, particular sorts of collection and measurements of data become very rapidly institutionalized, quite apart from their actual proficiency for programming and control. Whether, say, I.U.C.D. insertion rates are a relevant measurement for programme performance or not, it is very likely that they will become set. Research and innovation about measurement itself are critical planning requirements.

Rates of environmental change must mean that times will vary when initially acceptable formulae should be evaluated in terms of their actual outcomes. The E.C.L.A. paper assumes a need for negative data where positive data may be misleading, and for one sort of measurement in the initial stages of a service which should not be relied on at later stages. Granted that the measurements used in administration need to be changed from time to time, we need to set up secondary criteria as a check on primary criteria for social programme performance.[19] Secondary criteria provide a check within administration on the other measurements which it uses, and at the same time are simpler or cheaper to operate. The problem is to detect the possible secondary criteria: for example, is the number of teachers with such and such a qualification available; if it is, is the change in the aggregate a possibly useful indicator or secondary criterion for public policy-making in Dror's sense?

But the problems of social planning in the sense of deciding about the organizing of the measurement system go beyond these points too. To begin with, one could distinguish between three aspects of data. One could be called a system aspect: aggregate, descriptive or objective in the sense that, by itself, it is seen to carry no implication for any particular action. Data about comparative equalities of distribution of a service would be an example. Secondly, there is a political aspect, that is to say information wanted by politicians, or people who are interested in gaining or keeping such institutions or prizes (like leadership roles) as are dependent on aggregates of support. What, for example, is going to be the impact on the aggregate of support of some specific re-allocation: building a teaching hospital, say, rather than increasing the number of medical auxiliaries? Alternatively, where are the scarcely looked-for demands, in fact, going to come from next? That happens to be exceptionally difficult with social provision in less developed conditions, partly because of the problem of diffusion discussed above. Thirdly, there is a policy aspect, for example some formula of association between education investment and economic growth. This again would even more obviously be especially difficult to create in these conditions. But these are mere aspects of data; they are not a control or an information system.

In decision-making for social policy different sorts of data communication or message flow will be needed, and therefore organization will have to be provided for them. Two things have to be done. One is to categorize the data so as to provide for the three aspects cited as they will happen, in fact, to be recognized by the actual decision-makers concerned, and so as to correspond with the samples of data which will be employed. The other thing is actually to secure the flow itself.

In one situation it may be possible, say, for decision-makers at certain levels to take into account the qualitative difference between officials in one or another authority at some other level. In other systems this may not be possible. Policy may suggest a formula of association (like greater output from allocation decisions) which take this sort of difference into account. But that aspect of data may not be available for building into an information and control system either because it has not been demanded thus far or for reasons of the costing of its consequences. Clearly a system of indicators, for the selection of referrals from field to other levels for routine measurement and control, is necessary for adaptive decision-making. On the other hand, the more hierarchical the organization the more reliant it is on this process of referral; so it may be that what is also wanted is a maximization of the occasions of control and even adaptive decision-making at the field level itself.

This is one key area for the use of secondary criteria once they have been discovered. For this a selection of types of data which can be used to set up information systems is needed which can be relatively cheaply and securely described to field workers and used by them. Some relationships between policy and system aspects can point to referral indicators. The difficulty with social policy in less developed conditions lies precisely with the discovery of such secondary criteria.

That is not at all the same as the data gap so often talked about by planners. The failure of planning in this sense is not a data gap but a failure to see what secondary criteria, for example, can be described and employed in this way. That is not simply listing all the things a planner might think it would be nice to know about. It is to ascertain a minimum number of secondary criteria, to cost the flow, to research for unanticipated consequences and to consider alternative decision-making styles which will actually limit the needs in any case.

The application of evaluation indicators will mean the relating of policy aspects to the referrals, or the actual data flow produced by the operation of the referral indicators set up in the first place for maintenance and control. Evaluations may indicate the necessity of adaptation and, even, in some instances, a case for innovation. They may anticipate the occasions for critical decision-making—that is when choices between adaptation and innovation in the service will have to be made. For example, referral indicators may show a certain turnover in primary teaching posts. That will indicate a specific routine need to recruit so as to maintain the existing service. But, in the second place, there may be a policy aspect like an association formula indicating some optimum rate of turnover. So there may be a need to adapt the recruitment systems rather than merely call them into play. That, in turn, may uncover a need to alter primary teachers' conditions either at a critical moment when the choice must be made about some such adaptations, or at a distant horizon when possibly there may also be need for more radical changes in the service itself. There may even be a political aspect about the general trend of support, from, say, a primary teacher's union. Crucial indicators will then be provided by a combination of the flow of data from the evaluative or critical indicators with political data. They will, in fact, anticipate what can be called crucial decision-making, as distinct from critical decision-making, when the choice is between defeat, the destruction of an institution, a service or an innovation. That is extremely dependent on a sensitive, easy and rapid two-way movement between policy and political data. Of course, the data information from evaluative or critical indicators may suggest a convenient way of providing a normative justification for some pragmatic political need. Equally, the political indicators may provide an extra motivation for some crucial innovation of which a need would, to some extent, already have been suggested in other ways.

There are at least two points, then, where the design of an information system is closely related to other institutional choices. At one point, one has to wonder how far the field workers themselves can be given a wider role in critical decision-making. At another point, one sees that the actual possibility of building a crucial indicator system will depend on the institutional relationship between the receipt of policy aspects and the receipt of political aspects of data. In any case, different categories of data and information have to be coded and organized into indicators. Putting it crudely, you have to have officials who know what to look for and, beyond that, the information has to be made to flow—that is, it has to be triggered. There are two broad alternatives here: time triggers and event triggers.[20] It is clear that various combinations of each category are possible with variations in frequency, normality, self-inducement, randomness and discretion. The choice of combinations would pattern the way in which the information will actually flow. That means it will pattern the control system, itself, the shape of the organization and the decision-making style. Putting it crudely again, you can have a factory foremanship system, a foreign office system or a research team system. If one need is for secondary criteria, another is for appropriate triggering.

Hence the problem is much more complex than merely providing for quantitative measures. There is the problem of categorization in the information system, of its relationship to some basic institutional choices, and of triggering, and there are specific problems in social policy under all these headings.

To a large extent decisions about this system will come to mean decisions about the performance or social provision itself: there will be an informal as well as a formal network.[21] One could take one aspect of this informal network as an example. There will, in fact, be political debate about the data and its administration. The rationalization or modernization of social administration can be seen partly as the secularization or depoliticization of its information, like population and employment statistics. But this has been consistently more hazardous, costly, controversial and erratic than one might have expected. Debate about a particular data measurement or indicators becomes deeply associated with debate about its administration as soon as it is seen as a distributive formula. Thus, federal or central financial assistance in social administration demands formulae for distribution; the data for the formulae tends to demand centralization and, indeed, independence in its administration. The tendency to centralization and independence in statistical administration in social policy inevitably, though sometimes obliquely, leads towards some standardization of the actual field administration of these services. Whatever its appropriateness in developed systems, the spatial problem of social administration in developing conditions is likely to make this inconvenient and expensive there.

## IV

Rather similar conclusions to those reached in this paper could have been reached from other starting points. One might actually start very well with, say, the demand groups being thrown up from the experience of urban migration, to give just one example. The administrative decision-makers, however, are at least one category of the actors. We do not identify with them as a group in recognizing how they come to see their problems and in discussing some of the means available for dealing with them.

NOTES AND REFERENCES

1. Compare C. T. Leys, 'The Analysis of Planning' in C. T. Leys (ed.), *Politics and Change in Developing Countries*, Cambridge University Press, 1969, on the confusion of conceptual or analytic phases of planning with a description of planning behaviour or with recommendations.

2. See *Economic Bulletin for Latin America*, Vol. XI, No. 1, April 1966, at p. 49. Footnote 13 says that 'summaries of twelve national plans and investment programmes in part III of the economic survey of Latin America, 1964, indicate that objectives classified as "social" are limited to education and health, or to these plus housing, in six instances'. Education, health and housing are the only areas taught in the Latin American Institute for Economic and Social Planning.

3. Fifteen years ago Balandier, for example, was already attempting to establish a general picture of the current situation. See, for example, his U.N.E.S.C.O. paper of 1955, *Consequences Sociales du Progrès Technique dans les Pays Sous-Developpés*.

4. For example, P. M. Hauser, 'Cultural and Personal Obstacles to Economic Development in the Less Developed Areas', in *Human Organization*, Vol. IIXX, No. 2, Summer 1959, 78–84. Some aspects of this are discussed in this book in chapters by R. Apthorpe and S. Ortiz, in particular about the generalizations on traditions, etc.

5. A very good recent example is M. Kiray and J. Hinderink, 'Inter-Dependencies between Agro-Economic Development and Social Change: a Comparative Study conducted in the Cukurova Region of Southern Turkey', in *Journal of Development Studies*, Vol. IV. No. 4, July 1968, 497–528.

6. H. H. Gerth and C. Wright Mills, *From Max Weber, Essays in Sociology*, Oxford University Press, 1948, 200.

7. J. F. Holleman, *Experiment in Swaziland*, Oxford University Press, London, 1964; for example, see especially Annexures, 10, Urbanization, 324 ff., which provides typically interesting data on, for instance, the dual home and on whether it is the more or the less economically successful Mbabane population who see themselves as permanent urban or returning rural residents. That is exactly the sort of evidence which the planning and administration of social provision requires.

8. On administration intervention and formal and informal co-optation, see P. Selznick, *TVA and the Grass Roots*, Harper, Berkeley, 1949, especially 259–62, in ed. N.Y., 1966.

9. Clifford Geertz's arguments for encouraging an 'institutionalization' which can 'keep people outside the work force but inside the society', *Encounter*, July 1969, 34.

10. For example, Sir Robert Thompson, *Defeating Communist Insurgency: the lessons of Malaya and Vietnam*, Chatto and Windus, London, 1966, 66: 'Nor should one underrate the stabilizing influence of such things as pensions and provident funds.'

11. It may be calculated, for example (to give a British instance) that the training costs of setting up the Land Commission effectively would have to have been something like £300,000. That was certainly never mentioned in in the debates and as far as one can see not taken into account in the effective decisions.

12. See note 21 infra. On network analysis generally, my discussion owes a great deal to Dr Philip Packard.

13. See Jason L. Finkle and Ruth Meade, *Organizational Adaptation and Social Change: the Administration of Population Planning in Developing Areas*, mimeo, Ann Arbor, 1967.

14. The literature on the problems of adaption and of innovation in organization administration and bureaucracy is considerable. See, for example, Victor Thompson, 'Bureaucracy and Innovation', in *Administrative Science Quarterly*, Vol. X, No. 1, June 1965, 1–20; E. M. Rogers, *Diffusion of Innovation*, Free Press, New York, 1962 and the general work of Peter Blau and Philip Selznick.

15. See B. B. Schaffer, 'The deadlock in development administration' in C. T. Leys (ed.), *Politics and Change in Developing Countries*, Cambridge University Press, 1969, 186–88.

16. See E. M. Rogers, *op. cit.*, 1962, and E. Katz, 'The Social Itinerary of Technical Change: Two Studies of the Diffusion of Innovation', in *Studies of Innovation and of Communication to the Public*, Stanford, 1962.

17. Research about village level workers in development administration is peculiarly thin. The studies by Inayatullan and Q. M. Shafi in the Peshawar area are, therefore, especially valuable.

18. 'Social Development and Social Planning: a Survey of Conceptual and Practical Problems in Latin America', *Economic Bulletin or Latin America*, Vol. XI, No. 1, April 1966, especially 48–61.

19. See Y. Dror, *Public Policy Making Re-examined*, Chandler, San Francisco, 1968.

20. The flow of particular categories of information is the essence of control; control is communications. The categorization of types of data communications or flows as types of messages, its coding and the setting up of various triggers—time triggers or even triggers, for example—is the essence of setting up a system of data measurement and control. For a further treatment of this, which is only touched on here, see S. Eilon, 'Taxonomy of Communications', in *Administrative Science Quarterly*, September 1968. 266–88.

21. See T. D. Weinshall in J. R. Lawrence, (ed.), *Operational Research and the Social Sciences*, Tavistock Publications, London, 1966, 619–33, quoted in Eilon, op. cit., 1968.

# The System of Administrative and Political Corruption: Canal Irrigation in South India

*The paper describes how some irrigation engineers raise vast amounts of illicit revenue from the distribution of water and contracts, and redistribute part to superior officers and politicians. It argues that the corruption 'system', which is centred on control of personnel transfers, is an important supply-side reason for poor performance of canal-irrigated agriculture. Insofar as the same system operates in other government departments, it may be more important for understanding Indian politics and the political influences on economic development than has previously been realised.*

> Just as fish moving under water cannot possibly be found out either as drinking or not drinking water, so government servants employed in the government work cannot be found out while taking money for themselves [Kautilya, the Indian statecraft scholar, in about 300 BC, transl. *Shamasastry, 1967 (1915): 71*].

> The tendency to subvert integrity in the public services instead of being isolated and aberrative is growing into an organised, well-planned racket .... It was reported to us that corruption has increased to such an extent that people have started losing faith in the integrity of public administration [*India, Government of, Ministry of Home Affairs, 1964: 12*].

Canal irrigation can be looked at in at least two ways: as a system for delivering a particular agricultural input; and as a specific context of government action in the countryside.[1] One can study canal irrigation in India either to contribute to knowledge of canal irrigation systems in general; or to illuminate more general features of Indian society and government. This paper approaches the topic from both of these angles.

Economic planners and farmers have recurrently been dismayed—not only in India—to find that canal systems operate substantially below the expected level of performance [*Wade, 1975; Wade and Chambers, 1980*]. The causes of canal underperformance are many, including technical as well as

---

* Institute of Development Studies, University of Sussex. I have benefited from comments by Freddy Bailey, David Booth, Ronald Dore, John Harriss, Susan Joekes, and Michael Lipton, and from discussions in seminars at Harvard, Cornell, and (especially) Sussex universities, and at the World Bank. I am grateful to Professor J. D. Montgomery, of Harvard, and to the Lincoln Institute of Land Policy for providing the first occasion to present the paper. The several people in India who cooperated in a spirit of scientific enquiry should be thanked by name, but prudence says otherwise.

institutional factors. But one consideration which is likely to be an important part of the explanation of the underperformance of many government programmes—a lack of correspondence with the interests of the dominant class in the countryside—is *not* likely to be directly relevant to irrigation. Since the effective functioning of a canal system increases the profitability of private agricultural capital and is not redistributive between classes, and since canals (of the sort of size we are considering here) could not be operated and maintained privately, the collective interests of big farmers would seem to correspond rather closely with good performance by the canal bureaucracy.

Canal officials, on the other hand, have great discretionary power: they allocate big money for maintenance contracts; they are responsible for rationing a valuable input between competing users, who have (officially) to pay much less than they would be prepared to pay for it rather than go without; and the officials make decisions which impinge heavily on the political prospects of politicians and on the economic well-being of local communities. This paper argues that if instead of taking for granted that canals are everywhere operated and maintained primarily in the interests of farmers, one assumes as an initial hypothesis that in some regions and countries they might be operated and maintained so as to raise large amounts of illicit revenue for their staff and for politicians, one is led to examine a set of causes of underperformance which is normally left unexamined. One has to look at the responses of officials to opportunities for capturing for themselves a portion of the value of what they allocate, and at the responses of politicians to the fact that officials have these opportunities.

Much of this behaviour will be, of course, 'corrupt' by the standards of modern bureaucratic and legislative codes. To keep the analysis in perspective, one should recall that behaviour somewhat akin to that to be described here was familiar in the public bureaucracies of seventeenth- and eighteenth-century Europe [*Swart, 1949; Anderson and Anderson, 1967*]; and that, as periodic corruption scandals in Europe and North America suggest, the conception of public office as a public trust is still slow to take hold. India's bureaucratic and legislative codes, like their British counterparts, define a sharp separation between the public and private interests of public office-holders, and between the civil service and the legislature. But given such conditions as acute scarcity of resources, the inherited traditions of a patrimonial-bureaucratic state [*Weber, 1968, Vol. 3*] and a wide educational and status gulf between officials and the mass of the population, it is hardly surprising if a sizeable gap between legality and practice persists.

More surprising, however, is that the resulting 'corruption'—a phenomenon which affects administration, politics, business, education, health and a host of other crucial areas of social life—has been so little studied [*Bayley, 1970 (1966); Wertheim, 1970 (1963); Andreski, 1970 (1968); cf. Scott, 1972*]. It is surprising, too, that those studies which have been made (in India and elsewhere) tend to treat 'administrative' and 'political', 'high' and 'low' level corruption as distinct and unconnected forms.[2] The intention of this paper is to show how, in the specific context of irrigation in one south Indian state, they are systematically interconnected. If, as is likely, the same mechanism is found more widely and in other fields of government activity, it may be a more fundamental influence on Indian administration and politics than has hitherto been realised. Perhaps it is important in other poor, 'soft state' countries also.

## SETTING

In our south Indian state, paddy (unhusked rice) is the main irrigated crop, followed by groundnut, hybrid sorghum and cotton. Roughly four million net acres are under gravity flow canal systems. Almost all of the canal-irrigated area is fed from systems constructed, operated and maintained by the state Irrigation Department. The Department also constructs and maintains small local reservoirs ('tanks').

Figure 1 shows a conventional picture of the Irrigation Department's structure. The principal unit of administration is the Circle, headed by a Superintending Engineer (SE); the unit of execution is the Division, headed by an Executive Engineer (EE). There are normally about four or five Divisions in a Circle. Both units have a geographical *and* a functional reference; in a given area, there might be a Circle for the 'regular' work—operation and maintenance (O & M) of existing structures, and construction of small structures—and another Circle for 'special' work—such as construction of medium and major projects, investigations of new projects, crop zoning under new projects, etc. Each Division will normally be specialised by function; so that in the same town one may find the headquarters of several Divisions belonging to either the same or different Circles, with partly overlapping geographical jurisdictions: a Division for construction of minor irrigation projects, another for O & M of a big canal system, and another for investigation of a proposed new project, for example.

Our concern here is mostly with Divisions for O & M of large canal systems. There are about 45 such Divisions, out of a total of about 350 Divisions in the Department as a whole.[3] Each O & M Division may have an irrigated area of anything between about 80,000 and 400,000 (gross) acres (the smaller Divisions may have more 'tank' maintenance responsibilities, by way of compensation).

Each O & M Division normally has a staff of about 300 to 350 people.[4] Ninety per cent or more of the staff are field workers (bankers and foremen). They have at most a high school education. Supervisors, responsible for an average area of 7,000 to 20,000 gross irrigated acres (a Section), have a two-year post high school diploma in civil engineering. Assistant Engineers (AEs), in charge of Sub-divisions of 30,000 to 100,000 acres, normally have a university degree in civil engineering. Field staff cannot be promoted. Supervisors are promoted (to AE) towards the ends of their careers, if at all. AEs in O & M posts are normally over 40 years old; they usually come to O & M only after quite a few years elsewhere in the department. EEs in O & M posts are normally fifty or more. In the following discussion the term 'officer' is used to refer to Supervisors and above—though it will be clear that initiative and control is in the hands of AEs and above, the Supervisor being the agent of the higher ranks.

FIGURE 1

CONVENTIONAL ORGANISATION CHART OF IRRIGATION DEPARTMENT

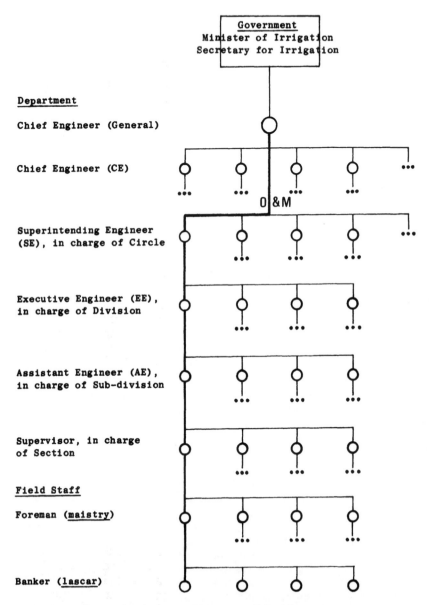

Note: The Chief Engineer (General) is responsible for O & M work.
Other Chief Engineers have responsibilities for individual
big projects, investigations, designs, drainage, etc.
... means pattern repeated.

Two other points of detail should be borne in mind. The year has two irrigation seasons: the rainy season (also called the first season), from June to December, and the dry (or second) season, from December to May, when crops are wholly dependent on irrigation. Official water rates are Rs.41 per acre per season for paddy, and Rs.28 for non-paddy crops (since 1978).

THE BASIS IN EVIDENCE

Given the extreme sensitivities at stake, it is necessary for the reader to be clear about the empirical basis of the discussion. Obviously one cannot work towards an understanding of the phenomena discussed here by the familiar methods of the random sample, the formal interview and structured questionnaire. One has to use, rather, more informal, more 'anthropological' means. The material on which the paper is based was collected in the course of six periods of fieldwork in the same small area of south India between 1976 and 1981, each of between one and four months' duration. The fieldwork has been directed towards understanding the way canal systems—two in particular, with some attention to a third (constituting three of the above-mentioned 45 canal O & M Divisions)—are actually operated and maintained, in the hope of contributing to a more informed discussion of how the performance of canal-irrigated agriculture might be improved from the supply side. As part of the wider study, a detailed investigation was made of local irrigation organisation in some 30 canal-irrigated villages, involving residence for several months in one of them.

It was certainly not part of the original intention to study the phenomena discussed here. Only gradually, from conversations with dozens of engineers, government officials from other departments and farmers did it become apparent that a 'system' was at work, which probably had an important impact on how canals are operated and maintained. In particular, once some degree of trust was established, farmers often volunteered information about how much they had to pay the Irrigation Department; and while one would discount their figures in one, two or three instances, the regularity in farmers' statements across many villages did suggest that something more than wild exaggeration or generalisation was involved. Yet if one accepted their magnitudes as approximately correct or even as 100 per cent exaggerations, the amounts of money being aggregated upwards were clearly large indeed.

This led to cautious, always informal enquiries of officers in other departments and of irrigation staff themselves, as part of wider conversations about the sorts of difficulties they saw themselves facing in doing their jobs well. These conversations, it should be noted, were with irrigation staff from outside the area of detailed fieldwork as well as with many serving within it; and covered the way 'the department' and 'the government' worked in the state as a whole, as well as in the specific district. Some of the engineers were thoroughly disgruntled at the situation they were caught in, and since disgruntled people tend to exaggerate the reasons for their discontent, one had to be cautious about accepting details from any one person at face value. Again, as with farmers, it is the regularities in the individual comments and incidents, and the consistency in the orders of magnitude (as between, for example, what a district Collector told me a Superintending Engineer had told him he had had to pay to get a one-year extension, and what an Assistant Engineer in one Division—in another district from the first case—said in strictest confidence his Executive Engineer had had to pay to get the transfer) that gives confidence in the correctness of the broad picture.

This method undoubtedly leads one to look for the common elements in what people say, and therefore perhaps to give an impression of greater regularity and less variation than is in fact the case. There is no way to deal with this problem except by more research which attempts to probe variations more systematically than was possible in an exploratory study. On the other hand it should be emphasised that the present essay is based on prolonged residence and repeated enquiry, on *both* sides of the farmer-official transaction.[5] And a few other studies, to be referred to later, have provided evidence which, even though fragmentary, is consistent with the argument to be made here.

IRRIGATION OFFICERS' SUPPLY OF REVENUE

Officers can use their office to raise large amounts of illicit revenue—some offices (or posts) being much more profitable than others. We begin by describing in some detail how the revenue is raised. Later we consider how it is redistributed, especially via the sale of transfers to particular posts. The emphasis is on the general features and procedures of the corrupt system; but it must be noted at the beginning that not all engineers participate in it, and discussion of what happens to those who do not take part is deferred till later. It will suffice to say here that they are unlikely to spend much time in O & M posts.

Officers have two main sources of revenue, from the works budget ('from works', as the officers say), and from irrigators directly ('from the *ayacut*', the irrigated area). We take each in turn.

*From the works budget*

Each canal Division gets a regular grant for annual maintenance work, calculated at so much per irrigated acre[6] plus a lump sum for each major structure (like a weir). The grant has to cover the cost of the field staff's salaries as well. The Division may also get grants at irregular intervals for 'special works'. The overall works grant is split into Sub-division budgets. The Supervisors of each Section prepare the estimates of annual maintenance works; their estimates are inspected and coordinated by each AE, and then approved (or not) by the EE. The works are put out to tender, to be done by private contractors following the department's plans and estimates.

*Kickbacks*: By long-established convention $8\frac{1}{2}$ per cent of each contract is kicked back to the officers and clerical staff of the Division—$2\frac{1}{2}$ per cent to the EE (as tender-accepting authority; for contracts of more than Rs.100,000 the SE is the accepting authority, so maintenance contracts are generally shaped to be less than this amount); one per cent to the clerical staff and draughtsmen; and five per cent to the Supervisor and AE to be split between them.

This however is the minimum kickback, on the assumption that the work is actually done according to specification. Then there are 'savings on the ground', as distinct from the earlier 'savings on the estimates'. If, for instance, the estimates call for six inches of gravel to be laid but the contractor lays only three, or if four inches of silt are to be removed but the contractor removes only one, the balance is split between contractor and officers, perhaps half and half, or one third to the contractor and two thirds to the officers.[7] Using less cement than called for in the estimates can be very profitable indeed, but is dangerous beyond a certain point—if the structure falls down in the next monsoon, samples can be sent for testing. In contrast, fiddling on 'earthworks'—removing or adding less than the stipulated amount of earth—is both profitable and safe.[8] (Since the contractor has an interest in removing even less earth or silt than was agreed informally with the AE, the art of desilting from the contractor's point of view is to judge how far to go from a cross-over road before removing virtually no silt; and also to judge the rhythm of the work so that it is completed and ready for inspection just before the water has to be released into the channel, to make inspection less likely.) If what are called 'supplementary works' have to be done to repair work done inadequately the first time round, by convention the contractor keeps the whole rake-off.

'Savings on the ground' is the part that is haggled over—both the percentage taken, and how it is divided. The officers want to increase the share going to themselves but also to ensure a minimum level of quality. The contractor wants to increase *his* share, not least because of the increasing cost of labour and also because on top of what he pays the officers he may have to pay something to the local Member of the (state) Legislative Assembly (MLA), especially near election times and especially if the MLA uses his influence to help secure him contracts. But 'savings on the ground' are normally sufficient to bring the total rake-off to the officers (including the $8\frac{1}{2}$ per cent) to at least 25 per cent of the value of what is meant to be put on the ground, and sometimes to as much as 50 per cent.[9]

In the late 1970s the annual maintenance grant (for all canals in the state) was Rs.10 per irrigated acre, plus an amount for each major structure which varied according to size. In an upland Division this might total Rs.4,000,000. Between about one-third and a half of the total,[10] say 40 per cent, goes as salaries to the field staff, leaving (in this example) some Rs.2,400,000 for works.

From savings on the estimates the EE gets $2\frac{1}{2}$ per cent of the value of works contracts, or in this example about Rs.60,000 a year. By prior agreement with the AEs, the EE gets normally five per cent of each Sub-division's total works budget (including what has to be paid as field staff salaries), or in our example, another Rs.200,000 a year. Therefore the EE can expect roughly Rs.260,000 in additional income a year, *at least*.[11] The average EE official salary, including allowances, is Rs.28,500 a year (Rs.8 = US$1 approximately, at the exchange rate of the late 1970s).[12]

*Subversion of tendering*: We consider shortly how the AE manoeuvres to raise the EE's five per cent of the works budget plus his own profit. In the meantime let us pursue the question of how the public rules for protecting the impartiality of tender-awarding and preventing kickbacks are subverted. The tenders have to be opened simultaneously and in public, and the EE would have to show good cause for not accepting the lowest.

Preparation of the estimates is the job of the Supervisor in whose Section the work will be done. As he prepares each estimate he also fixes the contractor who will do the work, in consultation with the AE (who will himself be following the EE's guidelines as to which contractors are to be favoured). The estimate will include the payments to go to the officers and clerks. The Supervisor then gives the estimate to the contractor, who will henceforth spend much time at what is called 'travelling with the estimate'. (Hence one is always likely to find contractors hanging about a Division or Sub-division office, ready to pick up the bill when the officer orders coffee for a visitor.) The contractor takes the estimate to the AE, who passes it on to the EE with his recommendation. If the EE sanctions it, the contractor sits with the draughtsman while it is properly drawn up.

Tenders must be notified publicly. But while several contractors might apply, the designated one will normally get it (though he may have to tip the others in recompense). The reason is that no contractor of the small size interested in maintenance contracts can long survive without the approval of the EE. The EE is the only man in the Division authorised to sanction estimates and pay bills.[13] An uncooperative contractor simply finds that his bills are not paid—part of the art of the EE is to decide which bills should be paid and when, in order to keep his contractors in hand. And the EE may make some extra income from the contractors in return for speeding up, or not delaying, payment of the bills.[14]

The EE can also control the contractors through loans. Contractors need credit, and the EE may be prepared to lend at cheap rates of interest. He lends not primarily to get the interest, but to have the very large amount of money he collects each year held not in his own hands (where it might be discovered), and not all in a bank (where it might leave traces for the possible attention of the Anti-Corruption Bureau), but in the hands of people over whom he has tight control. Often the contractors are little more than the EE's dummies (to use the word of an engineer informant); he lends them money to do the works, they present him with their bills, he (legitimately) encashes the bills at the bank and pays them—and then directs the contractors what to do with 'his' portion of the funds.

In practice, there are far too many contracts held by separate contractors for the EE to deal with each individually. He works mostly through his AEs, and also through a number of intermediary contractors, a few big ones and a sprinkling of medium-sized ones covering different parts of the command area. Some of them may hold sizeable amounts of 'his' money. A small contractor may borrow directly from one of these banker-contractors, with the EE's approval. When—as explained below—the Minister calls for money, the EE may tell one of his banker-contractors to pay the Minister's agent (the Minister too never touches the money; ministerial tours of the districts are useful occasions for these transactions to be made). When the EE wants to give a senior officer a gift he never carries the cash from his own headquarters; he tells one of his banker-contractors to meet him and hand over the money just before he meets an agent at the officer's headquarters or the man himself at his residence (he will have booked a 'personal call').

Furthermore, the EE may be in a legal business partnership with some contractors—a so-called *benami* partnership, in which his interest is registered in the name of someone over whom he has close control. He can use his privileged (if often still difficult) access to cement, a rationed commodity, to get supplies for his partners at discount rates. In these ways the EE can exercise control over very large amounts of money without having the incriminating evidence on his hands.

This description has shown the contractors as highly dependent on the EE. But when big (and therefore 'special', not 'regular') contracts are involved, class A or B contractors have to be used, and such men are often able to exert much independent influence over Ministers and MLAs. They obtain their influence by paying the Ministers and MLAs large amounts of money (or by being their kinsmen). As the engineers say, 'He (a big contractor) has X and Y (names of Ministers), they are his men'. The EE has to be careful of such contractors (unless he is a *benami* partner); they can get him transferred out if he refuses to alter accounts or is uncooperative in other ways.[15] Furthermore, the local MLAs depend not only on big contractors but also on the myriad small contractors for funds and help at election time, and may use their influence over the EE and AE to put contracts with the right ones. Yet while these points qualify the earlier picture of the EE and AE determining the allocation of contracts, it remains true that the EE can normally exert great independent influence; especially because the great bulk of the work is done in very small contracts, by small local contractors.

Let us now take up the question of how the AE goes about raising the money he has to pay the EE, plus his own profit. The EE, as noted, gets most of his income from the $2\frac{1}{2}$ per cent savings on the estimates, plus the conventional five per cent of the total works budget of each Sub-division. When the Minister demands more money the EE divides the amount to be raised between his AEs. It is very unlikely that an AE will be able to meet his obligations to the EE *and* raise enough for his own uses (which include, as we shall see, the 'cost' of his next posting) from his works budget alone. He makes up the deficit 'from the *ayacut*' (irrigated area)—by selling water or promises of water. While the EE may take an active part in his AEs' efforts on the works budget, he generally leaves them to raise money from water as they will, limiting his role to broad oversight.[16]

*From the irrigators*

*Organisation*: The canals are 'continuous flow' (water normally flows through each outlet continuously, not in rotation), but it may often happen that land towards the end of a distributory is not getting enough water, either because too little water is reaching the lower part of the distributory or because particular sluices are not sufficiently opened. In some cases it is possible for farmers (against the rules) to open the sluices themselves, or obstruct the flow immediately downstream of their outlet to increase the discharge through it, or break the channel bank. But they run risks if they persistently interfere with the structures; the irrigation staff may refuse to help them subsequently, or may even cut off their water by way of punishment. If insufficient water is reaching the lower part of the distributory these options are in any case not open to farmers of lower-down villages. They may have no alternative but to approach the irrigation staff with a request for more water.

A second reason why irrigators may approach the irrigation staff has to do with the zoning of land for irrigation [*India, Government of, Ministry of Irrigation and Power, 1972, Vol. 1: Chapter 6*]. Very large areas of land under most south Indian canals—often running into tens of thousands of acres per canal—are being irrigated unauthorisedly, in the sense that they are not entitled by the crop zoning to any irrigation at all, or are zoned for non-paddy but are growing (water-intensive) paddy, or are taking water in the wrong season. Farmers taking water for out-of-zone irrigation may want an assurance from the AE or Supervisor that they will continue to get water. In many cases they will have to pay for that assurance. Since the stiff financial penalties which are meant to be collected for out-of-zone irrigation are not in fact being collected anywhere in the state, the out-of-zone irrigators have only this extra (and illicit) charge to bear on top of the official water rate. And in any case they are often not too worried about paying something for a water assurance. While the first reason applies more to farmers towards the tail-ends of distributories than to farmers higher up, the second applies wherever unauthorised irrigation is taking place, provided that the irrigation staff might be able to cut off the water.

The interaction between farmers and officers commonly goes something like this: a few farmers representing one village, or perhaps (less commonly) several nearby villages, will approach the AE in charge of the Sub-division in which their land is located, and put to him a request. The AE tells them, as they expect, 'No, I cannot agree. You please see Supervisor and see what he can do'. The AE, now informed, tells the Supervisor his price for giving them what they want. The Supervisor in turn tells the farmers how much it will cost them, perhaps with an initial show of reluctance. If the farmers do not agree some bargaining may follow, with the Supervisor sending them away with a coded refusal meaning that they should see him again after he has consulted the AE. If the AE does not agree to come down, he may even order the Supervisor to reduce the water flow through the sluice or into the distributory until they meet his demand. (Note that the AE takes care never to be seen asking money of farmers.) Not uncommonly however the farmers' representative is himself a local contractor for the Irrigation Department. Between the AE or Supervisor and some of these contractors develop relations of special intimacy, in which the bargaining will be more direct and more surreptitious. The AE can use the promise of works to induce the contractor to get his co-villagers to pay up.

Of course, with the AE often under pressure to raise revenue for the EE and for his own purposes, he does not always wait for the farmers to approach him. The distinction between a bribe, offered by farmers to get the officer to do something he might not otherwise do, and extortion money, demanded by the officer in return for not inflicting a penalty, is often difficult to draw in practice. The officer need not extort directly; he may simply ensure the farmers know they might suffer if they do not 'offer' a bribe.

The farmers organise the collection of the money amongst themselves.[17] The amount from each requesting (or extorted) village may run into several thousands of rupees. The AE may tell the Supervisor to ask the farmers to pay the money directly to a named contractor, or the Supervisor may take the money and immediately pass it to the contractor. The only person with any money (evidence) on his hands is thus the contractor. If by chance he should be investigated by the police and large sums of money found in his possession he can say he has taken out loans for his works.[18]

At the time of meeting the farmers' request the Supervisor will strike his own bargain with the farmers. This will always be much less than the AE's amount. Though the Supervisor is the man on the spot, he has no power independently of the AE and EE, and if his demand is in the farmers' opinion excessive they may complain to the AE or EE about him and they, ever watchful to maintain the hierarchy, may discipline him.

*Price*: Price in these water transactions seems to be related to the following:

(1) Season: In the second, dry season the crop is completely dependent on canal water (in most of the state conjunctive use of surface and groundwater is not common); and yields are higher and more secure than in the first season *if* canal water arrives. Hence more money is normally raised on the second season crop than on the first.

(2) Drought in the first season: Since the first (wet) season rainfall normally provides roughly one-third to a half of the paddy crop water requirement (under upland canals), and since canal supplies can be increased only a little (if only because of carrying capacity constraints), some areas must go short of water, and/or management inputs must be increased substantially during a drought [*Levine, 1977; Wade 1980*]. If the drought comes after the transplantation, farmers by then have a sizeable investment to protect. They will rush to protect their crops by offering money, either in response to an actual shortfall in their supplies (perhaps because irrigation staff are favouring other villages) or in anticipation of one. Even a short period without rain at the time of ear-head formation may induce farmers to approach the Irrigation Department, for at that time in the growth cycle water stress will cut yields sharply.

(3) Whether the water favour is for zoned or out-of-zone land: Other things being equal, out-of-zone irrigation has to pay more than zoned (authorised) irrigation. Recall the point made earlier, that tens of thousands of acres under each canal are typically unauthorised.

(4) Crop: Paddy normally pays more than other crops, because it needs more water. Groundnut (which is grown mainly in the dry season) is also

expensive, because it needs water at the time of harvesting in late April and May, when canal supplies are normally short.

(5) Locational difficulty of meeting a request for more water: Tail-end villages will normally have to pay more for water than upper villages on the same distributory, because it is more difficult for staff to get them water (more work will have to go into patrolling the upper section of the distributory).

(6) Locational ease of cutting off water: Some villages, even if in upstream, good water supply locations, may be placed in such a way that it is easy for irrigation staff wholly or partly to cut off their water supply. Such villages will have to pay more than villages whose water supply is less easy to disrupt without disrupting that of many other villages.

(7) Whether the village is known as politically powerful: In the extreme case, no engineer would insist on money from the native village of an MLA.[19]

*Types of payment*: One can distinguish two kinds of transaction (in addition to 'gifts' of grain which we come to later). One is a flat rate, normally in cash but sometimes in grain, for an assurance of water for the whole season; it is collected especially from areas of unzoned paddy, and the rate will be higher in the second (dry) season than in the first. More exactly, it is an assurance that the Irrigation Department will not try to cut off water supply to the area; how much it also entails an obligation on the part of the Supervisor and AE to intervene actively if water runs short varies from case to case, depending partly on the personality and revenue needs of the staff, and partly on the influence of the villagers. The whole amount is paid over at the start of the season, and there is no rebate if the crop fails because of lack of water.

The second type of transaction involves payment in return for more active intervention by irrigation staff to improve an area's water supply, and is more contingent on the immediate state of crop water need and overall water supply. For example, during a first season drought, and most years towards the end of the second season, many tail-end areas, zoned and unzoned, will run short of water. Villages will then try and negotiate with the Irrigation Department wetting-by-wetting (or for, say, three wettings at x day intervals). Farmers call these emergency irrigations 'life irrigations'.

*Water distribution as a market*: In this second type of transaction, how is discrimination in favour of payers exercised? It is true that the physical control structures and communication facilities of south Indian canals are not good enough for discrimination to be possible on a *wide* scale without much more intensive management inputs than normal, and that compliance methods within the bureaucracy are not strong enough for these higher management inputs to be provided from the field staff alone. However, when the officers are on the canal it is often not difficult for them to discriminate in favour of a *minority* of villages or distributories. Note that the unit of discrimination and payment is the village or the distributory, not individual irrigators; only very exceptionally could discrimination be exercised in favour of particular people below the sluice outlet as against others below the same outlet. It is mainly at times of water shortage that officers come onto the canal to patrol, to ensure that sluices are not interfered with by farmers or by field staff acting on farmers' orders. It is then that they can most easily run a kind of water market. They themselves can stand guard by a sluice and see that farmers from lower down do not lower the gate to its proper level or remove the cross-bund;[20] or more likely they will place one or two field staff there and return frequently to make sure their orders are being followed. Vice versa for lower sluices: the officers can make sure the upstream sluices are not opened, so that more is available for lower down (whereas the field staff on their own might find it difficult to keep the upstream sluices lowered).

The use of a rotational delivery rule can provide a pretext for highly discretionary, predatory behaviour by irrigation staff towards farmers, and this point is worth elaborating because the introduction of rotational delivery is often regarded in the literature as a step forward in canal management [Levine, 1977; Levine et al., 1976]. While the normal water delivery rule in south Indian canals is 'continuous flow' (all outlets in the system are open simultaneously), in recent years some attention has been given to the use of rotational delivery during the dry season, such that parts of the canal command area receive water in turn rather than simultaneously [Wade, 1975, 1980]. There has also been slowly growing pressure from economic policy-makers and some politicians to reduce the area under water-consumptive paddy in the dry season, so that the available supply may irrigate a larger area of less water-consumptive crops. The irrigation engineers have been encouraged to set long rotational periods, such that the interval between irrigations in any one block is too long for paddy to be grown.

In practice, what may happen is that the Irrigation Department keeps farmers uninformed about the likely water supply in the dry season; farmers go ahead and plant paddy over large areas; the EE announces a 'turn system' which has intervals too long for paddy; the farmers with paddy rush to pay the AE in return for assurance of adequate and frequent supplies; and in implementation the irrigation staff make the supposedly rigid turn system highly flexible, depending partly on price. The uncertainty created by the flexibility may prompt irrigators of non-paddy crops, too, to try to get privileged supplies. Or even where the official rotational interval is short enough for paddy (as in a rotation during a wet season drought, for example) the engineers may inform farmers in certain villages that they must pay to have their full entitlement; if the rotation is eight days on and eight days off, the Supervisor may tell a village that (to take an actual but extreme case)[21] unless it pays Rs.50 per acre it will get only four days on and 12 days off. Where the unit of discrimination is the distributory (which may serve several villages or more) one should be able to check to what extent this happens by looking at the gauge reading records for the gauge at the distributory offtake (though for small distributories serving only 3–4,000 acres or less, there will probably be no gauge, even if the distributory takes off directly from the main canal). However, the gauge registers are commonly left with gaps during periods of acute water shortage, on grounds of 'pressure of work'; even if entries are there, falsification of gauge readings is so easy and common (at least for small gauges) that one cannot have much confidence in their accuracy [*Wade, 1981*]. A flexible rotation is thus a lucrative and fairly safe source of revenue.

The above account suggests that water distribution can be understood in terms of a simple market model—price is related to the scarcity of water, the certainty of yield, the ability of the irrigation staff to discriminate against non-payers, and so on. But one must note that the 'market' is highly imperfect, because the farmers cannot be sure in advance that they will get what they paid for, or that when they get it, it will be worth what they expect (if heavy rains fall in the meantime, the value of additional irrigation water may be small). If the AE takes money for assuring a village of sufficient water for, say, unzoned second season paddy, he may then not be able to supply it with enough—perhaps because he is responding to bribes from other villages; perhaps because the upstream AE is not releasing as much water to his Sub-division as he should be (the upstream AE may falsify the gauge readings); perhaps because with a certain degree of shortage he simply cannot exert enough control over the upstream sluices of a long (say 15-mile) distributory to get enough water down to a paying tail-end village; or perhaps because there is an overall shortage in the reservoir (which may be not only for natural reasons, but also because other canals fed from the same reservoir take more than expected). Whatever the real reason, the AE can nonetheless tell the farmers of the paying villages that there is a general shortage, that he is helpless, that they are getting more than they would have got had they not paid.

Hence one understands a senior engineer's comment that 'rumour mongering' is one of the tricks of canal operation: merely by rumouring a shortage money can be raised.[22] If farmers scramble to increase their supplies, the rumour can be self-confirming. More generally, the point is that a good deal of revenue can be raised from farmers with little work on the part of irrigation staff, by rumours, threats (especially to cut off water for unzoned crops), and occasional appearances by officers in their jeeps along the canal.[23]

This last point needs particular emphasis if the impression is not to be given that the large amount of revenue raised from irrigators indicates that the irrigation bureaucracy has the system much more under control—albeit for purposes of revenue collection—than is commonly supposed. To raise large quantities of revenue does not require tight control over a wide area (raising money by agreeing *not* to cut off water supplies to unzoned crops *may* mean less rather than more work for the irrigation staff, and looser rather than tighter control, at least in upstream Sub-divisions). When tighter control *is* required to raise money, that control can be exerted in quite specific locations, not across-the-board. A general improvement in water control over a whole canal system, in the interests of improving the performance of its agriculture, would require bigger changes in the management *system* and in physical structures than are needed to make these temporally and spatially more limited interventions.

*Politicians*: A further qualification to the simple market model concerns the role of politicians. One might suppose that the AE would discourage farmers from approaching politicians, for in so doing they might shortcircuit the flow of bribes. In fact, however, the AE may sometimes encourage farmers to approach the MLA, perhaps to gain protection against complaints from other farmers who see themselves disadvantaged by favours done for the first group, or perhaps to build up the politician's obligation to the AE himself, to be called upon at the time of his next transfer ('I have obliged you then, you please help me now').[24] Further, a favourite way for an MLA or Minister to enhance his support—or prevent its erosion—is to order the AE to be very strict on water releases (in particular, to release none to out-of-zone land), wait till the farmers start clamouring, accept their and the AE's invitation to come and 'solve problem', be seen to order the AE to give them what they want, and take the credit.

*Grain gifts*: 'Gifts' of grain constitute a third type of water payment (in addition to the assurance payment, and the wetting-by-wetting payment). Grain gifts are made *after* the harvest, usually in paddy; they occur mainly after the *wet* season harvest, and (in this case) are more regularised than the money payments, less subject to bargaining, less dependent on the degree of water scarcity; and go mostly to the field staff. They are seen by villagers as a tip rather than a price; and are likened by them to *jajmani* payments [*Bailey, 1957; Epstein, 1962*]. In some villages, village servants collect the grain from farmers on a per acre basis, and give it to the field staff who cover that village; in others, the field staff themselves have to collect from each household. Some grain is also given to Supervisor and AE. For field staff these payments are their main source of extra income. Under one upland canal, field staff are able to get the equivalent of another one to three months' salary out of these payments, which is an important supplement but nothing like the monetary revenue of the officers. Hence the complete absence of rags-to-riches stories amongst field staff. For Supervisors and AEs, too, the total grain gifts might come to something like one or two months' salary.[25] What is surplus to household requirements they can sell to friendly traders.

*Total revenue*: It is hard to make even a rough estimate of how much is typically raised 'from the *ayacut*'. The amounts from each village and Sub-division depend on how favourable are all the factors listed earlier as determinants of price; and also on such matters as how big is the works budget of the Sub-division (a function not only of irrigated area but also of number of big structures)—the bigger the works budget the less needs to be raised from irrigators.

However some modest points can be made. Payment of money (the following discussion excludes grain gifts, which are made in most villages) is a practice well known to all irrigators. But in the study area not all villages have to pay all the time—some almost never do (perhaps because of features of their location in relation to water supply), others have to pay only in an occasional severe drought in the first season and for one to three 'life irrigations' towards the end of the second season, while others have to pay for assurances in both seasons and for additional wettings as the need arises. The most common payment is for an assurance for the second season paddy area, plus payment for additional wettings in either the first or second season for paddy and non-paddy as the need arises. In this case costs to irrigators would commonly amount to Rs.10–25 per acre per year. If it is a matter of giving an assurance to, say, an out-of-zone block of second season ground-nut, the cost may rise to as much as Rs.50 per acre. But bribe/extortion payments of more than Rs.50 per acre are rare in the study area; this can be taken as the upper limit of the per acre price. With Sub-divisions normally having over 50,000 gross irrigated acres, one can be confident that a figure of Rs.50,000 per year from the irrigators in each Sub-division would be a rather conservative estimate. (Payments for changes in crop zoning are not included in this figure; see note 19.)

Following through the earlier illustration, we have the AE and his Supervisors getting five per cent of the works contracts by way of 'savings on the estimates'; if they split it half and half, each AE will end up with Rs.15,000.[26] He will probably be able to at least double that with 'savings on the ground'. If he gets Rs.50,000 from irrigators, his additional income for the year will be around Rs.80,000, a total based on even more conservative assumptions than the EE total given earlier. The average official AE income is Rs.23,000 a year.[27]

THE RELATIVE DESIRABILITY OF POSTS

It is safe to say that engineers can, and many do, earn many times their annual official income in these various ways. Our illustrative figures given above are from an upland area, and there is reason to think that on the more fertile, intensively irrigated coastal deltas the profitability of O & M posts is commonly considerably higher. One can, indeed, think of a rank ordering of posts in terms of their profitability, including not only O & M posts but also those in construction, investigations, design, etc. Investigations and design posts are at the relatively unprofitable end; while construction posts also *tend*, at AE and EE level, to be less profitable than O & M posts (in Construction units, initiative and control is normally higher in the hierarchy, at SE, CE and Ministerial levels). But profitability is only one factor in desirability. Looked at more comprehensively, the main determinants of desirability seem to be the following:

(1) How much money can be raised, which is a function of how much money is being spent through the post, and how much can be raised from outside the budget (mainly from farmers). O & M posts differ from one part of the state to another in how willing the farmers are to pay for water. Generally, O & M posts are less lucrative than construction posts in terms of money from the works budget (as distinct from farmers' payments)—unless the O & M post is in a badly drought-prone area where a drought can plausibly be declared often, thus making available a generous flow of Food for Work and other relief funds.

(2) How safely the money can be raised. O & M posts generally have an advantage over construction posts in this respect, since quality control is

minimal. O & M contractors will also usually have no reputation to protect, unlike some of the big contractors for canal construction. On the other hand, *if* an O & M engineer is caught raking off the works budget, his contractors are too small to be able to help in the ways canal construction contractors might.

(3) Living conditions. O & M posts generally do better in this respect too, since the posts are usually in well-established towns where, in contrast to many construction, and even more, investigation posts, clean drinking water is not a problem and one's children can be given a headstart in the qualifications race by attending English language schools.

(4) Prestige of the project. A construction post on a big dam site carries prestige for an engineer which no O & M post can confer.

(5) Nearness to native place. This is obviously idiosyncratic. Its weight depends on such things as whether a man has land to administer in his native place or brothers who might administer it in his absence. But in general, engineers at AE and EE level do value strongly being within half a day's journey of their native place. It is worth noting, conversely, that postings to the state capital are *not* widely sought after.

By rule officers must be transferred within three years, and can be transferred to any post in the Irrigation Department—there is no functional specialisation. No-one can expect to spend most of his career in O & M, for the number of such posts in relation to demand is too small. (Many senior engineers have no more than a few years' experience of O & M.)

Averaging out the above (and other) factors, most engineers will have distinct preferences about what type of work they wish to do, and where. They naturally want to influence their transfers in line with their preferences. There is enough overlap between individuals' preference rankings, for reasons to do with potential gain, schools, comfortable living, relatives, and the like, to ensure that for most O & M posts several people are likely to be interested at any one time. So as a man comes towards the end of the second year in a post he will study the vacancy listings with care. He knows he will be moved within three years, and he wants time in hand to allow himself some manoeuvre. If he wants to stay near a certain place, he may accept a temporary move away, thus satisfying the transfer rule; and then press hard to be transferred back to the first place after a year. But others may also be pressing hard for the same posts . . . .

THE SALE OF POSTS AND THE OFFICERS' DEMAND FOR REVENUE

It has not escaped the notice of politicians that irrigation engineers can earn large amounts of additional income in some posts. While it is difficult for them (or others) to manipulate who is *promoted* from one rank to another, it is not difficult to manipulate who is *transferred* into which post. Likewise, it is not difficult for senior officers to manipulate the same decision. Politicians and senior officers are able to obtain for themselves part of engineers' additional income by auctioning the transfer, and imposing additional demands as a condition of the successful bidder's not himself being transferred out before the normal term.

The normal term in practice is about two years. During an officer's tenure of a particular post (referring now to AEs and EEs—Supervisors are discussed separately) he will want to recoup what he paid out to get it, plus whatever extra he has to pay to senior officers and politicians during the tenure, plus his own profit—which has to include some of what he is to bid for his next post. This sets the amount of revenue he will try to raise.

Notice that the officer does not try to recoup a fee for entry to the irrigation service; for in most years since the mid-1950s there has been a shortage of engineering graduates and diploma holders, and no (illicit) payment for entry into the Irrigation Department has been needed.[28] Promotions are also not generally paid for, because for reasons we come to, a precise and public order of promotion is in fact generally followed, so discrimination between payers and non-payers is not possible. Let us consider the amounts involved in securing a transfer to a particular O & M post, and an aspirant's strategy for doing so.[29] The procedures differ for EEs and AEs.

## Transfers and Politicians

(i) *Executive Engineers*: For transfers at EE level the sanctioning authority is the 'government'—the (elected) Minister of Irrigation, and the Secretary of Irrigation (the senior-most civil servant in the Irrigation Ministry, an IAS officer).[30]

The contenders for a particular EE's post normally deal with the Minister through a go-between, perhaps the Minister's Personal Assistant (PA). The applicant may wait in the ante-chamber to the Minister's office while the PA shuttles between him and the Minister inside, a meeting taking place only once price and other conditions are agreed. The Minister then issues transfer orders, the old incumbent is moved elsewhere (he may have been going through the same procedure over his next move), and the new EE takes charge.[31]

News of who is in the running for a particular post and the price paid travels fast within the relevant Division. Posts acquire price reputations—'X is a one *lakh* post, Y is a five *lakh* post', the engineers say (one *lakh* equals Rs.100,000). This refers to the amount it costs to get the transfer orders. On top of this the EE has to promise to meet the Minister's demands for more money (or for 'gifts' in kind—'you give my brother-in-law a fridge') from time to time during his tenure; and to respect the Minister's wishes on who is to get major contracts (though the latter condition is less important on O & M posts, where contracts tend to be small, than on construction posts). While most or all of the transfer price goes to the Minister for his personal purse, this second, more contingent component tends to be more for party funds,[32] and its size varies with the electoral cycle.

Normally the EE does not have to pay the local MLAs, but he will most likely visit the more powerful of them[33] before taking charge to obtain their approval, a condition of which is that he respect their wishes on choice of contractors. But if an EE is noticeably 'without influence' he may have to pay more, not only to the Minister but also to the MLAs and senior officers, in order to get the post. A Low Caste engineer, or an out-of-state Brahmin (recruited in the 1950s when the state's irrigation service was taking applicants from wherever it could find them) may well be without influence. In the mid-1970s, for example, one particular EE 'without influence' found that he had to pay a total of $1\frac{1}{2}$ *lakhs* to get a certain post, for which his predecessor and successor both paid one *lakh*; in his case, one *lakh* went to the Minister, and another half *lakh* had to go to local MLAs and senior officers to get their support.

On the fertile coastal deltas, where canal irrigation has been practised extensively for over a hundred years, an EE's (O & M) post may cost up to 3 to 4 *lakhs*.[34] On the uplands O & M posts cost considerably less, agriculture being less productive, canal irrigation more recent, and farmers more resistant to paying irrigation bribes. In the middle to late 1970s, some posts on the uplands could be had for as little as Rs.50,000, others for Rs.100,000.

So on the deltas an EE may pay up to 14 times his annual salary (about Rs.28,500) for the two-year tenure of certain O & M posts; on the uplands, three times or less. Nevertheless, in terms of our earlier example, the EE who pays Rs.100,000 for an O & M post and another Rs.50,000 over the course of the period to meet supplementary demands and gifts can expect an additional income of some Rs.260,000 a year from the post: a most pleasing profit.

(ii) *Assistant Engineers*: For AEs the transfer strategy is different, because the sanctioning authority is their own CE and the SE too has more of a role.[35] Further, the local MLAs will be at least as concerned about who their AE is as about the EE, since the AE is more influential in allocating water to their actual or potential supporters.

An AE wanting a certain post may begin with the local MLAs and the relevant EE. He visits the EE to obtain his consent, and confirms his willingness to pay over to the EE an agreed proportion (traditionally five per cent) of the Sub-division's works budget *and* to pay over additional amounts during his tenure depending on the EE's demands. He also visits the concerned MLAs (normally only one or two will have major parts of their constituencies in his Sub-division).[36] Unless he is a man of unusual influence he will pay them for help with the CE and SE, perhaps Rs.10,000 each.[37] As well, he may have to go direct to the CE's office and pay the agent there to secure the transfer orders. Notice the neat division of revenue opportunities from transfers: at Ministerial level for EEs, at Departmental and MLA level for AEs.

In a typical O & M post on the uplands, if the prospective AE cannot raise at least Rs.25,000 before he takes charge he should not waste time trying for it; but the amounts required are often considerably more.[38] If AEs or EEs want an extension beyond two years they may have to bid for it against other contenders. Even before the two years are up they can be removed at any time on the Minister's orders (the Minister can easily mobilise some petitions or letters against them to justify his action). They have no effective appeal[39]—and of course lose what they paid for the post. In one case in the late 1970s an AE paid a very senior politician Rs.40,000 (payments by AEs to very senior politicians are unusual) to secure transfer orders to a certain post, only to be transferred out less than a week after taking charge to make way for a man known to have paid Rs.50,000 (to the same politician). This sort of instant transfer swindle is, however, not common.

Though AEs and EEs in fact normally stay in place for two years they are preoccupied with being removed before time. If a new Irrigation Minister comes to power (on average only once in two or three years) the EE may rush him a payment to ensure that the Minister does not put his own man in his stead. And if a big public works programme (Food For Work, for example)[40] comes under his charge the EE may, even without being asked, pay out large amounts to the Ministers and senior officers throughout his tenure to ensure he stays in the post. Normally the supplementary demands on the EE from the Minister and senior officers might total roughly half a *lakh* in cash and kind over the two years, in a one *lakh* post; but in the run-up to an election the demands are commonly much higher.

(iii) *Supervisors and field staff*: Supervisors normally have to pay nothing for transfers within an O & M Circle, unless the EE of the Division they want to move to particularly does not want to have them. 'Crow catching' is enough—to 'yes sir whatever you say sir' the EE and the SE at every opportunity. But transfer into an O & M Circle may cost, on the uplands in the late 1970s, about Rs.5,000—though some SEs (who are the sanctioning authority at Supervisor level) are reputed not to take money for this sort of thing from Supervisors.

Foremen (*maistries*) and bankers (*lascars*), the field staff, normally do not pay anything; rather they have to promise the AE into whose Sub-division they wish to move always to be obedient. Perhaps the reason why they do not have to pay relates to the fact that they normally benefit rather little from the revenue-raising system. As the earlier discussion showed, the system is not one in which collections are made by the lowest level staff, then aggregated upwards, each rank taking its cut, but rather one in which the revenue transactions are made at the middle levels (especially Supervisor and AE), from where the upward re-channelling begins. On the other hand, it is often said by officers that their field staff are 'corrupt fellows'.

*Inflation in the cost of posts*

The prices of posts have gone up sharply in several periods, for reasons relating either to departmental or to wider political events, or to a combination of both. The first period of rapid increase, around 1966–68, was linked to a struggle for power within the old Public Works Department between two CEs, which led to its bifurcation into the Irrigation Department (now with Power added on) and the Roads and Buildings Department. This was accompanied by a sharp increase in the involvement of politicians in transfer matters. At about the same time, changes in national political leadership were linked by several informants to tougher demands on state level politicians for revenue for national politicians. The price increase of

1973 was attributed by these informants to another major, if informal, change in national political leadership.

Towards the end of the 1970s prices (and supplemental demands) rose again. A certain *AE*'s post on the uplands which cost Rs.30,000 at the end of 1977, two years later cost the same for a *one* year extension; and the man who succeeded to it in 1981 (beating three other contenders) reputedly paid one *lakh*. In the same area, inter-Circle (O & M) transfers for Supervisors have jumped from about Rs.5,000 to about Rs.10,000 in 1981,[41] divided between senior officers. The rises in the late 1970s may be related to the fact that this state was one of the few to retain a Congress government during the period of Janata Party rule at the centre, so its bureaucracy became an important means of raising money for the Congress Party nationally and in states where the party had lost office. Departments such as Irrigation and Forestry had an important financial role in the party's re-emergence in national power. The sharp increase in 1981 may be related to the sudden closure of a number of Construction Circles and the consequent increase in demand for O & M posts.[42]

The steady decline in the real value of engineers' salaries—by about half since 1965, the same as for all state civil servants of these ranks—may also be a factor in the upward movement of transfer prices, as engineers seek to compensate for the fall in real salaries by moving to more lucrative posts. But as one retired Chief Engineer observed when this argument was put to him, the engineer's salary is, even in the relatively less profitable posts, rather small in relation to what can be earned illicitly, so it is doubtful that the decline in real salary has been a *major* factor.

CONTROL FROM WITHIN THE IRRIGATION HIERARCHY

It is very important for the careers and comfort of many engineers that the process of revenue-raising should go smoothly and without undue interruption by uncooperative or inefficient subordinates. The Supervisor, as the front man in the AE's water negotiations, is extremely vulnerable. The AE can always deny he issued orders to release more water to sub-distributory X or cut off water to Y and have the Supervisor punished for disobeying orders—nothing is written down. The AE has no sanctioning power over works (with an exception to be mentioned later), and is therefore dependent on the EE; if relations break down, the EE can make his life difficult by refusing to sanction some of his works, or (in some locations) by withdrawing water from his Sub-division without informing him. The EE can in turn be transferred out on the Minister's say-so. If he resists the Minister's demands for extra revenue he is likely to be transferred within the two-year term, to make way for someone who has promised to be more obliging. A man who refuses to bend to the farmers' or MLA's or superior officer's illegal request—say, to release water down a distributory when it is supposed to be closed—can easily be charged with trying to extort money, with holding back until paid. As Bayley says, writing of the Indian bureaucracy more generally, 'Even the honest official may be blackmailed by the threat that unless he act unfairly he may be charged publicly with being corrupt' [*1970 (1966): 528*].

DS.R—M*

There are, moreover, normative justifications, heard within the community of engineers (though never voiced in public), for taking money from farmers. A man who has qualms can be appealed to by his fellows and superiors in terms of how hard they, the engineers, have to work to supply farmers with water, how difficult and prejudicial to their children the living conditions are, and how inequitable the discrepancy between the incomes of uneducated contractors and their own. If the farmers or contractors want to give them something by way of gratitude, who are they to refuse? In this way the line between 'taking gifts' and 'corruption' is blurred—especially because part of the maintenance budget rake-off is well institutionalised and an engineer would have to go out of his way to avoid receiving the money. Hence one can understand why, from the point of view of farmers and contractors, an 'honest' engineer is not one who does not take money, but one who takes no more than the normal rate, who does not haggle, and who having taken your money at least tries to help you in return.

Recalcitrants may find themselves transferred to one of several well-known dumping grounds—such as the Investigation Circles, concerned with preliminary design of new projects (the extent to which their work finalises the location of canals is neither firm nor fine enough for them to provide revenue by discretionary conferring of enhanced land values); or even worse, 'leave vacant postings', replacing individuals who have gone on leave, a situation in which one has neither power nor respect. (Husbanding the 30 days' annual paid leave allowance is part of the art of post hunting; if you don't like your transfer orders you go on leave and mobilise your forces to get them changed.) Even construction posts can be a punishment, when they provide less or more risky revenue than O & M postings at AE and EE level, and are in disagreeable locations.

There are also instruments of control over the EE which fall short of transfer. In particular, CEs have come to make use of what is called the Letter of Credit (LOC) technique. Every three months each Division has to submit a budget showing its expected expenditure in the next period, and the CE writes a LOC on which the EE is authorised to draw. If an EE is failing to satisfy the extra revenue demands, the CE can (perhaps at the request of the Minister) cut back his credit, thereby slowing down and greatly complicating the work of the Division.

However, it would be wrong to portray the irrigation hierarchy as a tightly organised, internally disciplined apparatus for collecting revenue. The cross-pressures on any Supervisor, AE or EE are often complex. Local MLAs may push hard on behalf of particular contractors or particular locations. The MLA may have disagreed with the CE's choice of AE, or may fall out with him subsequently, perhaps because the AE is not being responsive enough to his wishes; he may then harrass the AE by mobilising letters of complaint about the AE's work and then making representations to the CE or the Minister . He may even induce the contractors to do very poor work, under the promise of his protection, in order to provide the evidence that the AE is inefficient. It is said that contractors are becoming more closely identified with politicians than in the past, and less obedient to the engineers. The AE may be more beholden to the MLA than to the EE; if the MLA in the head-reach Sub-division is very powerful, he may be able to protect the AE who lets down less water to the remaining Sub-divisions than he is meant to (the AE may cover himself by falsifying the gauge readings or even the gauge itself). This makes the job of the EE and the other AEs more difficult. If the EE tried to rectify the situation or get the AE transferred, he might find himself transferred. It is this complex field of forces that engineers have in mind when they say, in the words of an EE, 'Water management is all human relations, adjusting to the various pressures'; or in the words of another, 'Water management is 25 per cent water and 75 per cent people, you have to soothe people and you have not to displease the politicians also'. They make such remarks apologetically, because 'human relations' seems the antithesis of hard-nosed, rational engineering.

It is clear, then, that the pressures on any one individual to behave in a 'corrupt' manner, whether in response to demands from superiors in the irrigation hierarchy or to satisfy the expectations of politicians and farmers, are very strong. Many engineers find the pressures to which they are exposed from all sides (especially on O & M jobs) very trying, and find the behaviour needed to stay in the post in varying degrees distasteful. Morale in the Irrigation Department is certainly low. Why do not some of these individuals express their resentment at the way they are being treated by taking action against those who harrass them, perhaps by complaining to the Secretary of Irrigation, or to the Anti-Corruption Bureau? In the words of an EE, 'I would be crushed, I have my family to support, so I just keep quiet'.

When this particular EE first took charge of a certain O & M Division he discovered that the sluice openings in the stretch of the canal which passed through the constituency of a powerful MLA had been enlarged, with the result that this part of the canal took far more water than intended, squeezing the areas lower down; he ordered them to be put right in the next maintenance period. As soon as the work started the MLA got on the 'phone to the CE saying 'my people will suffer'; the CE ordered the EE to stop, and within a week the EE received transfer orders, having arrived only a few months before. The EE acted quickly to mobilise the MLAs of lower down constituencies (whose irrigators would have benefited from the sluice-narrowing programme); the transfer orders were withdrawn, but the sluice-narrowing programme was stopped. And the EE was still transferred three months before the normal term ended (dilatoriness in meeting the Minister's supplementary revenue demands contributed)—transferred to the worst possible posting, outside the Irrigation Department. The pressures on any one individual to conform are all the stronger because few alternative civil engineering jobs are available. The outflow of engineers from the Irrigation Department is very small.

CHECKS

*Official procedures*

What stops irrigation engineers from taking more than they do? There are, first, a number of bodies to exercise continuing scrutiny of government departments. One is the Accountant-General's Office, which routinely scrutinises all financial accounts from each Division—sufficiently effectively to make correct charging for bad structures, rather than over-charging for good structures, the most promising strategy, since neither this office nor any other independent body makes checks on *physical* quantities. Another institution for continuing scrutiny is the Legislative Assembly. But the sort of information it gets on each canal is quite inadequate to allow it to perform a public interest monitoring function. The lack of routine public monitoring of the performance of canal systems is, indeed, one of the main problems.

Then there are means of conducting special investigations and disciplining offenders. The superior officer has to fill in 'Confidential Reports' on his subordinates each year, one column of which is titled 'Integrity'. Remarks in this column (or other communications) can bring into action the department's own investigative machinery—its Vigilance Cell—or the state Anti-Corruption Bureau (ACB) and Vigilance Commission.

However, in India as in many other countries, the gap between scandalous administrative and political conduct and specifically indictable offences is large. Disciplinary cases can drag on for years, and since the relevant provisions of the Indian Constitution place overwhelming stress on protection of the individual officer, the cases are not infrequently declared void. Even to put an adverse remark on an individual's annual confidential report is hazardous. The elaborate series of safeguards in the Anti-Corruption Bureau-Vigilance Commission mechanism tends to break down at the 'government' stage—the Minister or Secretary can easily intervene if he has a mind to, to ensure that a case does not go forward. If the Minister sold an EE his tenure and subsequently put the screws on him for more money, he may be a bit ambivalent about allowing an ACB investigation to proceed.

Nevertheless the possibility of investigation, even if remote, probably does act as a check on the proclivities of officials to exploit their powers to the full. Even if an engineer has powerful allies he can never be sure he will not be investigated if he behaves too flagrantly. Often investigations are triggered as part of a struggle for power and spoils. A senior officer may, for example, fall out with the Minister; then the Minister, previously his colluder, may order the ACB to investigate. Or the Minister may change, and especially if the new man and the old man are rivals, the new man may approve investigations which the other was squashing.

Since engineers are normally very careful to conceal their receipt and passing on of illicit funds, investigative bodies are likely to look for indirect signs, particularly for evidence of living far beyond official income. Engineers are well aware of the need to conceal extra income and its uses, and have many ways of doing so. Savings may be placed in a bank account under the name of a woman over whom the engineer has close control (police investigation of women's bank accounts is said to be less likely than of men's). Daughters can be given lavish dowries. Children can be provided for generously in private schools. A *benami* partnership can be formed to operate private buses in the next district, or to sell fertilisers and pesticides. A shop may be opened in the name of a family member back in the engineer's native place; the shop may in fact stay closed most of the time but can provide an excuse for living beyond official means. Donations to temples are a most attractive use, being both safe and productive of incalculable spiritual returns, as well as a natural form of thanksgiving for God's help in a successful venture. Finally, money needs to be accumulated for the special and limited purpose of buying the next post. In these and other ways, it is possible for some engineers to have incomes many times their official salary, yet not appear in daily life to be living extravagantly.

*Farmers and politicians*

But in the normal course of events, the main check on the engineers comes from the farmers whom they are meant to serve. It is true that the farmers themselves are often willing partners to bribery; as we have seen, they will rush to pay if their crops are at risk, and they will, in some locations at least, be willing enough to pay for water for unauthorised irrigation. However, if an engineer comes into a post and starts demanding significantly *more* from farmers and contractors than was usual previously, then they may try to take action to check or avoid his demands. They may in some locations break the channel banks or sluice gates to by-pass his control (which not only directly checks his power, but may also attract attention to their situation from higher officers), and/or visit their MLA, and/or write letters of complaint about him. The letters, probably anonymous (hence called generically 'anonymous petitions'), will go to the CE, to the Minister, to the MLA, to the ACB, to anyone the authors think might be able to harm the man—perhaps with a copy to the man himself. The local MLA may encourage constituents to do this, and armed with copies will make representations to the Minister 'on behalf of public'. If a man really is behaving extortionately to many people, especially if he is also patently living beyond his means, the flow of such letters and their level of detail, and the interest of the MLA in placating his constituents, may be such that the normal excuse for such complaints— that the officer is being made the object of a vendetta—cannot be used.

But this mechanism is limited to the extent that farmers fear that the engineer and local staff will strike back at them, perhaps by cutting off their water supply, if they complain.[43] It is also limited by differential willingness of MLAs to act. A village which has some wealthy, influential farmers can expect to have its complaints receive more attention than a village of poor, low caste farmers. Or, in the complacently-spoken words of an AE, 'Villages of small farmers just have to suffer, they won't dare approach Ministers or MLAs. Only the middle classes will have easy access to meet Ministers'.

*Transfer*

If a sizeable volume of complaints starts coming to MLAs or the Minister or the CE about a particular engineer, the easiest way to 'keep the peace', to use the engineers' phrase, is not to mount an investigation, with the possibility of disciplinary proceedings at the end, but simply to transfer him out at the first opportunity. No reasons need be given; no messy business of finding hard evidence need be contemplated.

The usual way to punish an officer is thus to transfer him before the usual two-year term is up, and /or to transfer him to an undesirable post and place.

So transfer is used both to punish someone who is taking 'too much', and to punish someone taking too little; it checks both the excessively corrupt and the insufficiently corrupt—both types 'threaten the peace'. Of course the transfer weapon is not always effective, in the sense that a corrupt man might have powerful allies who can ensure that the transfer orders are overturned. (And an MLA has to restrict his use of the transfer weapon; he will use up too much influence if he uses it frequently.) But it is clear that fear of transfer does check the extortion of engineers who buy themselves into lucrative posts; not only because of where they might end up, but also because the balance of their receipts over outlay to get the post will be smaller the sooner they are transferred.

*Morality*

These various points relating to punishment help to explain why the engineers take such care to conceal what they do. How much they are also checked by a feeling that what they are doing is wrong, morally reprehensible, is difficult to say, partly because an engineer talking about it with a stranger will always say it is wholly wrong, and also because even within the same person, remorse, shame and compunction are subject to alteration and ambivalence. However, it is clear that revenue-raising is *not* a matter for boasting—even AEs chatting amongst themselves in private would be very wary of discussing their revenue-raising exploits.

Second, in the irrigation context it seems likely that engineers discriminate between situations according to *how far* they are acting contrary to the law (as the farmers certainly do). For example, they would probably feel less of a sense of wrongdoing for taking money to supply an unauthorised crop, especially if the crop is paddy, than for demanding money to supply a village its full official turn during a rotational schedule. And in the case of unauthorised paddy and groundnut, one may have some sympathy with the engineers:[44] they know that large areas under these crops in the dry season mean they will have to work hard towards the end of the season to supply them with enough water; on the other hand, they know the farmers will not be made to pay the tough financial penalties which unauthorised irrigation is meant to incur. One can understand why they say, in effect, 'All right, if you want to grow paddy where it is not supposed to be grown, you will cause a lot of extra work, so you pay us something for our trouble'. This is distinct from active manipulation of the water supplies such that farmers have to pay for what they are fully entitled to. It would be wrong to suppose that all O & M engineers are actively engaged in the latter: some (a minority) try to limit their revenue collections to 'obliging', perhaps occasionally making smash-and-grab raids when a daughter's dowry has to be raised, then returning to principled or timid correctitude.

*Promotions*

The fact that promotions are insulated from money power or particularistic pressures helps to explain why the principled or timid *can* nevertheless rise to the top ranks, and sometimes do. The order of promotions is assigned at the start of a man's career by the Public Service Commission and is very rarely altered, either to move a man up or to hold one down. Lists showing promotion order are published in the annual departmental diaries the engineers carry around with them, and each batch of promotions is avidly studied to see if anyone has been passed over (the case of advanced promotion virtually never arises). A man who finds himself passed over will go to court, where he has a good chance of getting the decision reversed. The fact that promotion order is protected in law (while transfer procedures are not) and that the judicial process is not determined by particularistic demands is the short answer to the difference in 'rule-boundedness' between promotions and transfers. The only familiar manipulation of promotion is for the Minister to keep, say, 10 EEs' positions vacant until the 10 AEs next in line pay up. But there is a limit to how many positions can be kept vacant, and what the Minister cannot do is to promote number 11 or 12, say, in place of one of the first 10 AEs who refuses to pay.

This means that a man who gets a good position in the initial ranking, perhaps because of excellent examination results, can be fairly confident of rising to SE rank, even if he incurs the wrath of superior officers and politicians on the way. This can cut both ways, of course; but it undoubtedly does help some men to be less responsive than others to the pressures and opportunities to be corrupt. These people simply accept, more or less, that they will probably spend much of their careers in investigations and designs, or in difficult and out-of-the-way construction projects. At the same time, the highly bureaucratised procedures for promotions are a source of considerable frustration, because the engineers know that even if they consistently do very good work they will not be advanced in the promotion queue.[45]

Yet the normative checks are weaker than they might otherwise be because of the absence of any training for engineers in the principles of canal operation and maintenance. Their training is in the design and construction of hydraulic and other structures, and they simply have to learn operation and maintenance on the job. The explicit principles of operation and maintenance which they learn are few and rudimentary, and give no precise guides to decisions in many actual situations. Not knowing clearly how they *should* be deciding (when, for example, water is too limited to supply all their area at once, how to devise sensible rotational schedules?) they are more likely to give way to the pull of money or influence.

It bears repeating that the general public interest checks on the Irrigation Department are rather weak. The legislative scrutiny of canal performance is poorly developed, and the Accountant-General's Office confines itself to scrutiny of finances. The district Collector is too remote and too ignorant of the local situation to intervene.[46] In addition, the practice of investigative journalism is too rare for the press to provide a general check. In practice, how much an engineer is checked beyond his own conscience depends heavily on particular local circumstances.

EFFECTS ON IRRIGATION PERFORMANCE

It is clear that the demand-side effects of irrigation corruption are not significant, in the sense that farmers' production incentives are *not* much affected by illicit water payments. Net profits (including hired labour costs) are of the order of Rs.900 per acre (late 1970s) for paddy, and much more for groundnut; pre-harvest costs of cultivation are about Rs.900 per acre for paddy, and somewhat more for groundnut. Corruption costs of the order of magnitude indicated earlier—not more than Rs.50 per acre per crop, commonly Rs.10–25 per acre over two seasons, and sometimes much less (especially in villages with ample water supply)—form too small a part of cost of production to have much effect on production decisions: on which crops are grown, and how much they are irrigated. The gains to farmers from their elimination would be tiny in relation to potential gains from the elimination of Betterment Levy[47] and increases in paddy procurement prices (issues on which widespread farmers' agitations in 1980 were based). The worries, rather, are on the supply side.

A large part of the problem is that canal managers have no incentive to manage and maintain systems well when this would conflict with the generation of illicit income, which may be many times the official salary. On the water supply side, maximum surplus is extractable when water supply is insecure (in the short term); yet the ostensible function of the irrigation staff is to make it more secure. On the maintenance side, maximum surplus is extractable (in the short term) when the quality of maintenance is poor; yet the ostensible function of the irrigation staff is to ensure that the system is well maintained. If in some contexts the view that 'corruption oils the wheels' has some validity, canal irrigation does not seem to be one of them. The engineers' and politicians' pursuit of illicit income not only alters the discretionary allocation of individual (or village) benefit, but actually subverts the pursuit of public purposes. More specifically:

(1) Productivity and equity: If farmers know they will be provided with reliable supplies, the possibilities for engineers to earn bribes are reduced. Bribes are high where uncertainty is high. To get money, engineers may *create* scarcity and uncertainty, by cutting off supplies to a vulnerable village until they are paid, or as a by-product of diverting water from one area to another to respond to bribe-backed requests. Greater uncertainty of water supplies reduces the productivity of water. In particular, engineers persist with flexible, *ad hoc* and unannounced rotational delivery schedules partly because these practices facilitate revenue-raising (during a first season drought, for example). This is not to say that such behaviour is to be understood entirely as predatory. The engineers do face very real difficulties in meeting the demands upon them, and, as noted, are given no training in how to do so on a 'scientific' basis.

The point about the revenue-raising potential of rotational irrigation is worth re-emphasising; as was indicated, the introduction of rotational irrigation both above and below the outlet is normally seen in the literature as a step forward in canal management. Indeed, the key point of the World Bank's new thinking on canal irrigation over the next two or three decades in South Asia is that canals have to be built to ensure 'flexibility' of operation— to ensure that varying quantities of water can be delivered through each outlet over the crop season in line with changing crop water requirement below that outlet. If this is to be done, then the question of how the much enhanced discretionary power in the hands of the engineers is to be disciplined needs careful thought [*Wade, 1982a*].

However, it is certainly possible that tail-end villages can offset to some extent their locational disadvantage by offering bribes, and that this makes for a spatial re-allocation from upstream areas where the marginal productivity of water is lower, to where it is higher—a re-allocation which would not be made in the absence of an (illicit) incentive to irrigation staff to patrol upstream sluices more vigorously than they would otherwise. In this sense the corrupt system *could* promote efficiency and equity. One *can* identify tail-end villages or distributories which almost certainly would not have received water during a shortage had the irrigation staff not worked much harder than usual to bring water down—because they were being paid to do so. If—and there do seem to be cases—upstream villages did not suffer corresponding losses of yield because of the sending of more water downstream, this would be a gain for efficiency as well as equity.

However, my strong impression is that this pulling in of water to tail-end villages by means of bribes does not happen on a *big* scale, sufficient to offset the adverse effects of the *general increase in uncertainty* which it is in the engineers' interest to promote.[48] It must be remembered that the prospect of additional income from working hard to push water to tail-end villages is not a *sufficient* condition for such extra effort by irrigation staff, because they can make plenty of money 'from works' with little effort and plenty more 'from the *ayacut*' merely by cutting off or threatening to cut off supplies to vulnerable areas (upstream as well as downstream), or even just by rumouring a shortage.

(2) Interest in scientific principles and operational reform: The preoccupation of the EE and AEs with running a vast financial enterprise would seem likely to blunt their interest in canal operation as a serious and demanding professional and intellectual activity. They can make plenty of money without running the system well. For the same reason they can be expected to oppose any reform which might weaken their hold over O & M decisions [*Ali, 1980*]. For example, the Irrigation Department has shown no interest in involving farmers more systematically in major O & M matters; and has often been lax to the point of negligence in informing farmers about changes or expected changes in water supply. Relatedly, in one southern state where a new department of Command Area Development was set up (at World Bank prompting) to concern itself with ways of improving the performance of existing canal systems, the Irrigation Department has opposed it tooth and nail, even in its activities below the outlet and still more so in its attempts to influence how the main systems are being run.

(3) Credibility of Irrigation Department: In the eyes of farmers, the Irrigation Department's announcements on matters such as when the canal will be opened at the start of the first irrigation season, when it is to be closed, and how much water is available, are not to be trusted. Farmers are liable to take the EE's warnings that water will be short in the second season as a signal to start coming forward with bribes. Thus the *workable* authority of the

Irrigation Department is undermined, with probably adverse effects on productivity.

(4) Water rates: The longest-running policy proposal in the irrigation business is to increase water rates. So they have been, occasionally, though much less than the increase in the average value of the crop. Neither the Irrigation Department nor the mass of MLAs are enthusiastic about increasing water charges. Perhaps this lack of enthusiasm is not unrelated to a fear that farmers might be unwilling to pay both the official water charge at the higher rate and the unofficial charge at a rate no lower than before. If so, increasing the water rate would mean encroaching upon the flows of money through these alternative circuits, at cost to officers and politicians alike.

(5) Maintenance: Maintenance suffers badly, and hence so do both productivity and equity. (a) EEs and AEs make poor quality controllers, because they benefit from sub-standard work. (b) But the contractor has a further incentive to do sub-standard work, because on 'supplementary works' done to correct first-round mistakes he gets all the profit. (c) The contracts are divided into very small units (for example, one contract might be for maintenance of one mile, six furlongs of a long distributory), to keep good relations with as many contractors as possible, not least because the contractors are useful agents of the Irrigation Department in the villages for helping the AEs to raise money from the *ayacut*. (In other words, raising money 'from works' and 'from the *ayacut*' are not as distinct as the earlier discussion implied; the AE can use the promise of works to induce a contractor to help lever money 'from the *ayacut*', if need be.) Maintenance down the length of a distributory is often badly coordinated as a result. (d) The AE is empowered to sanction rather small 'emergency works' in certain circumstances, and these he makes use of to achieve revenue-raising objectives, as in (c). Again, patchwork, uncoordinated maintenance is the result. (e) Between 25 and 50 per cent of the resources meant to be spent on maintenance goes elsewhere. Off the main canal, sizeable distributories may not be maintained (except perhaps to replace broken structures) for 10 to 15 years at a time. The engineers say the government must give them more maintenance money.

(6) Effectiveness of new canal projects: Investigation of new canals, the preparation of project proposals to go for funding (perhaps to the World Bank) is being done by men whose chief aim is generally to get out of Investigations as fast as possible. The likely effect on the quality of project plans can readily be imagined. The quality of construction work is affected by the demand for rake-offs and lack of quality control. Add to this the politics of project approval—the exaggeration of expected irrigated area and the concealment of costs to raise the projected benefit/cost ratio high enough—and one has some of the reasons for the recurrent dismay of economists and farmers at the 'poor' performance of canal irrigation projects, in addition to all the factors described above at the O & M stage.

One should be careful, then, about the argument which says: corruption payments make a negligible difference to farmers' incentives, and help to make water allocation work more like a market. All the more should one be sceptical of the argument which says that corruption allows farmers to make government actions more predictable, and hence 'corruption can increase the rate of investment' [*Leff, 1970 (1964): 515*, speaking about the desirable economic effects of bribe payments by businessmen in Less Developed Countries].

There are, however, some points which have to qualify the generally adverse effects noted above. It would certainly be mistaken to advocate merely that corruption payments should be eliminated and the crop zoning pattern strictly followed; for the zoning itself not uncommonly makes no ecological sense. Second, in a political environment where politicians are interested less in long-term development goals than in the disbursement of short-term material benefits to those who support them, the consistent political commitment to irrigation investment, which in some Indian states accounts for over half the state's development budget yet has a gestation period of five to ten years or more, needs explaining. Perhaps the answer has something to do with the way in which irrigation investment *does* provide an abundant stream of short-term material benefits able to be profited from by both politicians and state officials. Thirdly, the elimination of officials' corruption incomes would generate pressures for salary increases, which if financed out of higher taxes would probably worsen income distribution.[49] These points are not intended as a comprehensive qualification of the adverse effects listed earlier, but only as an indication of the complexity of making an overall assessment of the economic effects.

IRRIGATION IN OTHER STATES

Several bits of evidence suggest that the practices described here are not confined to our particular state. A recent enquiry in another southern state indicates a similar mechanism of sale of irrigation posts there.[50] Pant's study of the Kosi canal system in Bihar reports that contractors normally give about 30 per cent of the bill to Supervisors and above, and 10 per cent to office staff; about 10 to 20 per cent they keep as their own profit, leaving only 40 to 50 per cent to be spent on the actual works [*1979: 127*]. The same study reports, without elaboration, 'Postings in places of choice or from non-work (design or investigations) to work units involve transactions of huge amounts of money' [*1979: 128*]. The *Report* of the Santhanam Committee, set up by Government of India to investigate ways of preventing corruption, states:

> We were told by a large number of witnesses that in all contracts of construction, purchase, sales, and other regular business on behalf of the Government, a regular percentage is paid by the parties to the transaction, and this is shared in agreed proportions among the various officials concerned. We were told that in the constructions of the Public Works Department [of which the states' Irrigation Departments are offshoots—RW], seven to eleven per cent was usually paid in this manner . . . . In all cases, failure to pay the percentage results invariably in difficulty and delay in getting the bills paid [*India, Government of, Ministry of Home Affairs, 1964: 10*].

One would expect the precise ways by which engineers raise revenue in O & M posts to depend on such things as crop type, the degree and location of water control made possible by the physical structures, rules for crop zoning (if any), extent of conjunctive use of canal and groundwater, and the character of political competition. The canals of Punjab-Haryana (often taken, mistakenly, to be the typical type of Indian canal in structure and operation) differ from those of the south in several relevant ways [*Reidinger, 1974*]:

(1) Crop zoning ('localization') is not used in the northwest, so the possibility of earning revenue from supplying out-of-zone land does not exist.

(2) There is more conjunctive use of groundwater (by private well) with canal water, so farmers are less dependent on public water supply authorities.

(3) Paddy has traditionally not been grown in the northwest; the main crops do not require such intensive irrigation and their yields are less adversely affected by a (smallish) shortfall of water supply below potential evapo-transpiration level [*Levine, 1977*].

(4) Outlets on the northwestern canals are normally not gated—they are ungated 'proportional modules', which release a discharge proportional to the discharge in the canal, and so at outlet level there is less water control capacity and less scope for discrimination between outlet groups or villages [*Gustafson and Reidinger, 1971*]; in the southern uplands outlets are commonly gated.

(5) On the other hand, the Irrigation Departments in the northwest assess and collect water rates, while this is done by the Revenue Departments in the south.[51]

## POLITICAL DIMENSIONS

It seems likely that long before elective political institutions became important irrigation staff not uncommonly used their power over water and contracts to multiply their own income and that of their bureaucratic superiors [*Krishnaswamy, 1980*]. If so, Marx's dictum, 'There have been in Asia, generally, from immemorial times, but three departments of Government: that of Finance, or the plunder of the interior; that of War, or the plunder of the exterior; and, finally, the department of Public Works' [*1853*], might plausibly have been still more damning. Perhaps the mechanism of public works plunder described here gives hints about the cyclical collapse of reigning dynasties in the hydraulic societies not only of India, but of Egypt, Mesopotamia, and China as well—about the ways by which an increase in bureaucratic corruption was translated into worse maintained canals and dikes, extra unreliability of water supply, and lower production.[52]

However, it is likely that elective institutions have amplified the pressures towards corruption and made it more systematic. Amplification has come especially because of the spiralling cost of fighting elections and nursing a constituency between elections. In our area it is said that a man needs to have at minimum one *lakh* rupees available before it is worth even thinking about contesting an MLA's seat (except perhaps in the case of seats reserved for a Scheduled Caste candidate). Votes are commonly purchased, especially from Low Caste and Scheduled Caste voters (voting within the politically dominant but numerically inferior castes is more likely to follow factional alignments). In the local government elections of 1981, a serious candidate even for village headship (*sarpanch*) would have to reckon on spending something of the order of Rs.30–50,000 in an average-sized village, if the election was contested.[53] And Ministers may have to pay the Chief Minister to get the portfolio they want (which is perhaps part of the reason for the expansion in ministerial portfolios). Money is not the only requirement, of course; favours for supporters must be obtained from the bureaucracy too, but there is no doubt that the rupee price of successful politics is very high.

Politicians have been able to make use of the bureaucracy to help meet the costs of electoral competition. We have seen how they do so in the case of Irrigation; and one would expect that Irrigation would be an especially valuable department to control, not only because it spends big money but also because its decisions greatly affect the political prospects of politicians and the economic prosperity of local communities. However, it is clear (though I shall not go into the matter here) that similar mechanisms operate in other government departments as well, including such apparently 'clean' ones as Agriculture and Labour Welfare.

The transfer is the politicians' basic weapon of control over the bureaucracy, and thus the lever for surplus-extraction from the clients of the bureaucracy. With the transfer weapon not only can the politicians raise money by direct sale; they can also remove someone who is not being responsive enough to their monetary demands or to their requests for favours to those from whom they get money and electoral support—in particular, contractors. One is thus led to visualise a special circuit of transactions, in which the bureaucracy acquires control of funds, partly (in this case) from farmers in the form of variable levies, and partly from the state's public works budget, then passes a portion to MLAs and especially Ministers, who in turn use the funds for distributing short-term material inducements in exchange for electoral support. These funds, it should be noticed, do flow through the public domain (in one sense); but they are neither open to public scrutiny nor available for public expenditure programmes [*Wade, forthcoming*].

This 'transfer model', with its systematic linkage between top-level and bottom-level corruption and between administrative and political corruption, is, I think, quite plausible once spelled out. One wonders whether the processes it describes are not more common in poor countries than its absence from the political science literature would suggest.[54]

POLICY RESPONSES

In the specific context of canal O & M, what should reformers press government to do to improve the situation? One line of solution which appeals to many economists is to institutionalise a market, as with some canals of Spain, Italy, and the United States [*Maass and Anderson, 1978; Wade, 1979*]. But the enforcement problem would be extremely difficult to overcome: Indian canals are typically many times bigger than where water markets are used (500 to 1,000 outlets in a typical canal system) and each outlet irrigates a much bigger area (perhaps 200 acres or more), belonging to many more farmers, who are much more unequal in wealth and power. At present canal managers are not able to deliver a *constant* discharge to each outlet down each distributory, let alone one which varies from outlet to outlet depending on demand. (With bribe or extortion payments, as we have seen, only a limited number of outlets or distributory offtakes need be controlled; the rest can get the residual.) Secondly, where paddy is a major crop, the response time—the time between when farmers ask for water and when it arrives—would have to be very short, because paddy yields fall off sharply if water supply is below potential evapotranspiration; and this would call for very high quality management and communications. Thirdly, in the first season, when canal water supplements rainfall, it is difficult for farmers to know the value of canal water much in advance, so the quantities demanded may fluctuate greatly within short periods depending on rainfall, making main system operation more difficult. Finally, one should remember that nowhere in Asia has volumetric pricing of water been adopted; not even in Taiwan where canal management and water use is said to be much more effective than in India [*Levine, 1977*].

A second line of solution is to inspect, audit, check and double-check the Irrigation Department, by giving the Indian Administrative Service more control over it and by giving stronger powers to the Anti-Corruption Bureau and Vigilance Cell; these measures would be coupled with stricter definition of the rights and duties of officials, and stronger complaints procedures before a strengthened Administrative Tribunal. Suffice it to say that this is a familiar direction of administrative reform in India, especially popular in the eyes of Indian Administrative Service officers; but on its own it is unlikely to make matters better and may make matters worse—a stronger Administrative Tribunal, for example, would quite possibly be engulfed in a mass of litigation which the Indian judicial process is ill-equipped to handle.

A third line of solution seems more promising. It would attempt to strengthen the user side of the irrigator-official relation, both by the familiar device of user organisation—councils of irrigators covering 20 or so villages, or a Section, for example—*and* by monitoring of the performance of each canal system by an independent monitoring organisation whose reports would be made public [*Wade, 1980a, 1982a; Seckler, 1981*]. Aerial or satellite photography could help to make the monitoring objective. Opportunities for the exercise of 'voice', if coupled with a non-partisan source of information, could be much more effective in curbing the arbitrary exercise of authority than the record of government-sponsored 'cooperatives' in India would lead one to expect.

This strengthening of the user side might be supplemented by two other sorts of measures, one of which has to do with the work motivation of canal managers. It is difficult to see how a closer link can be made between conscientious effort and reward than exists at present, especially because promotion and salary rules cannot be altered for the Irrigation Department as long as canals are run by civil servants, because of civil service parity issues. But at least canal managers can be given a clearer notion of what they should be doing by means of professional training—a training which should include not only engineering and agronomy but also management science, and which should aim to foster the development of an ethos of professional service around O & M work. At present, operational skills and professional norms in our state are so weak that the training prescription—often as ineffective a prescription for bureaucratic improvement as it is familiar—does seem pertinent in this particular case.

The other measure is technical: to build many more 'on-line' reservoirs along the length of a canal system, to provide storage intermediate between dam and fields. They would be filled according to a pre-determined, well-advertised schedule, and irrigators would themselves have more responsibility for allocating water to the fields (as they now do under 'tanks'). This solution is constrained by ecological and economic factors (for example, the cost of land acquisition); but arguments in its favour on engineering grounds are clearly reinforced by the argument of this paper.

Clearly though, one of the main reasons for the illicit payments system lies outside the irrigation sector, and reform of irrigation will be difficult without also reform of electoral competition. This is *not* to say that politicians should be prevented from interfering in irrigation—economists and others are too prone to accept at face value the engineers' own definition of political interference as a problem; merely to exclude politicians would in many cases expose irrigators to even worse extortion than they face at present. Nevertheless, some check on the cost of electoral competition would clearly be desirable. Electoral reform proposals in India have generally been based on the argument that India cannot afford such expensive elections, while the widespread ramifications of the politicians' drive to raise revenue have been inadequately recognised. Yet just because these ramifications are so wide, it is difficult to talk of electoral reform in isolation, without also talking of the need for political rejuvenation by means of one or more mass parties able to insist upon performance standards from the bureaucracy.[55]

## NOTES

1. I assume a canal managed 'above the outlet' by a government department or parastatal agency, and 'below the outlet' by farmers, such as is normal throughout Asia for all but very small systems (say, less than 5,000 hectares irrigated area). I have applied this same dual perspective to irrigation in South Korea, in a way that encompasses both the technical characteristics of irrigation systems in that environment and, at the other extreme, the role of the bureaucracy in South Korea's rapid industrialisation [*Wade, 1982*]. For a comparison of South Korean and south Indian irrigation, which provides more detail on technical and organisational aspects of the south Indian case, see Wade [*1981a*]. For an analysis of the relevance of climate for understanding variations in irrigation institutions (including the incidence of corruption) see Wade [*1981b*].
2. Note the absence of such connections in two major works on corruption, Scott [*1972*] and Heidenheimer's selection of 58 readings [*1970*].

3. It proved difficult to get detailed information on such matters, though I tried at several points in the Irrigation Department. To the best of my knowledge, there is no organisation chart for the Department. The headquarters in the state capital has no information at all on how many field staff are employed throughout the state, and its aggregate information on number of employees above field staff level is, for AE and EE level, out of date and in any case available only for each rank as a whole, not broken into functional categories.

4. The figure excludes clerical staff, who may number about 50. The variation in staff numbers is less than in irrigated area, partly because Divisions with a relatively small irrigated area may be given more tank maintenance responsibilities, and partly because the crop zoning results in some canals having their irrigated area spread out in scattered non-contiguous blocks, with a relatively high ratio of channel length to irrigated area; such canals will need a higher density of staff per 10,000 irrigated acres.

5. I have checked the argument by presenting it in detail to two engineers, with experience in different parts of the state and of very different rank. I have also presented it in detail to an Indian economist long familiar with the state and its politics (his brother is closely involved in state and national politics). At the same time, it should be said that a few people from the sub-continent who have heard the paper in seminar have felt deeply affronted by the argument, and are not convinced it is not a tissue of exaggeration and half-truths. 'How many engineers did you interview, what percentage of them were corrupt?', they wanted to know. I hope that the earlier discussion shows why these questions are difficult to answer and why it is nevertheless worth making the argument.

6. The figure taken for irrigated area may be several years out of date—in 1980 the figure for 1974/75 was still being used.

7. One engineer said the division varies from half and half to one-third to contractor and two-thirds to officers; a retired engineer who since retirement had worked as a consultant to contractors said half and half was usual.

8. Even the formal stipulated procedures for quality control in the Irrigation Department are very weak—weaker than, for example, in the Roads and Buildings Department.

9. On big construction projects the percentage may well be lower. Over the summer of 1981 a Commission of Enquiry has been hearing evidence on the causes of the rupture of the Barna Dam, in Madhya Pradesh. A contractor has filed an affidavit alleging that contractors have to hand over 15 per cent of the contract value to the officers.

10. The percentage fluctuates, because increases in the maintenance grant and in field staff salaries do not occur at the same time.

11. It must be made clear that no engineer told me directly how much he was making. The income figures (as for the AE figures later) are arrived at indirectly, in the EE case from the size of the works budget, plus informants' statements about the way it is divided up. The income inferences can then be compared with what informants say about the price of posts (in specific instances, and in general). One can then see to what extent the figures tally.

12. This is the mid-point in the range, after the 1978 revision. The figure includes a cost-of-living allowance (Dearness Allowance) and a housing allowance.

13. In the case of big contracts, the *SE* is the payer of bills.

14. 'Speed' money is of course one of the oldest and most familiar forms of corruption. *The Northern India Patrika*, 30 July, 1981, reports that an EE of the Public Health Department of Uttar Pradesh was caught taking a Rs.1,000 bribe from a contractor; the contractor had complained to the Collector that the EE was demanding the bribe in return for paying a Rs.40,000 bill, and a trap was set up. Note that the bribe amounted to $2\frac{1}{2}$ per cent, the same as our EEs are said to get on 'savings on the estimates'.

    The speed money (as well as other types of payment which alter the allocation of benefits) is increasingly in the form of consumer durables. Krishnaswamy reports that a businessman told him that 'officials who have to pass bills ask for domestic durables to be purchased on the installment system in their names' [*1980*].

15. One EE related that he had been transferred early from being in charge of construction of a medium project for refusing to alter the accounts of a big contractor who turned out to have more influence with the Minister than he thought. Into his place was promoted his own AE, who though next in line for promotion would not usually have been given such a big responsibility immediately; but he had already demonstrated to the contractor his willingness to comply. Of course the Department could always argue that the AE's

experience with the project suggested he could proceed faster than could an older EE brought in from outside.

16. My guess is that on the coastal deltas the EE commonly is more actively involved in raising money from the *ayacut*, and that he has more direct ways of sharing in it than is the case on upland canals. If so, this might help explain why delta posts tend to be more 'expensive' (see below).

17. Biplab Dasgupta suggests (personal communication) that in many West Bengal villages such village-wide organisation would be difficult to achieve because of the greater degree of class-based organisation within villages than is normally the case in our state.

18. Occasionally incautious contractors are caught with huge sums of money on their hands, and such incidents may get small bylines in the press. For example, on 19 July 1980, *The Hindu* noted that the Income Tax Department had seized Rs.34 *lakh* from the residence of a contractor who owed even more in income tax arrears, plus another Rs.1$\frac{1}{2}$ *lakh* from the residence of a clerk of a private engineering college which bore the same name as the name of the contractor (the contractor comes from an adjacent state where private colleges have been permitted). I thank Jeremy Jackson for this reference.

19. These factors are relevant to variation over time and place within any canal command area. There is also variation between canals, especially between canals on the uplands and on the coastal deltas. Delta farmers tend to be prepared to pay more. When delta farmers come to the uplands (buying a bigger area with the proceeds of the sale of their delta land) they continue to be more willing to pay the irrigation staff—they become the 'price leaders'.

A further qualification: Although the zoning of land for irrigation ('localisation') is intended to be once-and-for-all, some flexibility is permitted—villages can have their water rights changed. Such desired changes may well have to be paid for, and obtaining them may entail several trips by village representatives to the state capital, as well as to the Division and Sub-division offices. Their price would normally be several times the price of a one-season assurance; and even if the villagers are prepared to pay this sort of amount their request may not be granted.

20. The cross-bund increases the discharge through the sluice, thus reducing what is available for lower-down sluices.

21. This case occurred in 1977. The village was near a tail-end, so could be easily discriminated against; it had few families of the dominant caste of the region; and was clearly in the poorest quarter of villages in the district.

22. He actually said that rumour-mongering is one of the tricks of being a field staffer (banker or foreman); senior engineers are quite prepared to admit, in general terms, that the 'lower down fellows' accept bribes.

23. If the farmers lose confidence in the willingness or ability of a Supervisor or AE to deliver on promises, and also think him 'weak kneed', they will be more likely to resort to breaking the structures, by-passing the irrigation hierarchy. This checks the extent to which the officers can promise without delivering.

24. One engineer said there is what he called a 'vicious circle' between engineers and politicians: 'The engineer gives more water to the lands of a politician, that fellow obliges at the time of transfer'.

25. Assume conservatively that the wet season paddy area, about 160,000 acres or so, pays 1 kg/ac, and assume, as in the village where I lived, that each village gives about one-third to the Supervisor and AE, and two-thirds to the foremen and bankers who directly serve it. Then over the whole canal, if the 330 or so field staff divide the collections equally, they will each get about 320 kgs of paddy (which can be roughly valued at Rs.1.2 per kg), compared to a monthly salary of between Rs.300 and 700. Each Supervisor and AE will get roughly 2,000 kg (if they share equally—in practice the AE would get more, the Supervisor less), compared to an AE's average monthly salary of about Rs.1,900, and less for Supervisor. The plausibility of the assumptions is strengthened by the absence of rags-to-riches stories amongst field staff, and by the fact that the grain payments do not arouse anything like the same resentment amongst farmers that the money payments sometimes do (depending on what the payments are for, as well as on their level). In the dry season the grain payments are less common, less institutionalised, more at the discretion of individual households; and more of the dry season irrigated area is under non-food crops.

26. Rs.2,400,000 × 5% × 25% (to reduce to a Sub-division basis) × 50%.

27. See notes 11 and 12.
28. However, in states where private engineering colleges are now permitted, very large fees for a place in a private college are now common; and authorisation of private education in engineering and medicine is being opposed in some states by people who argue that the graduates of such colleges who get jobs in the public sector will have a strong incentive to recoup the fee on the job, perhaps in illicit ways.

    For some years in the late 1960s and first half of the 1970s the supply of graduates and diploma-holders wanting to join the Irrigation Department exceeded the expansion of places, and it is said that joining payments *did* then have to be made. The engineers of whom I speak all joined before this time.
29. The strategy varies from case to case depending on a whole range of factors, such as the political complexion at the place to which the engineer wishes to go, and the engineer's own 'influence'. What follows is a typical pattern, as I understand it.
30. I ignore the complication that (since the early 1970s) there are Ministers for each of Major Irrigation, Medium Irrigation and Minor Irrigation, and several Secretaries for different parts of Irrigation; one Minister and one Secretary are clearly senior to the others. I shall also ignore the role of the Secretary (who is an Indian Administrative Service officer) in the following discussion. I further ignore the distinction between members of the state legislature and members of the national legislature.
31. Two qualifications: If he can, the EE may take a very influential man with him to see the Minister, someone to whom the Minister will find it difficult to say no. This will help the negotiations. Second, on big construction projects the CE is in charge of several Circles, and is the sanctioning authority for EE transfers *within* this set of Circles.
32. This, at least, is how the engineers understand the matter—though given that political parties tend to be weak as corporate organisations, the distinction between personal use and party war-chests may not be sharp.
33. Normally only the one or two most powerful MLAs will be visited, though six or seven or more may have significant parts of their constituencies irrigated by the canal. In the state in which this study is set, the local government structure (*zilla parishad, panchayat samithi,* village *panchayat*) was more or less moribund from 1970 to 1981. In states where elective local government structures function, people like the *samithi* president may also be involved in transfers as well as the local MLAs.
34. Some Superintending Engineer posts on the deltas cost 12–15 *lakhs* (for what is normally a two-year term of office), or 38–48 times the average annual SE salary. Three specific posts are known to cost in this range, all within the area considered to be the nerve centre of state politics. It is common knowledge that the incumbents of these posts can 'make millions'. Building sumptuous retirement houses is a favourite use of the profits—a use much facilitated by engineers' privileged access to scarce cement at below free market prices. (One reason why engineers like canal-lining programmes is because, as one said, cement is a gold mine'.)
35. The relative authority of the CE and SE depends on whether the transfer is inter- or intra-Circle.
36. Three complications: In some areas there is a big farmer-contractor who, in the selection of the MLA, is known as the kingmaker; the AE may well visit him. Second, where excess water from an upland canal runs into a coastal reservoir, the MLAs and Ministers under that reservoir can have a distinct interest in having an AE who is sympathetic to their needs at the critical point of the upland canal where the amount of 'excess' is determined. In this way, interest in what goes on in one watershed is by no means confined to the people and politicians of that watershed, so the patterns of influence can be spatially quite complex. Third, the local MLA may be of different party, or different faction, to the Minister, and this again leads to more complex patterns of influence.
37. This figure comes from a canal where the EE's post cost about one *lakh* in the late 1970s; where the price of the EE's post is higher one would expect the payment to MLAs to be higher also. If however the man is of unusual influence he may not pay the MLAs—'they have to come to him, he does not have to go to them', said one informant describing an actual case. In this case, although the man had a great deal of influence—'he had four Ministers on his side'—he still had to pay a lot of money to get the post, but the payment went to senior officers, not to the Minister or MLAs.

38. It is said that if an AE wants to stay in the same place and in order to do so has to transfer to a separate Circle, he sometimes has to pay the SE of his own Circle, especially if it is an O & M Circle, for *release*.
39. They can appeal to the Administrative Tribunal, to which all service disputes relating to government employees may be referred; but the procedure is bothersome and the Tribunal's decision is not binding on the government, so it is little used by irrigation staff.
40. 'In the Food for Work programmes, inflated muster rolls with fictitious names, utilisation of foodgrain for purchase of crockery and furniture and upkeep of government buildings have come to light' [*Krishnaswamy, 1980*].
41. The three Supervisors who came in the first half of 1981 all reputedly had to pay this amount.
42. Well over 100 AEs found themselves having to take compulsory one-month holidays in order to share out the shortfall of posts, and presumably (since the normal ratio of Supervisors to AEs is 4:1) well over 400 Supervisors. Occasional imbalances between the supply and demand for staff must be normal in any big construction organisation, and one wonders how they are handled in irrigation departments elsewhere in the world.
43. Hence farmers commonly do not want gates on their sluices, because if the sluices are ungated it is more difficult for the staff to cut off their water. On the other hand, farmers in tail-end locations *do* want upstream sluices to be gated, so that they can be closed and more water sent down to them. This sort of divergence between what irrigators want for themselves and what they want for the rest of the system is a fundamental feature of canal irrigation.
44. One has sympathy where the farmers could grow some crop other than paddy. But in some areas which are not zoned for paddy the land is too saturated by seepage from the canal, or from (zoned) paddy areas higher up, to grow any other crop; which reflects poor zoning, and failure to provide adequate drainage. In this case the engineers have much less justification.
45. A few engineers who reach SE or CE rank still find intolerable the pressures to be corrupt, to do a mediocre job and to keep quiet in the face of wrongdoing, and simply retire early. One SE appointed to a big new World Bank-aided project was appalled at the poor standard of design and construction, and said openly at meetings of engineers and senior government officials that if the minor distributories had been properly designed and constructed in the first place, the large amounts now having to be spent to upgrade them would have been unnecessary. He was harrassed so fiercely by his colleagues (it is said) that he retired early. I know at least one CE who did the same, for similar reasons. Both men were outstandingly talented and dynamic, and one suspects such people are more likely to take this course, depleting the Irrigation Department of a potential internal constituency for reform.
46. Collectors average less than two years in a place before being transferred. A correspondent, chiding me for not giving the Collector a central place in the checking mechanism, writes:
    It is the Collector that would normally be expected to control the system. In some states he is very, very powerful—for instance in Maharashtra. It seems to me that his interests are overwhelmingly in *not* letting corruption get out of hand; the risk to him, if he is seen to knave at it, is enormous [loss of career and disgrace], and the gains from taking bribes himself are relatively small in this light.
    This is not my impression for the area I know; especially because of the distinction between what the Collector's interests are, and what he is able to do.
47. Betterment Levy is a levy on the increase in land values which the bringing of land under command is expected to result in.
48. This difference in the 'partial equilibrium' and 'general equilibrium' effects of the corrupt system in irrigation is similar to the probable effects of 'speed money' in the bureaucracy as a whole. Speed money, if common, probably has the effect of slowing down the overall work performance of the bureaucracy, as officials cut back their work effort in order to invite the payment of bribes, by means of which individuals are able to accelerate officials' effort from this reduced level to deal with their particular cases.
49. This holds because the higher taxes would likely fall on items of mass consumption, while bribery and extortion payments come disproportionately from the landed.
50. An agricultural economist with detailed knowledge of a large irrigation canal in the uplands of another southern state, to whom I put questions similar to those addressed in this paper, replied as follows:

An AE working in the investigations or dam can get transfers in the canals by paying some amount or directly by political pressures through MLAs and then through concerned ministers. The money to be paid will be ranging from Rs.5,000 to 10,000 normally, depending upon the exact location in the canal system. In [his state], the political pressure is more dominant than direct influence through officials . . . . The staff in general are actually watching the vacancy position in different places and then get their transfer by giving money directly or through political pressures.

Normally money is given by the farmers for certain benefits. The money thus received is invested in purchase of real estates in different places, purchase of lands for cultivation, starting up of business shops like fertiliser and pesticide shops where the engineers can control a sizeable number of farmers for the business. Most of the investments will be in the wives' names only, so as to avoid any legal complications if any one complains of malpractices in the canal system . . . . The engineers are normally getting more in kind and they will dispose of them through close businessmen for cash.

The figures he gives for AE transfers to canal O & M are lower than the orders of magnitude under our canals; but still come to a quarter to a half of an AE's average annual salary. And as far as one can judge, the basic mechanism is the same.

51. A British ex-Chief Engineer in Punjab related (personal communication, 1976) that prior to Independence his field staff used to make money with a pile of bricks: they would place the pile next to an outlet, the farmers came running with money to prevent 'remodernisation' (effectively, narrowing the outlet), and the pile was moved on to the next village or sluice, and so on; the next incumbent of the post repeated the procedure.

52. See, for example, Ch'ang Hu [1955]. The scale of corruption in the Yellow River Administration in China during the eighteenth and nineteenth centuries dwarfs the scale described here for a south Indian state. Ch'ang Hu reports that the YRA received about 10 per cent of the central state's total budget, and that 'hardly one tenth of the regular and extraordinary appropriations was spent for actual water conservancy' [512]. He quotes a top civil servant writing in 1812, 'The important river works are manipulated as a means of political favoritism, and treasury funds are either squandered or used as bribes; hence the river officials have become fops and dandies, while the sites of river work have become places of flower and wine' [510]. Ch'ang Hu links the decreasing effectiveness of the YRA directly to the collapse of the Ch'ing dynasty.

53. The figures in this paragraph come from conversations with farmers and others in the study area.

54. I am preparing a paper on the 'transfer' model which discusses it in a more general, non-irrigation-specific context.

55. International development agencies potentially have a role in reducing the mismanagement of development projects. But at present the official position of both the agencies and the recipient governments is that the agencies are to concern themselves with increasing the inputs to development, while it is for the host government to worry about the outputs from development projects. Indeed, there is perhaps no subject in the international development community so sensitive and suppressed as the mismanagement of development programmes (an observation for which I thank David Seckler).

## REFERENCES

Ali, H., 1980, 'Practical experience of irrigation reform, India', Institute of Development Studies *Discussion Paper* No. 153, September.

Anderson, E. and P., 1967, *Political Institutions and Social Change in Continental Europe in the Nineteenth Century*, Berkeley: University of California Press, pp. 166–67, 206–19, 230–35. Reprinted in Heidenheimer, 1970.

Andreski, S., 1968, 'Kleptocracy or corruption as a system of government', in *The African Predicament*, New York: Atherton. Reprinted in Heidenheimer, 1970.

Bailey, F.G., 1957, *Caste and the Economic Frontier: A Village in Highland Orissa*, Manchester University Press.

Bayley, D., 1966, 'The effects of corruption in a developing nation', *Western Political Quarterly*, XIX(4). Reprinted in Heidenheimer, 1970.

Ch'ang Hu, 1955, 'The Yellow River Administration in the Ch'ing Dynasty', *Far Eastern Quarterly*, 14.

Epstein, T., 1962, *Economic Development and Cultural Change in South India*, Manchester University Press.

Gustafson, W. and R. Reidinger, 1971, 'Delivery of canal water in North India and West Pakistan', *Economic and Political Weekly* (Bombay), 6(50): A-157-162.

Heidenheimer, A., 1970, *Political Corruption: Readings in Comparative Analysis*, New York: Holt, Rinehart and Winston.

India, Government of, Ministry of Home Affairs, 1964, *Report of the Commission on the Prevention of Corruption* ('Santhanam Report'), New Delhi.

India, Government of, Ministry of Irrigation and Power, National Irrigation Commission, 1972, *Report* (4 vols.).

Krishnaswamy, S., 1980, 'Wide range of corruption', *The Hindu*, 30 August.

Leff, N., 1964, 'Economic development through bureaucratic corruption', *American Behavioral Scientist*, 8(3). Reprinted in Heidenheimer, 1970.

Levine, G., 1977, 'Management components in irrigation system design and operation', *Agricultural Administration*, Vol. 4, No. 1.

Levine, G., L. Chin, and S. Miranda, 1976, 'Requirements for the successful introduction and management of rotational irrigation', *Agricultural Water Management*, Vol. 1.

Maass, A. and R. Anderson, 1978, '... and the Desert Shall Rejoice: Conflict, Growth, and Justice in Arid Environments', Cambridge: MIT Press.

Marx, K., 1853, 'The British rule in India', reprinted in *Karl Marx and Frederick Engels, Selected Works*, Vol. One, Moscow: Progress Publishers, 1969.

Pant, N., 1979, 'Some aspects of irrigation administration (a case study of Kosi project)', mimeo, A.N.S. Institute of Social Studies, Patna, Bihar.

Ram, M., 1981, 'Ferreting out the black money', *Far Eastern Economic Review*, 6 Feb.

Reidinger, R., 1974, 'Institutional rationing of canal water in Northern India: conflict between traditional patterns and modern needs', *Economic Development and Cultural Change*, 23(1).

Scott, J., 1972, *Comparative Political Corruption*, Englewood Cliffs: Prentice-Hall.

Seckler, D., 1981, 'The new era of irrigation management in India', mimeo, Ford Foundation, New Delhi.

Shamasastry, R., 1967(1915), *Kautilya's Arthasastra*, Mysore: Mysore Printing and Publishing House.

Swart, K.W., 1949, *Sale of Offices in the Seventeenth Century*, The Hague: Martinus Nijhoff, pp. 112-127. Reprinted in Heidenheimer, 1970.

Wade, R., 1975, 'Water to the fields: India's changing strategy', *South Asian Review*, 8(4). Reprinted in E.W. Coward (ed.), 1980, *Irrigation and Agricultural Development in Asia: Perspectives from the Social Sciences*, Ithaca, N.Y.: Cornell University Press.

Wade, R., 1979, 'Collective responsibility in construction and management of irrigation canals: case of Italy', *Economic and Political Weekly*, Review of Agriculture, Vol. XIV, Nos. 51 & 52, Dec. 22-29.

Wade, R., 1980, 'Substituting management for water in canal irrigation: a South Indian case', *Economic and Political Weekly* (Bombay), Vol. XV, No. 52, Review of Agriculture, 27 Dec.

Wade, R., 1980a, 'Water users' associations: sociological principles and government practice', mimeo, Institute of Development Studies, University of Sussex.

Wade, R., 1981, 'The information problem of South Indian irrigation canals', *Water Supply and Management*, 5.

Wade, R., 1981a, 'Employment, water control and irrigation institutions: canal irrigation in South India and South Korea', paper prepared for the Asian Regional Team for Employment Promotion (ARTEP), International Labour Office, Bangkok.

Wade, R., 1981b, 'Climate and irrigation institutions', mimeo, Institute of Development Studies, University of Sussex.

Wade, R., forthcoming, 'The politics and economics of India's state accumulation policy: review of J. Toye, *Public Expenditure and Indian Development Policy 1960-1970'*, *Economic Development and Cultural Change*.

Wade, R., 1982, *Irrigation and Agricultural Politics in South Korea*, Boulder: Westview Press.

Wade, R., 1982a, 'The World Bank and India's irrigation reform', *Journal of Development Studies*, Vol. 18, No. 2.

Wade, R. and R. Chambers, 1980, 'Managing the main system: canal irrigation's blind spot', *Economic and Political Weekly* (Bombay), Vol. 15, No. 39, Review of Agriculture.

Weber, M., 1968, *Economy and Society: An Outline of Interpretive Sociology,* Vol. III, New
    York: Bedminster Press.
Wertheim, W., 1963, 'Sociological aspects of corruption in Southeast Asia', *Sociologica
    Neerlandica,* 1(2). Reprinted in Heidenheimer, 1970.

# ORGANISATION OF PRODUCTION
# AND EXCHANGE

# The Theory of the Optimising Peasant[1]

## By Michael Lipton*

'Peasant conservatism' is out. Economists of under-developed countries are beginning to realise that the farmer is no fool. A non-fool, in a static environment, learns to live 'efficiently': to optimise, given his values and constraints, and to teach his children to do the same. Moreover, food-grain output per worker has stagnated, secularly, in many poor countries;[2] that seems to support Professor Schultz's startling conclusion that underdeveloped agricultural com-munities — not just the individual farmers — are 'efficient but poor' (p. 38).[3] Each farmer, by maximising utility, prevents 'any major inefficiency in the allocation of tradi-tional factors' (p. 39).

Schultz's policy conclusion is that 'no appreciable in-crease in agricultural production is to be had by reallocating the factors at the disposal of farmers who are bound by the traditional agriculture' (p. 39). This follows from individual utility-maximisation only under perfect competition. In particular, a perfect market in factors and products must exist, and each farmer must be able to predict, with rea-sonable confidence, the outcome of each array of production, consumption and sale decisions at his disposal.

Schultz's two main sources of evidence are shot through with perfect competition: Dr. Hopper implicitly, Professor Tax explicitly. Thus Hopper: 'Are *the people* of Senapur realising the full economic potential of *their* physical re-sources ? *From the point of view of the villagers, the answer must be 'yes' for* in general *each man comes close to doing the best that*

---

* The author is Reader in Economics, University of Sussex, and Fellow of the Institute of Development Studies.

*he can* with his knowledge and cultural background' (pp. 45-6, my italics). This follows for 'the villagers', from individual optimisation, only under perfect competition. And Tax's Guatemalan '*market*... tends *to be perfectly competitive*' (p. 43, his italics).

With what sort of perfect competition are we dealing? Not, apparently, with linear-programming (LP) with fixed proportions in each activity and factor substitutions possible only by shifting activities. Schultz's thesis is to be tested, we are told, by the truth or falsity of its 'implications', and a key implication is that 'no productive factor remains unemployed' (p. 40). This implication does not follow in LP. In product-space, we may optimise at a vertex *on an axis*. Hopper's model appears to have only four constraints (land, labour, irrigation-water, bullock-time) and four activities (barley, wheat, peas, grass: p. 46). If it were reinterpreted in LP terms, an axis-vertex optimum would thus be extremely likely. Then at least one factor constraint is not binding, and at least one factor is not fully employed. If that factor is labour, it has zero marginal product — a hypothesis that Schultz spends a chapter in refuting (pp. 53-70).[1]

In any case an LP recasting of Hopper's evidence scarcely supports the 'efficient but poor' hypothesis. Reallocation of factors in Senapur, implies Hopper, could raise foodgrain output 10 per cent, without more inputs or loss of other outputs[5] — suggesting substantial 'inefficiency'. Incidentally, it is no disparagement of Hopper's pioneering work to point out that he omits some inputs. If he had measured (and priced) a key input — dung — his conclusions might have been very different.[6]

So Schultz is arguing for something close to neo-classical perfect competition (NCPC): neo-classical because the LP assumption of fixed factor proportions contradicts his own (and the LP evidence does not support his conclusions), perfect competition because otherwise his individual equilibria cannot add up to a social optimum. Agriculture, as a textbook paradigm of NCPC,[7] initially referred to advanced, temperate, monetised and literate agricultures.[8] Can NCPC be applied to underdeveloped, climatically uncertain, subsistence, largely illiterate farming communities? If the peasant in traditional agricultures is a NCPC-optimiser, he must allocate productive factors so as to *equate the marginal value-product of money* in each use.

Some economists with experience of underdeveloped countries have reacted vehemently against the theory of marginal value-product equalisation (hereafter MVPE). They suggest that it is a wicked attempt to retard growth in order to appease free enterprise dogmatism.[9] Right or wrong, MVPE needs a fuller treatment. Some of its supporters — not Professor Schultz, with his pleas for vast extension of State educational provision[10] — may delude themselves that MVPE is a laissez-faire weapon against creeping socialism; but it is the opposite.

MVPE is a doctrine of revolutionary pessimism. Private enterprise has done its best with the old factors, says this doctrine; but, as we know, the result is secular stagnation. For cultivators have not, of their own volition, introduced new factors on a big scale. The new factors needed — irrigation, education — are huge and indivisible; initial capital costs lie beyond the biggest private cultivator; pay-offs are too long-term to be financed by private loan capital; benefits are too diffused, in space and time, to be recoverable by the providers through betterment levies. Thus MVPE implies massive State intervention as a necessary condition for agricultural progress in underdeveloped countries. This writer, while accepting the implication, rejects MVPE.

Opponents of MVPE should thank Professor Schultz for a lucid, non-tautologous and testable statement of his case. That a peasant maximises utility — i.e. does what he wants to do, under the given constraints — is a tedious tautology. Or Schultz might have made his thesis, efficient use of existing factors, tautologous by redefining any improvement in factor allocation as a new technology — or (as when dung becomes compost) as a new factor. Short of tautology, the thesis could have been weakened into unexceptionable dullness. Schultz does not waste time asserting the truism that some incentives affect some farmers; the evidence against the backward-sloping supply curve was needed only by remaining True Believers in subsistence mentality (who, however, will not be swayed by mere evidence).[11] Again, nobody seriously believes that, after centuries of experience, peasant communities can suddenly be taught, by visiting experts, how to double output without increasing any input. But Schultz has not merely advanced a dull tautology, demonstrated that peasants wish to live better, or rejected the wilder claims of the office agronomists. MVPE, the assertion that under-developed cultivators are 'efficient but poor', is interesting because it is extreme. The following arguments try to show that it is mistaken.[12]

(a) Owing to rainfall variability, there is no unique marginal physical product (MPP) associated with any factor (for given inputs of all other factors), but only a probability-distribution of MPPs. By acting as if he used the calculus of expected values, an optimising peasant can nevertheless find a long-run profit-maximising algorithm analogous to MVPE. However, in the non-equatorial tropics, rainfall variance is much higher than in most temperate agricultures, so that — for rainfall and hence for MPPs — expected value is a much poorer predictor of actual value. In particular, the smaller is mean rainfall, the greater is the coefficient of variability.

The greater the *impact* of future rainfall upon optimal policy, the smaller is *knowledge* of that rainfall, and the likelier is MVPE to lead to disaster. In two senses, therefore, MVPE has dubious logical status. First, policy is critically dependent on information of which the tropical peasant is deprived in direct proportion to its importance. Second, MVPE for expected values is necessarily a long-run sequential algorithm (as it is not under certainty). Compared with a lower-mean, lower-variance policy, MVPE substantially reduces its practitioner's prospects of surviving to complete the sequence. The more 'underdeveloped' the peasant, the stronger are both objections to the logic of MVPE.

(b) Assuming away this logical problem, and allowing all uncertainty to be reducible to risk, MVPE is possible; but it is not optimal, even for the individual cultivator. He requires risk premium, and the risk is abnormally large owing to the high rainfall variance, and of an abnormally severe outcome, starvation. Utility maximisation can allow for some trade-off between variance and expected profit; MVPE cannot. The constraints or weighting required by such a trade-off, even for a utility-maximiser, ought to be unacceptable to Schultz. His evidence (Hopper, Tax) is relevant only to simple profit maximisation. His policy conclusion — that State measures, from forward pricing (applauded on p. 14) to collectivisation, could scarcely improve allocation of existing factors — also cannot survivea probabilistic, utility-maximising reformulation of MVPE.

(c) Even under certainty, imperfect factor markets (especially for land and, in India, for labour) render it impossible, even secularly, for a utility-maximiser to acquire that set of factors allowing him to approximate as closely to profit maximisation as his utility function allows. The role of taste in determining which crops are grown, different degrees of aversion to labour, different access to free supplies of otherwise scarce factors (e.g. dung), and the unification of production and consumption decisions, combine to render this discrepancy especially serious to MVPE.

(d) Even if factor markets were perfect, inter-farm differences in output from identical inputs, and hence thc likelihood that any apparent maximising behaviour results from 'cancelling errors', would still be greatest in underdeveloped agricultures: partly because of differing assets and hence trade-offs between risk and profit, but mainly owing to the fact that some farmers' economic behaviour is trammelled by constraints — hereditary job allocation, land inheritance rules — that prevent the full expression of economic rationality.

(e) The *secular* constancy of environment in underdeveloped countries, needed for learning any optimising algorithm, has been disrupted by population growth and (much less) by development planning. Added to the disruption of *annual* constancy by high rainfall variance, this suggests that an optimising peasant seeks survival algorithms, not maximising ones. Different peasants learn, and stick to, different algorithms. This hypothesis accords with peasants' descriptions of their own conduct and explains the wide inter-farm differences in the use of similar bundles of resources. MVPE does neither.

(f) In an underdeveloped agriculture, with all its risks and market imperfections, assume that each peasant adopts MVPE and that it maximises the constrained utility function of *each*. The adoption of MVPE by each would still not be optimal for *all*. A planner would reject MVPE in

favour of factor allocations allowing for risk, for the effect
of income distribution and monopoly on relative prices,
for inter-farm differences in reinvestment rates, and for
economies of scale to the plot. Even if prices were the only
variables directly altered by the planner, these aims would
not, in general, be best approximated by setting Langean
MVPE price-relatives.

In brief, MVPE is (a) impossible under true uncertainty;
(b) even if uncertainty were reducible to risk, not optimal
for the peasant; (c) even under certainty, especially diver-
gent from utility-maximisation in the imperfect factor markets
of underdeveloped agriculture; (d) even with certainty and
perfect factor markets, impeded by the framework of custom
and law, and demonstrably not adopted; (e) dependent on
the untenable assumption of a static environment; (f) socially
inefficient even if privately optimal. Evidence for assertions
(a)-(f) is provided in sections II to VII, mainly from
Indian experience.

## II

If climatic uncertainty prevails, no resource has a unique
marginal physical product (MPP) in any use. Instead there
is a probability-distribution of MPPs over states of nature.
If price variability is independent of the climate on a particular farmer's land, so that MPPs can stand proxy for
MVPs, the policy corresponding to MVPE (long-run profit
maximisation) is to equate the marginal-to-expected value-
productivity of money in each use.[13] Call this policy MEVPE.

There seems to be no periodicity in yearly rainfall data,
however local, in monsoon India.[14] At sowing time, therefore, the best estimate of this season's rainfall, $R_s$, is $E(R)$,
the average of seasonal rainfall over the longest period for
which data are available. However, the smaller $E(R)$,
the greater (i) the impact of $R_s$ on this season's output, (ii)
the coefficient of variability of $R_s$,[15] and hence (iii) the unreliability of $E(R)$ as an estimate of $R_s$. Hence, the greater
the impact of R on optimal choice of factor allocations and
amounts, the less accurately can $R_s$ be predicted. MEVPE,
therefore, has certain purely logical limitations in the highly
variable climates of monsoon Asia.[16]

First, the less $E(R)$, the more likely is an *ex ante* rational policy of MEVPE to be regretted *ex post*. MEVPE asks the farmer to learn from experience, but not to learn the dangers of learning from experience. Since MEVPE maximises profit only in the very long run, this is particularly serious.

Second, the putative long-run maximiser in India and Pakistan is usually a small farmer, with few grain stocks. In extreme cases, long-run MEVPE farmers are dead in the short run, if their risky experiments meet a low $\dfrac{R_s}{E(R)}$ in the early years. Much more often, this forces sale of land. Small wonder that farmers choose less risky (if ultimately less 'profitable') procedures.[17] MEVPE maximises only in the very long run; yet it shortens the probable 'run' over which the would-be maximiser owns, and hence derives benefit from, his factors of production. This blend is logically odd.

The root of the trouble is that MEVPE, in face of variable climate, yields predictions of rainfall which become less accurate as they become more important (i.e. as $E(R)$ falls). At sowing time, the peasant must employ (or imply employment of) most factor inputs; $E(R)$ is his best estimate of $R_s$; and the reliability of this estimate falls as its importance in picking MEVPE allocations rises.

If all MPPs varied with rainfall in similar proportions, this would matter less in practice (though the logical problem would remain). The climatically critical choice, however, is between (a) crops robust in face of poor rains, but with low average yearly value, and (b) crops with higher average value but worse hit by poor rains. This choice must be made at or before ploughing time — with information that falls in reliability as it rises in importance.

Again, this would matter less if price and output were contravariant for the individual farmer. However, especially in hilly areas, climate can vary drastically between villages. In a typical year, for each crop, some farmers will enjoy favourable $R_s$ and others poor $R_s$, but 'average' prices will prevail for all. Whatever may apply to country-wide data, the individual farmer cannot rely on price variability to offset rainfall variability.

Uncertainty is confounded and compounded by variations in the price of manufactured goods. Even if the farmer could predict all MVPs, and hence allocate any *given* outlay among productive uses, he would not know how much he could buy with the resultant income. So he could not select the optimal *total* outlay.

All this does not imply that tropical farming is impossible to organise rationally. The alternative to the optimising peasant need not be the pessimising optant. Some practices — covering manure pits, ploughing across the slope — produce more output for almost any Rs, with hardly any increase in inputs. Some allocative decisions — higher seed-rates on poorer soils, appropriate mixed legumes on marshy ground — are similarly always indicated. That, however, is because such decisions and practices reduce the variance of profit, as well as raising the expected value.

## III

Suppose that an Indian farmer forms the best possible estimate of monsoon rainfall when he ploughs his land. Suppose, further, that he knows the probability-distribution of rainfall about its likeliest mean value, and can associate with each rainfall-level a probability-distribution of outputs, competitors' outputs, and prices both of his outputs and of the goods he might later want to buy. Even then MEVPE would not be best for him. India is not a welfare state; the collapsing extended family and related caste-panchayat systems have not been replaced by public protection from private disaster. True, improved communications (and universal suffrage) render starvation unlikely. But if an MEVPE-farmer is punished with a poor harvest, he must still expect gambler's ruin, i.e. one or more of (a) a crippling burden of debt, (b) the need to sell land at well below normal market prices, (c) attached labour, amounting to bond-slavery for himself and for his family. While Government and cooperative lenders are unable or unwilling to give consumption loans, unenforced legislation to depress interest rates is powerless against market forces.

Thus the risk of harvest failure, associated not merely with MEVPE but with any uninsured risk, assumes immense proportions. Arguments about optimal policies, based on false analogies with the humane, rich and risk-cushioned agricultures of the West, do not impress the subsistence farmer. A bad year or two, in an optimal policy sequence, will not prevent the Western farmer from retaining land and other assets sufficient to follow through the sequence; they will ruin the Indian farmer. His first duty to his family is to prevent such ruin; with growing population, fewer and fewer have enough land left for subsequent optimising experiments. Risk premium is an increasing function of risk *and a decreasing function of assets*.[18] A well-off American farmer can safely prefer a 50-50 chance of $5,000 or of $10,000 to a certainty of $7,000 per year. An Indian farmer, offered a 50-50 chance of Rs X or Rs. 1000 as against a certainty of the Rs. 700 a year with which he barely feeds his family, cannot set X far below 700. An optimiser maximises utility, not profit. The utility, now, of symmetrically-distributed expected harvest is the more reduced by variance about expected value (a) as assets and 'welfare cushions' fall, and as expected value declines — i.e. in poor countries, and (b) as variance increases — i.e. in tropical agricultures. The reduction in family holdings, as India's population grows, will increase the sensible safety-first propensities of the Indian farmer — and probably the annoyance of the agricultural economist who observes them.

## IV

Divergence of utility-maximising policy from MVPE policy is a familiar problem of economics. When (as in the above section) it is due to risk, not much can be done through factor sales and purchases. Within limits, farmers with relatively low risk aversion can acquire land with high expected value-product, but also high variance, from less MVPE-oriented farmers. Each farmer can, in effect, acquire land with greatest comparative advantage for his particular attitude to security vis-à-vis profitability. This, however, merely reduces the divergence between actual and MEVPE policy.

Under certainty, the prospects for equating utility-maximising and profit-maximising allocations might, in the long run, seem hopeful in a community of small family farmers. The standard reconciliation problems concern leisure and tastes. If I inherit land yielding high profit but needing much work, and like an easy life, I can sell the land to a more Puritan spirit, and use the proceeds to buy land producing lower-value output but requiring less managerial effort. If my father's land is suitable only for maize, while I prefer wheat-flour (but wish to go on farming), and you are in the opposite position, we shall exchange land. The transaction will raise psychic income, as well as real output of both crops.

In the Indian village, however, factor markets are seriously imperfect. Farmland hardly ever comes into the market in many cases. The prevailing fragmentation of holdings into numerous tiny plots — which could be consolidated to the advantage of all — demonstrates the inadequacy of the market in reallocating Indian farmland. Ownership is a tenaciously guarded family right, and an insurance policy; because there are substitutes for land in neither function, its price-elasticity of supply is tiny. The labour market (while becoming less imperfect as urban contact and population pressure weaken hereditary job assignments) is still dominated by caste. In some parts of India, a Brahman cannot plough. In almost none would he become a cobbler.

These imperfections in the factor markets have three main effects. They increase the divergence between profit-maximising and utility-maximising factor allocations; they impede (or at least delay) the allocation of productive factors according to the principle of comparative advantage; and they perpetuate a pre-capitalist market structure, in which a few profit-maximising farms exist alongside many risk-avoiding farms, without bankrupting or absorbing them — almost, in many cases, without competing against them.

If there were a perfect land market, differences in taste (i.e. relative utility of different food crops) between farm families would not affect output volume much. Suppose family farmers A and B inherit, respectively, plots X and Y of identical area. Each year X yields 1 bag of millet per man but 7/8 bag of maize; Y yields 1 bag of maize but 7/8 bag of millet. Maize and millet have identical market prices per bag, and producers' marketing costs (including storage) are 1/7 of production costs. Suppose that A and B each have just enough family labour to feed the family on the crop with the comparative disadvantage. Now if A's family strongly prefers maize and B's millet, production of both crops will be sub-optimal. Marketing costs are such that

A will grow maize and B millet; the socio-hereditary role of land makes it unlikely that they will exchange plots; and a sub-optimal factor allocation persists. With many different plots, crops and farmers, the possibility of simple barter declines further. Transport and storage costs (especially for the initial capital needed for the transition from subsistence production) impede even perfect product markets from compensating for imperfect factor markets.

The virtual non-transferability of land titles, then, causes utility differences to impede production (a similar case occurs if in the above example X-land is 'profitable but hard' and Y-land is 'low-profit but easy', but the marginal rate of substitution of leisure for income is higher for A than for B at all relevant levels of labour-input). The social restraints on job transfer mean that many reallocations of labour towards greatest comparative advantage would reduce utility. Like non-transferability of land, this cause of divergence between utility-maximising and profit-maximising also exists in rich countries; extra time spent in Government employment has low marginal utility to many economists who, in such service, would outperform both their colleagues in Government and themselves on campus. Both for land and for labour, however, traditions of factor allocation are backed by strong sanctions in very poor agricultural societies. Hence both factors are especially likely to be allocated in a way that, to attain social harmony (utility maximisation), sacrifices much potential output.

It is vital for advocates of steady reform, whether by planning or by competition, to recognise that imperfect factor markets in very poor countries are not relics of ignorance and conservatism, ready to collapse at the slightest incentive (or executive order). They fulfil a precise function in a tightly knit social structure. The function is to permit the inheritance of security, both of tenure and of employment. The structure is a socio-religious ecology in which tolerance of traditional factor uses alone preserves the harmony between oppressor and oppressed — and hence the acceptance of some residual responsibilities by the oppressor.

The rootedness, the inherence of imperfect factor markets explains many of the disappointments of developmental gradualism, planned or marketeering. It accounts, more-

over, for the persistence within a typical Indian (far more
than in a U.S.) village of totally different attitudes to farm
management. Schultz might well ask, in reply to the arguments of pp. 10-12, 'Why don't MEVPE-farmers drive out
or buy up the rest?' Over the years, for a farmer strong
enough to survive poor harvests, MEVPE must bring an
ever-rising share of a village's output. The whole notion of
'taking over' non-traditional occupations and applying
MEVPE to them — or even of buying up more land for
management (as opposed to rent) may, however, be alien
to him. Thus entrepreneurial MEVPE farmers and leisure-
oriented risk-averters can exist side by side in a single
village.[19] The latter either concentrate on different crops
or are eventually 'infected' by the technical advances of the
former, and thus survive somehow, but very seldom do they
*voluntarily* sell their land, even when sale would be profitable.
The likeliest culturally practicable use of capital, raised by
such sale, is for moneylending; the ex-landowner would then
work on others' land. Agricultural labourers (and small
moneylenders) suffer worst in bad seasons; sale of land thus
raises risk as well as expected income; hence it is unlikely
to be adopted by a risk-averter, especially if he is concerned
for his sons.

V

Apart from the imperfections of factor markets, many
aspects of the customary and legal framework militate against
the adoption, survival or (vis-à-vis other algorithms) 'victory' of MEVPE. Experience in many villages does not
suggest that it was adopted. If these facts can be demonstrated, we must ask why the factor allocations in
Hopper's study, cited by Schultz, seems to be so close to
MEVPE. In 1965 I spent seven months in a typical dry
Indian millet village of 800 persons, Kavathe. There, it was
hard to identify either MEVPE or any other optimising algorithm. The framework of accounting, enabling the calculated
risk-taking necessary for MEVPE, and the institutions of ownership that would support such a framework, are lacking.
Where farmers adopt different practices, they are often
unrelated to resource differences; when they adopt identical
practices, they are often wrong, but based on 'long expe-

rience'. An examination of one or two of the major agricultural operations indicates what happens.

Ploughing is a case of failure to push labour and bullock inputs near the optimum, MVPE or any other. In Kavathe, with well-developed bullock-hire and bullock-exchange systems, the reason is not the usual one of fixed labour/bullock ratios and imperfect bullock markets. But each generation of fathers has split its land into ever-thinner strips, one for each son, from top to bottom of the slope. Soil quality varies from high to low land according to water inputs, but very little along a contour facing in one direction; and fathers want each son to have some land of each quality. This saddles each generation of sons with longer, thinner sloping strips, increasingly costly and inconvenient to plough properly, i.e. repeatedly and across the slope. Most farmers realise the virtues of such ploughing (soil conservation, water distribution) and claim they adopt it; but many do not.

This story has two morals. First, cultivators fail to adopt fully understood optimising technologies even when extra input-costs fall far short of expected MVP. Second, institutions restrict optimising possibilities; here, inherited landholding needlessly raises the labour input required to plough a given land area correctly. Specialised ploughing agencies, cooperative or capitalist, would disregard jealously-protected strip partitions and are thus seldom practicable. Incidentally, the share of land occupied by the partitions increases with each generation, widening the rift between private and social optima.

If ploughing illustrates how inputs stop well before (committed) marginal cost falls to (expected) marginal revenue, sowing in Kavathe shows how inherited survival algorithms are preferred to maximising allocation procedures. The standardised sowing practices are traditional, without logical explanation, and not based on remembered experience or experiment. Thus agronomists advocate leaving 12 inches between lines of *bajra* millet (the main monsoon crop), but the seed-drills prepared by the Carpenter all have 9 inch gaps between holes. Confident in the survival value of their sowing practice, the farmers do not press him to change. The mixing rate — three rows *bajra* alone, one row half *bajra* and half pulse-crop — is similarly sacrosanct. So is the 'normal' *bajra* seed rate of 3 kilos per acre.

Some aspects of sowing practice do show inter-farm differences, but these exemplify profit maximisation as little as do the agreed forms of behaviour. The choice of which, among several suitable pulses, shall be mixed with *bajra* millet is partly constrained by soil type, but within these constraints depends on family tastes and cultivating habits (there being hardly any market for these pulses). 'From long experience', about half of my sample of 62 farmers sow 3 kilos of *bajra* seed on good soil, just as on normal soil; one-third raise the rate on good soils; one-sixth (rightly, according to most agronomists) lower it. All three groups may be adopting survival algorithms; but it is impossible that all three are adopting MVPE. The huge variability among deciles in farm efficiency, noted by Hopper himself,[20] supports this evidence.

Manuring practice illustrates the role of custom in prising utility-maximising behaviour away from MEVPE. Most farmers heap up manure; a few bury their manure properly in a pit. The second group is best represented among the *Dhanger* (Shepherd) caste, some two miles distant from the distractions of village social life. In May, while the main body of villagers celebrate each other's marriages, the *Dhangers* give their land a second ploughing and prepare compost pits. The families in this caste, incidentally, have a milk surplus, but regard it as against their *dharma* (customary religious duty) to sell it, though they give it away readily. None of this behaviour is MEVPE; nor, given the values that prevail, is it 'irrational'.

Such a structure of custom helps to explain why, in most villages, the 'progressive farmer' is a myth. There is a progressive ploughman, a progressive sower, a progressive composter — but no mechanism to unite the three in a single farmer. On the contrary, the search for a *survival algorithm* leads each family to pick up a bundle of practices, some 'progressive' and others 'conservative', and to show great reluctance to modify part of the bundle. To explain this, we do not need to invoke the peasant's alleged reluctance to interpret events as causal sequences. He may well know that his entire complex pattern of farm practices determines his output level; but how is he to know which element to modify, or which ones must be changed together, to bring improvement? Scarcity sometimes provokes increasingly desperate insurance measures, rather than more accurate allocative procedures. In reply to a question about allocation of manure among crops, I was informed 'There is not nearly enough manure; therefore (*mhanun*) we do not trouble to fix any special division among crops'.

Paradoxically, both the institutions and the reforms of tenancy impede MEVPE. For such few tenancies as exist in Kavathe, the law fixes rent in cash terms, at a value around 20 per cent of average crop. Custom, land shortage and the tenant's preference for safety set actual rents around 50 per cent, crop-share. Thus, even if marginal cost falls below *guaranteed* marginal revenue, landlord and tenant must agree on how that cost is to be borne. The delay, friction and mistrust involved in such agreements in a semi-literate world are costs too.

As the man/land ratio rises, crop-share agreements increasingly commit the tenant to paying all improvement costs. On a half-share basis, marginal revenue must then be double marginal cost (more under uncertainty) before the *tenant* will incur the outlay. Of course a rational MEVPE landlord and tenant would combine to share the cost of investment till its marginal cost rose to the level of expected marginal product!

Selectively enforcable tenancy reform can inhibit MEVPE as effectively as custom. Near Kavathe is the village of Vadagaon, where the numerically dominant Maratha caste is unwilling to work for the Brahman landowner. He cannot easily escape the laws against tenancy at market rents, but he can (and does) exceed the legal ceiling on land holding by *mala fide* transfers to his relatives. Lax laws and strict laws combine to produce half-farmed land.

All this is not a reversion to the Pessimising Optant, the ignorant or stupid peasant conservative. Closely similar farm families with similar resources can *sensibly* adopt different survival algorithms — especially with different tastes, leisure preferences, risk aversions, tenancy arrangements and castes. Many superficially odd village practices make sense as disguised forms of insurance. In Kavathe, most farmer-borrowers prefer to pay interest in grain rather than in cash, though the standard grain-rate, in a year of normal harvest, is almost double the cash-rate; higher interest buys the borrower an insurance against low crop prices. Share-rent, on the other hand, insures mainly against low crop outputs. The survival of caste rigidity, too, represents *inter alia* a communal sacrifice of income for security.

## VI

Schultz derives his belief in MEVPE from the long constancy of traditional agricultural environments. 'The economic acumen of people in poor agricultural communities is generally maligned... people have been doing the same things for generations. Changes in products and factors have not crowded in on them... The factors of production on which they depend are known through long experience and are in this sense "traditional"' (pp. 36-37). We have seen that 'long experience' *plus* substantial cultural isolation of (and different preferences among) heads of families in fact produces (a) distinct survival algorithms comprising different practices within a village, not all MEVPE; and (b) agreement on demonstrably non-MEVPE practices to preserve security, ease, etc. We must now ask whether the secular constancy of environment is, in fact, so great as to permit the peasant to learn (and transmit to his sons) what is, for him, best practice.

Schultz writes, 'In modern times, the most pervasive force disturbing the equilibrium of agricultural communities is the advance of knowledge useful in agricultural production. Any poor agricultural community that is adjusting its production to one or more of these circumstances is thus excluded from traditional agriculture to which the *efficient but poor hypothesis* applies' (p. 38). This would still leave many communities where the hypothesis is alleged to apply. However, much more powerful disturbers of community equilibrium in poor tropical agricultures — population growth and planning for development — vastly reduce the number of communities where the secularly constant agricultural environment of (say) 1600-1930 offers adequate lessons to the would-be optimiser in 1950-1975.

The attack on malaria and yellow fever means that most agricultural communities are increasing their numbers by

2.5 to 3.5 per cent yearly. In a few environments (slash-and-burn regions of Eastern Zambia, waterholes used by nomadic tribal herdsmen of the Eastern Sudan, the extensible settlement frontier in Colombia), this does not invalidate the assumption of constant environment, since new possibilities of cultivation exist for which the old lessons apply. In most tropical agriculture, however, each new generation of rural decision-takers inherits a man/land ratio about double that of its immediate predecessor — not only because population is growing but because generations are lengthening. In so far as the peasant learns the cheap-land, dear-labour lessons of 'long experience', he is *dis*qualified as a Schultzian.

The political and economic changes since decolonisation, too, have altered the environment. Schultz points out that his hypothesis is not relevant to peasant communities assimilating new knowledge or new factors. Apart from the huge inputs of both, planning provides new opportunities of exerting political pressure, and these require radical revision of the conceptual framework within which the farmer applies *traditional* knowledge to *traditional* factors. If fertiliser is distributed by a cooperative instead of a firm, more or less corruptly; if Indian 'democratic decentralisation' alters the balance among castes, or substantially strengthens or weakens landlords or moneylenders; if improved transport of grain or water renders security against drought less important relative to expected-value maximisation — all these 'ifs' suddenly alter optimising procedures for ever, and in the last twenty years they have come in a rush, whatever one may think of their conception or implementation. Again the man who merely 'learns from experience' is sunk. Just as the year-to-year variability of the climatic environment forces peasants to adopt practices other than MEVPE, so the dramatic shift in man/land ratios and the changed political framework force them to change these practices.

## VII

Suppose that the objections so far raised are not valid. Assume that climatic information is equally reliable everywhere, instead of varying in usefulness inversely with its importance; that perfect markets, and supporting social institutions and attitudes, bridge the gap between a peasant's utility-function and a policy of MEVPE; and that such a policy is, in fact, carried through. Optimisation by each will not, in general, produce optimisation for all.

First, transfers of land could raise output without variations in input levels, or in MEVPE policy. This is because huge scale economies exist — not, as Professor Schultz rightly argues (pp. 110-124), to the firm (i.e. the farm), but to the plant (i.e. the plot). While land ownership retains its prestige and insurance value, population growth renders the loss of output from tiny, partitioned plots worse in each generation. The potential gains from consolidation correspondingly increase. In theory, voluntary land exchange to consolidate *plots* (with compensation by side-payments) is compatible with MEVPE, provided there are no economies of scale to the *holding*. In practice, however, systematic plot consolidation in a village — as opposed to random mergers as mortgages are foreclosed — requires public encouragement and organisation. Thus, even if each farmer is on his production possibility surface (PPS), the totality of farmers is almost certainly not.[21]

Second, market structures in underdeveloped countries (UDCs) push relative prices far away from any 'optimum', whether defined by Schultz, Lange, Mahalanobis, Friedman or Marx. Of at least five relevant processes, (i) to (iii) are familiar to economists. In UDCs as compared to rich nations,

(i)     relatively, and increasingly, inegalitarian income distribution raises wheat and rice prices relative to those of millets, especially as urban incomes grow;

(ii)    relatively high inter-product differences in the degree of monopoly raise domestic tea and cotton prices relative to those of foodgrains;

(iii)   relatively low, slow factor mobility and high time-preference make labour-intensive crops too expensive compared to land-intensive crops, since relative prices over-reflect the past and under-anticipate the future;

(iv)    an aspect of the prevailing urban bias, systematically stronger monopoly in the non-agricultural sector, prevents Governments from allowing foodgrain prices to rise to market levels, and fear of political instability underlines this decision;

(v)     backdoor price effects combine with urban bias when busdrivers strike and riot for lower rice prices, but offset it when farmers (especially cash-crop producers) obtain relief through fertiliser subsidies.

These five effects imply that, even if each farmer produces where his PPS is tangential to the price plane, and even if (which does not follow) the community is on its PPS, it will be at the 'wrong' point on the PPS, however 'wrong' may be defined.

Third, even if all individuals and the community are at a point on the PPS tangential with a socially agreed price plane, this is not even a static social optimum. This point is picked without considering variance, and hence is likely to be subject to a good deal of it. A rational planner in East Pakistan, acting on the above highly unlikely assumption, and seeking to maximise the expected value of output from jute and rice together, would not simply adopt MEVPE with only factor constraints. He would be as unwise as the peasant to disregard maximin survival policies. MEVPE maximisation should be his policy on most land, but some should be set aside for cultivation on a maximin basis. Then 'low-world jute price + poor rice harvest', as a strategy by malevolent Nature, cannot prevent the survival of the planner's population to complete his maximising (MEVPE) policies on the rest of the land area. The selection of the right areas to choose for the maximin policy is an interesting problem.

Fourth, operation at a static optimum, even under certainty, is not sufficient for dynamic optimisation. The weighting of the utility functions of individuals (implicitly by the market together with initial distribution of income and monopoly power, or explicitly by the planner) implies a social utility function, including a rate of time preference and a rate of diminution of utility. Together with production functions, this implies an optimal rate of investment in each time-period.[22] However, the rate of reinvestment will vary among optimising farm units. The reallocation of resources from low-reinvestment to high-reinvestment farmers would usually imply more wheat tomorrow, even if it reduced the total value of wheat today by reallocations from consumption towards seedcorn violating the MEVPE preference of each and every farmer-consumer.

Finally, the concessions of the first paragraph of this section give too much scope to MEVPE as a translator of private into social optima. The institutional constraints upon MEVPE also inhibit its translating powers. In Ruritania, the king decrees that each man shall cut off the right arm of his first-born son. Subject to this irrational constraint, each peasant is an MEVPE-optimiser. Conversion into a static social sub-optimum requires the central organisation of training for the left-handed, but such training impedes the urge to remove the decree. The analogy with India's programmes for improving milk-yield from sacred cows, as a second-best to their impossible slaughter but making it impossible for longer, is obvious.

## VIII

How, then, did MEVPE gain any acceptance? Can it have had significance for policy? Can it be replaced by a better theory?

MEVPE gained some acceptance for two main reasons. First, many people accepted the argument that a peasant learns to optimise in a secularly constant environment. Second, quantitative evidence suggested responsiveness to price movements. In particular (and much more surprisingly) it seemed to show that market price-ratios of factors and products stood close to MPP-ratios. Previous discussion has concentrated on the theoretical argument. We have shown that the environment is not secularly constant, that its annual variation makes MEVPE unobtainable, that imperfect markets and institutions render the application of learning difficult, that private optimisation does not imply MEVPE, and that private MEVPE does not imply social optimisation. So how can we account for the quantitative evidence?

The inevitably selective nature of Schultz's data has been justly, if somewhat vigorously, attacked.[23] However, it is now generally agreed that cross-elasticity of supply of acres-sown-to-crops, with respect to last year's relative prices, is positive.[21] It is not obvious that this is rational; two years of continuous rise in the price-ratio of crops requiring similar land, in many observed pairs of Indian price-series, fore-shadow a fall in the third year.[25] Schultz rightly puts little weight on such cross-elasticities. The special case of MEVPE needs much stronger evidence.

The sort of evidence provided is, I hope, not caricatured by the following description. Collect a cross-section of physical inputs and outputs of farms or villages. Fit these into a homogeneous production function, imposing constant returns to scale. Differentiate the function with 'best fit' parameters, for each crop, with respect to each physical input. The ratios between derivatives then represent relative input prices under MVPE; the price of a kilogram of Crop X is the value of the output of the factors making the marginal kilogram of X if re-allocated to their next best use; this price is equal to the sum of the marginal value-products of all factors making Crop X, each multiplied by its input per kilogram. (Euler's homogeneous-function theorem implies product exhaustion).[26] If market prices are 'sufficiently close' to Euler prices, MVPE is not refuted. Analogous tests hold for any homogeneous first-degree production functions, including those implicit in linear programming.

The last sentence contains the implicit weakness of all such testing: its inability correctly to specify the production function. Owing to collinearity (among the majority) of factor inputs, a wide variety of different production functions gives excellent fits. If one picks a function corresponding to an incorrect engineering relationship, the derivatives of such a function cannot be 'marginal products'. Such a function can give an excellent fit to the input data because of their collinearity, but wildly misrepresent the engineering relation. The production functions used by Hopper (and cited by Schultz) omit dung, a factor worth about 4 per cent of total input value in much Indian agriculture[27] — and, of course, capable of making far more than 4 per cent difference to ratios between MPPs of other inputs. Even if all factors of production were included, however, we could never choose among the many production functions with satisfactorily high $r^2$-values. Hence the ratios between derivatives of an arbitrarily chosen function, while theoretically pleasing if it takes Cobb-Douglas form, have no operational significance.

MEVPE is neither wicked nor absurd. It has plainly convinced many key policy-makers. In 1965, India's former Minister of Agriculture, Mr. Subrahmaniam, outlined his agricultural strategy for the Fourth Five-Year Plan.[28] Peasants on unirrigated land, he argued, had learned to make the best use of their resources in thousands of years of unchanged environment; outlays must be concentrated on the 10 per cent of farmers with the best prospects of raising their output.

The concept of the *survival algorithm*, outlined in this paper, is unlike MEVPE. It would not induce Mr. Subrahmaniam to spurn possible low-cost opportunities of raising output by bringing each peasant's ploughing, sowing, manuring, weeding and harvesting practices to the level of the best of his neighbours. It suggests why, in the identical environment of a single village, peasants may develop and inherit various, yet rigid, patterns of farming. It proposes an explanation of 'rational', security-centred peasant conduct remote from the self-confirming tests of collinear production functions, but close to the farmers' accounts of their own conduct.

Finally, the concept of the survival algorithm suggests policies for the use of existing factors, from forward pricing of outputs and crop insurance for innovations to consolidation schemes and demonstration farms. It also suggests the rejection of some policies. In an inadequately watered region, fertilisers raise the variance of net output as well as its expected value. They are thus likely to be wasted or, if adopted, to destroy the peasant's confidence in innovations so irrelevant to his scale of preferences. Their high rate of expected return over cost, therefore, has to be set against their hardening effect on security-centred survival algorithms.

[1] I am particularly grateful to Professor T. W. Schultz of Chicago University for careful and incisive criticism of an earlier draft of this paper. I am also grateful for valuable comments on earlier drafts by Professor V. M. Dandekar and Dr. Sharad Sapre, Gokhale Institute, Poona; Professor J. L. Joy and Dr. Lesley Cook, University of Sussex; Dr. Bennett MacCallum, Rice

University, Texas; Professor A. A. Walters, University of Birmingham; and Drs. Tom Weisskopf and Vahid Nowshirvani of M.I.T. Dr. Nowshirvani suggests an additional objection to marginal-value-product-equalisation as a privately optimising policy: the inappropriateness of point-input point-output assumptions for agricultures where one borrows, to buy seed and fertilisers, four to six months before the harvest is sold. In this period interest of 10-15 per cent of the value of the loan can mount up.

This article is in part based on observations in a Maharashtra village, Kavathe, Khandala Peta, in Satara District, Maharashtra, India. Kavathe is a non-irrigated village (on 90 per cent of land) but has enough moisture to permit double-cropping on slightly over half the plots. Almost all heads of households own land, and cultivate about four acres each, split on average into eight or nine plots. Soil quality is poor because — despite nitrogen deficiency — inadequate, seasonally concentrated rainfall limits fertiliser use. The population is about 800, some 70 per cent of Maratha caste, though the influence of caste on the agricultural economy is small. The village has a primary school, is a mile from the nearest doctor, and has a daily bus service to Poona (three hours' run) outside the monsoon season. Agricultural and animal-husbandry officers from *Peta* headquarters visit the village yearly, but have time only to distribute fertiliser and inoculate cattle — not to give advice or help.

My research in Kavathe, designed to isolate the effect on farming efficiency of physical and attitudinal variations among cultivators, was supported by the U. K. Ministry of Overseas Development and by the University of Sussex. Substantial research assistance was given by the Gokhale Institute of Politics and Economics, Poona. None of the persons or institutions mentioned is responsible for the views expressed, or for any errors.

[2] F.A.O., *The State of Food and Agriculture 1966*, Rome, 1966, p. 17.

[3] All page references in the text are to T. W. Schultz, *Transforming Traditional Agriculture* (paperback edition), Yale, 1964 (hereafter *TTE*). Schultz's chief sources are Sol Tax, *Penny Capitalism*, Chicago, 1953, and D. Hopper's work in Senapur, summarised in D. Hopper, 'Allocation Efficiency in Traditional Indian Agriculture', *Jnl. Farm Econ.*, Vol. 47, No. 3, 1966, pp. 611-624.

[4] The refutation is convincing. It is usually unclear whether the 'zero marginal product' is of *man-hours* or of *workers*. If *man-hours* are meant, then either people are putting in their last, most tired hours of work for nothing in the burning tropical sun, or (which has to be shown, but never is) the reduction of man-hours will produce exactly offsetting increases in the intensity or efficiency of those still worked. If *workers* are meant, then either the 'removed' marginal workers have been working for nothing within their families, or employers have paid them to produce nothing, or the mere fact of their removal will cause those who stay in the village to work longer, harder or better. None of these possibilities makes sense. Moreover, the urbanising peasant, usually a literate male aged 18-30, withdraws the best (not average, let alone marginal and barely employed) units of labour-input.

[5] Shown by J. L. Joy in a paper to the Honolulu Conference on the transformation of traditional agriculture (not yet published).

[6] See note 27 below.

[7] A paradigm still found in the best contemporary textbooks: Samuelson, *Economics: an Introductory Analysis*, 6th Ed., McGraw-Hill, 1964, pp. 399, 476; Lipsey, *Introduction to Positive Economics*, Weidenfeld and Nicolson, 1964, p. 55.

[8] Even as early as 1811, 65 per cent of the U.K's families were principally employed outside agriculture (B. R. Mitchell and P. Deane, *Abstract of British Historical Statistics*, Cambridge, 1962, p. 60). The proportion in India, both in 1951 and in 1961, was only 30 per cent (Census data). The adult literacy rate in India in 1961 was under 25 per cent; in the U.K. as

early as 1839, over 55 per cent (R. Williams, *The Long Revolution*, London, 1961, p. 166; Indian Census Data).

9 T. Balogh, *Economic Journal*, Dec. 1964, pp. 996-999. Few persons with field experience of underdeveloped agriculture could dissent from the conclusions of Dr. Balogh's writings on poor countries; but the Schultzian model is a serious (if perhaps misconceived) *ally* in his struggle against blind reliance on market mechanisms, not a frivolous or malicious 'Chicago dogma'.

10 T. W. Schultz, *The Economic Test in Latin America; TTE*, ch. 12.

11 Nobody has ever found such a curve. The latest of many refutations is E. R. Dean's work on Malawi tobacco farmers (North-Holland, 1966).

12 These arguments are not directed at Dr. Hopper's empirical work. The use of production functions, specified like his, to derive shadow prices will be considered in Section VIII below.

13 I am grateful to Professor Walters for showing that this is the proper formulation, and to Dr. MacCallum for formalising it and for showing that it is not, in general, equivalent to the more plausible one that I initially chose: equating the expected value of the marginal product of money in each use. What must be equated are the additions to expected value made by the final penny spent on each factor, and in each activity.

14 H. H. Mann, *Rainfall and Famine*, Poona, about 1950.

15 S. Naqvi, 'Coefficient of Variability of Monsoon Rainfall in India and Pakistan', *Pakistan Geographical Review*, Pt. IV, no. 2, 1949; O. H. K. Spate and A. K. Learmonth, *India and Pakistan*, London, 1967, p. 47.

16 These limitations would apply also to much of Central Africa, and with even more force to areas almost too arid for cultivation (e.g. in West Pakistan). They would not apply to equatorial rainforest regions such as Indonesia.

17 A finding confirmed by Mrs. S. Das Gupta's Ph. D. thesis (unpublished, but available in London School of Economics Library). She shows by a quadratic programming formulation that, of a number of possible crop combinations 'efficient' in the sense that higher expected profit implies higher variance, farmers almost always choose the lowest profit, lowest variance policy. A mixed strategy minimax approximates the policy of Jamaican fishermen in W. Davenport, *Jamaican Fishing: a Game Theory Analysis*, Yale, 1960.

18 M. Kalecki, *Theory of Economic Dynamics*, London, 1954, pp. 94-6.

19 Dr. Hopper, in an unpublished paper for the Indian Intensive Agricultural Development Programme, showed that top-decile farmers in Indian villages around Delhi usually outperformed research stations. In his analysis, he incidentally showed inter-decile variations of output per acre far larger than the data in, for example, E. Heady, *Economics of Agricultural Poroduction and Resource Use*, Prentice-Hall, 1964, ch. 7. Data are far too fragmentary as yet, but the following hypothesis is advanced here: the less developed an agricultural community, the greater is the inter-farm coefficient of variability of output in the normal year.

20 See note 19 above.

21 The whole PPS analogy implies, incorrectly, that each factor input is fixed in total but perfectly transferable among uses. The analogy is used merely for convenience of exposition, and the arguments are equally relevant where either or both implications fail to hold.

22 Either time preference (justifiable by the uncertainty of the future and technological improvements) or a finite planning horizon must be specified. Otherwise, however fast returns-to-scale and utility diminish, the fact that infinity is a long time generates a famous paradox: it always pays to cut consumption to the bare minimum now, so as to grow even faster 'for ever'; but 'for ever' never comes.

23 Balogh, *loc. cit.*

24 D. Narain, *Impact of Price Movements on Areas under Selected Crops in India*,

Asia, 1965, esp. pp. 158-162; E. Dean, *Supply Response of African Farmers*, North-Holland, 1966, esp. pp. 74-79.

[25] M. Lipton, 'Should Reasonable Farmers Respond to Price Changes?', *Journal of Modern Asian Studies*, 1966.

[26] Henderson and Quandt, *Micro-economic Theory*, McGraw-Hill, 1958, pp. 64-6. Hopper's production functions (*loc. cit., Jnl. Farm. Econ.*, 1966, p. 615) are of less than first degree — they exhibit decreasing return to scale. Thus if all factors are paid their MVPs, some of the value of the total product is unaccounted for — as much as 19 per cent in the case of gram. In other words, profit maximisation is incompatible with product exhaustion. This is why the 'implicit prices' calculated by Hopper are above market prices for the factors of production in Senapur, but below them for the products (*ibid.*, p. 621).

[27] Private communication from Professor Schultz, relating to Punjab. See also *Studies in Economics of Farm Management in Bombay: 1954-5 to 1956-7*, Ministry of Food and Agriculture, Delhi, 1962, pp. 86, 88.

[28] 'Panorama', B.B.C. Television, 1965.

# Price Control in Underdeveloped Countries

## By P. T. Bauer *

In Western Europe, North America and Australasia the war-time and post-war price controls were largely dismantled in the 1950's. But in many parts of Asia, Africa and Latin America they have been retained or reimposed. This article discusses certain implications and results of these controls.[2] It is chiefly concerned with price controls in conditions where they are more effective at one stage of distribution than at others.

The problems and situations discussed have been suggested largely by the experience of West Africa and India, and to a lesser extent Pakistan and Cyprus in the 1940's and 1950's. But the analysis is more generally relevant.

## I

Certain features of the economic scene of many poor countries bear on this discussion.

Although sustained or substantial monopoly or monopoly profits are unusual in trading in these countries because of the comparative ease of entry and the ineffectiveness of market sharing agreements, there is often a high degree of concentration in the import and export trades, and to a lesser extent in the local wholesale trade.[3] This reflects chiefly the advantages of substantial capital in the conduct of long-distance trade. Much of this trading activity is in the hands of people different in nationality, language or race from the majority of the population. They are sufficiently distinct from most of the local population for the

* Professor of Economics (with special reference to underdeveloped countries and economic development) in the University of London at the London School of Economics.

distinction to be habitually recognised in public life and social intercourse. Such differences, at times unnoticed by external observers (for instance, membership of different African tribes), are often clearly and habitually recognised locally. The prominence of foreigners, strangers or other ethnic groups distinct from the local population reflects advantages derived from the possession of human and natural resources (including commercial aptitudes) and from wider commercial contacts.

In this article importers are referred to as *merchants;* they are the first stage in the internal distribution system. In this context they include wholesalers who obtain supplies at controlled prices from producers, from the government or from other domestic sources. Firms and individuals operating in the distributive chain between the merchants and the ultimate consumers will be termed *intermediaries.* Reference to *traders* may be either to merchants or to intermediaries, according to the context.

Effective rationing at the final consumer stage is rarely possible in these countries. This is partly because the majority of consumers are illiterate, and also because the ideas behind rationing often conflict with the mores, values and customs of the community. As a result, the ultimate consumer, especially in the rural areas, almost invariably pays the open market price, that is the price at which the quantity on offer and the quantity demanded balance. This price will be referred to as the open market price, and it may be quite unrelated to the controlled price. Indeed, most of the transactions *after* the stage of sale by the merchants to their customers (usually the larger intermediaries) are at this open market price, that is either at the price paid by the final consumer, or at a price differing from this only by the costs of transport and distribution to the point of final sale. This is at times implicitly recognised in the arrangements for price control, in that prices are often not fixed beyond the wholesale or semi-wholesale stage. But whether or not formal price control extends beyond the wholesale stage rarely affects the prices actually paid by the majority of the, usually numerous, small-scale intermediaries or the bulk of final consumers.[4]

Chiefly because of the dispersal of consumers and the poverty of the individual consumer, ultimate retail transactions are on a very small scale. For these and certain other

reasons, there are a large number of successive stages in the
distributive process, and a large number of traders at each
stage. Most of the sales of merchants are to intermediaries,
especially large intermediaries, who are a small proportion
of the *total* number of intermediaries operating in the
country.[5] This is partly because consumers and the smaller
intermediaries often buy in smaller individual quantities
than the minimum quantities which it is economic for
merchants to sell; and also because many of the consumers
are far from the merchants' establishments. Some of the
merchants' sales, however, are to final consumers, especially
to certain categories whose position is considered in section
VI below.

In many of these countries specialisation, especially
occupational specialisation, is as yet imperfectly. developed.
In trade there is usually no clear cut specialisation by
stages, at any rate after the merchant stage; traders are
likely to operate at each of several successives stages. Further, large numbers of people are apt to shift at short notice
from other occupations into trading, both full-time and
part-time, and they equally readily shift their activities
from one commodity to another.

Lastly, intermediaries and the larger-scale traders generally
are among the most vocal and politically influential elements
of the local population. They tend to be literate, or at any
rate more literate than the population at large; they are
often closely connected with the local newspapers, and their
views are prominent in the local press and in political
assemblies.

## II

Before 1939 supply and demand conditions of imports
into poor countries rarely changed so rapidly and discontinuously as to bring about sudden sharp increases in either
retail prices or the profit margins of merchants. There
were no substantial short-period fluctuations in the condition of supply of imports. There were wide fluctuations in
demand according to variations in the flow of money
incomes. But the elasticity of supply of imports into any one
country was high, and increased supplies of imports were
readily forthcoming. And when import prices did rise,
this was part of a general rise in the prices of these commodities, and did not result in a significant increase in

profit margins of merchants. Again, increases in the prices of imports in a boom tended to be less marked than those in the prices of exports, or in the incomes of the great bulk of the local population. Lastly, such increases in the prices of imports were on the whole gradual. This was chiefly because of the high elasticity of supply of imports. In these circumstances such increases in prices of imports as did occur were usually gradual and were not accompanied by such high profit margins as to yield obviously abnormally high returns, nor did they impose serious strain on any substantial section of the local population. Accordingly they did not usually result in demands for price control.

Since 1939, however, there have been frequent, rapid and substantial changes in the supply of and demand for imports in many poor countries. Many of these changes bring about discontinuous sharp increases in the local open market price of imported commodities. Such situations have resulted either from a sharp contraction in supply and/or an expansion of demand. The principal reasons for these changes are familiar. During the Second World War and the first post-war decade they were chiefly the temporary eclipse of certain sources of supply; enforced reliance on higher cost sources of supply because of licensing of foreign exchange or scarcity of shipping; longer delivery dates for imports, especially from sources not subject to licensing; expansion of money demand; and discontinuous variations in producer prices subject to official determination.[6] Since about 1955 domestic inflation and changes in import licensing and exchange control policies have been the principal factors bringing about discontinuous changes in the supply-demand relationships of imported commodities in underdeveloped countries. The resulting sharp increases in the local prices of imported commodities have often affected adversely the interests, notably the standard of living, of influential, though not necessarily large, groups of consumers.

### III

A rise in the local equilibrium price of imported commodities may or may not be accompanied by abnormally high profit margins of merchants. It may reflect simply a general rise in the cost of imports, i.e. a shift of the supply curve to the left, without abnormal profits. This situation does not raise issues of analytical interest, nor does it usually issue in the imposition of price control.

But a change in supply may take certain forms under which the new equilibrium price will secure abnormal profits to merchants, which may be more than accidental or short-term, since there are no, or practically no, elements of self-correction in the situation. Such instances have been frequent since 1939; and although they all belong substantially to one genus, for the purpose of this discussion they may be considered under two headings.

First, there are arrangements (case A) under which a certain amount of the goods is made available at a given import price, and additional supplies are unobtainable. This occurs when the volume of the commodity to be imported is fixed by direct control, or indirectly by control of the issue of foreign exchange, or the allocation of shipping space.

Case B is a variant of such arrangements. Under this certain strictly limited supplies may be available from some sources, while additional supplies are obtainable at higher cost from other sources.

During and since the Second World War both these types of arrangement have been frequent in the import trade of many underdeveloped countries, notably in many British colonies. Locally, their counterpart is a system of licensing or allocation of supplies among merchants, usually on some basis of past trading performance. Frequently, however, a proportion of licences or of supplies is reserved for members of the local population, who had not previously been merchants; the favoured individuals usually are from the ranks of past or present intermediaries.

Both cases A and B imply that (in the absence of effective price control) merchants who obtain supplies at a cost (including their own selling expenses) below the new local open market price will secure abnormal profits, which may be very large. In both these cases the abnormal profits have their roots in the system of allocation or licensing of supplies; or in other words, in the inability or unwillingness of the original sellers and/or the authorities to raise the cost of these supplies to the merchants, or to impose or raise taxes to equate supply and demand at the merchant stage. These profits arising from the difference between the supply price and the open market price will be referred to as *windfall profits.* This term seems more appropriate than monopoly profits, or profits of scarcity, or abnormal profits.[7]

## IV

Recipients of licences (a term used here to include allocations of supplies) are generally subject to price control of varying degrees of effectiveness. The declared aim of price control is generally to skim off the windfall profits inherent in any system of licensing, and to reduce margins to a level yielding no more than normal profits. It is, however, rarely, if ever, possible to achieve this; for various reasons the licensees are almost certain to be left with more than normal profits. First, the permitted profit margins are likely to err on the side of leniency, since otherwise there is a danger that the service might not be forthcoming. Further, it is very difficult to allow for the various indirect advantages accruing from the receipt of licences or supplies in times of general stringency and in conditions of riskless trading. Thus even if price control were effectively enforced, it would be unlikely to eliminate windfall profits completely.

But price control is unlikely to be completely effective even over the sales of the larger merchants; and it is much less likely to be effective over the operations of those local intermediaries who have been promoted to the status of merchants through the receipt of licences. Thus even if the recipients are subjected to price control, there is likely to be an insistent demand for licences for amounts far in excess of those the applicants would want to handle in the absence of windfall profits.[8]

These aspects and results of import licensing are familiar. There are other results which are particularly characteristic of the economic, political and administrative scene in many underdeveloped countries. Certain important and characteristic repercussions arise from the differing degree of effectiveness of price control over the various classes of trader, notably its much greater effectiveness over merchants, especially foreign merchants, (or those who are at any rate ethnically distinct from the majority of the population) than over intermediaries.

Price control is likely to be at least partially effective when applied to the transactions of merchants, both to their sales in bulk and to their sales in smaller quantities. There are various political and administrative reasons for the

comparative effectiveness of price control over merchants.
These are generally substantial firms who keep regular accounts, and who employ large staffs. Thus control of their
activities is comparatively easy, while evasion is more likely
to be detected or denounced. Moreover, the political risks
of evasion tend to be great.[9]

But price control is often ineffective even over the transactions of the larger merchants. This is partly because of the
difficulty of effective control over the actions of the employees of merchants, either by the employers or by the
authorities. However, there is another and more important
reason. It will be recalled that the bulk of the sales of
merchants (including sales through stores as well as ex
warehouse) are to intermediaries, that is to customers who
are themselves re-sellers and not final consumers. These
re-seller customers of the merchants dispose of the commodities at open market prices, since for reasons stated in
Section I price control is usually inoperative beyond the
stage at which the merchants operate.[10] As their customers
re-sell in markets in which price control is inoperative,
merchants and their employees are strongly tempted to
evade price control. Indeed, pressure by their customers for
the allocation of supplies at controlled prices may be so
insistent that some evasion of price control may be well-nigh
unavoidable; and even when avoidable, evasion might
involve merchants in less trouble and unpopularity than
observance.

Not much can be said in general terms about the form
and extent which the evasion of price control is likely to
assume, except perhaps that the device of conditional sales
is often used. This amounts to a restriction of sales of the
price controlled commodity to buyers who undertake to
purchase another commodity or range of commodities,
which otherwise they would not buy, or at least not at the
price which they are required to pay. This type of evasion
is generally difficult to prove formally; and further, as
merchants usually sell a range of imported commodities
in their normal course of business, it is easier to subject their
customers to conditional sales than if trading were more
specialised.[11]

Of the total windfall profits inherent in a situation in
which the supply price of imported goods is kept below the
open market price, the merchants generally can secure a

part only, and often the smaller part. The balance accrues to the intermediaries to whom the merchants sell at prices below the open market price, which is the price at which the intermediaries can generally dispose of the commodities. While the distribution of the windfall between the merchants, their employees, and the intermediaries is often not easy to assess, it seems generally true that both the first and the last secure a significant share; and further, where the merchants are foreigners (or, at least, ethnically distinct from the majority of the population), and relatively vulnerable to political pressure, the share of the intermediaries is generally considerable. These are safe approximations; and they are sufficient for our analysis.

In such circumstances the demands for price control, which might in any case arise if vocal sections of the population (as consumers) find that the prices of important items in their expenditure have risen substantially, are likely to be reinforced by two factors.

First, it is likely to be widely realised that, in the absence of price control, the merchants (many of whom, it will be recalled, are often clearly distinct from the rest of the population) secure windfall profits which are likely to persist while licensing continues. Secondly, the intermediaries will appreciate that price control, if imposed, would be ineffective at the later stages of distribution so that its (more effective) operation over the transactions of merchants will secure for them (the intermediaries) an appreciable part of the windfall profits inherent in the situation. They will thus press vigorously for its imposition. Plausibility is lent to these demands by the rise in the prices of imports and the emergence of windfall profits for merchants.

## V

Thus, in the circumstances of many poor countries, the windfall profits inherent in cases A and B are likely to result in three types of demand or pressure: demands for licences; demands for the imposition of price control over the merchants; and demands for the allocation of supplies by merchants at controlled prices. As many intermediaries operate on such a small scale that they cannot hope to secure import licences (even under preferential treatment of the local population), their demands tend to be largely for price control and for allocation; and these demands may be more vocal and prominent than demands for import licences.

Price control, unless it is completely ineffective or redundant, implies a situation in which the quantity demanded is in excess of the quantity offered. As in these countries there can generally be no effective system of rationing, and often there is not even formal rationing, the merchants have to ration informally the price-controlled commodities. This in turn brings about an inflation in apparent demand, a speculative shift in the demand curve, i.e. over-statement by customers of their requirements at particular prices in order to secure larger quantities than they would otherwise obtain. For several distinct reasons this familiar phenomenon tends to emerge much more readily, and to be quantitatively more important, in underdeveloped countries than in more advanced countries.

First, as already stated, a large proportion of the beneficiaries from the difference between the controlled price and the equilibrium price are likely to be re-sellers who secure a cash gain from any allocation of supplies at less than the equilibrium price.[12] Thus the demands of individual re-sellers, unlike those of individual consumers, have practically no saturation point at the controlled prices (up to the point where the open market price is reduced to the controlled price by additional supplies). Further, the gains accruing from securing commodities at controlled prices and re-selling them at open market prices are manifest and easily calculable. Indeed, the allocation of the commodity at the controlled price (or more generally at any price below the equilibrium or open market price) is tantamount to a cash gift. In conditions of imperfect specialisation the possibility of this obvious gain brings about the appearance of large numbers of *ad hoc* traders[13] applying for supplies of the price-controlled commodity. In these conditions the apparent excess of demand over supply at the controlled price is much greater than the actual excess of effective final consumer demand.

Such a situation conduces to political tension. The merchants are likely to be accused of evasion of price control, conditional selling, and of favouritism towards particular individuals and groups, especially towards intermediaries and of their own nationality or race. In the circumstances there are many disgruntled traders and would-be traders.

## VI

The effects of price control on the ultimate consumer are very different from what is usually implied by those demanding its imposition. In case B the great majority of consumers do not benefit. They buy at the open market price which is not reduced by price control, however effective or ineffective at earlier stages.[14] Indeed, it may even be increased slightly. The transfer of windfall profits from merchants to intermediaries may increase total money expenditure. The merchants' profits are less likely to be spent locally than are those of the intermediaries; and further, they are usually subjected to heavier taxation (often *de jure* and very generally *de facto*). If the transfer of the windfalls from merchants to intermediaries results in an appreciable increase in money demand, the general level of prices is likely to be higher than it would be otherwise, and consumers paying open market prices would be worse off as a result of price control.[15]

There are, however, certain classes of consumer who are likely to secure supplies at controlled prices. These include civil servants, members of the police force, politicians and public men generally, and employees of the merchants. These favoured consumers, together with the intermediaries buying from the merchants, are generally a small proportion of the total population.

They are, however, politically, socially, and administratively influential groups. As they benefit appreciably from price control, they are likely to favour it, even though open market prices are unchanged or may even have been raised; and their advocacy of price control is not likely to be affected by its political and social results. Moreover, they rarely understand the factors behind the situation. Alongside other sections of local opinion, they are likely to ascribe these results to the selfishness and malice of the merchants.

Under case B the reasons and motives of demands for price control are likely to be very similar to those under case A: a sharp rise in the local prices of imported goods and the emergence of large profits for some merchants. And most of the results of the imposition of price control are similar to those observed in case A: excess of demand over supply, inflation of demand, informal rationing by merchants, and obvious discrepancy between the open market price and the controlled price.

But there is one significant difference. The open market price will now certainly be higher than it would have been without price control. The supply of imports is now not completely inelastic; additional supplies can be obtained from higher cost sources. Unless price control is completely ineffective over the operations of merchants, some merchants will not be able to realise such high average prices as they would otherwise, and it will not pay some merchants to tap certain high cost sources which they would have tapped without price control.

## VII

Even wide fluctuations in aggregate money incomes in the importing countries, or wide fluctuations in the supply of imports, need not require, or even render desirable, intervention in the markets for particular commodities. Thus if the cost of imports rises greatly, but the supply is elastic, the only way to assist consumers is by direct subsidy. Even if situations designated as case A or B threaten to emerge, it may still be possible to deal with them or forestall them without intervention in particular markets. It may be possible by suitable fiscal or monetary action to deflate aggregate money incomes sufficiently to equate demand and supply for imports. Or again in certain circumstances it may be thought desirable to leave the traders with windfall profits. Thus somes licences may be granted to members of the local population, and the high profits may be thought desirable to strengthen the resources of these traders in their years of apprenticeship in foreign trade, even though they represent windfall profits secured at the expense of the rest of the population.

But in many instances these courses would not be practicable, desirable or sufficient. The fiscal machinery or the monetary mechanism may not be sufficiently developed or responsive for a general control of the flow of incomes. Auctioning of licences might serve to increase further an already high degree of concentration. Complete non-intervention may secure very high and persistent windfall profits to the recipients of licences.

Thus other measures may have to be adopted, affecting particular commodities or those dealing with them. In practice it will be necessary to consider the effects and relative merits of price control (sections VIII and IX), of the imposition of particular indirect taxes and of the taxation of merchants' profits (section X), and of government purchase and sale of the imports affected (section XI).

## VIII

There is a certain superficial political and administrative attractiveness in a system of licensing combined with price control. It is usually demanded by influential sections of the local population. The merchants are also likely to favour it. In spite of price control they will make larger (and relatively riskless) profits than they would in more usual conditions. Moreover, licensing shields them from competition from new entrants. These demands are reinforced by superficial rough justice, since one class of beneficiaries (the favoured groups of consumers who succeed in buying at the controlled prices) include individuals who are generally adversely affected when priees have risen, especially if their money incomes have not risen correspondingly. Governments may also often welcome a system of licensing to promote the entry of local traders into direct importing. For political reasons participation of some members ·of the local population in external trade may be deemed desirable and in the absence of licensing the entrants may be unsuccessful.[16] Again, the salaries and wages of government employees are often linked to cost of living indices based on cohtrolled prices, so that governments have a financial interest in formal price control, even when it is ineffective. And lastly, a system of licensing and allocation may appeal to influential groups for political and administrative reasons, as facilitating or heralding a closer official control over various branches of economic life; and also because it tends to lead to the creation of important and influential positions.

## IX

In spite of these attractions there are severe disadvantages in such a system, some of which are familiar under any system of licensing with or without price control. Others are peculiar to underdeveloped countries, and stem chiefly from the fact that price control is so largely ineffective at the final consumer stage.

A system of licensing tends to freeze the pattern of trade.

This may be modified to some extent if licences are not confined to established firms. In this case, however, they are likely to be given to politically influential members or groups of the local population who would not be able to survive in trade without licensing.

The system tends to ensure riskless windfall profits to the licensees. Price control may remove some of these. But the more effective is the price control over the activities of merchants, the greater are the riskless profits accruing to the intermediaries at the next stage. This poses problems peculiar to the operation of price control in many underdeveloped countries.

For reasons discussed in section II, the differential effectiveness of price control over merchants and intermediaries respectively largely inflates the demand of the customers of merchants, with the result that frequently only a small fraction of the expressed demand can be satisfied.

The more rigorously the merchants observe price control, the greater and more obvious is the profit accruing to intermediaries, and the larger becomes the excess demand, and the smaller the fraction of the demand which can be met. The merchants will be accused of favouritism, illegitimate preference, and possibly also corruption. If, on the other hand, they evade price control by conditional sales or similar devices, they will be accused of profiteering by those who are disappointed of part of their expected profits. A further concomitant of such a situation is an increase in the volume and stridency of the demands by the local population, especially intermediaries, for a larger share in supplies.

The operation of these forces is intensified by a genuine failure of public opinion to appreciate essential features of the situation, in particular the reasons for the absence of effective rationing at consumer level and the consequent ineffectiveness of price control at that stage. The prominence among merchants and their employees of foreigners, strangers and of members of other ethnic groups distinct from the local population, tends further to exacerbate the situation.[17] These circumstances can help to bring about severe political tension.[18]

Such a situation is also likely to engender misleading ideas about the nature of trading activity and the sources of trading profits. It is likely to be believed that trade is a fixed quantity in which an increased share for some necessarily implies a smaller quantity available to others. Trading profits take on the appearance of riskless and almost effortless windfalls or monopoly profits. This serves both to attract large numbers into trading activity, while at the same time it discredits the work of the merchants.

Lastly, there is the familiar result of self-perpetuation under any system of licensing. In the circumstances described, there are special factors reinforcing the familiar tendency. The local traders and intermediaires who receive licences or supplies below the open market price from the merchants may not be able to survive in business without these favourable conditions. They will emphatically oppose their removal.

## X

Taxation may serve to avert some of the difficulties just described.[19] Where no further supplies are available or admitted (case B), the imposition of taxes to raise the supply price to the equilibrium price will not raise the latter, and may even lower it; and as the bulk of consumers pay this price they cannot be affected adversely.

The imposition or raising of taxes to reduce or eliminate the gap between the supply price and the open market price is certain to be strongly resisted by those affected. Even in more sophisticated communities such measures are often resisted on the argument that they would raise retail prices. In underdeveloped countries the opposition is likely to be much stronger, from merchants, from intermediaries, and from favoured consumers. Between them these groups are often much the most important section of vocal public opinion.

The opposition to this use of indirect taxation is likely to be even stronger if it is imposed before the emergence of the windfall profits and of the short supply situation. The rise in the open market price will be ascribed to the higher taxation. This view is less likely to gain currency if the gap between equilibrium price and the supply price has persisted for some time.

But even if the imposition of sufficient additional indirect taxation is politically practicable, it will not be the most effective instrument in dealing with the short supply situation of case A.

Indirect taxes cannot easily be altered frequently, and rarely more than once a year. If they are levied at rates designed to skim off the entire difference between the supply price and the open market price at the time of their imposition, supplies may disappear if subsequently there is a fall in the equilibrium price. Thus even if political conditions permit the imposition of indirect taxes to equate the quantities supplied and demanded, this may be inadvisable. It may be thought preferable to leave the merchants with slightly more than the normal profit margin, and leave it to profits taxation to deal with any surplus profits which it is desired to remove.

In case B the tension and difficulties brought about by price control are very similar to those under case A, with the added factor that the open market price itself will have been raised by the operation of price control. The resistance to the removal of licensing and price control, and to its replacement by additional taxation, are also likely to be very similar. In this case, however, the open market price will also be affected by the imposition of additional indirect taxation. It will clearly be higher than it would have been in the absence of price control and the absence of indirect taxation. In this type of situation it may be preferable to rely principally on income and company taxation to skim off the abnormal profits of those who have secured intra-marginal supplies to which access is barred to others. If this form of taxation is not highly developed, it can be supplemented or even replaced by the imposition of additional indirect taxes, which will, however, raise the open market price.

## XI

Government purchase of supplies for resale may be used as an alternative method for bridging the gap between open market prices and supply prices.[20] In substance this is, of course, closely similar to additional indirect taxes. It differs from it in certain aspects which may be important in the conditions prevailing in many underdeveloped countries.

First, while indirect taxes can usually be changed only once a year, the selling prices of commodities handled by the government can be altered frequently. In rapidly changing conditions of supply and demand this is important, especially in countries where, for reasons already stated, a relatively small discrepancy between supply price and open market price may result in a tense situation.

Secondly, in case B this method could deal with the situation without raising the open market price. For reasons suggested in sections IX and X, both the imposition of price control and of additional taxation is bound to raise the open market price when it discourages supplies from higher cost sources; and where consumer demand is inelastic, the rise in the equilibrium price may be substantial. Government trading may make it possible to avoid raising the open market price, and it may even be possible to lower it, since there need be no contraction of supplies from marginal sources. Moreover, the profits on the sale of supplies from lower cost sources (which, it will be remembered, cannot be expanded) may be used to subsidize purchases from higher cost sources, thus reducing the open market price.[21]

Third, the political opposition to this method may be less pronounced than to the imposition of indirect taxes. This attitude may be irrational, but it may nevertheless be present; witness the very different attitude of the British public to the trading profits of the British Ministry of Food, and to the suggestions for using the purchase tax to deflate the excess demand for motor cars in the early post-war years. Conversely, of course, the opposition of traders may be stronger if they see in this measure not only a device for skimming off windfall profits, but the beginning of permanent state trading.

The disadvantages and difficulties of the adoption of this method stem essentially from obvious political and administrative considerations. The machinery may not be equal to the task of organising and operating the scheme. Or the integrity of the local civil service, especially at the middle or lower levels, may be unequal to the evident temptations.

This method may also clearly set up strong influences of self-perpetuation or extension. It creates influential and remunerative positions yielding to their holders incomes or power far greater than they would enjoy otherwise. This is likely to retard the adoption of other measures for dealing with the situation whether by the deflation of aggregate money demand and/or by the development of new sources of supplies. Indeed, once established the scheme may be

so attractive to those in administrative and political control
that they may seek to extend it to other activities.

If these political and administrative dangers and defects
could be avoided, this method may prove the least disad-
vantageous solution in some underdeveloped countries for
dealing with a situation of excess demand for a range of
commodities.

## XII

The factors behind the short supply situation, that is the
situation of excess demand, and the principal implications
both of the situation and of the methods for dealing with it
are generally reasonably clear. But the choice of different
measures requires delicate assessment of political conditions
and of economic effects. Measures affecting specific activities or commodities are likely to be more effective and cause
less friction if the discrepancy between aggregate money
demand and the total volume of supplies is small, so that the
burden of adjustment borne by particular indirect taxes or
the taxation of merchants' profits is not too great. Thus
other things being equal, these measures are likely to be most
effective when used in conjunction with more general measures for deflating aggregate money demand.

[1] I am indebted to Professor B. S. Yamey for help in the preparation of this
article.

In accordance with current practice the term 'underdeveloped' is used
here to refer to most of Africa, Asia and Latin America; it is in fact a synonym
for 'poor'. The line of distinction between developed and underdeveloped
(i.e. rich and poor) countries is arbitrary and imprecise. This imprecision
does not, however, affect the discussion. The characteristics of under-
developed countries relevant to the argument are set out in section 1, and
they will be found to apply widely in the conditions of these countries.

[2] The discussion is mostly in terms of price control over imports, as this throws
into clearest relief certain issues of practical interest. Most of the discussion
would, however, apply also to price control over locally produced commodities, including manufactured goods.

This article is not concerned with, and therefore disregards, the possibility
that effective price control over a monopolist producer or distributor can
serve to increase his output. The usual type of price control over commodities in underdeveloped countries is not introduced for this reason, but to deal
with situations, often called colloquially short-supply situations, in which
the relevant supply (usually total supply, but at times supply from certain
sources) is fixed; cf. section 3 in the text.

[3] The concentration in the import and export trade of West Africa in the
early 1950's, and the reason for its high degree there as in many under-
developed countries, are discussed in my book, *West African Trade*, especially
chapters 5, 7, 8 and 17, and also in an article in *Economica* in November

1953, where it is argued further that a high degree of concentration furnishes an imperfect index of monopoly power or profitability in these conditions.

The following passages from a thesis submitted by Mr. B. G. Kavalsky for the M. Sc. degree at London University illustrate the ineffectiveness of price control in Northern Rhodesia in the 1940's, besides other aspects of economic life there.

'The case of Mufulira in 1944 provides an interesting example of the operation of price control. The control price was set for grain and meal and immediately evaded through a change in the measure given to customers. The management then introduced special cups and dishes, which when filled with grain or meal gave the correct weight, and enforced their use. The marketeers next step was to cut round pieces of cardboard of the same colour as the meal and fit them as a shelf some inches up from the bottom of the mug. When the authorities cottoned on to this, the marketeers switched to beating up the bottoms of the mugs, and when this was stopped, they cut down the tops gradually over a long period, so as not to be immediately noticeable. The effect of all this was that in 1945 none of the measuring cups bore any relation to the original size, and the price had been restored to its earlier level.

Other managements tried similarly to control the price by the introduction of scales. The figures on the scale were quickly scratched out and the old prices charged till eventually the matter was settled by the breaking of the scales. When the controlled price of fish was made 8d. a lb. as against the actual selling price of 2/- a lb. and the riverside price of 6d. a lb., the fish sellers simply left the market and refused to operate at that price. The customers were most unhappy about the situation and asked the management to stop the controls as they would rather have higher prices than no fish at all'.

The passages are Mr. Kavalsky's transcript of a longer discussion of this subject in W. V. Brelsford, *Copper Belt Markets*, Lusaka, 1947, pp. 22-3.

[5] Meaningful specific quantitative estimates of this point are difficult to secure because the occupational statistics of most poor countries are very wide of the mark, chiefly owing to the incomplete occupational specialisation in these countries where a significant proportion of the people not classified as traders nevertheless do ·trade, at least part-time or intermittently. This subject is examined in P. T. Bauer and B. S. Yamey 'Economic Progress and Occupational Distribution', *Economic Journal*, December 1951, and also in *West African Trade*, Ch. 2. However, it was found in 1950 that the number of traders operating in three markets of Eastern Nigeria was about 14,000, which was more than the total number of the regular customers of the eight merchant firms which at the time handled about five-eights of all commercial imports into Nigeria.

[6] The distinction between an increase in demand and a contraction in supply, though often important both for analysis and for policy, is not directly relevant to this article. For simplicity of exposition, the discussion is confined to a contraction of supply with an unchanged demand.

[7] It should be clear from the context whether the reference is to profit margins or to rates of return on capital.

[8] This type of situation is vividly described in certain official reports, especially locally published reports. Examples include the *Report of the Commission on Enquiry into the Distribution and Prices of Essential Imported Goods*, Accra, 1943; the *Report of the Commission of Enquiry into Conditional Sales*, Lagos, 1948; and also the *Report of the Commission of Enquiry into Disturbances in the Gold Coast*, London, 1948.

[9] These considerations apply much less to the transactions of local traders specially promoted to the status of merchants by the operation of import licensing, i.e. traders who would not normally import directly, and who are

attracted into this activity by the operation of licensing and enabled to participate in it by the allocation of licences.

[10] Scattered information on the level of controlled and open market prices in India will be found in R. G. Agrawal, *Price Controls in India*, New Delhi, 1956, and in B. R. Shenoy, *Indian Planning and Economic Development*, Bombay, 1963.

Some information on controlled and actual prices of consumer goods in West Africa in the late 1940's is presented in *West African Trade*, p. 437. There is also some sporadic information on this subject in the reports mentioned in footnote 8.

[11] The beneficiaries of conditional sales, as indeed of other types of evasion, are often the employees of the merchants rather than the merchants themselves. Where the beneficiaries are employees belonging to the local population, their position under price control and their interest in its maintenance are analogous to those of the local intermediaries.

[12] There are certain favoured groups of consumers who benefit from price control; they are considered in section VI.

[13] These may either be individuals who are not usually engaged in trade at all, or traders who do not normally deal in this particular commodity. In West Africa in the 1940's and 50's schoolboys often acted as *ad hoc* intermediaries either individually or in small groups. The same phenomenon seems also to have occurred in some other underdeveloped countries, including Pakistan.

[14] We are considering here Case A, that is, instances in which the supply is perfectly inelastic beyond the quantity already imported. When additional supplies are obtainable at higher prices (Case B) the open market price will certainly be *raised*. This is considered later in this section.

[15] This neglects any satisfaction they may get from the knowledge that some windfalls have been transferred from foreigners to compatriots.

[16] This might to some extent counteract the advantages to established merchants from the operation of licensing. However, the merchants rarely oppose restrictive licensing on this account.

[17] Many books and reports could be quoted showing the failure to understand the essentials of this type of situation, especially the reasons for the discrepancy between the open market and the controlled prices and the resulting pressure on merchants for additional supplies which makes conditional sales or other types of evasion practically unavoidable. Locally published official reports are particularly revealing on these points; the reports listed in footnote 8 above are examples.

[18] The disturbances in the Gold Coast in 1948 which culminated in the Accra riots in which more than twenty people lost their lives were closely connected with such a situation.

[19] In principle, similar effects can be secured by the auctioning by the authorities of the limited supplies or the licences to import. However, in the conditions of many underdeveloped countries this may have results undesired by the authorities, for example an increase in the degree of concentration in the import trade.

[20] State trading is, of course, no novelty. The discussion is intended only to examine its merits and defects compared to the other principal methods of dealing with certain specified problems.

[21] Such purchases could, of course, also be subsidized out of general revenue if this were thought desirable.

# DEFINITION AND DEFENCE

# The Frontiers of Development Studies: Some Issues of Development Policy

## *By Paul Streeten*

This paper discusses five issues:

(1) the view that there is a development process which can be dissected into comparable stages of development;
(2) the role of education in development;
(3) the role of agriculture in development;
(4) the use of shadow prices in development planning;
(5) the view that there are single barriers to development.

(1) The view that each country passes through comparable stages of growth is not tenable, because the co-existence of rich and poor countries alters the prospects of the poor countries. Favourable effects are obvious. Twelve reasons for unfavourable effects are given.

(2) To make school curricula more agricultural, vocational and technical is not enough to accelerate development. The solution is more complex and requires a number of other simultaneous measures outside educational reform. A number of unsettled questions in educational policy are raised.

(3) Six reasons are given for the need for an agricultural breakthrough. The distinction between agricultural knowledge and its application oversimplifies the problem. So does the emphasis on one or two strategic measures. Even 'packages' often leave out essential components, like land reform.

(4) Shadow-pricing requires a number of artificial assumptions: one should avoid disguising rough value judg-

ments and even rougher factual estimates as a precise, objective basis for decisions. Some presentations are circular.

(5) Development cannot be understood as a natural tendency which is kept in check by specific barriers. It is more helpful to regard it as a social process, in which a number of economic and non-economic conditions interact. A possible classification into six such categories is given. The question is discussed whether the notion 'investment' can be widened to embrace expenditure under these categories. The social system is illustrated by a discussion of the prerequisites of agricultural reform.

STAGES OF GROWTH

Deeply embedded in current thought on development is the view that each country passes, at different times, through a series of comparable stages of development; that there are basic similarities in this process; and that we can therefore learn from the pre-industrial phase of now industrialised societies lessons which are applicable to under-developed societies today.

I wish to question this belief on the ground that at any rate some of the conditions crucial to development at any particular stage depend on the stages which other societies have reached at the same time. Since the co-existence of a number of different societies, each at a different stage of development, crucially determines the development prospects of the least-developed ones, an essentially historical feature must form part of any valid analysis and prognosis. The fact that advanced industrial societies already exist when countries embark on development, makes a number of important differences to the development prospects of under-developed societies.

Some of these differences, and perhaps the most obvious ones, clearly benefit under-developed countries. A stock of scientific, technical and organisational knowledge has been accumulated, on which the under-developed countries can draw. They do not have to go through the laborious process of acquiring this knowledge for themselves and can therefore avoid a number of errors and false starts. The high level of income and its growth creates a demand for the products of the under-developed countries and enables them to benefit from wider international specialisation than was possible for the pioneers. Private investment, financial aid and technical assistance contribute to the transfer of resources from the rich countries to the poor and thus enable these to draw on a bigger pool of resources. These benefits were not available, or available only to 'a smaller extent, when the now industrialised countries embarked on their development.

On the other hand, the co-existence of rich and poor countries has also a number of drawbacks for the under-developed countries:—

(1) The most important difference is that the advanced state of medical knowledge makes it now possible to reduce deaths cheaply and rapidly, without contributing to an equivalent reduction in births. This has upset the population equilibrium and has caused the large and accelerating rates of population growth, which present the under-developed countries with much more difficult obstacles than those which the now advanced countries faced in their pre-industrial phase.

(2) Although a stock of scientific and technical knowledge is available on which under-developed countries can draw, this technology is ill adapted to the conditions and the factor endowments of the under-developed countries. Modern technology was evolved in conditions of labour scarcity and its purpose is therefore to save labour in relation to capital. The transfer of these sometimes inappropriate methods, which is encouraged by attitudes towards modernisation and by the prestige of Western technology, tends to aggravate the gross under-utilisation of labour from which the under-developed countries are suffering. The transfer of inappropriate technology, together with the rapid growth of the labour force, has created obstacles which are fundamentally different from those which the now industrial societies had to overcome in their pre-industrial phase.

(3) Not only knowledge of techniques of production, but also knowledge of organisations and institutions is ill-adapted to the needs of the under-developed world. Trade Union structure and attitudes, like technology, have evolved in conditions of labour scarcity and can therefore be damaging

if transferred to conditions in which labour is not fully utilised. The demand for the adoption of social welfare services developed in advanced industrial welfare states, has often proved an impediment to development and, far from contributing to greater social justice, has strengthened vested interests and pockets of privilege. Large public expenditure on curative medicine, on higher education and on subsidies to other public services and to consumption goods has absorbed scarce resources and reinforced attitudes and practices hostile to development.

Large-scale business organisations do not create the spread effects which smaller-scale enterprise would. Even political institutions, such as parliamentary democracy, are not always adapted to the needs of developing countries and, under the guise of constitutional democracy, reinforce the reluctance to touch vested interests and to use compulsion for development.

(4) As Dudley Seers has recently shown,[1] high levels of remuneration for professional skills in advanced countries raise obstacles to development in under-developed countries which go beyond the losses through emigration. By the creation of an international market in these skills, not only are internal inequalities without functional justification increased in under-developed countries, but obstacles are put into the path of development. International inequality has an impact on internal income distribution in under-developed countries which, like the impact of modern technology and modern institutions, impedes development.

(5) Systematic scientific research, which is reflected in the annual growth of productivity characteristic of growing economies, has tended to be concentrated at best on those activities which are not suited for production in under-developed countries such as temperate zone agricultural production, or at worst, as in the case of synthetics, has harmed the trade prospects of under-developed countries. Technical progress has reduced the need for the imports of the staple products of developing countries

(a) because synthetics have been substituted for natural products,

(b) because there has been increasing economy in the use of raw materials, and

(c) because demand has shifted towards products with low primary import content.

For such reasons, as well as because of protectionist policies, the trade opportunities of under-developed countries have been reduced. These reductions go beyond the often bewailed trend in the terms of trade.

(6) Whereas in the pre-industrial phase of now-industrialised societies (with the exception of Japan) areas rich in natural resources were still unsettled and were able to receive immigrants, the world has now been parcelled up and immigration is severely restricted. This, together with accelerated population growth and growing under-utilisation of labour, greatly increases the obstacles to development.

(7) For a number of reasons the attraction for capital and skilled men, including those of the under-developed countries, is greater to the rich industrial societies than to under-developed countries. As a result, some of the scarcest resources are drained off to the rich centres and away from the poor periphery.

(8) While it is true that foreign private enterprise can help to transfer material resources and human skills from rich to poor countries, it also creates greater difficulties than those which were presented by borrowing from abroad to industrialised societies in their pre-industrial phase. Then money was borrowed at fixed interest rates of between 5 and 6 per cent and default was not uncommon. Now almost all long-term private capital takes the form of equity at 15 — 25 per cent pre-tax and 10 — 15 per cent post-tax and default on short-term private and long-term official loans is hardly ever allowed to occur. Servicing profits, interest and dividends creates or aggravates the balance of payments problems of under-developed countries.

(9) Advance has meant national progress and national consolidation in the industrial countries. The benefits of the welfare state are largely confined to its citizens. National consolidation has encouraged nationalism in underdeveloped countries and their own attempts to integrate the nation have tended to lead to international disintegration. Prohibitions imposed by one under-developed country on the movement of men, money, goods and services of others have

reduced the benefits to be derived from the international division of labour or even from regional communities and have inflicted harm on other under-developed countries.

(10) Not only are technical and organisational knowledge ill-adapted and not only can their transfer be harmful to the under-developed countries, but also Western economic concepts and theories, and policies based on them, are often inappropriate and misleading when applied to current development problems. Analysis has tended to focus on investment (whether in fixed capital assets or in an aggregate called 'education') to the neglect of essential reforms of human attitudes and social institutions; and it has tended to formulate categories of aggregates which obscure the relevant distinctions.

(11) Some people have argued that even government aid has obstructed progress towards development by supporting and upholding feudal or conservative regimes which are unwilling to carry out the social and political reforms necessary for progress. Such policies are encouraged, intellectually, by the escape mechanism provided by Western economic theorising and, politically, by powerful vested interests on both the donors' and the recipients' side.

(12) While for these reasons the opportunities to develop have been reduced, the sense of urgency has greatly increased. Seeing opulence and rapid growth abroad means feeling the pain of their absence all the more acutely. It is true not only that what you *don't know doesn't hurt* you, which must have helped the now industrialised societies in their pre-industrial stage, but also that what you *do know does hurt*. This clearly reduces the patience with which the development process is viewed in the under-developed world.

It is this co-existence of rich and poor, rather than the intentional or unintentional colonial or neo-colonial exploitation, which can have detrimental effects on development efforts. And it is this co-existence which sets limits to the ready transfer of the lessons of one historical setting to an entirely different one. No analysis can be valid which does not contain an essentially historical element. No policy can be sound which does not place the development efforts against the activities in the rich countries and points to the need for mitigating the detrimental effects.

In addition to the co-existence of rich and poor, there is also (as Professor Meier pointed out), the more glaring co-existence of poor and poor, all making efforts to lift themselves out of poverty. Competition in exports of a narrow range of primary and manufactured goods, competition for a limited amount of capital and skilled services, competitive nationalism and the refusal to sacrifice sovereignty for gains in production, beggar-my-neighbour tax concessions, tariffs and other import restrictions have led to the mutual impoverishment of a group of countries which should set an example in mutual help.

## THE ROLE OF EDUCATION

Current doctrine awards the highest priority to agricultural, vocational and technical education. It insists that the main task is to link education with agricultural improvement. To make farmers literate will raise their productivity. Progress in primary education does not, however, guarantee literate farmers. In Africa rural children, educated at rural primary schools, will seek jobs in towns, which are paid twice or three times as well as what they could hope to earn if they returned to their farmstead. But not enough town jobs are available. To attract them back to the country, the modernisation of agriculture and the growth of rural schooling must be kept in step. Conclusion: concentrate on agricultural education and restrict universal primary education.

There is a danger that the doctrine of the high priority to be attached to agricultural, vocational and technical education is about to become vulgarised into the *simpliste* belief that more expenditure on this kind of schooling and a reform of the school curriculum are a *sufficient*, a *basic*, or at any rate a *strategic*, condition of development. The originator of the doctrine, Dr. Thomas Balogh, has not been guilty of this simplification,[2] but some of his latter-day disciples have.

First, the provision of vocational, agricultural and technical education is certainly not enough to accelerate development. Equally important is the provision of employment opportunities for technicians and agriculturists, both in the private and in the public sector. The present fault lies not only, and perhaps not mainly, with the type of training provided, but with the educational requirements of the public service. While the public sector rewards academic' qualifications and penalises technical, the wrong incentives will be perpetuated in the educational system. The appearance of white-collar unemployment must not be taken as *ipso facto* evidence of unfilled vacancies in technical and agricultural activities. It may simply be a symptom of general unemployment — or under-utilisation of labour — which would be shared by those educated technically if more were turned out by the educational system.

Second, changes in schooling must be accompanied by higher relative pay and status of technicians and agriculturists. Even if employment opportunities existed, the attractions to clerical jobs of higher prestige, status and pay will continue, unless fundamental reforms are instituted. In order to enable higher wages and salaries to be paid, productivity must rise. Although, therefore, vocationally trained men will be more productive, productivity and pay must be raised in order to provide the incentives for such training. Breaking out of this vicious circle is much more difficult than reforming the schools.

Third, facilities and amenities in rural and technical occupations must be improved. Like status and pay, these are necessary to create the correct incentives. Mr. Kiichi Aichi, chief Cabinet Secretary to Mr. Sato, the Japanese Prime Minister, is reported (*The Times* 13 Sept. 1966) to have seen one of the most important problems in agriculture in its failure to attract good brides — thus adding to the general gloom of the countryside. The government proposed a series of social welfare and amenity reforms to stimulate an influx of desirable brides' into the countryside.

Fourth, even more important than changing the content of education is the conduct of research into crops and animal and plant diseases and the dissemination of this research. It is interesting to note that the contribution of the American land grant colleges lay mainly in this field and not in training farmers.

Fifth, in view of the unreliability of projections of manpower requirements and of the continual advance of technical and agricultural knowledge, schools must lay the foundations for the ability to acquire and use further knowledge. They should provide the general basis for specialist training, not provide this specialist training itself. They should train for mental flexibility and insure against intellectual obsolescence.

Finally, there are social, political and long-term economic reasons for universal primary education of a fairly general type.

The conclusion is that the solution of the problem is much more complex than a change in curriculum. It depends upon a concerted attack on a system of interdependent factors determining agricultural and industrial productivity. An isolated attack on education may be as wasteful or counterproductive as the academic curriculum which has, rightly, been criticised. Although the need for balance between schooling and agricultural reform is obvious, the conclusion should be more rapid and more radical agricultural reform, rather than less and a different kind of schooling.

Dr. Balogh and I have attempted[3] to show that calculations of the returns to education, based on correlating income with educational attainment in the U.S.A., cannot be applied to underdeveloped countries for at least three reasons: first, differences in earnings do not reflect differences in productivity; second, even if they did, education is highly correlated with other causes of higher productivity, such as intelligence, motivation and environmental influences; third, it cannot be assumed that an underdeveloped economy can absorb the educated irrespective of the type of education and irrespective of a host of other measures, and in particular agricultural modernisation and industrialisation. The marginal returns on education by itself may often turn out to be negative.

For the rest I propose to set down only a number of questions:

(1) Are we justified in continuing to support efforts for better remuneration and higher status for teachers? The ratio of a teacher's salary to average income is already two to three times as high in an under-developed country as in a rich one. (A teacher gets seven times the average income or more in Africa compared with one-and-a-half times in the U.S.A.). The proportion of the population aged five to

fourteen is 25 per cent in the former and only 15 per cent in the latter — putting a heavier burden on educational expenditure. This is a complicated question, which raises other questions about the general level of civil service salaries (including teachers'), the relation between qualification of teachers, quality of teaching and salaries and the desirable scale and distribution of the educational effort.

(2) What is the correct balance between capital expenditure on building and recurrent expenditure on staff? Does capital budgeting and project aid-giving reinforce waste and attitudes hostile to development by drawing a false distinction between 'investment' (brick and mortar) and 'consumption' (teachers' salaries)?

(3) What are the causes and cures of over-education?

(4) Should University students be sent to Britain or America (or Moscow or Peking) to be educated or should they be educated, often at greater cost, locally?

(5) What is the correct strategy for a literacy and numeracy campaign?
Should it be directed at children or adults or both?

(6) Where and how has the search for emulating educational standards of the West — whether in content or in length and quality of training — been detrimental to development?

(7) Should research be pure or applied? How should its results be disseminated? What are the barriers to acceptability?

THE ROLE OF AGRICULTURE

It has become part of the current orthodoxy to say that agricultural reform must be given the highest priority. It is however not always made clear why precisely this breakthrough in agriculture is considered to be so crucial, nor how advance on this front is related to advances on other fronts.

A breakthrough in agriculture is necessary for at least five reasons: —

(I) It is necessary in order to feed and supply with raw materials the rapidly growing and indeed increasingly rapidly growing population and in particular the growing proportion of the labour force in industry. This requires a *marketable agricultural surplus*, which must be distinguished from:

(II) the need to provide an *investible agricultural surplus* i.e. provide a source of savings for investment. Industrial workers produce industrial consumer goods as well as industrial producer goods. The marketable surplus is used in exchange for the former; the investible surplus is used to contribute to the finance of the latter.

(III) Agricultural reform is also needed in some cases to reduce balance of payments strains. This can be done by raising the supply of exports, either directly by producing cash crops or indirectly by producing domestic food and raw materials for those engaged in exporting manufactured goods. Or it can be done by substituting domestic food and raw materials for imports.

(IV) The ability of the rural sector to supply food and raw materials to industry implies that the rural sector provides a market for industrial products. The higher the productivity of the rural sector, the higher will be its demand for industrial products. If industry adopts methods of mass production and exploits economies of scale, a prosperous rural sector, by providing an ever widening market, is a condition for progress in industry.

(V) Agricultural development must also provide employment opportunities for the rapidly growing labour force. The need to provide employment opportunities in agriculture and in rural industry calls for technological research, because the available technology is adapted to a shrinking not to an expanding rural labour force. It also calls for land reform, extension services, irrigation and drainage, improved seeds, fertilisers and pesticides, improved storage, transport, credit and marketing facilities and more reliable prices for the produce sold. It would be quite illusory to believe that urban industry can wholly absorb the growing labour force. If we assume that the rate of population growth is the same in agriculture as in industry, say 3 per cent, that the labour force grows at the same rate as population and that 80 per cent of the labour force are in agriculture and 20 per cent in industry, urban industry's demand for labour would have to grow at 15 per cent in order to absorb the whole growth of the labour force. The high growth rate of the labour force will continue for the next 30 years, however effective birth control were to become now. The need for the creation of employment opportunities in the rural sector is aggravated by the fact that population grows more rapidly in the rural sector than in the urban sector, that there is already substantial rural under-utilisation of labour and that the technology used in the urban sector saves labour in relation to capital. It follows that the emphasis on agricultural employment opportunities, far from presenting a case against industrialisation, shows the importance of agricultural advance as a necessary condition for industrialisation.

Rural under-utilisation of labour damages in a number of ways the prospect of successful industrialisation.

(VI) Finally, there is the need to improve the diet and to raise levels of living, both because these are objectives worth pursuing for their own sake and because this would improve the quality of the labour force by reducing apathy and increasing health, strength and vigour. In particular, there is a crying need to improve the diet and level of living of the rural population who constitute the large majority of the working population in under-developed countries and who, while ministering to the basic needs of life, suffer from the most depressed levels of consumption. It is they — the landless labourers, the small tenant farmers, the share-croppers and the peasants with tiny plots of land — who form the proletariat of the world today. Compared with them, the employed industrial workers in the under-developed countries are an aristocracy. Rural reform would therefore, in addition to breaking the main development bottleneck, contribute to a reduction of the most glaring social inequality.

When it comes to saying how the breakthrough in agriculture is to be achieved, there are two schools of thought. There are those who say that the necessary knowledge is available and that it only has to be applied. Existing knowledge would, if used, transform agriculture. It is a failure of will, not a lack of knowledge, which is responsible for agricultural stagnation. The other school does not deny that much available knowledge is not implemented, but emphasises also that existing knowledge, both of methods of production and of organisations, has evolved in conditions of different climate, soil conditions and factor endowments and that we need to know much more about methods of cultivation in tropical conditions where the labour force is likely to continue to increase. This school emphasises that much more research remains to be done on soil conditions in tropical regions, reactions to patterns of rain-fall, drainage, irrigation, fertilisers, improved seeds, animal stocks, cropping patterns, the use and adaptation of agricultural implements, the prevention of plant and animal diseases, the storage of perishable products, the appropriate irrigation schemes, the use of energy from wind, sun and the tides, etc.

But to some extent the dispute between the two schools is a sham dispute. There is no valid line of division between 'knowing' and 'doing'. 'Doing' also is 'knowing', for knowing is not confined to 'knowing that' but compromises 'knowing how'. If there are — as is generally agreed — obstacles to the acceptance and implementation of existing knowledge, research is needed into the reasons for this lack of impact. Here again, as I have stressed in a previous context, we assume too readily that the stock of knowledge in existence in the rich temperate North is there to be drawn upon by the poor arid South. But some resistances may be rational. We should find out whether it is motivation, different reactions to uncertainty, lack of complementary policies, deterrents created by systems of land tenure or attitudes such as those reported by Kusum Nair[1] which prevent implementation.

Another dispute concerns the manner in which the breakthrough in agriculture is to be achieved. At one extreme is the Ford Foundation package: agricultural colleges, extension services, veterinary services, plant breeding, better marketing, control of insect pests, advanced horticulture, fish culture, provision of storage capacity, and several other things must all be done together in order to get anywhere. At the other extreme is Professor Galbraith who believes that the secret is to identify one strategic decision. He illustrates this with the Eyrie Canal and the opening of the American West through the railways. But the analogy has limited value when Galbraith applies it to Asian conditions because capital, skills and complementary

inputs are not available in highly elastic supply to Asia, as
they were to America. W. W. Rostow considers four conditions necessary and sufficient:

  (i) reliable and fair prices;
 (ii) cheap credit;
(iii) technical assistance on the spot;
(iv) input of fertilisers, insecticides, farm tools and incentive
     goods.

But when he says 'putting aside infrastructure and minimum education and assuming a backlog of knowledge',
he puts aside quite a lot.

## THE USE OF SHADOW PRICES IN PLANNING FOR DEVELOPMENT

The call for the use of shadow prices (or accounting prices)
in planning for development stems from the obvious fact
that actual market prices do not reflect social benefits and
social costs. Some are fixed by administrative *fiat*. Others
are 'free', but influenced by restrictive practices or monopolies. Others again are determined by quantitative
controls. The shadow price is the price which would prevail
if prices were equilibrium prices, reflecting marginal social
benefits and marginal social costs.

But such a definition creates a spurious precision. In
order to establish the equilibrium price for *any one* factor or
product, full equilibrium would have to prevail in *all*
markets. Knowledge of the full equilibrium conditions for a
whole economy which, *ex hypothesi* is suffering from a number
of fundamental disequilibria, is not easy to get, even if
determinate meaning could be given to such a concept.

But the assumption of full equilibrium in the whole
economy is ambiguous, and, unless further specified, indeterminate. In order to discover equilibrium prices, we must
know demand and supply curves and the underlying production and consumption functions. But these functions
will be different according to what institutional arrangements
and what human responses we assume. Land prices will
depend upon the system of land tenure and on agricultural
policy generally. The supply price of labour will depend
upon the motivation and education of potential workers,
on the acceptability of employing women and on the attitudes to different kinds of work. The price of capital will

depend upon degrees of monopoly in the economy. The prices which are intended to guide policy are therefore themselves a function of public policy.

The next difficulty is to specify the time dimension of the equilibrium price: are we considering instantaneous, short-term, or long-term equilibrium ? If we postulate instantaneous equilibrium, the price will be altered in the short run, if short-run equilibrium in the long run. If we eliminate a scarcity by using a scarce factor, its short-term shadow price may make its use prohibitive, whilst its long-term shadow price would not show up its present scarcity value. Obviously inputs and outputs must be valued at consistent shadow prices, and benefits and scarcities at different times must be properly discounted, but nevertheless the different valuation may give contradictory results according to which time span is considered.

Another difficulty is that the notion of 'shadow price' becomes indeterminate if a lumpy project A uses an input which is complementary to, or a substitute for, an input into (or an output of) a lumpy project B, which is complementary to, or a substitute for, A. The decision to construct a power station and to electrify a railway line or the decision to construct a railway line and a road, raise the question as to the shadow prices of inputs of labour, capital and foreign exchange. These prices will be different according to which decisions are taken and cannot therefore be a guide to the decisions themselves. Non-infinitesimal decisions are typical of development planning and shadow prices reflecting marginal valuations are therefore not always useful.

To these theoretical difficulties must be added the practical difficulty of using shadow prices in an economy in which businessmen pay actual market prices, workers receive actual wages and money lenders lend at actual interest rates.

None of this is intended to detract from the importance in development planning of modifying judgments of profitability by considerations of social policy. But the impression of spurious precision must be avoided, and it should be made clear that the policy objectives are implicitly contained in the use of shadow prices and the latter can therefore not be used to justify the former.

SINGLE BARRIER THEORIES OF DEVELOPMENT

There is no scarcity of economic theories which attempt to explain the absence of development or its difficulties. Many of them share certain presuppositions. The reasoning commonly takes the following form. It is assumed that all men prefer higher incomes and therefore higher production to lower incomes. Since the knowledge of advanced methods of production is available and need only be transferred from the industrialised countries of the West, there is a presumption that these methods would be adopted everywhere. Since in fact we observe many countries which have not adopted these methods and therefore do not enjoy high incomes, there must be obstacles to development. Many of these theories then single out one obstacle.

Marxian versions see in colonialism and imperialistic exploitation the chief barrier. It is the vested interests of powerful monopolies which prevent the transfer of modern technology and the rise in incomes. But it is not difficult to point to countries and periods where development did not occur, although they were not dominated by colonial powers.

Non-Marxian theories have stressed a number of economic barriers. According to one group of writers, lack of savings keeps down investment, which in turn confines production to primitive techniques, which result in low productivity, low incomes and inability to save. The vicious circle of poverty can be broken only by somehow raising the savings ratio to the point of take-off'. Yet, in many of these societies distribution is very unequal and there should be no difficulty in extracting savings from the richest groups. There is also evidence that even the poorest set aside a part of their income for non-essential purposes, spending it on gold, jewellery, festivities, etc. Very poor countries are known to have been able to save quite considerable proportions for defence or war, for building cathedrals, temples, pagodas or pyramids. All this suggests that in few societies are levels of income so low that all income must be devoted to current expenditure on essentials.

A refinement of this argument says that it was easier for the Egyptians to build pyramids and for mediaeval princes and kings to build cathedrals because they did not have to keep up with any rich Joneses whose consumption levels made their mouths water and weakened the sinews of saving. It is the so-called international Demonstration Effect — the evidence of high living in rich countries — which presents a barrier to higher savings in poor countries. In particular, the elites in the less developed countries, it is argued, take their bearings from the high consumption societies of the West, emulating them on the beaches in the South of France or in Miami, on yachts, or in cadillacs in Paris or Rome. But this theory leaves unexplained why the elites seek to imitate luxury living but not habits of scientific research, experiment, hard work, rational management and entrepreneurial initiative. Savings, as well as consumption, are higher in advanced countries and the demonstration effect could apply to either.

Another theory sees the main obstacle to development in the lack of incentives to invest in productive plant and equipment. According to this theory, savings are, or would be, available, but they are wasted on non-productive invest-ment, such as the acquisition of land, the maintenance of a large number of useless retainers, on palaces and luxury housing, or they are tucked away safely abroad. The in-centive to invest, according to this theory, is weak because productive equipment must be put up with a minimum capacity to be efficient, but markets are too small to justify this minimum capacity. Once again, there is a vicious circle: low incomes cause small markets and small markets prevent the installation of capacity which would raise productivity, and incomes and which would widen the market.

But first, it is possible to find many countries in which domestic markets could quite easily be created by cutting off imports. Second, there are numerous manufacturing activities which can be carried out economically in quite small-scale enterprises. Third, many of these countries pride themselves on having development plans. They could co-ordinate the investment decisions and ensure that markets are provided for large-scale investment projects, by their being undertaken jointly.

Another theory attributes the blockage to the difficulty of constructing overhead capital. Roads, railways, harbours, power stations, require large lumps of capital. Poor countries cannot afford these. But without them, development cannot proceed. Although such projects can be very useful in promoting development, they can often be constructed with labour-intensive methods and, initially, on a relatively small scale and piecemeal. Where large-scale projects have been carried out with foreign aid, they have often turned out to be badly managed and under-utilised.

A more recent group of writers, impressed by the inadequacy of explanations that concentrate on physical capital as the main condition for accelerating development, has stressed 'inadequate investment in human resources', or, more simply, lack of education ana skills. Yet, it is evident that many under-developed countries spend too much on the wrong kind of education and, failing to take other necessary measures, have produced a class of educated unemployed who provide a fertile ground for reactionary rather than economic activity.

Others again have attributed considerable responsibility to deteriorating terms of trade and trading opportunities generally. Yet, countries which enjoy large oil revenues or have a plentiful supply of foreign exchange for other reasons have not been more successful in accelerating development.

The argument so far has been that, although many of these theories point to important obstacles, and although some may be true for certain regions at certain times, they certainly do not show that the removal of these barriers is a sufficient condition for development. In addition, it is possible to point to successful development which occurred in spite of the presence of many of these barriers. Development has taken place even though trading opportunities were unfavourable, even though no foreign loans were available, where the populaton had not been educated, etc. Even although rising savings and investment ratios have normally accompanied development, it is as plausible to argue that they were the *result* of development as it is to say that they were its *cause*.

Such considerations suggest scepticism towards any single-barrier explanation. Obstacles are numerous and interrelated, though clearly some are more important at certain times and in certain places than others.

It is helpful to look at the situation in under-developed countries as a social system. In this system a large number of 'conditions' are causally interrelated, in the sense that a change in any one condition will cause changes in some or all the others. It is possible to group these conditions into the following six broad categories:[3]

(1) Output and Incomes.
(2) Conditions of production.
(3) Levels of living (including nutrition and housing and facilities for health, education and training).
(4) Attitudes to work and life.
(5) Institutions.
(6) Policies.

The first three categories comprise what are usually called 'economic' conditions, while categories (4) and (5) would normally be called 'non-economic', psychological, social, and cultural conditions. Category (6) is a mixture and is regarded as 'economic' if policies aim at changing categories (1) (2) and (3), but not if they aim at changes in human attitudes and social institutions. Sometimes only categories (1) and (2) are considered proper topics of 'economic' analysis.

This particular ordering is arbitrary. Since conditions are interdependent, there can be no 'primary' and 'secondary" conditions, no categories that are more fundamental than others. For certain purposes entirely different categories may be appropriate.

When we speak of an 'under-developed society', we imply that the conditions (1) to (6) are undesirable, judged from the point of view of the ideal of development.

This is not the place to discuss the manner of interaction of these conditions. A change in any one condition can change others either in the same or in the opposite direction and a very great variety of different outcomes are possible. Some of these give rise to a stable equilibrium, others to an unstable equilibrium (a cumulative process upwards or downwards). The types of questions which one would wish to discuss include the following:-

(I) Is this particular classification the most convenient? Does it cover the ground or does it omit any important category? In particular, is it convenient to include facilities for health, education, and training in 'levels of living'?

(II) Is it possible to use quantitative indexes for these

categories and will it be possible to assign coefficients
of interdependence to the relationships ?

(III)   Can these relationships be studied independently of
        the direction of change, the previous history of the
        system and the simultaneous conditions in other
        social systems which have reached higher stages of
        development ?

(IV)    Is the distinction between 'economic' and 'non-eco-
        nomic' conditions tenable ? If not, does this distinc-
        tion contain a systematic bias which is liable to be
        reflected in biased policy recommendations ?

One important advantage of presenting the conditions of
development in this way is to reduce the emphasis laid a
decade ago on the accumulation of physical capital. But,
from another point of view, it is possible to widen the concept
'capital' so as to include anything that yields a stream of
production and income over time. All forms of income-
and product-yielding activities can be interpreted as creating
'assets' whose value can be determined by capitalising the
expected production stream at an appropriate rate of
interest.

Investment in 'human' capital is already generally
treated in this fashion. Raising levels of living by better
feeding, education and health measures, and reforming
some human attitudes by the creation of incentives, are
nowadays treated as investment, although, as in the case of
physical investment, the need for an appropriate composition
is sometimes neglected in the act of aggregation and the
need for complementary activities is occasionally forgotten.
The question remains whether the reform of institutions
(category 5), of *all* relevant attitudes (category 4) and of
policies (category 6) can be approached in the same way —
i.e. as the creation of 'capital' in an even wider sense than
that embracing both physical and human capital.

The answer depends on whether these measures require
the application of current resources and whether the costs
incurred can be subjected to the economic calculus. It can
be argued that the implementation of a land reform or of an
effective birth control campaign depend only to a small
extent on the amount of money spent and that such propositions as 'a pound invested in birth control is a hundred

times as effective as a pound devoted to physical investment '⁶ are pointless. One can admit that costs in the widest
sense must be incurred in order to reform attitudes and institutions, but that these costs are social and psychological
and cannot be subjected to the measuring rod of money.

To this a number of replies can be made. First, even if
these psychic and social costs were entirely unmeasurable,
usually *some* resource cost is involved and it is of interest to
planners what these costs are. Second, the fact that these
'investments' are not embodied either in physical or in
human capital does not *ipso facto* preclude calculation.
Investment in some forms of activity has been transformed
from an arbitrary routine to something calculable. Firms
try to make estimates of the yield of their expenditure on
advertising and the creation of goodwill — activities directed
at changing human attitudes. Similarly, a rough estimate of
the returns on the reform of attitudes, institutions and
policies may be possible, at least in some cases.

Third, the main difficulty arises not because investment
is not 'embodied' in a visible assets, but rather because the
concept 'investment' assumes substitutability between different forms of investment, both in production and consumption — so that the investment yielding the highest
returns can be selected — whereas many investments are
complementary — e.g. equipment, training for a skilled
labour force, social overheads, breakdown of caste prejudices and reform of trade union structure.

At the same time, this way of looking at development
avoids certain kinds of fault: it is no longer possible to say
that labour is a plentiful factor in under-developed countries
and capital is scarce, when it is seen that people have to be
trained, educated, motivated and given the institutional
framework before they become productive agents and these
forms of investment may be even more costly, and may yield
lower returns than investment in certain types of equip-
ment.⁷

While the 'returns to investment' approach tends to
overemphasise the opportunities for substitution (a bias it
shares with marginal productivity theory), the manpower
planning approach has the opposite bias. By assuming
fixed coefficients between skills, other factors of production
and output (and often also between teachers and pupils),

it transfers all the errors of using fixed capital coefficients from planning physical to planning human investment. A generalised approach to capital accumulation may help to correct both biases. It may help to approach different investment complexes (the components of which are complementary) as substitutes in a strategy for development. The returns of such complexes or packages, could, in principle, be compared. But it would amount to the evaluation of different large strategic decisions, not of marginal or infinitesimal moves.

The system may be illustrated by asking what are the prerequisites for the breakthrough in agriculture discussed in a previous section.

(1) Agricultural output and incomes depend upon:
(2) Conditions of production:
    assuming an adequate infrastructure of roads, irrigation, etc., it is necessary to increase inputs such as chemical fertilisers, insecticides and farm tools; and to improve the skills of farmers by training.
(3) Levels of living:
    it is necessary for the farmer to have a minimum level and the right kind of education, health and nutrition. Housing must be in the right place.
(4) Attitudes to work and life:
    it is necessary to increase availability of incentive goods, i.e. things which the farmer and his family would work harder to get; the resistance to work in the country on the part of urban youth and technicians must be broken down.
(5) Institutions:
    there must be a system of land tenure which permits the farmer to reap the benefits of his efforts; credit must be available at low rates of interest to make him change the composition of his crops and raise productivity; the marketing organisation should prevent middle-men from creaming off so much as to leave the farmer inadequate incentive to switch from export crops to domestic food production; diversification often depends on more efficient marketing.
(6) Policies:
    the farmer must be assured of a steady and remunerative

price; technical assistance relevant to his soil, weather conditions and change in technology must be made available *on the spot.*

It can be seen that these conditions interact. Better education, of the right kind, makes farmers more receptive to technical assistance and ready to use irrigation, better seeds, fertilisers and tools. The result of their improved efforts must be marketable at a stable and remunerative price, which reinforces confidence in further improvements and strengthens inducements to undergo the right kind of training.

---

[1] Dudley Seers, 'The Transmission of Inequality' unpublished paper read at the Haile Selassi I Prize Trust Conference in Addis Ababa, October 1966.

[2] T. Balogh. 'Catastrophe in Africa' *Times Educational Supplement,* Jan. 5th 1962 , p. 8 and Feb. 9th, 1962, p. 241. 'What Schools for Africa ?' *New Statesman & Nation,* March 23rd, 1962, p. 412. 'Misconceived Educational Programmes in Africa' *Universities Quarterly,* June 1962, pp. 243-49. 'The Problem of Education in Africa' *The Centennial Review,* Fall 1962, pp. 526-52. 'Education and Economic Growth. Comments on Professor Tinbergen's Planning Model.' *Kyklos,* XVII, 2, 1964, pp. 261-73. 'Land Tenure. Education and Development' International Institute of Educational Planning, *Problems and Strategies of Educational Planning in Latin America.* 1964. 'The Economics of Educational Planning: Sense and Nonsense', *Comparative Education,* October 1964, pp. 5-10.

[3] T. Balogh and P. P. Streeten, 'The Coefficient of Ignorance', *Bulletin of the Oxford University Institute of Economics and Statistics,* May 1963, pp. 99-107.

[4] Kusum Nair, *Blossoms in the Dust,* Gerald Duckworth & Co. 1961.

[5] See Gunnar Myrdal's forthcoming *Asian Drama,* Twentieth Century Fund.

[6] S. Enke, 'The Economic Aspects of Slowing Population Growth', *Economic Journal,* March 1965.

[7] A. Harberger, 'Investment in Man Versus Investment in Machines: The Case of India' in C. A. Anderson and M. J. Bowman, eds., *Education and Economic Development,* 1966.

# The Meaning of Development

*Dudley Seers**

Why do we confuse development with economic growth? Surely one could hardly say that the situation depicted by a set of projections was preferable to that shown by another set simply because the former implied higher *per capita* income. After all, in what sense is South Africa more developed than Ghana, or Kuwait than the U.A.R., or the United States than Sweden?

One explanation is that the national income is a very convenient indicator. Politicians find a single comprehensive measure useful, especially one that is at least a year out of date. Economists are provided with a variable which can be quantified and movements in which can be analysed into changes in sectoral output, factor shares or categories of expenditure, making model-building feasible.

We can, of course, fall back on the supposition that increases in national income, if they are sufficiently fast, sooner or later lead to the solution of social and political problems. But the experience of the past decade makes this belief look rather naïve. Social crises and political upheavals have emerged in countries at all stages of development. Moreover, we can see that these afflict countries with rapidly rising *per capita* incomes, as well as those with stagnant economies. In fact it looks as if economic growth not merely may fail to solve social and political difficulties; certain types of growth can actually cause them.

Now that the complexity of development problems is becoming increasingly obvious, this continued addiction to the use of a single aggregative

* Director of the Institute of Development Studies at the University of Sussex. The first third of this paper is derived from 'The meaning of development' published in the *International Development Review* (Vol. 11, No. 4, 1969), and republished in I.D.S. Communications Series, No. 44; *Revista Brasileira de Economia*, (Vol. 24, No. 3); *Internationale Spectator*, (Vol. XXIV, No. 21); *Ekistics*, 1970; *Sociological Abstracts*, U.S.A., 1970; *The Political Economy of Development* (ed. Ilchman and Uphoff) 1971; and *INSIGHT*, July 1971. I am grateful for comments from Hans Singer on a draft of this part, which was also discussed at seminars at the Universities of .Boston and Toronto, and formed the basis of a lunch talk at the 11th World Conference of the Society for International Development (New Delhi, November 1969). The remainder was written specially for this collection.

indicator, in the face of the evidence, takes on a rather different appearance. It begins to look like a preference for avoiding the real problems of development.

## THE DEFINITION OF DEVELOPMENT

In discussing the challenges we now face, we have to dispel the fog around the word 'development' and decide more precisely what we mean by it. Only then will we be able to devise meaningful targets or indicators, and thus to help improve policy, national or international.

The starting-point is that we cannot avoid what the positivists disparagingly refer to as 'value judgements'. 'Development' is inevitably a normative concept, almost a synonym for improvement. To pretend otherwise is just to hide one's value judgements.

But from where are these judgements to come? The conventional answer, which Tingerben accepts for his system of economic planning, is to draw our values from governments. But governments have necessarily a rather short-term view, in some cases discounting the future at a very high rate. More seriously, some governments are themselves the main obstacles to development, on any plausible definition, and once this is conceded, where is one to obtain the yardsticks by which government objectives are to be judged? Even supposing that governments represented faithfully, in some sense, popular attitudes, these are endogenous to the development process and therefore cannot provide a means of assessing it.

Another approach is to copy the development paths of other countries, which implicitly means aiming at thir present state as the goal. This is what model-builders, for example, are really doing when coefficients are taken from an international cross-section analysis, or from functions that fit the experience of an industrial country. Yet few if any of the rich countries now appear to the outside world as really desirable models. Some aspects, such as their consumption levels, seem enviable, but these are associated, perhaps inseparably, with evils such as urban sprawl, advertising pressures, air pollution and chronic tension. Besides it is by no means obvious or even likely that the rest of the world could trace the history of the industrial countries even if they wanted to.

If values are not to be found in politics or history, does this mean that we are each left to adopt our own personal set of values? This is fortunately not necessary. Surely the values we need are staring us in the face, as soon as we ask ourselves: what are the necessary conditions for a universally acceptable aim, the realization of the potential of human personality?

If we ask what is an *absolute* necessity for this, one answer is obvious—enough food. Below certain levels of nutrition, a man lacks not merely bodily energy and good health but even interest in much besides food. He cannot rise significantly above an animal existence. If anyone has any doubt on the primacy of food, they should reflect on the implications of recent research [*Scrimshaw and Gordon, 1968*] showing that if young children are not properly nourished the result may well be lasting impairment not merely of the body, but also of the mind.

Since foodstuffs have prices, in any country the criterion can be expressed in terms of income levels. This enables it to take account also of certain other minimum requirements. People never spend all their money (or energy) on food, however poor they are. To be enough to feed a man, his income has also to cover basic needs of clothing, footwear and shelter.

But I am not talking about consumption needs in general; I am talking about the capacity to buy physical necessities.

Peter Townsend and others who support a 'relative' concept of poverty describe those in any society as poor if they are unable to 'participate in the activities and have the living conditions and amenities which are customary in that society. These activities and customs have to be described empirically. In addition to food and clothing customs, they include, for example, in the United Kingdom, such things as birthday parties for children, summer holidays and evenings out' [*Townsend, 1970, p. 42*]. This concept of poverty as social deprivation implies that the poverty standard would rise as living conditions improve, and indeed that poverty could *never* be eliminated, except perhaps by making the distribution of income very equal. But to see one's child doomed by malnutrition to lifelong physical and mental inferiority or to be unable to buy a blood transfusion to save one's wife's life is surely a different sort of poverty from being unable to afford the cakes for a children's party or to take one's wife out to the pictures.

What I am asserting is that below the level at which a man can in some sense provide 'enough' food for his family, the marginal utility of income is much greater than it is above that level. This is of course an old-fashioned view, and it raises many problems of concepts and measurement to which I return later. But wherever there is serious poverty, a normative approach to development, which I have argued to be inevitable, implies a utility function of this general shape.

Another basic necessity, in the sense of something without which personality cannot develop, is *a job*. This does not necessarily mean paid employment: it can include studying, working on a family farm or keeping house. But to play none of these accepted roles, i.e. to be chronically dependent on another person's productive capacity, even for food, is incompatible with self-respect for a non-senile adult, especially somebody who has been spending years at school, perhaps at university, preparing for an economically active life.

It is true, of course, that both poverty and unemployment are associated in various ways with income. But even a fast increase in *per capita* income is in itself far from enough, as the experience of many economies shows, to reduce either poverty or unemployment. In fact, certain processes of growth can easily be accompanied by, and in a sense cause, growing unemployment.[1]

The direct link between *per capita* income and the numbers living in poverty is *income distribution*. It is a truism that poverty will be eliminated much more rapidly if any given rate of economic growth is accompanied by a declining concentration of incomes. Equality should, however, in my belief, be considered an objective in its own right, the third element in development. Inequalities to be found today, especially in the Third

World where there is massive poverty, are objectionable by any religious or ethical standards. The social barriers and inhibitions of an unequal society distort the personalities of those with high incomes no less than of those who are poor. Trivial differences of accent, language, dress, customs, etc., acquire an absurd importance and contempt is engendered for those who lack social graces, especially country dwellers. Since race is usually highly correlated with income, economic inequality lies at the heart of racial tensions. More seriously, inequality of income is associated with other inequalities, especially in education and political power, which reinforce it.

The questions to ask about a country's development are therefore: What has been happening to poverty? What has been happening to unemployment? What has been happening to inequality? If all three of these have become less severe, then beyond doubt this has been a period of development for the country concerned. If one or two of these central problems have been growing worse, especially if all three have, it would be strange to call the result 'development', even if *per capita* income had soared. This applies, of course, to the future too. A 'plan' which conveys no targets for reducing poverty, unemployment and inequality can hardly be considered a 'development plan'.[2]

Of course, the true fulfilment of human potential requires much that cannot be specified in these terms. I cannot spell out all the other requirements, but this paper would be very unbalanced if I did not mention them at all. They include adequate educational levels (especially literacy), participation in government and belonging to a nation that is truly independent, both economically and politically, in the sense that the views of other governments do not largely predetermine one's own government's decisions.[3]

As undernourishment, unemployment and inequality dwindle, these educational and political aims become increasingly important objectives of development. Later still, freedom from repressive sexual codes, from noise and pollution, become major aims.[4] But these would not override the basic economic priorities, at least for really poor countries, with large numbers of undernourished children. A government could hardly claim to be 'developing' a country *just because* its educational system was being expanded or political order was being established, or limits set on engine noise, if hunger, unemployment and inequality were significant and growing, or even if they were not diminishing. Indeed, one would doubt the viability of political order in these circumstances, if one didn't consider the claim *prima facie* somewhat suspect; on the other hand, certain political patterns may well be incompatible with development.

Before leaving this issue I must make it clear that the national income is not totally meaningless, just because it is an inappropriate indicator of development. It has some significance as a measure of development *potential*. Suppose that two countries start a decade with the same *per capita* income and one grows faster than the other over ten years, but that the increase in income in the former goes entirely to the rich, and that, because growth has been due to highly capital-intensive techniques, unemployment rates remain unchanged, while in the latter growth has been slower but has meant lower unemployment and thus benefited the poorest class. Then, although the country with faster growth has, on my criteria, developed least—in fact not developed at all—it has achieved greater potential for developing later.

In the first place, the fiscal system could bring about development more rapidly the greater the income available for transfer to the poor. Moreover, a fast growth rate implies a greater savings capacity, which could more easily mean true development in the future. Indeed the faster-growing country may well already have a higher level of investment *per capita*; if this investment is in agricultural projects which will raise food production and provide more rural employment, or in rural schools, genuine development could already be foreshadowed for the future.[5]

From a long-term viewpoint, economic growth is for a poor country a necessary condition of reducing poverty. But it is not a sufficient condition. To release the development potential of a high rate of economic growth depends on policy. A country where economic growth is slow or negligible may be busy reshaping its political institutions so that, when growth comes, it will mean development; such a country could develop faster in the long run than one at present enjoying fast growth but with political power remaining very firmly in the hands of a rich minority. It will be interesting to compare, for example, what happens in Cuba and Brazil in the remainder of this century.

PRIORITIES IN THE SOCIAL SCIENCES

It may help us to withstand the strong intellectual attraction of the national income as a yardstick of development if we look back a little.

By about 1950 the great economic problems had been brought largely under control in the industrial countries. Unemployment had been reduced to historically very low levels; absolute poverty in the sense I use the word had been largely eliminated; taxation and educational advances had reduced economic inequalities, and, though a good deal of what remained was associated with race, this was not a source of great political at that time, and it was largely overlooked by the social scientists, especially the economists.

We could say that these countries had managed in various ways to meet, in some degree at least, the challenges they had faced in the 19th century. One reason, of course, was that they benefited from world economic leadership and political power—to this I'll return later. But another was that social scientists such as Booth, Towntree, Boyd-Orr, the Webbs, Keynes, Beveridge and Tawney focused attention sharply on poverty, unemployment and inequality in the first half of this century. (I hope I am not being excessively nationalistic in choosing British examples: the names *are* rather significant.) Most economists, even Pigou, took greater equality as an obviously desirable objective.

With the easing of the big problems, however, economists turned their attention to innovations in professional techniques. In as far as they retained interest in current affairs, it was mainly in the progress of the nation conceived as a whole. The national income seemed ideal for comparing growth rates of a country during different periods, or for constructing an international league table. Moreover, it has maintained its role as a predictor of the level of employment—if the economy is diversified and the labour force is mobile, big short term changes in the national income are closely associated with changes in employment.[6]

We now see that even in the industrial countries basic economic problems had not really been cured. Their social scientists, notably in the United States, have been rediscovering their own poverty. Moreover, unemployment has recently grown, and inequality may well have done so too.

But the fundamental problems have never even started to disappear from sight in the Third World. In Africa, Asia or Latin America, development had been very limited on any of the three economic criteria until 1950. Since then, there has certainly been some reduction in the proportion, even if not in absolute numbers, living in poverty. But it has recently been estimated by Francis Keppel that seven out of every ten children in the entire world are 'affected by the apathy typical of chronic protein deficiency, an apathy which translates into diminished learning potential' [*Scrimshaw and Gordon, 1968*]; the fraction among many countries of the Third World, such as India, must of course be higher. Unemployment seems to have grown, judging from the countries for which data are available. It is probable, though data are extremely poor, that in most countries inequality has not been reduced; in many, it may well have increased. A paper by A. J. Jaffe [*1969*] on five Latin American countries for which comparable studies over time are available concludes that all showed increasing inequalities, with the possible exception of Mexico. It is even possible that, were the data available, we would find economic growth to be directly associated with growing unemployment and increasing inequality. If that has indeed been the case, there has been a negative correlation between growth and development. Even if that were not so, it is clear that the connection between them is not at all as straightforward as was once believed.

CONCEPTUAL AND MEASUREMENT PROBLEMS

One defence of the *national income* is that it is an objective, value-free indicator, Yet it is in fact heavily value-loaded: every type of product and service is assigned its own particular weight (many being zero). This weight is mainly determined by market forces, which reflect the country's income distribution. A familiar question in economics—how adequately income measures demand when its distribution is unequal—gets additional point when the distribution is as highly concentrated as it is in the countries of the Third World. Another question—how objective demand is when it is partially determined by salesmanship—appears even more cogent when tastes are to some extent imported from abroad. But, in addition, official policies, e.g. fostering import substitution by controls, often increase the prices of luxuries much more than of necessities. There are often egalitarian reasons for such policies, but the outcome is paradoxically that increases in production of luxuries count very much more highly in the estimation of rates of economic growth than they do in industrial countries.[7] While prices of staple foods and clothing may be comparable between poor countries and rich, perhaps lower in the former, prices of cars, refrigerators, etc., are several times as high. The absurd consequence may be that in a country where there is serious poverty, a car counts for more than ten tons of rice.

To estimate or use the national income also implies a set of judgements about what activities it should cover—what are the 'final' products, as against 'intermediate' products which are not considered intrinsically valuable and only produced because they make possible the products of other, more desirable, products. This raises the basic question: what activities are we trying to maximize?—a question once posed by Kuznets and now revived by Sametz [1968].[8] The issue of distribution can be raised in these terms too—are the luxuries of the professional classes a 'necessary cost' of raising the incomes of the poor, the real maximand?

It has also been argued on behalf of national income as a development indicator that it could at least be quantified. But what are all the voluminous tables of national income accounts really worth? So far as the Third World is concerned, much of what they ought to cover is virtually outside the scope of official statistics. This applies above all to output of domestic foodstuffs, even the staples, let alone subsidiary crops which come under the general heading of 'market gardening' (American 'truck farming'), not to speak of fish, forest products, etc. Extremely rough methods of estimation are often used, much of the output being assumed to rise in proportion to the increase in rural population, an increase which is in turn assumed to be some constant arbitrary rate in the absence of registration of births and deaths, or data on migration.[9] Secondly, we know very little about construction in the countryside by the farming community itself; this apparently amounts to a good deal if one takes account not only of building houses, but also clearing land, digging wells and ditches, constructing fences and hedges, etc. Thirdly, there are practically no basic data on domestic service and other personal services, even those which are remunerated.

We should ask national income estimators conceptual questions such as: which of the activities a farm family does for itself without payment, such as haircutting for example, have you included in the national income? And why? And practical questions such as: how many fishes were caught in Province A in the years concerned? How many huts were constructed in Province B? How many barbers worked in Province C? And how do you know?

We should also ask those who quote the national income, for example in a planning office or a university, how much time they have spent with the estimators? It is unsafe and therefore unprofessional to use national income data until one has personally satisfied oneself on how such questions have been handled.

I have examined the worksheets in about twenty countries; the blunt truth of the matter is that when one takes into account the difficulties of allowing for inventory changes and depreciation, and of deflating current-price data, the published national income series for a large number of countries have very little relevance to economic reality.[10] In many countries, any reasonably competent statistician could produce from the meagre basic data series showing the real *per capita* income either rising or falling. Decimal places are fantasy. Some series are in fact in a way more misleading than sets of random numbers would be, because they *appear* to have a significance. It would, of course, be very convenient if the national income data published in such quantities had objective meaning, but unfortunately this does not make them meaningful.

It might be argued that some numbers called national income series are at least available, whereas data on poverty, unemployment and inequality are very scrappy. This is, however, the result not so much of basic differences in estimation possibilities as of attitudes to development. The type of data collected reflects priorities. What work is done by a statistical office depends in practice partly on what its own government demands, partly on the advice it receives from various U.N. agencies, especially the U.N. Statistical Office. As a realization of the importance of social problems spreads, statistical offices will put less weight on national income estimation, more on preparing appropriate social indicators.[11]

I do not deny that there are conceptual problems with development indicators too. The difficulties in assessing *poverty* standards, or even minimum nutritional standards, are well known.[12] For a household these should reflect the ages and also the physical activities of its members.[13] Moreover, many households which can afford to exceed the nutritional minimum expenditure will not in fact do so, because they spend their money in a sense unwisely (whether because of conventional expenditures on non-essentials, lack of information or personal taste).[14] The recognition of this is indeed implicit in the official U.S. poverty line which allows $750 a head, of which about $250 is for food.

But we need not give up. When as in India, an official poverty line has been established, the resultant estimates of the proportion with incomes below a specified poverty line are not without meaning.[15] However rough, they have some significance as a yardstick for measuring development over time—certainly such comparisons convey more than changes in the *per capita* national income.

There are other well-known measures of poverty which I can only mention briefly here. One is the infant mortality rate (though this reflects in particular the effectiveness of health services, as well as diet, housing, etc.). Data on protein consumption and the incidence of diseases of undernourishment, such as rickets, are further clues on development, as are the height and weight of children.[16] However, they are only clues, and may well be misleading if used to compare nations of very different genetic stock, dietary habits, etc.

*Unemployment* is, of course, notoriously difficult to define in non-industrial societies. An urban unemployed person can be roughly identified by the usual test questions designed to reveal the last occasion when work was sought (though this means excluding from the unemployed those who would only look for a job if they thought there was any chance of finding it, and on the other hand including those who would in fact only accept particular types of work). In addition there is involuntary short time working, and people are more or less idle, at least for most of the day, in jobs which are more or less fictional (from superfluous posts in government to shining shoes). The volume of this is hard to measure; so is disguised rural under-employment because of seasonal variations in activity. One needs much more detail by sector, by region, by sex, by age, by educational qualification, to throw light on the nature of unemployment and underemployment in any country and on the attitudes of people to work.[17]

*Inequality* can be measured in many ways—by size, race, region, or by factor shares. All have their uses for different purposes, and they are of course all interconnected. They are also all limited in one important respect, namely that there are other sources of inequality than income. One's standard of living may be affected by access to free cars, for example. (An ambassador may well have a higher level of living than somebody with ten times his salary.) It also depends on access to public services such as health (especially important in urban-rural comparisons). More fundamentally, political power may greatly influence the inequality of people in terms of their ability to develop their personality, even to speak their minds.

Even concentration of income by size can be measured in many ways. If one wants a single measure, the Gini coefficient, derived from the Lorenz curve (showing cumulative proportions of income received by cumulative proportions of recipients), is probably still the most useful, for either income or wealth. But, if we are mainly concerned with inequality as a cause of poverty, a more meaningful measure may be to express (say) the lowest decile as a fraction of the median (following the general approach in a recent study by Harold Lydall [*1968*].[18] We are after all not greatly interested in changes *within* the top half of the income ladder.

Of course, all these measures of distribution raise the same conceptual problems as national income measurement—for example, where to draw the boundary between activities which are marketed and those which are not. In addition, such measures take no account of the price structure, which may well affect the concentration of *real* income—an important point in, e.g., countries where the burden of protection is borne mainly by the rich.

All in all, however, the conceptual problems of these indicators do not seem to be more formidable than those of the national income—we have just grown accustomed to ignoring the latter. And many of the practical problems are the same as those that face the national income estimators. But indicators of any of the elements of development I have mentioned also require supplementary information. Thus to measure the proportion of the population above a poverty line one needs to know how many people share each household income (and whether they are males or females, adults or children). To measure unemployment meaningfully, one needs to know what jobs people would be prepared to take (and at what income), and what hours they work. To measure distribution in any of its dimensions, one needs to know more than the national estimator about who receives various types of income.

But again we must not be diverted by such technical problems from attempting the assessment which really matters. There is one possible source for all of these measures, surveys of households designed to provide them; these can yield the necessary cross-classifications by region, race, income, etc. The systematic development of the information required to study trends in poverty, unemployment and income distribution in any country requires pilot surveys in depth to clarify the conceptual issues in their local context and guide the construction of indicators. This is best achieved if a permanent sampling organization, such as India has in its National Sample Survey, is established to collect the necessary information professionally, systematically and regularly.

I can only mention briefly indicators for the educational and political dimensions of development. In as far as education is provided by the formal educational system (which is very much open to argument) the main source is, of course, inputs and outputs of various levels of education. A technique for combining these in a diagram showing trends over time has been developed by Richard Jolly [*1969*].

Measurement of the extent to which the political aims have been achieved is of course much more difficult; possible clues include the number of prisoners held for political or quasi-political reasons, and the social and racial composition of parliaments, business boards, senior public administrative grades, etc., and also of those enjoying secondary and university education.

More general indicators of welfare, reflecting political and other influences, include the rates per million people of crimes of violence, suicide, alcoholism and other types of drug addiction. Here the main problem is to cope with the consequences of different standards of reporting, stemming from differences in definition (what is an alcoholic?) and in coverage (e.g. comprehensiveness of police records, death registers, etc.). Interpretation raises further problems. Thus is rural violence to be treated as a reflection of intolerable living conditions or of envy—or is it to be considered a necessary cost of a desirable social change?

Clues on the degree of national independence include the proportion of capital inflows in exchange receipts, the proportion of the supply of capital goods (or intermediates) which is imported, the proportion of assets, especially subsoil assets, owned by foreigners, and the extent to which one trading partner dominates the patterns of aid and trade. But there are also qualitative indicators such as the existence of foreign military bases and overflying rights, and the extent to which the country follows the lead of one of the great powers in the United Nations.

## THE COMPATIBILITY OF INDICATORS

This section raises the problem of weighing and comparing different indicators, a major indicator problem. It is, of course, impossible to explore all its aspects here, but it may be useful to indicate some major possibilities of inconsistency and how serious these seem to be.

On the face of it, there is a strong causal interrelation between the three leading indicators. Development on any of them implies, or helps bring about, or may even be a necessary condition for, development on one or more of the others. To reduce unemployment is to remove one of the main causes of poverty and inequality. A reduction in inequality will of course reduce poverty, *ceteris paribus*.

But are other things equal? Does lowering the concentration of income imply a slower rate of economic growth—and growth is, as we have seen, in the long run a necessary condition for eliminating poverty. And would slower growth impair employment prospects? There is a well-known, indeed classical, argument that inequality generates savings and incentives and thus promotes economic growth and employment.

I find the argument that the need for savings justifies inequality unconvincing in the Third World today. Savings propensities are after all very low precisely in countries with highly unequal distributions; the industrial countries with less concentration of income have, by contrast, much higher savings propensities. Savings are, of course, also affected by the absolute level of incomes, but the explanation of this paradox must in part lie in the high consumption standards of an unequal society.

Moreover, the rich in most countries tend to have extremely high propensities, not merely to spend, but to spend on goods and services with a high foreign exchange content, and, for countries suffering from an acute foreign exchange bottleneck, this is a major obstacle to development.[19] It is true that import demand can be held in check by administrative controls, but this leads to the elaboration of a bureaucratic apparatus which is expensive, especially in terms of valuable organizing ability, and which in some countries becomes riddled with corruption. In fact, the result of import control is often to create a protected and highly profitable local industry, which itself depends heavily on imports of intermediate products and capital goods, and remits abroad a large flow of money in profits, interest, royalties, licence fees and service charges of various sorts.[20] In any case, in a highly unequal society, personal savings often flow abroad or go into luxury housing and other investment projects of low or zero priority for development, or even for growth.

The argument that only inequality can provide the incentives that are necessary is also obviously of limited validity in a country where there are barriers of race or class or caste to advancement. Still, we cannot dismiss it out of hand. The needs for private entrepreneurial talent vary according to the circumstances of different economies, but there are very few where this need is small. Countries relying on growing exports of manufactures, as many do, depend heavily on the emergence of businessmen with the drive to penetrate foreign markets. All countries depend in some degree on the appearance of progressive farmers. Will these emerge without financial rewards on a scale that will make nonsense of an egalitarian policy? Are rising profits of companies, especially foreign companies, an inevitable feature of growth in many countries? Or are we exaggerating the importance of financial incentives? Can other non-financial rewards partially take their place?[21] Can social incentives be developed to a point where people will take on such tasks with little or no individual reward (as the governments of China and Cuba are trying to procure)?

The compatibility of growing equality and rising output and employment has recently become doubtful for an additional set of reasons. Can the people who are professionally necessary be kept in the country if they earn only a small fraction of which they could earn elsewhere? How much un-employment will their departure involve, because their labour is comple-mentary to that of the rest of the labour force? Yet what are the costs in terms of human welfare and even efficiency if they are prevented from leaving?[22]

On the other hand, there are also very serious reasons for questioning the compatibility of *in*equality and the growth of income and employ-ment. One is implied by the discussion of the composition of consumption above. Can a manufacturing industry be created to correspond to the struc-ture of demand that arises in a highly inequitable society (leaving aside the question of whether it *should* be created)? Will production rise rapidly if the proportion of the labour force which is too badly nourished for full manual and mental work is only sinking slowly? Can the government obtain the co-operation of the population in wage restraint, and in many other ways that are necessary for development, if there is visible evidence of great wealth which is being transmitted from generation to generation, so that the wage earner sees his children and his children's children doomed indefinitely to subordinate positions? Or if there is little prospect of reducing unemployment? Can political leaders under such circum-stances mobilize the energies of the population and break down social customs which obstruct development, especially in rural areas?

I do not pretend to know the answers to this complex of questions, which point to a set of 'internal contradictions' in the development processes more severe than those to which Marx drew attention. Any answer must in any case be specific to the country concerned. All I would say is that such questions have usually been ignored in the past, leading to a failure to appreciate the damaging consequences of inequality.

Yet another set of questions arises out of the potential inconsistency between employment in the short-run and employment in the longer term—which is often formulated as a conflict between employment and growth. There has recently been much discussion of this [*Stewart and Streeten, 1971*]. All I would say is that here too the conflict has been ex-aggerated. It would after all be surprising if the mobilization of all the above labour in a typical economy caused anything but a big rise in output.

My original paper, to which I referred in the first footnote, went on to discuss the consistency between these economic objectives and those mentioned above, in the political and social planes—political order and liberty, independence and education. I will not go over this ground here—it would take us rather far from the subject of development indicators (the interested reader can turn to the references given in that paper—though this is not to deny that political and economic dimensions of development are connected, certain political systems are incompatible with progress towards equality, because of the relationship between the distribution of income and political power.

IMPLICATIONS FOR PLANNING

The most important use of development indicators is to provide the targets for planning. The realization that the national income is in itself an inadequate yardstick of development implies a recognition that national income targets are not very relevant. We need instead targets for poverty, employment and income distribution, specifying some of the dimensions of the structure of society at which we are aiming.

The difference in approach is more profound than it seems. Formerly the basic technique consisted in extrapolating past trends and choosing investment patterns that would produce an acceptable increase in national income in a five-year period, tacitly assuming many constraints as given— thus consumption patterns were projected in a way that assumed little or no change in income distribution or in tastes or attitudes. Now we must try to envisage what might be a satisfactory pattern at some time in the future, in terms not only of production and employment structures, but of the patterns of income distribution, consumer demand and jobs, and then work backwards, to see if there is any plausible path for getting there.

The econometrician searches for planning models with multiple objectives, in response to this challenge. But perhaps the task is much simpler: to lift every family above a poverty line, based on food requirements, bare minimum though it may be. To achieve this must imply the elimination of poverty and unemployment and (especially if the time span is short) a reduction in inequality. It implies setting target incomes for various sizes of families and working out what measures would be needed to achieve these (the measures may include not only employment creation, but also welfare schemes such as special food programmes for children, pensions, etc.). The final step is to estimate what measures need to be taken in policy areas such as taxation and incomes.

This approach raises statistical problems. In the first place, sufficiently detailed income and expenditure studies are rarely available; even if they were, there would be problems of relating poverty lines to household composition, referred to above. Further, it would be hard to incorporate complicated indicators in development models and one might have to settle for something as crude as a minimum household income. Converting targets into policies raises further problems because of the many different influences on the income of the poor and because typically there is no machinery for straightforward fiscal redistribution. But the approach is nevertheless worth pursuing—its difficulties are no excuse for persisting with inappropriate, even dangerously misleading, planning models designed to maximize economic growth.

To concentrate on the elimination of poverty implies that increased income for the rest of the population is irrelevant so long as there is undernourishment, especially of children. So be it. We must however, recognize the risk that some redistributive strategies *may* in some circumstances hamper economic growth and thus the more fundamental long-term solution of the problem of poverty.

INTERNATIONAL DEVELOPMENT

The criteria suggested above can in principle be applied to any unit—a village, a province, a nation, a continent or the world. Let me in closing refer briefly to indicators of world development. Basically the same concepts of poverty and employment apply, but in the case of inequality we are now primarily concerned with comparisons between incomes of different nations, as a guide to the policy tasks which face the rich countries if they are to contribute to the development of the poor.

There has been progress, especially since the 1930s, on the poverty criterion; the proportion of the whole human population living below any subsistence line must have fallen. But total overt world unemployment must have grown, since the emergence of unemployment in the Third World must numerically outweigh the decline of unemployment in the industrial countries. In recent years, in any case, unemployment has risen in the latter too, so there can be no doubt of the world trend (though it is not very meaningful to add together national statistics for something like unemployment which takes so many forms). Moreover, since the middle of the last century enormous gaps have opened between rich countries and poor: inequality on the present scale is an entirely new phenomenon, as papers by Simon Kuznets [*1971, pp. 27ff.; 1966, pp. 390–400*] and Surendra Patel [*1964*] have brought out.

Economic inequality between nations, like inequality within them means differences in status and power, poisoning the attitudes of men towards each other. This, again as on the national level, means growing tensions between races, broadly in this case (as also inside many countries) between the whites and the remainder. Moreover, the incompatibility of inequality with the elimination of poverty is clearer for development on the international than on the national plane. The seepage, through many channels, of the consumption habits of rich countries has contributed to unemployment in poorer countries (see above), and probably also meant slower economic growth. The transfer of technologies designed for rich countries has had similar effects; available technologies are becoming increasingly inappropriate for the worlds needs. The growing difference in *per capita* incomes also stimulates the 'brain drain' and exerts an upward pull on professional salaries in poor countries. Thus national and international inequality are linked.[23]

When we consider the world scene, it is wrong to talk about 'development', on the criteria suggested above. One cannot really say that there has been development for the world as a whole, when the benefits of technical progress have accrued to minorities which were already relatively rich. To me, this word is particularly misleading for the period since the war, especially the 'development decade' when the growth of economic inequality and unemployment may have actually accelerated. (The prospect of a 'second development decade' is daunting: a repetition of the 1960s with unemployment and inequality rising still further, would be socially, economically and politically disastrous whatever the pace of economic growth!)

The measurement of international inequality raises its own set of conceptual problems. Egalitarians like myself face a theoretical paradox. If we argue that the national income is an inappropriate measure of a nation's development, we weaken the significance of a growing *per capita* income 'gap' between rich nations and poor. However, there is really no alternative—a world income distribution by size, showing the magnitude of absolute poverty, would be immensely difficult to construct.

There are, moreover, special conceptual difficulties about international comparisons of income. Comparisons of incomes have limited significance when life styles are so different (affecting among other things the proportion of activity covered by cash transactions and thus included in 'income'), and when there are differences in climate.

A familiar measurement problem is the inapplicability of exchange rates as means of converting incomes in different currencies to a standard of comparison (such as the U.S. dollar). Attempts have been made to prepare exchange rates more appropriate for measuring the true purchasing power of different currencies, but these run up against well-known problems of weighting.[24]

Still, we must not fall into the familiar trap of criticizing statistics to the point where we deny them any meaning. Despite all its limitations (including the additional one of defining a 'rich' country) the statement that during the first 'development decade' the ratio between the average income of rich countries and poor has increased from about 12:1 to about 15:1 is not entirely lacking in content, either morally or analytically. It illustrates the widespread impact on poor countries of increasingly inappropriate salaries, consumption patterns and technologies, aggravating their own intractable problems of inequality and unemployment.

One thing this critique suggests the need for the continued worldwide development of subsidiary indicators mentioned above, such as infant mortality rates, calorie and protein consumption, and the incidence of diseases of poverty and under-nourishment.

There are of course political dimensions to international as to national development. A big step was taken in the first post-war decade with the creation of a whole system—the United Nations and its agencies. But since then progress has been very gradual, due basically to the unwillingness of the rich countries to limit their sovereignty and accept the authority of international organizations. The continued eruption of wars is an eloquent indicator of a lack of political progress which goes far to explain the negative development of the world as a whole.

NOTES

1. Thus in Trinidad the growth in *per capita* income averaged more than 5 per cent a year during the whole period 1953–68, while overt unemployment showed a steady increase to more than 10 per cent of the labour force.

2. Suppose, for example, that a perspective plan specified that *per capita* income of Brazil doubled in the next thirty years, but assumed no change in distribution or in the proportion unemployed. Then at the turn of the century, a big landowner in the Matto Grosso could run four cars, instead of two, and a peasant in the North-East could eat two kilogrammes of meat a year instead of one. His son might well be still out of work. Could we really call that 'development'?

3. These dimensions are discussed in Mrs Baster's introduction.

4. Even for countries at a high level of development in any sense, the use of national income as an indicator is being widely challenged, e.g. by Mishan [*1967*], on the grounds that the environmental costs are ignored.

5. In an interesting paper Divatia and Bhatt [*1969*] put forward a different index of development potential, based on fundamental factor inputs such as capital and skills (though it is misleadingly described as a measure of the 'pace of development'). Movements in such an index could foreshadow what the future pace of economic growth could be. The index for India, for example, is encouraging because it shows a rate of increase twice as fast as the real national income. But, of course, it does not follow that growth potential *will* be released, let alone that development will take place.

6. This use of the national income had been developed by Colin Clark [*1937*]. In fact the great spurt forward in national income statistics in the 1930s and 1940s was due largely to the unemployment problem, although also to the need to quantify alternative wartime policies.

7. In addition, indirect taxes of various kinds on luxuries are relatively heavy, so such biases are particularly severe when market prices are used as weights.

8. For example, is a journey to work really an end product, as national estimators assume (especially a journey on a metropolitan underground railway!)? Additional issues are now being posed in industrial countries by the failure of national income to allow for the costs of environmental destruction, i.e. to be a sufficiently 'net' concept in that sense.

9. Every so often a researcher tries to draw conclusions about trends in *per capita* food consumption, which of course simply means revealing the implications of assumptions made by official statisticians.

10. There is an upward bias as well. The share of output covered by official statistics, and included in the national income, tends to rise, partly because a growing proportion of output passes through the hands of organized business, which is more adequately covered by official statistics, but also partly because of the general improvement in data collection.

11. The U.N. Statistical Office's 'A Complementary system of Statistics of the Distribution of Income, Expenditure and Wealth' is a useful starting-point.

12. Various poverty lines in India, where there has been much work on this question, are discussed by Fonseca [*1970*].

13. See papers by Abel-Smith, Bagley, Rein and Townsend in Townsend [*1970*].

14. This problem was first recognized by Rowntree [*1901*] in his classic enquiry in York, leading him to distinguish between 'primary' and 'secondary' poverty—the latter referring to the poverty of those who could afford the nutritional minimum but do not in fact attain it.

15. See, however, an interesting pair of articles by Minhas [*1970*] and Bardhan [*1970*], which show that even using the same criterion of poverty (one proposed in 1962 by a distinguished group of economists to the Planning Mission) very different conclusions can be reached on trends in the proportions lying below the poverty line through using different sources of consumption data, different allowances for price changes and different interpolation procedures.

16. Several indicators can be combined to give us an indicative profile of the prevalence of poverty in a nation, such as the U.N. Research Institute for Social Development has been experimenting with in Geneva. In fact they have taken a step further and produced a tentative 'development indicator', a weighted average of various series. The Institute's investigations of multiple associations are interesting and worth while, but we should not fall into the trap (as we could, although the Institute's Director warns us against it) of treating this indicator as 'normative'. It simply measures the extent to which a country has advanced along a path indicated by data from countries at different states of progress; see UNRISD [*1969*].

17. See I.L.O. [*1970*]. The point is made there that the measurement of unemployment depends very much on the dimension of the problem that concerns one—unemployment as a cause of personal frustration, low income or loss of output.

18. The Pareto coefficient, on the other hand, which long had its advocates, is expressly limited to measuring distribution among higher incomes.

19. To draw the conclusion that the income distributions should be changed, one has to assume that Engel curves are non-linear, but this seems not to need specifying. Consumption of such luxuries is zero over a considerable income range.

20. See I.L.O. [1970] for a discussion of the compatibility of a high concentration of income with full employment. Unfortunately most theoretical texts concentrate on the relation between income distribution, savings and growth, ignoring the more important effects via the composition of.consumption.

21. Though, of course, these imply inequalities of other types, even if only of social prestige.

22. I have dealt with these issues elsewhere [Seers, 1971].

23. See Seers [1971] and Jolly and Seers [1970].

24. Although this problem takes the form of finding the right expenditure weights for a price deflator, what we are actually doing is obtaining price weights for quantity comparisons, and this is extremely hard when price structures vary so much (see above). Analogous difficulties arise whenever comparisons are made between regions of a country (due to geographical variations in prices and consumption patterns) but much less severely.

## REFERENCES

Bardhan, Pranab K., 1970, 'On the Minimum Level of Living and the Rural Poor', *Indian Economic Review*, Vol. 5, April.

Clark, Colin, 1937, *National Income and Outlay*, London: Macmillan.

Divatia, V. V., and Bhatt, V. V., 1969, 'On Measuring the Pace of Development', *Quarterly Review*, Banco Nazionale del Lavoro, No. 89, June.

Fonseca, A. J., 1970, 'The need-based Wage in India: A Computerized Estimate', reprinted from *Wage Policy and Wage Distribution in India*, Bombay: University of Bombay.

I.L.O., 1970, *Towards Full Employment*, Geneva: International Labour Office.

Jaffe, A. J., 1969, 'Notes on Family Income Distribution in Developing Countries in Relation to Population and Economic Changes'; paper given at meeting of International Association for Research in Income and Wealth, August; to be published in *Estadistica*, Inter-American Statistical Institute, No. 104.

Jolly, Richard, 1969, *Planning Education for African Development*, Nariobi: East Africa Publishing House.

Jolly, Richard, and Seers, Dudley, 1970, 'The Brain Drain and the Development Process', proceedings of the International Economic Association Conference to be published in E. A. G. Robinson (ed.), *The Gap Between the Rich and the Poor Countries*, London: Macmillan.

Kuznets, Simon, 1966, *Modern Economic Growth*, Studies in Comparative Economics No. 7, New Haven: Yale University Press.

Kuznets, Simon, 1971, *Economic Growth of Nations: Total Output and Production Structure*, Cambridge, Mass.: Belknap.

Lydall, Harold, 1968, *The Structure of Earnings*, Oxford: Clarendon Press.

Minhas, B.S., 1970, 'Rural Poverty, Land Redistribution and Development', *Indian Economic Review*, Vol. 5, April.

Mishan, E. J., 1967, *The Costs of Economic Growth*, London: Staples Press.

Patel, Surrendra, 1964, 'The Economic Distance Between Nations', *Economic Journal*, Vol. 74, March.

Rowntree, B. Seebohm, 1901, *Poverty: A Study of Town Life*, London: Macmillan.

Sametz, A. W., 1968, 'Production of Goods and Services: The Measurement of Economic Growth' in E. Sheldon and W. B. Moore (eds.), *Indicators of Social Change: Concepts and Measurements*, New York: Russell Sage Foundation.

Scrimshaw, N. S., and Gordon, J. E. (ed.), 1968, *Malnutrition, Learning and Behaviour*, Cambridge, Mass.: M.I.T. Press.

Seers, Dudley, 1971, 'The Transmission of Inequality' in Robert K. A. Gardiner (ed.), *Africa and the World*, London: Oxford University Press.

Stewart, Frances, and Streeten, Paul, 1971, 'Conflicts between Output and Employment Objectives' in Ronald Robinson and Peter Johnston (eds.), *Prospects for Employment*

*Opportunities in the Nineteen Seventies*, London: Her Majesty's Stationery Office.

Townsend, Peter (ed.), 1970, *The Concept of Poverty*, London: Heinemann.

UNRISD, 1969, *Research Notes No. 2*, July, Geneva: United Nations Research Institute for Social Development.

*Post Script*

# The New Meaning of Development

The republication of this article provides an opportunity for self-justification. Yet rereading the paper, I cannot avoid the impression that it was written by someone else. So of course it was. It was composed by somebody living nearly a decade ago who had only recently returned to academic life after many years spent mostly in 'operational' roles. Its author had naturally no foreknowledge of the rapidly evolving world of the 1970s, nor of the professional jobs that would modify once more his attitude to 'development'. I shall take this opportunity to draw the lessons of what has happened in the intervening years for how we should view 'development', and to suggest the practical implications.

———

GROWTH AND DEVELOPMENT

It seems much more than a decade since 'The Meaning of Development' was published. The common basis of development studies and policy-making was still very simple in 1969: in order to solve social problems, such as unemployment, and achieve respectable status as modern nations, poor countries needed 'development', which could be measured by GNP. In fact, economic growth *was* development: this could be accelerated with the help of trade and aid and/or private capital from countries already 'developed'. If growth was in fact not fast, the reason must lie in 'obstacles', such as economic nationalism. Questions of distribution tended to be brushed aside: 'We must bake a bigger cake before discussing how to cut it up'. Inequality was (regrettably) necessary to generate savings and provide incentives. If growth were fast enough, income could easily be redistributed later—indeed that would happen automatically.

This basically neo-classical paradigm had been already losing credibility in the 1960s. To generalize very drastically, the social problems of 'developed' countries were being rediscovered and concern was spreading about the environmental costs of economic growth. The gap between *per capita* incomes of 'developed' and 'developing' countries was apparently growing even in relative terms, despite large transfers of capital and technology.[1] Even those developing countries enjoying fast growth had not after all achieved the political status or the social equity that had been expected and hoped for. Pakistan was a conspicuous example. Income distribution apparently remained highly concentrated,[2] not merely in very poor countries, but also in those of Latin America where *per capita* income was approaching 'European' levels. Power was increasingly concentrated in the hands of those who benefited from growth, and used more and more repressively to preserve these benefits. Even open unemployment was refusing to wither away, which was politically embarrassing: so questions were being raised about the appropriateness of consumption patterns that required heavy foreign exchange expenditures and of labour-saving techniques that accompanied both aid and private investment.

Cultural lags protect paradigms long after they have lost relevance. The neo-classical growth paradigm has been remarkably tenacious—in fact, it still survives in places. It has suited so many interests. It has been highly acceptable to governments that want to slur over internal ethnic or social problems. It has offered (not only in the hands of Walt Rostow) a basis for aid policies to inhibit the spread of communism. It has provided international and national agencies with an 'objective' basis for project evaluation, and goals for what should be called the Second Growth Decade. It has generated almost endless academic research projects and stimulated theorists to construct elaborate models. It has not been fundamentally unacceptable to economistic modernisers across a broad political spectrum, including Marxists as well as members of the Chicago school. Above all, as a paradigm it is very simple.

The author of 'The Meaning of Development' could have taken the position that to use 'development' as a synonym for growth had so debased the word that it could no longer be used by honest people. But he decided, probably correctly, to propose that it should be redefined rather than abolished. 'Development' still carried much goodwill and political force; besides it had been incorporated in the titles of research institutes and international and national agencies.[7] So this article, 'The Meaning of Development', said, in a nutshell, that growth was in itself insufficient, indeed perhaps socially damaging: a country was not enjoying 'development' unless in addition inequality, unemployment and poverty were declining.

Not really very original. The paper should be seen as just one articulation in a period of drastic change in professional attitudes. If it attracted some attention, this was partly because it was presented at an SID World Congress—and one function of such gatherings is to legitimise unorthodox attitudes whose hour has arrived. It also seemed rather shocking: wasn't the over-riding importance of economic growth *obvious*?

REDISTRIBUTION AND DEVELOPMENT

But attitudes had already started to change. Work on social indicators had been gathering momentum in the 1960s. In 1970, the ILO launched the first of its series of missions under the World Employment Programme, which were basically about distribution. A number of models were subsequently devised to draw the policy implications from distributive goals, with much discussion of the trade-off between growth and distributional or employment objectives.[3] Their general theme was summed up in the title of the IBRD-IDS study 'Redistribution with Growth'.[4] The message to aid agencies was to take account of the social consequences of aid and to try to reach the poorest, especially in rural areas. For planning departments, the implication was to concentrate on the satisfaction of 'basic needs', defined in rather narrowly material terms, and for statistical offices to measure the incidence of poverty.

Yet there is already an air of unreality about this whole approach. Governments (even in countries which have received the ILO comprehensive missions—Colombia, Sri Lanka, Iran, Kenya, Philippines) have done little to change distribution.[5] The basic assumption of the development profession is that they need technical help to do so. Radical critics, on the other hand, pointing to political interest rather than technical capacity, have repeatedly posed quite a simple question in one form or another: why should those with economic and political power give it away, as these policies require, especially to the rural poor?[6] The implication drawn by some is that social progress will be indefinitely prevented by a homogeneous ruling class until it is in due course overthrown in a revolution.

That seems to require an even more simplistic political model. Still, the question about the feasibility of redistribution does lead one to the sources of power both inside and outside countries, and to not merely economic and political influences, but also cultural ones. Indeed, cultural forces obviously (*pace* Karl Marx) shape the way people perceive their material needs. Elites, in particular, including those deciding and administering policy, are clearly determined to enjoy styles of consumption far beyond the reach of the great majority of their fellow citizens; and architects and engineers almost as obstinately prescribe completely inappropriate techniques.

Actually, the author of 'The Meaning of Development' did touch on the main source of these cultural forces. Human requirements, he said (but only in a footnote), are not purely economic; 'they include ... citizenship of a nation that is truly independent, both economically and politically'.[7] Why did he not see the link? The inertia of consumption and production patterns was obviously in part attributable to external links. True independence was not merely one of the intrinsic objectives, but also a *condition* (though insufficient in itself of course) for achieving the rest.

SELF-RELIANCE AND DEVELOPMENT

The 'oil crisis' of the 1970s really shook the conventional paradigm. It revealed starkly the cost of the continued economic and technological dependence of most countries, and underlined warnings about the limited capacity of the earth to sustain fast economic growth of the old type.

The time is indeed ripe for another critical look at the meaning of development. One could—even more easily than in 1969—defend the view that the word 'development' is too tarnished to be usable. The political and institutional reasons for retaining it still apply, however, and once more the way forward is to redefine it rather than reject it completely. The essential element to add—as is being widely recognized—is self-reliance.

We do not yet understand much about what self-reliance implies for development strategies,[8] but some of the economic aspects are obvious enough. They include reducing dependence on imported necessities, especially basic foods, petroleum and its products, capital equipment and expertise. This would involve changing consumption patterns as well as increasing the relevant productive capacity. Redistribution of income would help, but policies would also be needed to change living styles at given income levels—using taxes, price policies, advertising and perhaps rationing. In many countries, self-reliance would also involve increasing national ownership and control, especially of sub-soil assets, and improving national capacity for negotiating with transnational corporations.

There are other implications as well, especially in cultural policy. These are more country-specific, but as a general rule, let us say that 'development' now implies, *inter alia*, reducing cultural dependence on one or more of the great powers—i.e. increasing the use of national languages in schools, allotting more television time to programmes produced locally (or in neighbouring countries), raising the proportion of higher degrees obtained at home, etc.

On this approach, 'development plans' would henceforward not put the main emphasis on overall growth rates, or even on new patterns of distribution. The crucial targets would be for (i) ownership as well as output in the leading economic sectors; (ii) consumption patterns that economized on foreign exchange (including imports such as cereals and oil); (iii) institutional capacity for research and negotiation; (iv) cultural goals like those suggested above, depending on the country concerned. The Third Malaysian Plan (1976) partially reflects this approach, though it has of course been the basis of Japanese development strategy for a century.

Self-reliance has its own implications for the work of statistical offices.[9] These would need to concentrate less on 'national accounts' than on tables for key sectors and for the transnational corporations; less too on patterns of production than consumption; not so much anyway on economic, or even 'social', indicators as on technical and cultural statistics.

Of course, an emphasis on reducing dependence does not necessarily mean aiming at autarchy. How far it is desirable or even possible to go in that direction depends on a country's size, location and natural resources; on its cultural homogeneity and the depth of its traditions; on the extent to which its economy needs imported inputs to satisfy consumption patterns which have to be taken—at least in the short term—as political minima. The key to a development strategy of the type suggested is not to break all links, which would almost anywhere be socially damaging and politically unworkable, but to adopt a *selective* approach to external influences of all types.

One may well query whether this is any more feasible politically than 'redistribution with growth'. Why should the elites be any more willing to co-operate in this sort of 'development', which would also deprive them of many of the goods and services they consider essential to being part of the modern world? Basically, the answer is that such a programme may appeal to what seems in many countries to be a stronger force than social conscience—nationalism. This may be more likely to outweigh short-term material interests, as is shown by wartime experience in many countries.

Moreover, whereas redistributive policies provoke countervailing forces which often succeed in turning the clock back, moves towards self-

reliance may become cumulative.[10] Increased cultural independence not
merely has direct economic effects, it also strengthens the political leadership's motivation to make further reductions in dependence and weakens
the internal opposition to these.

There is an additional implication, which is perhaps more important
still. For if 'development' is now not primarily about *per capita* income,
but also about distribution, and even more about the national capacity
to negotiate with transnational corporations, and to cope with their
technological innovations and their cultural impact, then it is not just
needed in 'developing' countries, but in *all* countries.

This shift of emphasis is really crucial. It relieves us in 'developed'
countries (following the increasingly misleading UN terminology) of
paternalism. We would cease offering to solve other people's problems;
instead, 'development', on this definition, involves our all working on
*common* worldwide problems, while, paradoxically, keeping national
interests (long-term of course) firmly in mind. The door would, moreover,
be opened for the transfer of theories and experience from 'developing' to
'developed' countries, a possibility merely hinted at in 'The Meaning of
Development'. This would be most obviously helpful in countries of the
European periphery, such as Portugal and Greece, but also nearly as
obviously in Italy and Britain, countries suffering from typical symptoms
of 'underdevelopment': chronic inflation alongside chronic unemployment, and therefore resistant to Keynesian or monetarist remedies.[11]

The simple step of redefining development in this way is thus not by
any means purely semantic: it changes one's whole perception of the world.
For most professional purposes, to talk of the 'Third World' becomes
almost meaningless, although the political alliance between OPEC
members and the ex-colonies still has some vitality, so the concept has a
few years of life yet.[12]

In any case, the cultural lag before this new definition is accepted is
likely to be particularly long. Besides challenging a political alliance which
is not ineffective, and powerful commercial interests, it threatens the
comfortable academic ghetto of 'development studies' and it is also much
more difficult for aid officials (and members of aid lobbies) to accept. It
implies that the main way in which they could improve the world is not
through increasing aid (though this is still needed in some countries), or
even channelling it to people in greatest social need, but by curbing the
power of the transnational corporations and limiting cultural pressures of
which they themselves are a part.

I realize I am striking some notes that may seem even more shocking to
some readers than 'The Meaning of Development' (and this article is not
likely to be so extensively reprinted). Many, especially of the older generation, will find uncomfortable the implicit scepticism about the power of
humanitarian motives and the explicit endorsement of nationalism, including our own—which ceases to be an 'obstacle' to development, and becomes instead part of the very essence of it. However, this new definition

would not be at all incompatible with the praiseworthy reform of SID now in train.

September 1977                                    DUDLEY SEERS
                                    *Institute of Development Studies*


NOTES

1. However, as was suggested in 'The Meaning of Development'—perhaps not forcefully enough—economic growth cannot be measured in predominantly rural countries because of the lack of data on rural economic activities. See 'Seers versus Lipton on Urban Bias' (IDS *Discussion Paper* 116, 1977).

2. Income distributions are also (unfortunately) impossible to measure in most countries for the reasons given in the previous footnote. The evidence seems, however, overwhelming, if one also makes use of various types of data—social indicators, household budget surveys, etc.

3. Actually, since many goods and services included in the national product carry price weights which it would be difficult to defend for welfare comparisons (some goods and services are of negative social value), the policy dilemmas may not be so acute as they seem.

4. Oxford 1974. The first person to use this phrase was Hans Singer, co-leader with Richard Jolly of the ILO Mission to Kenya. The strategy proposed in this mission report was summarised as 'Redistribution from Growth'; later generalised in the IBRD/IDS study.

5. There was also a mission to Sudan, but it is too early to say yet whether its recommendations will also be shelved.

6. See, for example, 'The politics of redistribution with growth' by Colin Leys (IDS *Bulletin*, Vol. 7, No. 2, 1975) and the reply in the same issue by Richard Jolly.

7. The same footnote also referred to freedom of speech. Like political independence, this might be included as one of the 'basic needs'.

8. We could do with a study which might be called 'Greater Independence with Redistribution and Growth'. There are of course complex connections between distribution and independence (and possible trade-offs): I do not have the space to discuss these here.

9. See 'Statistical Needs for Development' (IDS *Communication* 120, 1977).

10. Unless blocked by external military intervention (a possibility always to be guarded against and requiring adequate defence expenditures to make such intervention expensive).

11. See 'North Sea Oil: The Application of Development Theories' by some of the faculty and students on the Sussex M.Phil course of 1975–77 (IDS *Communication* 121, 1977). Also, "Back to the Ivory Tower? The Professionalisation of Development Studies and their Extension to Europe" (IDS *Bulletin*, Vol 9, No 2) and *Underdeveloped Europe: Studies in Core-Periphery Relations,* ed D. Seers, M-L. Kiljunen and B. B. B. Schaffer (Harvester Press, 1978).

12. See 'A new look at the 3-world classification' (IDS *Bulletin* Vol. 7, No. 4, 1976). A revised version is due to appear as 'Patterns of Dependence' in *Transnational Capitalism and National Development; Studies in the Theory of Dependency,* ed J. Villamil (Harvester Press, 1978).

# Modernization Theory and the Sociological Study of Development*

## By Henry Bernstein†

**SUMMARY**

The focus of this article is methodological and macro-sociological. Its purpose is to disentangle some of the issues which arise in the sociology of development, and to question the assumptions and implications of a particular mode of conceptualization based on the notions of modernity and modernization which has provided the characteristic *theoretical* framework of the sociology of development. The principal assumptions of modernization theory as understood here—often enough made explicit by those who use this approach—are (1) that modernization is a total social process associated with (or subsuming) economic development in terms of the preconditions, concomitants, and consequences of the latter; (2) that this process constitutes a 'universal pattern'. Obviously among various writers there are differences of emphasis with respect to the meaning of modernization, partly due to its relationship with—or derivation from—that most contentious concept 'development'. For Lerner modernization is 'the social process of which development is the economic component' (Lerner, 1967, p. 21); while Apter sees development, modernization and industrialization as terms of decreasing conceptual generality (Apter, 1967, pp. 67–9). Some writers stress structural aspects while for others 'the concept of modernization has to do with a transformation of culture and of personality in so far as it is influenced by culture, rather than of some aspect of social organization or of human ecology' (Stephenson, 1968, p. 265). It is hoped that the following discussion is both specific enough to convey the essential aspects of the type of theory under review, and flexible enough to allow for some of the variants on the basic theme in what is a highly condensed survey of a substantial body of literature.[1] The critical approach adopted reflects certain ideas about societies and hence the questions social scientists should ask; these preoccupations cannot be discussed fully within present limits but are indicated in the suggestions contained in the concluding section. The first section serves to outline the context in which the concept of development studies arose. This is followed by a schematic outline of the central concepts and conceptual procedures of the sociology of development, and more specifically of modernization theory, which are then criticized on a number of counts. These criticisms lead on to an argument for the use of a historical perspective—moreover, one which results in a re-examination of the concept of underdevelopment, relating it to the expansion of Western

* The author would like to thank Rita Cruise O'Brien and Leslie Sklair for encouraging him to commit to paper his views on this subject, and Ronald Dore and Donal Cruise O'Brien for their extensive comments on an earlier draft.

† Lecturer in Interdisciplinary Studies at the University of Kent, Canterbury. This article was written while the author was a Research Assistant, Institute of Development Studies, Sussex.

capitalism and the effects of this process on the diverse indigenous societies of what is now called the Third World. The relationships of dependence and exploitation created by the process are exemplified in the colonial situation as narrowly defined though this is by no means the only situation characterized by such relationships. This perspective, developed in the work of certain political economists, can serve as the basis of a sociological approach which would prove more fruitful both in understanding the nature of underdevelopment itself, and in assessing the range of possibilities of development in the Third World, than that generally employed in the sociology of development at present.

## ENTER SOCIOLOGY OF DEVELOPMENT

Development—as aspiration, ideology, and field of study—became an issue of urgent priority following the end of the Second World War in the context of internal events in the colonial countries and the economic and political realities of a changing international situation. This is not to deny both the antiquity and continuity of the notion of development in Western thought, as pointed out by Professor Nisbet (Nisbet, 1969), nor a tradition of concern with 'growth' and 'improvement' on the part of many social observers and participants including colonial administrators. In some respects, the aspirations and goals of the 'modernizing élites' of today's underdeveloped countries appear to have a compelling precedent in the case of post-Mejii Japan. The' advice and information' offered by a group of 'prominent Americans' on the effects of education on a backward country, requested by Japan's first diplomatic representative to the United States in 1872, remains strikingly familiar to contemporary audiences. Education they reported,

> . . . would awake isolated peasant minds to new possibilities, tie Japan into a world exchange economy, stimulate new appetites requiring new industries and expanded trade to satisfy, improve the quality of peasant as well as technician, instil loyalty so that government can rule benignly rather than harshly; in short, it would lay the basis for prosperity and prestige among the nations of the world (Passin, 1965, p. 7).

However, the post-1945 preoccupation with development expressed in the vocabulary of decolonization and government planning, institutionalized in a proliferation of international agencies, and studied by Western, and notably American, social scientists, takes on a character and an intensity derived from a specific historical and global context, as clearly indicated by Robert S. MacNamara in presenting the case for the American foreign aid programme:

> Roughly 100 countries today are caught up in the difficult transition to modern societies. There is no uniform rate of progress among them, and they range from primitive mosaic societies—fractured by tribalism and held feebly together by the slenderest of political sinews—to relatively sophisticated countries, well on the road to agricultural

sufficiency and industrial competence. This sweeping surge of development, particularly across the whole southern half of the globe, has no parallel in history.

It has turned traditionally listless areas of the world into seething cauldrons of change.

On the whole it has not been a very peaceful process. . . . Given the certain connection between economic stagnation and the incidence of violence, the years that lie ahead for the nations in the southern half of the globe are pregnant with violence.

This would be true even if no threat of Communist subversion existed—as it clearly does. . . .

Whether Communists are involved or not, violence anywhere in a taut world transmits sharp signals through the complex ganglia of international relations; and the security of the United States is related to the security and stability of nations half a globe away.[2]

When it became clear, in the early 1950s, that the development of poor countries demanded a special attention from social science, the inability of economic theory to meet this demand by itself was soon appreciated:

Its neglect of culture, of disciplines such as history, sociology and anthropology, meant that it never produced a theory of economic development and of industrialization. Naturally the theories set forth tended to have some explanatory power for Western development, because it was the historical and sociological factors in that process which were the premises for model building. It was only when these theories were applied outside of the Western nationals that their premises became painfully obvious (Weinberg, 1969, p. 3).

The participation of other social science disciplines in the discussion of development was recognized as necessary, often being expressed in the 'social conditions of economic growth' or 'non-economic barriers to economic growth' types of formula. The extent of fruitful interdisciplinary activity in the resulting field of development studies is doubtful, but the contributions of social psychologists, historians, anthropologists and political scientists, as well as economists and sociologists, did ensure an occasionally useful eclecticism.[3] A decisive landmark in terms of a more systematic theoretical approach within sociology proper was Daniel Lerner's *The Passing of Traditional Society*, published in 1958, of which Bendix has observed: 'The great merit of Lerner's study consists in its candid use of Western modernization as a model of global applicability' (Bendix, 1967a, p. 309). It will be argued that this aspect of modernization theories is inextricably involved in practice with the other features indicated above. Within the conventional area of discourse of sociology certain criticisms of the 'grand theory' approach to development have been advanced, some of which are referred to in the framework of the broader critique attempted here.[4]

This necessarily brief outline lists the principal elements of the sociology of development and indicates in a broad way their application to analysis. The headings (1) to (5) represent the salient uniformities of the approach under review and are not to be understood as an attempt to summarize the work of the whole field, the variety of which is acknowledged in the additional comments following (5).

## (1) *Theory of social change*

The recognition that development represents a particular kind of social change stimulated an interest in social change which had been generally neglected as a macro-sociological preoccupation, certainly in American sociology. The treatment of social change was accommodated in varying degrees with the prevailing mode of structural-functional analysis, although involving some modification of the latter with the introduction of concepts of strain and tension into its basically static perspective. The classic sources of functionalism, Spencer and Durkheim, were drawn on to provide the dynamic of the differentiation-integration model of social change (Smelser, 1968).

## (2) *Conceptualizing the modern*

Given that development or modernization denotes a particular kind of social change in the contemporary context, it was necessary to find a heuristic designation of the beginning and end points of the process. Nineteenth-century sociology, which was primarily concerned with the disruptions and new social forms resulting from industrialization, again provided a number of concepts in a range of dichotomous ideal-types such as status-contract, sacred-secular, mechanical-organic, and community-association, to which were added later formulations such as Redfield's folk-urban concepts and the pattern variables of Talcott Parsons.[5]

## (3) *Evolutionary schema*

The characterization of a process of change in terms of these ideal-typical end points—usually subsumed under a more general traditional-modern dichotomy—and the differentiation model of social change both involve an evolutionary rationale which is further emphasized by the super-imposition of the former on the latter.[6] It seems customary to express various *pro forma* reservations concerning social evolution, possibly because of what are felt to be the excesses of its nineteenth-century protagonists, but despite such reservations an evolutionary rationale is implicit in the conceptual procedure under review here.

## (4) *Achieving development*

Within the framework established by the polar ideal-types and the differentiation-integration model outlined above, the sociology of development becomes a question of identifying and analysing the social, cultural and psychological conditions, concomitants, and consequences of economic development. The transition from the traditional (economically backward) to the modern (economically advanced) society can be treated with a primarily negative emphasis in terms of removing institutional obstacles to development, or with a positive emphasis in terms of creating the cultural environment necessary for development. These approaches are analytically complementary, but the former tends to rest on an 'economic man' postulate, assuming that development will occur once effective incentives are perceived;[7] the latter tends to assume that the necessary motivation has to be instilled, as, say, a sufficient level of need for achievement or a suitably progressive (e.g. future-oriented and rational) world-view, as a precondition of development.[8]

### (5) *Modernizing élites*

Whether the 'will to be modern', in Edward Shils' phrase, is held to be ubiquitous or not, it is generally regarded as finding its most strategic expression in the role of the modernizing élites. It is these groups—political, bureaucratic, intellectual (and often military)—which are charged with the articulation of development goals and supervision of development strategies for their countries, and with the task of 'nation-building', i.e. of creating viable national societies from their socially and culturally diverse populations.

Several additional points can be made to supplement this very brief outline. Within the basic assumptions and methodological procedure of modernization theory, there is a considerable variety of emphasis on different levels—according to whether conceptual priority is assigned to personality factors, institutions, cultural orientations, or social processes: according to the substantive designation of what is ideal-typically modern (e.g. 'empathy' or 'need for achievement' at the personality level), or what are regarded as the crucial mechanisms of modernization (e.g. urbanization, mass communications or political mobilization at the level of social processes); according to the concrete areas of social action focused on—the family, religion, education, demographic trends, the role of intellectuals, and so on. The total social transformation and 'universal pattern' assumptions of modernization theory encourage the attempt to relate to each other the different types of changes, within and between levels, through organizing principles derived from the core definition of the modern that is adopted, and certain *a priori* theoretical assumptions.

One significant trend in particular is worth noting, namely the school of political modernization or development which became so prominent in the 1960s, the central preoccupation of which has been with modernization as the progress towards a functionally integrated national political system.[9] Several salient features of the political development approach can be indicated briefly in anticipation of what follows, to show that it rests on similar assumptions, and is subject to similar criticisms, as other modernization theories. In the first place there is the designation of the 'destination' of the process of modernization which is based on a model of the American political system. In relation to this end point, the starting point is defined negatively—'the non-Western political process'. Conceptually structured in this way the modernization process is analysed in terms of the 'problems', 'conditions', 'determinants' and so on, of progress towards its ideal-typical destination.[10] This procedure raises the kind of questions which inform the following discussion, such as—are these models abstracted from Western (or Soviet, or Japanese) experience conceptually accurate or exclusive? Are they relevant as the basis of comparison? Even if accurate, is it desirable that they be emulated?[11] While there are political questions of obvious intrinsic interest as well as of great relevance to economic development, this does not explain the enormous resources devoted to the study of Third World politics nor some of the major forms this study has assumed which are divorced from problems of economic development. Lionel Tiger has suggested that 'the considerable scholarly attention . . . focused on problems of political integration' has been prompted by 'reasons as much connected with Cold War politics as anything else' (Tiger, 1967, p. 189). This point can be expanded in that in the West the conflict with the socialist countries, whether the U.S.S.R., China, Cuba or North Vietnam, is conventionally expressed in political terms, i.e. democracy or freedom *vs.* totalitarianism, even when this involves including the right kind of military dictatorship in the 'free world' and sacrificing some of the specifically parliamentary connotations of democracy.[12] In addition, an alternative politically derived definition of modern status was useful in a development decade characterized by a general failure to achieve economic targets.[13] Finally, in a period marked by the imagery of independence, decolonization and national self-assertion, it may not have been discreet to preach the virtues of capitalism as a way of life to the governments of former colonies, most of which at least proclaimed some form of socialism.[14]

MODERNIZATION THEORY: SOME BASIC OBJECTIONS

(1) *The traditional-modern dichotomy*

The first objection to be noted concerns the methodological procedure by which the traditional is simply defined negatively in relation to the modern, so that, even omitting the contentious question of what is modern, differences between empirical societies allocated to the residual category of the traditional are ignored. For example, Raymond Aron writes that Rostow's concept of the traditional society is

> of little use because it is supposed to be applicable to all underdeveloped communities. All past societies are put into this single category, whether they be the archaic communities of New Guinea, the Negro tribes of Africa, or the old civilizations of India and China. But the only feature

they have in common is that they are neither modern nor industrialized (Aron, 1964, p. 30).

A further objection concerns the cluster of traits making up the ideal-type of the traditional which often simply reflect the ethnocentrism underlying the formulation of modernity. Thus Lerner characterizes modern society as 'the Participant Society' (Lerner, 1964, ch. 2 and passim). As some 'traditional' societies were participant in a meaningful sense this leaves two alternatives—either such a traditional society is an exception (and exceptions accumulate), or it may be participant but not in the same way that modern societies are, a tautology rendered inevitable by the dichotomous procedure of definition. In any case, the nature and extent of 'participation' in modern societies is by no means clear. A further illustration of this kind concerns the ascription-achievement dimension of the traditional-modern dichotomy. Empirical investigation shows that there are traditional societies which have an achievement orientation in important areas of social life, just as ascription plays a major role in the organization of modern societies.[15] It is significant that often a first step in the operationalization of concepts in anthropological fieldwork is the clearing away of stereotypes of traditional society imposed by abstract deductive categories compounded with ethnocentric bias. While tending to be more reticent in macro-level theorizing about modernization (or perhaps because of this), anthropologists have produced some of the most interesting work in the field of contemporary social change.[16] Finally, it should be emphasized that the traditional-modern dichotomy in itself has only a heuristic function, designating an ideal-typical destination. In so far as it can serve as the basis of a dynamic approach, this is only by the banal means of depicting modernization as a process in which modern elements accumulate and traditional elements are displaced.

### (2) Ethnocentrism

The question of ethnocentrism becomes central when it is asked from which historical source the paradigm of modernization is abstracted and universalized. Eisenstadt, a leading modernization theorist, is quite explicit:

> Historically, modernization is the process of change towards those types of social, economic, and political systems that have developed in Western Europe and North America from the seventeenth century to the nineteenth and have then spread to other European countries and in the nineteenth and twentieth centuries to the South American, Asian and African continents (Eisenstadt, 1966, p. 1).

Leaving aside the question of 'spread', which is presumably to be interpreted as programmatic rather than actual, it appears that Eisenstadt regards the Western experience (culminating in the nineteenth century) as producing the model of modern society. Even admitting the possibility of different 'routes' there is but one 'destination'.[17] The general pattern of 'modernization' is derived from what can be characterized alternatively as a particular type of development which was industrial-capitalist, and which in itself encompassed a range of important differences—economic as well as social and political.[18] There is an obvious implication of this mode of conceptualizing modernization for empirical analysis; as Nettl has pointed out—'. . . the methodological approaches of Western social and political scientists . . . often assume that developing countries are infant or deviant examples of the Western experience and can be studied in terms of a shortfall from a norm. (Nettl, 1967, p. 193 and ch 7 passim). When (in what may be called the Weberian syndrome) the type becomes ideal in an evaluative as well as a conceptual sense we are liable to encounter those medical metaphors still beloved by some social scientists. Thus for W. W. Rostow communism is a 'disease of the transition'.[19]

Ethnocentrism is most overt when modernization is rendered synonymous with Westernization, a typically nineteenth-century equation exemplified in Macaulay's proposal to staff the new Indian Civil Service by creating a 'class of persons Indian in blood and colour, but English in tastes, in opinions, in morals and in intellect.'[20] Ali Mazrui, in tracing the connections between political modernization theories and Social Darwinism, remarks that ' . . . in the modern theories of modernization Darwinism has been "debiologized" . . . What is now involved is at the most ethnocentric cultural pride.' (Mazrui, 1968, p. 75). To identify ethnocentrism solely with cultural pride (with the additional disclaimer 'at the most') is disingenuous. It is clear that ethnocentric notions of modernization have a valuable ideological, i.e. legitimating, function in relation to the activities of certain economic, political and cultural interests. Although the extent to which social scientists actually influence policy is difficult to ascertain, the least that can be said is that a conceptual framework articulated by modernization theorists has its uses for government, military and intelligence agencies, as well as for the corporations and finally for export to underdeveloped countries. Since 'Project Camelot' days an increasing amount of evidence has been unearthed of services performed directly for such agencies by social scientists, of which 'counterinsurgency' work has gained the most notoriety. In the words of a specialist engaged on 'Project Agile' at the Thai-American Military Research and Development Centre in Bangkok: 'The old formula for successful counterinsurgency used to be ten troops for every guerrilla. . . . Now the formula is ten anthropologists for each guerrilla.'[21] With the independence fervour of the late 1950s and early 1960s many social scientists waxed lyrical on the 'revolution of rising expectations' in 'the new states', this phenomenon being central both to the conceptual framework of the sociology of development, and to the potential role of an enlightened U.S. policy in helping to establish effective economic growth and viable democracies. However, in the light of subsequent events, another kind of priority is gaining emphasis —or at least is being made more public:

In the Congo, in Vietnam, in the Dominican Republic, it is clear that order depends on somehow compelling newly mobilized strata to return to a measure of passivity and defeatism from which they have been aroused by the process of modernization. At least temporarily, the maintenance of order requires a lowering of newly acquired aspirations and levels of political activity. (Quoted by Chomsky, 1969, p. 33).

This prescription by Ithiel da Sola Pool, a political scientist and prominent 'new mandarin', while replacing liberal sentiment with a Realpolitik interest in suppressing popular aspirations, is expressed in the same ethnocentric vocabulary which refers to the 'passivity and defeatism' of traditional society.

### (3) Reductionism

One apparent means of avoiding the ethnocentrism of historically specific models of modernization is to universalize certain traits at the level of personality mechanisms. In this way the type of innovative and dynamic personality designated is not necessarily tied to any particular set of economic, social and political institutions, such as those of Western capitalist development, but can be identified in a number of different contexts. This approach is found in an extreme form in McClelland's concept of 'the need for Achievement' or n. ach, which denotes 'a desire to do well, not so much for the sake of social recognition or prestige, but to attain an inner feeling of personal accomplishment' (McClelland, 1963, p. 76 and passim). McClelland's formulation produces what may be called a moral (as opposed to a hedonistic) theory of entrepreneurship which still embraces the market-oriented acquisitive activity of capitalist society, but also claims to be able to explain the advances made by the Soviet Union and China in terms of rising levels of n. ach. Depsite the sophisticated techniques used to analyse a wide range of data, at a more fundamental level McClelland's theory is riddled with contradictions. In the first place it is subject to the logical criticism of reductionism which is that the attributes of social structures and processes cannot be derived from statements about individuals.[22] Furthermore, McClelland makes an unwarranted leap from correlation to a causal explanation of economic development, this being facilitated by his lack of any social or historical perspective (Rhodes, 1968, p. 393 and passim). Despite the obligatory nod in the direction of Weber's thesis the latter's basis in a sociological and historical method is ignored (Weber, 1930). As need for achievement is the motivation to comply with internalized standards of excellence, these are derived necessarily from a given social and cultural context in the first place. In the final analysis, McClelland cannot avoid relating changes in the level of n. ach. to the operation of concrete social forces, including revolutions, even if mediated for him through ideologies—for which read communism. So, although 'China was politically free under Chiang Kai-Chek, . . . it lacked the dynamic of a really self-sacrificing achievement effort until it was taken over by the Communists'. The rest of the passage is worth quoting as it was directed to a particular audience— the readers of the *Harvard Business Review*—and illustrates an alarming ideological crudity concerning development:

> Unless we learn our lesson and find ways of stimulating that drive for achievement under freedom in poor countries, the Communists will go on providing it all around the world. We can go on building dikes to maintain freedom and impoverishing ourselves to feed and arm the people behind those dikes, but only if we develop the entrepreneurial spirit in

those countries will we have a sound foreign policy. Only then can they look after their own dikes and become economically self-sufficient (McClelland, 1964, p. 176).

SOCIOLOGIES AND HISTORY: THE BASIS OF AN ALTERNATIVE APPROACH

The purpose of this section is to relate some of the issues previously discussed to questions of different sociological perspectives and the use of a historical method, together with some of the elements of an alternative interpretation of the historical context of modernization and development. Social scientists

> persist in using the term (modernization) not only because it is a part of popular speech, but also because they recognize that these many changes (in individual attitudes, in social behaviour, in economics, and in politics) are related to one another—that many countries in the developing world are today experiencing a comprehensive process of change which Europe and America once experienced and which is more than the sum of many small changes. (Preface to Weiner, 1966).

This statement by Myron Weiner usefully recapitulates the basic assumptions of modernization theory first referred to, as a departure point for the following discussion.

One basis of an explanatory theory of modernization as a 'comprehensive process' rests on the specification of necessary relationships, or at least relationships of an order of probabliity, between changes in different parts of a social structure and/or changes at different levels of social structure. This requirement is formally met, for example, in a crude way by the avowed psychological determinism of McClelland, or by a hierarchical conceptualization of social structure such as values/goals/norms/collectivities/roles in the work of Talcott Parsons. In functionalist theory, these relationships are formalized horizontally as well as vertically in the core concept of 'social system'. Originating in organic analogies, the concept of system in sociology has become increasingly sophisticated through the influence of cybernetics, communications theories, and so on. There is not the space here to go into its intricacies, but the fundamental problem it raises concerns the way in which the substantive referents of modernization theory, however arrived at, are tied in at the level of theory-formation with the 'pure' requirements of systemic interdependence or complementarity, and functional reciprocity.[23] The result is a theory both highly abstract and deductive—features which present obvious difficulties when it is applied to the analysis of what is, on any empirical criteria, the extreme heterogeneity of a field of study called the 'underdeveloped areas'. In the face of this diversity the abstract and deductive nature of modernization theory has been criticized by writers who have advocated alternative strategies of theory-formation and research based on a conceptually more flexible and empirically more sensitive comparative method.[24]

A related question concerns the conceptual status of the substantive component of modernization theory, more precisely the ideal-typical dichotomization of tradition and modernity. The notion of ideal-type itself has caused a series of problems in sociological theory ever since its formulation in the rather tortuous methodological writings of Max Weber.[25] Parsons has pointed out that Weber used ideal-types in two ways according to level of generality, rather than according to their function, which is that of concept formation and not description or explanation.[26] The individualizing ideal-type is synonymous with what Weber otherwise termed 'historical individuals', for example, the capitalist ethos in the modern history of north-west Europe and North America. On the other hand, an example of the generalizing ideal-type is Weber's formulation of bureaucracy. Now it is interesting that critics of Weber as different in other ways as Carl Friedrich and Isaac Deutscher have seen the ideal-type of bureaucracy as reflecting the values of the Prussian state to which Weber subscribed (Friedrich, 1952; Deutscher, 1969). In other words, for them it is culturally specific (not to say morally dubious), and the same criticism has already been applied in this paper to the ideal-types of modernity and modernization abstracted from the process of Western capitalist development. It is sometimes argued that the Western experience represents only the first historical example of modernization, and therefore can provide a paradigm for the study of the process in non-Western societies. This argument rests on what might be called an 'original state' view of underdevelopment and development, which is discussed below. The essential point is simply that what are in fact empirical generalizations or concepts of limited applicability ('historical individuals') have assumed the status of generalizing ideal-types, with certain consequences both for the characterization of 'destination' and for the analysis of types of social change, or lack of change, in the underdeveloped countries which fail to conform to the model. The several points made here have been illustrated by Bendix with reference to urbanization:

> Recent observations in India suggest that the generalizations and expectations we associate with the term 'urbanization' may be excessively culture-bound . . . what began as a definition has subtly turned into a prediction based on generalization about 'urbanism' though this prediction is hazardous.

Citing some of the evidence relating to urbanization in India, he continues:

> To dismiss all this as a transitory phenomenon that will give way to more familiar features to city life *presupposes what we need examine*, namely that the cluster of attributes constituting 'urbanism' represents a valid generalization of a pattern of interrelated social changes (Bendix 1963, pp. 534–5). [Emphasis added].

The dynamics of modernization theory consist of mechanisms such as the introduction of a market economy, monetization, urbanization, industrialization, the spread of mass communications and of literacy, and so on, which are subsumed and related at the theoretical level in the differentiation-integration model of social change.[27] It is instructive at this point to note an example of an explanation offered for evidence which contradicts the expectations of a theory in which definition fuses with prediction. This is also of interest in relation to the piety habitual among sociologists concerning the 'ongoing process' of reformulating theory in the light of research findings. Two facile ways of interpreting contradictory evidence have been mentioned briefly—one is to characterize it simply as 'pathological' in terms of the model, à la Rostow; the second is to view it as transitory, as pointed out in the above quotation from Bendix. Another possibility is to explain 'disturbances' in terms of 'lags' in the operation of integrative mechanisms relative to those of differentiation.[28] It is hardly surprising that modernization theorists have had to try to accommodate 'disturbances' and 'breakdowns of modernization' in the light of what is actually happening in the underdeveloped countries, but whether this evidence has resulted in any serious reconsideration of the assumptions of the theory is another question. Daniel Lerner writes:

> The most conspicuous symptom of the contemporary disorder is what has happened to urbanization in the developing areas. Every student of development is aware of the global spread of urban slums— from the *ranchos* of Caracas and *favellas* of Rio, to the *gecekondu* of Ankara, to *bidonvilles* and 'tin can cities' that infest the metropolitan centres of every developing country from Cairo to Manila.
>
> The point that must be stressed, in referring to this suffering mass of humanity displaced from the rural areas to the filthy peripheries of the great cities, is that few of them experience the 'transition' from agricultural to urban-industrial labour *called for by the mechanism of development and the model of modernization.* They are neither housed, nor trained, nor employed, nor serviced. They languish on the urban periphery without entering into any productive relationship with its industrial operations. These are the 'displaced persons', the D.P.s, of the developmental process as it now typically occurs in most of the world, a human flotsam and jetsam that has been displaced from traditional agricultural life without being incorporated into modern industrial life [emphasis added].

How does Lerner explain this phenomenon?

> . . . the modernizing lands are societies-in-a-hurry. Emulating what the advanced Western societies have become today, they want to get there faster. Accordingly, they force the tempo of Western development. Even more serious, as a result of their hurried pace, they often disorder the sequence of Western development (Lerner, 1967, p. 24).

In this last statement Lerner is referring to the disassociation of what he has designated as the two 'basic' variables in the development process, urbanization and industrialization. Two features of his explanation can be discerned. The first is that it is predicated on a statement about the underdeveloped countries as 'societies-in-a-hurry' which is symptomatic of a sociology that (like the speeches of politicians) assumes that societies have interests and goals, as opposed to investigating the crucial question of the interests and aspirations of different groups within societies, and the latent or manifest conflicts which exist.[29] Apart from population increases, a primary factor in the displacement of people from the rural areas and their consequent migration to the urban shanty towns is the widespread encroachment of rationalized capitalist production and/or marketing systems into peasant agriculture within the framework of *laissez-faire* agricultural policies. In this situation, who is 'in-a-hurry' with regard to what? That the 'flooding of great urban centres by people who have no work there' constitutes a problem of the greatest urgency is not disputed. What is questionable is the second feature of Lerner's explanation, namely the assumption that the Western process of development can (and must) be imitated in the underdeveloped countries, which leads on to an examination of the 'original state' view of underdevelopment and development.

What is termed here the 'original state' view has been concisely and explicitly expressed by Hoselitz—'If there are "developed" and "advanced" countries in the present they must have at some time been "under-developed" ' (Preface to Hoselitz, 1952). Two related historical arguments can be opposed to this view: (1) that it is distorting to classify today's underdeveloped countries with the pre-industrial societies of the West— 'The now developed countries were never *under*developed, though they may have been *un*developed' (Frank, 1966, p. 18); (2) that underdevelopment was *created* as an intrinsic part of the process of Western capitalist expansion—'underdevelopment is . . . a discrete historical process' 'due to the penetration of modern capitalistic enterprises into archaic structures' (Furtado, 1964, pp. 129, 138 and passim). These two statements indicate basic elements in a historical perspective within which certain points of contrast can be made between modernization theory as criticized here, and an alternative approach that addresses a different set of questions to problems of development.

First, several ways in which modernization theorists have dealt with historical dimensions can be mentioned briefly. One kind of problem concerns the origin of modernization in the West. Although a serious historical debate has been conducted over the nature and origins of European capitalism *qua* 'historical individual', and the names of Pirenne, Sombart, Weber, Tawney and Dobb spring to mind, the treatment of origins by those general modernization theorists who care to tackle it degenerates into a game of pick-and-choose with the centuries according to the particular aspect of modernity emphasized. In so far as the different historical situations of contemporary underdevelopment and the development of the West are explicitly acknowledged, this tends to be expressed in the notion of the 'advantages of backwardness' which usually refers to two arguments, neither of which is worth pursuing here—that under-developed countries today can modernize at much less social and human cost than was exacted by the development process in the West by heeding the excesses of the latter;[30] and that the store of skills and technology accumulated in the Western industrial countries is available ready-made for the use of the underdeveloped countries. A potentially more useful distinction is that between spontaneous and induced change, but in practice too often this receives a facile expression in the notion of different 'models' of the latter such as the Soviet Union, Kemalist Turkey and, most popular, Japan.[31] Stage theories should not be ruled out *a priori*, and various suggestions have been advanced for constructing them on a careful comparative basis which would avoid the customary stigma. However, once again in practice the stage theories advanced prove to be little more than exercises in 'comparative statics'.

If we refrain from discussing modernization as such and ask what we mean by the 'modern world' and what the historical processes were which formed the modern world, certain themes emerge which cut across the distorted comparative perspective and atrophied dynamics offered by modernization theory. First, the modern world as an inclusive international structure of economic, political and cultural relationships represents a novel situation in the history of human society; secondly, this situation was created principally 'through the midwifery of European imperialism' in Peter Worsley's phrase.[32] An explicit recognition of these factors is essential therefore to an understanding of the historical environment of contemporary underdevelopment and development. Jamil Hilal has expressed this succinctly:

> ... societies which previously existed only as—to use phenomenological language—'contemporaries' (that is, living at the same period of history and thus sharing a community of time but *not* of space) have become—often through the violence of a colonial situation and a process of 'compulsory familiarity'—'consociates'. That is, they have to encounter one another in the course of 'daily life'—they share, however briefly and superficially, a community of space and time and have become involved in each other's biography (Hilal, 1970, p. 2).

Thus the nature of the relationships between the developed and underdeveloped countries becomes a primary consideration in any macro-level discussion of development. These relationships are, however, ignored in modernization theory—'social theory has utterly failed to grapple with the outstanding feature of the last hundred years—the emergence of a world system of social relations' (Worsley, 1965, p. 374). The alternative starting point outlined here specifically confronts modernization theory with the question of the historical context in which the impact of 'modernizing forces' on indigenous 'traditional' societies is first located and this is 'in large measure the context of colonialism' (Rhodes, 1968, p. 397 and passim). Although important contributions to a political economy of colonialism have been made by a number of writers, a systematic and comprehensive sociological theory of colonialism has yet to be formulated. It is suggested that such a theory is indispensable to a critical and more fruitful sociology of development. Following Georges Balandier, one of the basic elements in the theory would be the concept of the colonial situation as a historical and 'total social phenomenon' characterized by certain forms of exploitation—economic, political, cultural and racial—which polarize the colonial and colonized societies.[33] This conceptualization, both substantively and as reflecting a different tradition of sociological analysis, stands in direct contrast to that derived from modernization theory which is precluded from identifying the dynamics and contradictions of the colonial situation as *sui generis* by a commitment to analysis in terms of 'traditional' and 'modern' elements which can only yield a dynamic in the concept of 'transition', or movement along a tradition-modernity continuum.[34] For this reason the notion of the 'dual society' is convenient for modernization theory as it neatly divides underdeveloped countries into backward (traditional) and advanced (modern) sectors without considering the symbiotic relationship between the two which can be analysed in terms of the creation of underdevelopment.[35] However, it is precisely the inaugural mechanisms of 'the modernization process', namely the intrusion of a market economy and the imposition of a modern administrative and tax structure (Kilson, 1963, p. 426 ff.), which are the basis of the creation of underdevelopment within the framework of the political economy of imperialism. The nature of the economic and cultural impact of 'modernization' is tied in with the metropolitan imperatives of imperialism and results in processes of change which defy the prescriptions of modernization theory.[36] Indigenous economic enterprise is destroyed, denied outlets, or a large part of its surplus appropriated for metropolitan purposes. The 'formation of a labour force'—a central theme in modernization literature—generally means cheap and expendable unskilled labour compelled by various means to work in European-owned mines and on European-owned plantations. Urbanization becomes the creation of racially segregated and essentially parasitic centres of administration and expatriate dominated mercantile activities. A post in the colonial bureaucracy or in the office of an expatriate company becomes the occupational ideal for those with a little education, and the 'middle class' which emerges on this basis is itself underdeveloped 'not engaged in production, nor invention, nor building, nor labour'.[37]


CONCLUSION

In criticizing modernization theory the intention is not to replace one abstract and rigid schema with another, and the broad generalizations advanced are not to be understood as the necessary and universally applicable elements of an ideal type of the colonial situation. Rather the example of the colonial situation is suggested only to illustrate in a summary way the differences between two sociological approaches and to show how modernization theory can be stood on its head by a mode of analysis which (1) approaches the study of development with a historical method; and (2) is informed by questions more relevant to the pressing needs of the present situation than those on which modernization theory is predicated, which is to say questions that do not disassociate the common concern with poverty, illiteracy and unemployment from the structural analysis of power and exploitation in their various forms. If this approach can be termed Marxist, all it means is that on the above criteria Marxism as a perspective in the social sciences displays a potential for the analysis of the underdeveloped world that is lacking in conventionally more acceptable procedures. This by no means implies that all analysis termed Marxist or neo-Marxist is either correct or *critical*. Indeed, the crude application of Marxism to problems of development often replicates some of the features of modernization theory which have been criticized here.[38] However, the proper use of a Marxist method, which is to say, one that is intrinsically critical, enables the ideological smokescreen of political 'independence' and 'decolonization' to be penetrated; and the kinds of questions addressed to the colonial situation are seen to be just as relevant and necessary for the analysis of underdevelopment and development in the post-independence setting, such as—who really rules? Who gets what benefit from ruling? *Who will benefit from the overthrow of the existing system?*[39]

NOTES

1. The following criticisms do not apply to (1) a 'revisionist' formulation such as that of Nettl and Robertson, 1968, which eschews any reliance on a tradition-modernity dichotomy; (2) the use of 'traditional' and 'modern' as analytical shorthand for empirically specified traits in a particular study, as in Vidich and Bensman, 1968; and Stephenson, 1968, who bases the definition of modernization in any given context on the perceptions of the subjects under study, arguing that this procedure yields an empirically meaningful scale of traditionalism and modernism at the expense of a basis for comparison and any assumption of sets of universal traits. It is perhaps significant that these two studies were concerned with aspects of American society.

2. Quoted in Magdoff, 1969, pp. 116/17. MacNamara was speaking on this occasion in his role as U.S. Secretary of Defense and not as President of the World Bank.

3. See the pioneering volume edited by Hoselitz, 1952; and the more recent symposium edited by Weiner, 1966, based on a series of talks in the Voice of America 'Forum' series.

4. For a frankly empiricist comment on modernization theory, see Dore, 1969.

5. Hoselitz, 1963; Riggs' 'theory of prismatic society' is an attempt to counter this 'propensity for dichotomous categories without imaginative intermediate concepts'— Riggs, 1964, p. 69 and passim.

6. Parsons 1964, 1966; it has pointed out that 'when Professor Parsons turns to what he calls "total society", he too gives us as unilinear a panorama of evolutionary change as did any of those evolutionists of the nineteenth century whom Parsons has often criticized for their monistic, necessary, and universal schemes' (Nisbet, 1969, p. 227). The question of the 'convergence' of industrial societies is also relevant here—see Feldman and Moore, 1962; Weinberg, 1969.

7. Scepticism concerning 'cultural inhibitions' and a call to 'put economic man back on the stage' are expressed by Anderson, 1963.

8. E.g. 'In the economically more developed nations, economic growth is a self-sustaining process of continuous innovation, change, and development. It is predicated on a particular view regarding the significance of life on this earth, on the acceptance of the idea of progress, that is, of a present better than the past and a future potentially better than the present. It assumes the perfectibility of man and society as a continuous possibility; it assumes man's ability to control and improve his natural environment, as well as the legitimacy of man's desire to do so.' Soedjatmoko, 1965, p. xii.

9. See the series *Studies in Political Development* sponsored by the Committee on Comparative Politics of the U.S. Social Science Research Council (Princeton, N.J. 1965-); and the preceding volume—Almond and Coleman, 1960.

10. Almond, 1960; Apter 1963a; Pye, 1963; Shils, 1965. It is hardly surprising that 'the Anglo-American polities most closely approximate the model of a modern political system' described by Almond and Shils (Coleman, 1960, p. 533), as this model is derived from them!

11. With reference to political 'modernization', see Bay, 1969. It is significant that the branch of political science devoted to the study of political development is often termed 'comparative politics'—the premises of the evolutionary conception of 'Comparative Method' are examined by Nisbet, 1969, Ch. 6.

12. 'Modernity entails democracy, and democracy in the new states, even where it is not representative, must above all be egalitarian' Shils, 1962, pp. 9/10.

13. This may reflect as much on the character of the targets as on anything else. Seers, 1970, makes some telling points about the nature of the conventional statistical indicators of economic growth.

14. Just how nominal this 'socialism' could be is indicated by the appreciation of its expression in the ideas of Senghor and Kenyatta by American ambassadors Mercer Cook and William Attwood (Senghor, 1964; Attwood, 1967). The 'Colloquium on Policies of Development and African Approaches to Socialism' held in Dakar in December 1962, represented the early nadir of this 'ideology'. Jean Lacouture observed that 'The distinction, always somewhat artificial between "revolutionary" and "reformist" Africa now seems altogether obsolete. . . . What is even more striking is that nobody challenged the necessity of calling upon foreign aid and investment'. Quoted in Arrighi and Saul, 1968, p. 158; see also Zolberg, 1964.

15. For observations on the use of this and other Parsonian pattern variables, see Frank, 1967, p. 24 ff.

16. See, *inter alia*, the monographs of Epstein, 1962; Hill, 1963; Belshaw, 1964. Recent theoretical essays relating to modernization by anthropologists are Belshaw, 1965; Nash, 1966.

17. The notion of different 'routes' to modernity is most clearly seen in the construction of typologies of modernizing élites—this is illustrated with reference to industrialization in Lamb, 1952; and, notably, Kerr et al, 1964. Typologies of régimes have constituted a major analytical tool in the political modernization literature—see Coleman, 1960; Shils, 1965; Apter, 1963b, 1967.

18. Differential economic and financial mechanisms related to 'degrees of backwardness' within the pre-1914 European economy are analysed by Gerschenkron, 1952, 1962. Barrington Moore, Jr., 1967, is an outstanding wide-ranging comparative study which deserves to have a major influence in 'bringing back history' into the sociology of development.

19. Rostow, 1967, pp. 162/4; Andreski, 1968, although in this case the characterization of what is 'pathological' stems from the idiosycratic and highly irascible perspective of the author rather than from the dictates of an explicit model of modernization.

20. Quoted in Worsley, 1964, p. 52; Kiernan, 1969, provides a wealth of references in a fascinating historical survey of ethnocentric attitudes, many of which remain unnervingly familiar.

21. Quoted by Gough, 1969, p. 144. See also Africa Research Group, 1969; Chomsky, 1969.

22. See the excellent résumé by Lukes, 1968. This type of reductionism, of course, militates against the rationale of any *social* science. The 'sociologism' of Émile Durkheim, for example, expressed a reaction against the analytical individualism of much nineteenth-century thought.

23. For a theoretical discussion, see Gouldner, 1959.

24. Moore, 1963; Bendix, 1963, 1967b. Moore, the foremost American sociologist of industrialization, is really a critic within modernization theory, as, say, Robert Merton, is within functionalism. Bendix is a historical and comparative sociologist in the Weberian tradition.

25. See, *inter alia*, Shils and Finch, 1949; and for interpretations of Weber's methodology, Aron, 1968; Freund, 1968; Parsons, 1968.

26. Parsons, 1968, pp. 601/10—'The Ideal Type and Generalized Analytical Theory'. Parsons' criticism of Weber is that the latter was too hesitant to go beyond a certain level of abstraction.

27. Industrialization, of course, may be the crucial mechanism in many cases. However, there has been a reaction against the tendency to overemphasize the role of industrialization—see, for example, Nettl and Robertson, 1968, pp. 38/42.

28. Smelser, 1963; and the comments on the differentiation model by Nettl, 1967, p. 110 ff.

29. This tendency in the work of Parsons has been criticized by, among others, Lockwood, 1956; Mills, 1959, Ch. 2; van den Berghe, 1967, Ch. 11.

30. Some 'modernizers' themselves have used this argument but looking to the

Soviet Union rather than to the West—for example, Nkrumah, 1963, pp. 166/7.

31. For a cautionary statement on Japan, see Dore, 1964.

32. Worsley, 1964, p. 10 and Ch. 1 passim; see also the excellent historical survey by Barraclough, 1967.

33. Balandier, 1963, Ch. 1—'La Notion de "Situation" Coloniale'; also Balandier, 1952.

34. It has been said that intellectually the distance across the Channel is greater than that across the Atlantic, and this is evident in the differential concern with the meaning and methods of a historical sociology. See Lefebvre, 1953; Goldmann, 1969; and the comments on the former by Sartre, 1964, pp. 51/2. Lefebvre and Sartre are cited by Balandier with reference to his formulation of the colonial situation as a historical and total social phenomenon. Among rare statements on behalf of a historical sociology by those conventionally regarded as sociologists in the Anglo-American concept of the discipline, are Mills, 1959, Ch. 8; Barrington Moore Jr., 1963.

35. See Rhodes, 1968; Frank, 1969; Stavenhagen, 1967; also the interesting critique of Malinowski's *The Dynamics of Culture Change* by Gluckman, 1947.

36. 'In a colonial state, the source of the social position of its power holders is, of course, the metropolitan socio-political system; and any comprehensive analysis would have to take account of this system' Kilson, 1963, p. 428.

37. Fanon, 1967, p. 120 and passim. See, *inter alia*, for part of the wide range of historical evidence Rhodes, 1968; Frank, 1969; Barratt Brown, 1970; Arrighi, 1970.

38. See the pertinent comments in a forthcoming piece by Hamza Alavi, 1970.

39. Barrington Moore Jr., 1967; and the reference to his work in Nettl, 1969, p. 28.

REFERENCES

Africa Research Group, 1969, *African Studies in America: the Extended Family*, Cambridge, Mass.

Hamza Alavi (forthcoming), 'The Army and Bureaucracy in Pakistan Politics', in A. Abdel-Malek (ed.), *L'Armée dans la Nation*, Paris.

Gabriel A. Almond, 1960, 'Introduction: a Functional Approach to Comparative Politics', in Almond and Coleman.

Gabriel A. Almond and James S. Coleman (eds.), 1960, *The Politics of the Developing Areas*, Princeton, N.J.

C. Arnold Anderson, 1963, 'The Impact of the Educational System on Technological Change and Modernization', in Hoselitz and Moore.

Stanislav Andreski, 1968, *The African Predicament. A Study in the Pathology of Modern-isation*, London.

David E. Apter, 1963a, Introduction to Part IX, 'Non-Western Government and Politics', in Eckstein and Apter.

David E. Apter, 1963b, 'Political Religion in the New States', in Clifford Geertz (ed.), *Old Societies and New States. The Quest for Modernity in Asia and Africa*, New York.

David E. Apter, 1967, *The Politics of Modernization* (paperback edition), Chicago.

Raymond Aron, 1964, *The Industrial Society* (English translation), London.

Raymon Aron, 1968, *Main Currents in Sociological Thought*, Vol. II (English translation), London.

G. Arrighi, 1970, 'Labour Supplies in Historical Perspective: a Study of the Pro-letarianization of the African Peasantry in Rhodesia', *Journal of Development Studies*, Vol. 6, No. 3.

Giovanni Arrighi and John S. Saul, 1968, 'Socialism and Economic Development in Africa', *Journal of Modern African Studies*, Vol. 6, No. 2.

William Attwood, 1967, *The Reds and the Blacks*, London.

Georges Balandier, 1952, 'Contribution à une Sociologie de la Dépendance', *Cahiers Internationaux de Sociologie*, Vol. 12.

Georges Balandier, 1963, *Sociologie Actuelle de l'Afrique Noire* (revised edition), Paris.

Geoffrey Barraclough, 1967, *An Introduction to Contemporary History*, Harmondsworth.

Michael Barratt Brown, 1970, *After Imperialism* (revised edition), London.

Christian Bay, 1969, 'The Cheerful Science of Dismal Politics', in Roszak.

Cyril S. Belshaw, 1964, *Under the Ivi Tree. Society and Economic Growth in Rural Fiji*,

London.

Cyril S. Belshaw, 1965, *Traditional Exchange and Modern Markets*, Englewood Cliffs N.J.

Reinhard Bendix, 1963, 'Concepts and Generalizations in Comparative Sociological Studies', *American Sociological Review*, Vol. 28, No. 4.

Reinhard Bendix, 1967a, 'Tradition and Modernity Reconsidered', *Comparative Studies in Society and History*, Vol. 9, No. 3.

Reinhard Bendix, 1967b, 'The Comparative Analysis of Historical Change', in Tom Burns and J. B. Saul (eds.), *Social Theory and Economic Change*, London.

Noam Chomsky, 1969, *American Power and the New Mandarins*, Harmondsworth.

Frederick Clairmonte, 1960, *Economic Liberalism and Underdevelopment. Studies in the Disintegration of an Idea*, Bombay.

James S. Coleman, 1960, 'Conclusion: The Political Systems of the Developing Areas', in Almond and Coleman.

Isaac Deutscher, 1969, 'Roots of Bureaucracy', in Ralph Miliband and John Saville (eds.), *The Socialist Register, 1969*, London.

Ronald P. Dore, 1964, 'Japan as a Model of Economic Development', *European Journal of Sociology*, Vol. 5.

Ronald P. Dore, 1969, 'On the Possibility and Desirability of a Theory of Modernization', Institute of Development Studies, *Communications Series*, No. 38.

Harry Eckstein and David E. Apter (eds.), 1963, *Comparative Politics*, New York.

S. N. Eisenstadt, 1966, *Modernization: Protest and Change*, Englewood Cliffs, N.J.

T. Scarlett Epstein, 1962, *Economic Development and Social Change in South India*, Manchester.

Frantz Fanon, 1967, *The Wretched of the Earth* (English translation), Harmondsworth.

Arnold S. Feldman and Wilbert E. Moore, 1962, 'Industrialization and Industrialism. Convergence and Differentiation', in *Transactions of the Fifth World Congress of Sociology*, Vol. II, Washington.

Andre Gunder Frank, 1966, 'The Development of Underdevelopment', *Monthly Review*, Vol. 18, No. 4.

Andre Gunder Frank, 1967, 'Sociology of Development and Underdevelopment of Sociology', *Catalyst* (University of Buffalo), No. 3.

Andre Gunder Frank, 1969, *Capitalism and Underdevelopment in Latin America. Historical Studies of Chile and Brazil* (revised edition), New York.

Julien Freund, 1968, *The Sociology of Max Weber* (English translation), London.

Carl J. Friedrich, 1952, 'Some Observations on Weber's Analysis of Bureaucracy', in Robert K. Merton *et al* (eds.), *Reader in Bureaucracy*, Toronto.

Celso Furtado, 1964, *Development and Underdevelopment* (English translation), Berkeley, California.

Alexander Gerschenkron, 1952, 'Economic Backwardness in Historical Perspective', in Hoselitz.

Alexander Gerschenkron, 1962, 'Typology of Industrial Development as a Tool of Analysis', in *Second International Conference of Economic History: Aix-en-Provence*, Vol. II, The Hague.

Max Gluckman, 1949, 'Malinowski's "Functional" Analysis of Social Change', *Africa*, Vol. 17.

Lucien Goldman, 1969, *The Human Sciences and Philosophy* (English translation), London.

Kathleen Gough, 1969, 'World Revolution and the Science of Man', in Roszak.

Alvin W. Gouldner, 1959, 'Reciprocity and Autonomy in Functional Theory', in Llewellyn Gross (ed.), *Symposium on Sociological Theory*, New York.

Jamil Hilal, 1970, 'Sociology and Underdevelopment', Department of Social Theory and Institutions, University of Durham (mimeo).

Polly Hill, 1963, *Migrant Cocoa-Farmers of Southern Ghana. A Study in Rural Capitalism*, London.

Bert F. Hoselitz (ed.), 1952, *The Progress of Underdeveloped Areas*, Chicago.

Bert F. Hoselitz, 1963, 'Main Concepts in the Analysis of the Social Implications of Technological Change', in Hoselitz and Moore.

Bert F. Hoselitz and Wilbert E. Moore (eds.), 1963, *Industrialization and Society*,

Paris.
Clark Kerr *et al*, 1964, *Industrialism and Industrial Man*, New York.
Martin Kilson, 1963, 'African Political Change and the Modernization Process', *Journal of Modern African Studies*, Vol. 1, No. 4.
V. G. Kiernan, 1969, *The Lords of Human Kind. European Attitudes to the Outside World in the Imperial Age*, London.
Robert K. Lamb, 1952, 'Political Elites and the Process of Economic Development', in Hoselitz.
Henri Lefebvre, 1953, 'Perspectives de la Sociologie Rurale', *Cahiers Internationaux de Sociologie*, Vol. 13.
Daniel Lerner, 1964, *The Passing of Traditional Society. Modernizing the Middle East* (paperback edition), Toronto.
Daniel Lerner, 1967, 'Comparative Analysis of Processes of Modernisation', in Miner.
David Lockwood, 1956, 'Some Remarks on "The Social System"', *British Journal of Sociology*, Vol. 7, No. 2.
Steven Lukes, 1968, 'Methodological Individualism Reconsidered', *British Journal of Sociology*, Vol. 19, No. 2.
Harry Magdoff, 1969, *The Age of Imperialism. The Economics of U.S. Foreign Policy*, New York.
Ali A. Mazrui, 1968, 'From Social Darwinism to Current Theories of Modernization. A Tradition of Analysis', *World Politics*, Vol. 21, No. 1.
David C. McClelland, 1963, 'The Achievement Motive in Economic Growth', in Hoselitz and Moore.
David C. McClelland, 1964, 'Business Drive and National Achievement', in Amitai Etzioni and Eva Etzioni (eds.), *Social Change*, New York.
C. Wright Mills, 1959, *The Sociological Imagination*, New York.
Horace Miner (ed.), 1967, *The City in Modern Africa*, London.
Barrington Moore, Jr., 1963, 'Strategy in Social Science', in Maurice Stein and Arthur Vidich (eds.), *Sociology on Trial*, Englewood Cliffs, N.J.
Barrington Moore, Jr. 1967, *The Social Origins of Dictatorship and Democracy. Lord and Peasant in the Making of the Modern World*, London.
Wilbert E. Moore, 1963, 'Introduction: Social Change and Comparative Studies', *International Social Science Journal*, Vol. 15, No. 4, *The Sociology of Development in Latin America*.
Manning Nash, 1966, *Primitive and Peasant Economic Systems*, San Francisco.
J. P. Nettl, 1967, *Political Mobilization. A Sociological Analysis of Methods and Concepts*, London.
J. P. Nettl, 1969, 'Strategies in the Study of Political Development', in Colin Leys (ed.), *Politics and Change in Developing Countries*, London.
J. P. Nettl and Roland Robertson, 1968, *International Systems and the Modernization of Societies. The Formation of National Goals and Attitudes*, London.
Robert A. Nisbet, 1968, *Social Change and History. Aspects of the Western Theory of Development*, New York.
Kwame Nkrumah, 1963, *Africa Must Unite*, London.
Talcott Parsons, 1964, 'Evolutionary Universals in Society', *American Sociological Review*, Vol. 29, No. 3.
Talcott Parsons, 1966, *Societies. Evolutionary and Comparative Perspectives*, Englewood Cliffs, N.J.
Talcott Parsons, 1968, *The Structure of Social Action* (paperback edition, 2 volumes), New York.
Herbert Passin, 1965, *Society and Education in Japan*, New York.
Robert I. Rhodes, 1968, 'The Disguised Conservatism in Evolutionary Development Theory', *Science and Society*, Vol. 32, No. 3.
Fred W. Riggs, 1964, *Administration in Developing Countries. The Theory of Prismatic Society*, Boston.
W. W. Rostow, 1967, *The Stages of Economic Growth. A Non-Communist Manifesto*, (paperback edition), London.
Theodore Roszak (ed.), 1969, *The Dissenting Academy*, Harmondsworth.
Jean-Paul Sartre, 1964, *The Problem of Method* (English translation), London.

Dudley Seers, 1970, 'The Meaning of Development', Institute of Development Studies, *Communications Series*, No. 44.

Léopold Sédar Senghor, 1964, *On African Socialism* (translated and with an Introduction by Mercer Cook), New York.

Edward Shils, 1962, 'The Military in the Political Development of the New States', in John J. Johnson (ed.), *The Role of the Military in Underdeveloped Countries*, Princeton, N.J.

Edward Shils, 1965, *Political Development in the New States*, The Hague.

E. A. Shils and H. A. Finch (eds.), 1949, *Max Weber: Essays in the Methodology of the Social Sciences*, Glencoe, Illinois.

Neil J. Smelser, 1963, 'Mechanisms of Change and Adjustment to Change', in Hoselitz and Moore.

Neil J. Smelser, 1968, 'Toward a General Theory of Social Change', in Smelser, *Essays in Sociological Explanation*, Englewood Cliffs, N.J.

Soedjatmoko, 1965, 'Memorandum on Scope and Purpose of Seminar', in R. N. Bellah (ed.), *Religion and Progress in Modern Asia*, New York.

Rudolfo Stavenhagen, 1969, 'Seven Erroneous Theses about Latin America', in Irving Louis Horowitz *et al* (eds.), *Latin American Radicalism*, New York.

John B. Stephenson, 1968, 'Is Everyone Going Modern? A Critique and a Suggestion for Measuring Modernism', *American Journal of Sociology*, Vol. 74, No. 3.

Lionel Tiger, 1967, 'Bureaucracy and Urban Symbol Systems', in Miner.

Pierre L. van den Berghe, 1967, *South Africa. A Study in Conflict*, Berkeley, California.

Arthur J. Vidich and Joseph Bensman, 1968, *Small Town in Mass Society* (revised edition), Princeton, N.J.

Max Weber, 1930, *The Protestant Ethic and the Spirit of Capitalism* (English translation), London.

Ian Weinberg, 1969, 'The Problem of the Emergence of Industrial Societies: a Critical Look at the State of a Theory', *Comparative Studies in Society and History*, Vol. 11, No. 1.

Myron Weiner (ed.), 1966, *Modernization*, New York.

Peter Worsley, 1964 *The Third World*, London.

Peter Worsley, 1965, 'Bureaucracy and Decolonization: Democracy from the Top', in Irving Louis Horowitz (ed.), *The New Sociology*, New York.

Aristide R. Zolberg, 1964, 'The Dakar Colloquium the Search for a Doctrine', in William H. Friedland and Carl G. Rosberg, Jr. (eds.), *African Socialism*, Stanford, California.

# Commentary

# The Disparaging of Development Economics

## by John Toye*

**Equality, the Third World and Economic Delusion.** By P. T. Bauer. *London: Methuen*, University Paperbacks 791 (paperback edition of book published in hard covers by Weidenfeld & Nicolson in 1981; received for review December 1982). Pp. viii + 293. £5.95. ISBN 0 416 34230 2.

## I. INTRODUCTION

No reasonable student of development economics claims that the subject is free from error. Mistakes are constantly being made and some, indeed, are repeated after having been convincingly shown to be mistakes. This is the common condition of the social sciences. However, a senior figure among development economists has recently published an attack on development economics which suggests that it is much worse in this respect than other branches of economics [*Bauer, 1981: 259*]. It is further suggested that the mistakes made by development economists are 'simple and readily demonstrable errors', the exposure of which has been frustrated by an effective phalanx of professional colleagues 'ready to shield the perpetration of even the crudest lapses' [*ibid: 261*]. The gravamen of these charges is serious professional misconduct by development economists. It is clearly implied that they have failed to root out obvious errors for essentially political reasons.

Why should one be perturbed by accusations of this kind? First, they were intended to be taken seriously by their author. They have been repeated over a long period [e.g. *Bauer, 1972*] and those which were originally published in minor sources have now been republished in the format of a university textbook. This indicates that a major statement is intended, with widespread impact on university students. Second, the book concerned and its author are advertised as having received high praise from the most senior professor of political economy at Oxford University. A. K. Sen is quoted on the book's cover to the effect that Bauer is 'one of the most distinguished development economists in the world'. The cover gives no hint of restraint or qualification in that accolade, although a full reading of Sen's review would reveal how little he agrees with Bauer [*Sen, 1982*]. This publisher's trick of selective quotation gives Bauer's views a fair prospect of achieving the wide

* Professor of Development Policy and Planning and Director of the Centre for Development Studies, University College of Swansea. Helpful comments and other assistance by David Booth, Michael Lipton, John Sender and Sheila Smith are gratefully acknowledged. Remaining errors are the author's.

and favourable reception which they seek, by trading on the great respect in which Professor Sen is held. Third, Bauer has received political recognition. He is the only development economist to have been ennobled by the present Conservative Government in the UK. This is in any case a rare honour: Lord Balogh is the only development economist similarly honoured to come to mind.

The fourth reason for being perturbed by Bauer's disparagement of development economics is explained in the course of this paper. It is that, in my opinion, the critique advanced of development economics is profoundly flawed. Indeed, it exhibits precisely those low standards of logic and evidence which Bauer, with tedious repetition, lays at the door of others. It is a defective piece of work, not just in details but in its central propositions, contributing nothing new empirically and interpreting existing material at best selectively and at worst with clear logical inconsistencies. The bulk of this paper is designed to substantiate these judgements.

The final reason for perturbation is that the current disparagement of development economics has a wider intellectual, and indeed political, context than appears from the book itself. It is part of a larger effort by academics of a conservative persuasion to denigrate the standards and standing of those whose study of society has led them to criticise existing social arrangements. This does not appear on the face of the text. Its appearance as a disinterested academic assertion of high intellectual standards is disingenuous. A political purpose of influencing the allocation of government funds for teaching and research is never acknowledged. But it is all the more important to point out if, as is argued here, the conservative claim to superior standards is baseless.

## II. POPULATION AND COMMODITY POLICIES

To avoid unnecessary misunderstanding, it should be stated at the outset that the argument presented here does not require us to reject all of Bauer's views on development and development policy. Some of them, for example on population policy and on commodity stabilisation schemes, are basically correct and unexceptionable. In these cases, what has to be rejected is the implication that the great bulk of development economists have gratuitously persisted in advocating contrary views for essentially political reasons. This implication is not at all correct.

First, let us look at the question of population policy. Bauer believes correctly that the so-called 'population explosion' has been greatly overrated as an obstacle to economic development and that drastic policies of population control are therefore unjustified. There are, of course, people who take the opposite view and who are alarmist about population growth inhibiting development. But they tend to be politicians and not development economists, whatever their political values may be. The instances cited by Bauer are Lester B. Pearson, the former Canadian prime minister and Robert S. McNamara, the former US Secretary of Defence. The development economists to whom Bauer refers were all engaged in either producing useful empirical studies of demographic behaviour or trying to arrive at valid general theories of the varied empirical discoveries. Thus, there is no evidence for a charge of serious professional misconduct here. But Bauer's complete failure to discriminate between the pronouncements of politicians and those of development economists whom he criticises for politically-motivated errors is highly significant. This confusion is at the heart of his method of argument and will be seen again in the discussion of income redistribution.

But perhaps there *are* politically motivated development economists, whom Bauer has simply forgotten to mention, but who hold the Pearson-McNamara view on population and development? If one looks at the famous names of left-inclined development economists, this does not appear to be so. Paul Baran is one such who is attacked by Bauer for his errors [*Bauer, 1981: 66-7*]. On population and development, we find Baran saying, as early as 1957, that attempts to discredit development planning

> are assisted by the neo-Malthusians who explain the backwardness of backward countries as the inevitable result of their 'excessive' population growth and who therefore denounce all attempts at economic development in these areas as utopian, so long as the population increase has not been brought to a halt. However, since a reduction of the population growth – assuming for the sake of argument that such a reduction is necessary – can only be achieved as a *result* of an all round development of the backward societies, the neo-Malthusian position renders economic development a hopeless task, made insolvable by the very nature of the human animal. [*Baran, 1973: 125-6*]

For the last thirty years, opposition to neo-Malthusianism has been a staple view of the left-inclined development economists [*Gurley, 1979: 210-2*].

One of the more recent examples is the late Bill Warren, who claimed that

> future historians will likely consider the population explosion one of the crucial causes of the unprecedented advance in human welfare achieved during the twentieth century, its effects in stimulating the reorganisation of human society (especially backward societies) so as to produce an ever greater volume of output far outweighing any initial per capita stagnation or decline .... Such deleterious effects of population growth were comparatively rare – and certainly localised. [*Warren, 1980: 131, note 10*]

This triumphalist view of the question now perhaps seems a little unsophisticated. Traditional anti-neo-Malthusianism now sits side by side with interpretations which attempt to present a more complex picture of demographic variation over time and space; drawing, in fact, on the same seminal contributions as those drawn on by Bauer [*Secombe, 1983; Cassen, 1978*]. But, simple or complex, there is precious little justification for the view that development economists as a group have persisted with Malthusian doctrines for political reasons, as Bauer implies.[1]

Equally slight is the justification for the view that development economists as a group have advocated commodity stabilisation schemes for political reasons. The defects and difficulties of such schemes are a familiar academic topic and Bauer's own treatment, though a good summary, does not break new ground. Again, it is necessary to distinguish clearly between political organisations, such as UNCTAD, which adopt an optimistic official view and the views of academic development economists. The latter have typically been at variance with the former. UNCTAD's inability to cope with independent economic analysis of the commodities issue has been properly described and criticised [Brown, 1980: 139-65]. The successes and failure of post-war international commodity agreements have been carefully appraised [MacBean and Snowden, 1981: 111-31]. The question of whether the benefits of such schemes reach the poor – which rightly concerns Bauer – has been pointedly raised [Smith and Toye, 1979: 15; Desai, 1980: 171-2]. Since Bauer does not cite any development economists who have mis-analysed commodity stabilisation schemes, it is difficult to come further to grips with the suggestion that development economists, as opposed to political organisations, have made unfounded claims for them.

## III. INTERNATIONAL INCOME COMPARISONS

In making his case for 'important transgressions encountered in academic writing and notably in mainstream development economics' [1981: 4], Bauer places considerable weight on the issue of comparisons of national income between widely different societies. He claims that such comparisons are still widely used 'two decades after Professor Dan Usher had shown that such comparisons are worthless' [ibid: 4, 119-20, 261, 274 note 28]. Since this alleged 'transgression' is referred to so often, it is worth examining it more closely.

Professor Usher made two quite separate and quite correct points about international income comparisons. The first was a conceptual point. Because relative prices differ in the two countries being compared, there is not one, but several different comparisons that can be made, each answering a different question. The second was that to convert rich and poor country incomes into a single *numeraire* by using foreign exchange rates gives a highly exaggerated indicator of real income differences and, in any case, does not have an unambiguous meaning in terms of the comparative questions which it is sensible to ask [Usher, 1968: xi-xxiii]. Thus, Usher's contribution did not prove, *pace* Bauer, that all international income comparisons are worthless. He showed that one popular method was worthless, and that alternative methods require a precise assumption about which country's relative prices are to be used, in order to be meaningful. In fact, the bulk of his book is concerned with deriving alternative estimates of the ratio of Thai and UK incomes [ibid: xxi].

It was pointed out at the time of Usher's contribution that the academic literature of the 1950s had in fact been well aware of the dubiousness of converting incomes through a foreign exchange rate [Toye, 1969 citing inter alia, Hagen, 1960]. Insensitive use of such statistics seemed to be limited to UN agencies and one well-known development economist writing a popular textbook [Bhagwati, 1966]. But any attempt to discriminate between political bodies on the one hand and the mainstream of academic development economists on the other has been entirely overlooked by Bauer. Indeed, in his latest writing, he is still trying to confuse the two in the public mind.

The fact that, by the time Usher's work was being published, the international agencies had themselves taken steps to produce more informative international income comparisons is also not acknowledged by Bauer. By 1975, the UN Statistical Office and the World Bank were publishing the first results of their International Comparison Project. Even when Bauer himself uses the results of phase II of this project, he does not give a full source citation and does not make it clear that the UN was one of the major sponsors and executors of the project [Bauer, 1981: 101, 273 note 13; Kravis, Heston and Summers, 1978: 1-3]. To do so would further undermine Bauer's claim that development economists work with international agencies to give a misleading impression of the size of international income differences.

Bauer's approach to the question of statistical refinement is anomalous and opportunistic. When international income differences are being discussed, he is all scepticism and (rightly) full of demands for the greatest statistical refinement. However, when it suits his argument, he flips over into childlike credulity. Here is a choice example, culled from a discussion of foreign 'aid':

> If there is a sensible and objective measure of wretchedness of life felt by the people who experience it rather than as envisaged by outide observers, it is the suicide rate. This is much higher in the West than it is in the Third World. [Bauer, 1981: 115]

The virtual certainty that international comparisons of suicide rates are vitiated by huge culturally determined differences in reporting practices does not for a moment deflect Bauer from his conclusion that wealth transfers should flow *from* the Third World, not *to* it. Very convenient, but not likely to inspire confidence in his initial statement of intentions:

> I do not intend to advance anomalous or paradoxical views to attract attention .... Much of my argument rests on simple reflection, analysis or observation, the validity of which the non-technical reader can verify readily. [Ibid: 2]

But the focusing of statistical scepticism on methods of comparing incomes internationally does not succeed in disposing of the fact that very large differences exist. Even on the revised UN figures, the per capita GDP of Kenya and India in 1973 was only about six per cent of that of the United States [Kravis, Heston and Summers, 1978: 10]. Bauer himself concedes that 'although Third World poverty is often much exaggerated, it is nevertheless true that people at large are much poorer than in the West' [1981: 253]. Thus, the question of what response is appropriate to this admitted fact remains, after all, very much on the agenda.

## IV. THE RATIONALE OF REDISTRIBUTION

One of the central complaints levelled by Bauer at development economists is that they have given a veneer of intellectual respectability to policies of income redistribution, both within countries and between countries. Unlike the previous issues discussed, there is no question here of Bauer's misrepresenting the tendency of mainstream development economics. It has emphasised redistribution, both nationally, as in the IDS/World Bank project on *Redistribution with Growth* [*Chenery et al., 1974*], and internationally, as in the Brandt Commission's *North-South: A Programme for Survival* [*ICIDI, 1980*]. The question is therefore whether this has been an appropriate response to the substantial differences in incomes which, by common consent, exist in the world today.

Opponents of redistribution rely on two different lines of argument. One is an argument about rights: people have a right to 'their' incomes, because they have earned, produced or otherwise created them. The other is a pragmatic argument: the costs of redistribution – in lost output arising from disincentives, administrative costs of transfer and other political costs of 'increased coercion' – outweigh the benefits. Bauer pursues both lines of attack but both prove to be nebulous and inconclusive.

The first runs into the objection that in a society, as opposed to a desert island inhabited by Robinson Crusoe, no one actually creates his or her income all alone. They do so under a set of laws and social conventions which regulate the forms of economic co-operation with other people. These laws and conventions are historically specific and may be the legitimate object of moral criticism. Bauer himself objects to laws and conventions which allow people to gain incomes by the exercise of monopoly power or from other sources of 'windfall' profit [*Bauer, 1981: 12-3, 174*]. Others may criticise other laws and conventions which permit incomes to be earned from activities that cause, for example, permanent environmental degradation or irreversible damage to human health and safety. Whatever the precise criticism, the fact that such criticism is possible and is frequently recognised as legitimate, nullifies the attempt to establish a right to retain income (or wealth, for that matter) howsoever it is come by. The retention of *all* forms of income or wealth cannot itself be a matter of principle.

As an important corollary to this, we must note that Bauer's attack on development economists for advocating 'state economic controls' is much too simple-minded. If one objects to monopoly, as Bauer does, it is inconsistent to object to all state economic controls. The reason for this is that some state economic controls, particularly controls on the prices of industrial products in developing countries, are actually necessary to neutralise the effects of monopoly power. It may be argued that the liberalisation of imports is an important method of checking industrial monopolies in poor countries, and this is so. But it is not the case that the anti-monopoly impact of price controls can always be achieved by import liberalisation, as those who oppose state economic controls *as such* and continually advocate increased external contacts seem to believe. Import liberalisation, assuming that this policy is a real political option, is ineffective against monopoly where the product enjoys natural geographical protection from imports and reduces economic surplus where the product's production process exhibits economies of scale [*Whitworth, 1980: 92-3*]. Bauer does not seem to be familiar with these propositions.

If one is seriously opposed to monopoly, one must logically be in favour of effective anti-monopoly measures. But such measures are an instrument of income redistribution. Although much of the discussion by Bauer and other conservative writers appears to assume that income redistribution derives only from taxation and public expenditure, this is a fallacy [*Chenery et al., 1974: 73-4*]. Thus, it is inconsistent of Bauer to oppose both monopoly *and* income redistribution policies.

Turning now to the pragmatic argument against redistribution, it should be clear that for this argument to be convincing, some quantification is required. The argument is that the costs of redistribution exceed its benefits. How can one be convinced of this in the absence of any attempt at measuring costs against benefits? One is entitled to take a minimalist position on the possibility and relevance of quantification in economics, as Bauer does [*1981: 22, 265*], although, in my opinion, such a position is much too extreme. But it is inconsistent both to adopt a minimalist position and to expect people to accept propositions of the form 'A is larger than B'. It is equally illogical to take development economists to task for ignoring the costs of their policy proposals while, at the same time, embargoing the use of all the standard methods by which economists take costs into account and balance them against benefits.

Quantifying the costs of state economic controls or income redistribution measures is not impossible. One will not achieve the perfect measure first time but it is quite reasonable to begin with a relatively crude measure and then progressively refine it, so that our estimates approximate the true position more closely after each refinement. (This is what has happened with international income comparisons.) Returning to the example of anti-monopoly devices, since these are the redistribution measures which Bauer himself favours, one policy often employed is the licencing by government of new or additional production capacity in certain industries. The costs of such a policy consist of the opportunity costs of the civil servants who administer the policy, including salary and non-salary elements, plus the loss of economic surplus caused by administrative delays. The former needs data from the government budget, adjusted if necessary by shadow wage rates and shadow commodity prices. The latter needs information on the length of delays, the size of the investments delayed, the marginal rate of return on the investments and their expected economic lives. For some developing countries at least, either actual data or good approximations are available to allow such a calculation to be made. Thus, an interesting estimate of the cost of this particular policy could be made to establish the order of magnitude, if not the exact amount. But no calculations of this, or of any, kind are offered by Bauer, just dramatic general assertions that the costs are high.

Equally, no estimates are offered of the benefits of income redistribution. This may be designed to give the impression that the benefits are always zero, so that any positive cost makes redistribution an undesirable policy. But that is not so. It is reasonable to believe that the value of a unit of income is greater for a poor person than a rich person, the difference in value being a positive function of the size of the initial difference in income levels. There are various methods of calculating the weighting that makes a unit of income

equally valuable to rich and poor alike and this weight can then be used to
calculate the probable benefits that accrue from redistribution of given size
between given initial income levels. This is never attempted. The claim that
costs of redistribution always exceed the benefits remains untested.

As the late Professor G. M. Jenkins of Lancaster University remarked:

> The line of demarcation between science and non-science rests not on
> whether a proposition is sensible but whether it is *testable*. If it is not,
> then its current status has more to do with theology than with science.
> If economic theory is to provide better guidelines for policy-makers,
> then there is a greater need for *testing specific economic hypotheses* and
> for attempting to discriminate between hypotheses. [*Jenkins, 1977:
> 560*]

## V. INTERNATIONAL REDISTRIBUTION THROUGH FOREIGN 'AID'

If the proportion of his book's pages devoted to it is a reliable guide, the most
serious accusation being levelled by Bauer against mainstream development
economists as a group is that they have persistently advocated programmes
of international 'aid', despite the many possible objections to such programmes. Bauer claims to see 'an umbilical link between development
economists and foreign aid'. He evidently believes also that 'the expansion
of development studies serves to promote political systems favoured by
mainstream development economists' [*Bauer, 1981: 145*].

This is surely a gross exaggeration of the political influence of development economists. Because 'aid' has endured as a political fact and because
many development economists have been supporters of the principle of
international redistribution of income, it does not follow that they are
responsible for the durability of foreign 'aid' programmes. The best way to
see this is to consider a different issue of economic policy, on which development (and other) economists are actually more united in their view than
development economists are on 'aid'. An example would be tax holidays as
an investment incentive. Very few economists of any political persuasion
have a good word to say for this particular policy device. Yet it turns out to
be overwhelmingly popular with governments of developing countries and
developed countries alike.

The practice of foreign 'aid', as opposed to the principle of international
redistribution, has been much criticised by development economists of all
political persuasions. Bauer himself represents the conservative strand of
this criticism and he notes that development economists of the far left have
also been critical [*Bauer, 1981: 148*]. What then of those on the middle
ground? The late Professor Dudley Seers surely comes as close to being a
representative figure of the middle ground as any. Recording his life's work,
his obituary notes:

> 'The Prevalence of Pseudo-Planning' (1972); 'Why Visiting Econom-
> ists Fail' (1962); 'What Types of Government Should be Refused What
> Types of Aid' (1977); demonstrated another strand (sc. of his work),
> his protest at the inappropriateness of much of the western world's aid

> effort and advice; this series included 'The Tendency to Financial
> Irresponsibility of Socialist Governments and its Political Conse-
> quences' (1981) and 'Muddling Morality and Mutuality' (1980), his
> characteristically robust quarrel with the conclusions of the Brandt
> Commission. [*The Times, 1983*].

Little evidence here that Professor Seers created 'an effective claque which
has managed to silence discussion of the subject, including worthwhile
reform of aid' [*Bauer, 1981: 148*]. Practical discussions of new initiatives in
aid policy, such as poverty-focused aid, appear frequently in the professional journals of development economists. Their criticism of aspects of aid
policy is not purely negative, however. The identification of defects is but a
preliminary step to suggestions for further reform [e.g. *Mosley, 1981*].

The sad fact is that a great deal of the informed criticism which development economists of all persuasions have produced over the years has not
been effective. This is hardly surprising in view of the substantial vested
interests that are involved: these are, as Bauer points out with others, the
industrial and commercial interests in developed countries and the governmental and bureaucratic interests in developing countries. In addition,
the governments of developed countries have their own distinct interests in
the exercise of power which discretionary 'aid' permits and its uses in gaining
assent to policies of immigration control and trade restriction. Where government departments, such as the UK's ODA, *do* attempt to evaluate the
impact of 'aid', development economists are regularly to be found partici-
pating in this detailed and difficult work [*ODA, 1983*].

Significantly, although Bauer promises to examine the argument that 'aid'
is a restitution for present wrongs of the aid donors, he does not actually get
around, in his very long essay, to doing so [*Bauer, 1981: 87, 120-2*]. That
would certainly be an interesting argument to look at. One could then
grapple with a rather different set of facts than those which are highlighted.
For example, the UK government last year collected a profit of £3 million
from the fees paid by applicants, mainly in the Third World, for UK
citizenship; most of the applications were refused. Or, at the other end of the
scale, many thousands of millions is added to the debt owed by the Third
World every time the level of interest rates rises by one percentage point;
and rising interest rates are an essential policy instrument of conservative
Western governments who are determined to decrease inflation whatever
the consequences.

The fact that interest rates on commercial Third World debts are flexible is
an important fact about the current financial position of developing countries which Bauer seems to have missed. But it does have a significant
implication for one argument that is frequently used to criticise 'aid'. It is
that the requests for the re-scheduling or cancellation of debt which Third
World governments have made from time to time, and are now making with
increasing frequency, are *ipso facto* evidence that 'the capital was supplied to
governments who have wasted resources they received, or who refuse to
honour their obligations' [*Bauer, 1981: 96*]. The charge of wasting 'aid' is
surely true of some developing countries at some times, but a general case

that they are guilty *either* of folly *or* of knavery does not stick, once it is recognised that developing countries' current debt problems arise in part from the unsound lending of developed countries' commercial bankers, combined with flexible interest rates. Bauer's critique had more relevance to debt re-schedulings being sought ten and more years ago. It has been well and truly overtaken by the events of the 1970s.

The claim that aid is most unlikely to be productive anyway is based on speculation rather than empirical studies. It is true that such studies are rather rare but they have been done and they have shown, for example, a five per cent rate of return on aid funds supplied to Egypt in the 1960s and 1970s [*Levy, 1982; cf. Bauer, 1981: 110*]. This is certainly no more than modest but it is not evidence that foreign resources are inevitably wasted.

Among the welter of anti-aid arguments often used to criticise development economists who favour the principle of equalising international transfers, one more may be noted. It is that such tranfers are actually regressive, not progressive in their impact. At first glance, this might appear to be a powerful blow to the case for international transfers. Imagine development economists, of all people, advocating a policy with bad distributional consequences! They who are always so fussy about equity! Before the cries of 'shame' become deafening, two things should be said. Bauer is thereby pre-supposing correctly that equity is important, contrary to much of his earlier argument that economic differences are a matter of indifference, because they are merely part of a natural order. Also, he is implying, quite falsely, that international transfers are advocated by development economists without concern for the low income taxpayer in developed countries who willy-nilly contributes to them. In fact, exactly the same people who are concerned about international equity are also concerned about the regressive tax structures of the developed countries. The fact that many developed countries have set up for themselves 'poverty traps' is a reason both for removing them and for giving equalising transfers to developing countries; it is not a reason for doing neither.[2]

## VI. THE CONTRIBUTION OF INVESTMENT TO DEVELOPMENT

The case for international (and, indeed, intra-national) transfers would be gravely weakened if it were true that capital investment made no contribution to the development of the recipient country. Development economists generally have not believed such a strong proposition, although they have disputed how great a contribution investment makes and what emphasis to put on different forms of investment to gain the largest possible contribution to development from a given stock of investible resources. However, now development economists are being criticised for not assenting to the strong proposition of a zero or negligible contribution [*Bauer, 1981: 248*].

The criticism rests on a particular interpretation of the sources of growth analyses which were made for developed countries, mainly the United States, in the 1950s and 1960s [*Bauer, 1981: 242, 280 note 2*]. These are accepted as showing that overall economic growth in such countries has been much greater than can be accounted for purely in terms of the increases in the volume of 'capital' and 'labour' used as inputs to produce it. What Bauer does not mention is that these analyses were extensively commented on in the 1960s by general economists and development economists and were, on the whole, found wanting. Today, this seems to have been conveniently forgotten.

The theoretical construct which underlies sources of growth analysis is the aggregate production function. Even those who produced the original analyses were highly ambivalent about the real validity of this abstraction. Revealingly, Solow says in his seminal article: 'I would not try to justify what follows by calling on fancy theorems on aggregation and index numbers. Either this kind of aggregate economics appeals or it doesn't. Personally, I belong to both schools' [Solow, 1957: 213]. What helped to give the aggregate production function plausibility was its prediction – admittedly based on a series of highly unrealistic neo-classical assumptions – that the shares of income accruing to labour and capital during economic growth would remain constant, which has been broadly true. But it was pointed out long ago that there are other less unrealistic theories which are also consistent with this result [Salter, 1960: 137; Fisher, 1969].

Ralph Waldo Emerson thought that a petty consistency was the hobgoblin of little minds. If, like Solow, one wishes to belong to both schools and persist with the aggregate production function approach to growth, one faces the famous problem of the 'residual', the economic growth that apparently cannot be accounted for by increases in capital and labour. The indestructibility of the residual is more apparent than real. Without elaborating all the detail of their accounting adjustments, one may nevertheless take cognisance of one of the more thorough-going demolitions, by Griliches and Jorgenson. After adjusting for errors of aggregation, price deflation and the definition of capital services and labour, they concluded that 'if real product and real factor input are accurately accounted for, the observed growth in total factor productivity (i.e. the "residual") is negligible' [Jorgenson and Griliches, 1967: 272].

Thus, development economists are aware of many reasons why the original sources of growth analyses cannot simply be accepted at their face value. But even if they could, they do not necessarily bear the extreme interpretation that capital is unnecessary for economic growth. Everything then depends on what one thinks the 'residual' represents. Solow, for example, thought that it represented technical progress which had to be embodied in each new vintage of capital equipment, a progression of improvements in the design of capital goods. If that were true, it would be impossible to have technical progress and, thus, economic growth, without a continuous process of capital accumulation. Bauer holds that the 'residual' represents something quite different – his conception of the true determinants of development, discussed in the following section. But this is merely a supposition. It is not based on the sources of growth analysis, any more than is Solow's alternative supposition.

It is surely necessary to move on from single-factor explanations of the 'residual' and from a method of analysis, the simple regression model, which tries to measure the contributions to growth of machine design changes, education and improved resource allocations as if each were determined independently of the others. There are obvious interactions between educational progress and design improvement and between the latter and resource allocation improvements. It is these which need further investigation and modelling. This is very different from propagating a simple supposition that capital accumulation is not required for growth [cf. *Nelson, 1964: 590-7*].

It is very odd indeed that these famous discussions have been overlooked when development economists are accused of 'investment fetishism', since they were elegantly summed up over a decade ago:

> The wheel has turned 360°: an implication of Solow's findings in 1957 was that the traditional economic factors, capital accumulation and deepening, had bit parts only in the growth saga. The backlash ... has come, first, through embodied technical progress and, now, through the Jorgenson-Griliches script. The traditional economic factors and neo-classical processes are again the stars and the other factors have been left with virtually no role at all – they have been written out of the script. [*Harcourt, 1972: 83*]

Today, economists emphasise the role of capital formation in explaining the slowdown in productivity growth in developed economies since 1973 [*Lindbeck, 1983: 28-9*]. Although, for various reasons, including problems of concept and measurement of 'capital services', the revolution does not any longer appear quite as dramatic as stated by Harcourt, it is clear that Solow's original position was at the time, and still remains, highly problematic. It is not, and never was, an authoritative statement of truth about the role of investment in developing countries.

The wasteful character of much investment spending in both developed and developing countries is then brought forward by Bauer as evidence that investment is not necessary for development. But the truth or otherwise of the first proposition is not logically related to the validity of the latter. If all the investment ever made had been wasteful, it would still be true that some further investment is necessary for economic development. In the real world, there is not, nor can there be, any guarantee that investment will be productive. Certain very simplified and abstract economic models of long-run equilibrium have the property that investors' expectations are always fulfilled, but we actually make economic decisions in a disequilibrium world. That is why, for national accounting purposes, investment is defined purely negatively: that part of the income of a period which is *not spent* on goods and services that are 'used up' within the period. These 'left over' goods and services may or may not generate revenues in excess of their costs in future time periods: there is nothing in this definition that takes a position on their future productivity [*Toye, 1981: 68-9*].[3] And, in a world of uncertainty, peopled perhaps by myopic managers as well as conservative trade unionists, one thing is certain – a share of investment spending will *always* be wasted. But that does not imply that development will take place without a continued attempt to invest productively.

VII. PSYCHO-SOCIAL DETERMINANTS OF DEVELOPMENT

The denial of a significant role of capital accumulation in the process of development opens the door to a wide range of alternative explanations of the determinants of development. Popular alternatives in the past have been formal education, learning by doing and processes that prompt efficient resource allocation. At present, popularity tends to favour even more ethereal and less well-defined formulations. Bauer, for example, puts it thus: 'personal qualities, social institutions and mores, and political arrangements which make for endeavour and achievement' [1981: 194-5], or 'people's capacities, attitudes, values and beliefs' [ibid: 118]. It is with disregard to 'evident determinants of economic achievement, such as personal qualities and social and political arrangements' that development economists are taxed [ibid: 259].

Although Bauer's more recent formulations have become vaguer, this explanation is not entirely tautological and contentless. If we go back to his earlier versions, examples are given of specific attitudes that are, from the point of view of material progress, favourable (personal responsibility, curiosity, experimentation, assertion of individual rights, desire for acquisition and achievement, dislike of begging) and unfavourable (asceticism, passivity, leisure preference, fatalism, superstition, reverence for animals, purdah of women) [Bauer, 1972: 76-9]. The basic unit of the theory is not the nation or the individual, however. It is the ethnic group. Some groups have favourable attitudes, and they make material progress; others have unfavourable attitudes and they do not. There you have it. That is why incomes differ. Population policies, international transfers, capital accumulation do not matter, it is said.

The similarity of this vision to colonialists' images of their subject populations is clear enough [Greenberger, 1969: 42-54; Alatas, 1977: 70-81]. But such images were faulty in that they were based on imperfect understanding of the culture of subject groups and combined with psychological need for rationalisations and justification for colonial domination. Despite the activities of nineteenth-century physical anthropologists, these images lack any scientific basis, thus achieving only the status of group stereotypes put together from the casual observations of foreigners.

The problem here is that one gets the clearest impressions of the places where one has lived longest, and the longer one lives in one place, the less opportunity one has to live in others. Inevitably, mere impressions are biased and the process of generalising from impressions is subject to no form of scientific control. Impressions of differential group behaviour stemming from West Africa, Malaysia and Hong Kong form the backbone of the theory of the psycho-social determinants of development [Lipton, 1983]. But, even for these, the causal link running from, for example, the holding of certain attitudes to material success is invariably assumed, but never established, even tentatively. Attempts to link economic performance with ethnic origin have indeed proved inconclusive and with psychological characteristics have yet to be made [Kilby, 1983: 107].

Because there is so little that is concrete to say about this theory, one ends up learning more about certain European cultural tensions than one does about the non-European cultures which are supposedly under examination. Bauer, in particular, exhibits the tension between a dynamic utilitarianism and a romantic anti-industrialisation creed. This is evident in the way he uses the term 'development'. On the one hand, he identifies it with material progress (and the alleged favourable attitudes to material progress), while on the other he persistently abstains on the question whether material progress is desirable [*Bauer, 1972: 149*]. This ambivalence is deep-seated in European, and especially British, culture. This sets him somewhat at odds with the ultra-conservatives who are his current political allies. They have no doubts that industrialisation ought never to have been allowed to happen.

What are the policy implications that emerge from this psycho-social account of the determinants of development? Something that looks like a policy implication would be an exhortation not to persecute or expel minority groups who possess the attitudes allegedly favouring material progress. Third World governments are certainly harshly condemned for doing the opposite [*Bauer, 1981: 79, 84, 94, 106, 112, 250*]. The principle here is that one should not persecute anybody, whether their attitudes favour material progress or not. But, leaving that aside, the picture is usually infinitely more complex and tragic than the simple black comedy of Third World governments cutting off their noses to spite their faces, which Bauer presents to his audience.[4]

The other policy implication which the 'favourable-attitudes-of-groups' theory carries is that external contacts should be expanded. This one seems merely confused and foolish. It derives directly from J. S. Mill's views of the 1840s, which were formed *before* the major modern examples of the fatal impact of Europeans on aboriginals were fully understood [*Hirschman, 1982: 1471, note 3*]. Should external contacts be expanded regardless of whether they are good or bad, fortunate or unfortunate, or are all external contacts by definition good? To affirm the latter is self evidently not true. The sale of Nestlé's powdered baby milk to African mothers whose poor knowledge of hygiene made bottle-feeding deadly to their children is just one of many possible examples of the way in which external contacts *can* have dire consequences for those contacted.

Large-scale tragedies that can occur through external contacts are littered through modern history, ranging from nineteenth-century Tahiti to twentieth-century Kampuchea. Other modern examples of virtual extermination or genocide are the aboriginal populations of North America and Australia. Bauer's treatment of these two classic cases is so inconsistent as to be almost schizophrenic. On the one hand, he acknowledges the facts [*1981: 45, 189, 192, 194, 196*]. On the other hand, we are told, and presumably meant also to believe, that:

> the level of material achievement usually diminishes as one moves away from the foci of Western impact. The poorest and most backward people have few or no external contacts: witness the aborigines, pygmies and desert peoples. [*Ibid: 70*]

If today's aborigines have few or no external contacts, it is because there are now so few of them left, the great majority having met with a terminal accident (otherwise known as an external contact) some while ago.[5]

The absence of policy implications of any significance from the theory of the psycho-social determinants of development is, in one way, quite appropriate. If 'development' is seen, as it is by Bauer, as a morally neutral concept, we can all rest easily in the knowledge that there is nothing much that the developed countries of the world can do to advance it. Thus, Bauer gives us, at least, a perfectly consistent complacency.

## VIII. COMPARISONS WITHIN ECONOMICS

Bauer's fundamental criticism is that intellectual standards are lower in development economics than other comparable branches of economics. It is common ground that development economics, being of fairly recent origin, will show some of the confusion and patchiness of a new sub-discipline. What is asserted beyond that is that development economics is *more* intellectually defective than other new sub-disciplines, and that this results from the political commitments of its practitioners.

To make this point, Bauer contrasts development economics unfavourably with other new departures within economics in recent decades, as follows:

> There have been major, genuine and undisputed advances in recent decades. They have been genuine in that they have helped us to understand real phenomena and sequences. They are undisputed, in that their significance is recognised regardless of differences in political position or in preferred methodology. An incomplete list of such areas of progress would include ... the economic analysis of major political and administrative processes; and the examination of the economic implications of different kinds of property rights. There is no need to elaborate on these well recognised advances ... [*Bauer, 1981: 256*]

In a brief paragraph, this sounds very impressive and convincing. But is there really no need to elaborate? It would be pleasant indeed to report such unanimity, but it would also be factually incorrect. Considerable dispute has taken place about the significance of applying utilitarian marginalist analysis to politics and legal rights over the last twenty years. It focuses precisely on the scientific validity of these exercises and expresses a high degree of doubt that they in any way help us 'to understand real phenomena'.

As long ago as 1961, C. B. Macpherson was questioning the attempt to interpret political processes by analogy with economists' marginal analysis of markets [*1973: 185-94*]. He concluded that:

> political theorists have paid too much attention to the superficial analogy between the market and the political process at the operative level and not enough attention to the market concept at the deeper level of the postulates about the nature of society and the nature of human freedom ...

having previously commented that 'equilibrium is a nice tune for whistling in the dark' [*ibid: 194, 192*].

The scientific validity of the work of Downs and Breton on economic theories of politics has been examined by asking whether their predictions in the field of public finance either have been or can be tested. The answer was that they had never been tested rigorously, usually because they were formulated in a way that would make them virtually impossible to test [*Toye, 1976: 433-47*]. It is interesting to note the response which this paper met from the scholars of Bauer's 'major, genuine and undisputed advances'. It was paraphrased without any acknowledgement of source. None of the substantive criticisms advanced in it was rebutted. Instead, they were met with the following comment:

> It would be unwise to ignore the partial justice of each of these criticisms. ... Public choice is a young discipline (at least in its modern form), and it encounters all the well-known problems of straddling diverse disciplines. Certainly, its theoretical structure has been developed from relatively primitive initial forms, and the tests to which it has been exposed have been fairly simple and subsequently often proved unacceptable. But this is true of any emergent discipline. [*Rowley, 1978: 38-9*]

Rowley then proceeds to validate this type of theory 'by the market test itself', the fact that its journal 'is highly-rated by ambitious faculties and by academics striving to make their way within a highly competitive profession' [*ibid*]. So much for the intellectual standards of Bauer's achievers of authentic knowledge. They represent a return to Callicles' argument in the *Gorgias* that the philosopher 'however gifted, is bound to lose his manly qualities, if he keeps away from the centres of public resort, the market place ... where famous men are made' [*Cornford, 1941: xx*]. This was the prototype of all subsequent claims for the priority of politics over philosophy.

Dissent, too, has been expressed about the use of economic theory to analyse legal problems and make legal policy. The gist of the doubts has been well expressed as follows:

> [The] method of analysis makes sense *only if* the existing distribution is accepted as proper ... increasing efficiency is not necessarily the most effective means of increasing welfare .... Given a concern for either welfare or freedom (the meaning of which cannot be determined by technical economic analysis), the content of analytic categories and the proper scope of the market were shown to present problems properly answered in the public or political realm. Thus, it seems that economic efficiency is not an adequate basis from which to assess and make suggestions concerning the law. [*Baker, 1975: 47*]

At best, the economic analysis of law *may*, if applied correctly, codify the biased and dominant ideology of the historical period during which the laws under analysis were developed. The better understanding to be gained from it is that the 'common sense' of that period is all too frequently nonsense, from a wider perspective of the meaning of human welfare [*ibid: 48*].

The utilitarian marginalism of neo-classical economists has for many years demonstrated its imperialist designs on other areas of social science. Apart from politics and law, the topics which it has 'rationalised' have included marriage, divorce, extra-marital sexual relations, suicide, capital punishment, racial and sexual discrimination, child-bearing and friendship [*Harcourt, 1979: 244*]. But the light that all of this has thrown on the way that the real world works is very dim indeed, because social relations cannot be reduced to the sum of the actions of a set of individualist, rational maximisers. As a model for what development economists should be doing, it is bald and unconvincing.

## IX. CONCLUSION

After this extensive review of the main heads of evidence adduced by Bauer, one hardly hesitates in rejecting as unproven the claim that development economists, relative to economists practising other new sub-disciplines of economics, have shown greater proneness to error, greater failure to right error or greater politically induced dogmatism.

This conclusion rests on a detailed examination of flaws in the reasoning used to advance the claim. The fundamental source of these flaws is carelessness in establishing the attribution of views to development economists, in setting out the full background of academic debates and in ensuring consistency between positions taken on the same topic at different places in the argument.

More specifically, as has been shown, the defects include the following:

(a)  persistent failure to discriminate between, on the one hand, professional statements made by development economists and, on the other, varied utterances of politicians, spokesmen of international agencies and even newspaper leader writers and students;

(b)  the presentation of a very partial picture of the academic debate on international income differences, the theory of capital and productivity growth and the validity of economic analysis of politics and law;

(c)  inconsistent argument in relation to critical issues, such as the reliability of quantitative comparisons, the acceptability of racial discrimination and the value of external contact to aboriginals;

(d)  simple mistakes of logic, as that involved in opposing both monopoly and all state economic controls, in attributing the durability of 'aid' to 'aid' advocacy by development economists and in not recognising that, in disequilibrium, some investment will always be wasted;

(e)  reliance on unscientific generalisation from very few cases – Malaysia, West Africa and Hong Kong – as a basis for a theory of ethnic group stereotypes.

Bauer admits that his project is ambitious. It now readily appears to have been over-ambitious. The requirements of proof of the thesis of a 'conspicuous and disconcerting hiatus between accepted opinion and evident reality in major areas of academic ... economic discourse since the Second World War' [*Bauer, 1982: 1*] substantially outrun those resources of 'simple reflection, analysis and observation' and 'evidence and logic' which he has been able to bring to bear on it. This is not at all surprising. Momentous issues of world-wide scale are unlikely to be definitively resolved using only intellectual devices 'the validity of which the non-technical reader can verify readily' [*ibid: 2*]. What is much more likely to issue from this is the clever cultivating of prejudices. It is worth noting, at this point, that this is precisely what intellectuals of a certain political persuasion advocate as a worthwhile activity [e.g. *Scruton, 1980: 119*].

This is an important book, as Amartya Sen has said. It does 'apply and extend a view that is widely held' and is important because, in doing so, it reveals the frighteningly flimsy intellectual foundations on which that view rests. It is frightening because the beam in Bauer's own eye never deters him from talking up the motes in the eyes of his professional colleagues. It is frightening because this kind of disingenuous disparagement of development economics and development economists is only a small part of a much wider campaign of thetorical denigration in the UK at present, which extends to sociologists, architects, planners, ecologists and teachers of peace studies, to name only the most prominent. On current political trends, this campaign could be very successful in draining public resources away from all of these 'target groups' if not from aid recipients in the Third World.

Bauer has not 'lost his manly qualities' by pursuing philosophy and contesting the prejudices of his place and age. He has instead opted for a voice in the centres of public resort. He is now one of the famous men whom the market place has made.


NOTES

1. Ironically, the spectre of 'over-population' still seems to haunt the thinking of the conservative intellectuals. See, for example, Scruton [*1980: 43, 121*].
2. In the UK since 1979, the personal tax system has been made more regressive at the same time as its 'aid' programme priorities have been reordered away from the previous focus on overseas poverty and towards greater service to UK commercial interests. Since 1979, the average rate of tax (income tax, national insurance contributions and indirect taxes less child benefits) on a family earning three-quarters of national average earnings has risen from 34.7 per cent to 36.9 per cent. At the same time, taxpayers earning £29,567 per annum or more will pay *less* income tax and national insurance contributions, in real terms, than they paid in 1978–79, despite increases in real earnings since then. The general background to the evolution of the 'poverty trap' in the UK is given in Field, Meacher and Pond [*1977*].
3. This point was originally made in criticism of Myrdal's concept of 'productive consumption'. Bauer seems to be involved in the same misunderstanding of the meaning of 'investment' as Myrdal, with whom he evidently thinks that he strongly disagrees. It is no 'anomaly' that unproductive investment is recorded as investment in national accounts, once the principles on which the accounts are drawn up are understood [cf. *Bauer, 1981: 249*]. It is indeed hard to see how it could be otherwise, given that investment spending has to be recorded as *something* well in advance of the time when it will be known whether it proved to be productive or not. Like Myrdal, Bauer failed to appreciate this elementary point. Consequently, at the end of his argument, Bauer finds himself endorsing the Myrdalian concept of productive consumption [*ibid: 253*] and denying that consumption and investment are

mutually exclusive alternatives [*ibid: 254*]. The misleading nature of this latter contention has been examined elsewhere [*Toye, 1981: 69-70*].

4. To witness a personal or collective tragedy, and to describe it as such, is not to condone or approve of the actions of the protagonists. Thus, there is no question here of excusing the inhuman or discriminatory acts of Third World governments on the grounds that they are only following the European colonial example [cf. *Bauer, 1981: 84*]. But it follows from this, as Bauer does not appear to realise, that European discrimination and brutality also cannot be excused on the ground that 'discrimination on the basis of colour and race is not a European invention. In much of Africa and Asia, and notably in India, it has been endemic for many centuries' [*ibid: 79*]. Here is another example of opportunistic inconsistency in argument which matches beautifully with deep-seated European, and particularly British, cultural prejudices. Although many of today's persecutions and expulsions have to be understood in the context of colonial history of the West, other similar examples appear in different historical contexts. The revocation of the Edict of Nantes in 1685 is often cited as an example of counter-productive folly. It is often forgotten that the Huguenots had been waging intermittent civil war against the French monarchy for the preceding hundred years, yet had failed, because they shared the royalism and social conservatism of their opponents, to expand beyond their very limited numerical, social and geographical base [*Parker, 1978: 11-30; cf. Bauer, 1981: 16, 44*]. Again, this is emphatically *not a justification* for their expulsion. Rather it is a warning against a too-simple view of the role minorities play and against the hindsight assumption that the Huguenots would have been as socially, politically and economically valuable, had they stayed in France, as they subsequently became in their countries of refuge. The same comments apply to the Vietnamese expelled at the conclusion of the Vietnam War.

5. The moral here would seem to be: sitting on abundant resources in ignorance of the capitalist ethic can seriously damage your health. But, no, it turns out that the Navajo are actually the victims of US Government generosity: 'official handouts to improve their economic conditions'. Heavily subsidised by the United States Government for many decades, they are a familiar example of the way that whole societies can be pauperised [*Bauer, 1981: 113*]. This should be stopped forthwith:

> Should present-day Americans be taxed to make amends to American Indians when most of the taxpayers are descended from immigrants who entered the country long after the time of any wrongs perpetuated against the ancestors of the Indians? A statute of limitations on historical wrongs is more than just: it is unavoidable. [*Ibid: 122*]

It is certainly necessary, as Edmund Burke was aware, to underpin conservative philosophies of land ownership rights. But this illumination is sidestepped by another rhetorical question:

> The recent practice of referring to the poor as deprived ... again helps the notion that the rich owe their prosperity to the exploitation of the poor. Yet how could the incomes of ... people in ... North America have been taken from ... aborigines of Papua, or the desert peoples or pygmies of Africa? [*Ibid: 74*]

It is not clear why the North Americans have to exploit Papuans or Africans for the possibility of deprivation and exploitation to be validated. Does not their expropriation of their own aborigines suffice?

## REFERENCES

Alatas, S. H., 1977, *The Myth of the Lazy Native*, London: Frank Cass.

Baker, C. E., 1975, 'The Ideology of the Economic Analysis of Law', *Philosophy and Public Affairs*, Vol. 5, No. 1, Fall.

Baran, P. A., 1973, *The Political Economy of Growth*, Harmondsworth: Penguin Books.

Bauer, P. T., 1972, *Dissent on Development*, London: Weidenfeld and Nicolson.

Bhagwati, J. N., 1966, *The Economics of Underdeveloped Countries*, London: Weidenfeld and Nicolson, World University Library.

Brown, C. P., 1980, *The Political and Social Economy of Commodity Control*, London: Macmillan.

Cassen, R. H., 1978, *India: Population, Economy, Society*, London: Macmillan.

Chenery, H. B., et al., 1974, *Redistribution with Growth*, Oxford: Oxford University Press.

Cornford, F. M., 1941, *The Republic of Plato*, Oxford: Clarendon Press.

Desai, M., 1980, 'Stabilisation of Primary Product Prices: The Lessors of the International Tin Agreement', in A. Sengupta (ed.), *Commodities, Finance and Trade*, London: Frances Pinter.

Field, F., M. Meacher and C. Pond, 1977, *To Him Who Hath: A Study of Poverty and Taxation*, Harmondsworth: Penguin Books.

Fisher, F. M., 1969, 'The Existence of Aggregate Production Functions', *Econometrica*, Vol. 37, No. 4, October.

Greenberger, A. J., 1969, *The British Image of India: A Study in the Literature of Imperialism*, Oxford: Oxford University Press.

Griliches, Z., and D. W. Jorgenson, 1967, 'The Explanation of Productivity Change', *Review of Economic Studies*, Vol. 34.

Gurley, J. G., 1979, 'Economic Development: A Marxist View', in K. P. Jameson and C. K. Wilber (eds.), *Directions in Economic Development*, Notre Dame and London: University of Notre Dame Press.

Hagen, E. C., 1960, 'Some Facts about Income Levels and Economic Growth', *Review of Economics and Statistics*, Vol. 42, February.

Harcourt, G. C., 1972, *Some Cambridge Controversies in the Theory of Capital*, Cambridge: Cambridge University Press.

—— 1979, 'The Social Science Imperialists', *Politics*, XIV (2), November.

Hirschman, A. O., 1982, 'Rival Interpretations of Market Society: Civilising, Destructive, or Feeble?', *Journal of Economic Literature*, December.

Independent Commission on International Development Issues, 1980, *North-South: A Programme for Survival*, London: Pan Books.

Jenkins, G. M., 1977, Review in *Journal of the Royal Statistical Society*, Series A.

Kilby, P., 1983, 'An Entrepreneurial Problem', *American Economic Review*, Vol. 73, No. 2, May.

Kravis, I., A. Heston and R. Summers, 1978, *International Comparisons of Real Product and Purchasing Power*, Baltimore and London: Johns Hopkins for the World Bank.

Levy, V., 1982, 'The Savings Gap and the Productivity of Foreign Aid to a Developing Economy', mimeo.

Lindbeck, A., 1983, 'The Recent Slowdown of Productivity Growth', *Economic Journal*, Vol. 93, No. 369, March.

Lipton, M., 1983, 'Comment on Bauer's Paper', in D. Seers and G. Meier (eds.), *Pioneers of Development Economics*, World Bank (forthcoming).

MacBean, A. I., and P. N. Snowden, 1981, *International Institutions in Trade and Finance*, London: Allen and Unwin.

Macpherson, C. B., 1973, *Democratic Theory: Essays in Retrieval*, Oxford: Clarendon Press.

Mosley, P., 1981, 'Aid for the Poorest: Some Early Lesson of U.K. Experience', *Journal of Development Studies*, Vol. 17, No. 2.

Nelson, R. R., 1964, 'Aggregate Production Functions and Medium-range Growth projections', *American Economic Review*, December.

Overseas Development Administration, 1983, *The Lessons of Experience: Evaluation Work in O.D.A.*, London: HMSO.

Parker, D., 1978, 'The Huguenots in Seventeenth-Century France', in A. C. Hepburn (ed.), *Minorities in History*, London: Arnold.

Rowley, C. K., 1978, 'Market "Failure" and Government "Failure" ', in *The Economics of Politics*, London: Institute of Economic Affairs. Readings 18.

Salter, W. E. G., 1960, *Productivity and Technical Change*, Second Edition, Cambridge: Cambridge University Press.

Scruton, R., 1980, *The Meaning of Conservatism*, Harmondsworth: Penguin Books.

Secombe, W., 1983, 'Marxism and Demography', *New Left Review*, Number 137.

Sen, A. K., 1982, 'Just Deserts', *New York Review of Books*, 4th March.

For Product Safety Concerns and Information please contact our EU representative GPSR@taylorandfrancis.com Taylor & Francis Verlag GmbH, Kaufingerstraße 24, 80331 München, Germany

Printed and bound by CPI Group (UK) Ltd, Croydon, CR0 4YY

11/04/2025

01844010-0020